The rise of modern police and
the European state system from
Metternich to the Second World War

The rise of modern police and the European state system from Metternich to the Second World War

HSI-HUEY LIANG

Vassar College

CAMBRIDGE
UNIVERSITY PRESS

Published by the Press Syndicate of the University of Cambridge
The Pitt Building, Trumpington Street, Cambridge CB2 1RP
40 West 20th Street, New York, NY 10011–4211, USA
10 Stamford Road, Oakleigh, Victoria 3166, Australia

© Cambridge University Press 1992

First published 1992

Printed in the United States of America

Library of Congress Cataloging-in-Publication Data

Liang, Hsi-huey, 1929–
    The rise of modern police and the European state system from
Metternich to the Second World War / Hsi-huey Liang.
        p.   cm.
    Includes index.
    ISBN 0-521-43022-4
    1. Police – Europe – History – 19th century.   2. Police – Europe –
History – 20th century.   3. Europe – Politics and government – 1815–1871.
4. Europe – Politics and government – 1871–1918.   5. Europe – Politics and
government – 1918–1945.   I. Title.
HV8194.A2L53   1992
363.2'096 – dc20   92-17111
                                                                        CIP

A catalog record for this book is available from the British Library.

ISBN 0-521-43022-4 hardback

Für Francette

Da stellen wir Menschen aus Angst
voneinander Staaten auf, umgeben uns
mit Wächtern jeder Art, mit Polizisten,
Soldaten, mit einer öffentlichen
Meinung, aber was nützt es uns?

Friedrich Dürrenmatt
Der Richter und sein Henker

Contents

Abbreviations used in footnotes

AA	Auswärtiges Amt (German Foreign Ministry)
ADdBR (Strasbourg)	Archives départementales du Bas-Rhin, Strasbourg
ADdHR (Colmar)	Archives départementales du Haut-Rhin, Colmar
AMAE (Paris)	Archives des relations extérieures, Ministère des Affaires Etrangères, Paris
AN (Paris)	Archives Nationales, Paris
APD (Vienna)	Archiv der Polizei-Direktion, Vienna
APP (Paris)	Archive de la Préfecture de Police, Paris
ASRK (Berne)	Archiv des Zentralsekretariats des Schweizerischen Roten Kreuzes, Berne
AVA (Vienna)	Allgemeines Verwaltungsarchiv, Vienna
BA (Berne)	Schweizerisches Bundesarchiv, Berne
BA (Frankfurt a.M)	Bundesarchiv (Aussenstelle), Frankfurt-am-Main
BA (Koblenz)	Bundesarchiv, Koblenz
BA–MA (Freiburg i.B)	Bundesarchiv–Militärarchiv, Freiburg im Breisgau
BYB	The British Year Book of International Law
CDJC (Paris)	Centre de documentation juive contemporaine, Paris
EJPD	Eidgenössisches Justiz- und Polizeidepartement (Swiss Federal Department of Justice and Police)
EPD	Eidgenössisches Politisches Departement (Swiss Federal Political Department)
GP	Die Grosse Politik der Europäischen Kabinette, 1871–1914. Sammlung der Akten des Deutschen Auswärtigen Amts, 40 vols. (Berlin 1922–7)
GPStA (Berlin)	Geheimes Preussisches Staatsarchiv, Berlin
HHStA (Vienna)	Haus-, Hof- und Staatsarchiv, Vienna
HICOG	United States High Commission for Germany
Hoover Inst.	Hoover Institution on War, Revolution and Peace, Stanford, California
KA (Vienna)	Kriegsarchiv, Vienna

LA (Berlin)	Landesarchiv Berlin
NA (Washington)	National Archives, Washington, D.C.
PA (Bonn)	Politisches Archiv, Bonn
SPD Library (Berlin)	Library and archive of the Social Democratic Party of Germany, Berlin
StA (Basel-Stadt)	Staatsarchiv, Basel-Stadt
USDC (Berlin)	United States Document Center, Berlin
VfZG	Vierteljahrshefte für Zeitgeschichte

Preface

The historical period in the title of this book is approximate, because it indicates very broad developments in the social and political history of Europe from the onset of the modern age of nation-states to the eclipse of the European state system following the outbreak of the Second World War. The term European state system, itself, is a convenient shorthand reference to the network of relationships of a handful of continental powers in the police structure of the Continent. For reasons of space the police relations between France, Austria, Germany, and Switzerland are examined most closely; Russia's police influence in Europe is treated peripherally. Great Britain and the United States have been omitted because they were not deeply involved in the continental balance of power in our period. Bohemia is mentioned in our discussion of the Austrian Empire's police problems in the nineteenth century because in the last chapter we deal with Czechoslovakia's struggle against Nazi subversion.

The bulk of my evidence, much of it in the form of excerpts from documents, explains why I am sparing with the space I give to general historical narrative. Police records exist in abundance in many European archives, but they are voluminous and ill-sorted, so that I was forced to proceed by mere sampling more often than I had wanted. Unlike diplomatic papers, whose complete publication after an interval of some thirty years has become routine, many police documents still remain unread despite the wealth of information they contain on the concerns, the conflicts, and the habits of mind of past generations.[1] Their significance for the international situation of a country can sometimes only be guessed at. When I asked a senior official of the Austrian ministry of interior in 1979 why this was so, he explained that decisions on the cabinet level concerning national security were mostly made by way of confidential exchanges between ministers

---

[1] "Welch schauerlichen Abgründe von Verworfenheit, Unglück, Elend längst vergessener Menschen, welche Einblicke in die dumpfe Psyche der kleinen Leute von ehemals, wenn man nur irgendein Paket vornahm und blätterte." Friedrich Meinecke on being initiated to the holdings of the Prussian Secret State Archive in 1887 and leafing through Repositur 49, "Schwerverbrecher." See his *Erlebtes 1862/1919* (Stuttgart, 1964), p. 93.

"selbstverständlich ohne Protokoll." To be on the safe side I have quoted long passages from the protocols that I did find and which I thought relevant. I am responsible for all translations except where otherwise stated. Often I have wished to keep the text in the original because the "flavor" is unattainable in English. In such instances I have left at least some of the original words in parentheses. Readers unfamiliar with basic police terminology and police methods will find a brief explanation in the Introduction.

My thanks are due to my students at Vassar, who over the past years have smilingly endured my growing involvement with the "police" side of the historical questions discussed in class; to my colleagues Professors Donald J. Olsen, David L. Schalk, and Carole K. Fink, who have helped me with much encouragement and advice; and to Vassar College for granting me a year's sabbatical leave in 1984–5, during which time most of the documentary research was done, and two more semesters in the fall of 1988 and 1990 to write down the bulk of the manuscript.

Two earlier exploratory trips to Europe were made possible by outside donors: a summer trip to Vienna in 1979 financed by the Kenan Foundation and the Austrian ministry of science and research; and a three-week trip to Paris in 1981 funded by the American Philosophical Society. A few reflections on the collapse of Communist police dictatorship in East Berlin and Prague in 1989 were added following visits to East Germany and to Czechoslovakia in March and August 1990.

I would like to thank the following persons who most courteously assisted me during my visits abroad:

In Austria: Police President Dr. Karl Reidinger, Dr. Anton Schulz of the ministry of interior, and Sektionsleiter Dr. Erben and Regierungsrat Dr. Köck of the Austrian national bureau of Interpol. At the archive of the Polizei-Direktion Wien, Dr. Hochenbichler and Herr Ebner; at the Haus-, Hof- u. Staatsarchiv, Dr. Anna Benna and Dr. Christiane Thomas; at the Kriegsarchiv, Dr. Allmayer-Beck and Dr. Kurt Peball; and at the Allgemeines Verwaltungsarchiv, Dr. Lorenz Mikoletzky. Very supportive also were the historians, Dr. Gerhard Jagschitz and Dr. Wolfgang Maderthaner; Dr. Triska of the Institut für Kriminologie; and two old friends, Dr. med. Franz-Klemens Feiks and Lisl Feiks; and Frau Rosemarie Starlinger.

In Germany: Dr. Weinandy and Dr. Keipert at the Politisches Archiv in Bonn; and at the Bundesarchiv Dr. Bauer (Koblenz), Dr. Schenk (Frankfurt a.M), and Drs. Fleischer, Neugebauer, and Ringsdorf (Freiburg i.B.). Dr. Hans Umbreit of the Militärgeschichtliches Forschungsamt and Professor Bernd Martin of the University of Freiburg are thanked for their friendly encouragement. In Berlin I received help from Dr. Letkemann at the Geheimes Preussisches Staatsarchiv; Drs. Wetzel, Reichardt, and Drogmann at the Landesarchiv; Dr. Thomas Lindenberger of the Free University; and President Dr. Georg Schertz and Regierungsdirektor Gerhard Simke of the Police Presidium in West Berlin. In East Berlin, very informative were Professors Fritz Klein, Frank Hadler, and Stefan Wolle of the Akademie der Wissenschaften, Professors Harry Nick, Harald Neubert, and Eberhard Fromm of the Akademie für Gesellschaftswissenschaft beim ZK der SED, Herr Matthias Maier of the Bürgerkommittee Berlin, and Frau Evelyn Zupke of the Initiative Freiheit und Menschenrechte.

In France: In Paris, the staff of the Archives Nationales and Monsieur Dethan at the Archives des relations extérieures; also Monsieur Poisson and Mademoiselle Charmais at the Archives de la préfecture de police. On my visits to Interpol, I was assisted by Commissaire Principal Gérard Laheuguère and Dr. Karunatilleke. Two retired *commissaires de police*, Jacques Delarue – himself a historian – and Louis Séverin, are thanked for their generous hospitality and stimulating talk. In Strasbourg, Jacques D'Orléans guided me through the departmental files, and in Colmar I was received by Monsieur Wilsdorf.

In Switzerland: My chief sponsors were Dr. Ulrich Barth of the Staatsarchiv Basel-Stadt and Dr. Christopher Graf of the Bundesarchiv in Berne. I was also aided by Nicolas Buckhardt of the International Red Cross, Mr. William Reid of the Union Postale Universelle, and by Dr. Markus Mohler, who commanded the police in Basel, and his assistant Dr. Robert Heuss. Mrs. Margaretha Winzenried, an old family friend, provided many valuable introductions.

In Czechoslovakia: My inquiries were greatly facilitated by the helpfulness of Mrs. Dagmar Havlová and Dr. Tomas Pštross of Občanské Fórum, and of Mrs. Dagmar Burešova, chairwoman of the Bohemian National Parliament. Valuable information was offered by the historians, Professors Josef Harna, Jiři Kořalka, and Zdenek Šolle.

I am happy to extend my appreciation to Cambridge University Press, specifically to Frank Smith for his valuable help and Herbert A. Gilbert for copy-editing the final text.

Although I am deeply indebted to the many persons listed here, they are, of course, in no way responsible for any errors and misjudgments that may be found in this book.

Introduction: How do we define "modern police"?

Definitions in police literature

The literature on government of the past two centuries is rich in definitions of police. But many of these definitions are pompous and simplistic, and none of them tells us about the role the police played in the modern history of Europe. They are useful at best to make us see how the general concept of police has gradually changed during this period. Thus, under the influence of enlightened rationalism Joseph von Sonnenfels, the Austrian political economist, in 1765 called police a "science that teaches us how to create and cater to the domestic security of the state."[1] His contemporary, the Hanoverian publicist Johann von Justi, while basically of like mind, preferred to stress the benevolent side of royal despotism: "Police in the strict sense refers to everything needed for the maintenance of civil life, thus for discipline and order and well-being among the subjects in the towns, and for the growth of the peasantry."[2]

Today, these eighteenth-century definitions strike us as implausible because of their ready assumption that man has the intellectual power to devise a harmoniously policed society. (If Adam Smith can postulate an "economic man" to teach us how to increase the wealth of nations, they seem to say, why might not cameralist postulate a "policeable man" to explain the best way to free society from civil disorder?) During the Napoleonic wars, for example, Günter Heinrich von Berg's *Handbuch des teutschen Polizeyrechts* (1809) cast the police in the role of the ultimate guardian of civilized life: "Police is not only that branch of state power responsible for preventing harm in the interior of the state, but furthermore that part which is charged with promoting the security and welfare of the subjects *in every instance where other branches of the state power prove ineffective.*"[3]

---

[1] Joseph von Sonnenfels, *Grundsätze der Polizei, Handlung und Finanz* (Vienna. 1765), as quoted in Friedrich C. B. Avé-Lallemant, *Physiologie der deutschen Polizei* (Leipzig, 1882), p. 10.

[2] Johann Heinrich Gottlob von Justi, *Grundsätze der Polizeiwissenschaft* (Göttingen, 1756), as quoted in ibid.

[3] Geheimrat Günter Heinrich von Berg, *Handbuch des teutschen Polizeyrechts* (1801–9), as quoted in ibid., p. 12. My italics.

1

Still, von Berg was surpassed by the Prussian official, Dr. Wilhelm Abegg, who, following the yet more devastating war of 1914, ponderously proclaimed that, "Every single police decree must constitute a step forward in the progress of culture."[4]

True, in the nineteenth century definitions of police have spoken less about what police can or should do for mankind, and drawn more on legal history and constitutional law to inform us of the police's statutory powers and responsibilities. But like eighteenth-century authors, these theoreticians have mostly maintained the fiction that police is the key to the improvement of society.[5] Thus the General Prussian Code of Law (Allgemeines Preussisches Landrecht) of 1794 was regularly hailed by all German police authors for more than a century as the charter of Prussian civil rights, because it ended the license of the royal police to treat the king's subjects as immature wards.[6] But did it really? When fifty years later Heinrich Heine wrote *Deutschland, ein Wintermärchen* (1844) – his scathing denunciation of German servility to authority – had Prussia a courteous and fairminded police?

It was left to the twentieth century to raise searching questions about police because in our own times the need for elaborate social protection has become more urgent than ever before. At the same time the most frightening visions of totalitarian police regimes have also become possible through the latest advancements in science and technology. Far from evoking the vision of a society free from want and crime, writers like Aldous Huxley and George Orwell offered their readers the nightmarish prospect of future worlds enslaved through total programming or through merciless degradation.[7] Orwell's police state was actually realized if not surpassed by the police terror of Stalin and Hitler in the 1930s and 1940s. If most of the Western European countries were spared a similar fate they owe this not least to the civic courage of countless judges, civil servants, politicians and intellectuals who, while recognizing the police as an institution beyond the power of any government to abolish, exposed it in newspaper articles and books as a machine to be closely watched because of its inherent disposition to tyranny.

Finding a useful definition of modern police that we might want to quote at the outset of this book thus poses some difficulty. We might as well recognize that police is better understood through an examination not of its doctrine and legal status but of its methods and procedures.[8] A police director in Metternich's or

---

[4] Foreword to H. Degenhardt and M. Hagemann, *Polizei und Kind* (Berlin, 1926), pp. 21–2.

[5] F. W. Maitland, in his *Constitutional History of England* (London, 1956) (Lectures delivered at Cambridge in 1887–8), p. 415, emphasized the power of the public administration including the police as "that most powerful engine of government."

[6] Paragraph 10, Part II, Article 17 of the Allgemeines Preussisches Landrecht reads: "Die nötigen Anstalten zur Erhaltung der öffentlichen Ruhe, Sicherheit und Ordnung und zur Abwendung der dem Publikum oder einzelnen Mitgliedern desselben bevorstehenden Gefahr zu treffen, ist das Amt der Polizei." Paul Riege, *Kleine Polizei-Geschichte* (Lübeck, 1959), p. 25.

[7] Aldous Huxley, *Brave New World* (1932); and George Orwell [Eric Blair], *Nineteen Eighty-Four* (New York, 1949).

[8] Attempts to distinguish between the police of different nations in professional police circles concentrate on technical details of organization, like budget, salaries, promotions, and union rights.

Louis Napoleon's time did not aspire to create a utopian community, but rather to build a force capable of dealing from day to day with the problems of a restless and dangerous world, himself closer to a Jeremy Bentham than to a John Stuart Mill. In our own century it was the revolutionary romantic, not the professional policeman, who glorified the omnipotence of Lenin's security chief, Feliks Dzerzhinsky; the layman, not the specialist, who dreamt of a government so meticulously engineered that its police could monitor the conversations of all passengers on every express train criss-crossing the Continent at any given hour.[9]

We have heard least from the historian in regard to what police is and what police does. Police history has yet to become a field of study as fully established as diplomatic or constitutional history.[10] But are not historians most likely to capture the endlessly shifting interplay between rulers and ruled, the leaders and the led, performers and critics, rivals and enemies? Who if not the historian can tell us which of these roles the police assumed when and under what circumstances? And are not historians most likely to tolerate an approximation to the truth when scientific exactitude is impossible, and to shun definitions of police that are either inspired by self-complacency or blinded by excessive distrust?

The time of modern police: A historian's definition

The modern police as a historical phenomenon falls between the beginning of industrialization, one hundred and fifty years ago, and the rise of the ideological world of the twentieth. To study it takes us from the Metternich period to the outbreak of the Second World War, a period during which all Europe underwent a complicated process of change that required constant and elaborate monitoring and endless adjustments both inside particular sovereign states and in their relations to one another – in short, that called for a policing system covering the whole Continent and responsive to local needs as much as to the strategic shifts in the international balance of power.

As part of my definition I stress the periodization from the early nineteenth century to the end of the 1930s. I thus exclude from the modern police the praetorian guards and secret spies used by all royal courts under the ancien regime. By the same token I draw a clear distinction between the modern police and the police in the European dictatorships between the two world wars and which

But such information has little bearing on our analysis of police as a factor in international relations. See for example Union Internationale des Syndicats de Police, "Panorame sur la police en Europe" (Koblenz, 1977).

[9] This simile for Fascism is from Karl Mannheim, *Diagnosis of our Time* (New York, 1944), p. 103. For the idealization of Dzerzhinsky, see the short novel by Somerset Maugham, *Christmas Holiday* (New York, 1939). On the task of police to cater to a world full of imponderable dangers, see Johann Friedrich Karl Merker, *Handbuch für Polizeybeamte im ausübenden Dienst* (orig. 1818 East Berlin, 1984), Erster Abschnitt, paragraphs 18, 19.

[10] This remark does not apply to the many splendid monographs on the police of individual European countries for particular periods by scholars like Sidney Monas, Donald E. Emerson, Howard C. Payne, Dieter Fricke, and Robert Conquest.

continued to exist in Eastern Europe until very recently.[11] The collapse in 1989 of the Communist bloc has vindicated the "modern police," for the time being at least. But is still remains to be seen whether the Gestapo, the SS, the NKVD (or KGB), and the Stasi represented a more advanced stage of police development temporarily defeated, or a corrupt offspring of modern police, now happily discredited.

As a parallel development to the new bourgeois civilization arising in the towns in the nineteenth century (like street pavements, public elementary schools, railway companies, hospitals, and banking houses) modern police institutions contributed to the steady improvement in the quality of life and the standard of living. The fact that police in the nineteenth century was compatible with liberalism and the promotion of material well-being has given the modern police a relatively positive image compared to its eighteenth-century predecessors and its totalitarian rivals in our own time.[12] Indeed, the modern police was often seen as an instrument of progress, consistent with the idea of free enterprise, academic freedom, and constitutional protection against arbitrary government. Its basic principles may be summed up as follows:

1. Police must operate on a legal basis only and prosecute suspects solely on objective (material) evidence.
2. Police should regulate the behavior of individual persons rather than of collective groups and should not use terroristic methods, like hostage taking.
3. Police must apply no more physical coercion than is absolutely necessary in any given situation. Torture to exact confessions is inadmissible.
4. Police serves the European state system by assuring the minimum of damage to civilian society during all the violent clashes – wars and revolutions – that inevitably accompany its perpetual movement toward improvement and reform.[13]

[11] David H. Bailey has also tried to define modern police by periodization, but his method of tracing the police styles of several countries individually backwards in time is bewildering and in the end inconclusive. David H. Bailey, "The Police and Political Development in Europe," in Charles Tilly, ed., *The Formation of National States in Western Europe* (Princeton, N.J., 1975). Brian Chapman's analytical essay, *Police State* (New York, 1970), comes closest to my attempt at imposing a structure on European police history through periodization and national differentiation in police styles. But although I owe Chapman a number of refined aperçus, which I acknowledge in footnotes, our nomenclature ("modern police," "police state") and our conclusions differ, presumably because Chapman's approach is more that of the political scientist analyzing forms of government, whereas mine approaches that of the diplomatic historian.

[12] "Experience has taught us that public security can be maintained only when authorities and inhabitants share a common agreement [Uebereinstimmung]." Merker, *Handbuch für Polizeybeamte*, Erster Abschnitt, paragraphs 16, 17. The Germans learned in two world wars the difficulty of policing hostile populations in conquered territories. André Siegfried, "Conférence d'ouverture du stage de l'A.M.F.A.," (faite en Sorbonne) (pamphlet used by French occupation forces in Germany, 1945, courtesy Louis Séverin.)

[13] The term "modern police" as explained here does not apply to the European colonial police in Africa or Asia in the nineteenth century, where the exploitative relationship of colonial masters to native inhabitants was frankly admitted. See, for example, Guy Fernand, *Les Indigènes fonctionnaires à Madagascar. Etude historique de législation et de politique coloniale* (Paris, 1939).

The territoriality of police jurisdiction came with the rise of the independent state at the end of the Middle Ages. It put an end to the universalist concept of justice, as it also superseded the idea of a justice founded on blood loyalty, vassalage, and clientage, and of punishment meted out as vendettas and public spectacles. In its place came criminal law and criminal procedure administered by the state, applicable exclusively inside the territory of the state, and serving the purpose of exalting state authority.[14] The exemption of foreign diplomats from the jurisdiction of territorial states was literally a matter of "the exception confirming the rule": It was deemed wrong to submit representatives of foreign countries to local laws precisely because the moral force of law was seen as founded on local historical tradition.[15]

The growth of the modern territorial state has been the subject of many scholarly treatises – some of them classics in historical literature, all of them too elaborate to present in this study. But one idea about the rise of territorial politics must be mentioned because it explains the different ways in which police ideas developed in the modern period in Western Europe and in Eastern Europe, with Germany and Austria uneasily poised between the two. The Western European states were generally smaller and more densely populated, with tightly knit social–political organizations resting on a pragmatic rationale of economic and administrative efficiency, and in perpetual need to defend their existence by participating in the exacting game of the balance of power. The Eastern European States consisted of geographical expanses with sparse populations, few towns, and poorly endowed with natural frontiers. Their societies were not bound by complicated ties of individual rivalry and mutual dependency. Danger of foreign subjugation came not from a decline in the solidarity of state and society, but more simply from the political mistakes, or the misfortune, of the rulers.

The Western development manifested itself for the first time in the life of the city-states of Renaissance Italy in the fifteenth century. A "hothouse phenomenon" according to Herbert Butterfield, these small states during their short and dramatic history developed in an exaggerated form the very same modern rationale for political behavior that we shall see in the larger nation states of late nineteenth-century Europe: tsarist Russia functioning like the personal tyranny of Milan, France like the republican state of Florence, and England like the commercial oligarchy of Venice.[16] Similarly Jacob Burckhardt has pointed to the "modern mentality" of the Renaissance states by stressing their secular thinking and their predilection to found authority on selfish manipulation and calculation – on too much manipulation and not enough ideological concern, perhaps, for the

---

[14] Michael R. Weisser, *Crime and Punishment in Early Modern Europe* (Hassocks, Sussex, 1979), pp. 24, 100–32.

[15] W. E. Beckett, "The Exercise of Criminal Jurisdiction over Foreigners," in *BYB* (1925), pp. 45, 51.

[16] Herbert Butterfield, lectures on the Renaissance delivered at Cambridge University, Lent term, 1950. See also Herbert Butterfield and Martin Wright, eds., *Diplomatic Investigations. Essays in the Theory of International Politics* (Cambridge, Mass., 1966), ch. 6.

small states, liable to swift extinction in one afternoon's unlucky military engagement had no chance to develop into communities founded on mutual loyalty.[17] Their peoples were no more than "simply a disciplined multitude of subjects" policed by outside mercenaries "deaf to the cry of misery and careless of the ban of the Church."[18] The rulers, in turn, insecure because of the narrow territory they held, fearful of assassination from one day to the next, were inclined to be tyrannical, suspicious, and domineering, more given to instill awe than respect among their subjects by extravagant displays of luxury and symbols of reverence. Niccolò Machiavelli's advice in *The Prince* (1513) on how to survive as the ruler of a newly acquired state can serve as a police manual only for ill-policed, if not for unpoliced, territories. If the modern police has rejected despotism, this is because despotism is but a short-term method of ruling.

The Italian city-states were suboptimal as military and as police units and quickly succumbed toward the end of the fifteenth century due to the onset of economic decline, the revolt of the German princes against Rome, and the political and military encroachments of France and Spain. They succumbed also because, as Eduard Fueter has explained so well, the model of the Italian city-state had migrated north out of the narrow land neck of Italy across the Alps to the valleys of Switzerland, where the idea flourished much better under the protection of Alpine mountains and patriarchal cantonal democracy.[19] In the sixteenth century it was the Swiss cantons but not yet the vaster territory of the French kingdom which were optimal for the development of effective defense and police control. The cantons supervised their people so well that outsiders could not bypass them to recruit local men for mercenary service. The Swiss pikemen whom the cantons hired out to foreign princes were furthermore good because the effective police order in the Alpine valleys made possible systematic recruitment and standardized training. Larger states than the Swiss cantons had less effective communal control and could not match the Swiss troops either in drill or in discipline. Finally, Switzerland also benefited politically from the Protestant revolt against papal power. Martin Luther's "Here I stand" version of the police principle of right by emergency (force majeure) was a challenge to all like-minded men to accept the imperious demand of the hour and rise against prescribed law and prescribed doctrine. It was morally a stronger political claim of authority than what a Renaissance tyrant could produce.

However the Swiss advantage was broken with the coming of heavy artillery and heavy fortifications designed for siege campaigns. The new military technology of the seventeenth century favored countries large and wealthy enough to afford long-term investments in costly arms production and the training of military architects. Geographically, a successful state henceforth also needed a large

[17] Jacob Burckhardt, *The Civilization of the Renaissance in Italy* (Oxford, 1945), pp. 2ff.
[18] Ibid., p. 3.
[19] Eduard Fueter, *Geschichte des europäischen Staatensystems von 1942 bis 1559* (Munich, 1919), pp. 30ff., 231–8.

hinterland to support its military frontier with agricultural produce and man-power. Finally, it needed a domestic police order sophisticated enough to make it unnecessary for military resources to be squandered on internal fortifications.[20] All these conditions explain the rapid rise of France under Louis XIII and Louis XIV to the foremost position among the powers of Europe. And having staked out the territorial limits that France was to claim as her rightful domain to the twentieth century, the French wars of 1668 to 1701 must then be regarded as border wars along France's only vulnerable frontier facing the Lowlands, designed less to expand French territory into the Germanic Rhineland than to prod her eastern neighbors into matching France's accomplishment with comparable efforts at state building. By promoting the development of Brandenburg–Prussia into a disciplined state of soldiers and bureaucrats, the French improved their own state security while contributing to the expansion of the modern state system eastward into the vast plain of Central Europe.

During this same period from the fifteenth to the seventeenth centuries the large territories east of the Elbe river suffered from the liability of poor communications, economic stagnation, and the absence of sufficient challenge either from home or from abroad to construct efficient political state machines. Stanislaw Andrzejewski has argued that as late as the eighteenth century geography militated against the provision of the people in Eastern Europe with the sinews of territorial police states.[21] The political order in the East relied on the imposition of religious orthodoxy on a submissive peasantry, on dynastic alliances and on military campaigns, which military campaigns however resembled punitive expeditions into no-man's-land more than modern conquests followed by permanent subjugation. Because of the technical difficulty of holding and administering the vast stretches of sparsely populated territory of Poland and West Russia, a prince was easily tempted to accept the aid of *fortuna* (i.e., a profitable marriage alliance, a chance victory on the battlefield) to enlarge his domain without regard to the strategic usefulness of his acquisition for the consolidation of his state. Jerry-built, his empire was liable to collapse under the impact of later and unforeseen circumstances. The social chaos produced when whole regions changed hands time and again because of the chance outcome of military engagements was dramatically demonstrated in the agonizing experience of Germany during the Thirty Years' War. "Peace," Roland Bainton wrote a few years ago about the wars of religion in Europe, "can exist only between smaller well-governed entities."[22]

Given the very different forms of state building in Eastern Europe, the rise of Russian power in the eighteenth century owed much to the fortuitous decline of Sweden and Turkey, the inefficiency of the Polish state, the unbridled ambition of

[20] Gustav Roloff, "Hauptstadt und Staat in Frankreich," in Friedrich-Meinecke-Institut, *Das Hauptstadtproblem in der Geschichte* (Tübingen, 1952), pp. 249–65.

[21] Stanislaw Andrzejewski, *Military Organisation and Society* (London, 1954), p. 38.

[22] Roland H. Bainton, "The Responsibility of Power according to Erasmus of Rotterdam," in Leonard Krieger and Fritz Stern, eds., *The Responsibility of Power* (Garden City, N.J., 1967), pp. 56–7.

Peter the Great, and to his empire's remoteness at the eastern periphery of the European state system. The Austrian Empire also benefited from the decline of Turkey after its last attempt to storm Vienna in 1683. Like Russia, too vast and also too varied in language, culture, and religion for effective central government, the Austrian monarchy had the advantage, however, of possessing in Central Europe smaller autonomous regions with excellent natural frontiers and held together by advanced and homogeneous cultural ties. Neighboring Brandenburg–Prussia by contrast was poor in natural resources and its territorial possessions were dangerously scattered. That this small state should successfully challenge the house of Habsburg for the control of Central Europe in the coming century was to a large extent the result of historical accidents: French military and economic assistance, a victory over Sweden at the battle of Fehrbellin (1675), and between 1640 and 1786 a succession of four hardworking monarchs.

The period when the whole Continent became subject to the rule of one interlocking balance of power – following Napoleon's campaign to Moscow in 1812, and the entry of Russian cossack troops in Paris two years later – coincides with the rise of what we call "the modern police" in Europe. Over the decades they became as indispensable for the functioning of the international state system as the standing armies and navies and as necessary as the permanent diplomatic missions in all the capitals of Europe. No international treaty could be concluded unless all the signatory parties were reasonably secure at home, for, as William Pitt the Younger said about the French Directory in 1799: "What trust can one place in a government which is at the mercy of a pistol shot?"[23]

To be sure, the balance of power assumed of its member states no more than material effectiveness in an overall military competition for survival. International law, which was the theoretical expression of this system, offered, in essence, no higher justification for the individual state than its capacity to maintain itself by its own strength. Indeed, for the balance of power to work as it should, no bonds should be formed between states that were not subject to immediate revision given a change in the political situation. Each state presumably was to be ruled by men constantly watching out for their country's best interest and ready to switch its foreign alignments from one day to the next with the same lack of scruples as a stockbroker playing for high stakes.[24]

This left the European state system with one higher purpose to serve. To divide Europe into smaller territories was to make possible the administration of justice and the promotion of human welfare in accordance with the particular needs and inclinations of their local inhabitants. The European state system could be said to

---

[23] Jean Galtier-Boissière, *Mysteries of the French Secret Police* (London, 1938), p. 73. It is remarkable that police power is little mentioned in the classical texts of the modern law of nations, except indirectly in regard to the vicarious responsibility of states for the actions of their officials; the obligation to assist one another in the pursuit of fugitive criminals; the right to grant asylum (to avoid having to judge the merits of another government's demand for the extradition of a political dissenter); and in reference to the conduct of war.

[24] David Hume, "Of the Balance of Power," in his *Theory of Politics* (New York, 1951), pp. 190–220.

make possible a higher level of moral community *within the territory of each single state* by offering to each of them a reasonable measure of safety against outside interference in their internal affairs; in other words, in the making of their domestic police condition. When Jean-Jacques Rousseau tried to advance the system of the balance of power as the foundation of his project for *Perpetual Peace* (1765), he was hard pressed to endorse it with his customary wit and eloquence.[25] Compared to his more famous treatise on *The Social Contract* (1762), Rousseau's argument on behalf of the balance of power was weak. Rousseau instinctively sensed the dynamic quality of domestic politics over foreign affairs in the approaching age of democracy. His concept of the "general will" portrays a moment of perfect police control founded on an absolute consensus beyond anything ever imagined by Machiavelli, and unattainable in the relations between the states who made up the European system in the modern period.

We shall in Chapter 1 describe the national police styles of five states with particular reference to their response to revolutionary disturbances in the early nineteenth century. The five states are the Austrian Empire, Switzerland, France, Prussia, and tsarist Russia. Our comment on Russia is the briefest of all, because Russia, strictly speaking, was not served by modern police. But because Russian political police played an important role in international relations during the late nineteenth century, we want to remark on tsarist Russia's image in the West as a police power. Another special case is Prussia (later Germany), a military state really, whose most interesting role in the history of the European state system is its police work in occupied territory during the wars of 1870, 1914, and 1939. In this chapter we limit ourselves to a description of Prussia's preoccupation with readiness for war, culminating in the Prussian invasion of Alsace in 1870. However, because for a short time in the twentieth century Prussia's police strategy resembled that of France under its constitutional monarchy, we use our discussion of the French police between 1815 and 1848 to point to some similarities with the police of Weimar Germany.

In Chapter 2, we follow the maneuvers of France, Germany, and Russia in the period between the end of the Franco-Prussian War of 1870–71 and the onset of a paralyzing crisis in the balance of power in the 1890s, the first signs of the European-wide conflict that was still to come. In this chapter we explain how France recovered from its defeat in 1871 with the help of its special police. Switzerland also began to reassess its role in the European state system in response to the shift of the balance-of-power's center of gravity from the West to Central and East Central Europe and because of the growing radicalism of the revolutionaries who came to seek refuge on Swiss territory.

Chapter 3 describes the modern police caught in the whirlpool of the European-wide crisis at the turn of the century, when the idea of a future international police system first arose, intent to safeguard Europe against chaos as

---

[25] Jean-Jacques Rousseau, *A Project of International Peace*, trans. by Edith M. Nuttall (London, 1927), pp. 27–9.

its multinational state system neared the end of its usefulness. The opportunity for experimenting with international police collaboration arose in conjunction with new problems such as international crime and anarchism and the danger of revolution in Russia.

It was not to be. Instead, as we see in Chapter 4, the police in all European countries were given the job to prepare their nations for total mobilization. It ends with the police of Western Europe at the end of four years of war trying to establish a common front against Bolshevik subversion from Leninist Russia.

Chapter 5 deals with the rise of Nazism in Germany as the most terrible challenge to its integrity yet faced by the modern police. There is no attempt here to tell the story of the Holocaust, which is so much better covered in specialized monographs and in the memoirs of survivors; instead we seek to understand why officials of modern police forces in Europe permitted themselves to become associated with totalitarian institutions either through direct participation or indirect collaboration. Were they, we ask, even then covered by the duty of the modern police, to provide civilian society with protection as far as is possible against the destructive forces of wars and revolutions?

The Epilogue is a comment on, rather than a detailed study of, the almost half century since the end of the Second World War. It attempts to show why we should review modern police systems in Europe over the past one hundred and fifty years, the better to anticipate the many problems we face on a global scale in the century to come.

Police terminology

Security police: political police

Security police consists chiefly of the political police, also known as the high police, secret police, or simply, for example in Austria, as state police. Its task is to protect the political state (often identified with the regime) against dangers from within. In quiet times political police work often requires nothing more sinister than routine scanning of newspaper editorials, censoring books and theatrical plays, and watching electoral meetings but in times of trouble the political police has resorted to extralegal preventive measures on the assumption that the safety of the state has absolute priority over the rights of the individual. Of particular importance in the nineteenth century was the political police of France (the *police spéciale*) and of Russia (mainly the foreign operations of the Third Section and the Okhrana), while Switzerland established a political police in 1889 only reluctantly and then to deal mainly with the foreign revolutionaries on its territory.

While political police usually operates in plain clothes and uses methods resembling those of the ordinary detective force, following 1848 every country stationed uniformed police brigades in its principal cities to be prepared for political riots and insurrections.

Order police or low police: Precinct, administrative, and criminal police

Officials who go on street patrol are the mainstay of order police. Their work is supplemented by the officials performing routine administrative tasks like registering inhabitants and licensing commercial establishments inside local precinct stations (administrative police). Order police officials also inspect factory sites and public fairs, conduct the first inquiries at the scene of an accident or a crime, and since the turn of the century deal with the growing volume of road traffic. The criminal police (also called judicial police or detective force) deals with common crimes, mainly in the towns. All branches of the order police also serve as the eyes and ears of the government to alert it to local developments that can affect general security.

At the end of the nineteenth century, the modern police, with all its liberal connotations, found its mainstay in countries where the low police played an important role in domestic security. Switzerland remained a democracy because her political police was really no more than an aliens police and did not infringe on the liberties of native Swiss citizens. In France, Georges Clemenceau in 1907 called the detective service the only police that a true democracy should require.[26]

The two designations, criminology and criminalistics, have been used varyingly in professional literature. In this book "criminology" refers to the scientific study of criminal behavior and "criminalistics" to the science of combating crime.

Other branches of police

The gendarmerie is rural police, in the past mounted on horseback, today moving on motorcycles and trucks, with a certain military capacity to use against mass disorders. Generally the gendarmerie is subordinate to the ministry of war but for operational purposes it is placed at the disposal of the ministry of interior. Its importance was reduced in the last hundred years by the creation of additional police forces for guarding frontiers, railway installations, airports, and coastal waters.

Private police refers to gamekeepers on landed estates, company police, or private detective agencies. They have not played a role in the involvement of police with the European state system but their existence has been taken as a sign of a low level of government surveillance. In most countries (as, for example, in the United States) this may be taken as a cause for public relief; in nineteenth-century Russia the "self-justice" (*samosud*) practiced by peasants after emancipation to curb thievery in the countryside was a dangerous sign of the tsarist regime's incompetence as the guardian of civil order.

Espionage and counter-espionage belong to the police functions of the European countries because the work they do is vital to the security of their states. In nineteenth-century Russia and Austria, foreign espionage was carried out by the

[26] Jean-Marc Berlière, "La guerre des polices," in *L'Histoire*, no. 117 (Dec. 1988), p. 40.

political police itself, and also in France, where the special police did much intelligence gathering outside France.

Police regimes and police situation

Self-police. There are three principal styles of police authority: (1) coercive police, like the French *dragonnades* against Protestants who refused to reconvert to the Roman Catholic faith in the 1680s; (2) welfare police, much favored in the eighteenth century by benevolent despots though in practice equally harsh on the population, and (3) self-police. Of these three, only the last one requires some elaboration because it best represented what "modern police" aspired to achieve: a willing acceptance of police rule by a community that understands and endorses its mission. Self-police is often associated with "democracy," though what a community wishes is not necessarily always "democratic." Self-police is usually found in smaller localities or in countries with very strong national cohesion, like Spain. The ability of a government to fall back on the assistance of civilians for police work plays an important role in emergencies. Detectives might appeal to local residents in a town for leads to solve a crime; in a national crisis the entire people might be asked to form civil-defense teams.

Police states. Technically speaking, every state has a police. But not every state is called a police state. Colloquially the designation police state has the pejorative meaning of country under arbitrary police rule, unchecked by law and exempt from any accountability to the public. For the purpose of this study, however, the term police state is more usefully understood as the alternative to a state ruled along military conceptions. It designates the predominant tendency of a given state to rely on order enforced through good information, intellectual persuasion, and intervention with the behavior of single individuals as opposed to massive punitive force. A police state usually is considered more sophisticated than a military state. The designation "police state" was worn with pride in the eighteenth century by France, Austria, and Russia, Europe's three foremost police states.

Police situations. A police state may or may not enjoy what we call a "well-policed situation" because there are efficient and inefficient police states. Historically the establishment of such well-policed situations from a situation of chaos has mostly fallen on soldiers. States assumed the form of military regimes during the time it took to consolidate a territory and bring it under effective control. Once civil order achieved, the military gave way to the police which then perpetuated the new order through daily supervision and periodic corrective measures or preventive interventions. It is true the conversion from military rule to civil (or police) rule has often been difficult to bring about. A well-policed situation, moreover, can never be expected to remain so indefinitely. It is always prone to become troubled and effective policing calls for endless building and rebuilding of well-policed situations.

Police other than national public security forces

Parallel-police and counter-police. Police power depends on the existence of a measure of resistance from the society. Sometimes the police can even find itself in need to help such a resistance to organize itself (for example the workers' unions sponsored in the 1890s by the police in Moscow and St. Petersburg), in other words, help the inhabitants to develop some policing power of their own with which to counter the power of the state. If this opposition force duplicates the efforts of the public police, we call it parallel police. If it is used against, or in rivalry to, the police, we call it counter-police. Russian revolutionaries in exile organized a counter-police to protect themselves against the tsarist Okhrana agents. After the Second World War, the Soviet MGB performed the role of parallel police to the security services of the people's democracies in Eastern Europe.

International police. The most obvious example of non-national police work is, of course, international police work. Many countries quietly conducted police actions abroad and in turn suffered some police actions by foreign governments on their territory – clandestinely, if possible, or disguised as part of consular activities. In the twentieth century this practice has become increasingly overt, in particular in regard to combating international terrorism. Three different kinds of international police work now exist:

1. Joint intervention by the armed forces of several countries in the police situation of a third country without resorting to war. This method was much advocated by the Holy Alliance of 1815; by the end of the century it was chiefly used by the European powers against non-European countries like China during the Boxer War.
2. International surveillance and guard duty in potential trouble spots, for example the dispatch of London bobbies to secure order at the Saar referendum in 1935. To this we also count the joint control of the navigable portion of the Danube after 1856, and the health police practiced by the consuls of the great powers in the port of Alexandria after 1881.
3. Unofficial police activities outside the national territory with or without the permission of the governments concerned: The best known instances are the collaboration of French and Russian police in the time of the Dual Alliance from the 1890s to the First World War, and in the 1930s the policing of Reich Germans living abroad through the foreign branch of the Nazi Party. Espionage activities also belong to this category, combated in each country by counter-intelligence, but recognized under international law as belonging to international usage.

Among international revolutionary secret societies in the nineteenth century the existence of an "international police" organization to suppress them was recurrently denounced as an affront to the law of nations. A French police spy in

Geneva reported to his superior in 1884, that "the Russian Nihilists complain that an agent of the International Police has taken the liberty of stealing letters from their mail boxes outside their houses."[27]

International bodies created to deal with certain European-wide problems were mostly endowed with a limited police authority. The international postal service has the power to investigate mail thefts without assistance from the public police, and the International Red Cross Society can impose some emergency rules in disaster areas. In the twentieth century the International Criminal Police Commission and its successor, Interpol, and the peacekeeping forces of the United Nations are in fact performing police duties.

Police methods

Divide and rule

To divide the inhabitants into suitable compartments for better control and manipulation the police can follow a number of different criteria, separating them by locality, social provenance, occupation, wealth, religion, age, sex, race, and so on. There are, however, some rules to the method of dividing a society into compartments which we must note here:

There must be enough differences in the particular rights and duties of every group, so as to create a disparity, if not a scale of, desirability between them. Unless the members of the various groups are all to some extent dissatisfied with their lot, or apprehensive about not being able to hold their current place in society, the police is deprived of that social ferment which, through manipulation, produces its authority. Lacking everything else it may be necessary to create an artificial rivalry in society. A roomful of children are easier to control if they are given a ball and taught the rules of soccer: the delight of this competitive game will make the children positively want an umpire to police them.

Membership in his or her particular group must be linked to a personal attribute which the individual cannot discard, or can alter only with much effort and at great sacrifice. A good Lutheran, seeking spiritual salvation, will not lightly renounce his faith; an illiterate man cannot deliver a Cambridge lecture because learning cannot be faked; and an African *évolué* will not pass as a metropolitan Frenchman because skin color is permanent.

At the same time the government's hold over subjects so trapped in their particular enclave, will be enormously enhanced if a slim chance always remains open to anyone who very badly wants to evade the strictures of his or her social standing. Hermann Göring's announcement, "I decide who is a Jew!" was a clever bid for yet more policing power. (A Russian court favorite who asked Nicholas I to "make him a German" was, perhaps unwisely, turned down.)

[27] Report by agent "Loth," Geneva, 14 Nov. 1884, in APP (Paris), Carton B A/196, "Le socialisme en Russie de 1872 à 1889."

The rules dividing the society into different groups must periodically be revised, and sometimes completely overhauled, to prevent the social stagnation that comes from perfunctory obedience and general indifference. (A German police handbook advised that police decrees should be of short duration, "to keep police rules from going stale" (zwecks Frischhaltung des Polizeirechtes).)[28] Tsarist Russia under Alexander III and Nicholas II suffered from the complacent self-indulgence of the privileged, the apathy of the unfavored multitude, and the dull resentment of the police by everyone.

Fear of the police's secrecy

Hiding the mechanism of its power from public view is surely one of the chief sources of the police's influence; only in the twentieth century have public memorials been put up for police heroes and have police detachments marched in festive parades. In 1851 the police instructions for the canton of Zurich laid down in all candor the following:

> The police must be careful to cover up all its internal activities. No one must be clear as to the real extent of its power and influence. It is in the interest of the police to appear powerful even where it knows itself to be weak. Operations that turn out successful must be used to define the police's mission so as to advertise its effectiveness. Spectators among the public should at all times be kept from discovering the internal workings of the police machine. The police must never show feverish activity [*zappelnde Geschäftigkeit*] which is liable to attract public attention and watchfulness. Loud and hasty activity on the part of police personnel wastes time and energy and attracts crowds of observers.[29]

Violence and deceit justified by "force majeure"

The third method that we may call inherent to the definition of modern police is the use of violence and subterfuge against disturbers of domestic public peace. However, violence, as Hannah Arendt has told us, takes two forms: there is the actual infliction of physical punishment, and there is the threat of using such punishment. Only the latter, Arendt tells us, can be said to contain the seeds of a future political understanding between hostile parties and consequently belongs to the normal functions of police. Ongoing combat is devoid of a spiritual nexus between the contestants.[30]

The police has used not only violence but also deception in what it claimed was a situation of dire need ("force majeure") when subsequent investigations found its tactic ill-conceived or illegal. The following very frank statement on the police's right to proceed in an emergency with nearly any method that promises results is again taken from the police instructions of Zurich in 1851:

[28] Dr. Erich Klausener, et al., *Das Polizeiverwaltungsgesetz vom 1. Juni 1931* (Berlin, 1931) pp. vii–ix.
[29] *Kurze Anleitung im practischen Polizeidienst* (Zurich, 1 May 1851), pp. 3–4.
[30] Hannah Arendt, *On Violence* (New York, 1969), p. 37.

The defense of the country and of the society's welfare may call for the use of otherwise reprehensible means by the police. The police must discover all the roads travelled by vice and crime. In the face of danger all is permitted: no price is too high when the state, the fatherland, or the public weal are threatened by destruction or perdition.

The police instruction did admit that "dubious means should be applied only if the goal cannot be attained with forthright methods. Meticulous and conscientious calculation as to what to do must come before the police resorts to ruses and dissimulation." It nevertheless went on:

Flattery, cunning and deception, and exploiting other people's treason and cowardice are admittedly disreputable means. But they are justified against the enemies of the public good. Since practice has taught us that the most refined and dangerous criminal plots can only be uncovered with the help of bad people, there can be no more scruples about catching thieves with thieves. It is not despicable for the police to use crooks to learn the truth.[31]

The fourth and final method of modern police that needs to be mentioned is the reliance by the police on popular myths.

Myths

There are many historical antecedents to the modern development of the "single idea" on which the entire complicated police structure of a country might rest. The moral foundations of the Respublica Christiana was derived from the scriptures, Professor John Figgis once explained, so that the concept of divine rights of kings is ultimately responsible for what spiritual inducement to respect the law we still have in Western civilization.[32] Frantz Funck-Brentano, in turn, has told us of the elaborate spiritual edifice of the ancien regime, whose *ordre fondamental* depended on the punctilious fulfilment of symbolic etiquette and ritualistic procedures, with His Most Christian Majesty himself the prisoner of its elaborate machinery.[33] So important was the maintenance of this myth that the abortive attempt of a disgruntled lacquai to knife Louis XV in 1757 prompted religious ceremonials of repentance as far away as Eastern Europe.[34]

Wilhelm Reich, the psychologist, attributed Fascism to the self-deception of bourgeois morality – self-enforced a thousand and a million times over by the private fears of every inhabitant that his thoughts were not pure. The culprit, to his mind, was the bourgeois moral code of the nineteenth century, a gigantic house of cards, magnificent but vulnerable to the criticism of the Freudian

---

[31] *Kurze Anleitung im practischen Polizeidienst*, p. 5.
[32] John Figgis, *The Divine Right of Kings* (Cambridge, 1914).
[33] Frantz Funck-Brentano, *L'Ancienne France. Le roi* (5th ed., Paris, 1913), passim.
[34] Philip J. Stead, *The Police of France* (New York, 1983), pp. 24–31; and Pierre Rétat, ed. *L'Attentat de Damiens. Discours sur l'évènement au XVIIIe siècle* (Paris, 1979), p. 110.

iconoclast.[35] Victorian sexual taboos were a major source of that bad conscience that makes individuals so acutely policeable, a powerful reason for every bourgeois's obsessive concern with reputation and good name. Yet the same "myth" also gave rise to sexual blackmail, a very "bourgeois" crime used not only for private gain but also for political power, as illustrated by the way Hitler used it to defame the Jews and to destroy the leader of the S.A. and the Wehrmacht in the 1930s. The Nazis resorted to ceaseless improvisations to tap every hidden mental disposition in the German people's collective psyche that could be used to shore up their contention that Hitler and National Socialism represented Germany's deepest wishes until, with the outbreak of war and its escalation into mass destruction, the illusion was broken in 1945.

[35] Wilhelm Reich, *The Mass Psychology of Fascism*, trans. by Vincent R. Carfagno (New York, 1970), ch. 1.

1

Five national police styles in response to popular unrest in the nineteenth century

The Austrian police: The Metternich system and its decline after 1848

General remarks

Austria's performance in the nineteenth century came closest to serving a perceived need for a European-wide police order. All the other countries followed their own national interest, especially after the revolutionary year 1848 when the Concert of Europe was replaced by an increasingly bellicose confrontation between the great powers. By contrast, the police control imposed by Metternich on the German Confederation after the murder of the Russian state councillor, August von Kotzebue, in 1819, was the forerunner of many more Austrian sponsored attempts at building bridges between the police authorities of the sovereign states of Europe.

With Austrian police at the height of its European influence in the immediate post-Napoleonic period, it is no wonder that Austrian police – like the police of France – to this day take pride in the length of its historical tradition, including its attainments under absolutist rule. The Hofpolizeistelle in Vienna, which kept the Habsburg rulers directly informed of daily police developments until 1848, dated back to the police ministry of Count Johann Anton von Pergen in 1793. Feudal titles like *Hofrat* for high police officials were continued into the republican era, as were (at least until the 1920s) the injunctions to the Austrian policeman to defend the good name of the monarchy and to give "obedience to his legitimate ruler."[1]

---

[1] See the objection of the Austrian chancellery in 1937 to the treaty allowing Czechoslovak officials access to police files dating from the imperial period, mentioned in Chapter 5, and the report of the Disziplinarkommission at the Polizei-Direktion Vienna on the trial of Oberwachtmeister A. of Abteilung Mariahilf "wegen Vergehens gegen den Paragraphen 21 der D.P.," 15 July 1927. Paragraph 21 of the *Dienst-Pragmatik* begins: "Der Beamte ist verpflichtet, dem Kaiser treu und gehorsam zu sein und die Staatsgrundgesetze sowie die anderen Gesetze unverbrüchlich zu beobachten." Document available in AVA (Vienna), S. D. Parl. Klub/67, folder 43: "1927 Polizei." Also Karl Springer (Wirklicher Hofrat und Polizeidirektor), *Die österreichische Polizei. Eine theoretische Untersuchung* (Hamburg, 1961), passim.

The Austrian police took pride in the number of police officials who held advanced law degrees and carried the designation *Konzeptsbeamten.*[2] Perhaps the high level of education of its leading officials was meant to compensate for the fundamentally undemocratic disposition of Austrian police before 1945. As in tsarist Russia, the Austrian low police was less sophisticated than the high police, but both were equally authoritarian. Ordinary civilians had no legal recourse against a police order.[3] In the 1850s, civilians who showed disrespect to the ruling house could still be punished by police with physical beatings. The police could also summon any member of the public it pleased for questioning about happenings in a neighborhood.[4] Candidates for police service needed testimonials of good character from teachers and priests, but confidence between policemen and members of the public was not encouraged.

Metternich's supranational police system should not only be contrasted to Bismarck's *realpolitik* in the 1860s – every country for itself, with only the fortunes of war to regulate their relations – but also to Russian police behavior under Alexander I and Nicholas I. Acting more often than not as a "Glaubenspolizei"[5] to defend the principle of legitimate monarchy, Metternich's political police worked for ideological compatibility throughout Europe, which (in a more democratic version) to this day is understood as the prerequisite for international police collaboration. Russian police agents went regularly on official missions to the West since the early 1830s, but always in defense of the Russian Empire's interests alone, never on behalf of a larger European cause, as did Austrian agents.[6]

The Central Investigations Commission, 1819–29

The German confederation's Central Investigations Commission (Central-Untersuchungs-Commission, or CUC) was established by decision of the Federal Diet on 20 September 1819. Seven out of thirty-nine federal states were chosen by the Diet to appoint the members of the CUC, whose seat was to be at Mainz.

---

[2] Dr. Karl Hauss, "Der Polizeijurist in Oesterreich und sein Nachwuchs," in *Oeffentliche Sicherheit* (Vienna), 12. Jhg., Nr. 2 (Feb. 1932), p. 1. Before the First World War, "Konzeptsbeamte" were listed as embracing Polizeipräsidenten (Rangklasse IV), Polizeidirektoren (V or VI), Hofräte (V), Oberpolizeiräte (VI), Polizeiräte (VII), Polizeioberkommissare (VIII), Polizeikommissare (IX), Polizeikonzipisten (X), and Polizeikonzeptspraktikanten (no rank). See "Verzeichnis der in Oesterreich bestehenden besonderen landesfürstlichen Polizeibehörden" (March, 1914), in HHStA (Vienna), F52, Karton 20: "Beschwerden 1896–1918," folder: *Publikationswesen Marokko.*

[3] Johann Pezzl, as quoted in Viktor Bibl, *Die wiener Polizei. Eine kulturhistorische Studie* (Leipzig, 1927), pp. 253–4.

[4] "Every subject is obliged to comply with the summons to such interrogations and to provide the information that is requested of him." Josef Ullrich, *Grundzüge des österreichischen Polizeirechtes* (Prague, 1881), p. 7.

[5] Bibl, *Die wiener Polizei,* as reviewed in "Die Polizei der Habsburger. Aus der Geschichte der Wiener Polizei," in *Arbeiter Zeitung,* 25 Dec. 1926.

[6] For police surveillance at the Congress of Vienna, see August Fournier, *Die Geheimpolizei auf dem Wiener Kongress. Eine Auswahl aus ihren Papieren* (Vienna, 1913). On Russian agents in Europe, Sidney Monas, *The Third Section. Police and Society in Russia under Nicholas I* (Cambridge, Mass., 1961), p. 232.

Though they were to study in detail several hundred political cases of the last ten years (among them the murder on 23 March 1819 of August von Kotzebue, the popular playwright who also held the title of Russian state councillor), they were to leave all judicial action against individual persons to the appropriate authorities of the German states. Their chief mission was to report on the overall unrest in Germany since the Napoleonic occupation (1806–14) by comparing and analyzing the many acts of subversion in recent years.[7]

As one of the earliest modern attempts at joint political policing by separate state governments, the CUC suffered from all the weaknesses of an experimental undertaking: lack of self-assurance, improvisation, a tendency to exaggerate its achievements and at the same time to shirk ultimate responsibility. But German *Kleinstaaterei* and some personal wrangling aside, the CUC acquitted itself surprisingly well. It demonstrated a remarkable perspicacity and open-mindedness.

We do not have the record of the terms of appointment for the seven CUC commissioners, but we do have the text of the terms of employment for the secretaries and clerks (*Aktuare*) on the staff of the CUC.[8] We find to our surprise that the secretaries were not required to take an oath of allegiance to the Confederation or to the ruling houses of the Confederate states, and that the authorities also showed great tolerance and forgiveness toward clerks who belonged to clandestine political clubs so long as such connections were renounced forthwith. Equally remarkable was the Commission's dispassionate understanding of "revolutionary activities," which were simply defined as: "Efforts . . . whose intentions it is to produce from below and in violation of existing laws changes in the established constitution contrary to the will of the governments or at least without their participation."[9]

One of the first tasks the commissioners set themselves was to discover the character and the motives of the men who were engaged in revolutionary work. Here their judgment ranged from an almost clinical analysis of the psychology of Carl Sand, the murderer of Kotzebue, to an admission of implicit admiration for the idealism and courage of the philosopher Johann Gottlieb Fichte. But while Sand's case evoked at best the commissioners' pity for a young life wasted,[10] the revolutionary career of Fichte was recounted in a tone bordering on frank admiration. Professor Fichte, the CUC reported, had arrived in Berlin from Königsberg in 1808 to deliver his "Reden an die deutsche Nation" to a large and mixed audi-

---

[7] "Bericht der Central-Untersuchungs-Commission über die gesammten Resultate der bisherigen Untersuchungen" (Mainz, 1826), p. 7, available in HHStA (Vienna), Deutsche Akten alte Reihe 120, alt 47 d 1–3.

[8] Protokoll der Untersuchungs Commission, III. Sitzung, Mainz, 15 Nov. 1819, in ibid., 103 alt 40.

[9] Ibid., vol. 1, p. 3. "Total Uebersicht der gesammten Resultate der Central-Untersuchungen zu Mainz," Ite Periode, Iter Band. Hereafter cited as "Total-Uebersicht."

[10] Ibid., vol. 3, pp. 1131–4. Concerning Sand's character: "Unter dem Einflusse verzärtelnder Schwärmerei erzogen . . . und von Kindheit auf gewöhnt, . . . die erste Autorität, die sich ihm bei dem Eintritte in's Leben in der Person seines Vaters entgegenstellte, als ihn und seine Gefühle zu begreifen unfähig gering zu achten. . . ."

ence at the university: "These addresses could not but move and excite his lis-
teners and his readers at that time, so noble was the power of their ideas, so
forceful their language, and so impressive the speaker's courage as he stood up in
public under the eyes of the foreign conqueror."[11]

Carl Sand and Johann Gottlieb Fichte were of course two well-known figures
in the German revolutionary scene. As the commissioners turned to the examination of less prominent individuals (many of them students from the universities
of Tübingen, Heidelberg, and Giessen) their selection was determined by the
need to discover the political strategy of the German revolutionaries: How did
they intend to bring down the established authorities? What kind of government
would they put in place of the Confederation? How would they justify such a new
government and enlist the necessary support for it at home and abroad?

The answer arrived at by the CUC is of importance not only for our study of
Austria's police but also because it gives us a preliminary idea of the police problem in nineteenth-century Germany, which in turn influenced the police strategy
of the Prussian kingdom.

According to the CUC report of 1828, (a) the revolutionary pressures in Germany were almost exclusively intellectual in origin (there was scant mention of
economic or social distress); (b) the chance for a successful revolution in Germany
was expected to come in a national crisis originating from outside the Confederation and so beyond the power of any German authority; and (c) nothing definite
could be established about the new order that a German revolution might seek to
establish. Thus while most revolutionaries deplored Germany's partition into separate small states, many also doubted that the liberty and the unity they dreamt
of were truly realizable in Europe. "Believe me, my friend!" a criminal judge in
Dillenburg was quoted as having written to a friend about to leave for North
America, "many a good and free-minded man will yet follow you to the palm
forests of the New World. In Europe, humanity has lost its vitality through its
confinement in obsolete, rusty forms. I have no more hope for a new soaring of
the spirit and for powerful free actions in Europe."[12]

The CUC paid much attention to political movements that were spontaneously
formed during the Napoleonic invasion, each with a built-in discipline that gave
it the capacity to police itself: notably the gymnastic movement of Friedrich Ludwig Jahn in association with the *Kriegspolizei* (the war police) of Justus Gruner and
the *Tugendbund* (Society of Virtue).[13] "Vater Jahn" was the prototype of a potential
new kind of authority in Germany, the leader-by-popular-acclamation. He was
the inventor of the gymnastic movement which, in the words of the CUC, "won
so much prestige and importance under the name of gymnastic art [*Turnkunst*],"
not least because its membership included numerous state officials, army officers,
and university professors. The CUC had the names of 30 members, but assumed
that their total number in 1828 was around 140. What Jahn's plans were is not

---

[11] Ibid., vol. 1, pp. 37–8.   [12] Quoted in ibid., pp. 445–6.   [13] Ibid., vol. I, p. 70.

reported by the CUC, but inferences could be drawn from his connection to Justus Gruner. During the war years 1811–12 the Prussian secret state councillor, Justus Gruner (after 1815 Justus *von* Gruner), held the post of *Chef der Hohen Polizei* for all Prussia. Both men apparently tried to benefit from the other's organization: Gruner in 1811 tried to use the gymnasts as informers, and to this end joined the Charlottenburger Verein himself; Jahn wanted to keep Gruner in Berlin so he could have the assistance of his secret police. Moreover, Gruner, like Jahn, had become a *frondeur* because he violently disagreed with the Prussian king's decision in 1812 to join Napoleon's campaign against Russia. Gruner reentered Prussian service after Napoleon's defeat in 1815 to direct the Prussian political police in occupied Paris, and in 1816 he served briefly as Prussian minister to the Swiss Confederation.[14]

Neither Jahn nor Gruner (who died in 1820) posed a continuing threat to the German Confederation in the 1820s, yet the CUC saw what power a disciplined movement, like Jahn's gymnastic society, could wield when coupled with an intelligence service like Gruner's. The Sokol organizations in the second half of the nineteenth century, which, following Jahn's model, advanced the cause of Slav nationalism were to confirm the CUC's fears. The Sokols were to be followed by the Wandervogel movement and the political armies of young Fascists and Communists, who constituted a particularly dangerous revolutionary force after the First World War. The secret of the success of Jahn's *Turnerschaft* (and of the Nazi storm troopers and the SS one hundred years later) was their appeal to the principle of force majeure: the justification of self-arrogated police authority that insurgents can derive from a situation of emergency which they claim has arisen from circumstances beyond their control. In 1806 such an emergency existed because of the arrival of Napoleon's armies. In the 1920s Germany's national distress was blamed on the Peace of Versailles. Seeking a new legitimacy for political authority in the German Confederation, the young German nationalist rebels of the 1820s focused their attack on Germany's princes who, they charged, had incompetently exercised their right to make war.

The Tugendbund (founded in 1808) was particularly vociferous in its claim to the right to wage war against an external enemy, with or without an order from the sovereign prince. In the words of the Commission's report:

According to the testimonial of informed witnesses which we have in our files, the more violent members . . . demanded that [the Tugendbund] intervene directly in the administration of the state and incite the people to launch an attack against the enemy even if this is opposed by the government. . . . One member . . . called it 'the first practical example of the idea that the armed force of the state can also act independently [from the government] to accomplish ends which it is [legally] supposed to attain only under orders [*das*

[14] Wolfram Siemann, *"Deutschlands Ruhe, Sicherheit und Ordnung." Die Anfänge der politischen Polizei 1806–1866* (Tübingen, 1985), pp. 63–71; and Werner Knopp, "Berliner Stadtgeschichte am Beispiel des Polizeipräsidiums," in *Der Tagesspiegel* (24 Feb. 1985), pp. 52ff.

erste ausübende Beispiel der Lehre von eigenwilliger Erhebung der bewaffneten Gewalt für Zwecke, denen sie nur gehorchend dienen soll].[15]

Metternich's commissioners understood that spontaneous bursts of war enthusiasm emanating from the civilian society could create a new moral basis of political authority, challenging legitimate monarchy. Anticipating the coming of Carl Schmitt's doctrine of "Dezisionismus" in the twentieth century (which asserts that decisions over war and peace belong to the most intensely charged political actions and confer supreme authority to whoever can invest it with true existential meaning for the nation),[16] They warned that German nationalist leaders during the wars of liberation had in fact dreamt of a new form of government for Germany through popular dictatorship. "In Arndt's *Phantasien für ein zukünftiges Deutschland*," the commissioners wrote,

the idea of a dictator appears, who would assume supreme power during a general uprising under the title of *Ruhewart* [Peace Warden]. His would be the power to decide over life and death. − 'To you I shall show a man' − Arndt has God say − 'who will be just, bold, powerful, and fiery, who instills courage in the good and fear in the wicked and surpasses all others in strength and glory. Him you shall elect when he appears in your midst, and to him shall you swear allegiance as he, in turn, will hold fast to honor and loyalty.'[17]

Perhaps of greatest interest to us is the CUC's far-reaching explanation for the origin of the revolutionary disturbances in Germany as well as in Europe.

What has caused the changes in the European spirit [Gemüth] during approximately the last fifty years and the disposition to search for political innovation must be answered with reference to the discoveries made over the past three centuries in regard to the nature of politics and the means of wielding political power − also discoveries in the art of war, in the communication of ideas and their dissemination, and in the volume of metal used as monetary currency . . .[18]

The Commission's perspective (whose full text is several pages long) resembled in breadth a complete survey of Western civilization since the fifteenth century. Yet its political implications were unmistakable: (a) No police authority in Germany could be expected to control forces engendered throughout Europe by historical changes dating back several centuries; and (b) whatever in the future might be done to harness these forces to the cause of orderly progress would require the effort of more than one country's police, in other words would require some sort of international police collaboration.

---

[15] "Total Uebersicht," vol. I, p. 55.
[16] See Carl Schmitt, *Nationalsozialismus und Völkerrecht* (Berlin, 1927); and Hans Krupa, *Carl Schmitts Theorie des "Politischen"* (Leipzig, 1927).
[17] "Total Uebersicht," vol. I, pp. 175–6. For another example of an appeal for a German dictator, see idem., pp. 43, 233–4, 237–8. On the other hand, as Otto Pflanze said about Bismarck's ethics: "The possession of an active conscience, grounded in religious faith, is never a sufficient substitute for legal and institutional checks on the use of power." Otto Pflanze, *Bismarck and the Development of Germany* (Princeton, N.J., 1963), p. 14.
[18] "Total Uebersicht," vol. I, pp. 14–16.

Austria's response to the Revolution of 1848

It is difficult to overestimate the impact of the revolutionary year 1848 on the relationship of the European states as police powers. For a good part of that year over half of them were paralyzed by an unprecedented outburst of civil disobedience in dozens of major towns. What happened shocked all the cabinets of Europe into a new awareness of the importance of the police. Nearly every country reinforced its police during the next two decades. And yet, no country's domestic peace could henceforth be fully assured by its own security forces. The unrest had swept across the Continent from city to city in a matter of only days and weeks without stopping at state frontiers or slowing down in the rural regions.[19] The revolutionary message was carried by the new railways and telegraphs, by propaganda leaflets from all parts of Europe, and it fed on the widespread discontent since the end of the Napoleonic wars over residual absolutist rule, growing factory exploitation, and unfulfilled dreams of nationhood. Though the old order was largely restored by 1849, nobody believed that the causes of the discontent had been laid to rest. Alone or together, how were the governments to improve their domestic security if the currents of change covered so many states at once and yet affected each one of them differently? Until now the European powers had relied on the Metternich principle of joint intervention against isolated outbreaks of popular violence. Now such intervention was proven futile against broad shifts in the structure of society and impracticable against a chain of revolts extending from Italy to Poland and from Belgium to Hungary.

Austria was different from France and even from Prussia in one respect: it lacked an effective capital city which either a government could use for vigorous centralized control, or rebels capture in a swift bid to seize power. The fact that insurgents in Vienna twice drove the Habsburg family from the city – in May 1848 and a second time in October – did not mean that they ever came close to substituting themselves for the Habsburg regime.[20] Because Vienna was a royal residence rather than a center of power, it played no decisive role in helping either the revolution or the reaction to victory. The troubles in the city beginning with the violent demonstrations of 13 March 1848 were an infuriating nuisance to the government, but all the same a nuisance more than a disaster; they were resolved when Prince Alfred Windischgrätz and his troops recaptured Vienna on 1 November. Far more dangerous to the monarchy than the radical burghers and students of Vienna were the national rebels of northern Italy, Bohemia, and Hungary, because they commanded sufficient territory, inhabitants, and natural resources to break away from Austrian rule. Against them only deft diplomatic contacts to friendly outside powers and extensive military operations, but not police actions, could save the day. Austria returned to stability when Windischgrätz

---

[19] A. J. P. Taylor, in François, Fejtö, ed., *The Opening of an Era. An Historical Symposium* (London, 1948), p. xvi.
[20] R. John Rath, *The Viennese Revolution of 1848* (Austin, 1957), pp. 327–9.

marched his troops into Prague in June 1848, Marshal Radetzky pacified Italy in March 1849, and in the spring of that year, with Russian assistance, also broke the resistance of the Hungarians.

The Czech revolutionary movement in 1848 is particularly interesting to us because of the role that Czechoslovakia in the twentieth century was to play in Austria's security problems. The Czech rebels in 1848 did not rely on military organization and fighting spirit as much as on their national solidarity made possible by the optimal policing conditions in Bohemia – a small plateau surrounded on three sides by mountains in whose midst Prague was the natural capital city – conditions that were exploited by the Czech nationalists far better than by the Austrian ruling class. The latter, according to the French historian, Ernest Denis, was "so ignorant about the common people's longings, and had so little chance of winning the people's support, that it was inevitably reduced to inaction and cowardice when the revolution [of 1848] came."[21] As in Vienna, the police in Prague was strong in the political sector but not formidable on the level of order police; Denis called it *"une police d'opérette."*[22] It is a measure of the Czech people's self-control that despite the feebleness of the Austrian police in Bohemia they avoided political extremism in the midst of the European turmoil of 1848 and – somewhat like the contemporary Berliners – before long welcomed the return of the old authority on the principle: "Before demanding political and administrative equality, let us win moral equality. The moment will surely come when the government must recognize the change that has taken place."[23]

On being reconquered Vienna was placed under martial law for nearly two years. But this measure was meant to pacify rather than to intimidate the population. The death of the minister of war, Baillet de Latour, at the hands of a lynch mob on 6 October 1848 was not countered with an armed assault on the workers' quarters, similar to the military operation during the June days in Paris of that year; instead detectives of the Viennese Sicherheitsbüro patiently looked for the one workman in the lynch mob who had struck the fatal blow and actually found him.[24] Nor were the people of Vienna kept ignorant about their government's difficulties in Hungary, though the murder of Latour ostensibly was in protest against the dispatch of garrison troops from Vienna to fight the armies of the rebel, Louis Kossuth. On the contrary, the public's sympathy was solicited through candid reporting about the government's repeated setbacks in the field. Thus, on 26 May 1849, the minister of interior requested of Freiherr von

---

[21] Ernest Denis, *La Bohême depuis la Montagne-Blanche* (Paris, 1930), vol. 2, p. 205.

[22] For the organization of the police in Prague, see Ullrich, *Grundzüge des österreichischen Polizeirechtes*, p. 3. Also Denis, *La Bohême depuis la Montagne-Blanche*, vol. 2, p. 189; and Adam Wandruszka and Peter Urbanitsch, eds., *Die Habsburgermonarchie 1848–1918*, vol. 2: "Verwaltung und Rechtswesen" (Vienna, 1975), pp. 125–8.

[23] Denis, *La Bohême depuis la Montagne-Blanche*, vol. 2, p. 376.

[24] Kurt Frischler and Peter Zehrer, *Kriminalwalzer. 120 Jahre Wiener Sicherheitsbüro* (Vienna, 1979), pp. 27–9.

Pillersdorf, chairman of the council of ministers, the immediate announcement of the fall of Budapest.

It appears to me of great importance that the Viennese papers publish the sad news of the loss of Ofen [the western part of Budapest] without delay. The authorities have repeatedly promised not to suppress any news, however unfortunate. The mood of bitterness, which usually follows upon bad news will turn against the government if the people are given grounds to complain about [official] secretiveness.[25]

By 1850 the ministry of interior furthermore urged an end to the state of siege in Vienna and demanded the restoration of civil police order in that city:

[T]he main objective of a state of siege is to concentrate all political, judicial, and military power in one person. But this cannot be achieved in Vienna. *There are too many important affairs taking place concurrently here, each of them affecting too many diverse interests.* . . . The state of siege means no more than military control of the police and the existence of a military tribunal. As a result we have legal insecurity in Vienna's administrative and judicial life. . . . The state of siege has already been lifted in all the other countries that were shaken by the revolution. . . . Austria is the only one to retain it for a considerable time. This creates the impression abroad of lack of internal security and stability and must hurt Austria's international prestige. Two years ago [in 1848] we had to pay dearly for new armaments and a new army in order to convince a skeptical Europe of our domestic strength. Prussia would never have gone as far [as to propose a new German Empire under its direction] had it not believed that Austria's internal weakness prevented it from waging a foreign war. . . . It is also clear, that an unfavorable opinion abroad will have a negative influence on our credit standing since foreign capitalists will shy away from investing in Austria.[26]

Most significantly, after careful study the monarchy decided to raze the fortifications around Vienna. By an imperial decree of 1857, Emperor Franz Josef ordered the razing of the city's defense walls and their replacement with magnificent boulevards – the Ringstrassen – adorned by public buildings, parks, and monuments. The new Vienna was to become an architectural celebration of the glory of the house of Habsburg and of the cultural sophistication of the city's bourgeoisie.[27] This decision was at first resisted by the military and the police.[28] In the view of Archduke Maximilian von Este: "Once the proletariat of a capital city . . . has succeeded in one rebellion, it can no more be trusted than a wild animal after tasting blood. It is absolutely impossible to govern a country from a city which is accessible to this proletariat."

---

[25] Letter, Austrian minister of interior, 26 May 1849, No. 3809/M.I., in AVA (Vienna), Ministerium des Innern, Präsidiale 19/4, Karton 690.

[26] Anonymous draft memorandum, available in ibid., italics mine. On Prussia's abortive plan to found a German empire under its direction in 1849, see Heinrich Friedjung, *Oesterreich von 1848 bis 1860*, (Stuttgart, 1912), vol. 2, books 1–2.

[27] Carl E. Schorske. *Fin-de-Siècle Vienna. Politics and Culture* (New York, 1980), pp. 69–81.

[28] This passages is based on Walter Wagner, "Die Stellungnahme der Militärbehörden zur Wiener Stadterweiterung in den Jahren 1848–1857," in *Jahrbuch für die Geschichte der Stadt Wien* (1961–2), pp. 216–85; also Gunther E. Rothenberg, *The Army of Francis Joseph* (West Lafayette, Ind., 1976), p. 45.

He consequently proposed to divide Vienna into two cities by a wall with the eastern half (including the inner city, the Imperial Castle, and all government buildings) turned into a citadel defended by artillery. But Prince Windischgrätz, the liberator of Vienna, and Count Caboga, chief of the engineer troops, submitted another, more flexible plan. They recommended securing the lines of communication from Vienna's inner districts to Hungary and Italy with *Defensionskasernen* (fortified barracks) and with gunboats on the river Danube to make possible the rapid evacuation of the imperial family in a future emergency. Windischgrätz argued that a rabble could never be deterred from street violence by artillery fire; cannons, he said, could scare the conservative bourgeoisie who had homes to lose and understood the cultural value of palaces and monuments, but not destitute workmen. Against the latter the only protection were iron grills around public buildings and half-way up their interior staircases, defended by small arms fire. Failing that, a city in the throes of mob violence should be evacuated by the government and later retaken from the outside.

It was surely Vienna's good fortune that neither of these two military plans was implemented. The razing of the fortified walls, already contemplated by architects since the eighteenth century, was ordered by the emperor in 1857 and acquiesced to by the army, no doubt because by then the fear of renewed popular rebellion had largely abated.

In the spirit of the city's commitment not to advertise the military confrontation of government and people, but rather to promote a reconciliation of state and society in a common Habsburg culture, Vienna in 1867 also introduced a new civil police, the Sicherheitswache. Again, this was not what the city fathers had wanted immediately after the suppression of the revolution. After 1849 few Austrian bureaucrats at first trusted the lower classes. "The local inhabitants lack the necessary respect for the law," a commentator wrote in 1851 about the people of Graz. "The police cannot expect any assistance from these inhabitants and must frequently apply force to overcome popular resistance to its authority."[29] And because this same suspicion also applied to "unpoliceable Vienna," it appeared preferable to keep the police in the imperial residence under military-style command. Police soldiers, so the argument ran, were in any case easier to lead and less corruptible because they expected less pay. Many police recruits in postrevolutionary Vienna were Czech or Moravian peasant lads who barely understood German and had no ties to the local inhabitants and their past traditions. This was done in pursuance of the "principle of ahistoricalness" (*das Prinzip der Geschichtslosigkeit*), which saw in the absence of common historical memories between police and public a welcome guarantee against fraternization.[30] But all this

[29] "Entwurf einer Dienstes Instruktion für das k.k. Grazer Militaire Polizei Wachkorps (August 1851)," in AVA (Vienna), Ministerium des Innern, Präsidiale, Karton 707.

[30] As late as 1924, policemen born in Bohemia and Moravia were by far the two largest nationality groups in the Viennese street police and made up nearly half the Sicherheitswache: 708 Czechs and 553 Moravians out of a total of 2,687 policemen. *Jahrbuch der Polizeidirektion in Wien. Mit statistischen Daten aus dem Jahre 1924* (Vienna, 1926), p. 137.

changed after the decision to open Vienna to architectural embellishment was made in 1857 so that ten years later a *Civil*-Polizeiwache was finally introduced with a mission more compatible with the idea of modern police in the age of bourgeois civilization.[31]

In keeping with the liberalization of its domestic administration following the Prussian victories at Sadova (1866) and Sedan (1870), the Vienna government even cut back on domestic political espionage in favor of more conventional detective services to protect the Empire against treason and sedition. The importance of this change was not lost on later diplomatic historians searching for the causes of the First World War: "The large defensive machinery of the secret police, equipped with habits and skills of espionage or sedition activities . . . was progressively dismantled after 1870, and while it remained formidable, it was never after that day the mainstay of the regime."[32]

On the eve of the war of 1914, the political police in the *Polizei-Direktion* in Vienna consisted of no more than four to five senior officials, assisted by about fifteen detectives.[33] This meant that the Austro-Hungarian Monarchy in its most critical hour depended on a system of domestic security which so far only democratic countries like England and Switzerland had been able to afford.

Another example of Austria's liberal police style at the end of the nineteenth century was its relaxation of the censorship laws. In 1902 Ernst von Koerber, the prime minister and minister of interior, issued instructions to free theatrical performances from petty (*chicanös*) obstructions by the lower police:

> Where serious questions over the advisability of certain passages arise, the authorities may seek to remedy these through deletions in consultation with the playwright or the theatrical director. Under no circumstances shall unilateral deletions be made by the censors. In the future, no theatrical play can be banned by the lower ranks of the political police or the general police. . . . In principle the stage is open for the discussion of all conflicts in society, provided the ethical bases of these conflicts are made clear. . . . Many economic and cultural changes are taking place in our times, and all efforts at blocking them in the past have proven unsuccessful and pointless. On the other hand, an unprejudiced discussion of these changes [in a theatrical play] can lead to peaceful transitions.[34]

[31] *Instruktion für die kaiserlich-königliche Civil-Polizeiwache* (Vienna, 1854), p. 3; and Oberkommissar Ehrenfreund, *Fünfzig Jahre Wiener Sicherheitswache* (Vienna, 1919), pp. 32–3.

[32] Laurence Lafore, *The Long Fuse. An Interpretation of the Origins of World War I* (Philadelphia, 1965), p. 72.

[33] "Warum die Polizei im Kampf gegen die Verbrecher versagt. Das Urteil eines Polizeifachmannes," in *Arbeiter-Zeitung*, 16 Mar. 1928, p. 5. See also Otto Stolz, *Grundriss der Oesterreichischen Verfassungs- und Verwaltungsgeschichte* (Innsbruck, 1951), p. 171; and Othmar Schreiber, "Die historische und modene Organisation des Sicherheitswesens mit besonderer Berücksichtigung der österreichischen Verhältnisse," (Diss., University of Vienna, 1935), p. 29.

[34] Circular, Dr. Ernst von Koerber to all Landeschefs, Vienna, 2 Apr. 1902, in AVA (Vienna), Ministerium des Innern, Präsidiale, Karton 1982: "Polizeibefugnisse, Theater u. öffentliche Schaustellungen, 1900–1918." See also the appointment of a Czech poet to the Theatrical Board of Censors in Prague, as described in letter, Statthaltereipräsidium in Böhmen to k.k. Ministerium des Innern, Prague, 18 Nov. 1907, in idem, Präsidiale 20/9. Karton 1986.

The Austrian decision to dismantle the fortified walls of Vienna went together with a general disenchantment with warfare. This can be discerned in official Austrian documents from the decades following the revolution of 1848. Istvan Déak argues that the external splendor of the Austrian army before 1914 served the "police purpose" of keeping alive the myth of Habsburg greatness, but not to fight foreign wars.[35] One early hint of this pacifist disposition can be found in a letter addressed to the minister of interior, Dr. Alexander Bach, by the governor of the Banat, dated Temesvar, 16 July 1850. It was in reply to an inquiry by Bach to all governors, asking their opinion about a plan to compensate private persons who had suffered losses in the Hungarian civil war from the confiscated property of convicted high traitors.[36] The governor of Banat argued against compensation.

[General compensation] would make war appear less evil than it is. . . . It would diminish that capacity innate to all natural catastrophes to serve [mankind] as a warning and an inducement to reform. . . . No. Let everyone who has suffered at the cruel hand of war accept it as the punishment of God and redouble his moral and physical effort to redeem this evil and to prevent its repetition. In this way he will learn to suffer his misfortune and perhaps even turn it into a good lesson.[37]

Similarly, the Austrian attitude in mid-century toward army deserters and draft evaders suggests a softening of views about the war duty of Habsburg subjects. As an old participant in the European balance of power, Austria, of course, respected the right of every country to the military service of its subjects. Thus by an imperial decree of 18 September 1837, subjects of foreign states could not serve in the Austrian army without proof that they had satisfied their military obligation at home or had the explicit permission of their government.[38] And from 1847 to 1851 the Austrian government took great pains to apprehend one common thief for extradition to Russia after learning that this thief was also a deserter from the Russian army.[39] But the Austrians were remarkably lenient toward their own deserters. During the civil war in 1848, one August Brunner from the Steiermark abandoned his unit. As part of his punishment, the government confiscated his property. But when, on 23 March 1850, Brunner petitioned the ministry of interior for its return, his petition was endorsed by the ministry of war, which wrote on his behalf: "Since the petitioner did not flee abroad and has paid for his delinquency by submitting to corporal punishment, and in view of

---

[35] Istvan Déak, "The Habsburg Army in the First and Last Days of World War I: A Comparative Analysis," in Bela K. Kiraly and N. F. Freisziger, eds., *East Central European Society in World War I* (New York, 1985), p. 304.

[36] Following the suppression of the revolution in Hungary, about 100 insurgent leaders were executed.

[37] Document available in AVA (Vienna), Ministerium des Innern, Präsidiale 19/4, Karton 690. See also the answers by the Governor of Siebenbürgen, dated Hermannstadt 8 Feb. 1851, No. 28.029/ C.M.K. 1850; and by the governor in Pesth, dated 17 Sept. 1850, in ibid.

[38] Document available in ibid., Karton 669, folder 82/1855. See also dossier concerning Adolf Huber, in ibid., folder 11414/1855.

[39] See the case of Carl Georg Beck, in ibid., Ministerium des Innern, Allgemeine, Karton 362, folder: "Deserteure 1848–1869."

the fact also that he subsequently resumed his service in the k.u.k. Army until the end of the year 1848, when he was released for invalidity, the Ministry has decided . . . to grant him his wish."[40]

The Austrian authorities were particularly moved toward leniency by the fact that many Austrian deserters sought refuge from the law in the remotest corners of the monarchy, in Siebenbürgen and near the borders of Wallachia, more often than not also beyond the frontier, thus necessitating requests for extradition by Moldavia and Wallachia. The primitive conditions in the Balkans – reflected in the persistency of brigandage and the requests by Austrian traders in 1852 that their government obtain for them permission from the Turkish authorities to carry arms[41] – made it difficult for the Austrian officials not to feel some solidarity with Austrian draft dodgers and deserters as "fellow Europeans."[42] How successful the Austrians were in producing change in a region of Europe where transportation was still largely on foot or by ox cart and local policemen were illiterate peasants, is another question. In 1872, when Romania was found to convey Austrian deserters back home chained together in treks that lasted from thirty to forty days, the Austrian consul in Galatz complained to Foreign Minister Andrassy: "Since these deserters *are not criminals*, this treatment hits them very hard."[43]

Rather than preparing for future wars, Austria after 1848 tightened control over its territory through closer border surveillance and more police contacts to other countries. This involved better protection for the newly established telegraph lines[44] as much as frequent checks on all travelers at railway stations and on country roads near the border. Foreigners were taken into custody as spies when their clothes or their behavior struck a local gendarme as suspicious. Their cases were subsequently disposed of with greater or lesser courtesy depending on Vienna's relations to their home governments. In 1859 a Swiss ambulant trader in time pieces named Kraemer was held in jail without trial for three months, the victim of Austria's displeasure with Switzerland for having sheltered foreign insurgents in 1848.[45] On the other hand, in 1860, an English traveler in the Tyrol was hastily released with apologies after being held for only one day when the British ambassador in Vienna inquired about his fate, and the local district cap-

---

[40] Ibid., folder 2.
[41] Letter, ministry of trade to ministry of foreign affairs, Vienna, 29 Sept. 1852, in HHStA (Vienna), Administrative Registratur F52, 1, *Politische Flüchtlinge 1835–1845*, fols. 937–40.
[42] HHStA (Vienna) Administrative Registratur F52, "Schubwesen," folders 102–3.
[43] Available in ibid., Karton 47, "Schubwesen 1871–1918," my italics.
[44] On the stiff penalties for damaging telegraph lines and the need to solicit the help of clergymen to educate the peasants about their usefulness, see letter, k.k. Minister für Handel, Gewerbe u. öffentl. Bauten to Ministerium des Innern, Vienna, 30 July 1849, in AVA (Vienna), Ministerium des Innern, Allgemeine 192/a, folder: "Telegrafenwesen, 1848–1869."
[45] Report, Polizeiministerium to k.k. Minister Präsident Graf von Rechberg, Vienna, 1 Nov. 1859, 5445/B.M., in HHStA (Vienna), Administrative Registratur F52, 1: "Politische Flüchtlinge 1835–1845."

tain was reprimanded.[46] At the same time Austria made few war preparations against Prussia. The intelligence service (Evidenzbüro) of the army general staff, founded in 1860, and since 1861 instructed to collaborate closely with the police ministry's undercover agents abroad, concentrated its efforts against France, Italy, Russia, and the Balkan states before finally turning to Prussia in March 1866, three months before the outbreak of hostilities with Berlin.[47] Unlike Prussia, Austria also neglected to draw up systematic plans for the orderly withdrawal from border cities in case of a hostile invasion. The helter-skelter evacuation of Prague by the Austrian police in the war of 1866 further undermined the Habsburg monarchy's prestige in Bohemia.[48]

Austrian police communications to its close neighbors within the German Confederation were generally peremptory in tone. These were the states which until recently had accepted Metternich's leadership in the joint policing of Central Europe. With Saxony the Austrian minister to Dresden, Count Kuefstein, arranged in 1849 for the participation of the criminal judge Moritz Hoch and the police commissar Dedera of Prague in the investigation of local revolutionary conspirators. The Austrian government justified its interference by pointing to direct links between the uprisings in Dresden and Prague. To circumvent any legal obstacles the Austrian officials, though present at the interrogations, submitted their questions in writing to the Saxon officials.[49] In 1851 Austria and Saxony also concluded an agreement providing for periodic consultations between the gendarmerie of Bohemia and Saxony along the frontier. These conferences took place regularly until 1858.[50] Yet another way to develop contacts to the police authorities of the European states was collaboration against common crime and vagrancy. The Austrians concluded such a convention with Prussia in 1863. Article 7 of this convention gave the gendarmerie of both states the right to cross the border to continue the pursuit of dangerous persons so long as the authorities of the other state were notified and given the chance to take over the operation. Article 8 provided for regular contacts between the security organs of adjacent border districts and for joint patrolling; Article 9 for assistance across the border in case of natural catastrophes like fires and inundations even without prior invitation by the other country.[51]

---

[46] See the case of Edward Whitfield, in HHStA (Vienna), Administrative Registratur F52: "Fremde Polizeibeschwerden."

[47] Max Ronge, "Geschichte des Evidenzbüro des Generalstabs" (typescript, ca. 1942), in KA (Vienna), Nachlassammlung B/126, Nr. 1a, folder 117–26.

[48] *Geschichte der preussischen Invasion und Okkupation in Böhmen im Jahre 1866* (Prague, 1867), pp. 305–8.

[49] HHStA (Vienna), Administrative Registratur F52: "Fremde Polizeibeschwerden," folder 140.

[50] Report, "An das Kaiserl. Staatsministerium," (18 Dec. 1860) (ad. 14.773/2774.I.), in ibid.

[51] Draft convention between Prussia and Austria concerning the joint pursuit of common criminals, 21 Mar. 1863, in ibid., folder 3. A similar agreement was negotiated in the same year with the Grand Duchy of Baden. See report by Austrian chargé d'affaires in Karlsruhe, 20 June 1863, No. XXI AE, in ibid.

The Austro-Prussian Convention of 1863 later served as a model for Balkan countries seeking to suppress regional banditry.[52]

In the German Confederation, Metternich's old Central Investigation Commission was not revived. Instead, an organization of German police chiefs came into existence under the leadership of Karl Ludwig Friedrich von Hinckeldey, the police president of Berlin, and a Prussian police councillor named Dr. Wilhelm Stieber made a name for himself by his far-flung investigations of revolutionary agitation at home and abroad.[53] In an apparent effort to recover the initiative, the Austrians in 1852 launched the *Central-Polizei-Blatt*, a bulletin which amalgamated police news from throughout the Habsburg Monarchy and which was offered to neighboring police authorities in exchange for their bulletins.[54] In the ensuing decades the Austrian *Central-Polizei-Blatt* was sought after by more and more police authorities throughout much of Europe.[55] For obvious reasons exchanges of police bulletins across state borders first took place with countries adjoining Austria and belonging to the German-speaking part of Europe: Bavaria, Saxony, Württemberg, and Baden. In March 1863 the exchange of fifteen copies of every issue of the *Polizei-Anzeiger* of Prague was arranged in return for twenty-two copies of the *Sächsisches Gendarmerie-Blatt* of Dresden, the latter intended for all Austrian gendarmerie posts along the Austro-Saxon frontier.[56] By 1863, on the basis of a special Prussian-Austrian convention, the *Central-Polizei-Blatt* of Vienna went regularly to the police headquarters of major Prussian cities, and regional agreements were worked out over the next ten years for circulating the Viennese bulletin, or other regional police bulletins, among neighboring towns.[57]

An exchange outside the immediate radius of the German Bund between all the major capitals of Europe developed in the 1870s and 1880s, leaving only Russia, Russian Poland, and Italy not on the list of countries regularly exchanging police bulletins with Vienna.[58] In 1880 the Austrian government began negotiating with the Russian ministry of foreign affairs for similar cooperation between

---

[52] See for example Kr. dalm.-hrv.-slav. zemaljski vladni odjel za poslove unutarnje, to Austrian Foreign Ministry, 31 Dec. 1884, No. 50795; and note verbale, Romanian legation to Austro-Hungarian foreign ministry, Vienna, 26 June/8 July 1885, No. 701, in ibid., folder 8.

[53] On the German police association, see Wolfram Siemann, ed., *Der "Polizeiverein" deutscher Staaten. Eine Dokumentation zur Ueberwachung der Oeffentlichkeit nach der Revolution von 1848/49* (Tübingen, 1983).

[54] Leaflet, "Programm für das zu gründende Central-Polizei Blatt" (Vienna, 16 Sept. 1853), in HHStA (Vienna), Administrative Registratur F52, 1, "Politische Flüchtlinge."

[55] Report of the k.k. no. Statthalter to K.u.K. Mm des Aeussern, 4 Aug. 1882, in HHStA (Vienna), Administrative Registratur F52, Karton 8, folder: "Grenzsicherungsdienst."

[56] K.k. Staatsministerium to k.k. Minister des Aeussern, Vienna, 7 Mar. 1863, in ibid., Karton 3, folder: "Grenz-Sicherheits-Dienst. Verhandlungen mit deutschen Regierungen bet. Handhabung des Grenzsicherheitsdienstes & Austausch der Polizei-Blätter."

[57] For example, in the Prussian districts Breslau and Liegnitz, some townships subscribed to the Central-Polizei-Blatt of Vienna, others wanted the Polizei-Anzeiger of Prague, and yet other towns, the Polizei-Blatt Braunau or Polizei-Blatt Troppau. "Verzeichnis derjenigen österreichischen Polizeiblätter, auf welche seitens der königlich Preussischen Grenzbehörden Anspruch gemacht wird (1878)," in ibid., Karton 8.

[58] Request by k.k. Statthalterei Vienna to Min. d. Aeussern, Vienna, 18 Sept. 1880, in ibid.

the two countries' chief police authorities but the Russians showed themselves reserved, perhaps because the difference between their own police system (very refined on the level of high police, incompetent on the level of low police) and that of Western Europe was beginning to tell. Besides, the Nihilist wave in Russia was reaching its peak and Austria was not entirely trusted by Petersburg as a well-intentioned neighbor. On the other hand there was need for both countries to control the growing traffic along their very long frontier in Galicia, where rural crime and vagrancy, the spread of infectious diseases, not to mention the illicit coming and going of revolutionary agitators, made cooperation between border guards indispensable.

There was however the mounting cost of the bulletins which by the 1880s and 1890s not only spoke for the success of the Austrian venture but also marked its practical limits. When in 1884, the Austrian consul in Barcelona asked to receive the *Central-Polizei-Blatt* so he would know who among his daily visitors might be a fugitive from Austrian law, he was told the government could not afford this extra expenditure. Austria then maintained 153 consulates throughout the world. To supply every consulate with a police bulletin would have required too many additional copies.[59]

Although Austria's police collaboration with Saxony and Prussia served to suppress revolutionary unrest in the three territories, no such purpose is discernible in the lively exchange of information between the police of Vienna and Paris during the late 1850s. Austria's encouragement of this contact, which largely dealt with ordinary criminal and administrative matters, served no useful purpose that we can see, unless it was to strengthen the precarious foreign position of the Habsburg Empire.

Between 1856 and 1860 (thus, from the conclusion of the Crimean War in which the Austrian diplomats ended by taking France's side, through the 1859 war in which Austria fought against French troops in Italy) the French embassy in Vienna sent hundreds of Paris police bulletins to the Austrian ministry of foreign affairs for transmission to the ministry of interior and to the Vienna police, presumably on a basis of reciprocity. This exchange of wanted lists is puzzling since most of the French bulletins concerned common delinquents without any apparent interest to the Austrian government. The 609th bulletin of the French ministry of interior, dated 18 October 1860, contained the names of 141 individuals wanted by the French police, all of them French by nationality, nearly all of them of the lower class if not outright destitute persons, and none of them charged with a political offense. Twelve persons were not even wanted by the French authorities but by their families, the French police here providing an administrative service in aid of private citizens. None of the individuals on this list was suspected of being on Austrian soil or in any other way had the remotest connection to Austria.[60]

[59] K.k. General Consulate in Barcelona to the foreign minister, Kalnoky, Barcelona, 2 Sept., 1884, no. 1336, in ibid., Karton 8.
[60] HHStA (Vienna), Administrative Registratur F52: "Austausch."

The exchanges between the French embassy and the authorities in Vienna were invariably most polite, yet one cannot help but wonder whether the cordiality of this exchange may not have been the chief reason why the Austrians attached such value to this enterprise. True, the French and the Austrians may also have shared a common concern over the new tasks facing police in modern world cities like Paris and Vienna. A *note verbale* from the French embassy to the Austrian ministry of foreign affairs, dated Vienna, 4 February 1863, concerning the importance of maintaining an efficient postal service between the two countries anticipates our own century's insistence on rapid and punctual communications from one metropolitan center to the next.

The Imperial [Austrian] foreign ministry has surely remarked that there have lately been many interruptions in the regular postal service between Paris and Vienna . . . Public mail, telegrams, and newspaper deliveries are sometimes 24 hours late. This happened notably on 3 February – telegrams from France were not delivered until the following day – and last month this happened four or five times. The regular occurrence of these interruptions suggests faulty planning in the timing of mail departures, in the connection between postal trains, and in the overall organization of international communications. Because of these delays the public in fact loses the benefits of modern rapid communications and [the European states] one of the great opportunities for improving international relations.[61]

With the rebellions in Bohemia, Italy, and Hungary quelled, Austria in the second half of the nineteenth century still held center stage in the European balance of power. But it was unprepared to adopt a policy of forthright state egoism in place of the traditional Habsburg idea of universalism – this despite the fact that everywhere else in Europe restored governments were preparing for solutions to unresolved national or social problems by unilateral action from the top, and at the expense of their neighbors if necessary. While Louis Napoleon of France, and after 1862 Prime Minister Bismarck of Prussia, met the challenge of 1848 with dramatic new foreign political ventures the Austrian response remained largely passive if not outright negative: old assets were given up to make room for half-hearted reforms, the challenge of modernity was met by delays and diversions, setbacks in diplomacy and war accepted as irreversible defeats.[62]

The Swiss police: A public service to Europe?

General remarks

In the modern period, the Swiss police, like the English police, did not have to deal with major revolutionary changes in the structure of the political state, nor

---

[61] Ibid., Administrative Registratur F49, Karton 1, "Postwesen: Generalia 1862–1864," folder: "Beschwerden."

[62] Bismarck believed that Austria's slow response to the challenge of the modern industrial age might make possible Prussia's eventual ascendancy in Germany without the need to resort to war. Otto Becker, "Der Sinn der dualistischen Verständigungsversuche Bismarcks," in *Historische Zeitschrift*, vol. 169, no. 2 (Aug. 1949), p. 291.

with foreign invasions or the assimilation of conquered territory. The Swiss civil war (*Sonderbundkrieg*) of 1847 was too short to cause a genuine political interruption and it was fought exclusively by soldiers. As a result the Swiss police has been molded by a very different experience compared to its counterparts in Central and Eastern Europe. In these countries revolutions and territorial wars have made for increasing centralization of police command, and for the constant enlargement of police powers. Also in Germany, Austria, and Italy, the 1848 revolution ended undecidedly with none of the outstanding national problems resolved, whereas for Switzerland the Sonderbundkrieg of 1847 resulted in the triumph of liberal democracy.[63]

Switzerland was not a police state though it was one of the best policed countries in Europe. It was not a police state because, being so well run by the people acting as democratic communities, it had no need to be one. At the same time, Switzerland's domestic cohesion had its price inasmuch as the country had to keep the pace of reform moderate while other countries forged ahead. It also had to abstain from all international disputes and submit to numerous pressures by foreign governments.

The literature on Swiss police is not abundant compared to the literature on police for Germany and Austria. We may attribute this to the fact that Switzerland has no extensive national police bureaucracy with the need for theoretical education on its mission and elaborate instructions on procedure. Switzerland does not even possess training and research institutes in police science comparable to those in other countries.[64]

When in 1978 an American sociologist published a study on the low incidence of crime in Switzerland, his book drew some skeptical smiles from Swiss police officials.[65] Yet they had to agree with Clinard's general assessment of Switzerland's remarkably high level of law abidingness. Clinard cites several factors to explain Switzerland's fortunate situation. Of these, the following are of interest to this study:

1. Switzerland's rate of urbanization was slow and decentralized. In the absence of abundant coal and timber resources for fuel, Swiss industry, relying largely on water power and later on hydroelectric power, was dispersed to be close to available rivers and streams. Without large industrial centers like Leeds, Sheffield, and Birmingham, Switzerland was spared the development of urban slums and a proletariat prone to crime. In the mid-nineteenth century, only

---

[63] The French police in the nineteenth century also faced less drastic political changes than the police in Central and Eastern Europe. But the growth of the French royal government from Louis XIV to Louis XVI had already made for considerable centralization of police before 1789. Also, France, unlike Switzerland, in the period of our study repeatedly faced dangerous military threats from Germany that called for special police alertness.

[64] Interview, Dr. Markus Mohler, police commandant of Canton Basel-Stadt, Basel, 25 Jan. 1985.

[65] Marshall B. Clinard, *Cities with Little Crime. The Case of Switzerland* (Cambridge, 1978), pp. 158ff; his conclusions corroborate earlier findings in Erich Krafft, *Organisation und Tätigkeit der Kriminalpolizei des Kantons Luzern* (Diss. University of Zurich, 1938), pp. 37, 95–6.

6.4 percent of the Swiss population lived in towns and Switzerland's birth rate was low compared to that of Prussia.[66]
2. The cultural division of Switzerland by language, religion, and regional customs, Clinard says, inhibited urban migration for education and jobs. (This factor, we might add, does not illustrate the police method of "divide and rule" but the principle of "optimal policing units": the Swiss cantons over the centuries were able to maintain strong community bonds.)
3. Long years of militia service acted as a school of good citizenship for the male population. With the medieval industry of mercenary soldiers falling into desuetude by the 1840s the cantonal militia army after the 1850s became a symbol of Swiss neutrality and independence, rooted in local patriotism. "Antimilitarism" (refusal to serve in the army) never became the catchword of democracy except among a small minority of socialists at the end of the nineteenth century. But then Switzerland had no military caste like Wilhelmine Germany, and not the same barrack-square discipline in factories or in the civil service. The decentralization of the Swiss army in turn strengthened the decentralization of the Swiss police.[67]

To this day, the twenty-three cantons carry the main responsibility for police throughout the Swiss Confederation. Federal offices charged with police matters exist only since the late nineteenth century and arose mainly in response to Switzerland's need to meet its international police responsibilities in the face of growing revolutionary and warlike tensions gripping the European state system. To some extent we see a kinship between the police in the French, German, and Italian cantons with neighboring France, Germany, and Italy. The French cantons had a gendarmerie and a *sûreté* coordinated on the highest level (as in France, where all police work was ultimately controlled from Paris) and the police of the canton of Geneva, in the 1850s, corresponded directly with French police in political cases.[68] Conversely, the police in the German-speaking cantons had *Abteilungen* with cross-contacts at a much lower echelon, as in Germany, and those adjoining important frontier regions maintained immediate contacts with their German colleagues, as did the police of Basel-Stadt with the police in Lörrach across the border.[69]

The Swiss police was democratic in the sense that a close rapport existed between police and the people in the cantons. There was never a "barracked" police in Switzerland to keep the distance between police and public. At the same time, given the very conservative outlook of many cantons on what views and what be-

---

[66] Eduard Fueter, *Die Schweiz seit 1848. Geschichte-Politik-Wirtschaft* (Zurich, 1928), p. 17.
[67] On the Swiss militia as a constitutional guarantee of the citizens' freedom, see William E. Rappard, *Die Bundesverfassung der Schweizerischen Eidgenossenschaft 1848–1948* (Zurich, 1948), p. 220.
[68] Henri G. Mutrux, *La Police moderne au service du public* (Geneva, ca. 1950), p. 15.
[69] Thus the criminal code of Basel (1821) provided the death penalty equally to anyone disloyal to the Confederation and the canton of Basel. Dr. Robert Heuss, Polizeikommando Basel-Stadt, "Die Organisation des Nachrichtendienstes in der Schweiz," (lecture given at Landespolizeischule Freiburg i.Br., 1984), p. 5.

havior was acceptable in public, the cantonal and communal police, as their executive agents, also had to espouse conservative attitudes. To protect the closeness of cantonal life, the Swiss were very careful in regard to what kind of immigration, and how much of it, they would tolerate from the outside. By the turn of the century, some of this responsibility fell on the central police departments in Berne. But the democratic principles of local self-government remained strongly alive, with the police enforcing the community's decisions.

Switzerland's position in the European police system was determined by its neutrality as laid down by the Declaration of the Five Powers of 20 November 1815. This declaration placed it outside the international competition for power and so exempted it from having to maintain a police strong enough to prepare its people for national war efforts, either politically or economically. However, while Swiss neutrality was still relatively easy to defend with militia forces in the early nineteenth century, this was no longer true following German unification in 1871 and the emergence of a protracted revolutionary crisis in Eastern Europe.

In the game of the balance of power a number of European countries have used means other than war and diplomacy to exert the influence they needed for their security abroad. Dynastic alliances, monetary subsidies, even police assistance against crime and subversion come readily to mind. Switzerland, like England (though evidently under quite different circumstances) provided Europe with a place of refuge for political dissenters during much of the modern period. In due time, Switzerland's asylum policy had to be revised, largely because the circumstances attending the inception of this policy in 1815 no longer existed. But in the immediate post-Napoleonic period, Switzerland willingly offered asylum to foreign exiles because the great powers of Europe unanimously requested it to, and because the exiles Switzerland had to shelter were few in number and not very dangerous.

Switzerland and the allied powers, 1815–23

In 1815, Austria, Russia, England, and Russia jointly decided on the internment outside France of members of the Bonaparte family and important functionaries of the fallen French Empire. Switzerland was asked to guard the Duchesse de St. Leu, whose wish to remain in Switzerland the Powers respected. How obediently Switzerland assumed the part assigned to it by the Four Power Agreement is evident from this letter by the chancellor of the Swiss Confederation, Mousson, to the chamberlain of Emperor Alexander I, Baron de Krüdener, dated Zurich, 1 December 1815:

The Swiss Confederation, true to the principles that it has espoused from the beginning of the revolution that occurred in France [during Napoleon's brief return to power in 1815]; intent on removing from its bosom all seeds of disorder and agitation; anxious, finally, to cultivate the relations that it entertains with the allied Royal and Imperial Courts and with His Most Christian Majesty; *did not wait to be so invited* before adopting a rigorous police system in regard to individuals who have been noted for their part in the latest conspiracy against the Royal Government of France and the rebellion that arose from it.[70]

The case of Dominique Ettori (or Ettory), forty-five years old, who passed through Canton Basel in 1816, further illustrates Switzerland's willingness to provide the victorious powers with very specific police services, in this instance the surveillance of an individual who did not belong to a former ruling house. Ettori had annoyed the Austrian government for spreading the story that Vienna had known beforehand of Napoleon's plan to escape from Elba in 1814 and had failed to share this intelligence with its allies.[71] The Austrian minister to Switzerland, Schraut, and his Prussian colleague, Justus von Gruner, informed Mayor Ebinger of Basel on 18 May that Ettori, in their opinion, was an adventurer and a traitor. They asked the Basel government to have him closely followed by a police spy. On 19 June, after the Swiss had arrested Ettori and conducted him under guard to the Austrian frontier, a gratified Schraut wrote to Ebinger and the cantonal council of Basel:

We shall certainly not fail, Messieurs, to let it be known at our Courts . . . with what deference you have responded to our request. The promptness with which you have executed your decision [to accede to our demand] gives you renewed claims to our gratitude. . . . You will find, Messieurs, the most ample sentiment of reciprocity with our Monarchs.[72]

Switzerland was important as a transit territory for individuals who interested certain governments. It was also strategically placed as a potential safe haven for revolutionaries waiting for a chance to strike against a handful of neighboring countries. The same Schraut made no effort on 19 May 1821 to hide his displeasure with the Swiss in a letter to the burgomaster and the state council of Zurich (whose turn it was to represent the Swiss federal government) over an incident involving Piedmontese rebels fleeing into Swiss territory, 19 May 1821.

In all Europe, no other region is better suited for rebels whose principles and ideas tie them to seditious elements inside Italy, France, and Germany than is Switzerland: centrally located, neutral, *indifferent toward everything except its own welfare* – here they can safely hatch new plots and revive old ones. Surely [Switzerland] will not want to establish for itself a system [situation?] of self-isolation and unapproachability which in such a flagrant situation could put in question the strongest bonds of friendship and neighborliness![73]

The burgomaster and the state council of Zurich thereupon lost no time to reassure the ministers of Austria, Russia, and Prussia of Switzerland's unquestioning support of the Powers belonging to the Concert of Europe, and of its "high

---

[70] Document available in StA (Basel-Stadt), Rep. A11, Politisches EE4: "Politische Flüchtlinge in der Schweiz. Allgemeines u. einzelnes 1815–1833," my italics.

[71] Donald E. Emerson, *Metternich and the Political Police. Security and Subversion in the Hapsburg Monarchy, 1815–1930* (The Hague, 1968), pp. 50–1.

[72] Document available in StA (Basel-Stadt), Rep. A11, EE 4.

[73] Document available in ibid.

confidence in Their August Monarchs, who after having restored the long-awaited general peace in Europe through their victories and their generous ministrations, have yet once more in a great crisis saved Europe from the incalculable evils that threatened it."[74]

If the Swiss did sympathize with fugitive revolutionaries, their sympathy suffered a severe blow when in February 1834, Italian revolutionaries under Giuseppe Mazzini and aided by Polish, French and German refugees in Switzerland, mounted an armed invasion of Sardinia from Geneva. They struck at Annemasse, a small town just south of the border, and were quickly defeated. Austria, Bavaria, Württemberg, and Baden lodged complaints with Switzerland for its failure to prevent this raid.[75] Fortunately for the Swiss, the damage caused by the Mazzinists, given the limited scope of armed encounters one hundred and fifty years ago, could be quickly repaired with a ceremonial gesture of homage by a Swiss delegation to the King of Sardinia during a visit of Charles Albert I, near the Swiss border in June 1834.[76]

Two more documents will demonstrate Switzerland's willingness to shape its policy of asylum in accordance with the wishes of foreign governments. The first is a report on measures recommended by the Confederate Diet (*Tagsatzung*) to the cantonal diets, concerning freedom of the press and aliens police, dated 14 July 1823. It begins with praise for "Hospitable Switzerland, which has long performed the Christian duty of taking in the miserable victims of great convulsions . . ." from the wars of religion to the turmoil of the French Revolution:

But never was it a sanctuary for criminals. In a situation where a mere opinion can be tantamount to the commission of a crime, and where the one can surreptitiously lead to the other, some hard decisions must be made, however difficult this may be. The primary charge which foreign governments levy against us is that we abuse our right of granting hospitality.[77]

The European powers, so the recommendation of the Diet went on, also think Switzerland too readily allows its press to print news and opinions affecting the security of other countries without first checking the sources of these stories. The

[74] Document available in ibid. See also in the same folder the blunt request by Schraut to Berne in 1823, that certain individuals be deported forthwith from Switzerland to America by decision of the Congress of Verona.

[75] See folder, "Acta über die wegen des Aufenthalts der politischen Flüchtlingen [sic] der Schweiz angedachten . . . Massregeln von seiten der Nachbarstaaten, vom 21. Juni 1834 bis . . . ," in ibid.; also Johannes Langhard, *Die politische Polizei der Schweizerischen Eidgenossenschaft* (Berne, 1909), pp. 5, 148; and Berthold van Muyden, *La Suisse sous le pacte de 1815* (Lausanne, 1892), vol. 2, pp. 282–332.

[76] Document available in StA (Basel-Stadt), EE 4.

[77] "Kommissional Bericht über den durch das vorortliche Kreisschreiben vom 12. März (1823) *ad instruendum* gelangte Antrag an die Hohen Stände, zu Massnahmen in Beziehung auf Pressefreyheit und Fremden-Polizey" (Geheime gedruckte Abschrift), p. 2, available in StA (Basel-Stadt), Rep. A11, Politisches EE 4. *Vorort*, principal city, here means the seat of the Swiss federal government, which at that time periodically rotated between Zurich, Berne, and Lucerne when the Diet was not in session.

cantons consequently were told to institute preventive censorship. "To punish certain crimes after they have been committed cannot undo the damage that has been done."

The Diet also urged the cantons to require passports of all foreigners entering their territory and documents attesting to their "trustworthiness" (*Unverdächtigkeit*). Greater care was needed in registering each foreigner, they were told, since inefficient handling of such matters by local police in the past had made it difficult for some foreign governments to identify their refugees.

The Diet's next recommendation dealt with persons "designated as dangerous" by foreign governments. With no apparent concern for the subjective nature of such designations Berne recommended their "nonemployment as teachers or in other public positions [*die Nichtanstellung von Personen in Lernfächern und andern Aemtern, welche von den äussern Mächten als gefährliche Subjekte bezeichnet sind*]."

Finally, all foreigners were to be placed under surveillance if what they said and did and their condition in general could give rise to negative impressions abroad on the state of opinion in Switzerland.[78]

The second document lists the orders by the magistrate and council of Berne, dated 15 September 1823 for the policing of "dangerous aliens" in the cantons. We cite this document in its entirety, because it so nicely illustrates police procedures in Europe prior to the onset of large-scale industrial development.

In order to prevent the sojourn of persons who have in a friendly country committed a crime or disturbed the public peace and are now in flight, and in order to discover those who, after receiving proper permission to reside here, are found guilty of engaging in dangerous plots against the legal government and the domestic peace of foreign states . . .

1. No foreigner who is a fugitive for political reasons and whose guilt is officially asserted by a friendly power ["*dessen Schuld von einer befreundeten Macht förmlich angezeigt worden*"] shall be permitted to reside in this canton.
2. Foreigners seeking to reside in this canton must have valid passports issued by their home governments.
3. Foreigners whose governments maintain an accredited minister in Berne must have their passports visaed by them inside of 8 days if they want to stay in Switzerland.
4. Innkeepers must report the names of their lodgers every 8 days, these names to be sent to the Central-Polizey-Direction.
5. Foreigners traveling to the capital [Berne] must leave their passports with the gate-keeper [*Thor-Inspektor*] in return for a receipt.
6. During their stay in Berne their passports will be kept at the Central-Polizey-Direktion.
7. The receipt for the passport must be shown to the innkeeper.
8. Foreigners who are not allowed to stay must leave the country along prescribed routes.[79]

[78] Ibid., p. 5.   [79] Document available in StA (Basel-Stadt), Rep. A11, EE 4.

Franco-Swiss relations, 1815–38

The difficulty of Switzerland's position in the balance of power during the Restoration period becomes clearer still when we consider that before the end of the 1820s, the recovery of France already forced it to shift its attention increasingly from responding to the wishes of Austria, Russia, and Prussia to those of the French government. Franco-Swiss relations in the nineteenth and early twentieth centuries centered much on police affairs, chiefly on France's need to control French political dissenters in Geneva, and on Switzerland's desire to maintain its sovereign integrity against the presumptuousness of French police agents operating on its territory. And because war was never a serious likelihood between the two countries (both being far more concerned about their relations with Germany and to some extent Russia), police questions (but not questions of military defense) remained a major subject in their mutual dealings in this period. These dealings, let it be said from the outset, were less friendly than is often assumed. They were marked by petty suspicions and a muted ill-will which could result in pro-German behavior by Swiss authorities when tensions were high between Paris and Berlin and in French efforts to damage Swiss relations with either Germany or with Russia.

Franco-Swiss police relations had started on a note of technical hostility. In 1815 Switzerland had been summoned by the Allied powers to take part in the encirclement of France by means of a *cordon sanitaire*.[80] But by 1828 Switzerland signed a bilateral police treaty with the government of Charles X, thereby ending its participation in the European alignment against France.[81] Louis Napoleon's abortive coup d'état in Strasbourg (1836), which he launched from his home in Arenenberg, canton of Thurgau, had obviously compromised the Confederation's neutrality. But the French were slow in taking steps against Switzerland, if only because Louis Napoleon, after his capture and deportation from France, did not return to Switzerland until 1837. In the meantime the French sought less open ways to compromise Switzerland's standing among the European powers. One of them was to expose once more Switzerland's alleged role as an accomplice to various revolutionary plots against the monarchies of Europe.[82] It does speak strongly for Swiss courage that in August of 1838, when the French began to concentrate troops close to the Swiss border in order to force the expulsion of

---

[80] Close to the Swiss border, the French had to raze their fortifications at Huningue.

[81] Treaty of 18 July 1828. See report by Swiss chargé d'affaires Barmann to the federal council in Berne, dated Paris, 6 Feb. 1849, on the French practice in matters of extradition to Switzerland, in BA (Berne), Bestands-Nr. 21, Archiv-Nr. 24626, Bd. 1.

[82] See letter by the first secretary of the French embassy in Berne to prefect of département du Haut-Rhin, Berne, 28 Aug. 1836, in ADdHR (Colmar), 4 M 197, "Passage par la France de réfugiés expulsés de Suisse et dirigés vers la Grande Bretagne et les Etats Unis, 1834–1855," recommending the capture of a German fugitive who allegedly possessed damaging political information about the Swiss government.

Louis Napoleon from Arenenberg, they responded by mobilizing one battalion of infantry and one company of sharpshooters. As far as the Swiss were concerned, Louis Napoleon was one of their fellow citizen since 1832 and consequently entitled to protection. The military confrontation of France and Switzerland lasted less than a fortnight. It was defused by Louis Napoleon himself when, on 20 September 1838, he decided to leave for England.[83]

But though Louis Napoleon spared Switzerland a military clash with France by leaving the country, the Swiss position vis-à-vis France deteriorated steadily in the direction of an ill-defined dependency. In 1844 the Swiss sought to improve their relations with Paris through agreements on mutual extradition procedures,[84] but the opportunity for revising the police relations between the two neighbors only came under the Second French Empire, which will be treated below.

The French police: *défense du territoire*, the key to controlled change

General remarks

The French – and with good right – claim to possess the most refined system of central police in Europe. If France in the seventeenth century became the first country with diplomatic influence reaching as far as Madrid, Moscow, and Constantinople, it owed this achievement to the inner strength of its political civilization. The French kingdom thrived because the very elaborateness of its court, its many royal councils, and its multitude of bureaucracies made for a society where – as in ancient China – maintaining good order at home was already possible with the mere use of censorship of language and literature.[85] The Revocation of the Edict of Nantes in 1685 reaffirmed the importance of France's *"ordre fondamental,"* even though the exodus of so many Huguenots had the disadvantage of eliminating a useful loyal opposition. By extension, the Revolution of 1789 can be attributed to the failure of France's thought police to deal with the intellectual subversion of the Enlightenment philosophers.[86] Not surprisingly the French police state was also a pioneer in modern criminology: the campaign to abolish torture dates from the eighteenth century, and the use of criminal statistics from 1825 – more than one hundred and fifty years before Switzerland.[87]

---

[83] Letter, Louis Napoleon to *Landamann* Anderwert, président du Petit Conseil du Canton de Thurgovie, Arenenberg 20 Sept. 1838, in StA (Basel-Stadt) EE 8: "Louis Napoleon Bonaparte 1838"; also Langhard, *Politische Polizei*, pp. 18–30. For a detailed account of this affair, see Van Muyden, *La Suisse sous le pacte de 1815*, vol. 2, pp. 475–553.

[84] Report by chargé d'affaires Barmann, Paris, 6 Feb. 1849, in BA (Berne), Bestand-Nr. 21, Archiv-Nr. 24626, Bd. 1.

[85] Alan Williams, *The Police of Paris, 1718–1789* (Baton Rouge, La., 1979), pp. 9–10.

[86] Jean Galtier-Boissière, *Mysteries of the French Secret Police* (London, 1938), p. 23.

[87] Interview Markus Mohler, 25 Jan. 1985: "Until three years ago, Switzerland kept statistics on court convictions only, but no crime statistics."

A long police tradition is not the only reason why the literature on police in France is relatively abundant. Much writing about police was stimulated by the half dozen revolutions in France since 1789, which accelerated the growth of political awareness of the public. Since the reign of Louis XIV well protected for nearly two centuries against invasion from across the English Channel, the Pyrénées, or the Rhine, France never became a militaristic state. Even in the modern period political debates in France always concerned questions of principle rather than issues materially as irrevocable as the choice that nineteenth-century Germany had to make between unification under Berlin or Vienna. And because political opponents in France always assumed that they had to coexist permanently in one country, they also accepted some fundamental rules of political behavior and the need for a police service standing above factional disputes.

True, much of the literature on French police was written by lawyers, journalists, and politicians who, having themselves been the target of police surveillance, often saw the police in a pessimistic light. There were charges that the police manipulated public opinion and there were accusations of police corruption in high places, notably during the Chiappe administration in the 1930s. More disturbing perhaps, critics from outside the police ranks have put in question the loyalty of the Paris police during the two German invasions in the twentieth century. (In regard to this last charge, we should remember that police forces have different duties than military personnel in the face of an enemy invasion in time of war.)[88]

The most serious criticism of the French police was political opportunism, if not in the face of enemy troops then in the face of successive revolutionary upheavals. Yet in the long-range perspective, such political flexibility by the police may actually have been all to the good. Monsieur Goron, the chief of detectives in Paris in the 1880s, saw nothing wrong about a police agent who, after many years of watching republicans for Napoleon III, began tailing Bonapartists immediately after the Empire had collapsed.[89] While Nicolas de la Reynie, the first *Lieutenant-Général de Police* of Paris, was surely right when he uttered that famous homily, "It is much easier to defend an existing order than to build a new one once it has been destroyed" (1671), France had no choice but to undertake this difficult task time and again following 1789.[90] To some contemporary observers abroad, the image of the French police weathering one change of regime after the

---

[88] E. Cresson, the police prefect of Paris in January 1871, told in his memoirs that some Parisian hotheads wanted to burn Paris down rather than let in the Prussians, in imitation of the Moscow Fire of 1812, but that the prefecture would certainly not have carried out such a policy. Cresson, *Cent Jours du siège à la Préfecture de Police* (Paris, 1901), pp. 247–8.

[89] Marie-François Goron, *Les Mémoires de M. Goron. Ancien chef de la Sûreté* (Paris, n.d.), vol. 4, p. 126; see also for the early nineteenth century Louis Canler, *Les Mémoires de Canler, ancien chef du service de sûreté* (Paris, 1882), vol. 1, pp. 42–3.

[90] In Aubert and Petit's version: "Il est plus aisé de conserver la tranquillité que de la rétablir si elle est une fois troublée." Jacques Aubert and Raphaël Petit, *La Police en France. Service public* (Paris, 1981), p. 39.

other, however, suggested fickleness and corruptibility. In 1905 a Swiss Socialist publication in Zurich exclaimed: "Who can trust information provided by the French police? A country where yesterday's hunted revolutionaries are tomorrow's ministers of interior? Where a Camille Barrère is a wanted Communard today and a French ambassador the next?"[91]

We hasten to stress that the French police was never feared like the Russian political police was, perhaps because the French police in the nineteenth century never faced situations as precarious as Russia's police did from the 1870s on and consequently was never tempted to resort to terror. It did not bear as lonely a responsibility for the preservation of the political state as did the Third Section or the Okhrana, and was never cast in the role of a belligerent in a civil war.[92] Since the fall of Joseph Fouché (1799–1817), French ministers of interior have usually been accountable to a parliament, and the French police subject to close scrutiny by the press.

Admittedly, not even the communal police in France was ever as responsive to the people's wishes as the cantonal police in Switzerland. In France, in general, the maintenance of good order was the government's business and the people's that of criticizing when things went wrong. But for a century following 1789, the French people practiced a form of direct democratic action: popular demonstrations that ended in overthrowing regimes in 1830, 1848, and 1870. (In 1852, the Napoleonic Empire was restored but without popular initiative.) And in all these crises the police was needed as the arbiter. The police managed the crowds during the political turmoil; sometimes it sought to exploit the balance of power between rebels and reactionaries while, admittedly, pursuing a policy of wait and see. But it was the one who eventually had to escort the defeated government to the frontier, and the one who decided when the barricades should come down – thereby, in effect, minimizing the loss of life and property while the country underwent yet another constitutional adjustment. As the midwife of (moderate) revolutionary change whenever such change became unavoidable; in this capacity the French police can be said to have performed a service to democracy. Only when the revolutionary process in France threatened to undermine more than the regime in power, namely the very foundation of state and society, were strong coercive methods applied: The July days in 1848 were followed by the police dictatorship of the early 1850s, and the Paris Commune of 1871 was suppressed by a massacre in May of that year.

Thus, in France the continuous adjustment of political laws to social progress was not facilitated by decentralization as in England and Switzerland, but by political flexibility in the national leadership. It was also produced by the existence of a complex array of complementary but separate national police authorities

---

[91] Sozialdemokratische Fraktion des Zürcher Kantonalrates, "Politische Polizei und Spitzelwirtschaft," (Zurich, 1905), p. 18. Barrère, as ambassador to Italy, was also French delegate to the International Anti-anarchist Conference in Rome, 1898.

[92] S. Stepniak, *Russia under the Tzars*, trans. by William Westall (London, 1885), vol. I, p. 100.

which allowed for power shifts between parallel police institutions.[93] It was France's good fortune that for the most part police power was shared between the Sûreté Générale, the Paris police, the gendarmerie, and the Deuxième Bureau (army intelligence). Also, the government officials with the power to set rules that the police had to enforce (minister of interior, prefects, and mayors) were not identical with the officials who directly commanded police operations.[94] Equally important in preventing rigid police dictatorship was the clear separation in France between the executive, the legislative, and the judiciary.[95] As Richard Cobb said, France was not a country with very tight police control, only with a plenitude of police control.[96] And Louis Casamayor, a judge and frequent critic of the French police, has argued on behalf of France that "no country can afford a truly efficient, honest and relentless police. Such a police would destroy a society. If the various elements in society could no longer flow together through constant compromise and the granting of exceptions and privileges, could society survive?"[97]

Lastly, the French national police system may be characterized in its international strategy by the words *"défense du territoire."* The phrase originated with Georges Clemenceau, the Radical leader of the Third Republic, who in 1908, as minister of interior, took much interest in police organization. According to a spy report to Chancellor Bismarck, Clemenceau in 1879 made the following declaration:

We want to destroy the political police and replace it with an aliens police. What we want is a police for the defence of the national territory [*une police de défense du territoire*] which will extend [from the French frontier] to the interior and exterior to hunt down the enemies of France [*les ennemies du territoire*] and not [French] political parties.[98]

Translated into colloquial terms, Clemenceau's formula called for the elimination of all foreign interference in French domestic politics by means of strict border controls (the famous *police spéciale*) and close surveillance of all foreign travelers on French soil (through the railway police and daily checks on hotel registrations), supplemented if need be by offensive intelligence work outside France to discover the background of suspicious aliens. With the French nation, its sovereign body, thus protected from any unwanted influence from outside, France

---

[93] Richard C. Cobb, *The Police and the People. French Popular Protests 1789–1820* (Oxford, 1970), pp. 17–18.

[94] Georges Audebert, *Organisation et méthodes de la police française* (Diss., University of Poitiers, 1938), p. 12.

[95] The police in modern France, as an arm of the executive, has performed no judicial functions. Since the abolition of the "lettres de cachet," the *police judiciaire* in France was only a detective force placed at the disposal of the public prosecutor. In Austria and in tsarist Russia, the police exercised punitive powers until the end of the First World War. See Fernand Cathala, *Cette Police si décriée* (Saverdun, 1971), p. 25.

[96] Cobb, *The Police and the People,* pp. 17–18.

[97] Louis Casamayor [Serge Fuster], *La Police* (Paris, 1973), p. 133.

[98] Report by secret agent "A" (Belina?) from Paris, 4 March 1879, in PA (Bonn), Abt. IA B.c. 81, Acta betreff. "Nachrichten von politischen und Polizei Agenten über Verhältnisse in Frankreich."

could afford true political freedom at home (the right to free association and free speech), that its citizens might oppose one another without fear, and through democratic elections determine their country's future.

Against the multinational background of Europe we may well conclude that the French police strategy of défense du territoire – nationally self-centered though it was and politically opportunistic – contained nonetheless an element of idealism, the idealism of an Ernest Renan, who in Clemenceau's time coined the phrase of the nation as *"un plébiscite de tous les jours."*[99]

The French compromises of 1815 and 1830 with some anticipatory notes on the German police situation in the 1920s

To illustrate and amplify this general commentary on the French police it is useful to study several documents concerning two events during the early nineteenth century: the second and final restoration of the Bourbon monarchy in the summer of 1815, following Napoleon's unsuccessful return to power for one hundred days; and the establishment of the July Monarchy in 1830. The behavior of the French police on these two occasions set the pattern for its performance in most government crises in the modern period. But it also bears much resemblance to the behavior of the German police following the end of the First World War. The performance of the police in Paris in the early nineteenth century and in Berlin in the early twentieth century furthermore teaches us how police authorities ensconced in powerful capital cities proceed carefully when faced not with full-scale revolution but with the delicate task of supervising a limited change in regime.

The French defeat in 1815 and the German defeat in 1918 meant for both countries the temporary loss of all military strength in the face of strong hostile forces poised at the border and in partial occupation of important strong points. From this arose the need for the two countries to rely almost exclusively on police to control a very fluid internal situation. Neither the White Terror in France nor the free corps in Germany were recognized as police, both of them disqualified by their excessive violence.[100]

The police in Paris during 1815 and 1830, and the police in Berlin after the First World War, made similar appeals to compromise and moderation. On 28 June 1815 Louis XVIII had a poster printed and displayed all over France in which he presented himself as the savior of the people from all the calamities it had suffered since 1789:

I learn that a door to my Kingdom has opened, and I hasten to return. I return to gather together my subjects who have gone astray, to soften the sufferings that I had wanted to

---

[99] Ernest Renan, "Qu'est-ce qu'une nation?" (Paris, 1882).

[100] Ernst Jünger after the First World War recognized the dependency of all governments on the professional police as the true technicians of power. "Ohne sie würden die Revolutionen im Sande verlaufen, würde eine Mischung von Untat und Geschwätz bleiben." Ernst Jünger, *Gläserne Bienen* (Frankfurt, 1960), p. 74. For Berlin, see Hsi-Huey Liang, *The Berlin Police Force in the Weimar Republic* (Berkeley, 1970), ch. 2.

spare them, to place myself for a second time between the Allied Armies and the French people in the hope that the esteem that I may enjoy [among the Allies] can be used for their salvation.

Louis XVIII next acknowledged the difficulties in restoring public order in the country: "When I came back among my people I found them rent apart by conflicting ideas and emotions." He assured them that the principle of legitimacy would be restored: "My subjects have learned through cruel experience that the principle of royal legitimacy is one of the fundamental bases of the social order, indeed the only one on which a wise and orderly form of liberty can be established in the midst of a great people." The *dîme* will not be restored, nor the feudal rights of the nobility. "I don't need to refute these fables, invented by our common enemy." But would there be a purge?

I have in recent times received the same assurance of love and fidelity from subjects belonging to all the classes. I want them to know how much I have appreciated this; so it is from Frenchmen of every rank that I now want to choose those who shall approach my person and my family.

The Frenchmen who were misguided I forgive all that has happened from the day I left Lille among so many tears, to the day when I returned to Cambrai among so many acclamations.

But an act of treason [Frenchmen rallying to Napoleon on his return from Elba] unmatched in the annals of the world has caused the blood of my subjects to be spilled. This treason is why the foreigners today stand in the heart of France. I must then, for the sake of the dignity of my throne, the welfare of my people, and the peace of Europe, withhold my pardon from those who instigated and carried out this horrible plot. They will be relegated to the legal vengeance of the two tribunals which I propose to establish without delay.[101]

Louis XVIII's proclamation was a political masterpiece. It sought to assuage national patriotism – indignant toward a dynasty brought back by the foreigners – without relinquishing the theory of divine rights of kings. It overruled traditional social divisions in favor of new categories of political merit and political guilt (always a useful way to reinforce police control), with the king reserving to himself the right to determine who would be placed where on this scale. There would be due process by law, to be sure, but who was going to appoint the new judges? Modern ideas like tax equality were acknowledged as good, though in an off-hand manner, while the old courtly language was retained when speaking about the bestowal of the king's favors. The ultimate justification for this decree was cleverly distributed between the king's personal obligation toward his house, his moral obligation toward the French nation, and Europe's need for a lasting peace.

The king's proclamation was soon followed by an equally carefully worded explication in the *Gazette officielle* of 18 July 1815, of what the Restoration regime

---

[101] Poster, available in APP (Paris), Série A A/419, folder: "Evénements de 1815 (divers)."

expected from its administrative officials. The author was Pasquier, minister of justice *per interim*, and it was addressed to all the prefects of France:

> Your administration, *Monsieur,* must be marked by reason, calm, and firmness. You must never deviate from the constitutional line followed by the King, you must closely follow in all detail the duties of your office, see that all business is handled correctly and expeditiously, that you are just and benevolent toward all, and that you appease the minds of those who are distraught and worried. The support and the individual advantages enjoyed by every citizen under a regime of liberty and a well-regulated administration are the only way to produce *a reconciliation of all parties.* [102]

Both in France after the Restoration and in Berlin after 1918, the political police was at first abolished, only to be reintroduced with some haste when it was found that political intelligence gathering was vital for all governments in a time of insecurity following an upheaval.

In 1830 the Bourbon regime collapsed under Louis XVIII's successor, Charles X, who had lacked his brother's understanding for the need to reconcile France's political factions. He was replaced by Louis Philippe of the house of Orléans as the new head of state. France was spared foreign intervention thanks to the rapidity with which the Marquis de Lafayette and his friends arranged for a successor regime. But the work of the police in Paris was also important. Order was quickly restored after a few days of barricade fighting, the police for the first time assuming the role of the caretaker of society during a quick political change.

This time it was the police, not the king, who furnished the most eloquent proclamation posted on the walls of Paris. We cite from the preamble of an appeal by the prefect of police, A. Girod, presumably dated Paris, 16 August 1830:

> We, the prefect of police, believing that order is inseparable from Liberty; that there can be no good police, no individual security, no public peace, no property, [and] no commercial or industrial prosperity if everyone is allowed to place his own interest before the interest of the community; believing that the police rules that have survived provide adequately for the regulation of everything that falls under the general interest and that, pending any revision, they be carefully observed so that the basic needs of the population are met . . .

The message ended with the assertion that the people's attachment to order was equal to its devotion to liberty. In its anxiousness to rally all the parties in a national reconciliation Girod's appeal can only be matched by the proclamations of the Berlin police in the November days of 1918, when Police President Eugen Richter called on the "conscience" of the workers not to deliver the city to its criminal elements. [103]

But national reconciliation of a defeated country will always take some time, while a capable bureaucracy was something immediately needed to assure the country's swift return to normalcy. In post-Napoleonic France as in post-Wilhelmine Germany, the pressing question was what to do with the staff of the

---

[102] *Gazette officielle du* 18 Juillet 1815, available in ibid.
[103] Poster, available in APP (Paris), Carton A A/420, folder: "Evénements divers 1830."

defunct regime. The French and later the Germans soon found that a moderate revolution is difficult to effectuate without a police strong enough to supervise the establishment of a new social equilibrium. Would such a police not inevitably have to be made up of seasoned men – therefore of men with professional experience made in the previous regime? The following order of the prefect of the department of the Dordogne, Baron Ch. Didelot, and dated Périgueux, 16 July 1815, is almost identical to appeals in Germany for Royal Prussian police officials to return to duty under the new republic:

On receipt of this order, all subprefects, mayors, deputy mayors, commissaires, and municipal councillors who, for whatever reason, were removed from their posts since 1 March, *including those who were dismissed because of the events that occurred* [i.e. Napoleon's Hundred Days], are hereby required to resume their functions. [104]

Thus the first step toward the restoration of public order is to replenish the ranks of officialdom. Political peccadilloes might even be overlooked among subordinates whose submission for that very reason may turn out to be especially fervent. An example is furnished by the following directive of the minister of interior of the prefect of police in Paris, the Comte d'Angles, on 19 October 1815. On the one hand, monetary compensation was offered to police officials who had *not* served Napoleon during the Hundred Days: "In execution of the Royal ordinance of last July, five *commissaires* and two *officiers de paix* of Paris, who were relieved of their functions during the interregnum, should be indemnified for a total of 4,255 francs, to be paid by the City of Paris."

But what about the *commissaires* who had *entered* the police service on 20 March, the very day Napoleon had resumed power in Paris, and who had not been retained in the police service since the king's return? In principle, the minister said, they should not be paid anything: "But it is my wish, *Monsieur le Préfet,* that you send me a separate report on each individual case, so that I can lift this suspension of salary from those who can be shown to have done no more than to serve the public order." [105]

In 1830 the police was less troubled than in 1815 because this time the government had fallen for political reasons, not because of inadequate police protection. [106] It had less of a problem with staffing because the ideological difference between the fallen Bourbon monarchy and the new Orléans monarchy was minor and the constitution underwent only modest changes. Instead of a turnover of personnel the police sought to enhance its visibility in the capital to strengthen its authority. This is essentially what the Berlin Police also did at the end of the First World War. Both, for example, staged massive raids on criminal haunts to affirm the presence and vigilance of the security forces. On 25 August 1830, P. Malléval, the prefect of police in Paris, sent this order to all police commissars in the city:

---

[104] APP (Paris), Série A A/419. Italics mine.   [105] Ibid.
[106] Jacques Aubert and Raphaël Petit, *La Police en France. Service public* (Paris, 1981), p. 76.

In the current situation it is important, *Messieurs*, that nothing be left undone that could strengthen order and public security. I have reason to believe that simultaneous visits to certain lodging houses known to shelter malefactors and vagrants will not be without usefulness. [. . . These visits] will have the benefit of leaving an impression on the evil-minded elements by showing them that the police is watchful and active.[107]

Keeping in touch with the situation and showing the flag was one part of this strategy. The other was to demonstrate the police's openness to the changes that were expected under the new regime. Here again, the methods in Paris in 1830 were to find their counterpart in the Berlin of the 1920s: The Paris police saw to the ceremonial burial of civil war casualties (158 "victimes de la grande semaine" who were buried near the Champs de Mars on 30 July 1830), it collected money from the employees of the police prefecture "en faveur des Victimes des 27, 28, et 29 Juillet 1830," and helped the government to estimate the cost of compensating house owners whose property had been damaged in the course of the fighting.[108] Money was paid to the old *Garde du Corps* of the fallen monarchy if they had accompanied Charles X to Cherbourg on his voyage to England.[109] And rather than order the dismantling of the revolutionary barricades in the streets of Paris, the police prefecture in July 1830 recommended "as a measure of public sanitation" cutting small openings in the barricades to drain the pools of stagnant water, placing wooden planks over them as bridges for pedestrians, and seeing to a daily cleaning around the barricades with buckets of fresh water and brooms.[110] Intermingling the prosaic with high political issues of the day was always a useful device to dampen public excitement during a crisis, whether in France in 1830 or in Germany ninety years later.[111]

Still, appeals to moderation and displays of police presence can only see a police through the first turbulent weeks after a change in regime. As calm returns, the police is expected to show endorsement of the new political course if only with token changes in official titles, insignias, or forms of salute.

Curiously, the question as to what colors the postwar regime should adopt was an issue both in Bourbon and Orléans France and in republican Germany. For a time the Weimar Republic's Black-Red-and-Gold flew side by side with the imperial Black-White-and-Red, the latter stubbornly held to by die-hard monarchists. In France, the problem was how to substitute the royal white flag for the revolutionary tricolor in 1815 and back again in 1830. Flags are important in societies mature enough to rely on symbolic demonstrations of their political commitments. In Weimar Germany's *Flaggenstreit*, police commanders like Walther Stennes refused to fly the republican colors and got away with it, and in France

---

[107] APP (Paris), Carton A A/420.   [108] Documents in ibid.

[109] Samples of certificates of the "Royaume de France, Garde-du-Corps," which entitled the bearers to claim payment for having belonged to Charles X's escort to Cherbourg, are available in ibid.

[110] See folder, "Rétablissement de la circulation dans Paris et mesures d'hygiène," in ibid.

[111] According to the police prefecture, the events of 29 July 1830 also led to the evasion of 600 prostitutes from police control, which posed an additional problem to public health. See document issued by the police prefecture, dated 17 Sept. 1830, in ibid.

an "ordre du jour" to the National Guard of Paris on 8 June 1815 designated the *cocarde blanche* as France's emblem of national unity with this enjoinder:

At the same time, His Majesty wants to see those treated with indulgency whom error and exaltation prevent from immediately accepting back this symbol of union. Above all, he wants that none of his subjects use violence to enforce [the white flag] and that the magistrates do no more than apply the laws of the state. Consequently, the National Guard will equally place under arrest those who sport colors other than the cocarde blanche and those who disturb the peace pretending to make others wear it. On this occasion, His Majesty must more than ever count on the prudence and firmness of the National Guard, which he honors and cherishes for having twice saved the capital and twice extinguished in its bosom the fires of civil strife.[112]

We may wonder whether Louis XVIII's professed trust in Paris's 11,000 National Guardsmen was more a matter of caution or hypocrisy. Had not the Garde Nationale rallied to Napoleon at the return of the emperor in 1815, ostensibly to ensure the continuation of "dispassionate public service" during a time of incertitude, as it later claimed? (That was also how Berlin's *Sicherheitspolizei* rationalized its collaboration with the impostor government of Kapp and Lüttwitz in 1920.)

There is one more idea that is associated with French police: the use of *agents provocateurs* for political espionage. The fear of the agent provocateur goes back to the ancien regime though its most successful practitioner, Police Director Joseph Fouché, had served the French Revolution and Napoleon I. The use of political undercover agents continued in the post-Napoleonic period when the unpredictable behavior of the population, particularly in Paris, caused the government great concern. Democratic political life was in its beginnings and many political movements in their experimental stage sought security in anonymity. The leaders of these secret societies with very small memberships and scarce funds – a Raspail, a Blanqui – compensated for their lack of power with extravagant plans for immediate action. "Great political crimes require educated leaders," wrote the German sociologist Hans von Hentig in the 1920s, when Germany also faced many unknown sources of subversion at home,

It requires men with trained minds and some social manners. However, educated men are normally quickly dissuaded from undertaking such action after a closer look at the various forms of prevention [police!] within society. The ones who are not so dissuaded are the clinically insane, or the fanaticized imbeciles. That is why political criminals usually are negative personalities of subordinate rank.[113]

Hentig's remarks applied to lone fanatics like Fieschi, the Corsican ex-convict, who on 28 July 1835 tried to assassinate Louis Philippe with a contraption of twenty-five muskets.[114] These individuals were so dangerous because there was

---

[112] In ibid., Série A A/419; also Louis Girard, *La Garde nationale, 1814–1871* (Paris, 1964), p. 108.

[113] Hans von Hentig, *Fouché. Ein Beitrag zur Technik der politischen Polizeien in nachrevolutionären Perioden* (Tübingen, 1919), p. 39.

[114] Georges-André Euloge, *Histoire de la police et de la gendarmerie des origines à 1940* (Paris, 1985), pp. 172–3.

no way of predicting how many people – from friends of friends down to elements of the "classe dangereuse" – might become involved in such an enterprise. Like the Weimar Republic, Orléanist France lacked a strong political ideology. Louis Philippe's challenge to the middle classes, *"enrichissez vous!"*, benefited many bourgeois entrepreneurs just as republican Germany's liberalism opened the door to many talents. But neither the French "dynasties bourgeoises", nor the cultural elite of Weimar Germany were ready to repay their debts in the form of political loyalty.

Thus the condition of the July Monarchy made aggressive intelligence among the political underworld a necessity pending the evolution of more permanent and overt forms of political life in France. To protect the government of Louis Philippe the French police used entrapment to lure the most dangerous elements into the open. It was helpful to the police that the atmosphere of mutual distrust inside the secret societies made it difficult for their members to distinguish easily a true brother from a government spy. By the time of the Third French Republic, however, France no longer needed to fear secret and unpredictable revolutionary plots from its native malcontents. It is therefore ironic that at this same time France's principal potential partner in the European balance of power, tsarist Russia, should have entered a period of flux as volatile as the 1830s had been for France, only on much vaster a scale and with much graver implications for all Europe. Russia's decision to use the French method of agents provocateurs hurt France's reputation when the two countries became allies after 1891, because it rekindled the memory of Fouché's network of informers. By the 1870s and 1880s European political life was increasingly sensitive to public opinion, and the growing chasm between democratic and autocratic countries foreshadowed the coming of the ideological conflicts of the twentieth century.

From the Revolution of 1848 to the end of the Second Empire

We have drawn on some materials from the French Restoration period and the July Monarchy to illustrate police practices in times of political unrest. But France's chief contributions to the development of police relations throughout Europe came in the Third Republic, which will be discussed in the next chapter. The intervening years from 1848 to 1870 require only a comment to explain why the police dictatorship of Louis Napoleon, insofar as it foreshadowed the coming Fascist era in Europe, also put the French people sufficiently on guard to resist it when it overtook so many other nations in the twentieth century.[115]

The question whether or not the Paris police in the February Revolution of 1848 failed in its mission as the guardian of state and society is a moot point. Was the police wrong when it allowed the gathering of over a thousand guests at a reform banquet in the 12th arrondissement on the assumption that this would re-

---

[115] Jost Düffler, "Bonapartism, Fascism, and National Socialism," in *Journal of Contemporary History*, 11 (1976), pp. 109–28.

lease some pent-up popular feelings and at the same time convince more moderate banqueteers elsewhere in Paris to cooperate with the authorities?[116] Did it open the door to anarchy when Police Prefect Delessert gave way on 24 February to Marc Caussidière, a revolutionary hothead, who was then allowed as police prefect for the next two months to use his militia, the "Montagnards," openly to support every Socialist demand made to the provisional government?[117]

From the point of view of the French police a change in regime may have been acceptable and in 1848 even desirable, but surely not the destructive behavior of the unruly mobs led by a Blanqui, a Ledru-Rollin, or a Louis Blanc in Paris, thus at the very seat of France's highly centralized government.[118] In keeping with the pattern of the political pendulum in nineteenth-century Paris, Caussidière forfeited his popular mandate by 18 May and had to give way to Jacques Trouve-Chauvel, a former mayor of Mans. In June 1848, the Paris workers were mercilessly suppressed by the troops of General Cavaignac. The one important change that resulted from the February Revolution was the beginning of a slow but steady process of decentralization and deconcentration for the French state machinery. The Revolution of 1848 confirmed the great power Paris had come to exert over France's political life. This was now recognized as a source of danger, since Paris was easy prey to irresponsible radical elements who by besieging the government could hold the entire nation to ransom. Paris was to serve only one more time as the springboard for a rapid political turnabout: that was Louis Napoleon's own coup d'état in December 1851, in preparation for the restoration of the Bonapartist empire. Soon afterward, like Hitler after 1933, Louis Napoleon in the 1850s began to transform his capital from a strategical power center into something more innocuous: a showcase of his regime's grandeur. New public squares and wider, well-paved streets were to make popular uprisings almost impossible in the future, while some of the strong points of government authority were shifted to the *départements* through administrative reorganization.[119]

---

[116] Adrien Dansette, *Deuxième République et Second Empire* (Paris, 1942), pp. 22–3. On the king's refusal to heed the counsel of the police prefect, see Euloge, *Histoire de la police et de la gendarmerie*, p. 188; and André Castelot, *Le Grand Siècle de Paris* (Paris, 1955), p. 237.

[117] Canler's memoirs describe the calm that prevailed at the prefecture on the night of 22–3 Feb. 1848. He also praised Caussidière for retaining the services of most police officials, including scores of *sergents de ville* who at first went into hiding. On assuming his post as police prefect, Caussidière did say that the neutrality of the police rather than the survival of the regime was his first concern, an idea quite compatible with "modern police" in a time of revolution. Canler, *Mémoires*, vol. 2, pp. 219–37; and Patricia O'Brien, "The Revolutionary Police of 1848," in Roger Price, ed., *Revolution and Reaction. 1848 and the Second French Republic* (London, 1975), p. 142.

[118] On the police's failure to anticipate the chance for city-wide disturbances, see André-Jean Tudesq, "Police et état sous la monarchie de juillet," in Jacques Aubert, Michel Eude, Claude Goyard, et al., eds., *L'État et sa police en France (1789–1914)* (Geneva, 1979), pp. 74–5. The Paris police may also have been miffed by orders not to use force as long as the crowds went no further than throwing stones. Karl Schröder, "Strassen- und Häuserkampf," in *Die Polizei*, Heft 20 (Nov. 1927), pp. 490–1.

[119] Ted W. Margadant in his study of *French Peasants in Revolt. The Insurrection of 1851* (Princeton, N.J., 1979), dates the movement to break up the hegemony of Paris from 1848, but as in the case of Berlin in 1933, the decline of the city's political power came slowly.

True, the thesis that the rebuilding of Paris under Prefect Baron Haussmann served the purpose of improving police security is not supported by conclusive evidence. And yet, Paris for nearly a century after 1851 experienced no more spontaneous uprisings. The outbreak of the Paris Commune at the close of the Franco-Prussian War does not dispute this point for the insurgents in 1871 did not capture the city from the authorities in street combat; they seized a citadel that the government had already abandoned some months before in the face of approaching foreign armies. At the same time, we must admit that in the second half of the nineteenth century, not only Paris, but all European cities became more or less immune to popular uprisings, probably due to many other changes, among them the great improvement in the armament of government forces. If urban historians maintain that the beautification of Paris under the Second Empire was prompted mainly by aesthetic considerations not unlike the redesigning of Washington, D.C., they may well be right. [120] At the same time, transforming Paris into a world center of culture, business, and entertainment reminds us of what Emperor Franz Joseph did for Vienna in 1857, also in response to a recent experience with revolution. It was political propaganda of a novel sort, in itself a very modern idea of policing.

If we are to comment on the Second French Empire as a possible precursor of Fascist police states in our own century, we must also from the outset recognize the limits set to Louis Napoleon's police regime. Paris, for example, not only advertised the glory of his Empire, but helped to speed its eventual demise, a little like the *Weltstadt* Berlin, which served Hitler as the stage for his triumphant parades but whose people never fully succumbed to his spell. Paris, as the Englishman J. E. C. Bodley saw in the 1880s, was Napoleon's accomplice in his fatal follies and also his most merciless critic when the time for retribution drew near. [121] By virtue of its sheer size the city from the outset of his regime defied all attempts at thorough police surveillance. Its inhabitants defiantly returned republican legislators to the Assembly from as early as 1852. On the eve of the 1870 war its proletarian quarters were alive with anticlerical, Republican, and Socialist activity beyond effective police control, while the police prefecture itself was besieged by spies of a Republican counter-police watching the comings and goings of detectives and stool pigeons. [122]

The failure of the French police to secure even Paris against subversive activity was due to the simple fact that the Second Empire was not really a revolutionary regime, and certainly not totalitarian. The French police of the

[120] Donald J. Olsen, *The City as a Work of Art* (New Haven, Conn., 1986), pp. 44–6. Howard Saalman, in *Haussmann: Paris Transformed* (New York, 1971), p. 9, acknowledges that after 1789, "the state as the ultimate instrument and master of its newly created citizens was in the ascendancy and its prerogatives practically limitless," but Haussmann's goal for Paris was not security as much as making the city more livable for the middle classes. Aubert tells us that the increase in the size of the Paris police was prompted by Louis Napoleon's wish to imitate the excellent police service in London. Aubert and Petit, *La Police en France*, p. 106.

[121] J. E. C. Bodley, *France* (London, 1907), vol. V, pp. 532–3.

[122] Frank Jellinek, *The Paris Commune of 1871* (London, 1937), pp. 22–3.

Second Empire changed mainly in technical organization. There was now more centralization to strengthen state control, and also deconcentration for better police responsiveness to local needs. The key to this development was the improved system of departmental prefects. Most incumbents of these highly powerful posts were replaced in 1852 by men whom Louis Napoleon trusted personally. The prefects were given certain executive functions previously held by cabinet ministers in Paris, notably the control over the local police in the départements which thereby became a function of the central government but were located outside Paris.[123]

Only in regard to three kinds of police activities could the Empire be called a repressive police state: there was the very heavy political censorship under General Espinasse, there were many more undercover agents than before watching political malcontents (in Paris three *brigades politiques* were established in 1856 for this purpose with a total staff of sixty-three officials),[124] and the police was used to manipulate election results in the government's favor.

All the same one cannot help but conclude that the French dictatorship in the mid-nineteenth century was essentially benign. In the three months between December 1851 and February 1852, military tribunals throughout France passed sentences on thousands of political prisoners, condemning many to exile in Cayenne or Lambassa. Most convicts were ordinary civilians ranging from landowners to simple workers. It was a harsh measure to apply to political opponents as was the confinement in 1933 of anti-Nazis in concentration camps. Both the bagnard system and the KZ system gave rise to immediate protests and sometimes these protests resulted in the release of individual prisoners. But while the KZ system in Nazi Germany became increasingly intolerant and savage, the political deportations under the French Second Empire remained comparatively lenient. Political exiles, unlike common criminals, could submit petitions for clemency and were sometimes allowed to return to France on condition that they abstained from all further political activity. In one case of banishment from the year 1856, the *préfet maritime* of the police of Lorient pleaded for a warm coat for a young convict about to be deported to Océanie for having plotted to assassinate the emperor.[125] In April 1854 an inmate of St. Pélagie prison, Charles François Marie Deney, was permitted by the prison director to visit his dying father in Paris.[126] Other prisoners at St. Pélagie were given short furloughs to take care of their private affairs. A carpenter was allowed to go to his home to take care of his tools because they were to be his only source of livelihood when his prison sentence was up.[127] We

---

[123] Howard C. Payne, *The Police State of Louis Napoleon Bonaparte, 1851–1860* (Seattle, Wash., 1966), pp. 128ff. Two excellent studies are L. Trotabas, *Constitution et gouvernement de la France* (Paris, 1924); and Joseph Barthélémy, *Le Gouvernement de la France* (Paris, 1939).

[124] Aubert, et al., eds., *L'Etat et sa police en France*, p. 102.

[125] Letter, M. Lavaux to prefect of police in Paris, concerning one Edmond Bellemare, dated Lorient (Morhiban), 19 Sept. 1856, in APP (Paris), A A/434: "2ème Empire. Attentats et complots."

[126] Préfecture de Police, 3ème Bureau, 1ère Section, to minister of interior, 18 Apr. 1854, No. 33 208, in APP (Paris), A A/434.

[127] Letter by the prisoner Henri Paté to prefect of police, June 1853, in ibid.

must remember that in the first half of the nineteenth century most Parisians lived close to the subsistence level. The police instructed the city morgue to hand out the clothing of the victims of the recent fighting to their family members when they came to reclaim them – items of clothing remained in use for several generations. [128]

One of the cleverest innovations of the Second Empire was the creation by decree of 22 February 1855 of the commissaires spéciaux. This new category of police agents was deliberately meant to exploit the revolutionary impact which the coming of railways had had on France and Europe. Since the 1840s the chief artery of national and international political communication, it proved to be an ideal source for vital information about activities that potentially affected state security. [129] Thirty commissaires spéciaux were appointed in 1855, assisted by 70 inspectors. They were assigned to major railway stations, in particular along the frontier of France and in the capitals (chef-lieux) of the départements, and in towns known for their radical inhabitants. The men were chosen for their education, intelligence, and discretion and expected to report all their observations accurately, with discrimination and subtlety. [130] But it is precisely because of the political sophistication of the commissaires spéciaux that we have reason to believe that this police force was professionally too smart to commit itself unconditionally to the Bonapartist dictatorship, whose usefulness to France barely extended beyond the first few years.

There is no evidence that any high-ranking police official went to great lengths in defence of Napoleon III's regime in its declining years. True, Louis Napoleon had greatly depended on the 40 commissaires de police in Paris, the 800 *sergents de ville* and all the brigades of the Sûreté and the officiers de la paix to carry out his coup d'état in the night of 2–3 December 1851, which laid the foundation for his personal power. [131] But the men were not told the true objective of their operation and were lured into dismissing what political doubts they might have had by relieving them of all personal responsibility for their actions. Thus Emile de Maupas, the police prefect, issued the following circular to all commissaires in Paris:

The graver the situation, the greater the importance of your functions and of your obligation to devote yourself wholeheartedly to them. Preserve the public peace with courage and unflagging energy. Do not tolerate any gathering whatsoever by people anywhere in the capital. Do not allow any meetings to take place whose purpose seem to you suspicious. The slightest attempt to stirring up disorder must be broken immediately and with unyielding force. I rely on your devotion – you can count on my support. [132]

---

[128] Préfecture de Police, 1ère Division, to Monsieur le Greffier de la Morgue, Paris, 18 Dec. 1851, in APP (Paris), A A/433. "Coup d'état 1851."

[129] Payne, *The Police State of Louis Napoleon*, pp. 19, 222.

[130] Aubert, et al., eds., *L'Etat et sa police*, p. 105.

[131] A. Granier de Cassagnac, "Récit complet et authentique des événements de décembre 1851, à Paris et dans les départements," (Paris, 1851), p. 2, in APP (Paris), A A/433.

[132] Document available in ibid.

In 1933, Hermann Göring as Prussian prime minister and minister of interior during the Nazi seizure of power was to announce in similar terms the exemption of every Prussian police officer from personal responsibility for his performance of duty as long as he showed no hesitation in striking down all opposition to the Nazi Party. In a time of political uncertainty policemen are easily tempted with such offers of immunity, but the price can be their complicity in the illegal if not criminal actions of the new rulers.

The police of the Second Empire surely knew that all that was achieved by the censorship laws was to drive expressions of discontent with the current regime from the political columns of the newspapers to the weekly literary reviews. [133] As political restrictions prompted the launching of such scandal-mongering sheets as Villemessant's *Le Figaro* and *L'Evènement,* the atmosphere of cynicism and corruption they exuded spawned a literary reaction of denunciations and disgust. Which is not to say that the police authorities might not have welcomed the mutual antagonism of intellectuals and imperial establishment since tension between distinct social elements traditionally helps to keep everyone under better control. Emile Zola made his early fortune thanks to the censor who banned his two novels *Thérèse Raquin* and *Madeleine Férat,* and because his "scientific approach" offered bourgeois France some indirect comfort: his naturalism taught that human society can be studied dispassionately and its diseases, like alcoholism and crime, cured by police. [134]

There never was a truly dangerous opposition to Napoleon III. The election of Republican candidates in defiance of the prefects' wishes was not illegal, the literary expression of disdain for the regime by noted writers immaterial. And an attempt to kill Napoleon in the spring of 1853 was the work of a secret society and not the forerunner for a massive rebellion. The Paris police responded to this attack with professional detective work rather than with politically inspired reprisals and intimidation.

Franco-Swiss relations 1848–69

There were nine plots to assassinate Napoleon III. Only the Orsini plot of 1858 represented a foreign conspiracy and consequently has received some attention in modern international law. The perpetrator was the Italian nationalist Felice Orsini, and the attack, which took place outside the Paris Opera house on 14 January, failed. Two legal issues were raised by this event: (1) The responsibility of states for plots against the security of other states by persons residing on their territory. (Orsini had planned his attack while residing in England); and (2) the right of states to grant political asylum to fugitives who advanced revolutionary causes by assassination of foreign heads of state.

---

[133] Ernest A. Vizetelly, *Emile Zola: Novelist and Reformer* (London, 1904), pp. 85–7.
[134] Matthew Josephson, *Zola and His Time* (New York, 1928), p. 93. See also George Lukacs on the Zola centenary in his *Studies in European Realism* (London, 1950).

The Orsini case brought down one British cabinet and caused the passing of an Act of Parliament in 1861 making physical attacks on foreign heads of state a capital crime in England.[135] Belgium and Sardinia were forced to tighten their laws against all activities on their territory aimed against the security of foreign states. In Germany, the *Polizeiverein deutscher Staaten* made the Orsini affair the central theme of its meeting in June 1858.[136] In France a new *loi de sûreté générale* gave the French government the power to deport political suspects overseas without trial. Prefects were instructed to use the bagnard system more diligently in communities that were considered by the ministry of interior as hostile toward the regime.[137] Switzerland was obliged by France to move all Italian fugitives away from the French border and to allow the opening of more French consulates in Swiss towns, so that more French officials could keep foreign refugees in Switzerland under observation.[138]

During the revolutionary year 1848, the Swiss had given the cause of democracy no assistance beyond offering shelter to refugees, and not to all refugees who came to its door at that. Two cantons in particular were affected by the unrest outside Switzerland: Basel, facing the revolution in the Grand Duchy of Baden,[139] and Geneva, where many French revolutionaries came to seek shelter. But only Geneva caused the federal government in Berne great concern because in the mid-nineteenth century France was still Switzerland's most powerful neighbor.

The political climate in Geneva was in any event far more radical than in Basel. But Geneva's offer of sanctuary to French agitators could not continue long after Louis Napoleon's election as president of the Second French Republic. By May 1849, the Council of State of the Republic of Geneva was forced – if only by economic difficulties – to appeal to the federal council in Berne for assistance.[140] It found the government in Berne unsympathetic toward helping these foreign arrivals. On 30 November 1848 the Bundesrat had already cautioned the cantons that international law required fugitives to be placed under police surveillance and situated away from the frontiers.[141] To be sure, when in early August 1849 the French ambassador to Berne, Charles Reinhardt, asked for Swiss assistance to

[135] Manuel R. Garcia-Mora, *International Responsibility for Hostile Acts of Private Persons against Foreign States* (The Hague, 1962), pp. 89–92.

[136] Siemann, ed., *Der "Polizeiverein" deutscher Staaten*, p. 13.

[137] Charles Seignobos, *Histoire politique de l'Europe contemporaine* (Paris, 1924), vol. I, pp. 201–5.

[138] Langhard, *Politische Polizei*, p. 108.

[139] See reports by local Basel policemen, May 1849, in StA (Basel-Stadt) Politisches FF4,1: "Eidg. Politische Polizei (Dr. Gottlieb Bischof) betr. Vereine, Flüchtlinge usw. abgegangene Schreiben 1849–1850," vol. 1; and Paul Siegfried, "Basel während des zweiten und dritten badischen Aufstandes 1848/49," in *Neujahrsblatt der Gesellschaft zur Beförderung des Guten und Gemeinnützigen zu Basel*, vol. 106 (Basel, 1928), passim; and Langhard, *Politische Polizei*, pp. 45ff.

[140] Conseil d'état de la République et Canton de Genève to M. le Président et MM. les Membres du Conseil Fédéral Suisse, 19 May 1849, in BA (Berne), Bestands-Nr. 21, Archiv-Nr. 48, Bd. 1.

[141] Langhard, *Politische Polizei*, p. 45.

control French refugees in Geneva, he was at first rebuffed.[142] A moderate letter by Reinhard was answered by Berne with an array of figures which it had obtained from the Genevan government: only 110 French refugees were in that city, the Swiss government maintained, of whom 20 to 30 already had voluntarily left for other cantons in search of work. Only 30 of these 110 French refugees lacked proper papers and so could truly be considered as "refugees."

The Berne government then counterattacked, arguing that Switzerland was fulfilling its police duties toward its neighbors as best as could be expected:

Now that we have done with the question of how many of these refugees are here, allow us to tell you that most of them have no dealings with each other and that it is a fable to pretend that they are busy plotting the subversion of the social order. Let someone tell us of just one single fact, one subversive plot, or one meeting and we shall immediately intercede against those who seek to compromise our country. But no such events have come to our attention and we have granted asylum only to people who have positively assured us not to use our territory for conspiracies against other countries.

The Genevan government also observes that French officials from adjoining regions are in Geneva every day. The Genevan Government is in constant touch with them. They [the French officials] tirelessly praise the tranquility and order in that city. The Genevan Government suggests that the French Government inquire with the French authorities along the [Swiss] frontier to find out how things stand in Geneva.[143]

The defiant tone aside, the Swiss communiqué is interesting insofar as it touches on one persistent problem in modern police work on the international level: the distinction made between foreign police officials crossing the border in civilian clothes on factfinding missions, and foreign police officials coming over to carry out executive functions with legal consequences.[144]

By September 1849 the French government's patience with the Swiss had run out. Ambassador Reinhard repeated his demand for the internment of French and Italian refugees on 3 September. Thereupon, on 10 September, the Swiss political department (in charge of foreign affairs) recommended to the federal council that it yield to French pressures despite Geneva's objections. Some passages of this recommendation are worth quoting in full because, rather surprisingly, a copy of it was sent directly to Monsieur Reinhard:

We cannot deny that Switzerland had in the recent past actively endorsed the principle of internment whenever a considerable number of refugees settled in Switzerland close to the frontier, even in the absence of ostensible conspiratorial activity on their part. . . . Not to do this would have invited, at the very least, foreign military and police measures to the detriment of Swiss interests.

[142] Charles Reinhard, French minister to Switzerland, to President Furrer, Berne, 6 Aug. 1849, in BA (Berne), Bestands-Nr. 21, Archiv-Nr. 48, vol. Bd. 1.
[143] Draft of an answer by the Swiss Bundesrat to Minister Reinhard, Berne, 20 Aug. 1849, in ibid.
[144] See the case of two French police agents chased out of Geneva by a mob in July 1849, as reported in a letter, Le Procureur Général près de la cour d'appel de Lyon au Ministère de la Justice (in Paris), Lyon, July 1849, in ibid.

1. All Europe sees in Geneva the capital of political and social propaganda. This view may be exaggerated, but it is not entirely spurious if we consider the geographical location of this city, its people, and the perennial presence there of revolutionary leaders, above all the apparent tendency of the [Genevan] government to assist these people in every way and through them to become engaged in international developments and to involve Switzerland in French affairs.

2. It is notorious that a Socialist club has been opened in Geneva under the chairmanship of Galeer. What French Socialism stands for can be deduced from the various revolutionary experiments in France, none of which, so far, has submitted a rational plan to demonstrate its capacity to cure social ills. All that these revolutions show is that they undermine the existing society by inciting the have nots against the haves. . . .

3. The persistent official reports by French civil authorities [about radicalism in Geneva] cannot be groundless. They contain a considerable measure of inner probability [*innere Wahrscheinlichkeit*] and they have been confirmed by the numerous testimonials of trustworthy private persons. In the face of all this less credence can be given to the report of the Government of Geneva, which denies everything either because it is ignorant about many things or because it has a peculiar idea about what constitutes abuse of asylum.

The political department ended by saying Switzerland should accede to the French demands. Because the French refugees would be interned on orders of the Swiss Confederation, the Confederation would bear the cost, which would also ease the financial strain on Geneva.[145] The Genevan authorities thereupon submitted to the federal council, but did so under protest.

By the fall of 1849 the Federal government had the refugee situation well in hand. There were about 2,000 refugees in Switzerland, reported Dr. Gottlieb Bischoff, head of the Swiss political police from Berne, dated 26 January 1850: mostly German, French, and Italian political refugees, but also Austrian army deserters and "individuals of various nations whom their governments had ordered to go to Switzerland." This included "Poles, whose home authorities had given them passports valid for Switzerland together with an order to emigrate."[146] The man in charge of refugees was Federal Councillor Henri Druey, chief of the department of justice and police (EJPD) in Berne.[147]

Druey, in collaboration with the French police, saw to the transportation of inconvenient refugees out of Switzerland, if not out of Europe altogether. Local cantons like Basel and Zurich would report to Berne their expenses as they helped politically inconvenient foreigners to leave Switzerland (the latter were given clothing, railway tickets, sometimes pocket money) usually with the destination of Le Havre, the French port where many emigrants for America boarded ship.[148]

---

[145] Letter by Dr. Furrer, dated 12 Sept. 1849, available in ibid.

[146] Circular letter, EJPD to all police departments, Berne, 26 Jan. 1850, in StA (Basel-Stadt), Politisches FF4, 2.

[147] Circular letter, H. Druey, chief of the EJPD, to Cantons Basel-Stadt, Basel-Land, Solothurn, Aargau, Berne, Neuchâtel, Waadt, and Geneva, (n.d., but presumably 1850), in BA (Berne), Bestands-Nr. 21, Archiv-Nr. 48, Bd. 1.

[148] For example, report by Bundesrath Furrer, Berne, 23 Jan. 1851, in StA (Basel-Stadt), Politisches FF4,1, Bd. 2.

Some of these refugees carried pistols, which the neutral Swiss feared might compromise them because it was they who had issued their travel papers. On the other hand, as one refugee pleaded, "these arms are of very great use in America." In the end arrangements were made to send the pistols to the port of embarkation under separate cover.[149] In February 1850 Druey granted one German refugee 100 francs payable only by the Swiss consul in Le Havre.[150] Two others in 1852 he was willing if need be to have escorted by Swiss police as far as the French coast.[151]

Yet in spite of all this improvement in Franco-Swiss relations, the humiliation of General Dufour's trip to Paris to placate Louis Napoleon was still necessary in 1852. The main reason was the agitation by expatriate Frenchmen in Geneva in response to Louis Napoleon's coup d'état on 2 December 1851. On 5 December seven persons in Geneva issued an open call to arms to the French people. French language papers in Switzerland, among them the *Tribune Suisse*, published articles with invidious comments on President Louis Napoleon and his coming dictatorship in France.[152] For Switzerland the situation was aggravated by the strong support which Austria and England gave the Paris government shortly after the coup d'état of December 1851. W. S. Granville, the British minister in Berne, urged the Swiss to find ways consistent with their independence and dignity to meet all reasonable demands of their neighbors, so as "to prevent any military occupation of their territory."[153]

The Swiss government needed no such warning from London. Two days earlier, it already had decided that the French government had to be mollified. Fearing the French embassy in Berne might have contributed to the hostility of the Quai d'Orsay, the political department decided to send as special emissary to Paris Louis Napoleon's old military instructor, the Swiss General Guillaume Henri Dufour. Dufour accepted the mission to plead with his former pupil in a letter to Dr. Jakob Konrad Kern, president of the Swiss Confederation, dated 2 February 1852.

I interpret the note from the French minister the same way you do. Its character and the language it employs are such, that were the Federal government to accept it, it would give up our country's independence. No one but the Federal government should decide what measures must be taken to see that its decisions are respected and that its right as a neutral and hospitable country are upheld. The pretensions of this note are therefore exorbitant. We must reject it.

At the same time, I must admit that [the note] does not surprise me at all, because the cantonal governments (or at least some of them) have not done all they could have and – even more – *should* have done, to carry out the orders of the federal council whose purpose

---

[149] Letter, Gaston Carrière to Basel police, Manheim, 5 June 1852, in StA (Basel-Stadt) FF4,2.

[150] Letter, Bundesrath Druey to Dr. Bischoff, Berne, 2 Feb. 1850, in ibid.

[151] Letter, H. Druey to Dr. Bischoff, Berne, 19 Mar. 1850, in ibid.

[152] Schweizerischer Bundesrath, "Das öffentliche Recht der Schweiz über den Missbrauch der Presse gegen fremde Staaten." (27 April 1888), in BA (Berne), Bestands-Nr. 21, Archiv-Nr. 14447.

[153] Letter, Granville to W. S. Christie, esq., Foreign Office, 6 Feb. 1852, in ibid.

was to stop the criminal activities of certain refugees. . . . We therefore must become twice as severe toward these individuals and make sure that the orders of the federal council are not evaded as they have been to this date, and that its police measures are given full effect. Only this will calm the irritation of our neighbors and make them give up their pretensions. [154]

On 29 November 1869 the Swiss federal council gave an account of the development of Franco-Swiss relations over the preceding thirty years to a session of the Federal Assembly in Berne. France and Switzerland had signed an extradition agreement in 1828, the report began, but because of the rapid changes in the overall political and social conditions in Europe the treaty had required repeated amendments, adding more and more offenses to the list of extraditable crimes. In the early 1850s negotiations took place with a view of concluding a new extradition treaty whose coverage the French hoped would also include "betrayal of confidence by a salaried employee" and "abuse of confidence inside domestic households." During the years 1854–6 (the years of the Crimean War) success had seemed near, however, negotiations were broken off in 1856 because of the Swiss refusal to extend the treaty to political crimes. [155]

Had Napoleon III's declining political fortunes after the Orsini affair and the Italian war of 1859 against Austria stiffened the Swiss attitude towards France? When negotiations between Paris and Berne finally resumed in 1868 the Austro-Prussian war had been fought and Napoleon's position had become perilous in the face of a powerful opposition at home and a victorious Prussia across the Rhine. The Swiss justified the conclusion of a treaty with France on 9 July 1869 by the steady growth of social and economic relations between the inhabitants of the two countries. But still the Swiss adamantly refused to include assassinations of heads of state among the list of common extraditable crimes, stubbornly holding to a position which they said was dictated by their faith in democratic republican government. [156] Little wonder the French were distrustful of Swiss neutrality when, in the following year, Prussia and France went to war over the future of Central Europe.

Police in Germany. Prussia and the idea of "Burgfrieden"

General remarks

German literature on police is rich in theoretical writings and in tales of misfortunes and crimes. It is shorter on political and institutional history. The novelist Heinrich Böll discovered in the 1960s that there existed no adequate text on Ger-

[154] Ibid.
[155] Comte de Salignac-Fénelon to Swiss president, Berne, 25 Sept. 1854; and also Botschaft des Bundesrathes an die hohe Bundesversammlung, betreffend den Auslieferungsvertrag mit Frankreich (vom 29. Nov. 1869), in BA (Berne), Bestands-Nr. 21, Archiv-Nr. 24626, vol. 3.
[156] Ibid.

man police history for use in West Germany's police academies. [157] Many German police texts are also marked by a didactic tone that seems to confirm the cliché about the people's alleged submissiveness to authority, its *Polizeifrömmigkeit* and *Polizeihörigkeit*. [158] "There is no police writer," F. C. B. Avé-Lallemant, a criminal director in Lübeck, wrote more than a hundred years ago, "and were he but the editor of a miserable dictionary of criminal slang, who will not lecture us with the earnestness of one confiding a scientific secret, that the source of all police is contained in the Greek word politeia." [159]

If we turn to German literary references to police outside police publications, we find that the idea of German submissiveness to authority needs qualification. In the late eighteenth and early nineteenth centuries the police came in for much denunciation by writers of the stature of Gotthold Ephraim Lessing, Friedrich von Schiller, Hoffmann von Fallersleben, Heinrich Heine and not the least by Karl Marx, whose *Communist Manifesto* named as the worst persecutors of the workers "the Pope and the Tsar, Metternich and Guizot, French radicals and German police." [160] If the number of these critics was not very large, we must make allowance for the fact that not until after the Second World War did Germany begin to have writers seeking political influence. [161] A Heine who protested against police oppression made no proposal for police reform. He jeered at the police in the same irresponsible way students in his days jeered at the police. Perhaps this was so because there was no point in demanding a democratic police before Germany had a democratic socioeconomic foundation, and Germany was not likely to have a society with economic stability and political freedom until it attained military security through national unity. Though for centuries close to the cultural orbit of France, England, and the Lowlands, Germany, not unlike Russia, was conscious of having to catch up with the more advanced nations of the West, which could give state and people a common cause. [162]

Wilhelm Raabe's popular novel *Die Chronik der Sperlinggasse* (published around 1856) poked fun at the police in the person of the bumbling Berlin

[157] Ernst-Ullrich Pinkert, "Schriftsteller und Staatsgewalt in Deutschland" (Diss., Philipps-Univ. Marburg, 1979), p. 63.

[158] Heinrich Hoffmann's children's book, *Der Struwwelpeter* (1845) has often been called authoritarian, because its admonitions to good behavior consist of a mixture of appeals to conscience and threats of humiliation and punishment. For a recent indictment of the Germans' meekness in the face of uniformed authority, see a poem by Helga Novak, "vom Deutschen und der Polizei," in Klaus Wangenbach, ed., *Deutsche Literatur der sechziger Jahre* (East Berlin, 1968). See also the reference to the sycophantic behavior of German children toward police in Jerome K. Jerome's *Three Men on a Bummel* (1894), which surprisingly was published in H. Degenhardt and M. Hagemann, *Polizei und Kind* (Berlin, 1926), pp. 58–60.

[159] Friedrich C. B. Avé-Lallemant, *Physiologie der deutschen Polizei* (Leipzig, 1882), p. 4.

[160] Pinkert, "Schriftsteller und Staatsgewalt," passim; also Gordon A. Craig, "Friedrich Schiller and the Police," in *Proceedings of the American Philosophical Society* 9 Dec. 1968, pp. 367–70.

[161] Robert Minder, *Dichter in der Gesellschaft. Erfahrungen mit deutscher und französischer Literatur* (Frankfurt a.M., 1966), ch. I.

[162] See Hajo Holborn, "Der deutsche Idealismus in sozialgeschichtlicher Beleuchtung," in *Historische Zeitschrift*, vol. 174 (1952), pp. 359–85.

constable Stülpnase. But Raabe's description applied to the Biedermeier Germany before unification and industrialization. Novels written during or about the 1920s and 1930s treat German policemen with greater respect, or at least with serious attempts at understanding their difficult job. Since 1945 the rise of a rebellious youth movement in West Germany, and the spectacle of citizens courageously defying arbitrary police rule in the German Democratic Republic for forty years, have laid to rest the image of German men and women as incapable of standing up to defend their personal freedom.

Besides qualifying the image of the German people as consistently *"polizeifromm,"* we need to offer a reason why the German public until very recently has unquestioningly shown much propensity to obey the police. While intellectual historians give importance to the Lutheran influence on German political attitudes since the sixteenth century,[163] the police historian will emphasize Germany's long territorial fragmentation into small particularistic states and the resulting preponderance of low police in controlling public life. While France since Richelieu and Mazarin grew into a unified kingdom with a central police ministry in Paris, no city until 1871 could aspire to become Germany's capital and no German government build a national ministry of police until 1936. In the political culture of German *Kleinstaaterei,* where many rulers personally regulated pigeon keeping and chimney sweeping, "the relationship between princely authority and subjects could not be otherwise than humiliating and oppressive."[164]

The result was not only widespread petty theft in the German countryside in the first half of the nineteenth century,[165] but also a heavy burden of bureaucratic oppressiveness in the tightly controlled small towns, many of them still surrounded by protective walls until the 1850s. We read in Friedrich Rettig's compilation of the police laws in the Grand Duchy of Baden that to be admitted as a resident in a local township a candidate had to swear an oath of loyalty to the ruling house and demonstrate some knowledge of reading and writing. But more important, he had to behave with industriousness, sobriety, Godfearingness and instantly obey all military and police orders.

Whoever flaunts an order from the authorities or their representatives with the aim of subverting their intention will be punished with penitentiary. The same punishment applies to any person who is summoned to lend [the authorities] a helping hand and fails to do so, thereby causing the escape of a suspect or some other danger to public peace.[166]

---

[163] For an interesting discussion of this question, see D. Iwand, "Gott mehr gehorchen als den Menschen," in Bundeszentrale für Heimatdienst, *20. Juli 1944* (Bonn, 1954), pp. 140–6.

[164] Fritz Veljavec, *Die Entstehung der politischen Strömungen in Deutschland, 1770–1815* (Munich, 1951), p. 73.

[165] Friedrich C. B. Avé-Lallemant, *Das deutsche Gaunertum in seiner socialpolitischen, literarischen und linguistischen Ausbildung bis zu seinem heutigen Bestande* (Leipzig, 1858–1862), 4 vols.; and Friedrich Eberhardt, *Polizeiliche Nachrichten von Gaunern, Dieben, und Landstreichern nebst deren Personal-Beschreibungen. Ein Hülfsbuch für Polizei- und Criminal-Beamte, Gensd'armen, Feldjäger und Gerichtsdiener* (Coburg, 1828), p. 14.

[166] Friedrich Rettig, ed., *Die Polizeygesetzgebung des Grossherzogthums Baden* (Karlsruhe, 1826), p. 181.

It seems safe to say that most German small burghers in the time of the Confederation (1815–66) willingly accepted low-level police tutelage in return for the security of having a hometown to call their own.[167] "A police ban is no laughing matter," wrote Ernest Dronke (1822–91), himself a man hounded from Berlin, Leipzig, and Altenburg for "disrespect toward the authorities."

No need for a court decision or a legal order, yet it hurts much more than placing someone under arrest. . . . Wherever [the fugitive] turns he will find police waiting to refuse him the right to establish residence. No one who has ever been marked by police can escape the curiosity of petty police minds. They lurk in every locality, always pleased to find someone they can report. Germany lacks [political] unity, but its police forces work together.[168]

The Prussian police idea of the "Burgfrieden"

The Prussian kingdom – and after 1871 its de facto successor state, the German Empire – is the only power which we study in this book that must be categorized as a military state more than a police state. The priority its government assigned to external defense matters is understandable considering that throughout the first half of the nineteenth century Prussia's domestic life was exposed to the repeated interference of Vienna and St. Petersburg.[169] For the police historian this means paying special attention to Prussia's concern over its war readiness during this period. The files of the Prussian ministry of justice for this period offer various illustrations of this. Thus, between 1803 and 1840, Prussian lawmakers argued repeatedly whether and how far the practice of dueling among the nobility should be curtailed. Should courts of honor be instituted to dissuade contestants from resorting to combat? Should medical doctors be required to report patients with wounds sustained in a duel? While personal combat undermined the authority of the state the Prussians also feared that banning dueling outright would undermine the aristocratic and soldierly sense of honor. Their dilemma stood in sharp contrast to contemporary legal opinion in France, where a lawyer in an article published by the *Gazette des Tribunaux* in 1837 (and which was read by the Prussian lawmakers) dismissed duels as relics of the Middle Ages. "Duels were then seen by the common people as the judgment of God not unlike witch trials

---

[167] Mack Walker, *German Home Towns. Community, State, and General Estate 1648–1871* (Ithaca, N.Y., 1971), p. 307. Even the poet Goethe dutifully reported to the police of Saxony-Weimar the personal shortcomings of his house servants. Pinkert, "Schriftsteller und Staatsgewalt," pp. 38–9; and H. N. Houben, *Der polizeiwidrige Goethe* (Berlin, 1932).

[168] Ernst Dronke, *Polizei-Geschichten* (orig., 1846; Göttingen, 1968), p. 55. A lighter note is struck in Wilhelm Raabe's *Chronik der Sperlinggasse* (Hamm, 1954; first published 1856), p. 91, where the victims of police eviction decide to make a picnic in the forest outside Berlin and find a beautiful bird's nest: "Es ist doch prächtig, wenn einen die Polizei so früh hinausjagt in den Wald!"

[169] "Memorial des Kaisers Nikolaus über die preussischen Angelegenheiten von 1848," in W. A. von Eckardt, *Berlin und St. Petersburg. Preussische Beiträge zur Geschichte der russisch-deutschen Beziehungen* (Leipzig, 1880), pp. 17–56.

by water or fire," wrote Maître Dupin, and he denied that they still had a place in the modern civilization of Europe.[170]

Another worry of the Berlin government was whether exempting foreigners from military service would undermine the patriotism of rank-and-file soldiers – exempting well-to-do foreigners, that is, whose willingness to settle in the kingdom depended on the severity of Prussia's conscription laws. The question was debated on highest cabinet order in the royal state council in 1821 and resulted in a seven-to-three vote against exempting any foreigners from army duty, even at the risk of Prussia forfeiting some commercial advantages.[171]

A third way in which the Prussian government showed its nervousness about the prospect of war were the preparations made in mid-nineteenth century in anticipation of an enemy invasion along the border with France and Austria. Orders were prepared in Berlin in 1840, 1850, and variously in the 1860s for the evacuation of local civil servants, government property, and any movable goods likely to be useful to an invader. Only the judicial authorities and police were told to continue doing their work under enemy occupation and prison guards instructed to make sure no dangerous criminals escaped. Preparations were also made for the evacuation of the lower classes from important forts likely to come under enemy siege, with the use of force if necessary.[172] In 1862 the Prussian ministry of justice was told that in case of a French attack on the twin cities of Cologne and Deutz some 58,000 people would have to be evacuated because of insufficient food stocks. (By 1870 the number of would-be evacuees was estimated at 100,000.)

Those who will have to be evacuated will find themselves suddenly reduced from a more or less adequate (or at least tolerable) condition to penury and distress. They will also lose most of their possessions because there will be no transportation. As long as the enemy encirclement has not yet taken effect and the siege is not felt, it will certainly be impossible to persuade them to make this sacrifice. Rather, it must be assumed that the vast majority of those to be evacuated will refuse to leave unless force is used – and we mean extreme force. But if extreme force is used we must also expect bitter resistance, which could escalate into rebellion and so threaten the security of the fortress.

Even were it possible to evacuate these thousands of people there would be great difficulty in finding them new work. The general disruption of economic life throughout the country because of the war will endanger the livelihood of the entire working class, [but in particular] of workers driven from their hometowns on short notice.[173]

[170] Procureur Dupin in *Gazette des Tribunaux* (no. 3677), 23 June 1837, in ibid.
[171] "Gutachten der VI. II. und V. Abtheilung des Königlichen Staatsraths über die Militair-pflichtigkeit der Ausländer." Document available in GPStA (Berlin), Rep. 84a/2234, Justiz-Ministerium, Acten . . . betreff. "Die Militärpflichtigkeit der Ausländer, (1822–84)."
[172] Document in GPStA (Berlin), Rep. 84a/11603, Justiz Ministerium betreff: "Das Verfahren der Civilbehörde bei einer etwa eintretenden feindlichen Invasion 1840–1866."
[173] Votum, dem Königlichen Staats-Ministerium vorzulegen, Berlin, 6 July 1862, in ibid. After the armistice of 28 Jan. 1871, Bismarck complimented the police prefect of Paris on the perseverance of the city's inhabitants. "Any German general who exposed 2 million inhabitants to starvation in a city that is not a citadel would have been court martialled." Cresson, *Cent Jours du siège*, pp. 296–7.

The Prussian authorities rejected the idea of confiscating food stores from the rich for general distribution, as they also seemed to give no thought to means of alleviating the class war. Unlike the Swiss, they did not counsel against Prussia going to war in the first place because of the domestic problems war would create.[174] The idea of clearing the decks of external combat by simply evicting all domestic malcontents rather than by patiently seeking to reconcile conflicts within the society – this was what gave the Prussian, and later the German, police style its militaristic coloring. Mentally it amounted to the extension of the system of well-secured local hometowns to the state level. Bismarck applied this strategy between 1878 and 1890 when he evicted hundreds of "unpatriotic" Socialist leaders to Switzerland, and so did extremist nationalists after the First World War when they demanded the expulsion of all foreigners who had settled in Germany after 2 August 1914. The Nazi concept of the Volksgemeinschaft is derived from this territorial idea of ensuring domestic order, in this case escalated during the Second World War to insane proportions. While the term "Burgfrieden" is popularly known only as Kaiser Wilhelm II's appeal to national solidarity at the outbreak of the First World War, as a characteristic attitude of the Prussian police style it dates from the early nineteenth century.[175]

Prussia's military response to the Revolution of 1848

The popular uprising in Berlin in March 1848 was never attributed to a failure of the local police. Berlin in the pre-March period was not a town simmering with revolutionary discontent. A young city as European capitals go, Berlin counted just over 40,000 inhabitants in the 1840s, still small enough to possess some of the ambiance of a hometown where popular festivals were celebrated with the modest restraint befitting an impoverished kingdom under a mellowing absolutist regime. There was no class of very rich burghers as in the prosperous sea-trading cities like Hamburg or Lübeck, nor the perpetual menace of a pauperized class as in Paris. Adolph Glassbrenner, whose humorous stories of life among Berlin's servant and tradesman class popularized the common people's slang, helped to mitigate the industrial class conflict that was in the making. Bettina von Arnim (1785–1859) had written her volume of social protest, *Dies Buch gehört dem König* (1843), to denounce the poverty in Berlin's Voigtland, but by the accounts of local Berlin historians this was a slum area of no more than two or three blocks of houses.[176]

---

[174] Otto-Ernst Schüddekopf points to Switzerland's solution, which was to trade its liberty of action abroad for the freedom to run its home affairs as it liked, in *Die deutsche Innenpolitik im letzten Jahrhundert und der konservative Gedanke* (Braunschweig, 1951), p. 12.

[175] The suppression of domestic conflict was as important under the Second Empire as under the Third Reich. See Hans-Ulrich Wehler, *The German Empire, 1871–1918* (Dover, N.H., 1985), p. 130; and John G. Kormann, "U.S. Denazification Policy in Germany," (HICOG, 1952), p. 1–2.

[176] Walther Oschilewski, "Karl Marx als Student in Berlin," in *Jahrbuch des Vereins für die Geschichte Berlins* (Berlin, 1953), pp. 97–124; and Rudolf Stadelmann, *Social and Political History of the German 1848 Revolution*, trans. by James G. Chastain (Athens, Ohio, 1977), p. 26.

The worst disturbances in Berlin during the decades before 1848 were riots in 1830, 1835, and the "potato war" in 1847: Four days of disorders and plundering brought about by food shortages. They could not be compared to the bitter riots in Paris, Lyon, and Marseille in the early nineteenth century.[177]

Berlin was served by a royal police authority since 1742, which after 1810 functioned under the name Polizeipräsidium. The street police was surprisingly small: 40 sergeants in command of 110–20 gendarmes, plus nightwatchmen and market masters, and special sergeants for emergencies.[178] Obviously the Berlin authorities in the Biedermeier period did not anticipate large-scale political disturbances. After the March Revolution of 1848 the Prussian government blamed the turmoil on foreign agitators (Polish officers, Romanian students, and Swiss radicals) who allegedly had entered the city in large numbers during the preceding weeks. But local chroniclers who point to the advertisements outside news offices and the new newspaper cafés as dangerous political forums agree that the event was precipitated by tales of popular uprisings, especially those coming from France. The news of the fall of Louis Philippe reached Berlin on the day it happened, Saturday, 26 February, and provoked immediate discussion among the population at large. After two weeks of mounting political debate throughout the city, a demonstration of Berliners clashed with soldiers near the Royal Castle on 13 March, and within days Berlin was dotted with hundreds of barricades.[179]

The prompt capitulation of the royal authorities in turn militated against the transformation of this spontaneous insurrection into a true revolutionary force comparable to Kossuth's regime in Hungary. Like the Viennese burghers, the Berlin burghers had too much to lose from full-scale civil war. The citizens' guard (Bürgerwehr) which assumed police duty in Berlin on 19 March – with the Royal Police President von Minutoli himself in temporary command – quickly discredited itself by its incompetence and venality. In June, the military under General Friedrich von Wrangel, which had withdrawn to Potsdam in March, returned to disband the Bürgerwehr. In July the government was already building a new armed police, the Schutzmannschaft, this time 1,630 men strong and equipped with the latest infantry muskets plus sabers and pistols.[180]

By October Prussia was charged by the Confederation to use its armed force in a police operation to help other German states reestablish order in their respective territories. Reich Governor Johann (an Austrian archduke elected by the Frankfurt Parliament) appointed the Prussian major-general, Eduard von Peucker, as Reich minister of war. The Prussian soldiers' mission was to protect the life and

---

[177] Dirk Blasius, *Bürgerliche Gesellschaft und Kriminalität. Zur Sozialgeschichte Preussens im Vormärz* (Göttingen, 1976), pp. 51–4; and Wolfgang Ullrich, *Verbrechensbekämpfung. Geschichte, Organisation, Rechtssprechung* (Berlin-Spandau, 1961), pp. 39–43.

[178] Willy Feigell, *Die Entstehung des Königlichen Polizei–Präsidiums zu Berlin in der Zeit von 1809 bis 1909* (Berlin, 1909), p. 28.

[179] Ernst Kaeber, *Berlin 1848* (Berlin, 1948), ch. 3.

[180] Paul Schmidt, *Die ersten 50 Jahre der Königlichen Schutzmannschaft zu Berlin* (Berlin, 1898), pp. 17–35.

property of individual burghers against disturbers of the peace and to help local governments to restore the public order "whose legal and peaceful reform," so a proclamation of the Reich governor read, "is already underway everywhere."[181] The Prussian troops by all accounts acquitted themselves quite satisfactorily as defenders of law and order. Few communities complained about their behavior, though some found the cost of feeding and lodging them onerous.[182] Indeed there are documents in the German Bundesarchiv in Frankfurt a.M. from the events of 1848 which suggest that the Prussian soldiers went out of their way to give good treatment to the political prisoners they took in this operation.[183]

The mobilization of Reich troops under General von Peucker was made more attractive to German patriots by presenting it as an action in defense of German national sovereignty. In November 1848 Switzerland was accused by the Grand Duchy of Baden to give sanctuary to German insurgents in nearby Basel: The Swiss president, Furrer, in December, personally came to order their evacuation to the interior.[184] France was more difficult. Spies of the ministry of war of Baden related that German refugees in Besançon and Nancy were provided by the French with food, clothing, shelter, and a daily allowance, and also permitted to practice military drill (though not out of doors).[185] To the chagrin of the Frankfurt government, the Paris authorities also delayed the extradition of fugitives whom the German provisional government charged with complicity in the murder on 19 September 1848 of Prince Lichnowsky and General von Auerswald, two members of the German National Assembly. The French minister of justice, Marie, dismissed the German request with ill-concealed condescension: "I cannot see myself delivering [to another country] eighteen foreigners who have sought refuge on our territory as a result of civil war and who do not appear to be professional evil-doers, just on some vague assumption that they have committed murder." The suspects were not extradited until ten months later (June 1849) by order of the new president, Louis Napoleon.[186]

The Prussian response to the Revolution of 1848 did not emphasize police work but war making. First the Prussia king, on the advice of General Radowitz, proposed a new confederation under his own leadership and with the title Deutsches Reich, only to discover that such a bold move to forestall more uprisings by placing Prussia at the head of a unified German nation was unrealistic without the military preparation to overcome Austrian and Russian objections. We are therefore less concerned with the creation of the Prussian Schutzmannschaft in 1850

---

[181] Proclamation by Reich governor, Archduke Johann, and Reich minister of interior, Schmerling, Frankfurt, 2 Oct. 1848, available in BA (Frankfurt a.M.), Reichsministerium des Innern, DB 55/37.
[182] For example, complaint by the burghers of Göttingen, 4 Nov. 1848; and by those of Donaueschingen, 19 Nov. 1848, in ibid., Reichsministerium des Krieges, DB 56/42.
[183] Report by Lieutnant-General von Huser, Mainz, 20 Sept. 1848, in ibid.
[184] Report by Baden authorities to Frankfurt, 9 Dec. 1848, in ibid.
[185] See reports by agents of Baden dated 18 and 20 Nov. 1848, in ibid.
[186] Documents available in ibid., Reichsministerium des Innern, DB 55/37.

than with the use of the Prussian army for policing civilians in non-Prussian territory: as imperial soldiers in other states of the German Confederation during the
period of pacification in 1848–9, and in 1866 and 1870 as occupation troops in
Bismarck's wars of unification. The fact that Prussia sought a military answer to
the problems of 1848 meant that for the remainder of the nineteenth century the
army took precedence over the police as the chief executive arm of the state. Besides, the Prussian police, as we know, had long assumed that the revolutionary
unrest in Prussia was beyond the control of local security forces. The events of
March of that year had only reaffirmed to the Berlin police that cultivating tolerable relations with the inhabitants was no protection against revolutionary currents originating from elsewhere in Europe.

Bismarck on police

While the Frankfurt government resented French sympathies toward German
revolutionaries in 1848, the subsequent relationship of France and Prussia in the
time of Louis Napoleon was determined strictly by considerations of state interest
and power. Neither side sought to interfere in the domestic affairs of the other to
gain political advantage. This worked against the French because it meant that
they could not make full use of their more sophisticated police apparatus. What
France needed more than good police was military preparation for the coming
conflict with Prussia. But for various reasons Napoleon III's plan to introduce the
Prussian *Landwehr* system and other army reforms in France was fatally delayed
by disagreements among legislators and professional soldiers until it was too
late.[187] Of course, whereas Napoleon's gifts as a police director were useless in the
war against Bismarck, Bismarck's own talents as a diplomat no longer sufficed
after the German Empire was forged in 1871 and his empire, in turn, faced many
domestic security problems.

By reputation Machiavellians both, Louis Napoleon and Bismarck were radi-
cally different in character, temperament, and political thinking. Bismarck had
never, like Louis Napoleon, led the lonely existence of a conspirator scheming to
seize power and he disapproved of rebels like Brutus and Wilhelm Tell.[188] The
French emperor was an *idéologue* at least by disposition and as such anticipated the
thinking of totalitarian leaders of the twentieth century. While Louis Napoleon,
characteristically, had volunteered for constable work during the Chartist troubles
in London, Bismarck's own experience with low-level criminal courts during his
youth had not inspired him with a high regard for police work. Police President

[187] On the plans for army reform in France, see Napoleon III, *Oeuvres*, vol. II (Paris, 1856), pp.
299–323; and Emile Ollivier, *L'Empire libéral. Études, récits, souvenirs* (Paris, 1907), vol. XI, pp.
272–3. On their failure, consult Edwin Pratt, *The Rise of Rail Power in War and Conquest, 1833–
1914* (London, 1915), pp. 138–9; and General Jarras, *Souvenirs* (Paris, 1892), pp. 30–7; Bismarck's appreciation of Napoleon III's political talents is discussed in Otto Vossler, "Bismarck's
Ethos," in *Historische Zeitschrift*, vol. 171, No. 2 (Mar. 1951), p. 278.

[188] Otto Fürst von Bismarck, *Gedanken und Erinnerungen* (Stuttgart, 1898), vol. I, p. 15.

von Minutoli's cooperation with the Berlin rebels in March 1848 and his popularity among Berliners at that time appalled him.[189] He also disapproved of the peaceful disarmament of the Bürgerwehr by General Wrangel. A small but decisive armed encounter would have been better, Bismarck thought, because it would have publicly and unequivocally demonstrated where the preponderance of power lay.[190] All application of *materielle Polizeigewalt* presumes that a ruler knows where his country's interests lies and that he has the conviction to defend them.[191] Bismarck showed greater interest in police work as strategic military espionage. In May 1866 he ordered the Berlin police councillor, Dr. Wilhelm Stieber, who had transferred from the criminal police to the state police (*Sicherheitsabteilung*) in 1853, to organize a secret intelligence operation to find out how well prepared the Habsburg monarchy was for war; and a similar operation was launched by Stieber against France in 1869.[192]

Prussia's police problem was indeed complicated by the fact that it was subordinate to its foreign political situation. Not revolution in Prussia was what Berlin should be concerned with, Bismarck thought, but Russia's fear of revolution in any of the German states or revolution in Poland.[193] This meant Prussia should use its controlling influence over the revolutionary situation in Central and Eastern Europe to diplomatic advantage. Radowitz's plan of creating a new German Reich was wrong because it was founded on the legal consent of fellow German princes rather than on Prussia's military power. Had Prussia founded a German Empire by military force in 1849, Bismarck contended, it would still have had to fight Europe in order to win outside recognition of this *fait accompli*. Only the wars would then have been fought *in defense* of a new German nation, and not in anticipation of a German nation yet to be made. To Bismarck the soundness of a domestic police order depended not only on its legal structure but also on the historical process that brought it about.[194]

The German invasion of Alsace

Of the three wars that Bismarck fought for German unity, the war with France was the longest and the most dangerous to Prussia. Yet it belongs with the occupation of Bohemia and Moravia in 1938–9 to the only successes scored by the German military during the modern period in establishing German rule over

---

[189] Ibid., p. 29. [190] Ibid., p. 52. [191] Ibid., p. 56.

[192] The memoirs of Stieber, of which one version appeared in 1884 and another in 1978, have received very controversial reviews. But there can be no doubt about the massive use of low-level espionage by the Prussians in preparation for both campaigns, on the basis of documentary holdings in West German archives. See Wolfram Siemann, *"Deutschlands Ruhe, Sicherheit und Ordnung," Die Anfänge der politischen Polizei 1806–1866* (Tübingen, 1985), pp. 22–3, 372–3; and Stieber's textbook on criminal police work, in which he asserts that police depends on ruses like spying more than on brutal force. Dr. Wilhelm Stieber, *Praktisches Lehrbuch der Kriminalpolizei unter besonderer Berücksichtigung der Kriminologie und Kriminalistik,* (2nd ed., ed. by Hans Schneickert, Potsdam, 1921), pp. 20–21.

[193] Ibid., p. 75. [194] Ibid., p. 57.

newly conquered territory. The reasons may have been that in both instances the territories involved had formerly belonged to the Holy Roman Empire of the German Nation, and that the European powers on both occasions accepted these territorial gains by Germany as long as the transfer of jurisdiction took place in an atmosphere of relative order and moderation.

But more interesting for the purpose of this study, the German success in Alsace and Lorraine in 1870 can also be attributed to the invaders' use of various basic rules of modern police: the exploitation of existing rivalries and animosities within the population; the careful calibration of punitive sanctions to the gravity of each situation; the attribution of acts of resistance to individuals rather than to collective groups whenever possible; and the inducement of collaboration by means of rewards of various kinds, not the least of which was the granting of forgiveness to repentant inhabitants who merely were slow in redirecting their obedience to the new masters.

How well the German army knew how to police a frightened population by exploiting its social tensions and the personal weakness of local officials is reflected in the report of a Prussian captain to the German military *General Gouvernement* of Alsace, on 13 October 1870:

Napoleon [III] is hated everywhere, among all classes of people. He is blamed for France's defeat and he is above all accused of cowardice.

Very noticeable is the social gulf separating the propertied classes from the proletariat. Both sides feel this gulf. I often think that it is the fear of possible excesses by the non-propertied classes that keeps the propertied classes from supporting the levée en masse [*Volkskrieg*]. For in the course of such a national war communist excesses would be difficult to avoid. Typical for this is the statement by the mayor of Badonwiller, who said that in this war he had always feared the Prussians in his community more than the Prussians from Germany. This mayor of Badonwiller, a Herr Perret, may be worth the attention of the German authorities. As a very wealthy man he enjoys a considerable prestige in the locality; also he has the wisdom to adopt as his guiding principle obedience to whichever power happens to prevail.

[French] national pride, already deeply shaken by the number of severe defeats, is gradually giving way to a cool-headed assessment of the damages sustained. There is a growing desire for peace at any price. People are even beginning to get used to the idea that Alsace and Lorraine will now become German. Admittedly, people still hope that German territorial gains will not extend beyond the linguistic frontier.[195]

There were in fact few instances of determined popular resistance to the invaders. One such instance occurred in Lorraine at the fortified town of Thionville; it prompted Otto von Bismarck to write to the new governor-general of Alsace, the Count von Bismarck-Bohlen in Strasbourg, that he should submit Thionville "To severe treatment, beginning with the exaction of a heavy contribution. . . .

---

[195] Karl Popp to Generalgouvernement im Elsass, Sarrebourg 13 Oct. 1870, in ADdBR (Strasbourg), AL 87 (3920), "General-Gouvernement im Elsass. Acta betr. Ruhestörung, Renitenz, Ausweisung."

Treating a rebellious population with leniency creates from the outset the impression of weakness, especially if it has been accustomed to a French regime. [Severity, on the other hand] will make it that much easier for us, later, to attain our goals through a policy of moderation."[196]

For the most part, however, the resistance by the inhabitants in Alsace was minimal. To the Germans the police problem was not how to overcome the hostility of the population, it was how to win their active help to stop isolated acts of sabotage. One method was reprisals, including billeting soldiers in a locality and demanding that its inhabitants feed them,[197] another the imposition of a large monetary fine on a village or town – but always with the promise to rescind it as soon as the individual culprit was caught.[198] Sarrebourg was fined 500 francs for shots fired in the vicinity of German military trains. Had Sarrebourg been wealthier, the penalty would doubtless have been much higher.[199] The small town of Dornach, near Mulhouse, was fined 25,000 francs because "Dornach is a well-to-do community. Its mayor reports that the yearly real estate tax yields 8,000 francs in revenues."[200] As an alternative to punishment, the Germans also offered individual rewards of 25 francs to anyone who caught a sniper.[201] And shortly after the war, in a remarkable gesture of fair play, the Germans voluntarily paid the sum of 200 francs to the poor relief fund of Klingenthal to compensate that village for the beating of a civilian by unruly German soldiers whose identity the German authorities said they could not establish.[202]

The flexible response of the Germans to the behavior of the inhabitants encouraged the latter, in turn, to win their leniency with gestures of submission. Thus, the mayor of Rappentzwiller in March 1871 directed a plea for clemency directly to King Wilhelm I, asking that the village be forgiven the fine of 2,000 francs imposed on it after a local peasant had shot at a patrol of Prussian gendarmes. The petition pleaded the poverty of the community that already bore the burden of feeding German occupation troops stationed in its midst. "The Mayor and the members of the communal council make this appeal in the name of the entire community in a spirit of childlike confidence in Your Fatherly Goodness [*bitten mit kindlichem Zutrauen auf Ihre väterliche Güte*]."[203]

The use of fines agreed better with the police needs of the German army in nineteenth-century rural Alsace than did hostage taking, a method more readily applied by the German Wehrmacht in the Second World War when its troops

[196] Letter, Otto von Bismarck to Graf von Bismarck-Bohlen, Versailles, 4 Dec. 1870, in ibid.

[197] In January 1871, the village of Merzweiller was given a garrison of thirteen men in punishment for cases of "impudent poaching" and because suspicious marauders had been observed near railway and telegraph installations. Report available in ADdBR (Strasbourg), AL 87 (3920).

[198] Poster, signed von der Heydt, in ADdBR (Strasbourg), AL 87 (3288), "Acta des Civil-Commissariats in Elsass betr. Beschädigung und Störung der Verkehrsmittel."

[199] Ibid., AL 87 (3920).   [200] Ibid., AL 87 (3288).

[201] Decree by General-Gouverneur von Bismarck-Bohlen, Hagenau, 23 Sept. 1870, in ibid.

[202] Ibid. 5 AL 87 (3289), Ober-Präsidium von Elsass-Lothringen. Acta betr. "Feindselige Handlungen gegen deutsches Militair und deutsche Beamte, Excesse, Alarm-Nachrichten" (1872).

[203] Ibid.

could hold to ransom the highly integrated urban societies of Western European democracies. In the 1870 war, one rare case of hostage taking occurred in Dornach, the affluent community already mentioned above, which was ordered on 30 November 1870 to provide citizens to ride on German trains in order to discourage French snipers. This order led to some discussion among the Germans themselves, whether to use people from the upper or lower classes as hostages, since most saboteurs were likely to belong to the lower classes and might not care about the lives of their social betters.[204] In another case the municipal council of Mulhouse on 19 January 1871 responded to a German demand that it provide the names of prominent citizens as suitable hostages by drawing up a most ambiguous declaration:

The Municipal Council of Mulhouse,

Considering that this requisition does not arise from an immediate emergency;

That it is contrary to all principles of international law and an attack on the dignity and liberty of the citizen; and

That it is unsuitable for the Council to point out citizens to be submitted to such an outrageous demand;

Nevertheless considers that this measure is of concern to certain persons and that therefore [these persons] should be consulted. But since it is impossible in the absence of tax records to know who pays the highest taxes the Council will do no more than inform an indeterminate number of people who by reputation belong to the wealthiest inhabitants.

The Council most energetically protests against the requisition in question and declares that it will in no way share in its execution except in regard to the inhabitants whom it specially selects to decide for themselves what their course of action should be.[205]

Thus, while voicing its outrage, the council issued warnings to its most prominent citizens and thereby indirectly pointed them out to the enemy as suitable hostages. The resistance of the Mulhouse authorities cannot therefore be taken very seriously. When the Germans, on 2 February 1871, finally decided to draw up a list of notables on their own the local police actually gave them assistance.[206]

The German use of intimidation against the inhabitants of Alsace was intended to stop the operation of the French *francs tireurs*. The Germans did not approve of francs tireurs because if civilians out of uniform and without disciplinary control by a government participated in the fighting they threatened to escalate the war from a limited contest between professional armies to a conflict between rivaling societies – a conflict whose revolutionary effect on these societies the Germans had more cause to fear than the French. At the same time, the German treatment of captured francs tireurs was relatively mild, probably because the latter did not enjoy popular support in Alsace.[207] Novéant escaped punishment for a sabotage

---

[204] Order of Bismarck-Bohlen, Strasbourg, 30 Nov. 1870, in ibid., AL 87 (3288).

[205] Dr. Schultz to Bismarck-Bohlen, Mulhouse, 29 Jan. 1871, in ibid.

[206] Telegram, Dr. Schultz to von Kühlewetter, 2 Feb. 1871, in ibid.

[207] See surrender agreement signed by General Major von Schmeling and Lieutenant-Colonel de Kerkor at Neuf-Brissac, 10 Nov. 1870, and the similarly worded surrender agreement for the town of Schlettstadt, 24 Oct. 1870, in ibid.

act at the local railroad station by setting up a civilian patrol to assist the German sentinels.[208] A Monsieur Dolder, mayor of Hochwald, volunteered information on a detachment of French francs tireurs to the "Royal Command of the Occupation Troops" in the hope of sparing his people possible German retaliation:

> I have the honor to inform you herewith, that on 11th instant 3 francs tireurs came to my home. They demanded 6 loaves of bread, 15 pounds of smoked meat, and 40 francs in money. I refused, explaining that if I did what they asked all Hochwald would suffer punishment. They told me that they were 1,600 men strong and were on their way to Saverne to blow up a bridge.[209]

On receiving Dolder's denunciation, the Germans immediately sent reinforcements to Saverne.

If there was bitterness and frustration among the inhabitants of Alsace, these sentiments were sometimes equally directed against the French civil servants who were slow to leave. For as early as October 1870, the Germans had begun with the systematic evacuation of French officials and their replacement with suitable German officials.[210] In November some postal clerks and mailcarriers at Molsheim requested German protection against the hostility of the local people who resented their work under enemy occupation.[211] The smoothness with which the administrative transfer from French to German rule took place prompted the Italian legation in Berlin – while the war was still in progress – to request that "the competent Prussian authority that now had been established in Alsace" be instructed by the German foreign ministry to help Italian criminal police to stop the production of counterfeit liras in the Alsatian village of Rixheim.[212]

Following the easy occupation of Alsace and the fortuitous capture of Napoleon III at Sedan on 2 September 1870, the war against France turned for the Prussians into a long and sometimes anxious experience, prompting doubts about the tenability of the Burgfrieden strategy in the years to come. For what the German armies faced after the fall of the Second Empire at Sedan and the proclamation of the Third Republic was war with political dimensions foreshadowing the ideological struggles of the future. There was Léon Gambetta's call for a *levée en masse* against the invaders, which the Germans knew they could not match. There was

---

[208] Decision of Kaiserliches Gouvernements Gericht, signed Generalleutnant und Gouverneur von Loewenfeld (n.d.) in ibid., AL 87 (3288).

[209] Dolder to Königliches Commando der Besatzungstruppen, Hochwald, 12 Feb. 1871, in ibid., AL 87 (3920).

[210] General Gouverneur von Bismarck-Bohlen to General Gouvernement in Lothringen zu Nancy, Hagenau, 4 Oct. 1870, No. 846, in ibid.; and request by Civil-Commissar im Elsass to Justiz-Ministerium Berlin, Strasbourg, 1 Nov. 1870 for transfer here of German judicial officials in view of the "bevorstehende Lostrennung des Elsass und Deutsch-Lothringen von Frankreich," in GPStA (Berlin), Rep. 84a/574, betreff. "Die Verwendung preussischer Justizbeamten in den occupierten französischen Landestheilen 1870–71."

[211] Report by a Premier-Lieutenant and Compagnieführer to the General-Commando der Infanterie der Truppen im Elsass zu Strasburg, Molsheim, 30 Nov. 1870, in ADdBR (Strasbourg), AL 87 (3920).

[212] Letter by chancellery of North German Confederation to General Gouverneur im Elsass Bismarck-Bohlen, Berlin, 16 Dec. 1870, in ADdBR (Strasbourg), AL 87 (453), "Acta betr. Verbrechen und Vergehen 1870–1884."

the stubborn resistance of the Parisians to months of blockade and bombardment. And there was the growing concern among the European public about the perils facing the French nation and its magnificent civilization. Last but not least, the joint antiwar protest by German and French workers with the approval of Karl Marx's Socialist International in London sent a shiver through all the cabinets of Europe.

The professional Prussian approach to war, as we have seen, had worked well enough in rural Alsace and its German-speaking people. Before we turn to the continuation of that war in metropolitan France and the outbreak of the Commune in 1871, let us conclude this discussion of the Prussian police style with an excerpt from Field Marshal Helmuth von Moltke's account of the 1870–1 campaign, written shortly after the war. He did not say one word about Germany's long search for national unity, but he did write of Napoleon III's desire for a foreign political success to offset domestic problems. He did not attribute the German victory to the enthusiasm of Prussian and Bavarian soldiers but rather spoke of the French armies' technical shortcomings and of France's vulnerability to any attack on Paris. But Moltke did express apprehension about future international conflicts that he said would frustrate all military calculations because they would arise from unresolved domestic conflicts rather than from the clash of rivaling national interests:

As long as nations lead separate lives there will be disputes that arms alone can resolve. But in the interest of humanity we must hope that wars will henceforth become less frequent because they have become more terrible.

In any event, peace is no longer endangered by the ambition of princes. It is threatened by the passion of the nations, the restlessness caused by domestic conditions, and by the machinations of political parties and of their spokesmen.[213]

If unresolved domestic police problems could lead to future wars the principle of the Burgfrieden would lose its original justification as a call to patriotic solidarity and become instead a source of danger to the peace of Europe.

The Russian police and Europe

The Russian police has probably received more attention from historians than the police of any other European country. According to A. T. Vassilyev, the last chief of the tsarist secret police, the reason for this is that the Russian state had never been able to draw on an intelligent class of genuine patriots who upheld national institutions and consequently had depended far more heavily on police than countries like England, France, or Austria.[214] And because of its extraordinary importance to the state, the mentality, methods, and the goals of Russia's police also differed from that of modern police in Europe. At the same time, the Russian

---

[213] "Geschichte des Krieges von 1870/71," in BA-MA (Freiburg i.B.), Nachlass Moltke, N16/14–15.
[214] As quoted in Richard Deacon, *A History of the Russian Secret Service* (New York, 1972), p. 91.

government's persistent use of police agents to observe Russian subjects living in the West resulted in all European states following closely what news about Russian police affairs they heard and watching the presence of Russian police on their territory. Russia's vulnerability to subversive plots organized by its exiles preoccupied the governments of Paris, Vienna, Berlin, and London, and they all had detailed reports on the Russian army mutiny of 1818 and the Decembrist uprising of 1825. As Count Lebzeltern, the Austrian ambassador at St. Petersburg in 1825, wrote to Prince Metternich, that coup d'état *manqué* should absolutely have been prevented by the Russian police.[215] The Third Section, founded shortly thereafter, did successfully apprehend the Petrashevsky circle in 1849.

To be sure, following the revolutions of 1848 and the fall of Metternich Russia's continuous adherence to the police practices of the European Congress contributed to the rise of a popular Russophobia in many parts of Europe. Since the 1840s the image of Russia as an unenlightened police state and the chief obstacle to progress in the West was fed by the travel books of foreign visitors who told of being plagued by suspicious and intolerant police inspectors, customs officials, and even postal clerks. A German diplomat visiting Riga and St. Petersburg in 1883 was reprimanded for not taking off his hat in the post office where a picture of Alexander III hung on the wall; in the customs office in Riga he was lectured that "Within the house of the tsar, you are not allowed to utter a thought that might be displeasing to the master."[216] His contemporary, the American journalist George Kennan, claimed that almost no foreigner traveling through the Empire of the Tsars could avoid being arrested by the police at some point. The German Baron Alexander von Humboldt was detained in 1829 because his looks had displeased a police officer, and the great British connoisseur of Russia, Sir Donald Mackenzie Wallace, was arrested in 1872 on suspicion of espionage.[217] Even so sympathetic a scholar as the Frenchman Anatole Leroy-Beaulieu wrote, in the 1880s, that "In the calmest days of Alexander II, . . . you felt that . . . liberty was something precarious and unaccustomed, [that] under the aegis of the police and the 'blue-officers' there can be no true liberty – only tolerance."[218]

In fairness to Western travelers like von Humboldt, Wallace, and Kennan, it should be said that they were without fail highly educated men with a keen eye for Russia's enormous difficulties in coping with the challenge of Western European science and philosophy. They believed that the Russian police was not responsible for creating the repressive atmosphere in the Empire but that it was itself largely the product of Russia's unique civilization whose distinction from the liberal West since the French Revolution was each year becoming more apparent. Karl Nötzel,

[215] Constantin de Grunwald, *La Vie de Nicolas Ier* (Paris, 1946), pp. 1–19.
[216] Heinrich von Eckhardt, "Erinnerungen des Herrn Gesandten von Eckardt" (MS, 1943), p. 21. Courtesy of his grandson, Oliver von Mühlen.
[217] George Kennan, *Siberia and the Exile System* (London, 1891), 2 vols.
[218] Anatole Leroy-Beaulieu, *The Empire of the Tsars*, trans. by Zénaïde A. Ragozin (New York, 1903), vol. 2, pp. 144–5; on his skepticism toward a Franco-Russian alliance, see Georges Michon, *The Franco-Russian Alliance, 1891–1917* (London, 1929), p. 9.

a German scholar who admired the works of Paul Miliukov and Thomas G. Masaryk on Russia, and who himself had spent many years studying the confrontation of Gemandom and Slavdom in Eastern Europe, wrote about the Russians in the First World War that they were a people obsessively preoccupied with the state that shackled them to the point of glorifying their own servitude. Thus, like Masaryk, Nötzel predicted that a future Russian revolution would seek to impose democracy by despotic means. This was the result of the people's limitless subjection to omnipotent rulers and of "the absence of all practical experience with a well-regulated freedom for the individual, or freedom for private groups in society."[219]

Tsarist Russia's reputation as a police state rested mainly on the political police: from 1825 on the imperial chancellery's Third Section, and after Alexander II's death in 1881, the Okhrana, both reinforced by regiments of Cossacks. Political police in Russia, like the "Glaubenspolizei" in eighteenth-century Austria, was honed to the point where breaking the will of one obstreperous dissident was worth hours of concentrated energy by a highly placed personality, be it Tsar Nicholas I himself censoring Pushkin's writings or talking face to face with a repentant Bakunin, or the Okhrana chief Sergei Zubatov in Moscow sweet-talking a political prisoner into becoming a government spy.[220] In Russian police philosophy, controlling the attitude of a dissident could be more important than policing his behavior.[221]

The situation was somewhat different when it came to practical contacts between Russian and European police. Austrian and Russian low-level frontier police were in constant touch throughout the nineteenth century over several hundred kilometers in rural Galicia and Bucovina, with the officials on both sides mostly poorly educated and vastly understaffed. Collaboration had been difficult during the Polish rebellion of 1863. The Prussians at that time offered St. Petersburg much more effective help than the Austrians by simply sealing the frontier hermetically with soldiers. While Vienna and St. Petersburg were equally anxious that travelers between the two empires remained under police control, the bureaucratic procedure on both sides was so clumsy that it frequently resulted in long detention for simple traders and even to complications requiring resolution on the highest diplomatic level. Between April and July 1860, for example, the Russian embassy in Vienna and the Austrian foreign ministry were kept busy over the case of a Polish itinerant showman who had entered Austrian territory with his traveling papers improperly visaed; he was also unwelcome because the local

[219] Karl Nötzel, *Grundlagen des geistigen Russlands. Versuch einer Psychologie des russischen Geisteslebens* (Jena, 1917).

[220] Jeremiah Schneiderman, ed. and trans., "From the Files of the Moscow Gendarme Corps: A Lecture on Combatting Revolution," in *Canadian Slavic Studies* II, No. 1 (Spring 1968), p. 93.

[221] Daniel Balmuth, *Censorship in Russia, 1865–1905* (Washington D.C., 1979), p. 28; and A. T. Vassilyev, *The Okhrana. The Russian Secret Police* (London, 1930), p. 76. The Russian police thus shared with the Austrian police the same insistence on orthodox thinking among the subjects of the Empire, which was very different from the Prussian King Frederick II's insouciant attitude: "Raisonnier er soviel er will, aber gehorche er!"

Austrian officials had found his general appearance "not trustworthy enough."[222] Some Russian migrants were kept in detention cells for many weeks while their identification papers were taken to Lemberg for translation into German. When verification of documents was also demanded, this could further delay a case by several years. The problem became especially severe in the last three decades of the nineteenth century. Since 1870, a convention was in existence fixing the days in the week and the particular spots along the frontier where the two empires would expel each other's subjects to make sure there would always be gendarmerie from the other side on hand to take such persons into custody. Another agreement in 1886 provided for direct cooperation between the Austrian and Russian police for the mutual repatriation of undesirables.[223]

In their concern to control who enters and who leaves their territory the two old police states, Russia and Austria-Hungary, followed a similar policy. (By contrast, Switzerland was more anxious to protect the right of expellees – in particular political expellees – to choose the country to which they were dispatched; while Prussia's law of free movement – *Freizügigkeitsgesetz* – of 1 November 1867 required police escorts for returning Prussians only if they were repatriated in order to stand trial before a Prussian court.)[224] At the same time, the cumbersome procedure along the Austrian and Russian border did not necessarily strain the relations between the two parties. A common disposition of anti-Semitism made for some mutual understanding. The Austrians were not happy with having Russian Jews in their land, many of whom after 1881 refused to go home, and they felt it a burden to have to intercede countless times for Austrian Jews who got into difficulties with the Russian authorities. The Austrian chargé d'affaires Freiherr von Trauttenberg reported from St. Petersburg, 28 July/9 August 1881, that during the last two years the Austrian embassy had negotiated with the Russians on behalf of no less than thirty Austrian Israelites. The situation in his view was best left to negotiations from case to case, since so often there was no solution other than "*des accomodements avec le ciel et la police*," in other words, resort to prayers and bribery.[225] The Russians were also touchy about travels near military fortifications and in regions where army maneuvers were under way. Sometimes they demanded from the Austrian authorities the kind of police support that they also expected from other European governments, for example in 1887 a time-consuming survey of the personal circumstances of every single Russian subject living in Tarnopol, then a town in Austrian Poland.[226]

[222] This exchange of letters is available in HHStA (Vienna), Administrative Registratur F52, "Fremde Polizeibeschwerden."

[223] *Note verbale*, Russian embassy to Austrian foreign ministry, 30 Dec./11 Jan. 1881, in ibid., Karton 47, "Schubwesen 1871–1918."

[224] Austrian ambassador Szögyeny to Austrian foreign ministry, Berlin, 18 June 1902, in ibid., folder "Schubwesen–Preussen."

[225] Austrian chargé d'affaires Freiherr von Trauttenberg to Austrian foreign ministry, St. Petersburg, 10/22 Apr. 1882, in ibid., Administrative Registratur 97 F52: "Staaten R."

[226] Einsichtsstück des I.B. des M/m des Aeussern No. 2596/4 I.B., 11 Sept. 1890; and idem, note, Russian consulate in Brody to Bezirkshauptmannschaft in Tarnopol, 10/22 Aug. 1887.

If illiteracy and corruption on the part of the Russian police was at the source of many difficulties,[227] the solution lay not in improving police training, but ultimately in transforming Russian society. During a visit by King Carol I of Romania to Jassy, in 1904, an event attended by Prince Urussov, the governor of the neighboring Russian *gubernie*, and by the Austrian general in command of the garrison in Siebenbürgen, the discussion turned to the police in Western and Eastern Europe. King Carol proudly related how a new bill required a legal education of all Romanian police officers with the rank of district inspector and above. For Russia he recommended administrative decentralization and the wholesale conversion of that empire into a confederation of autonomous nationalities not unlike Austria-Hungary.[228]

How sensitive the tsarist regime was to foreign critics who classified the Russian Empire among the ill-policed regions of the world like Turkey and China is revealed by the vehement rebuttal of the Russian foreign ministry to George Kennan's book, *Siberia and the Exile System* (1891).

In 1884 the American journalist, George Kennan, was granted permission by the Russian government to visit colonies of political exiles in Siberia. The Russians did this after Kennan had publicly defended the tsarist regime in a lecture in New York City against what he then regarded as the biased reporting by Russian exiles like Stepniak and Kropotkin. But when Kennan's book appeared in 1891 it carried a message of resounding condemnation of the Russian police system as being arbitrary, unenlightened, and cruel. Kennan denounced the capriciousness with which hundreds of Russian students were banished to Siberia without proper court proceedings and without being formally charged. He asserted that offenses which in Austria-Hungary would be punished by a few days of detention in Russia easily drew ten to twelve years at hard labor. He ridiculed the political police for ruling as subversive Adam Smith's *The Wealth of Nations* (1776) or any history book that mentioned the French Revolution, and for fearing the power of any young people with high ideals:

Every one of [these young people], I think, would lay down his arms, if the Tsar would grant to Russia a constitutional form of government and guarantee free speech, a free press, and freedom from arbitrary arrest, imprisonment, and exile.[229]

Upon arrival in Semipalatinsk, he wrote:

I experienced for the first time something like a feeling of contempt for the Russian government. . . . The idea that a powerful government like that of Russia could not protect

---

[227] In the central provinces of Russia, as many as 80 percent of the local bureaucracy had no formal education whatsoever, according to David Footman, *Red Prelude. The Life of the Russian Terrorist Zhelyabov* (New Haven, Conn., 1945), p. 6; and Peter A. Zaionchkovsky, *The Russian Autocracy in Crisis, 1878–1882*, ed. and trans. by Gary M. Hamburg (orig. Moscow, 1964; Gulf Freeze, Fla., 1979), pp. 107–8.

[228] Prince Serge Dmitriyevich Urussov, *Memoirs of a Russian Governor*, trans. by Herman Rosenthal (London, 1908), pp. 137–8.

[229] George Kennan, *Siberia and the Exile System* (London, 1891), p. 179.

itself against seminary girls and Sunday-school teachers without tearing them from their families, and isolating them in the middle of a great Asiatic desert, seemed to me not only ludicrous, but absolutely preposterous.[230]

Cesare Lombroso, the Italian pioneer of criminal anthropology, was cited by Kennan as having found Russian terrorists, from the way they looked in police photos, as "true revolutionists," many with the physical traits of saints and geniuses, unlike French Communards whom Lombroso found to be 12 percent criminals and 10 percent lunatics; or Chicago anarchists, 40 percent of whom, in his view, were criminal types.[231]

Almost two decades later, at the outset of Russia's constitutional era, the Russian Government circulated an official answer to Kennan in a twenty-nine-page brochure sent to all the ministries of foreign affairs in Europe. The brochure charged Kennan's book as the source for the attempts of various foreign newspapers (*L'Humanité, Le Journal de Genève,* the *Arbeiter-Zeitung,* and *The Daily News*) to vilify the Russian government with mendacious reports about the mistreatment of prisoners in Russia. This was not true, the brochure insisted, because in Russia criminals were not merely treated as enemies of the social order but also as unfortunates who needed help. To underline this point it cited an ordinance of 9 August 1908 (more than a decade after Kennan's journey) which it said allowed prisoners in Russia more visits by friends and relatives than prisoners in England, Prussia, or Belgium. It then cited an Englishman by the name of Wyndt, who had visited exiles in Siberia and on Sakhalin Island ten years after Kennan and who had concluded that he would prefer banishment there to a jail sentence in England.

It needs to be said that Mr. Wyndt, the author of two books on Siberia, declared as unfounded most of the information about the horrors of deportation to Siberia that one finds in the description by G. Kennan, which at one point so aroused public opinion in Europe, and in England caused loud protests against the prison administration in Russia.[232]

The Russian brochure admitted that conditions in Russian prisons were not what they should be, but the reason for this was the doubling of the size of the prison population between 1906 and 1909.

The explanation lies in the rise of the crime rate in the Empire – a normal consequence when a society has been subjected to upheavals such as Russia's was in 1905. The promise of political reform was misunderstood by the masses and misinterpreted by mischievous people.[233]

On the other hand the crime rate in Russia has since fallen again, standing at 6 convicts for every 10,000 inhabitants compared to 7.8 in France, 10.0 in

---

[230] Ibid., p. 183.   [231] Ibid., pp. 454–5.

[232] Direction Générale des Prisons, "A propos des bruits sur les prétendues oppressions des détenus dans les prisons russes. Démenti officiel" (St. Petersburg, Imprimerie "Russo-Française," rue des Officiers, No. 6, 1910), pp. 4–5.

[233] Ibid., p. 8.

Austria, 12.0 in Switzerland, 16.3 in Prussia, and 16.7 in Belgium.[234] Besides, the brochure added naively, the condition of the prisons was more tolerable than would appear to foreign observers because the Russian people have a low standard of sanitation; personal hygiene is almost unknown to them (*"les mesures hygièniques et sanitaires lui sont à peu près étrangères"*). In 1892, the death rate in the prisons (30 per 1,000) had actually been lower than in the country at large (42 per 1,000).[235]

[234] Ibid., p. 10.   [235] Ibid. We must remember that 1892 was a year of famine.

2

Modern police and the conduct of foreign policy. The French police and the recovery of France after 1871

Foreign responses to the French debacle and the Paris Commune

As a small neutral country closely situated to the military operations in 1870–1, Switzerland reacted with greater sensitivity to the political and social implications of the war than von Moltke. While the federal government anxiously clung to a policy of neutrality, the citizens of Basel, Zurich, and Berne, moved by sympathy for the French people, privately organized the evacuation of several thousand non-combatants from beleaguered Strasbourg – with the consent of the commander of the German siege army, General von Werder, we might add.[1] Other Swiss citizens, long resident in France, petitioned the Berne government for permission to help the French war effort by joining the national guard. But because the Berne authorities forbade the enlistment even in such local forces (whose primary task was order-policing), Swiss citizens in Paris, Lyon, Marseille, and Le Havre set up ambulance services and fire brigades, and some joined the national guard in defiance of their government.[2] The Swiss volunteers were not alone in demonstrating sympathy for France. There were also young Americans serving in the Légion Franco-américaine[3] and some 16,000 Italians, Hanoverians, and Hungarians fought the Prussians under the command of Giuseppe Garibaldi.[4]

The politicians in Berne manifested a more calculating attitude than their private compatriots, with a hint even of satisfaction at the humiliation currently suffered by France. This at least is the impression conveyed by various letters which

---

[1] Gustav A. Wanner, "Das Strassburger Denkmal–Monument der Menschlichkeit," in *Basler Zeitung*, 4 Aug. 1984, p. 27.
[2] Swiss consul Rüffer in Lyon, Berne, 28 Sept. 1870; and Bundesrat to the Swiss consul in Marseille, Berne, 2 Nov. 1870, in BA (Berne), Bestands-Nr. 21, Archiv-Nr. 500. On the mutual rights of French and Swiss citizens to settle in each other's countries, see the Franco-Swiss treaty of 18 July, 1828, in Berthold van Muyden, *La Suisse sous le pacte de 1815* (Lausanne, 1892), vol. I, pp. 396–399.
[3] Letter, Dufour (a lawyer) to Bundesrath, 19 Dec. 1870, in ibid.
[4] Franz Herre, *Anno 70/71. Ein Krieg, ein Reich, ein Kaiser* (Cologne, 1970), p. 144.

were addressed by the political department, and in one instance by the Swiss president himself, to Swiss nationals living in France. A Dr. Perrochet in Montmorency was assured by the political department: "I am persuaded that the German army will do you no harm." A Swiss accountant, Alexandre Galland, was told by President Jacob Dubs: "Be assured the Germans will treat you with respect as long as you abstain from all hostile action against them." The Swiss Consul Rüffer in Lyon was calmed by his superiors in Berne that German soldiers would show him every consideration, "though we advise you to accept their consideration as a favor and not to demand it as a right." When the French police in Le Havre forbade a Madame Blaser to fly the Swiss flag from her window because they thought this would spread defeatism in the city, Berne advised her to hang out her flag only when the Germans actually entered the town.[5] Unlike the citizens of Berne, Zurich, and Basel, and many private Swiss residents in France, the Swiss government showed little sympathy for the French in their hour of defeat, and after the war promptly charged the French government twelve million francs for sheltering General Bourbaki and his 87,000 troops after they retreated into Switzerland.[6]

The provisional government of Adolphe Thiers, which succeeded to the Second French Empire after the battle of Sedan (2 September 1870), was in the beginning insecure, so much so that the Germans felt called upon to help it forestall social revolution or anarchy in France. In October 1870, the Germans had briefly flirted with Marshal François-Achille Bazaine, the commander of Metz, who on surrendering his fort proposed to march on Paris to save the French state from collapse by establishing a military dictatorship.[7] But in March 1871, they came to the aid of Thiers government when Paris, after the long winter siege, erupted in rebellion and proclaimed itself an independent Commune.

The revolt of the Paris Commune, aggravated by parallel outbursts of violence in other French towns, for a last time presented France's neighbors with the need to deal with the "French revolutionary tradition." This most savage of civil conflicts in any European city during the nineteenth century held little promise for a settlement by the methods of modern police. The reestablishment of domestic peace in the spring and early summer of that year involved armed force and a much wider array of participants: besides the French government and its administrative and judiciary agents in the provinces, the German military's General-Gouvernement in occupied France and the governments of European countries where fugitive Communards sought asylum after 1871.

The rapid agreement reached between the Germans and the French government in Versailles on joint measures against the Paris Commune can be followed

[5] Letters, EPD to Dr. Perrochet, Berne, 16 Sept. 1870; Swiss president Jacob Dubs to Alexander Galland in Massereaux, Alsace, dated Berne, 20 Sept. 1870; and to Consul Rüffer (Lyon) and Consul E. Wanner (Le Havre), Berne, 22 Nov. 1870, in BA (Berne), Bestands-Nr. 21, Archiv-Nr. 500.
[6] Herre, *Anno 70/71*, p. 189.
[7] Maurice Garçon, *Histoire de la justice sous la IIIème République* (Paris, 1957), vol. I, p. 120; and Herre, *Anno 70/71*, p. 142. There is also material on the police investigation of Bazaine's treason against the French Republic, 1870–3, in APP (Paris), Série B A/953, "Bazaine."

by reading the notes exchanged between Chancellor Bismarck, German General-Gouverneur von Fabrice, Adolphe Thiers, and French Foreign Minister Jules Favre in the spring of 1871. No doubt the partnership between the German soldiers and the French officials was a partnership *de convenance*. But it confirmed that in the European state system of the nineteenth century all states, whether at war with one another or not, still had a common stake in its continued existence, with each member state obliged to be defensible to the outside and effectively policed at home. On 20 March 1871, Bismarck informed Jules Favre that German forces were prepared to fire on Communards if they ventured near their positions outside Paris. "We do not doubt the loyal intentions of the government in power and want to remain on good terms with it in accordance with the preliminary peace terms *as long as this government remains in control*."[8] Thiers himself addressed a circular to all prefects, subprefects, and other senior officials of France to convince them how important it was that the German military believed in the provisional government's ability to restore order as quickly as possible: "The German army, turned menacing when there were grounds to fear the triumph of disorder, quickly changed its attitude and became peaceful when it saw the government recover its strength. It has conveyed very satisfactory explanations [for its conduct] to the Chief of the Executive Power."[9] Thiers's appeal was underlined by a stiff German warning in April that the German military government would not indefinitely respect the disorders in Paris as a French domestic affair.[10]

The Paris Commune and the communes in other French towns were put down by government troops in May 1871. In the period that followed Switzerland again submitted to demands from Paris that it cooperate in the police surveillance, if not in the neutralization, of French political dissidents. But it was to be the last time that Switzerland accepted such treatment from France. On 6 June 1871, the Swiss federal department of justice and police (EJPD) reported to the Bundesrat that the French legation in Berne was requesting the arrest in Geneva of six persons accused of participation in the recent events in Paris. Only three had been located so far, but since no specific criminal charges had been filed against any of them the EJPD had instructed Geneva to place them only under "provisional arrest" while reserving the decision on their extradition to a later time.[11] This did not please the French government. On 14 July 1871, the French legation in Berne sent a stern note to Swiss President Schenk concerning one of the three wanted men, one Félix Pyat, whose presence in Geneva the Swiss had denied.

The government of the French Republic is in receipt of information which persuades it that M. Félix Pyat is definitely in Geneva. This is made clear without any doubt in a report by the *commissaire spécial* at Ferney. This official informs us that he has furnished all the

---

[8] Telegram, Bismarck to General-Gouverneur von Fabrice, Berlin, 20 March, 1871, in PA (Bonn), Abt. IA. Europa Fasc. 1, No. 11, "Aufstand in Paris. Krieg 1870/71." My italics.

[9] Circular, 24 Mar., 1871, in ibid.

[10] Letter, von Fabrice to Favre, Versailles, 15 Apr. 1871, in ibid.

[11] Letter, EJPD to Bundesrath, Berne, 6 June, 1871, in BA (Berne), Bestands-Nr. 21, Archiv-Nr. 125, "Communarden Flüchtlinge aus Frankreich."

necessary details to the local [Swiss] police. Consequently, *Monsieur le Président*, I am charged by my government to ask Your Excellency kindly to renew to the government of the Canton of Geneva the orders that were issued to it several weeks ago concerning the arrest of M. Félix Pyat and to insist that Your Excellency will add to these orders the demand that they be executed without delay. [12]

The tone of the French communication to Switzerland showed no loss in self-assertiveness by France, in spite of its humiliating military defeat in the war and the recent chaos in Paris. French requests for Swiss police aid against fugitive Communards (in 1873 estimated by the Swiss as numbering 143 in the city of Geneva alone) and Bonapartists continued for the next few years. At the same time there was a resurgence of protests from the Swiss public against French police influence in their country. At the forefront stood a group that called itself "The People of Geneva Constituted as a Popular Assembly." On 29 May 1871, it petitioned the Berne government as follows:

We, citizens of a free country, ask the federal council that the refugees coming from France following the latest events be received as the victims of political misfortune with the right to asylum and hospitality, to protection against attacks and immunity from extradition, [for to extradite them] would be a deadly blow to our independence and to our Republic . . .

The petition went on to say that Switzerland had always without discrimination accepted the victims of violence (*proscrits*) of all persuasions and all parties. "Switzerland has never offered its aid to the victors of the day and turned against the vanquished, and under far less favorable circumstances in 1838, the whole country was ready to face the dangers of war rather than to accept humiliation by a French government." [13]

The petition of the Genevan citizens was obviously not heeded, for two months later, on 23 July, the *Association politique ouvrière nationale de Genève* (in whose eyes the Communards had not been rebels but belligerents in an international war against France) lodged a protest against the arrest of a number of refugees in Geneva "on the request of the Versailles government." To the *Association* the French refugees in Geneva had every reason to go into hiding since they were being "hunted by our police, doubling as agents for a foreign power." [14]

[12] French Legation to the Swiss president Schenk, Berne, 14 July, 1871, in ibid. The prestige of the French *commissaire spécial* in Ferney on the French border just outside Geneva, suffered a setback in 1873; however, when this official was forced to request the Geneva police to release an accused Communard who had been arrested on his demand. That Communard was actually a French police spy. See letter, Département de Justice et Police in Geneva to Bundesrath, Geneva, 13 May 1873, in BA (Berne), Bestands-Nr. 21, Archiv-Nr. 125.

[13] Petition to Bundesrath by "Le peuple de Genève réuni en assemblée populaire," 29 May, 1871, in ibid. On the war threat of 1838, see the discussion of the Swiss police in Chapter 4. The reference to helping the vanquished is of interest here because it mirrors Switzerland's diminishing faith after 1871 in the general progress of Eruopean society toward democracy.

[14] Document available in ibid.

In fact, the Swiss federal government responded only very reluctantly to the French pressures. At the end of May 1871, the EJPD proposed to the federal government a general policy to examine each individual French request for extradition separately and to distinguish carefully between political delinquents and ordinary criminals.[15] On 31 May, the Geneva police arrested Guillaume Chol, who for two weeks had acted as chief of police in Lyon on behalf of the Commune. But he was for apparently good reason wanted for embezzling public funds as well.[16] In July Eugène Razona, alias Marquez, a former member of the French National Assembly, was arrested on French request on charges of arson and participation in the Paris Commune. But the Swiss did not extradite him to France. In September 1874 they also refused to send home the well-known publicist Henri Rochefort, publisher of *La Lanterne* and in 1871 briefly a member of the Paris Commune. In 1874 he had escaped from his banishment to New Caledonia and taken up residence in Geneva, where he was seen consorting with Razona and the artist Courbet.[17] The EJPD in his case recommended granting him asylum because he was a political writer rather than a violent revolutionary. The French foreign minister Décazès thereupon expressed his displeasure to the Swiss minister in Paris, Kern. He denied that France had any intention of censoring a political publication.

No. I am talking about the need to interfere with a dangerous refugee who resides close to our border. To underline our legal right [to your cooperation] I am complaining about his abuse of the asylum he is granted [in Switzerland] by publishing a weekly journal of an insulting character. Now, cases of asylum are decided in Switzerland as they are in France administratively, as questions of international police work. I was talking about the application of higher police functions of this kind.[18]

It would therefore seem that with France's standing in Europe diminished after 1871 Switzerland no longer responded to French requests for police assistance with the same alacrity as before. But there were now other countries ready to help France, moved by their fear of international socialism. Belgium in 1871 quickly restored a law requiring all travelers coming from France to carry valid passports. Foreign travelers in hotels and inns were also placed under close control by the aliens police.[19] The Italian royal police in 1872 expressed the desire to exchange

---

[15] Bundesrath minutes of 26 May 1871, in BA (Berne), Bestands-Nr. 21, Archiv-Nr. 20875, folder concerning Dr. J. Langhard, author of *Das Recht der politischen Fremdenausweisung mit besonderer Berücksichtigung der Schweiz* (Leipzig 1891).

[16] See French arrest warrant against Chol, dated Lyon, 27 May 1871, and report of his arrest by the Genevan police, dated 31 May 1871, in BA (Berne), Bestands-Nr. 21, Archiv-Nr. 125.

[17] Department of justice and police, Geneva, to political department in Berne, Geneva, 3 Aug. 1874; and report by Genevan police on Rochefort, 23 Sept. 1874, in BA (Berne), Bestands-Nr. 21, Archiv-Nr. 20875.

[18] "Or, l'abris de l'asile est en Suisse comme chez nous une affaire administrative, une question de police internationale. C'est l'application de cette haute police que j'ai eu en vue." Report to Bundesrath by Swiss minister Kern, dated Paris, 5 Nov. 1874, in ibid.

[19] "Conférence internationale de Rome pour la défense sociale contre les anarchistes, 24 novembre–21 décembre, 1898" (Rome, 1898), p. 91, in ibid., Archiv-Nr. 14027.

information with Switzerland about the movement of agents of the International even though it considered the rumors about an imminent socialist insurrection improbable because of lack of money and arms.[20] The attitude of Rome in matters of political asylum was certainly far less liberal than Berne's. In May 1873 the Rome police expelled a former French Communard, Victor Cyrille, even though he had broken no Italian law. "However," the Italians explained, "M. Cyrille belongs to that category of individuals to which the Italian government has decided not to accord its hospitality in order to avoid the kind of international complications and disputes which other countries have experienced that have tolerated their presence."[21]

Budapest put on trial and executed one Communard of Hungarian nationality for the common crimes of murder and arson rather than extradite him to France,[22] and Russia sent Prince Gorchakov to Switzerland in 1872 to ask how Berne would respond to an invitation to join the Great Powers in collective steps against the Socialist International.[23] Spain took a stronger stand yet than Russia on the need for international police cooperation against Socialism, arguing that the most dangerous elements in the Paris Commune had been foreigners who had gone to France as soon as the Second Empire went down in defeat.[24]

The only country that took a moderate – even benign – attitude to the threat of international Socialism seems to have been England. According to a report to the Bundesrat by a private Swiss firm, Escher-Wyss of Zurich, Mr. Gould, a secretary of the British legation in Berne, was charged by Lord Granville in April 1872 to contact representatives of the International in Switzerland and to see whether they could not be bought off with money. (Escher-Wyss believed that the motive of the British government was completely selfish: It wanted to use the International to stir up labor troubles on the Continent so as to ease the pressure of foreign competition on Britain's export trade.)[25]

The stir made by the Paris Commune throughout the continent persuaded Switzerland to join with the rest of Europe in containing the Socialist International with police alertness. It helped the Swiss to resist the direct pressure from France for unilateral police assistance. The canton of Fribourg warned that a French legislative proposal in 1872, that sought to deprive Communards of French citizenship, could burden Switzerland with many permanent stateless refugees (*un nouveau heimatlosat*).[26] Neuchâtel reported that the French police was driving Communards across the Swiss frontier at Verrières without passports and refusing to take them back.

[20] *Pro memoria* (ca. 1872), in ibid., Archiv-Nr. 14004.
[21] Swiss legation to political department in Berne, Rome, 25 May 1873, in ibid., Archiv-Nr. 20875.
[22] K. k. Austro-Hungarian legation to Bundesrath, Berne, 8 Mar. 1876, in ibid.
[23] Swiss minister Charles Mercier to EPD, Petersburg, 24 Mar./5 Apr. 1872, in ibid., Archiv-Nr. 14004.
[24] Bonifacio de Blas, Spanish foreign ministry, political section, to Bundesrath, Madrid, 9 Feb. 1872, in ibid.
[25] Escher Wyss & Cie to Bundesrath, Zurich, 18 Apr. 1872, in ibid.
[26] *Conseil d'état* of Canton Fribourg to Bundesrath, Fribourg, 1 Mar. 1872, in ibid.

The French government relented and in 1872 Minister Kern was informed that France would not deprive the French members of the Socialist International of their citizenship, but instead place them under the surveillance of the French political police for periods ranging between five and ten years.[27] On 11 July 1880, the French government issued a general amnesty to all former Communards.

In the 1870s Switzerland's problems with foreign political refugees underwent a change as fewer and fewer Frenchmen sought sanctuary there from the persecutions of their government. In their place came Russian revolutionaries (some of them reputed quite dangerous, like Bakunin and Nechaev), and by German Social Democrats expelled under Bismarck's anti-Socialist law of 1878.

The French police and the recovery of France

Disposing of Bonapartism

The recovery of France under the Third Republic is so remarkable because it took place under the watchwords patience, toleration, compromise, and moderation. The Republic was the work of men whose names were associated neither with military glory nor charismatic leadership: a Thiers, a Ferry, and a Freycinet rather than a Gambetta, a Boulanger, or a Déroulède. (Georges Clemenceau's political career belongs to a later period already, even though the "Tiger's" alleged demand that France commit herself to a police of "défense du territoire" – a phrase that we have used to label the essential idea of modern police in France – dates from 1876.)

We begin with a brief word on the French police's success in disposing of the remaining Bonapartist faction in France, which the Republic effectuated with admirable tact and imagination, and practically no resort to coercion. When Emperor Napoleon III surrendered to the Prussian armies at Sedan on 2 September 1870, the French police, as in 1815, was called on to help consolidate a successor regime. Only this time there was no need to engage the assistance of the Concert of Europe, not even to banish all the members of the Bonaparte family from France. It speaks well for the political wisdom of the French authorities that they recognized Bonapartism as a cause that had run its historical course. French police agents in Geneva watched former Communards much more closely than self-exiled Bonapartists. The general policy of the French political police in the 1870s and 1880s was to apply only minimal restraint on the freedom of movement by members of the former imperial family and to promote instead the democratic mood in France through discreet censorship of books and plays and by relegating the Napoleonic legend to the realm of French historical saga.[28]

The task of the police was facilitated from the outset by the fact that after the Franco-Prussian War the protagonists of the Napoleonic cause had been reduced

---

[27] Letter by Minister Kern to Bundesrath, Paris, 22 Mar. 1872, in ibid.
[28] Ministère de l'Instruction publique des cultes et des beaux arts, *Bulletin administratif*, tome XIII, no. 252 (26 Oct. 1870), p. 455; and L.-Henri Lecomte, *Napoléon et l'Empire ractontés par le théâtre, 1799–1899* (Paris, 1900), pp. i–ii.

to silence by the magnitude of the recent defeat. For a time the fallen regime and the name of the two Napoleons were publicly accursed. The principal remaining attraction of the Bonapartist cause were the prince imperial (Loulou who was killed in Africa in 1879), and Prince Jérôme, whose meetings in Geneva during the summer of 1871 with marshals Bazaine and Canrobert, and with the one-time Paris police prefect Pierre Piétri were watched by an agent of the prefect of the department of Ain.[29] Like other members of his family Jérôme remained under police surveillance for several more years, each of his entries into France requiring prior authorization by the ministry of interior of Paris.[30] His vague idea of launching a political campaign with a program of state socialism (1875) and his consequent visits to factory towns like Le Creusot and Mâcon (1880) drew only perfunctory police attention. A Bonapartist banquet in Paris on 5 May 1878, at which the Comte de Murat brought a toast to "Napoleon IV!" was left undisturbed. "Nothing to report," wrote Lombard, the officier de paix of the Paris municipal police who was present.[31] Jérôme's last bid for political power was an open letter which he published early in 1886, claiming the right to rule France because seven million voters had endorsed Napoleon III in the plebiscite of 1869. On this occasion the commissaire spécial de police of the railway station at Saint Germain-des-Fosses (department of Allier) reported:

> There is some talk about Prince Napoleon's letter, but this document does not appear to have caused the public the slightest concern. A few people do think this action was a political demonstration and that it should be suppressed. But others, and I think they are in the majority, believe that Prince Napoleon's activities in no way compromise the existence of the Republic and that the government would do well to ignore this letter completely.[32]

Spies and traitors in France

The greatest danger to France in the early 1870s was not Bonapartism. But it was not Prussian spies and French traitors either, however diligently these individuals peddled information to the Wilhelmstrasse in Berlin. Rather the greatest danger was that a passionate patriot like Gambetta might rush the country into a hasty war of revenge. Insofar as France after 1871 needed peace above all, it was just as well that the image conveyed to Berlin in the 1870s by German secret agents was one of political disarray in Paris, continued military unpreparedness throughout the country, and of a totally inept police. The French writer Léon Daudet half a

---

[29] Report by *commissaire spécial* at Ferney (Ain), 29 July 1871, in AN (Paris), F7 12428, "Agissements bonapartistes, 1871–1891," folder: "1871–1873."

[30] See circular by ministry of interior, Direction de la Sûreté publique, Versailles, Oct. 1872, in ibid., folder: "Expulsion du Prince Jérôme, 1872–1886."

[31] Report by M. Lombard, *officier de paix*, Police Municipale, 4ème Brigade des Recherches, to Préfecture de Police, Paris, 5 May 1878, in APP (Paris), Carton B A/1, 510. The fourth brigade was in charge of political investigations. See L. Andrieux, *Souvenirs d'un préfet de police* (Paris, 1885), pp. 32–39.

[32] Document available in AN (Paris), F7 12428, folder: "Surveillance 1886."

century later even spoke of a secret collusion between the French *Sûreté Générale* and German police officials in France during the 1870s, with the French police cast in the role of humble subservience, but his charges are unsupported by evidence and colored by his personal and political vendetta against the Sûreté. Also they contradict the record of performance of the French police in the larger picture of the police as a tool of French foreign policy. Daudet's assertion that the Paris police prefecture and the Sûreté were in the pay of German intelligence is more than balanced by documents in the *Archives nationales,* the *Archives de la Préfecture de Police* in Paris, and in the German *Politisches Archiv* that indicate low-level German espionage in France as having been both unreliable and of poor quality. This, of course, may simply indicate the absence of serious war plans against France by Berlin at that time. But the documents also testify to long years of excellent service by France's border police superintendents and by French observers sent out to study conditions in other countries of importance for France's recovery as a great power.

The German military intelligence (*Nachrichten-Bureau im grossen Generalstab*) kept agents in France in the 1870s to observe its military. Most of them seem to have been well known to the French police. One of them was a Baron von Steger, twenty-eight years old, who passed himself off as a Swiss but lived with a German woman and openly entertained German guests at his home, among them a captain from the office of the German military attaché in Paris. The police prefecture had him listed as *"un agent militaire prussien à Paris."*[33] The quality of information obtained by such military observers may be put in question if we go by the so meager report of one agent from the year 1875, only three months after Europe was shaken by rumors of another war between Germany and France:

French plans of mobilization. The recent worries have prompted the ministry of war to tackle the question of mobilization for the French army. Pertinent instructions have been issued to corps commanders. It is said that mobilization is to be effectuated in five days. Mass transports to begin on the sixth day. I hope to have more details in a few days.[34]

Especially astonishing was the crude intelligence method employed by the German consul in Nice, a Major Hasperg, who in 1877 sought to buy information from the local police. The prefect of the Département des Alpes-Maritimes immediately reported this incident to the ministry of interior in Paris, though the prefect's own reaction to this German undertaking is somewhat astonishing too.

[Hasperg] has sent a circular letter directly to all police superintendents, asking them to draw up for him a chart showing all travels by foreigners [through this *département*], with indication of their nationality. He has even offered them a gratification.
This procedure is evidently quite irregular. He should have addressed himself to me.

---

[33] Report by agent "Jack," dated 28 Oct. 1873, in APP (Paris), Carton B A/1,287, "Tcherni-schewski, Tourgéneff."

[34] Note, dated Paris, 3 July 1875, in PA (Bonn), Abt. IA B.c.81, Acta betreff. "Nachrichten von politischen und Polizei-Agenten über Verhältnisse in Frankreich." The famous article, "Is War in Sight?" appeared in *The Post* of London and in the *Kölnische Zeitung* on 9 Apr. 1875.

I thought it best to authorize my agents to fulfill his request but also told them to refuse all gratification as a matter of course. At the same time I told them to scale down the figures for foreigners of Italian nationality.

I thought it inappropriate to comment [to Hasperg] about all this. The issue is relatively unimportant. Also, given the violent temper of the consul, he probably would have taken my remarks badly, however nicely I phrased them.

In any case I would rather he uses my agents than other ones. In this way we can follow the direction of his investigations.

Naturally I have told my superintendents never to contact him without first telling me, and not to give him any documents that are not first submitted to me.[35]

Another equally puzzling case occurred two years later. In 1879 the Sûreté Générale was mystified by hundreds of letters sent by a certain J. Heilbut in Hamburg to French village school teachers in a number of departments, asking them to name him the most prominent residents in their locality plus their professions and their exact addresses. The covering letter was remarkable for its tone of arrogant condescension and the total absence of any explanation of purpose:

M . . .

Assuming that it is easy for you to procure me the names of inhabitants in your village and in neighboring villages, I take the liberty of sending you, enclosed, the necessary forms for 300 addresses, which I expect to receive here as soon as possible but no later than in two weeks.

For every 100 addresses, clearly written and correctly spelled, I will pay you Frs. 2.-, thus for 300 addresses Frs. 6.-, which sum I will remit to you through an international postal order or in postage stamps of your country as soon as I receive the addresses.

I ask you, M . . . , to write down the richest merchants, artisans, innkeepers, and farmers.

Put down only the addresses on the forms. If you have other information to give me, please use the enclosed correspondence cards.

In case you carry out this work to my satisfaction I may be able to entrust you with greater tasks.

If you don't want to do the work yourself but someone you know is willing to do it, be so good to give to that person the forms and this letter.

Please be assured, M . . . , of my perfect consideration.

Upon inquiry, the Sûreté discovered that Heilbut was organizing a lottery scheme in Germany. But distrustful as it very well should have been, it ordered the prefects to advise the local teachers not to respond to Heilbut's letter.[36]

Given the clumsiness of German low-level espionage, the German government probably could not afford to ignore the many informers who presented themselves after the war from the most varied backgrounds.

[35] Préfet des Alpes Maritimes, to minister of interior, Nice, 15 Dec. 1877, in AN (Paris), F7 12566, "Relations Allemagne." France in the late 1870s was using much Italian labor for construction projects connected with the military fortification of Paris.

[36] Folder on "J. Heilbut, Gr. Bleichen Nr. 46, Hamburg," in ibid.

Between 1874 and 1877 an expatriate German merchant named August Laur fed the Wilhelmstrasse with political news from France which he collected through his numerous acquaintances in high places under the Third Republic. His initial letter to Chancellor Bismarck led to an immediate inquiry by the German *Auswärtiges Amt* to the Berlin police presidium, which reported favorably on him on 23 March 1874. Several of Laur's reports to Bismarck are preserved in the *Politisches Archiv.* They stress the rapid normalization of economic relations between France and Germany.

The adverse sentiment in Paris against us Germans has become much more bearable. Now we can speak in German here and no one will molest us. People in the provinces are more hostile, and Paris and the provinces equally try to exclude us from their social life. But business between us is now as lively and as cooperative as before the war. Even German manufacturers, who after the war were put off by French firms with *"nous ne recevons pas des Prussiens,"* have recently received handsome orders again, for example some velvet makers in Krefeld.[37]

Laur's contacts to French textile makers to collect information lends credence to a French police report from Berlin, dated 10 November 1877, to the effect that German army officers were being sent to France and Austria disguised as commercial travelers with instruction to send written reports to some innocent-looking address in Germany every four days.[38] Léon Daudet also asserted that the Germans used commercial activity as their cover for intelligence work. He pointed to an *Institut W. Schimmelpfeng* with head offices on the boulevard Montmartre in Paris and branch offices in Bordeaux, Lyon, Marseille, and elsewhere, and which since 1870 provided credit information on commercial houses to its customers and used this activity to collect elaborate files on all the regions of France: on their climate, the state of their communications, their inhabitants, economic produce, the local politicians, etc.[39]

But Laur was by 1877 replaced by the newspaper editor Léo Taxil, one of a large number of Frenchmen on record in the *Politisches Archiv* who in the 1870s and 1880s volunteered to act as informers for Germany. Léo Taxil wrote to Bismarck from Geneva on 22 May 1877:

Being anticlerical, *Monsieur le comte,* means more to me than being a Frenchman. I have always applauded your energetic struggles against Jesuitism. That is why I believe it my duty to inform you about some things that may be unknown to you, and why I herewith assure you that, should the present communication please you, I will place myself entirely at your disposal for more information of this kind. I do hold a fairly important position in the provincial press of France. I am editor of *l'Egalité,* the great daily paper of Marseille,

---

[37] See documents on August Laur in PA (Bonn), Abt. IA B.c.81.
[38] Report by "E. No. 9," Berlin, 10 Nov. 1877, in APP (Paris), Carton B A/323, "Allemagne."
[39] Léon Daudet, *L'Avant-guerre. Etudes et documents su l'espionnage juif-allemand en France depuis l'affaire Dreyfus* (Paris, 1923), pp. 8–19. See also report by the commissaire spécial de police de St. Etienne, 28 Oct. 1883, on German industrial espionage in French textile workshops, in AN (Paris), F7 12566.

of *La Jeune République,* another Marseille daily, of *l'Indépendant,* the daily paper of Perpig-
nan, of *Le Petit Méridional* in Montpellier, and I myself run the foremost satirical journal
in southern France. Because I have voluntarily retreated to Geneva (I left my country precisely because of my hatred for the Jesuitism that reigns there), I have the right to write
openly in whatever paper or journal I choose. I therefore have very good connections. Since
you have made yourself the champion of human progress, let me make myself useful to you
if you so wish.[40]

The German consulate in Geneva thereupon was instructed to investigate
Taxil. Three separate reports were sent to Berlin June 1877 by a certain Bachmann, who called on Taxil posing as a messenger. He found out that Taxil's real
name was Antoine Gabriel Tagand, that he was a native of Marseille, and that he
once held a high position in that city's police. Taxil struck Bachmann as intelligent but full of delusions, living with his wife in utter poverty. ("He surely will
do anything for money.") A study of several of Taxil's reports to Berlin suggests
that he was interested in hurting France by selling military secrets, though his
somewhat sensational news items make one suspect him of gratuitous exaggera-
tion to say the least. Thus he informed Berlin of an impending French invasion
of Italy in June 1877 that never took place, citing secret mobilization orders to
station masters along the railway lines between Paris and the Mediterranean; of
munitions trains rolling toward Italy; and of one French soldier in the garrison
of Sète, who, he said, committed suicide because he refused to fight against
his heroes, Garibaldi and Victor Emmanuel.[41] (This soldier, presumably, was
also anticlerical.)

Taxil was controlled by General von Roeder, then the German minister to
Berne. His reports were soon labeled "not valuable" and we must assume that his
career as a German agent was quite short. There was, however, another publicist
by the name of Henry de Vézian, who in 1879 also offered his services to Bismarck, giving as his reason no more than his "profound admiration for your profound spirit and your immense work. . . . Without you, without the fear that
you inspire in the leaders of the European-wide revolution, what would become of
this world?"[42] What he had to tell the Germans and how accurate his information
was matters less than the overall impression the Germans must have received from
the behavior of Taxil, de Vézian and other Frenchmen like them, of a France
whose elite was selling the country and giving up its self-respect for reasons of
individual political gratification. A rash of treason cases in the French army in the
1880s finally prompted the passing of a new espionage law in France under War
Minister Boulanger (1886),[43] but France's prestige had by then suffered so much

[40] Original text in French. PA (Bonn), Abt. IA B.c.81, vol. II. A penciled note, in German, dated
28 May, reads: "He is offering political information. He could be a spy [*mouchard*], on the other
hand his services could be useful."
[41] Documents available in ibid.
[42] Letter, Henry de Vézian to Prince Bismarck, Geneva, 26 Jan. 1879, in ibid.
[43] PA (Bonn), Abt. IA Frankreich No. 113 (Generalia): "Akten betreff. das Französische Spionagegesetz," vol. I.

that the *Daily Telegraph* of London wrote on 3 October 1888: "Traitors seem to abound in the French Army. At one time 'military plans' are stolen and sold; at another rifles of the 'new pattern' are offered by soldiers to foreign governments, and so it goes on until the War Office authorities are almost at their wits' end."[44] By 1888, the climate in France was already set for the explosion of the Dreyfus Affair.

Besides private citizens of various nationalities, the Germans were served by professional agents of obscure provenance. One such prominent agent was a Russian national who used the code signature "A," and sometimes was identified as "Belina." Belina was not rated as "trustworthy" by the German embassy in Paris.[45] His dossier in the *Politisches Archiv* nevertheless contains several lengthy reports dating from 1879, which are of some interest because they concern alleged corruption and mismanagement in the Paris police, closely resembling the allegations made by Léon Daudet after the First World War, and all of them prone to convey to the German government a picture of France on the verge of domestic chaos during a very critical year. This was the year when domestic tensions were high in Germany as Bismarck proceeded to suppress the leadership of the Socialist movement while in Russia the Nihilists began their single-minded campaign to assassinate Alexander II. The relationship between the two empires had further cooled over the results of the Berlin Congress and the conclusion of the German-Austrian dual alliance.

The crisis of the French police, alluded to in the reports by Belina, had its origins in a domestic confrontation of Republicans and Legitimists. Its reverberations, however, affected the international relations of police agencies throughout much of Europe because they all pointed to the common specter of a Socialist world revolution. According to both Belina (who sought to ingratiate himself with the Germans) and Daudet (who sided with the French royalists) the French Sûreté under Prefect Albert Gigot in February 1879 found itself in a state of dissolution, assaulted and practically reduced to immobility by the political attacks of the French Socialist and Radical press, among the latter notably Rochefort's *La Lanterne*, actively supported by the left-wing politicians, Millerand, Briand, and Viviani.

The cause of the trouble lay two years in the past, in the abortive attempt by President MacMahon to restore the Bourbon monarchy on 16 May 1877. The police prefect, Félix Voisin, had at that time reactivated the political police inside the prefecture (a service first disbanded under the Paris Commune, then quietly restored by the Republic in 1874) to move against hundreds of Republicans who were expected to oppose a Royalist regime, so much so that between 25 June and 14 October France witnessed what one historian has described as a return to the worst days of Napoleon III's police

---

[44] *Daily Telegraph*, 3 Oct. 1888, clipping in ibid.
[45] Von Hohenlohe, German embassy, to State Minister von Bülow, Paris, 5 June 1878, in PA (Bonn), Abt. IA B.C.81, vol. II.

dictatorship.[46] However, this period did not last very long. When the parliamentary elections in the fall returned a Republican majority once more, the national crisis for France was over.

Only the Paris prefecture was left in deep turmoil. Police prefect Félix Voisin was replaced by Albert Gigot who promptly dispersed the political police by reassigning its personnel to minor posts in the police administration and sought to dispose of its many political files. (The political police was eventually placed at the disposal of the departmental prefects in 1882, and in 1893 wholly assigned to the departments and charged with the overall *renseignement* service in their territories.)[47] It so happened that these files contained not only compromising materials on figures in the public limelight, Belina said, but also a list of forty-four German Socialists who were being expelled from Berlin and which the Police President von Madai had sent to Police Prefect Gigot on 23 December 1878.[48] Gigot allegedly returned these lists to Berlin in 1879 fearing that they would be found among the Sûreté files by his successor, who then might use them to provoke a scandal about collaboration between the Sûreté and German police. Already scores of police officials had left the public service and entered the employment of *La Lanterne*, Belina continued, which was mounting a "counter-police" to infiltrate the Sûreté with informers.[49] True or not, the crisis in the prefecture was said to have reached a point where the governments of Europe could no longer rely on the French police to supervise and control a forthcoming International Socialist Congress in Marseille:

The police, impotent and under close scrutiny, remains passive. The men no longer care. . . . All the chiefs of services are disheartened. They wonder whether the clamor outside will not reach such proportion of audacity that the German government will be obliged to intervene and to restore order here.[50]

Belina repeated the same point on 8 March 1879, this time with reference to an editorial in a French newspaper:

There is no doubt but that the prefecture is completely finished . . . I send you under separate cover this evening's *Courier*, which talks about a possible introduction [*ingérence*] of German police in the coming Marseille congress in the light of the dissolution of the French police. . . "We may not believe that Germany will be pretentious enough actually to send its own agents to supervise our public meetings and thereby mount a kind of secret invasion [of France], even under the pretext that 'Security Police' truly stands for a higher, conservative, international service, whose needs our [police] organization can no longer fulfill."[51]

---

[46] Georges-André Euloge, *Histoire de la police. Des origines à 1940* (Paris, 1985), pp. 233–5.
[47] Jacques Aubert and Raphaël Petit, *La Police en France. Service public* (Paris, 1981), p. 103.
[48] Letter, the police president von Madai to the prefect Albert Gigot, Berlin, 23 Dec. 1878, No. 4470 P.J.I., in APP (Paris), Carton B A/195, "Socialisme en Allemagne, 1871–1889."
[49] It is in this context that Clemenceau was reported by Belina to demand the replacement of the existing political police with an alien police to implement the concept of *défense du territoire*.
[50] Report by "A," Paris, 16 Feb. 1879, in PA (Bonn), Abt. IA B.c.81, vol. II.
[51] Report by "A," Paris, 8 Mar. 1879, in ibid., vol. III.

To complicate the pressure on the Paris prefecture, there was in addition to the campaign of the Socialists and *La Lanterne* the pressure of that ambitious politician Gambetta, who nursed grand projects for the day that he would come to power of creating a new political and military intelligence service for France (the military was increasingly seen as potentially important for quelling labor unrest) and to reorganize the Sûreté altogether. Daudet in 1925 asserted that Gambetta by 1879 had for personal reasons become the willing associate of Baron Henckel von Donnersmarck, in charge of German police operations in France just as Millerand, Briand, Viviani, and others, according to him, were by then in the service of "le bismarckisme policier."[52] The association of Gambetta and anything like treason to France is far-fetched and yet has a remote plausibility insofar as there exists in the files of the Paris police prefecture a report by a street agent, dated 14–15 July 1880, linking Gambetta to Rochefort and Léo Taxil, who by then was back in Paris running an "anticlerical bookstore."[53]

So much for the information to be gleaned from some of the holdings of the German foreign ministry archive in Bonn concerning secret agents in the service of Bismarck after the Franco-Prussian War. While there are grounds to believe that the political crises that shook the Third Republic between 1877 and 1879 affected the police prefecture, the suggestion that the French Sûreté was out of commission to the point where the governments of Europe might call for German police to deal with a labor congress in Marseille, not to mention the allegation that Gambetta was betraying French interests, are all unsupported rumors, though unsupported rumors that the historian cannot refute with direct evidence to the contrary. What he can do is to balance them against the undoubted achievements of the French police during the 1870s and 1880s in restoring France's position abroad. He can do this by studying, next, the offensive operations of the French police outside France in the two decades following the Treaty of Frankfurt.

French offensive police actions

French police operations abroad between 1871 and 1890 were directed at three principal targets: (1) Germany, including Alsace and parts of Lorraine, the prospective enemy in the next war; (2) Switzerland, a potential strategic threat to French national defense should, under the changed circumstances since 1871, the German Empire establish a political and military dominion over her; (3) Russia,

---

[52] Léon Daudet, *Magistrats et policiers* (Paris, 1935), p. 102, and ch. V, *passim*. On 10 Dec. 1886, Donnersmarck was praised in a letter by the Prussian Staatsministerium to Emperor Wilhelm I for his rich experience in industry and agriculture: "Derselbe . . . hat es sich, namentlich in letzter Zeit, sehr angelegen sein lassen, dieselben im öffentlichen Interesse nutzbar zu machen." See GP-StA (Berlin), Rep. 90/1885, Akten "betreffend das Gräfliche Haus Henckel von Donnersmarck," vol. I.

[53] Report, Préfecture de Police, Contrôle Général, Paris. Note supplémentaire du 14 au 15 juillet (1880), in APP (Paris), Carton B A/923, "Gambetta année 1880."

the most desirable military partner in the next war, but beset by revolutionary unrest and liable to seek accommodation with autocratic Germany rather than with republican France.

ALSACE-LORRAINE

The first task of French intelligence after the war of 1870–1 was to assess the situation in the territories so recently ceded to Germany. We may assume that scouting missions across the border by French commissaires spéciaux assigned to towns near the Alsatian border were routine, and that in the first ten years they were mostly limited to collecting information on the public mood and the administrative disposition made by the Germans. One such report, by the commissaire spécial at Avricourt, dated 14 November 1877, was written on the basis of casual conversations with local inhabitants on the German side of the border and the reading of newspapers on sale there. Still, this report was forwarded by the local prefect to the First Bureau of the Sûreté in Paris and from there reached the ministry of foreign affairs.[54] However, after 1887 the mission of the commissaires spéciaux changed from simple collection of information to preparing useful contacts for clandestine operations in case of mobilization.

The best-known commissaire spécial along the frontier with Alsace was Charles Schnaebelé, superintendent at the railway station of Pagny-sur-Moselle, whose arrest by German frontier guards in 1887 was to cause a brief international crisis. A native Alsatian, born in Pfaffenhofen in 1827 and in his younger days an elementary school teacher, Schnaebelé served as a political police officer in Pagny since 1872.[55] His many reports dating from the 1870s and 1880s speak well for the breadth of information and the sophistication of judgment of these elite officials in the French police, confined though many of them were for decades to duty in one small rural town far from Paris. We offer as one example Schnaebelé's report on local reaction in Alsace to the Russo-Turkish War and to MacMahon's unsuccessful coup d'état, dated 20 August 1877:

The failure of the Russian army has on the whole produced wide-spread satisfaction, because this may end the war more quickly and more smoothly than was expected. Everyone would welcome this in the interest of our country, which is not thought to be recovered sufficiently as yet to benefit from a European war or avoid another humiliation. Across the frontier the opinion remains unchanged, namely that German interests absolutely demand that France remains a Republic and that she cannot tolerate the "government of the clergy" of 16th May. The Prussian newspapers continue to insult the Marshal [MacMahon] and his cabinet while they sing the praises of MM. Thiers, Gambetta, etc., whom in the past they have treated with sarcasm.[56]

[54] Report by *commissaire spécial* d'Avricourt, 14 Nov. 1877, in AN (Paris) F7 12566.
[55] *Metzger Zeitung*, 22 Apr. 1887.
[56] Report, Schnaebelé to M. le Directeur, Pagny-sur-Moselle, 20 Aug. 1877, in AN (Paris), F7 12566.

Schnaebelé's persistent advocacy of correct and civil dealing between French and German officials is also remarkable. A German soldier who crossed the frontier in June 1883 to ask permission to live in France, where he wanted to work as a house painter, was treated with consideration: "He declined to enlist in the Foreign Legion, explaining that his sole reason for deserting was that he found the military life too hard. I arranged for his sabre to be returned to the German gendarmerie at Novéant."[57] Three years later Schnaebelé urged his government to be more liberal in its policy toward travelers who promoted cultural contacts between Germany and France. The Prussians had invited French scholars to the five hundredth anniversary of Heidelberg University and asked the composer Camille Saint-Saëns to direct a concert at Aachen, while the French had barred entry to a Dutch conductor from Amsterdam solely because two musicians in his orchestra were German. "Annoyances like these have a bad effect on the German public as a whole," wrote Schnaebelé, "including those Germans who, in spite of everything, still harbor a certain sympathy for us."[58]

Painstaking correctness and strict enforcement of disciplinary rules on everyone, including German personnel, were among the chief reasons for the success of the German Reich administration in the former French territories between 1870 and 1918. The Germans made clear their insistence on preserving an air of mutual respect between victor and vanquished from the first day of the occupation. When in 1870 the three superintendents and twenty *sergents* of the municipal police of Mulhouse to a man refused to serve under German command, the Germans accepted their resignation with good grace, though they had wanted to make use of the old staff's familiarity with local conditions. The *Unter-Präfekt* on this occasion found a word of praise for the old police: "The strict sense of civil obligation which is displayed here – as probably in no other French town – may augur well for the future development of a communal spirit of self-government."[59]

An order of forced military billeting in local houses, which the Prussian judicial authorities issued in January 1872 after a brawl between country boys and Prussian soldiers in a pub in Bittschwiler, was revoked by the *Kreis-Director,* Herr Hagemann. The true culprits may not have been local villagers, Hagemann objected, so that the punishment would not hit those who were really responsible. Military billets, in any case, were usually set up in the best houses, but the rowdies presumably belonged to the poorer inhabitants. So the Kreis-Director decided on a more suitable punishment: a 9 P.M. curfew imposed on all pubs on Saturdays, Sundays, and Mondays, to be strictly enforced by the gendarmerie. To justify his moderation Hagemann pointed to the absence of true anti-German

[57] Schnaebelé to M. le Directeur, Pagny-sur-Moselle, 3 June 1883, in ibid. A standard French procedure with all foreign deserters was to invite them to join the Foreign Legion.

[58] Schnaebelé to M. le Directeur, Pagny-sur-Moselle, 11 Aug. 1886, in ibid.

[59] Report, Dr. Sch—— to Freiherr von der Heydt, Mulhouse, 22 Dec. 1870, ADdHR (Colmar), 73842, "Les Anciens Personnels de la Police française 1870–1871."

feelings in Bittschwiler because local quarrels between natives and newcomers arose too often simply because Prussian soldiers did not understand the Alsatian dialect, and were given to sporting "arrogant" airs.[60]

At the same time German rule was harsh. A twenty-four year old Alsatian, who in 1871 had opted for French nationality and had been expelled from Alsace, was arrested by German gendarmerie on returning to his home town in the summer of 1877. On his way to prison at Gorze, he asked his escort to remove his handcuffs. The German gendarme consented after first warning him that he would be shot if he tried to flee. The young man then tried to flee and was killed on the spot. In Paris the affair was discussed between the ministry of interior and the ministry of foreign affairs, and the upshot was that the French government did not protest this action even though a French gendarme in a similar situation would not, in the opinion of the French war ministry, have acted in the same way. "Taking flight does not constitute resistance or rebellion."[61]

But the same harshness applied to the punishment of German constables in Alsace who were liable to immediate dismissal with forfeiture of all pension rights for even minor infractions of rules. A number of petitions for leniency from the 1880s and 1890s are on file in the departmental archive in Strasbourg, in which German policemen pleaded their cases on the strength of their long military service before joining the police. Everyone of these petitions was rejected. One case in 1894 concerned detective Karl Wilhelm Schmidt, since 1888 detailed to the political police in Strasbourg with rank of *Schutzmann*. Schmidt was dismissed with forfeiture of all retirement benefits because a private letter to his mother, which he inadvertently had left lying on a table in the police station, contained abusive words about his service superior. He was accused of gross violation of duty (*grobe Dienstvernachlässigung*) and insulting the police director. Schmidt pleaded his case as a veteran of the battles of Vionville, Gravelotte, and Metz in 1870–1:

> I have always conscientiously executed my duties [as a detective], and so have incurred the animosity of a large section of the local inhabitants who belong to the radical parties. Were I now to earn my bread in this town as a simple day laborer – and there is little chance that I will find another means to support myself – my lot will be made a hundred times harder than if I were just anybody else. It is known that people are very suspicious about hiring fired policemen.

Schmidt had a sick wife, a daughter, and a daughter-in-law to support; his two sons were dead. Despite this hard-luck story by a man in his fifties, his request for clemency was denied.[62]

[60] Kreis-Director Hagemann to Freiherr von der Heydt, Thann, 7 Feb. 1872, in ADdBR (Strasbourg), AL 87 (3289) Acta betreff. "Feindselige Handlungen gegen deutsches Militair und deutsche Beamte, Excesse, Alarm-Nachrichten" (1872).

[61] Report by prefect of Meurthe-et-Moselle to minister of interior, Nancy, 20 July 1877, in AN (Paris), F7 12566, folder: "Meurtres commis par des gendarmes allemands sur des Alsaciens-Lorrains ayant opté pour la nationalité française."

[62] Letter, Schutzmann Karl Wilhelm Schmidt, to Min. für Elsass-Lothringen, Strasbourg, 29 Nov. 1894, in ADdBR (Strasbourg), AL 87 (2142), Acta betreff. "Schutzmänner in Strassburg (1873–1907)."

The French were aware that the chief problem facing the German administration after 1870–1 was not so much the residual loyalty to France by the inhabitants of Alsace and Lorraine, but the steady progress of the modern industrial labor movement, thanks in large part to the excellent work done by the organizers of the German Social Democratic Party. Spontaneous demonstrations of sympathy for France were surely gratifying, such as the cheers that greeted three French gendarmes in uniform from the garrison of Doubs who in 1886 arrived in Colmar to testify as witnesses in a criminal case.[63] But popular sentiments were not politically effective tools in the hands of the French government. As early as 1877 a French secret agent reporting home to the police prefecture from his assignment in Germany had recommended that the civilian population in Alsace be released from any further obligation to show defiance toward Berlin:

This year's elections in Alsace-Lorraine are of particular interest. We must realize that the political life of the French provinces which were annexed by Germany has now entered a new stage. Most people in Alsace-Lorraine believe that the time has come to abandon their stance of pure and simple protest against the German conquest, that [this stance] has been maintained forcefully and long enough to satisfy national honor. In the long run it cannot serve as the *modus vivendi* for a population of 2,500,000 souls, nor as a protection of its vital interests.[64]

During the invasion of Alsace in 1870 the Prussians had willingly exploited what class conflict they had found among the population in order to neutralize civilian resistance to the occupation force, for example when meting out penalties among the richer and poorer inhabitants of towns and villages. But the socialist movement in Alsace had still been in its infancy. A report by the Kreis-Director of Mulhouse, in 1874, described the working-class movement in his town as no more than "incipient" on the eve of the Franco-Prussian War. In 1870 the question of joining the workers' International had been broached for the first time by a prominent agitator named Eugen Weiss who was known to possess direct relations to the International in Paris. Since the war, the same Weiss had established contacts to the German Socialists of the Eisenach faction under August Bebel and Wilhelm Liebknecht. But, wrote the Kreis-Director, the question of shorter working hours and the religious issue of ultramontanism still played a greater role than plans for a world revolution. The *Rixheimer Volksbote,* he said, attacked the factory owners of Mulhouse because they were Protestant and the workers Roman Catholic.[65]

By 1878, following the two attempts on the life of Emperor Wilhelm I by Max Hödel and Karl Nobiling, whom the Prussian political police accused of acting on behalf of Social Democracy, efforts were under way to establish direct

---

[63] Report, *commissariat spécial,* police sur les chemins de fer, gare de Belfort, 7 Mar. 1886, in AN (Paris), F7 12566.

[64] Report by "H. No. 3," Berlin, 16 Jan. 1877, in APP (Paris), Carton B A/323.

[65] Report by an unnamed Kreis-Director to Freiherr von der Heydt, Mulhouse, 21 Mar. 1874, in ADdBR (Strasbourg), AL 87 (400), Acta betreff. "Socialdemokratische Umtriebe." On the tardiness of the Socialist movement in Alsace-Lorraine, see Dan P. Silverman, *Reluctant Union. Alsace-Lorraine and Imperial Germany 1871–1918* (University Park, 1972), p. 121.

lines of communication between the political police of all administrative Kreis-Directorien in Alsace-Lorraine and the police presidium in Berlin.[66] These links were finally established in 1880, thanks to the growing importance of the German political police in Alsace to the Berlin police, but not on account of a dangerous workers' movement among the Alsatians, rather because the political police officials stationed in Alsace were well placed to keep an eye on the number of German Socialist agitators who began to arrive in Switzerland after 1878.[67]

BERLIN, 1871–8

More important than French police probes into Alsatian villages and towns were the intelligence reports reaching the police prefecture in Paris from deep inside Germany, notably from Berlin.

The French government, of course, obtained much information openly and with the full knowledge of the Prussian authorities through French diplomats and private journalists. G. de la Ferronays, a French military attaché in Berlin, undertook a study of the Berlin police in 1874 with the assistance of two German police officials assigned to him by Police President von Madai, and which eventually resulted in a bulky manuscript of sixty-eight pages.[68] Also the growing range and tempo of modern international life led to a mounting volume of official contacts between the police forces of all the European capitals including Paris and Berlin. In 1875 the Berlin police presidium, through the German embassy in Paris, urgently requested the help of the Paris police to trace the movements of three Irishmen who were believed to be on their way from London to Berlin via Paris to assassinate the German emperor.[69] In 1887 Sûreté commissaire Goron came to Berlin in person to hunt down a murder suspect whose trail had led him from Paris to Brussels, and from there to Cologne and Berlin. He was amused by the smug satisfaction of the Prussian detectives who were just as happy that the fugitive, though a German, was also a Socialist.[70]

Goron, in 1887, showed something less than admiration for the Berlin that he saw. Though from the vantage point of one century later we today recognize the solid strength of the German socioeconomic foundation in Bismarck's time, con-

---

[66] Letter by [name illegible] to Herr von Ernsthausen in Colmar, Mulhouse, 5 June 1878, in ADdBR (Strasbourg), AL 87 (400).

[67] See various reports by political police officials in the late 1870s and early 1880s on their frequent missions to Switzerland and the growing budgetary appropriations from Berlin. For example, Sommer, police in Mulhouse, to Kaiserliches Ministerium für Elsass-Lothringen, (no date), in ibid., AL 30 (109) Acta betreff. "Die Verhaftung des Polizei-Inspektors Wohlgemuth in der Schweiz 23 Apr. 1889–6. Dez. 1889."

[68] B. de la Ferronays, "Rapport sur la Police de la ville de Berlin," (Berlin, 28 Mar. 1874), in APP (Paris), Carton B A/1693, "Polices étrangers," folder: "Police en Allemagne."

[69] Ambassador von Hohenlohe wrote to police prefect Léon Renault on 15 Apr. 1875: "Je viens d'être chargé par mon Gouvernement de Vous faire part de tous ses remerciements pour l'obligeant empressement avec lequel Vous avez, comme de coutume, répondu à notre demande." Note, Chef du Cabinet to Chef de la Police Municipale, Paris, 23 Mar. 1875, in AN (Paris), F7 12566.

[70] Marie-François Goron, *Les Mémoires de M. Goron, ancien chef de la Sûreté* (Paris, n.d.), vol. II, p. 111.

temporaries in the 1870s and 1880s were alarmed by the state's heavy reliance on military and police protection on the one hand and the depth of class hostilities on the other. Henry Vizetelly in 1872 marveled at the constant traffic of helmeted aides-de-camp and smart-looking orderlies in downtown Berlin, where in the restaurants uniforms predominated over civilian dress and in other parts of the city the "Briareus-like institution of the police, whose hundred heads are supposed to provide for every exigency of civil life." By contrast, in the poorer sections of Berlin, he wrote, "the *proletariat* are more brutal and menacing than in any other chief city in Europe."[71]

French police agents in the 1870s tended to endorse this alarmist view about the Berlin workers. The situation in Berlin was closely watched by a number of French agents reporting to Police Prefect Lombard in Paris, their reports identified only by codes like "1," "Z. No. 3," "L. No. 3," "6," "12," or "13." A report by "Z. No. 3," dated 22 February 1877, and which confidently predicted the outbreak of serious troubles in the German capital, is startling.

Thirty thousand men are all that is needed for an uprising [*émeute*] in Berlin. And we must not forget that the women and children of these people would certainly join their ranks. Up to the present vagabonds, thieves, drunkards etc, did not belong on the side of Social Democracy. But in an uprising they will make common cause with it. And since the brutality and bestiality of the Berlin populace have become proverbial, you will easily understand that the continuous fear of an uprising by the affamished class weighs like a nightmare on Berlin society.[72]

In May 1878 Lombard was informed by agent "13" that the Socialist International was planning to reorganize itself with headquarters in Germany.[73] This was confirmed by one police agent who signed his reports "Labore" and on a tour of the industrial regions of Germany sought out labor leaders like Keunzel, Bebel, and Motteler. "I traveled to Germany in accordance with your instructions," he wrote to Lombard on 10 July 1878: "If revolution were to break out in Germany . . . all Europe will be affected. All the workers' organizations [in Europe] are directly in contact with the leaders of German Socialism."[74]

Bismarck's anti-Socialist law was passed by the Reichstag on 21 October 1878. Already by 29 November of that year, however, "L. No. 3" reported that, if anything, the security in Berlin had worsened:

The Berlin police, having known for about ten days about a cache of Orsini-style bombs somewhere in the Prussian capital without being able to find it, has now reported the matter to Prince Bismarck. At the same time the police president of Berlin, von Madai, has reported to the Chancellor on the consequences of the Socialist law, proving that while

---

[71] Henry Vizetelly, *Berlin under the New Empire* (London, 1879), vol. I, pp. 63. See also Victor Tissot, *Voyage au pays des milliards* (Paris, 1875), passim.

[72] Report by "Z. No. 3," Berlin, 22 Feb. 1877, in APP (Paris), Carton B A/323.

[73] Préfecture de Police, Cabinet, Note 5896 pour M. Lombard, Paris, 29 May 1878, in APP (Paris), Carton B A/195.

[74] Report by "Labore," Paris, 10 July 1878, in ibid.

[Socialist] agitation in public has ceased, it now has spread inside the factory workshops and into the homes of the workers.[75]

But "L. No. 3" was the only French agent who cast doubt on the necessity of the anti-Socialist law to prevent open rebellion in Berlin. He continued:

Bismarck had proposed the imposition of a state of siege, which yesterday had been proclaimed for Berlin and Potsdam. About forty Socialists were expelled from Berlin and Potsdam, among them some Reichstag deputies. One pretends that a plot has been discovered to assassinate all the crowned monarchs of Europe. Conferences are said to take place between Berlin and Vienna, Livadia, Rome, and Madrid. The arrival of Prince Gorchakov in Berlin is supposed to be connected to all this. Finally, there is talk of a common *démarche* against Switzerland because of the Swiss policy of asylum for international socialists.[76]

Bismarck's anti-Socialist law and German police activities in Switzerland, 1878–90

General remarks

The proletarian rebellion in Germany's capital, which contemporaries in the 1870s had predicted, never took place. Instead, Bismarck used the excitement produced by the two assassination attempts against Wilhelm I (Max Hödel's on 11 May, and Dr. Karl Nobiling's on 2 June 1878) to push an anti-Socialist law through the Reichstag that was meant to suppress that vast and well-organized propaganda among the industrial population which gave the Social Democratic Party so distinct an advantage over the other parties in the Reichstag. One large town after another, together with its surrounding areas, came under martial law. Hundreds of party members became unemployed. All the leaders with few exceptions lost their means of existence.[77]

The "law to ward off Social Democratic excesses" (*Gesetz zur Abwehr sozial-demokratischer Ausschreitungen*), of 21 October 1878, though a piece of domestic German law, produced movement in the European situation, which in turn enabled France to improve its situation in the balance of power. This movement came from the exodus of hundreds of German Social Democrats to other countries, some through voluntary emigration, others through expulsion decreed by local police authorities. Because most of the German Socialists continued their political work abroad, their arrival called forth responses by the police of their host countries, especially where militant working-class movements were already in existence.

[75] Report by "L. No. 3," Berlin, 29 Nov. 1878, in ibid.
[76] Ibid. See also report by "L. No. 3," Berlin, 30 Nov. 1878, on the foolishness of banishing Germany's best labor leaders from its cities, in ibid.
[77] A detailed dossier on the German anti-Socialist law of 1878 is available in BA (Berne), Bestands-Nr. 21, Archiv-Nr. 13929. See also Eduard Bernstein, ed., *Die Geschichte der Berliner Arbeiter-Bewegung* (Berlin, 1907–10), vol. II; and Reinhard Höhn, ed. *Die vaterlandslosen Gesellen. Der Sozialismus im Licht der Geheimberichte der preussischen Polizei, 1878–1914* (Cologne, 1964).

We might well ask today why Germany between 1878 and 1890 exported its unwanted Socialists instead of confining them in prisons and penitentiaries at home. The answer probably is the same as to the question why Bismarck did not outlaw the Social Democratic Party altogether and permitted the SPD Reichstag faction to continue in existence, or why the attempt to muzzle Socialist ideas during the following twelve years of legal proscription so often resembled a benign game of cat and mouse between gendarmes and "Sozis," hard on the individual labor leaders but no more than annoying for the common factory workers. The memory of radical elements leaving Germany in the early nineteenth century more or less freely for countries more receptive to their ideas was still fresh and it was positive. They included the German democrats who had emigrated to Pennsylvania after the War of Liberation, the Stephan Borns and Ernst Dronkes who had ended up doing well in England, not to mention the many "1848ers" like Carl Schurz whose brilliant careers overseas reflected some glory on their country of origin. What is most important, very few of them had come back and none had seriously tried to influence his old homeland politically from abroad.[78]

Had not the Prussian government reason to believe that in the new empire a policy of evicting dissenters on a moderate scale might suffice to ensure the desired domestic consensus at home? The inhabitants of Alsace-Lorraine were given four years to opt for French nationality and accept expulsion – the number of those who actually left did not reach alarming proportions. When Bismarck in 1885–6 ordered nearly 30,000 Polish Jews who were Russian and Austrian subjects evicted from the eastern borderlands of Prussia, he also met with little opposition by either Russia or Austria. The Austrian consul in Breslau, who was instructed by his government to intercede on behalf of one Chaim Kozicki, actually declined to do so:

Ch[aim] Kozicki is that type of so-called Galician Jew who inspires little confidence and is not welcomed by the authorities of Upper Silesia for good reason. Intercessions on behalf of people like him are regularly rejected. Were I to intervene on his behalf the chances of success would be minimal. The High k.u.k. Ministry [of Foreign Affairs] will surely agree with me when I say that I would do better to reserve my good services for the better elements where success is possible, and that I refrain from doing the same for more dubious characters.[79]

Austria's passivity may have been prompted by a note from Bismarck on 22 September 1885, which was transmitted to the Ballhausplatz through the Prussian chargé d'affaires in Vienna and which categorically stated that the removal of certain Polish elements from Prussian territory was a matter of "state security" that

---

[78] Cf. speech by Prof. Kühnemann on the occasion of the unveiling of Carl Schurz's memorial in New York, in Committee of the Carl Schurz Memorial, "Addresses in Memory of Carl Schurz" (New York, 1906). Against this see, however, the reference to Carl Sturz [sic] in a French police agent's report on tensions between Germany and the United States: No. 912, Berlin, 23 Feb. 1884, in APP (Paris), Carton B A/323, "Allemagne."

[79] Consul Stadler to k. k. Ministerium, Breslau, 18 June 1886, in HHStA, Administrative Registratur F52, Karton 66, "Staaten–Deutschland."

brooked no discussion. "Our special motive for, and the purpose of, this measure make it necessary that we impose it wholesale and without any attempt at sifting the inhabitants by categories, in other words, that we let it also fall on *individuals against whom there is no personal proof of any behavior endangering our state security."*[80]

Bismarck's note was one of the earliest indications that the German Empire, faced with much vaster military problems than Prussia had faced in the early nineteenth century, might not commit itself wholeheartedly to the modern police principles evolved in the West which gave priority to individual over massive intervention in society and to procedures based on legal evidence rather than on group characteristics – and of an Austrian inclination to acquiesce. The Austrian prime minister Taaffe on 22 October 1885 answered an interpellation in the *Abgeordnetenhaus* on this matter with the declaration that Austria recognized Prussia's full right to proceed in such internal matters in accordance with Prussian state interests.

A police-ordered transfer of Socialists in bulk from Germany to another country with the collaboration of the receiving country's government only developed with Switzerland. The reason for this may largely have been due to the circumstances in 1878. We must bear in mind that, for obvious reasons, no German Socialist emigrated to autocratic Russia, where a fierce police hunt on rebellious students gave foreign radicals very little chance of survival. Nor would the Berlin government have wanted to ask St. Petersburg to take in charge its most outspoken Socialists. Indeed, Bismarck understood his campaign against German Socialism as a contribution also to the Russian government's effort to subdue its own revolutionaries.[81] The Habsburg monarchy was a more likely country of emigration for German Socialists because of the close bond between the German and the Austrian Social Democratic parties at the founding congress at Eisenach, in 1869. At the same time the Socialist movement in the Habsburg monarchy had begun to take an independent turn since the founding of the German Empire in 1871, with many workers' associations such as the Czech unions encouraged to pursue an ethnic national rather than an international goal. The passing of Bismarck's anti-Socialist law shocked the Austrian Socialists as a frightening manifestation of the German police's power of suppression. Far from offering shelter to their persecuted comrades in the north, the Austrian Socialists began to divide into moderate and radical wings, arguing over the best course to follow while anxiously watching for signs of a possible Austrian counterpart to Bismarck's law of proscription.[82]

---

[80] My italics. Letter, Bismarck to German chargé d'affaires Graf von der Goltz in Vienna, Berlin, 22 Sept. 1885, in ibid. also A. O. Sarkissian, ed., *Studies in Diplomatic History and Historiography* (London, 1961), p. 258.

[81] Günther Roth, *The Social Democrats in Imperial Germany. A Study in Working Class Isolation and National Integration* (Totowa, N.J., 1963), p. 68.

[82] Helmut Konrad, *Nationalismus und Internationalismus. Die österreichische Arbeiterbewegung vor dem Ersten Weltkrieg* (Vienna, 1976), passim. On Taaffe's half-hearted attempts to follow Bismarck's example, see Karel Maly, *Policejní a soudní perzekuce delnicke tridy v druhe polovine 19. stoleti v cechach* (Prague, 1967), pp. 276–7.

A joint anti-Socialist campaign by Berlin and Vienna might have been possible in the light of earlier conferences between the two governments shortly after the Paris Commune, and in connection with the diplomatic agreements concluded by them between 1873 and 1879. But the policing situation in the two countries differed too widely, suggesting for each a police strategy that scarcely applied to the other. Germany, fully embarked on a large-scale conversion to industrialism and faced by a nation-wide well-organized labor movement, sought to contain it with sanctions against widespread propaganda among the masses, some progressive measures of state protection for workers against illness, invalidity and old age, and the eviction of the most radical leaders. Austria, by contrast, was a monarchy endowed with an old tradition of sophisticated political police and a society in which the industrial class conflict was muted by the unresolved rivalry of Catholic nobility and liberal bourgeoisie besides being broken up by national rivalries. The police here was well advised to emphasize the dispersal rather than the suppression of Socialism: the rustication of the most vocal Marxists out of Vienna into the provinces, where they would lock themselves in disputes with local landowners and clergy, liberal schoolmasters, and nationalist peasant leaders.[83]

The German police infiltration of Switzerland

The two attempts against the life of the German emperor in 1878 produced more than a German anti-Socialist law: It caused an immediate demonstration of solidarity among Europe's autocratic monarchies which left the more democratic countries like France, England, and Switzerland at a certain disadvantage, in particular Switzerland.

Switzerland was still seen by most governments as the traditional country of refuge for revolutionaries from different countries. Suddenly it became the object of a possible joint intervention by the great powers of Europe. The Swiss minister to Berlin, A. Roth, reported home on 29 November 1878, that many people he had talked with assumed that the German Socialists had long ago decided to go to Zurich should they ever be prevented from continuing their activities in Germany and that they would then press on with their propaganda campaign from Swiss soil. Roth also reported a rumor that the powers were preparing a collective demand to Switzerland that it tighten its surveillance of Socialists, Nihilists, Internationalists and other dangerous elements on its territory.[84] A few days later, Roth wrote home that the Spanish government was the strongest advocate of such an international demarche in Berne.[85] Indeed, at a reception given by the German emperor and empress in December, the Spanish envoy had said to Wilhelm I that the Madrid government had already intensified its security measures

---

[83] See reports to Berlin by the German ambassador von Reuss in Vienna, especially 4, 10, and 21 Jan. 1884, and 29 Mar. 1887, in PA (Bonn), Europa Generalia 82, Nr. 8: Acta betreff. "Die Sozialdemokratie in Oesterreich-Ungarn," vol. I.

[84] Swiss minister A. Roth to Bundespräsident, Berlin, 29 Nov. 1878, in BA (Berne), Bestands-Nr. 21, Archiv-Nr. 13929.

[85] Roth to Bundespräsident, Berlin, 3 Dec. 1878, in ibid.

because of the assassination attempts in Germany. "We hope the other states will imitate [our] example. It is sad indeed that this movement [Socialism] should chiefly be directed against the lives of sovereign rulers."[86]

More remarkable, Roth wrote in his report of 3 December 1878, was that republican France was inclined to support this move by the conservative powers against Switzerland. He attributed this to a current desire by Paris to improve French relations with Germany. We may assume that the French anxiety stemmed from the war tension between the two countries in 1875 whose repercussions are reflected in a report to the ministry of foreign affairs by the First Bureau, Sûreté Générale, ministry of interior, dated 12 July 1877:

In a war between Germany and France, which is a contingency [*éventualité*] that will inevitably take place sooner or later, Switzerland will acquire a fairly important role because of its geographical location, and this quite possibly from the very beginning of the fighting. It is therefore of very great interest to the French government to be exactly informed on the true state of Swiss public opinion and to influence it as much as possible in favor of France. This is difficult since for some years now Switzerland has been cultivated in the opposite direction. General von Roeder, the Prussian ambassador, is a very active and clever man. He never lets an opportunity slip by unused and always seizes on every chance that presents itself.

Several newspapers, especially in the German-Swiss cantons, have been bought and carry on a very active propaganda on behalf of German ideas. We must therefore not assume that this is also what the public thinks. Nor can we guess what the public thinks from the statements of the Swiss federal council, whose members are all enfeoffed to German ideas. . . .

If Germany mobilizes, it can make use of the Swiss railway lines that pass from Germany into Switzerland through Romansthorn, Constance, Schaffhausen, Waldshut, and Basel. . . . The [German] garrisons at Constance and Weingarten would suffice for the occupation of the above-mentioned railway stations by a *coup de main*. Massive reinforcements would then be brought from Ulm, Stuttgart, Ludwigsburg, Augsburg, Munich, etc. . . . It is remarkable that for the last two years [there has been much new construction] in Constance, Weingarten, Tübingen where nothing stood before, and that other [stations] have been much enlarged, several of them to twice their size. . . . It is not difficult to deduce from all this the existence of some surprise project, carefully planned and whose means have been put in place with much forethought. . . . The execution of this plan may still be far away. [But] we must seek more information on site in Munich, Ulm, and Stuttgart.[87]

With the French anxious to delay a confrontation with Germany, it may be understandable why the French police, though not at all displeased to hear that Germany faced serious labor problems, should have exchanged information with Berlin over the movement of Socialists from their respective countries. When German workers collected money at a Socialist meeting in Paris, in July 1878,

---

[86] Roth to Bundespräsident, Berlin, 8 Dec. 1878, in ibid.
[87] Note, Sûreté Générale, 1er Bureau, to ministry of foreign affairs, Paris, 12 July 1877, in AN (Paris), F7 12566, "Relations Allemagne."

the Paris prefect reported this to the German ambassador, Prince Hohenlohe.[88] The Berlin police, in return, offered the French information on Socialists and Communists from France if they would send to Berlin what photographs they had of them.[89] And as was mentioned earlier, the police president, von Madai, did, on 23 December 1878, send to the Paris police prefecture a list of forty-four Socialists who were being expelled from Germany.[90]

And yet, France was not the country Berlin could count on for loyal cooperation against Germany's domestic opponents – there was too much mutual suspicion between the two nations for that. Along the Franco-Alsatian border, commissaire spécial Schnaebelé in November 1878 reported heightened vigilance by the German police opposite Pagny. The Germans were now under orders to watch all foreigners with special care and to place under immediate arrest anyone heard expressing a seditious thought or criticizing the German government. Schnaebelé cautioned French military personnel off duty not to visit relatives in Alsace-Lorraine and French railway employees not to venture in their uniforms across the border anymore.[91] On 3 December 1878 the Swiss minister in Paris, Kern, talked with Monsieur Picot, the director of the criminal department in the French ministry of justice, who sought to cast France and Switzerland in the role of two potential victims of the Great Powers' suspiciousness: "We fear that one fine day the various countries, with Berlin at the head, will come to tell us that only the material order in France has been saved [in 1871], and that our republican form of government represents an incitement to social democracy against which France owes the monarchical states [of Europe] certain legal guarantees."[92]

Was this the reason why, three days later, Kern reported home that a number of French politicians, among them Léon Gambetta and Eugène Spuller, thought that Switzerland should bow to the Great Powers and consider changing its laws of asylum, in order to avoid becoming the subject of international pressure?[93] Was France throwing Switzerland to the wolves to gain time for itself?

Given this perplexing situation in which Switzerland was threatened by the large powers on account of a crisis in another country that she scarcely could have prevented, it is not astonishing that Berne proceeded with little compunction to offer Germany its full cooperation in surveilling expelled German Socialists who, under the circumstances, might as well be directed by the German police to its territory. England certainly was no help to Switzerland: the British minister to Vienna, Sir Henry Elliott, assured his Swiss colleague Tschudy that Britain would never join a common demarche against Berne, if only because Britain

---

[88] Prefect of police to German ambassador Prince Hohenlohe, Paris, 28 July 1878, in APP (Paris), Carton B A/195.

[89] Letter, Prince Hohenlohe to prefect of police, Paris, 11 June 1878, in ibid.

[90] See discussion of "Spies and Traitors in France" in this chapter.

[91] Report by Schnaebelé, Pagny-sur-Moselle, 4 Nov. 1878, in AN (Paris), F7 12566.

[92] Swiss minister Kern to Bundespräsident, Paris, 4 Dec. 1878, No. 1/3776 (*confidentiel*), in BA (Berne), Bestands-Nr. 21, Archiv-Nr. 13929.

[93] Swiss minister Kern to Bundespräsident, Paris, 6 Dec. 1878, in ibid.

followed a similar policy as the Swiss toward political refugees. But, Sir Henry added rather condescendingly, unlike Switzerland Britain of course could never be told by the Great Powers to change its laws.[94]

Most comforting among all the other statements by European diplomats perhaps was the attitude of Austria-Hungary, as reported by Tschudy:

No one [in Vienna] wants to support the proposition [of the Powers]. Social Democrats are not feared because in Austria they really don't constitute a danger, except perhaps in Galicia – to the Russians. And there is even less fear of "emperor killers" [Kaisermörder] because in no other monarchy is the bond between Kaiser and people as strong as in Austria-Hungary.[95]

To appreciate the nature of Swiss police cooperation with Germany it is best to examine the communications passed between Berne and certain cantonal authorities, and between Berne and Minister Roth in Berlin, from 1878 to the early 1880s. First, a notification by the federal department of justice and police to the police of the canton Basel-Stadt, dated Berne, 7 December 1878:

Due to various circumstances we have come to believe that a certain number of the promoters of Social Democracy are most likely to arrive in Switzerland because of measures taken against them in Germany, and that they will try to continue from Swiss soil their agitation against the governments and constitutional system of other states.

While the Bundesrath is in no way inclined to limit the right of asylum which Switzerland traditionally has accorded to political fugitives, it is nevertheless determined to interdict any activity by such fugitives – be it in written or oral form – which is likely to disturb the friendly relations between Switzerland and other states.

We ask you to watch the situation [in your canton] with the above consideration in mind and to keep us constantly informed by means of detailed reports. To this end we hereby convey to you a list of persons who have been expelled from Berlin as leading partisans of Social Democracy.

We would be very grateful for a report on the present situation in regard to this matter soon after receipt of this letter.[96]

Appended to this letter were thirty-four names of expellees who were expected to arrive in Basel. The open publicity attending the eviction of these Socialists and the matter-of-factness with which the German authorities accepted Swiss collaboration is as surprising as is the absence of evidence that any one of these Socialists was really a dangerous revolutionary. On 30 November 1878, for example, the Swiss legation in Berlin told Berne the names of the latest expellees on hand simply of a newspaper clipping from that morning's edition of the Nationalzeitung: "Among the Social Democrats who this morning received expulsion orders from the Police Presidium are Reichstag deputies Fritzsche and Hasselmann, the editor

[94] Report, Swiss minister Tschudy to Bundespräsident, Vienna, 1 Dec. 1878, in ibid.   [95] Ibid.
[96] Andermat (EJPD), to police department of Basel-Stadt, Berne, 7 Dec. 1878, in StA (Basel-Stadt), Politisches EE 12, 1. "Sozialisten, Anarchisten, Politische Polizei, Allgemeines 1878–1880–1884."

Auer, the bookseller Rackow. . . . . They have four days to leave the city, no appeals permitted."[97]

More formal, but surely by then routine, was a communication by Berlin police president von Madai to the Swiss department of justice and police in 1879:

> The police presidium has the honor to inform the Swiss department of justice and police most humbly that pub owner Joseph Schmidt of Berlin, whose personal description is appended, has been banned from the city of Berlin, the townships of Potsdam and Charlottenburg, as well as from the districts Teltow, Nieder-Barnim, and Ost-Havelland in accordance with the Prussian state ministry decree of 28 November of last year, based on paragraph 28 of the imperial law to ward off Social Democratic excesses of 28 October last year.[98]

In one rare instance a German worker was described by the EJPD as requiring the special watchfulness of the Basel police:

> The German legation has conveyed to us for confidential use a report on the circumstances of the well-known mechanic Franz Julius Schindler and his past record. [The legation] suggests the closest surveillance in his case, because people of his mental bent are precisely the ones who are most easily used by secret societies to carry out criminal acts. We enclose this report for you to read and perhaps to copy and ask you to keep Schindler under careful guard. Please return this report as soon as possible because we must also inform the Federal Council.[99]

Most of the expellees from Germany did not apparently warrant special care — not all of them were even German. There was one French Communard, named Henri Moertier, whom the German authorities sent to Switzerland, and one Russian Jewish medical student from Mohilev, Moses Aronson. There was even one expellee for whom Berlin police president von Madai furnished a recommendation of good character.[100]

For a number of years the Swiss uncomplainingly helped the Germans keep their Socialists under guard though, admittedly, the orderly behavior of these exiles made their task relatively easy. To illustrate the Swiss alacrity, we have the dispatch from the Swiss legation in Berlin, dated 3 April 1881, in which it reported that it had approached the German foreign ministry for the latest list of expelled Socialists and that the Swiss minister had apologized to the *Auswärtiges Amt* for bothering it with this trifle: "We could not obtain the names on our own

[97] Swiss minister Roth to Bundespräsident, Berlin, 30 Nov. 1878, in BA (Berne), Bestands-Nr. 21, Archiv-Nr. 13929.

[98] Polizei-Präsidium Berlin to EJPD in Berne. Journal No. 925.P.F.I., Berlin, 10 Feb. 1879, in BA (Berne), Bestands-Nr. 21, Archiv-Nr. 13999.

[99] EJPD to police department of Basel-Stadt, Berne, 14 Nov. 1879, in StA (Basel-Stadt), Politisches EE12,1.

[100] Letter, Swiss minister Roth to EJPD, Berlin, 22 Oct. 1879, concerning one C. A. Schramm, in BA (Berne), Bestands-Nr. 21, Archiv-Nr. 13999.

because the lists have not been officially published."[101] When workers from nearby German townships were invited to an assembly by the *Deutscher Arbeiterverein* held in Riehen, on Swiss territory, the Basel police sent *Polizeiburalist* Lippe to take careful notes for the German authorities.[102] These and many other such cases raise the question, had Germany after 1878 assumed the role of dominant protector of Switzerland, so recently still held by France?

Franco-Russian police relations, 1872–81

Three documents on Russia

The rapprochement between Germany and Switzerland over Bismarck's anti-Socialist law may have disquieted France. But the French government received much information also from police agents watching the revolutionary situation in Russia from observation posts elsewhere in Europe and in St. Petersburg. The Empire of the Tsars was on the one hand the only serious partner who over the years could help France reverse the dangerous drift of the balance of power in the direction of German hegemony. But Russia was also the one European power that faced a revolutionary upheaval serious enough to threaten its position in the family of nations. More complicated still, the energy and the ideology of the forces aroused by its social, economic, and political problems could deeply affect the future of much of the world and in France produce a conflict between sympathizers for the antitsarist rebels (because they appeared to be more democratic) and sympathizers for the tsarist regime (because Russia formed a military counterweight to Germany).[103]

Thus France in 1878–9 on the one hand lacked a convenient handle to interfere with the easy collaboration that developed between the Berlin police and the EJPD in Berne; on the other hand the assets France had at stake in the German–Swiss dalliance were dwarfed by the ominous forces that were gathering in Eastern Europe. We quote from three French police reports on the state of the revolutionary crisis in Russia around the time when Bismarck launched his anti-Socialist campaign in Germany.[104]

Our first document dates from the spring of 1877, a time when Tsar Alexander II's reform movement, so dramatically launched in 1861 with the emancipation of the peasants, had spread to reform efforts in the Russian army, the bureaucracy, and the universities. However, the tsar's enthusiasm for change was beginning to give way to the realization that he was opening the floodgates to a revolutionary groundswell that could sweep away traditional Russia and the Romanoff dynasty.

---

[101] Swiss legation to Bundesrath, Berlin, 3 Apr. 1881, in BA (Berne), Bestands-Nr. 21, Archiv-Nr. 13929.
[102] Report by G. Lippe, police department of Basel-Stadt, Basel, 26 Apr. 1880, in StA (Basel-Stadt), Politisches EE 12,1.
[103] Emile Haumont, *La Culture française en Russie (1700–1900)* (Paris, 1913), p. 429.
[104] All three documents are available in APP (Paris), Carton B A/196: "Le Socialisme en Russie de 1872 à 1889."

The Third Section of the imperial chancellery, which was the political police founded by Nicholas I in 1825, was struggling to find a way that would ensure Russia a controlled pace of liberalization.

Préfecture de Police, Cabinet, Paris, 10 April 1877
Information from Russia speaks of a very strong revolutionary movement at this time. The Nihilists and the Socialists demand a change in the government and the enlightened classes attack favoritism and want a constitution and a responsible ministry. The chief of the Third Section has sent a report to the Emperor saying that the demand for a constitution is even heard among members of the civil service and that there is need to divert these demands by means of a convenient war. The Russians say that if Emperor Alexander [II] has not yet begun hostilities with Turkey this is because he is not sure of Germany.

The second document is interesting because of the comparison it makes between the French and the Russian political state: the former is seen as a finite and coherent political machine controllable by police though needing constant supervision and repairs; the second is depicted as amorphous and the prey to relentless historical forces that police can contain only up to a point. Ultimately it requires military force to build a new political consensus on physical coercion. By the end of 1879 the political climate in Russia had changed; fear of chaos was beginning to replace what little hope existed two years earlier for modernization from the top: Russia's foreign policy in the Balkans had been checked at the Congress of Berlin; the Nihilist movement of rebellious students returned from universities abroad had demonstrated its growing ideological appeal when in the Vera Zassulich trial the tsar's own judiciary had acquitted the assailant of an imperial official; and finally the tsar had himself become the target of an open campaign of assassination, most recently on 19 November. At the Paris police prefecture interest in a Russian alliance was at a low ebb. The domestic resentment of clerical influence in high quarters (see Léo Taxil's letter to Bismarck in praise of the Kulturkampf) was seemingly more the kind of problem worth the attention of the French police.

Rapport Cabinet, Brussels, 12 December 1879
In the light of the most recent attempt at the tsar's life, we can find the reliability of our sources of information reaffirmed. . . .

We may still witness some alternating periods of agitation and calm before we see a complete turnover in the state of affairs in Russia. What is certain is that this agitation will not end, whatever happens. To think otherwise is not to understand human nature. We do, incidentally, believe as do certain Socialists, that revolutions are not produced on order. They arise from given circumstances, as in the case of the Paris Commune of 1871. We have said before that the Paris insurrection resulted from carelessness by the government and the authorities of the time, who showed a weakness and a continued hesitation that could only produce anarchy and its consequences.

The third document dates from only a few days later. It reiterates the argument that there was an unstoppable movement for change in Russia but draws more attention to its European-wide significance. The political illness of the Russian

Empire was shared by the central European empires Germany and Austria-Hungary, though in the latter two the crisis was much less severe and the symptoms were different. Would the empires of the Romanoffs, the Hohenzollerns, and the Habsburgs recognize their common difficulty as autocratic regimes, all three of them in need to win democratic support from their peoples without risking the collapse of the hierarchical edifice of birth and education, dynastic armies and police bureaucracies on which rested their survival as independent sovereign states? Would they seek ways to resolve this problem through collaboration (see their movement toward an international political police agreement 1898–1903, below), or through mutual rivalry, each trying to resolve its own problem at the expense of the others (as Germany did briefly in the Peace of Brest-Litovsk in 1918)? Everything depended on whether Russia chose an alliance with France to maintain the balance of power in Europe or joined Germany and Austria-Hungary in search of a common solution to their socioeconomic difficulties.

Copie, Rapport Cabinet, Bruxelles, 27 December 1879
What happens in Russia is not a revolt but a revolution. True, there is no civil war, where two halves of a nation slaughter one another in the streets and which ends in a few days. It is nonetheless true that there is in Russia a struggle between the government and the people and that this struggle is the more terrible as the revolutionary attacks almost always succeed in striking at their target despite the armed forces at the disposal of the authorities and despite the extreme severity with which they are used (or abused).

A revolution that takes place in the well-known fashion would certainly last only a short time. It would be more bloody [than earlier ones] but hold out little chance of success for the people because of the military strength available in all states today.

The way the Nihilists operate, therefore, represents a step forward and we would not be surprised if their example will be followed in other countries, especially in Germany, where the partisans of the revolution have too much to fear from the army.

The Nechaev affair

The French government must have recognized its inability in the 1870s to influence the Russian situation. Paris probably could not even decide whether to offer help to the embattled tsarist regime or to stand aside and let the events take their course, content to be no more than a distant onlooker watching from the banks of the Seine river.

The construction of a police alliance between the Third Republic and autocratic Russia may have come about on Russia's initiative more than on France's. An innocuous first step toward a Franco-Russian police entente took place in 1872, when the Russians asked a defeated and isolated France to lend a helping hand in a small, technical police undertaking: the capture of the much wanted Nihilist and self-proclaimed world revolutionary, Sergei Nechaev, then about twenty-two years old and known to be living in Switzerland. The affair merits mentioning because of three questions that it raises: (1) If Nechaev was in Switzerland, why did the Russians ask the French police to help them in addition to the Swiss police? (2) Why did the Russians demand that French police agents go to Switzerland when they had their own agents on location who could penetrate Russian revolutionary circles much better than Paris detectives and could have identified Nechaev to the French police had he escaped to France? (3) Were the Russians perhaps using the Nechaev case, in which they had a technical edge over the French, chiefly to establish the precedent of a superior hand in some future Franco-Russian police collaboration?

To appreciate how the Russians, far from assuming the role of petitioners toward the French, managed instead to direct the French police during their joint search for Nechaev we must first look at the written agreement concluded between the Paris police prefecture and the Russian government in the summer of 1872:

Préfecture de Police
7, boulevard du Palais
Sécrétariat particulier
Paris, 9 July 1872
Summary of arrangement concluded between Count Levachov and the Police Prefecture of Paris in regard to the arrest of one Nechaev.

1. It is understood that the individual named Nechaev will be arrested wherever on French territory he may be found, and that he will be expelled from said territory at whatever point the Russian Government will have beforehand indicated to the Police Prefecture.
2. The Russian Government continues its surveillance of the above-mentioned individual during his entire stay in Switzerland and will notify the French Government by telegram of the departure and destination of that Nechaev.
3. If the Russian agents are in a position to point out the destination in France of that Nechaev, [the French] will take measures to arrest him at the place so indicated. In case the Russian agents can only signal Nechaev's departure but neither his destination nor his travel route, the [Paris] Police Prefecture will have the two principal railway lines between Lyon and Paris closely watched.
4. To implement this last arrangement the French Police Prefecture will immediately dispatch 2 agents to Zurich who will spend two weeks to familiarize themselves with Nechaev's outward appearance and his habits. After that they will return to Paris to await the signal from the Russian agents that the individual in question has left.
5. The telegram announcing the departure [of Nechaev] will be sent to Paris to a M. Perrot, 125 rue St. Jacques, and be signed Jacques. For obvious reasons the name Nechaev will not be mentioned. Letters from St. Petersburg concerning this same subject will be sent to the same address, signed P. H.–.
6. What information the Prefecture believes needs be sent to St. Petersburg will be addressed to M. Paul David, hairdresser, Nevsky Prospect 12.[105]

Between 11 July and 19 August 1872, a total of thirty-seven reports arrived from Zurich for Monsieur Lombard, officier de paix, Service des recherches at the prefecture, sent via the cover address of M. Perrot at 125, rue St. Jacques. The

---

[105] Document available in ibid., Carton B A/924, "Netchaïëf. Russe coupable d'assassinat politique."

senders were two of Lombard's detectives, Gautier and Sauvage. There is an involuntary comicalness to these letters since they make it so plain that these two policemen were quite unsuited to their task. Poorly educated, to judge by their many misspelled French words, they knew no German to help them find their way around Zurich, and no Russian to eavesdrop on the conversations of fellow diners after they were finally steered to the favorite hangouts of Russian students. To make up for their lack of success in finding Nechaev, they turned to reporting on whatever else they chanced to come across: on French freemasons they saw in Zurich, on a speech they heard Gambetta was to deliver in the city, and on Bakunin's looks when they happened to catch a glimpse of the famous anarchist ("big, corpulent, between 45 and 50, he is said to be a political exile deported from Russia"). [106]

After two weeks of frustration Gautier and Sauvage had to be directed to their prey by information provided by "P. H." all the way from St. Petersburg via Paris ("our friend has several passports, in Zurich he goes under the name Lamanche and poses as a French subject. . . . Hoping to contact the working class and Polish émigrés, he has made himself an apprentice to a house painter . . .") but not without first submitting them to a humiliating summons to report to a Russian police official in Basel:

Last Saturday, a higher official has left [St. Petersburg], arriving in Basel on Thursday, where he will take rooms at the Hotel Schweizer Hof. If one of your agents were to call on him he will be told how to find our friend. This meeting in Basel is indispensable . . . for the success of our undertaking. Your man merely has to ask for M. Nikolits and introduce himself with the words: "I am one of the two who came from France." [107]

The Russians in the end did not need French help to apprehend Nechaev; perhaps they had never really needed this help to begin with. Nechaev was arrested by the Zurich police on 1 August 1872, and three months later the Swiss government agreed to extradite him to Russia as a common criminal. [108] The ineptitude of Gautier and Sauvage, however, gave the Russian Chancellor Prince Gorchakov the excuse for sending to the French police a telegram from Interlaken, on 8 August 1872, which contained something like a reprimand:

The two French agents sent from Paris to find Nechaev nearly ruined everything in Zurich due to their imprudence, and now they have disappeared. Could you send us as quickly as possible two replacements who have more experience? They need only go to Basel and at the Hotel Schweizer Hof ask for M. Frédéric who will give them detailed instructions. These French agents should, like the earlier ones, be given the necessary legal powers to act in any situation. Please telegraph your answer to Berne. [109]

---

[106] Ibid. The description of Bakunin is in a letter dated 27 July 1872.

[107] P. H., St. Petersburg, 17/29 July 1872, in ibid.

[108] Report by Gautier and Sauvage of 19 and 21 Aug. 1872; and notice in *Le Figaro* (3 Nov. 1872), in ibid.

[109] Telegram, Prince Gorchakov to French Sûreté, 8 Aug. 1872, in ibid. In a letter to his superior, dated 12 Aug. 1872, however, Lombard defended Gautier and Sauvage as "intelligent, zealous, and loyal." Letter by "Perrot" (Lombard), Paris, 12 Aug. 1872, in ibid.

French police surveillance of Turgenev and others

More gratifying for the French police than the bungled Nechaev affair were the contacts developing in the 1870s with the Russian police in regard to Russian subjects residing in France, whom the agents of the Sûreté could watch with much greater self-confidence. This was the case with the writer Ivan Turgenev who had come to live in France in 1861. Turgenev was for several reasons an ideal subject for the French police to watch for the Russians. His literary reputation as the "father of Nihilism" gave him a certain importance. At the same time Turgenev was a gentleman who was basically loyal to the tsar, so that the French police did not risk endangering vital Russian interests should through some accident their surveillance of him break down. Turgenev also did not live submerged in a closed world of émigré Russians. On the contrary, his friendship with Madame Pauline Viardot and with noted French men of letters like Alphonse Daudet, Edmond de Goncourt, and Gustave Flaubert gave every advantage to the Sûreté agents over Russian spies, for whom the Paris of the upper bourgeoisie was not the native milieu.

The prefecture files contain two overall evaluations of Turgenev from the years 1873 and 1877. Composed by an agent who used the code name "Jack," Turgenev was portrayed as a literary man sympathizing with the Russian peasantry rather than as a revolutionary activist. His novel *Fathers and Children* was mentioned (the report also gave the original title in cyrillic letters), so was his correspondence with Russian exiles in Switzerland (Zhukovsky in Geneva, Bakunin and Golitsin in Vevey), and his literary friendship with Chernishevsky, the author of *What Is To Be Done?* While none of this information could have been news to the Russian police it served to demonstrate the thorough work of the French Sûreté.[110] More useful probably to the Russians were the French probes into Turgenev's private life in the house of Madame Viardot at 50, rue Douai: tidbits about the meals he ate, his servants, and his surprisingly good relations to M. Viardot, his mistress's estranged husband: "The life of the inhabitants in the Hotel Viardot is shrouded in mystery. No one in the neighborhood knows what goes on there and one can only speculate on the relationship between these three persons."[111]

There were sometimes meetings of Russian Nihilists at the house in the rue Douai, and sometimes Turgenev was reported by the Paris police at the Russian reading room in the rue de Corneille, an association that he also subsidized.[112] Yet following the attempt to blow up the train of Emperor Alexander II on 19 November 1879, the Brigade de Recherches also had the satisfaction of reporting

---

[110] Report, Préfecture de Police, Cabinet, 1er Bureau, 3 Mar. 1886; and report by agent "20," Paris, Oct. 1887, in APP (Paris), Carton B A/1,287. In 1886, the Sûreté purchased the books of Turgenev and Chernishevsky in French translation to improve its understanding of Nihilism.

[111] See report by "Jack," 28 Oct. 1873; and a report by Police Municipale, Service des Garnis, Cabinet, 1er Bureau, file no. 106,409, Paris, 10 Jan. 1877, in ibid.

[112] Report of 15 Apr. 1877, in ibid.

Turgenev's decision to return to St. Petersburg, to clear himself of all suspicion of collusion, or so it was believed.[113] Turgenev briefly preoccupied the Paris police again in connection with the expulsion of the Nihilist Pierre Lavrov from France shortly before the novelist died in Paris in 1883.

But far more important than the successful surveillance of Turgenev was the mounting gravity of Russia's revolutionary crisis in improving the Sûreté's standing within what by the mid-1870s was developing into a regular collaboration between the French and Russian police – albeit of a collaboration exclusively serving Russian security interests. By 1875 France's police agents abroad, who in the past were only used against French political refugees or to assess the danger to France of foreign countries, began to report in detail on Russian revolutionaries in Switzerland and Germany. Unmistakably the Russian revolutionaries were increasingly portrayed by the French in the tsarist perspective with an unfavorable bias, but then another slant would hardly have been suited for reports meant to be shared with Russian officials.[114] At the same time these reports also fed the Russians the impression that neither Switzerland nor Germany were doing enough to keep the Nihilists who lived there under control. When "Jack" in October 1878 reported that forbidden Russian books were secretly printed in Leipzig, the Paris municipal police ordered a full list of all the titles, presumably for transmission to the Russians.[115] In the same month another French agent, code-named "X," reported from St. Imier (canton Berne) that books praising Nihilism were being printed there "in considerable quantities and daily dispatched to Romania from whence they are smuggled into Russia hidden among different merchandise." "X" went on to warn that: "A perfect Nihilist 'counter-police' is at work in this city. Anyone suspected of being a *mouchard* is submitted to a very meticulous surveillance. And with such dangerous characters as Pressmakoff in charge (better known in Zurich by his given name André), woe to the Russian police agent who is found out."[116]

But if the available record on Franco-Russian police dealings between 1872 and 1878 suggests that the Russian tsarist police kept the upper hand (if not by giving instructions to French detectives as in the Nechaev case, then by the fact that all joint endeavors served Russian needs) this is not to say that the French government on the cabinet level was as yet ready to risk France's future in Europe on an alliance with the tsarist regime. French police reports continued to come in on the worsening situation in St. Petersburg in 1878 and 1879.

---

[113] Report, Préfecture de Police, 1er Brigade de Recherches, Paris, 3 Mar. 1880, in ibid.

[114] See for example the report by "Ludovic," dated 17 Sept. 1878, denouncing the "immoral" conduct among the Russian Nihilists in Geneva, and another report by a woman agent in Dresden, "3," dated 8 Dec. 1878, which portrayed women Nihilists in derogatory terms as adventuresses of the upper classes, in APP (Paris), Carton B A/196.

[115] Report by "Jack" as conveyed by Chef du 1er Bureau, Préfecture de Police, Cabinet, to Chef de la Police Municipale, Paris, 4 Nov. 1875, in ibid.

[116] Report by "X," St. Imier, 3 Oct. 1878, in ibid. For a general account on Russian students in Europe during the second half of the nineteenth century, see Alfred Erich Senn, *The Russian Revolution in Switzerland, 1914–1917* (Madison, 1971), ch. I.

1. In October 1878, in the case of Vera Zassulich, agent "X" reported that the majority of the jury had been intimidated by the revolutionaries or bought off, and that the director of the prison in St. Petersburg, Feodorov, had taken 50,000 rubles in bribes to let her escape.[117]

2. In November 1879, a report from St. Petersburg described the Russian police agents who had been assigned to live clandestinely among the Nihilist students as being ". . . either their accomplices or cowards. Thus, when last month someone openly distributed about 30 copies of the revolutionary journal at the University he was spotted by 4 or 5 police agents, but none of them took any action."[118]

3. On top of the suspicion of cowardice came the charge of ignorance and stupidity. Paris was told of a Russian police inspector who overheard two students in a railway carriage conversing in French (a language he did not understand), whereupon he had them arrested by the gendarmerie at the next station for "sedition."[119] Following the bombing of the tsar's train in November 1879, General Gourko, in charge of security, ordered that all students in St. Petersburg must leave their keys in the doors of their rooms so the police could enter and inspect their premises at all times.[120]

4. Concurrently the French informers in Russia described the tsarist authorities as weakening in the face of popular unrest:

It is said that a few days ago the Third Section received a fresh impulse, and that we might be told in another week that the Socialist leaders have all been arrested. In the meantime, there are news of more disturbances in the region of Kiev, where the peasants are said to have risen to demand bread. Here [in St. Petersburg] everything appears quiet but it is known that judges in the local courts have strict orders to side with the peasants against the landowners. While draconian laws remain on the books, the government has decided to follow the road of prudent indulgence. The students of the pedagogical institute (which is a nest of Nihilists) have just been granted permission to form an association.[121]

5. A final indictment of the Russian police was its opposition to Adjutant-General M. T. Loris-Melikoff's efforts to bring about constitutional reform in Russia. An Imperial ukase of 16 March 1880 had temporarily placed the Third Section under the direct control of Loris-Melikov as a first step to divest it of its judicial powers. For the gendarmes and police, so the French report, this was the cause of much resentment and of secret glee at the attempt by Mlodetski to shoot Loris-Melikov dead.[122]

Thus the turn from the 1870s to the 1880s presented the French Sûreté with a complicated foreign situation. How serious was Germany's labor problem? Did the Berlin police really face a potential civil war in the Reich capital? Did

[117] Report by "X," St. Imier, 3 Oct. 1878, in APP (Paris), Carton B A/196.
[118] Report from St. Petersburg, 12 Nov. 1879, in ibid.
[119] Report from St. Petersburg, 14 Nov. 1879, in ibid.
[120] Report from St. Petersburg, 22 Dec. 1879, in ibid.
[121] Report from St. Petersburg, 13 Nov. 1879, in ibid.
[122] Extrait d'un rapport Cabinet, St. Petersburg, 26 Mar. 1880, in ibid.

Switzerland deserve the threat of diplomatic sanctions by the European powers because it was a sanctuary of dangerous assassins (sanctions which France might be well advised to join) or was this the opportunity Bismarck needed to begin a German infiltration of Switzerland in anticipation of a future military strike at France through the Jura mountains? Should the French police welcome Russia's growing interest in French police assistance against Russian Nihilists in the West, even if the Russians were high-handed and the domestic situation in Russia was deteriorating?

The turning point in the French attitude towards Russia seems to have come in 1881. In 1881 Tsar Alexander II succumbed to the assassins of the *Narodnaya Volya*. But, much more important from the French point of view, Russia showed unexpected resilience in carrying on despite this disaster and the next tsar, Alexander III, was a man believed to harbor Francophile sentiments.[123] Slowly, the notion took hold that a Russia strong enough to survive the murder of its ruler and yet dependent on foreign help to proceed with modernization while keeping revolutionary assassins in Europe at bay, might after all make a reliable ally for France. Yet it took another decade for the official Franco-Russian alliance to come about and some luck to outmaneuver the German government which was no less interested than France in exploiting the Russian revolutionary situation to strengthen its national security.

13 March 1881

The Nihilist campaign to hunt down Tsar Alexander II had begun in 1879. By 1880 a number of European governments, the French government included, became aware of some shared responsibility for the safety of the Russian monarch. A scheduled visit to the south of France by Alexander II was canceled by the Third Section for security reasons.[124] In February 1879, two Frenchmen among the household staff of the Winter Palace came under suspicion of accepting bribes from revolutionaries to poison the tsar.[125] There was also a Russian employee in the French embassy in St. Petersburg who was accused of using the French diplomatic pouch to smuggle missives from Russia to Nihilists in France.[126]

The news of the assassination of Alexander II by two bombs hurled at him on a bridge in St. Petersburg on 13 March 1881 reached the Paris police around 10 o'clock that evening, local time. It was obtained, so it appears, by direct inter-

[123] On Alexander III's reputation of sympathy for France and dislike for Germany, see report by French agent "100," from Brussels, 17 Mar. 1881; report by agent "Michel," from Vienna, 15 Mar. 1881; and a report dated Paris, 15 Mar. 1881, saying Berlin newspapers were trying to hide the new emperor's Germanophobia. "Mais dans le public on se gêne moins et anecdotes sur Germanophobie du Czar sont à l'ordre du jour." In APP (Paris), Carton B A/1329, "Attentat du 13 Mars 1881 contre Alexandre II."

[124] Report by agent "100," Zurich, 3 Jan. 1880, in ibid.

[125] Extrait d'un rapport Cabinet, St. Petersburg, 16 Feb. 1880; and report by "100," Zurich, 20 Feb. 1880, in ibid.

[126] Note of the police prefecture, dated Apr. 1880, in ibid.

ception of the telegram from the Russian foreign ministry to its Paris embassy. ("I have taken this information from the very dispatch addressed to the ambassador," reported the police officer in charge of the *7e arrondissement.* "The area around the embassy is now being watched. There are many callers.")[127] In Paris as in other European capitals, there was excitement and worry. A police telegram to Montpellier on 17 March described the public mood as follows:

The most serious rumors about the situation in St. Petersburg are circulating in Paris tonight. A number of telegrams by [French] government officials [to Russia] have remained unanswered – it is said they have been intercepted. There are stories of another attentat, but this is not confirmed. A revolutionary movement is more likely and we have reason to believe that there are widespread disorders.[128]

More immediately, the French government had to worry about the spontaneous expression of jubilation which spread among the lower classes in Paris.

The death of the Emperor is the subject of discussion everywhere. The majority among the public is well pleased by this assassination. The most improbable speculations can be heard. Some people think war now inevitable, there is talk of an offensive alliance between France and Russia against Germany. The Socialists say that their cause has been vindicated: all other monarchs deserve the same fate and Gambetta also.[129]

Socialist posters hailing the murder went up in the *Xe* and *XIe arrondissements* and extra policemen were detailed to take them down again.[130] Eugène Rouher, the Republican elder statesman, considered taking legal steps against some radical newspapers that printed editorials attacking the Russian autocracy.[131] But there was compensation for what offense the left-wing publications could give the tsarist authorities in the equally heartfelt condolences expressed by conservative upper-class French who attended the daily services at the Russian church in the rue Daru, that landmark now under heavy police guard.[132] All Nihilist haunts in Paris were placed under surveillance, according to the Russian expatriate E. Cyon, and Russian students could expect being expelled for the most minor "seditious" action.[133]

When the first shock of the assassination wore off, there were questions about the future to be answered. Why had Russian security failed to protect the tsar? Could Russia prevent more such attacks against its ruling house? A report from agent "Droz" in Switzerland, dated 15 March, emphasized the leading part of the Nihilist committee in Geneva in the murder.

[127] Telegram, Police Municipale, 7e arrondissement, to Chef de la Police Municipale, 13 Mar. 1881, 10:10 p.m. (this item is accidentally misdated 13 July, 1881), in APP (Paris), Carton B A/1329.
[128] Telegram, Préfecture de Police to Toulouse, Paris, 17 Mar. 1881, in ibid.
[129] Rapport Cabinet by "Denis," Paris, 15 Mar. 1881, in ibid.
[130] Report by the police prefecture, 1er Bureau, Paris 17 March, 1881, in ibid.
[131] Extrait d'un rapport Cabinet by "Antonio," in Mar. 1881; and telegram, Agence Universelle, Paris, 19 Mar. 1881, 9:50 a.m., in ibid.
[132] Préfecture de Police, Cabinet, 1er Bureau, to Chef de la Police Municipale, Paris, 19 Mar. 1881, in ibid.
[133] Telegram, E. Cyon to Golos in St. Petersburg, Paris, 27 Mar. 1881, 2:30 p.m., in ibid.

The event that just took place in St. Petersburg was well known in advance in Switzerland, and certain revolutionaries in Paris also knew of the plot. Before Henri Rochefort left Geneva he often visited the Russian revolutionary colony. . . . Be assured that Alexander II's death is only the beginning of a chain of serious events beginning in Russia (where Alexander III will be no safer than his father was) and spreading from there to Italy, Germany, and Paris . . .[134]

The Russian paper *Novy Mir* seemed to concur with this line of thinking as it promptly revived the proposal of strong action against Switzerland already once advanced in 1878 after the attacks on Emperor Wilhelm I. This time *Novy Mir* wanted Russia to punish Switzerland with a series of retaliatory measures: first a rupture of diplomatic relations, next, the expulsion of all Swiss citizens from Russia, then prohibitive tariffs on all Swiss imports, and finally – if all this did not persuade the Swiss to stop offering asylum to Nihilists – an invitation to Germany to annex Switzerland.[135] But to the French police this particular idea of revising the map of Europe was surely less attractive a way of consolidating the European political order than individual police action against conspirators like Rochefort. On the day following the report by "Droz," an agent named "Grégoire" in Paris wrote a recommendation which directly coupled action against Rochefort with France's broadest national interests:

Rochefort left for Geneva last night where he will plot with the Nihilists. Against whom? I don't know. His activities must be watched because for the sake of France there must be no new disaster [*malheur*]. Our country will recover thanks to an alliance with Russia and we shall no longer fear war. But let the Radicals leave our country alone![136]

The prevention of disasters engineered by secret conspirators belonged to the domain of the political police *par excellence*. It made all conspiratorial explanations for the success of the revolutionaries on 13 March welcome to the police. A study of the assassination of Alexander II, submitted to the cabinet of the police prefect before the end of the month, claimed that "In all likelihood no more than six persons were involved in the plot of 13th March."[137] This finding reinforced an earlier report from St. Petersburg which had also emphasized that the Russian revolution could be controlled by good detective work:

It is clear that if only the Russian police can put its hand on the twenty-odd individuals who provide Nihilism in Russia with its leadership, that movement will suffer a severe blow. Given the tight legal control over all printing presses and over the sale of movable types, the Socialists will lose their best means of propaganda as soon as the one printing press they have left (and it is not in good repair) has been found. And this is about to happen. It is known [to the Russian police] that the second edition of the Socialists' revolutionary journal is to come out within a week, mailed in sealed envelopes. It is known in what quarter of town the envelopes will be placed in mailboxes. Now, on the sugges-

---

[134] Report by "Droz" of the Police Municipale, Paris, 15 Mar. 1881, file number 148900, in ibid.
[135] Unsigned telegram from Berlin to "République," Paris, 21 Mar. 1881, countersigned by sous-chef de section, in ibid.
[136] Report by "Grégoire," Paris, 16 Mar. 1881, in ibid.
[137] Report by "Stolz," Paris, Mar. 1881, file no. 148900, in ibid.

tion of one clever agent, the director of the high police and the director of posts have conferred and agreed to number all the mail boxes in that district and to have them staked out by police agents who will follow any person dropping envelopes of a certain size into these mailboxes. [138]

The confidence of this particular police informer in 1879 was both naive and premature, and yet in the course of the 1880s, under Alexander III, the Russian police did succeed in putting an end to the Nihilist movement. Russia was praised at the international conference to combat anarchism in Rome (1898) for its success against the predecessors of anarchism. How was that possible?

The Okhrana in Paris

The answer was better organization and competent leadership for the Russian police in Europe. It took the event of 13 March to shake up the Russian political police at home and abroad, resulting by 1885 in the replacement of the Third Section by the Okhrana and the dispatch of Active State Councillor Peter Rachkovsky to Paris (1884–1902), where he established a headquarters for all Russian police operations in Europe (the Foreign Agentura) at the Russian embassy in 79, rue de la Grenelle.

Rachkovsky's importance for the success of the Franco-Russian police alliance is apparent when we consider the difficulty of the French police before 1885 in knowing the precise authority of any high-ranking Russian personality arriving on a clandestine mission in Paris. There was General Seliverstoff who, after coming to Paris in March 1879, was first identified by the Paris police as "Adjutant to the Superior Chief of the Russian Police." [139] But when on 29 March 1881, the French telegraph office alerted the police that Seliverstoff had cabled a Russian frontier town about two travelers to St. Petersburg carrying false passports, the prefecture turned to the municipal police for help: "Request to the Chief of the Municipal Police to obtain with utmost urgency . . . information on the person named Seliverstoff, who seems to be a Russian government agent." [140] The answer, one week later, was hardly very satisfactory:

Seliverstoff has lived at the Hôtel de Bade, boulevard des Italiens 32, since 28 February. He is 50 years old, a retired pensioner from St. Petersburg, a wealthy landowner with a vast fortune. He holds the rank of a general in the Russian army and is an agent of the Russian government. When he headed the Third Section he was replacing Police General Mezentsoff who was assassinated. . . . No one knows where he spends his days and he is not talkative. His conduct and his mores give rise to no unfavorable comment. [141]

[138] Report from St. Petersburg, 13 Nov. 1879, in APP (Paris), Carton B A/196.
[139] Rapport Cabinet No. 6, Paris, 29 Mar. 1879, file no. 190.621 in ibid., Carton B A/878, "Seliverstoff."
[140] Préfecture de Police, Cabinet, 1er Bureau, to Chef de la Police Municipale, Paris, 31 Mar. 1881, in ibid.
[141] Report by an *officier de paix*, Paris, 6 Apr. 1881, in ibid. See also his murder in Paris, under "The Franco-Russian Alliance" in this chapter.

Another mysterious figure was Grand Duke Constantin, a brother of the murdered Tsar Alexander II. In March 1881, during the funeral of Alexander II, there was gossip in St. Petersburg about the new emperor's dislike of his uncle. It was said that Constantin, a grand admiral, had been implicated in the murder plot. Why on that fateful Sunday had he so strongly recommended this inspection tour to Alexander II when on the four previous Sundays that task had been left to the grand duke's own son, Nicholas Constantinovich?[142] However, the same grand duke, in disfavor with Alexander III, was also reported to be under "suspicion" of working "to bring about a Franco-Russian alliance."[143] His arrival in France, in 1883, could only leave the French police guessing as to the status that it should accord him:

Grand Duke Constantin, who is believed to be affiliated to Nihilism and to give much money to its most militant adherents, is presently at the Hôtel du Rhin, place Vendôme 4. He has just come from Nice accompanied by Admiral Romanoff, Lieutenant-Colonel Litvinoff, Count de Steinbock and Madame Poliokoff, who are all said to assist him with his Nihilist propaganda.[144]

Constantin, in turn was spied on in Paris by Elie Cyon, the Russian expatriate professor of physiology at the medical faculty of Warsaw University, who in 1881 acquired French citizenship. Cyon was a shadowy figure in Franco-Russian relations from the early 1880s to his death in 1912. The Paris police dossiers following the death of Alexander II give a confusing picture of his political associations and throw some doubt on his business ethics. He was linked to Prince Orloff as a Russian agent trying to penetrate Nihilist circles. He was also said to have dealings with German espionage, to be reporting to the Austrian embassy, to work for British military intelligence, and – perhaps most disconcerting of all – to be in touch with various figures in French political life: Léon Gambetta, the comte de Paris, and later General Georges Boulanger.[145] On 28 April 1882, the police learned that Cyon was accused of embezzling 210,000 francs which had been raised in France to help Russian Jews. Cyon then gave 18,000 francs to the Nihilists in Paris to support Russian refugees: "The money was accepted, but not Cyon, whom [the Nihilists] distrust because of his connections to Count Tolstoy, the Minister of Interior."[146]

Raising funds for Russian Jews in Western Europe during the 1880s meant trying to help the victims of the cruel pogroms unleashed as part of the Rus-

[142] Rapport Cabinet, Russie, 11 May 1881, in APP (Paris) Carton B A/196.
[143] Report by agent "36," Paris, 14 Dec. 1881, in ibid.
[144] Rapport du Contrôle Général, Paris, 16 Jan. 1883, file no. 124851, in ibid; and L. Andrieux, *Souvenirs d'un préfet de police* (Paris, 1885), vol. 2, pp. 125–30.
[145] See documents in APP (Paris), Carton B A/1023, "De Cyon, Elie, né a Hirtoskily (Russie) le 25 Mai 1843. Ancien directeur du 'Gaulois' et de la 'Nouvelle Russie,' " passim.
[146] Note dated Paris, 25 June 1882, in ibid. Tolstoy was Russian minister of interior 1882–9. Not until 1886 did the police finally decide that Cyon must be regarded as an agent of the Russian police on assignment to penetrate the Nihilist circles. Report by agent "20," Paris, 22 Oct. 1886, in ibid.

sian reaction to the murder of Alexander II. The harshness of the authorities in Russia did not help the image of the Russian police representatives in France. We quote from one rather caustic report filed at the Préfecture de Police in June 1881:

It seems there is in Great Russia, or in Central Russia, a caste or a class [of people] called the *kulakis* or *miroiedis*. Nearly all of them are Jews or Hebraics, usurers who as innkeepers or some sort of victuals merchants exploit the people, notably the peasants.

A movement will now be organized or has already been organized against this class, a movement that amounts to a Jew hunt. Nihilists in Paris tell that many Anarchists have returned to Central Russia to help rouse townspeople and country folk against the Jews. At the Café Soufflet, people openly say: you will soon see in the Center of the Empire the same unrest as in the South. Only this time the Government will pay a high price to halt the uprising.

The court judgments recently passed in the Kiev trials (following local pogroms) will serve to assuage all misgivings. People will be told: "Look! No one was sentenced to death! No one was executed! All these arrests merely served to keep up appearances, they were only a show. Every convict will be pardoned, the Tsar has formally promised it. So have no fear, beat [the Jews] in the name of the Emperor who is secretly on your side and shares your distaste of the *kulakis*."[147]

More news about the failings of the Russian police was not wanting. Whatever plans had existed over the past few years to modernize the St. Petersburg police along the lines of the police of London and Paris were scrapped after 3 March.[148] However strict the reputation of Russia's censorship system, there were now allegations of corrupt customs officials who for ten rubles closed their eyes to cases of explosives imported from Sweden by revolutionary students.[149] General Ignatiev, as minister of interior, continued to antagonize the public[150] and even the Russian judiciary, one of the chief bulwarks of Russian autocracy, was reported to turn against the Russian police.

They claim there is general and permanent antagonism between policemen and magistrates. The latter above all abhor the Third Section. They use every chance they can get to humiliate and disparage the cops and to lower their image in the public eye. Many of them make it their sport in court sessions to expose some poor little policeman to public ridicule. There are stories about presidents of judicial courts who tell their prosecutors not to treat the police in any other way but with disdain, to keep their distance from it, and to avoid all familiarity, in short to regard the Police as no more than a very humble servant of the magistrature.[151]

---

[147] Préfecture de Police, extrait d'un rapport Cabinet, Paris 13 June 1881, in APP (Paris), Carton B A/196.
[148] Rapport Cabinet, Russie, 11 May 1881, in APP (Paris) Carton B A/196. *op. cit.* See also Robert W. Thurston, "Police and People in Moscow, 1906–1914," in *The Russian Review*, vol. 39, No. 3 (July, 1980), pp. 320–38.
[149] Report by agent "36," Paris, 12 Oct. 1881, APP (Paris), Carton B A/196.
[150] Report by agent "..*..," London, 29 Dec. 1881, in ibid. (This French agent used a five-pointed star as his signature.) Ignatieff was minister of interior from 1881–2.
[151] Extrait d'un rapport Cabinet (A.M.), 27 June 1881, in ibid.

The same image of police incompetence coupled with vast arbitrary powers struck the American reporter George Kennan who traveled through Siberia in 1884 to study the Russian exile system with the tsarist government's permission, and who in the course of this trip turned into one of the Empire's most eloquent critics.[152] But the breakdown in the collaboration of the judiciary and the police in Russia, as predicted by the Nihilists, did not take place. The Russian government resorted to the classical strategy of linking its domestic emergency to international interests concerning the balance of power, in particular to France's concern for its own security against Germany. The head of the new Okhrana's Foreign Agentura in Paris was the perfect man for the job: "Rachkovsky was too intelligent not to understand that with all the difference between the political regimes of France and Russia and the great fear of terrorism in St. Petersburg, only a police alliance [*une alliance policière*] could bring about that diplomatic alliance which finally would have to be crowned by a military collaboration, that last step in the rapprochement of the two states."[153] It was the Nihilists who in the course of the 1880s were shown to be guilty of excessive optimism.

Triumph and decline of Nihilism

The Nihilists in Europe had barely one year in which to savor the *Narodnaya Volya's* victory of 13 March. For a few months they were at the height of their prestige in the West. Russian émigrés in London were overheard in June boasting that they would next kill Loris-Melikoff during his forthcoming journey to Wiesbaden because, as Alexander II's minister of interior, he had been responsible for the death of many political prisoners.[154] The most daring among them came up with a fantastic plan in October for a surprise air raid outside St. Petersburg. They would set fire to the emperor's palace at Gachina by dropping dynamite from a balloon, then storm the premises and capture Alexander III himself. "Though it is told with much graphic description the plan appears serious enough inasmuch as over the past few weeks the Nihilist party has sprung back to life from its previous somnolent state," wrote a French police informer in London.[155]

The Nihilists' self-confidence elicited some imitation by the opposition. In St. Petersburg, Grand Duke Vladimir was said to be founding a secret organization to protect the tsar and his family using the same tactics as the Nihilists.[156] It also

[152] George Kennan, *Siberia and the Exile System* (London, 1891). See also Russian police, in Chapter 1.

[153] Henri Rollin, *L'Apocalypse de notre temps. Les Dessous de la propagande allemande d'après des documents inédits* (Paris, 1939), p. 395.

[154] Report by "..*..," London, 14 June 1881, in APP (Paris), Carton B A/196.

[155] Report by "..*..," London, 26 Nov. 1881, in ibid.

[156] Report by "..*..," London, 8 Dec. 1881, and 14 Feb. 1882, in ibid.; and report by "Wladislas," Paris, 28 Dec. 1881, in ibid. Sergei Witte, the future finance minister, also joined a secret society of tsarist loyalists for a short time. See *The Memoirs of Count Witte*, trans. by Abraham Yarmolinsky (Garden City, 1921), pp. 22–5.

earned them a certain measure of social respectability. There were stories in circulation of liberal landowners in Russia who were now ready to assist hunted Nihilists to flee out of the country ("Refugee Nihilists in Europe are requested to
tell us where the frontier can be easily crossed by fugitives")[157] and – most surprising, if true – an allegation that the French prefect in Nice was uncommonly
friendly with revolutionary Russians living in his department.[158] Well-known
personalities like Vera Zassulich and Pierre Lavrov fueled the expectation of a
large-scale Nihilist offensive in the near future by publicly raising funds for a new
"Red Cross Society of the People's Will,"[159] while the dire warnings by Prince
Kropotkin and Lavrov, that a major revolution in Russia could ignite war in the
East and bring down the German and the Russian monarchies together, made the
Nihilist determination to strike out only that much more real.[160]

But parties also lose their credibility if their grandiose plans fail to material-
ize within a reasonable amount of time. If they are foreign they can provoke in-
tolerance by trespassing on domestic politics. On 12 February 1882 the French
government decided to expel the same Pierre Lavrov, whom it regarded as
the leading Nihilist in France comparable to Vera Zassulich in Switzerland.
Lavrov, formerly a teacher of artillery science at the Russian War Academy, was
now a man in his sixties, earning a living on the Paris left bank with language
lessons and translation work. He was said to have helped defend a Parisian
fort against Thiers's troops during the Commune. Because he was also a protégé
of Turgenev, his eviction from France became a political issue as Turgenev
mobilized a number of deputies to interpellate the government in the chamber.
The French members of the Socialist International made common cause with
refugee Communards in London and Nihilists like Kropotkin and Stepniak,
threatening to find ways to overthrow the Freycinet government in Paris with
the help of the old Gambettist party.[161] Lavrov left for London, but the affair
had stirred up the French authorities who remembered how in 1880 the expulsion of Stepniak (alias Hartmann) to London – but not to Russia – had brought
threats of assassination against the police prefect, Andrieux, and Frenchmen living in Russia.[162]

Threats are also counter-productive if the party making the threats begins
to suffer setbacks from defections and internal dissension. In 1884, a Russian
police colonel named Sudeikin succeeded in recruiting sixteen Nihilists in Paris
as secret informers against their own comrades. He was promptly murdered by

[157] Report by "Wladislas," Paris, 28 Dec. 1881, in APP (Paris), Carton B A/196.
[158] Report by agent "No. 4," Nice, 30 Dec. 1881, in ibid.
[159] Report by "..*..," London, 8 March 1882, in ibid.
[160] Report by "..*..," London, 21 Feb. 1882, in ibid.
[161] Report by "..*..," London, 14 Feb. 1882, in ibid.; and Préfecture de Police, Cabinet, 1er Bureau,
to Chef de la Police Municipale, Paris, 12 Feb. 1882, in APP (Paris), Carton B A/1,287; also
"Expulsion de P. Lavroff," in *Le Gaulois* (11 Feb. 1881).
[162] Report by "..*..," London, 12 March 1880, in APP (Paris), Carton B A/196. Curiously, Andrieux's reference to the Hartmann affair in his *Souvenirs*, pp. 185–200, is bland and
uninformative.

the Nihilists, but then the reorganization of the Russian police in France was only in its beginning. Rachkovsky arrived in 1884, and in 1886 an article on life among the Russian émigrés in France (by Lavrov, who had managed to come back) already described "the espionage to which all of them are submitted by the Russian embassy in Paris" as part of their daily existence.[163] By now five years had passed since the death of Alexander II and the revolution in Russia had made no visible headway. Instead, the French police noticed a growing financial distress among the Nihilists in Paris: "The Nihilists who live in Paris are suffering acute pecuniary embarrassment. Their parents send them less and less money and their better-off fellow believers [*corréligionnaires*] cannot meet all their needs."[164] The pressures of finding the means of existence from day to day gave rise to internal bickerings and undermined discipline: "Lavrov, who used to be acclaimed by the entire party as the leader, is losing followers. He is suddenly seen as too bland, too moderate. The younger ones especially no longer listen to him."[165]

The discouragement of the Nihilists was deftly exploited by the Russian government, who in the summer of 1886 reduced the penalty for Russian men who had gone to live abroad without obtaining a passport. Such Russian subjects were now permitted to return home if they would fulfill their military obligation there. "Many are taking advantage of this amnesty."[166] By 1887, neither the Russian library in the rue Corneille nor the restaurant Koch served as the favorite haunt of the Nihilists any more, and even the number of Russian students in Paris seemed smaller. Léon Bourgeois, as prefect of Paris, reported on 11 March 1888 to the minister of interior: "There is much economic misery among the refugees. The Russian students' mutual help society is in a very precarious financial situation. The Russian Library, their former meeting place, has run out of funds and its subscriptions to newspapers and journals have been canceled."[167]

A general report on "Nihilism and Nihilists" dating from this period may be worth summarizing because it expresses so well the belief of the French authorities in 1887 that the terroristic wave which had disturbed so much of Western Europe since the time of Nechaev was being brought under control: "[Russian] Nihilism is of foreign origin. Neither the political nor the social life of Russia actually contain the elements necessary for its origin and growth."

Nihilism arose in the 1860s through the transplantation to Russia of Western ideas, the report continued. This explains the monstrous forms that it assumed there – namely, terrorism – and also why so many of its adherents

---

[163] Report by agent "20," Paris, 20 May 1886, file No. 119365 (Lavrov), in APP (Paris),Carton B A/196.
[164] Report by agent "20," Paris, 17 Feb. 1886, in ibid.
[165] Report by agent "20," Paris, 22 Feb. 1886, in ibid.
[166] Report by agent "20," Paris, 5 July 1886, in ibid.
[167] Léon Bourgeois, Préfet de Police, to minister of the interior, Paris, 11 Mar. 1888, in AN (Paris), F7 125 19-20, "Révolution de 1905."

ultimately abandoned their efforts in Russia and joined the ranks of the anarchists in other countries.

Resembling parasite plants encircling the organic Russian state, the Russian Nihilists have no other intellectual equipment but some German books on Socialism which they translate and publish in very great numbers. . . . But in spite of a very active propaganda, experience has taught the Russian Nihilists that the ideas they took from these foreign books were absolutely useless for their country. In other words: what might make sense if applied to Western Europe's industrial cities with their proletarian inhabitants was not only inappropriate but absurd in the context of agricultural Russia, where every peasant is a landowner.

To be of service to Russia, the Nihilists would have to study the actual conditions prevailing in their country. But they are intellectually too lazy to make this effort. Most of them are school dropouts and young men shirking their military obligation. Terrorism is easier.

Terrorism has the convenience that it hides the absence of all political and social programs. It allows you to take the offensive by loudly shouting against despotism and denouncing the alleged atrocities in Siberia as described by Keanan [George Kennan] . . . (this last information also something borrowed from a foreign source, for once American) etc., etc.
  The idea of destroying the political order of so immense an Empire as Russia is so naive, even comical, that the Nihilists were forced to turn it into very personal missions of their own, identifying their subjective goals with the alleged will of the people.
  But the Russian Government is so sure of the loyalty of its people that it never resorted to the methods of suppression so characteristic of regimes which are imposed on a nation. This explains why the Nihilists were able to kill Alexander II, but could not shake the imperial power which is protected by the whole Russian people.[168]

The exact date of this report is not ascertainable, but it appears to have coincided closely with the following message of the French ministry of foreign affairs to M. Goblet, then French premier and minister of interior, dated 25 April 1887, to the effect that the Russian government had finally and formally requested France's help against the Russian Nihilists in the West: "While the Russian government asks us to refrain from expelling Nihilists [from French territory] − because it believes the intentions of the Nihilists are easier to follow in France than in Switzerland or in England − it is also anxious that we neglect nothing to assure that they are being watched as carefully as possible."[169]
  To explain how France rather than Germany at the end of the 1880s became Russia's chief partner for the policing of Nihilist revolutionaries abroad, we must return to the Berlin government's war against international Socialism in Switzerland following the passing of Bismarck's anti-Socialist law.

---

[168] Unsigned and undated report on "Le Nihilisme et les Nihilistes," presumably written around 1887, in ibid.
[169] Emile Flourens, minister of foreign affairs, to René Goblet, prime minister and minister of interior, Paris, 25 Apr. 1887, in ibid.

Switzerland and the murder of Alexander II

Switzerland's most immediate concern after 13 March 1881 was to prevent any public demonstration of satisfaction among the many Russian exiles in its cities, insofar as this was the most likely violation of Swiss laws that would force Switzerland to expel them. Minister Roth in Berlin reported on 25 March 1881, that an article in the Berlin paper *Nationalzeitung* had mentioned the numerous Russian police agents in Geneva who could not make the Swiss police undertake any steps against the Russian Nihilists like Vera Zassulich and Prince Kropotkin unless they broke a Swiss law. The Russian agents had so far failed to trap them into making a false move.[170]

Any rejoicing over the death of Alexander II was obviously inadmissible in Switzerland. A celebration at the Café Schiess in Geneva on 18 March 1881, prompted the EJPD to demand a full investigation of the event by the Genevan Police, in particular about the role played by Professor Zukhovsky, Prince Kropotkin, M. Dragomarov, and some others. In addition, the EJPD wanted to know how many Russians, Italians, and French in Geneva were more or less openly engaged in political activities.[171] The Genevan police, on 26 April, estimated the number of people who had attended the meeting in Café Schiess at about 200, but claimed that most of them had been Swiss. It then provided the EJPD with the number of foreigners living in Geneva, but said it had no precise knowledge of their political opinions.[172] As we shall see, the Genevan police, and the police of some other cantons as well, showed themselves much less anxious to cultivate the goodwill of the great powers than Berne was.

Besides the celebration in Geneva, there was another meeting held in Zurich on 3 April, 1881, in the *Schützenhaus*. But the Zurich police report, like the Genevan report, downplayed the gravity of the occasion.[173] Only one individual was expelled from Switzerland in the wake of 13 March, that one was Prince Kropotkin. The procedure took its time (as had the extradition of Nechaev) and the police interrogation was conducted by a *sous-inspecteur* A. Benoit of the Genevan police whose sympathies lay with the Russian émigrés in his town. We cite the protocol of his interrogation of the famous Russian Nihilist in the commissariat of police, Geneva, on 22 April 1881, which was simple and brief:[174]

---

[170] Swiss minister Roth to Bundesrath, Berlin, 25 Mar. 1881, in BA (Berne), Bestands-Nr. 21, Archiv-Nr. 20871.

[171] Letter, EJPD to the state council of Canton Geneva, Berne, 26 Mar. 1881, in BA (Berne), Bestands-Nr. 21, Archiv-Nr. 13905. The meeting at Café Schiess is mentioned as important in Johannes Langhard, *Die politische Polizei der Schweizerischen Eidgenossenschaft* (Berne, 1909), p. 195; see also the collection of Socialist leaflets celebrating the murder of Alexander II, in StA (Basel-Stadt), Politisches EE 12, 1.

[172] Report by the state council of Canton Geneva to Bundesrath, Geneva, 26 Apr. 1881, in ibid.

[173] Telegram, Polizeicommando Zurich to EJPD, Zurich, 3 Apr. 1881, in ibid.

[174] Protocol of Kropotkin's interrogation at the Commissariat de Police, Geneva, 22 Apr. 1881, in ibid.

I am Krapotkine Pierre, geographer, 38 years old, from Moscow, domiciled at route de Caronge 17.

Q: You declare that you have committed no insult [*outrage*] of a foreign government or violated the law of nations?

A: That depends on your interpretation; the law is laid down in very general terms.

Q: What are your thoughts on this matter?

A: I know the law and I believe I remained within the limits of the permissible.

(Signed): Pierre Kropotkine
(Signed): A. Benoit, *sous-inspecteur*

Nevertheless, the EJPD on 20 July proposed the expulsion of Kropotkin to the federal council, and his expulsion was decreed on 23 August, 1881, on three basic grounds:

1. Prince Kropotkin alias Lewaschoff, from Moscow, has in the journal *Révolte* advocated acts which the Swiss court of assizes has ruled to be contrary to international law: attacks on property and the murder of Alexander II.
2. Though the last-mentioned event took place outside Swiss territory, it was nevertheless instigated by a political refugee (Kropotkin) who resided in Switzerland and presumably still intends to return here and who continues to publish in Switzerland a journal that expresses his ideas . . .
3. Although Kropotkin has not succeeded in disturbing [the Swiss] domestic order, the federal authorities cannot tolerate his doings because, unless they are stopped, they are prone to disrupt our good relations to other states.[175]

Another Swiss response to the murder of Alexander II was the investigation in 1882 of ten foreign anarchists who had lived in Basel for some years. Nearly all of them belonged to the simple classes: they were carpenters, printers, tailors. One of them, the plumber Carl Theodor Weiss, was however found to be an informer of the Berlin political police. Another, the sculptor Vladimir Varovsky and the best educated of them all, was expelled. The expulsion of Varovsky took place on 20 November 1884. He was transported from Basel into Alsace and from there to France where, unaccountably, he died in Montbéliard on 24 January 1885. His death became the occasion for some inquiries by the federal government and a reprimand to the Basel authorities, which we bring here because it speaks for a renewed effort by Switzerland in the second half of the 1880s to defend its independence against the imposition of the great powers.

On reading the protocol concerning [Varovsky's] expulsion on 20 November, we noted with surprise that his travel route was laid down without asking him first to state his own preference. We take this occasion to remind you that . . . the principle has always been observed that a foreigner who is expelled from Switzerland for political reasons is granted

---

[175] Decree of the Swiss Bundesrath "an sämtliche eidgenössische Stände," requesting help to effect the expulsion of Kropotkin, Berne, 23 Aug. 1881, in StA (Basel-Stadt), Politisches EE 12, 1.

the liberty to choose the country that he will enter next. We absolutely must maintain this principle, and we entreat every canton to observe it in all future cases of this kind even without special instructions from us. [176]

That the Swiss in the face of a growing rivalry among the continental great powers should have wanted to reclaim their freedom from foreign interference in their domestic affairs was only natural. That they should have tried to make their point first with Russia may be due to the fact that Switzerland's political culture differed from that of Russia more than it did from that of France, Austria, or Germany. To be sure, the Swiss were always careful to maintain their basic obligations to Russia as a member of the European family of nations. In 1879, the Swiss president personally wrote to the Russian legation in Berne about the discovery of a secret bomb factory in Switzerland that could have been supplying Russian revolutionaries. [177] But the Swiss – principally the Genevan authorities – did not like the officers of the Third Section. There was even a certain sympathy for the Russian dissenters (other than violent Nihilists of the Nechaev brand). The same sous-inspecteur Benoit who in 1881 interrogated Prince Kropotkin had two years earlier sent the following confidential report to Berne on two Russian printing presses in Geneva:

These printers print the works of all the Russian *littérateurs* and authors who are of a liberal persuasion; also brochures. These works are smuggled by Prussian subjects across Prussia [to the Russian frontier]. Some also are sent to Romania, notably to Bucharest, where the Russian officers show much appreciation for them [*en font grand cas*].

All the *littérateurs* who write these works are highly placed people of social distinction. None of them recommends assassination but all of them devote themselves to furthering the cause of emancipating the Russian people.

Last year there was a marshal of the Russian army who wrote against his government. He has since died. Today we have a colonel of the Russian general staff on furlough in Geneva who also writes a lot against his government though he does not sign his works. There is a member of the tsar's own family in St. Petersburg who writes against the government.

The two printing shops in Geneva together receive 50,000 francs per year in order to support and win the reforms for their country.

The names of all the employees and all the authors of these print shops are known [to us]. But since they face an unjust repression from the Russian authorities if they return . . . they beg the Director of the Central Police [the EJPD] to respect their incognito, and they assure him that they have broken none of the laws of the country that is offering them its hospitality. [178]

[176] Bundesrath to president and Regierungsrat of Canton Basel-Stadt, (n.d., but presumably Jan. 1885). The federal government in February 1885 also instructed the Swiss legation in Paris to verify the information about Varovsky's death in France. See EJPD to the police department of Basel-Stadt, Berne, 16 Feb. 1885, in StA (Basel-Stadt), Politisches EE 12,1 "Socialisten Anarchisten Politische Polizei Allgemeines 1878–1880–1884."

[177] *Note verbale*, Swiss president to Imperial Russian legation in Berne, Berne, 16 Oct. 1879, in BA (Berne), Bestands-Nr. 21, Archiv-Nr. 14008, "Polizeiwesen 1848–1930."

[178] Report, A. Benoit to EJPD, Geneva, 30 May, 1879 (*très confidentiel*), in ibid.

Naturally, the Russian government wanted Switzerland to deport a number of the Russians living in Switzerland, and the British minister to Vienna and the Austrian minister of justice were particularly interested to know how the Swiss responded.[179] Recognizing that they were not receiving all the help they wanted, the Russians in 1879 tried to hire a Genevan policeman named E. Rochonnet to spy on a Russian resident. The Russian police official who offered to employ Rochonnet, a certain Nelmeyer, was promptly expelled by the Genevan police. The EJPD in Berne did not interfere though it did ask to be advised of all political expulsions by a cantonal government in the future "since such affairs can affect Switzerland's international relations."[180]

In 1873 a Russo-Swiss extradition treaty was signed.[181] It was concluded shortly after Switzerland had arrested Nechaev and, after much deliberation, had surrendered him to Russian police agents. But the situation remained unclear. Prince Gorchakov, the tsar's minister in Berne, wrote on 26 May 1873, that in the treaty Russia had agreed to a modification to the extradition clauses, which it had concluded with other powers "since the Imperial Government wanted to . . . show consideration for the principles permitted in Switzerland in matters of political delinquency."[182] The Swiss did in fact insist that their treaty with Russia should include a special provision not applied in their extradition treaties with France or Belgium:

A modification [in our treaty with Russia] in respect to the treaties [with France and Belgium] exists insofar as an absolute obligation to extradite arises [toward Russia] only if the criminal action involved is punishable by more than one year's imprisonment under the laws of both contracting states. This differs from [our] other extradition treaties, where only the law of the state requesting extradition counts. In these latter cases it means that the extraditing state must comply even if the delinquency in question is not punishable under its own laws.[183]

What the Swiss were anxious to avoid was having to extradite Russians for such offenses as insulting the sovereign (*lèse majesté*), as they already sought to exclude political crimes and even political murder. They did expel Prince Kropotkin for having favored the plot to assassinate Alexander II, but they did not extradite him to Russia. In 1887 the Russians, in turn, compensated for the reserved treatment they received from certain countries by curtailing public access to their court trials, so that some extraditing states could not control whether an extradited person was not tried for additional or different crimes than were listed in the original extradition request. The Swiss minister Roth in Berlin reported on this development from Berlin, citing Bismarck's response with obvious disapproval:

---

[179] Swiss minister Tschudy to EPD, Vienna, 20 Apr. 1879, in ibid.
[180] Letter, EJPD to department of justice and police of Geneva, Berne, 5 June, 1879, in ibid.
[181] EPD to Russian consulate general in Berne, Berne, 2 May, 1879, in ibid.
[182] Letter, Russian minister Gorchakov to Monsieur Knusel, Berne, 26 May, 1873, in BA (Berne), Bestands-Nr. 21, Archiv-Nr. 24650, Bd. 1.
[183] Ibid.

When the Reich chancellor learned two days ago about this "highest order" of Emperor Alexander [III], he made the explicit comment that in view of the fact that Prussia and Russia only extradited the nationals of the contracting party but not their own, he had no objections at all to this innovation. He is completely indifferent about how Russia treats its Russians. [184]

But Switzerland did not share this cynical view. The same issue also came up when in 1885 both Germany and Austria-Hungary approached Switzerland with requests for a revision of their extradition agreements with Berne in regard to political offenses. Berlin and Vienna proposed to Berne that henceforth every murder should be treated as a common crime, including murders committed for political reasons. But the Swiss remained adamant in their refusal. In a statement on 17 February 1885, the Swiss government recognized that a number of recent delinquencies perpetrated in Germany and Austria could have been common crimes hiding under the cloak of political activity. Nevertheless, Switzerland would insist that the exact nature of each crime be individually established before a proper court of law. A compromise was worked out in 1887: The Austrians had proposed that when a common extraditable crime was compounded by the commission of political delinquencies, the accused should be extradited but tried only for the common crime. The Swiss accepted this formula provided the court proceedings were held in public and the existence of additional political delinquencies did not aggravate the sentence meted out for the common crime. [185]

Thus Switzerland had a more serious disagreement with Russia than with Austria-Hungary or with Germany. But even between these three neighbors in Central Europe – one small, democratic, and neutral, the other two sprawling empires – there were disagreements on questions of political ideology. And in the course of the 1880s, as Switzerland collaborated with the Berlin police against German Socialists in Basel and Zurich, the question came up with increasing frequency: Why should Swiss policemen be made to enforce foreign laws that sanctioned actions that were permitted in Switzerland?

The breakdown in German–Swiss collaboration against the SPD

A brief mention of Switzerland's resistance to Russian pressures before and especially after the murder of Alexander II helps us to understand the deterioration in Swiss–German relations that also took place around the late 1880s. The immediate occasion was the German effort to stop the entry of Socialist publications across the Swiss border into Germany when these same publications were not illegal in Switzerland. But a more basic reason may have been Ger-

---

[184] Ibid.
[185] Protocol of Swiss Bundesrath session of 17 Feb. 1885, in BA (Berne), Bestands-Nr. 21, Archiv-Nr. 24624, Bd. 2.

many's support of Russian demands on Switzerland. Germany still hoped to outdo France as St. Petersburg's best partner against the Russian revolutionary movement abroad.

Smuggling Socialist papers from Switzerland and England to Germany was one of the chief fighting methods of the outlawed German Social Democratic Party between 1878 and 1890. Compared to the activities of the Russian Nihilists it was a peaceful propaganda war. Basel was one of the principal smuggling points across the Swiss–German frontier though by far not the only one. Rohrschach, further to the east, was another, and there is a document showing that at one point the Rohrschach policemen searched some Swiss houses on request of their German colleagues in Konstanz and even sent a copy of their report to the Germans.[186] The first smuggling case mentioned in the Basel police files dates from February 1882: The smuggler was an Austrian mechanic named Franz Zehetner. Then, two years later, German customs officials caught a little boy carrying forbidden Socialist papers from Basel to the German town of Lörrach.[187]

On 12 May 1888, the *Nord Deutsche Allgemeine Zeitung* announced that *Polizeikommissar* Schöne of the Berlin police was in charge of organizing a closer collaboration between the German and Swiss police to suppress the smuggling of Socialist literature.[188] However, in August of that year, the EJPD rejected a request by the German authorities in Lörrach for permission to investigate smuggling in the city of Basel itself. One German policeman nonetheless did come to Basel to interrogate a suspect and the Swiss official who assisted him was given a severe reprimand.[189] At this point, the resistance against German impositions chiefly came from the local cantonal police rather than from the highest Swiss police authority in Berne, the EJPD. The federal department of justice and police, while also wanting to uphold the principle of Swiss police sovereignty, preferred to placate the Germans by investigating these smuggling operations with Swiss police:

> The Swiss central authorities have an interest in knowing whether proscribed printed material is in fact being exported to Germany from Switzerland, or whether these are just rumors emanating from someone's provocative attacks on Switzerland. Consequently we think investigations are necessary, and we are in particular anxious to find out if the persons involved acted on their own volition or were induced by outsiders.[190]

The EJPD reiterated the same point to a session of the Swiss federal council on 14 September 1888:

[186] Draft report, EJPD to Bundesrath, Berne, 13 Sept. 1888, in ibid., Archiv-Nr. 14450.

[187] Report by EJPD to Basel police, Berne, 14 Sept. 1888, in ibid., Archiv-Nr. 14448; and letter, Grossherzoglich Badisches Bezirksamt Lörrach to Basel police, Lörrach, 18 Mar. 1884, in StA (Basel-Stadt), Politisches EE 12,1.

[188] Swiss minister Roth to EPD, Berlin, 13 May 1888, in BA (Berne), Bestands-Nr. 21, Archiv-Nr. 14451.

[189] Letter, chief of Basel police Burckhardt to EJPD, Basel, 14 Nov. 1888, in BA (Berne), Bestands-Nr. 21, Archiv-Nr. 14448.

[190] EJPD to Basel police, Berne, 28 Aug. 1888, in ibid.

The EJPD has submitted a report to the Bundesrat about its inquiries concerning printed material with provocative content that is smuggled into Germany. These inquiries were prompted by the arrest in various German towns of persons whose domicile is in Switzerland. Contrary to newspaper reports, the inquiries were not conducted on the request of German authorities. The sole purpose was to inform the Bundesrat about these occurrences.[191]

But Switzerland being a democracy, the government had to contend with criticism from the public, especially from the socialist wing. The *Basler Arbeiterfreund,* a workers' paper, carried an editorial on 18 September 1888, with the scornful title: "This is getting better and better!" [*Es wird immer schöner!*] "The same source which has launched so many lies over the past few months assures us that the inquiries in question were not undertaken on the request of German authorities but merely to inform the Bundesrat about what is happening. It is hard to imagine a more stupid excuse."

Why investigate only the smuggling of papers prohibited in Germany, not also papers that are prohibited in France or in Italy? the *Arbeiterfreund* asked. Why not investigate the smuggling of coffee or sugar? Is not the Swiss government trying to render the German government a friendly service? "The Bundesrat cannot possibly want to know what is happening unless it wants to inhibit or suppress the smuggling of Socialist literature into Germany in conformity with the interest of the Bismarck government."[192] The point of the Swiss Socialist paper was surely well taken. But worse still, the local police of Basel-Stadt also expressed concern over the services it was made to render a foreign, nondemocratic government. The chief of the police department of Basel-Stadt wrote two letters to Berne to express his deep unease:

Letter, Burckhardt, Police Department of Basel-Stadt, to EJPD, Basel, 7 September 1888:

We take this occasion to request your instruction how we should treat persons who are under suspicion of smuggling forbidden literature into Germany. Such smuggling mostly involves material whose publication is permitted in Switzerland, and which anyone can obtain by a subscription at the next postal office, for example the *Zürcher Socialdemokrat, Die Arbeiterstimme,* and *Der Arbeiterfreund.* Since the smuggling of printed materials into Germany concerns brochures which can be bought openly in Switzerland, we have until now assumed that we were not required to take action against these smugglers. We must now insist that we be given precise instructions by you in this matter. We have found none in any of your previous communications to us.[193]

Letter, Burckhardt, Police Department of Basel-Stadt, to EJPD, Basel, 8 September 1888:

We have the honor of drawing your attention to the article entitled, "The Basel Section of the Federal Political Police," which appeared in today's *Der Arbeiterfreund.* We assume that you will want to make a public declaration to the effect that the measures taken against

---

[191] Protocol of Bundesrat session of 14 Sept. 1888, in ibid.
[192] Clipping from *Basler Arbeiterfreund,* 7 Sept. 1888, in ibid.
[193] Letter, Burckhardt to EJPD, 7 Sept. 1888, in ibid.

persons suspected of smuggling Socialist literature to Germany took place on your explicit orders, and that there are no grounds for the reproach that the Swiss authorities have been used as helpers for the German police.

Such a declaration by you seems to us necessary because without it the exercise of political police functions in this canton will become very difficult to carry out, especially for the officials who are assigned to this work. [194]

By the time the Basel police wrote a third time to express its unhappiness at being assigned to monitor German Socialists in its canton the situation between Switzerland and Germany had already significantly changed. The cause was the capture in Zurich by the local police of two agents in the pay of the Prussian political police, Carl Schröder and Christoph Haupt. The incident, which caused much public outcry in Switzerland, also aroused the German Socialists in the Reichstag in Berlin. On 6 January 1888, August Bebel and Paul Singer, both members of the German parliament and well-known Socialist leaders, wrote a letter to the chief of the Zurich police, *Hauptmann* Fischer, asking him to confirm the arrest of Schröder and Haupt. Bebel and Singer showed that they were well informed about the two men. They knew that Schröder earned 200 marks per month and Haupt 250; that the Swiss police had found some dynamite in their rooms; that both were controlled by *Polizeirat* Krüger in Berlin; and that Haupt had already served the Berlin police as a spy for the last seven years, first in Paris, then in Geneva. [195]

What was remarkable was the answer by Fischer to Bebel and Singer, dated Zurich, 6 January 1888:

Since the Swiss authorities are keenly interested in this case, given the provocative nature of the activities of these two men, I will tell you – even though I am not obliged to do so – that the assertions in your letter (which I hereby return to you) are fully confirmed by the confessions of the accused and the testimonial of witnesses. The only detail that has not officially been ascertained as yet is your statement under question six. . . . [196]

Fischer's letter infuriated the Berlin authorities as a flagrant breach of confidentiality and a violation of professional conduct by the chief of the Zurich police. In the Reichstag debate of 27 January 1888, the Prussian minister of interior, von Puttkammer, demanded that a strong protest be lodged with the Swiss government: "To think that the Swiss authorities will provide information about an ongoing judicial inquiry to two private persons in another country, both with notorious reputations, and merely because they have asked for it – that surely is most curious," one newspaper quoted him as saying. Puttkammer wanted Fischer to be punished. But the Swiss government refused to be intimidated. Though the

---

[194] Letter, Burckhardt to EJPD, Basel, 8 Sept. 1888, in ibid. See also the letter by Regierungsrat of Basel-Stadt to Bundesrat Berne, 31 July 1889, in ibid., which protests the lack of a legal foundation for certain interventions that the police is ordered to execute.

[195] Letter by August Bebel and Paul Singer to *Polizeihauptmann* Fischer, Zurich, dated 6 Jan. 1888, in BA (Berne), Bestands-Nr. 21, Archiv-Nr. 13894.

[196] Document available in ibid.

German minister in Berne, von Bülow, delivered an oral protest to the Swiss government alleging that it had interfered in German domestic affairs and given support to revolutionary activities against a friendly neighboring country, Fischer received no more than a reprimand. Above all, the Swiss Bundesrat on 31 January 1888, announced its decision to create a Swiss federal political police to strengthen Switzerland's control over all political activities by foreigners on its territory.[197]

True enough, the Swiss refrained from proceeding severely against the two Prussian agents. Haupt was expeditiously returned to Germany on 27 January 1888. There were plans to prosecute Schröder because unlike Haupt he was a naturalized Swiss citizen. But the charges were eventually dropped for lack of sufficient evidence.[198] Another case of trespassing by a German police agent, however, occurred near Basel in the following year, and when the Swiss once more proceeded to arrest the suspect, Bismarck in a fury threatened to retaliate against Swiss travelers near the Basel frontier by taking them hostage.

The much publicized Wohlgemuth affair of 1889 took place on the eve of a Reichstag vote on the desirability of extending the anti-Socialist law for a third time for yet another three years. There were misgivings because the electoral returns for the Reichstag during the past nine years had shown the law to be ineffective in reducing the number of Socialist votes. Also, the discovery of a bomb plot in Zurich involving Russian Nihilists and German Socialists, and whose intended victim was believed to have been Bismarck, gave further weight to the argument that the policy of 1878 had been a failure. Far from undercutting the Socialist movement in Germany, the German Socialists, it was now believed, by going abroad were coming under the influence of more radical foreign revolutionaries like Russian Nihilists. Clearly, the time had come for a reconsideration of Germany's policy towards the Socialist movement.[199]

The Schröder and Haupt case had signaled Switzerland's growing determination to draw a line in the face of more and more foreign police operations on its territory. The German government often used the political police in the Reich territory of Alsace to monitor the activities of German Socialists residing in Switzerland. Police inspector August Wohlgemuth was in charge of political police in nearby Mulhouse. Because he was new at his post, he was especially anxious to do well. Learning that Socialist literature was continuously entering Germany from Switzerland, he decided to use an informer of his own rather than to rely on Swiss police help. He hired a tailor by the name of Lutz and personally met the man once in Lörrach (inside the German border), and once in Rheinfelden (on Swiss territory). Had the Swiss learned about Wohlgemuth's activity from Lutz him-

---

[197] Protocols of Bundesrath sessions of 31 Jan. and 7 Feb. 1888, in ibid.

[198] Swiss Bundesanwaltschaft, report on history of foreign police activities in Switzerland, Berne, 7 Mar. 1930, in BA (Berne), Handakten Häberlin, E 4001(a)1, Aktenband 39.

[199] On the German police's view about the failure of the anti-Socialist law, see Höhn, ed., Die vaterlandslosen Gesellen, p. 264.

self? Did the local police chief of Rheinfelden, *Bezirksammann* Baumann, trap Wohlgemuth in defiance of Berne's more cautious attitude because he personally sympathized with the Socialists? At a second meeting between Wohlgemuth and Lutz in Rheinfelden on 23 April 1889, the Basel police was waiting for him and he was arrested and put in the local prison.[200]

The Swiss must have trusted to the fact that they were on safe legal grounds in holding a foreign police official caught outside his sphere of jurisdiction. They took care to treat Wohlgemuth well. His wife was informed and his son was allowed to come from Mulhouse to visit him in prison. The German minister in Berne, von Bülow, was shown the Swiss police file on the case. Had it been left to the German foreign ministry the affair might have petered out quietly with the Swiss happy at having scored a small victory on behalf of their sovereign independence for, as one official in the *Auswärtiges Amt* wrote on this occasion, "It is most annoying when police officials go abroad for the sake of obtaining that kind of information. Bringing informants inside our country to report is worth the extra cost."[201]

But Bismarck's reaction was unexpectedly violent. He placed all the blame on the Swiss. "Germany is forced to maintain its own police on Swiss territory because the Swiss police provides no adequate guarantee that the activities against Germany's internal security on Swiss soil are kept under effective surveillance."[202] To the German minister in Berne he cabled:

According to the information we have, arresting Wohlgemuth was a reckless and hostile act because this official obviously was only after information and did not intend any provocative action. Firmly demand his release and indicate that, if this is not done, we shall have to proceed with the arrest of any Swiss public official or Swiss national (especially from the canton of Aargau) whom we encounter on German soil. We regret that our customary good relations [with Switzerland] are recklessly being undermined by democratic-minded subaltern officials.

To the governor of Alsace, von Hohenlohe, Bismarck gave instruction to make immediate preparations to place the railway traffic between Basel and Strasbourg under close surveillance. Both in Alsace and in Baden the German authorities began checking all travelers crossing over from Rheinfelden and in Mulhouse preparations were under way for the housing of detained Swiss citizens.[203]

Nothing very drastic happened, however, and German public opinion was not aroused. A Frankfurt paper, the *General Anzeiger*, urged calm: Wohlgemuth was unlucky to be caught, the paper wrote, but this should not have happened to a clever detective anyway, and if it does, he must bear the consequences of his

---

[200] Eduard Fueter, *Die Schweiz seit 1848* (Zurich, 1928), vol. 2, pp. 208–9. According to Fueter, Lutz betrayed Wohlgemuth to the local Swiss authorities.

[201] Auswärtiges Amt to governor of Alsace-Lorraine, Prince von Hohenlohe, Berlin, 24 Apr. 1889, in ADdBR (Strasbourg), AL 30 (109).

[202] See report by Bundesanwaltschaft to EJPD, 7 March, 1930 in BA (Berne).

[203] Telegram, Staatssekretär in Strasbourg to Kreis-Director in Mulhouse, Strasbourg, 23 Apr. 1889, in ADdBR (Strasbourg), AL 30 (109).

adventure without complaining. "He may not even say of himself, like a soldier . . . that he fell on the field of honor because, as a state official, he really has no business at all to be on foreign territory."[204] The negotiations between Berne and Berlin ended with the release of Wohlgemuth on 1 May 1889.

To the Swiss this confrontation with Bismarck nevertheless served as a rude shock. It taught them that being accommodating towards a great power would not earn them gratitude or reciprocal consideration. The Wohlgemuth affair played an important role in the modern history of Switzerland: (1) it made the Swiss reestablish the office of federal prosecutor in Berne and to put it in charge of all matters concerning aliens police on the federal level. (2) It furthered Switzerland's slow but steady dissociation from its old policy of offering asylum to Europe's political fugitives.[205]

Gambetta, Boulanger, Schnaebelé, and the Franco-Russian alliance

We must conclude our discussion of France's recovery after 1871 by returning to the work of the French police at home.

Paris had agents in Switzerland who no doubt observed with satisfaction the dilemma of the Swiss police in the face of German presumptuousness. We cite one *Extrait d'un rapport Cabinet (de Suisse) signé No. 301*, dated Paris, 7 July 1888 (or half a year after the Schröder/Haupt affair), when in Berlin Herrfurt replaced von Puttkammer as Prussian minister of interior: "All this leaves the German Socialists in Swizerland in no doubt whatsoever concerning what the Swiss federal and cantonal police have in store for them on the instigation of the Berlin police."[206]

At the same time, the same French informer (*"No. 301"*) expressed great confidence in the ability of the German Socialists who, he said, had a very efficient "counter-police" to continue with their work. In the following year the Wohlgemuth affair must have struck yet closer home, considering that the German political police agents involved were operating out of Alsace where French intelligence was well served. The Bismarck government's battle with the SPD must have given the French a special gratification on the occasion of their Universal Exposition in Paris, which was held on the centenary of the French Revolution. Seventy German Social Democrats arrived in Paris on the eve of the Quatorze Juillet, welcomed by the prominent French Socialist M. Valliant in his capacity as member of the municipal council of Paris.[207]

[204] "Deutschland und die Schweiz," in *General Anzeiger*, 10 May 1889, p. 1.
[205] Swiss Socialists took a less kindly view and suggested that the Swiss political police was founded in 1889 at the same time as the anti-Socialist law was being debated in the Reichstag in order the better to serve Germany's police needs in Switzerland. See Otto Lang, "Gegen die politische Polizei" (Zurich, 1898), in BA (Berne), Bestands-Nr. 21, Archiv-Nr. 13888.
[206] Document available in APP (Paris), Carton B A/195.
[207] Report, Préfecture de Police, Service des garnis, Paris, 13 July 1889, in ibid.

Gambetta

The French interest in what happened in Alsace and in Switzerland was no doubt also influenced by the resurgent national spirit in France more than ten years after Sedan. A new French nationalism was emerging, associated with names like Ernest Renan, the historian Albert Sorel, and later with Maurice Barrès – not to mention some lesser lights like Paul Déroulède. We must, of course, keep in mind that in Western Europe, the police was never in charge of making the decisions on war and peace. It seldom advocated war, though it always readily fulfilled the task of preparing their countries for the eventuality of war. In the 1880s, a time of popular revanchist excitement in France in connection with the brief political prominence of Léon Gambetta and Georges Boulanger, the police of Paris, if anything, exerted a restraining influence. A prefectorial cabinet report on 3 August 1880 sums up this attitude rather neatly:

People begin to say that M. Gambetta wants war with Germany and that he will succeed in having it. The idea is gaining ground and becoming accepted even though no one welcomes it. Everyone thinks it is a folly but is nonetheless prepared to do his duty when the time comes. The friends of Gambetta talk about it all the time and in the mess halls the army officers begin to take on bellicose airs.[208]

The police did watch Gambetta closely between 1880 and 1881, detailing spies to follow his movements who variously signed their reports "Ludovic" or "Grégoire" (we know some of their reports on Russia), "Howe," "Athanasse," "Antonio," and "l'Ami." In September 1880 "Grégoire" warned of a German preemptive strike as a possibility.

King Humbert [of Italy] has said to his brother-in-law that a Gambettist victory at the next legislative elections will be the signal for German troops to concentrate along the French frontier. Bismarck has not forgiven Gambetta his Cherbourg speech and thinks of him as the personification of *"revanche."* Maybe this troop concentration will even take place during the elections themselves in order to diminish Gambetta's chances of victory.[209]

More directly pertinent to the business of political police was Gambetta's alleged plans of a dictatorship that would overthrow the republican constitution. "L'Ami" reported in September 1880:

Concern about Monsieur Gambetta's dictatorial ambition is growing as more and more of his partisans fill ambassadorial posts and posts in all branches of the administration. It seems people are chiefly afraid that if M. Gambetta were to assume power this would lead to foreign complications and that England – always so ready with promises – will let us

---

[208] Extrait, rapport Cabinet (I), Paris, 3 Aug. 1880, in ibid., Carton B A/923; and more reports from September 1880 warning that a Gambetta cabinet would provoke war with Germany, in ibid.

[209] Report by "Grégoire," 10 Sept., 1880, in ibid. On Gambetta's Cherbourg speech, see Harold Stannard, *Gambetta and the Foundation of the Third Republic* (London, 1921), pp. 209–11.

down as it has done before. That is why it is hoped for the sake of external peace that Monsieur Grévy will continue as President of the Republic for some time.[210]

In the following month "Grégoire" also had news about the technique Gambetta might use to seize power: to stand for election in as many as 60-odd departments concurrently and then, should the results be satisfactory, demand a change in the constitution making the president of the republic eligible by direct vote of the people. The final step would be having himself proposed as candidate for the presidency.[211]

We are not forgetting that the police's task was to protect Gambetta's person against physical harm as well, in particular as both he and the police prefect, Louis Andrieux, were threatened by Russian Nihilists at the end of that year.[212] Gambetta's name regularly figured side by side with that of the tsar, Bismarck, and King Humbert on the target list of international terrorism, all these men allegedly obstacles to the advancement of humanity.[213] Following the murder of Alexander II, Gambetta was mentioned in Socialist leaflets in Paris as among the next personalities who would suffer the same fate. No wonder that when Gambetta finally formed his own cabinet later in 1881 – though not a dictatorship, as expected, and not even a cabinet that produced many changes – police agent "36" reported from St. Petersburg that the Russian government was well pleased to know that France had a new government more dedicated than earlier ones to order at home and more likely to restrict the right of asylum of foreign revolutionaries in France.[214]

Boulanger

Gambetta's political career as a militant patriot was cut short by his death in 1882. But France's growing mood of national reassertion found a new focus four years later in General Georges Boulanger. Once more, we must draw attention to the guarded attitude of the police in this political crisis. The political leaders of the police, of course, were more decided in their attitude than the rank and file. The minister of interior, Ernest Constans, and M. Lozé, the police prefect of Paris, were openly against Boulangism.[215] Léon Daudet, a fiery supporter of Boulanger, went so far as to charge that Constans worked hand in glove with "the German political police in Paris, then quartered inside the embassy but already able to influence the Police Prefecture and the Sûreté Générale. They dug into the private life of Georges Boulanger and finally brought him to fall over an old love

---

[210] Document available in APP Carton B A/923. One of these ambassadors was Camille Barrère, who later became, with Delcassé, one of the chief architects of the encirclement of Germany.
[211] Report by "Grégoire," classé au dossier 2710, Paris, 14 Nov., 1880, in ibid.
[212] Reports dated Dec. 1880, in ibid.
[213] Report of *officier de paix* Gaillot, classé au dossier 148900, Paris, 19 Jan. 1881, in ibid.
[214] Report by agent "36," Paris, 17 Nov. 1881, in ibid.
[215] Goron, *Mémoires*, vol. III, pp. 266–7.

affair from his lieutenant days."[216] But among the police staff at large there were at best some individual partisans of the general.[217] Perhaps Boulanger was even less reassuring to the police than Gambetta had been because he lacked the customary credentials of a politician. Had he seized power as minister of war he would have been hampered by the French army's tradition of neutrality in domestic politics. Nor had he a consolidated group of followers in the political constituency at large. This meant that the Paris police did not have to fear that the Boulanger crisis could erupt into civil war. Boulangism for the Paris police meant mainly unprecedented technical problems with crowd control in city squares and at railway stations, for example the throngs of thousands of sympathizers who milled around the Gare de Lyon on 8 July 1887 to cheer Boulanger, forcing the *gardiens de la paix* to send back situation reports every fifteen minutes.

Keeping abreast of the general's movements during the summer of 1887 (the celebration of Bastille Day had just been introduced as a national holiday) meant incurring the occasional wrath of his partisans. There were shouts of *"à bas la police!"* by several hundred people on 8 July 1887 at the Place de la Bastille. On the other hand, in the following year on 21 April 1888, people shouted, *"Vive la Police! à bas les étudiants!"* because they were getting tired of the daily demonstrations. In other words Boulangist partisans and police never opposed one another because of different political views, only because they got into each other's way in the streets. When a high-ranking police official was overheard in a crowd instructing the constables to keep people moving, bystanders called out goodhumoredly: *"Faites circuler ce monsieur et nous circulerons aussi."*[218]

Inasmuch as the Boulanger affair gave rise to a short but acute war scare in Europe we should note that while trying to stay neutral in questions of national politics, the reports by the Paris municipal police in 1888–9 did stress the public's basic wish for peace and ventured to offer some advice to its government, notably to the prefect of police himself and the president of the Republic.

M. Debeury, Officier de Paix, Police Municipale, 8e arrondissement, Paris 28 March 1888:

I have the honor to transmit to *M. le Chef de la Police Municipale* as requested some information on the current state of public opinion about the latest events. People seem to be much more aroused by the acquittal of M. Wilson than by the repeal of General Boulanger. . . . They think [Wilson] was acquitted because of his position [as son-in-law of President Grévy] and because he has influence. [By contrast] people who have served in the army understand that the army must have its discipline and that it must stand aside from politics. Consequently there is less unanimity in criticizing the second decision.[219]

[216] Léon Daudet, *Magistrats et policiers* (Paris, 1935), pp. 141–50.
[217] Goron, *Memoires,* vol. I, p. 171.
[218] Reports by *officier de paix* Garnot of the XIe arrondissement, Paris, 18 Apr. 1888, and by "Chevalier," 28 Apr. 1888, in APP (Paris), Carton B A/1644, "Général Boulanger 1887–88–89."
[219] Document available in ibid., the police prefect Henri Lozé actually openly opposed Boulanger. Goron, *Mémoires,* vol. III, pp. 266–7.

The police's enjoinder to caution became more insistent as the months went by. On 23 April 1888, the *2ème Brigade de Recherches* of the *Police Municipale* sent this report to its chief:

Résumé of observations made today in various quarters of the capital:

People are glad that Boulanger has decided to move from the Hôtel du Louvre to Neuilly – this will put an end to the daily demonstrations. Throughout Paris people have had enough of public disturbances. The prefect of police is also blamed because he does not act energetically enough to stop the students who take too many liberties and think they have the right to cause scandals and to break shop windows. In short, the majority of the people think it is high time to put an end to the current state of affairs.

By the spring of 1889 Boulangism was seen in decline not only in Paris but also in the smaller towns. There is an almost light-hearted note of relief in a long police account on Boulanger's visit to Tours in March, that showed the flimsiness of his support outside the capital. This report tells of local musicians who broke off playing the "Marseillaise" as they hurried to keep at the head of the procession, of street urchins (*voyous*) paid by some stranger to shout: *"Vive Boulanger!,"* of curious spectators from neighboring towns and old soldiers happy to salute a general and being saluted back, "a whole day of festive activities but barren of permanent results."[220]

The tone became even a little impatient after the elections of 28 July, 1889. The *4ème Brigade de Recherches* reported: "Some people demand that the General resume his place in the ranks of the army like everyone else and pay more attention to the laws than he has done so far. And at the next election let him put himself up as the candidate in only the one district of his choice and not in some 20 districts as he intends."[221]

The Schnaebelé incident

Boulanger had shown great interest in the army and none in the police. The only effect he had on the police was an order in 1887 to use the commissaires spéciaux for penetration into enemy frontier towns in case of danger of war. In April 1887, this plan had reached the point where the Sûreté Générale instructed all the commissaires spéciaux along the frontier to designate by name the particular agents they would send to the other side of the border within twenty-four hours of a declaration of mobilization in Paris.[222] To obtain a better idea of what procedures this involved we cite a set of instructions issued by the Sûreté Générale from a folder labeled "Circulaires 1887–1907," though the date of this particular document unfortunately is not given:

[220] Unsigned report dated Paris, 29 March, 1889, in APP (Paris), Carton B A/1644.

[221] The report, entitled "Exposé sommaire sur l'effet moral produit par le résultat des élections du 28 juillet 1889 auprès de certains personnalités du parti Boulangiste," Paris, 30 July 1889, is available in ibid.

[222] Copies of the circulaire are available in AN (Paris), F7 12648, "Circulaires 1887–1907."

Under this set of instructions French agents were to go into German towns close to the French border with the mission:

1. To learn the layout of the town;
2. To establish a few good contacts with local inhabitants without, however, disclosing their mission to them;
3. To discover places where they might stay in case of war (hotel, someone's home) and to identify the restaurants, cafés or other public places that are useful to frequent because of the kind of people or the information that can be found there;
4. To assess the importance of the local newspapers for local and national news;
5. To study the best way of collecting military information like enemy troop movements;
6. To study the safest and fastest way of sending information back to the French authorities;
7. In peace time where best to pick up military and political news;
8. To establish contacts at the railroad station.[223]

It cannot be a coincidence that in 1887 the Germans intensified their observation of the French frontier police – "prompted by the recent political develop ments" – as a German document put it.[224] The German authorities asked for detailed reports from all the Alsatian towns along the French border on everything they could find out about the French police agents facing them on the other side: their names, their physical appearance, their personal circumstances, and down to their private habits.[225] The German report from Metz, for example, reported on 8 February 1887: "The personnel of the French border police at Pagny consists at this time of Police superintendent Schnaebelé and three police inspectors Ismer, Fougère, and Venner. The first two [inspectors] frequently come on visits to our side."[226] The police post in Diedenhofen reported on 9 February 1887 that the French police superintendent Horbert at Audun-le-Roman, a native of Colmar, and Madame Horbert often crossed the frontier to visit the family of the bookseller Krier in Diedenhofen. The report read: "Since the Krier family has cultivated this kind of relationship with every preceding commissaire in Audun-le-Roman, there should be no doubt that this contact serves espionage purposes."[227]

The reports so collected by the Germans filled the German authorities with a very high esteem for the French frontier police. In a general administrative report for the district of Metz, the *Bezirkspräsident* wrote on 7 April 1887:

---

[223] Directeur de la Sûreté Nationale, "Instructions très confidentielles," (n.d.), in ibid.

[224] Report of Bezirkspräsident of Metz to Kaiserl. Min. für Elsass-Lothringen, Metz, 3 Mar. 1887, in ADdBR (Strasbourg), AL 30 (102), Acta betreff. "Die französische Grenzpolizei (1887)."

[225] The number of *commissaires spéciaux* at the end of the nineteenth century was about 480. Maurice Mathieux, "Le Rôle des commissaires spéciaux . . . ," in Société d'Histoire de la Révolution de 1848 et des Révolutions du XIXe siècle, *Maintien de l'ordre et polices en France et en Europe au XIX siècle* (Paris, 1986), p. 152.

[226] Report from Metz, 8 Feb. 1887, in ibid.

[227] Report by German police in Diedenhofen, 9 Feb. 1887, in ibid.

I cannot let this occasion pass without mentioning the extent to which our own police organization has been found wanting. . . . I refer you to my earlier report on the organization and efficiency of the French frontier authorities. On this side we have nothing that can compare with it. We don't even have an adequate control of traffic passing through the principal border crossing points. Even Avricourt, which is so important from the point of view of national security, is manned only by a police probationer whose doubtful command of the French language will only be submitted to an examination in a few days. Our gendarmerie is not good for frontier police work. Most of the police superintendents, even those directly along the border, know very little French and they regard their jobs as soft, administrative positions, not as policing functions.[228]

Not long after this report, on 20 April 1887, the commissaire spécial of Pagny-sur-Moselle was captured by Berlin policemen who for the past few weeks had been assigned to watch out for Polish conspirators seeking to pass from Germany into France. The arrest of Schnaebelé was reported by Mayor Hahn of Metz directly to Under State Secretary von Puttkammer in Berlin. However, the exact circumstances of the incident remain in dispute. Was there a mistake made because the Berlin official by the name of Marx was unfamiliar with the local situation? Was Schnaebelé seized on German territory or on French territory? We may assume that the Germans knew of Schnaebelé's importance as an intelligence officer specializing on Alsace and Germany. The text of the letter of invitation to him by a German official named Gautsch was cryptic enough to suggest Gautsch was trying to lure Schnaebelé onto German territory. But Bismarck's letter to the French ambassador in Berlin on 28 April 1887 – and which was released to the press a few days later – is important since it clearly shows that in 1887 Bismarck did not want war. According to Bismarck's letter, the Germans had for some time a warrant of arrest against Schnaebelé ready should he be apprehended on German territory because he allegedly had tried to incite German citizens to commit treason against their country.

Given the proof that we have against him, Schnaebelé will undoubtedly be found guilty by a court. His sentence is likely to be that much more severe as he has abused the prestige accorded to officials engaged in dealings across an international border where mutual trust is particularly important. Schnaebelé abused this trust . . . by seeking to incite German nationals to commit crimes against their fatherland for money. This abuse of office increases his culpability . . . even if he acted on higher orders.

If the undersigned nonetheless thought it his duty to beg the Emperor, his most gracious master, for Schnaebelé's release, he did so in consideration of the customary assumption under international law, that invited visits across the frontier to conduct official business are presumed to be covered by a safe-conduct.[229]

[228] Auszug aus dem Verwaltungsbericht des Bezirkspräsidenten zu Metz," 7 Apr. 1887, IA 4869, in ADdBR (Strasbourg), AL 87 (4812), Acta betreff. "Die Berichterstattung über wichtige ungewöhnliche und Aufsehen erregende Ereignisse (1870–1918)."

[229] Bismarck to French ambassador to Berlin, Berlin, 28 Apr. 1887, as published in *Landes-Zeitung für Elsass-Lothringen*, 2 May 1887, in ADdBR (Strasbourg), AL 29 (11), Acta betreff. "Die Verhaftung des französischen Polizei-Kommissars Schnäbele und das Verhalten des Pol. Kommissars Gautsch bei derselben (April 1887)."

The French public greeted the release of Schnaebelé as a national victory – Goron in his memoirs recalled *"l'héroisme qui firent la France si belle au moment de l'affaire Schnaebelé"* – while radical patriots of the *Ligue des Patriotes* vowed to administer physical punishment to Gautsch.[230]

The Franco-Russian Alliance

Fortunately for the peace of Europe the Boulangist movement petered out by 1889 after the general lost heart in a critical moment and instead of marching on the Elysée Palace fled with his mistress to Belgium – defeated by Bismarck's conciliatory disposition rather than by "the German political police in Paris," as Daudet claimed.

To clinch the rapprochement between French and Russia the French police in 1889–90 demonstrated its resolution to help put an end to the Nihilist movement in Western Europe. The occasion came when a bomb exploded accidentally on 8 March 1889, on the Zürichberg, wounding some Russian students.[231] On 7 May 1889 Switzerland ordered eight Russian Nihilists expelled. Because they opted to go to France they were escorted by Swiss police as far as Porrentruy, arriving in Paris at the Gare de l'Est on 17 May. The whole transfer was closely watched by the commissaires spéciaux of Annemasse, Delle, and Pontarlier.[232] Paris used this opportunity to stress how much more responsibly their police handled foreign revolutionaries than the Swiss. The commissaire in Annemasse reported: "Until yesterday, Russian nationals were specially well treated [*favorisés*] throughout Switzerland. Students and others simply had to say they were refugees and they were given permission to stay."[233] The commissaire at Delle concurred with his colleague by reporting on 15 May 1889 that the Swiss had shown much sympathy for the thirteen Nihilists. They were warned by employees of the Swiss government to leave Switzerland on their own so that their passports would not be stamped with the word "expelled."[234]

The year 1890 is usually considered the year when the French partnership with the Russian police was officially approved by Alexander III because of the success by the Paris police in March of that year in arresting seven Nihilists. In Goron's recollections, the Nihilists were caught in the possession of explosives which they intended to smuggle into Russia for use in an attempt on the life of Alexander III. The French police had been tipped off by a chemist where one of the Russians had

[230] Goron, *Mémoires*, vol. I, pp. 331–2. One threatening letter to Gautsch read: "Infame bandit. Vous ne serez pas pris en traître; vous êtes prévenu? Nous sommes 10 bons français de la ligue des Patriotes; qui iront vous casser la gueule l'un ou l'autre réussira. à bon entendeur. Salut." Available in ADdBR (Strasbourg), AL 29 (11).

[231] Report by *commissaire spécial* of Annemasse, 5 Apr. 1889, in AN (Paris) F7 12521, "Organisation révolutionnaire russe à l'étranger."

[232] Reports by *commissaire spécial*, gare de Pontarlier, 30 May 1889, and by prefect of police to minister of interior concerning the expulsion of Nihilists by Switzerland, Paris, 8 June 1889, in ibid.

[233] Report, *commissaire spécial* in Annemasse, 19 May 1889, and 6 Feb. 1890, in ibid.

[234] Report, *commissaire spécial* in Delle, 15 May 1889, in ibid.

ordered a test tube of an unusual thickness.[235] The Russian minister of interior personally called on the French ambassador in St. Petersburg, M. de Laboulaye, to tell him of the tsar's extraordinary appreciation.[236] According to French police reports, the public in France was equally pleased by this event. J. Simon, the commissaire spécial de police at the Grenoble railway station, reported in June, 1890: "The public strongly approves the decision of the minister of interior [Constans] to arrest the Russian conspirators who live in Paris. The public is happy that France is showing Europe that it keeps a close watch over dangerous foreign revolutionaries in its midst and that it does not grant them an inviolable asylum. Monsieur Constans is seen as having rendered France and the Republic a good service and this is beginning to earn him popularity even in the countryside."[237]

Half a year later, on 18 November 1890, General Mikhail Seliverstoff was murdered in his suite at the Hôtel de Bade, where he regularly spent two months of the year. The murderer was assumed to be Stanislaw Padlewsky, thirty-five years old, a Russian-Polish refugee who believed in propaganda by deed. Seliverstoff was thought responsible for several trials against Russian refugees who had returned home.[238] The ensuing hunt through Paris was personally conducted by the famous Paris chief of detectives, François Goron.[239] The French police did not find Padlewsky but ended by arresting and expelling Stanislas Mendelson (a great-grandson of the Prussian philosopher, Moses Mendelssohn) who was regarded as one of the principal Nihilist leaders. The body of Seliverstoff was transported back to Russia after a ceremony in the Russian church in Paris, with French army units providing military honors and police and *garde républicaine* special security.[240]

Conclusion

In retrospect the historian may ask whether the contribution of the French police to the Franco-Russian alliance had been worthwhile. Was not the value of a Russian alliance for France put in question a bare decade later with the beginning of Russia's advance into Korea that ended so disastrously in the battle of Tsushima and in revolutionary outbreaks throughout European Russia? France itself in the 1890s suffered the trauma of the Dreyfus Affair, which so dramatically brought to the fore the inherent conflict between the values of democracy and the virtue of patriotism. Caught in a dilemma – with Socialists like Jean Jaurès in 1909 de-

---

[235] Goron, *Mémoires*, vol. IV, ch. VIII.

[236] J. Simon, *commissaire spécial*, gare de Grenoble, 3 June 1890, in AN (Paris), F7 125 19-20, "Révolution de 1905."

[237] Report on Nihilists in Paris by Léon Bourgeois, prefect of police, to Directeur de la Sûreté Nationale, Paris, 11 March, 1888, in ibid.

[238] "L'Assassinat du général Michel de Seliverstof," in *Le Temps*, 20 Nov., 1890, clipping in APP (Paris), Carton B A/878.

[239] Goron, *Mémoires*.

[240] Report on the funeral of Seliverstoff by Contrôle Général de la Sûreté, 5 Dec. 1890, in APP (Paris), Carton B A/878.

nouncing as scandalous the presence of Russian police on French soil – the French government tried to hold fast to its Russian alliance while seeking ways to soften the harshness of tsarist rule. In March 1897 a French senator interceded with the Russian government to permit a Polish nobleman named Narcisse Sutkiewicz (exiled in France since the failed revolt of 1863 and now old and repentant) to return to his family estate in the government of Kovno; and two months later the faculty of natural sciences of the University of Nancy sent a collective petition to the president of the republic, asking him during his forthcoming visit to St. Petersburg to ask Nicholas II to allow a Russian-Jewish student named Schreyev to return to his family in Odessa.[241] We do not know how many Russian exiles wanted to return to their country at the turn of the century. But there were many signs in the air of a gradual mellowing in Europe's old civilization based on the rule of omnipotent states, including autocratic Russia.

This is not to say that insofar as the French police did not warn the government of the revolution to come it was guilty of a major piece of misjudgment. The French police in the 1870s had thought the Russian situation impervious to police control but after the murder of Alexander II changed its mind and assumed there was a chance that the revolution could be contained by police measures like hunting down agitators and assassins. It thought that containing the revolutionaries in Europe (Paris, London, Zurich, Geneva) would substantially contribute to the consolidation of the tsarist regime. It thought that economic progress and foreign political success might in time enable the Russian government to weather the current crisis and that police measures could buy the Russian government the time that it needed. It is not possible to say even today that this speculation was entirely unrealistic.

Of course it is also possible that the French police did not fully believe in its own prognosis of Russia's political future. But then the police was not responsible for making national policy. On the contrary, the police, especially in France, has a long tradition of service to a succession of political regimes for whose downfall it assumed no responsibility because such changes were caused by factors outside the range of police power, like military and naval developments throughout Europe, domestic affairs in Germany and Austria-Hungary, colonial relations with Britain, or for that matter social changes in France.

Did the French police get on well with the Russian agents in Paris? No police likes to share its turf with outsiders, but in this case the partnership presumably worked well because (1) the Russian government was generous with decorations and money awards to French officials; (2) the French realized they lacked the necessary staff to penetrate Russian student circles in Paris, (3) the Russians did not abuse their limited freedom to operate on French soil, (4) the French in principle used many of the same police methods as the Russians: paid informers, agents

---

[241] The correspondence concerning these two cases is available in the AMAE (Paris), correspondence politique Nouvelle Série 1879–1918, Russie, Carton 80: "Arrestations et expulsions, 1896–1917."

provocateurs, violation of the secrecy of mails, and banishment. True enough, these methods used in France did not produce police terrorism because of the political maturity of the French society whereas in Russia they impeded the growth of individual rights and democratic participation in government. But the point is that the similarity of police procedure facilitated collegial relations in Paris.

Had the French police warned about the imminence of a Russian revolution, would the French national government have changed its policy? It seems unlikely that the French government had the freedom to do so. To drop the Russian alliance after 1895 would have led to a rapprochement of Russia and Germany, and that would have been intolerable to Paris.

What conclusions can we draw? Perhaps that political ideologies, seen through the perspective of police, appear not as moral values but as tools to cement political movements or to form political communities. The French police had no reservations about collaboration with autocratic Russia and vice versa because (1) French parliamentary democracy and Russian autocracy were seen as two different systems serving two different societies, and (2) reports on critical situations can never be regarded as "objectively true." Their importance lies not in what they say but in what conclusions are drawn by those who must act on them. The same report can be read as negative and invite despair by one politician, and positive and invite endorsement by another.

3

International police collaboration from the 1870s to 1914

Professional contacts between police administrations

While France, Russia, Germany, and Switzerland maneuvered in the 1870s and 1880s to absorb the consequences of the 1870 war and the assassination of Alexander II, Austria-Hungary diligently continued to foster professional contacts between the police authorities of different countries. Besides the exchange of police journals and the conclusion of agreements on hot pursuit of fugitive suspects, Vienna also promoted comparative studies of police laws and organizations. In 1869 Austria inquired with a number of governments about their laws concerning the transportation of women across national boundaries for purpose of prostitution. While the governments of Prussia and Mecklenburg-Schwerin obliged with noncommittal statements concerning their laws on emigration,[1] the answer by the Romanian government, which was both polite and evasive, exposed the purpose of the Austrian demarche for what it was: an official communication on a police question nobody believed could be resolved, and which was made largely for the sake of the communication itself:

Having conveyed to the ministry of interior the question contained in the note of 14 December of last year which you were good enough to address to me, the ministry now informs me that the assistance which your esteemed agency has requested touches on a matter of domestic administration so that the Princely government finds itself unable to accede to it. Nevertheless, in the interest of humanity and the advancement of public morality, the government of His Highness, moved by the same sentiments as the Imperial and Royal government, is presently engaged to add yet more serious measures to those already in force so as to safeguard public morality.[2]

---

[1] Foreign ministry of the North German Confederation to Graf von Wimpffen, Austrian minister in Berlin, Berlin, 25 Mar. 1870; and foreign ministry of Mecklenburg-Schwerin to same, Schwerin, 19 Nov. 1869, in HHStA (Vienna), Administrative Registur F52, Karton 3, Fach 4: "Prostitution."

[2] Romanian foreign ministry to Austrian consul Ritter von Zulauf, Bucharest, 21 Jan./12 Feb. 1870, No. 582, in ibid.

The Austrian inquiry was well timed, as it fell together with many new social problems that would require handling by the European countries in the decades to come: problems arising from the introduction of social insurance laws, compulsory primary education, public health measures, universal military service, etc. By 1899 a *Bureau international pour la suppression de la traité des blanches* was actually founded in London, and an international conference to discuss measures against white slavery took place in Paris in 1902, leading to the conclusion of a first convention on this subject in 1910.[3]

In regard to the other inquiries from Vienna, most governments responded very courteously, probably knowing that information about matters like budgetary outlays or the ratio of street police to inhabitants did not in any way compromise their foreign commitments. In fact, it seems doubtful that any significant conclusions were drawn by anyone from these compilations of technical facts. European police officials on inspection tours were more likely to hail from Hamburg rather than from Berlin, from Manchester rather than London.[4] When the Vienna police in 1874 reported that the Austrian capital spent only one third as much on public security as did Paris and only one fifth as much as London, who was to say that Vienna could or should be policed like the other two capitals?[5] Countries that had only recently joined the family of nations, like Albania, were sometimes more willing to study the police practices of other countries; also non-Western nations without a stake in European power politics. High-ranking Japanese police officials who paid visits to the Vienna Polizei-Direktion in 1879 and 1889 were prompted by domestic motives as much as by the wish to learn foreign techniques.[6] The advantage of visitors from overseas was that they were more inclined to give high praise to what they were shown. The Vienna police had every reason to be pleased by the flattering reports of New York police officials like Colonel Theodore Bingham and Raymond Fosdick, who came on visits before the First World War, and by that of Police Commissioner Richard F. Enright in 1922.[7] During the last quarter of the nineteenth century police reports from nearly every European country were collected at the Viennese Polizei-Direktion. They are today of more interest to social historians than to police historians because they usually exclude anything that can be regarded as sensitive material. At best it suggests the diligence with which the Austrian police pursued the dream of a future European-wide police solidarity. Thus a "Report of the

---

[3] Lothar Philipp, "Weltpolizei," in *Die Woche* (8 Sept. 1928), p. 1146.

[4] Consul general von Stephani to Austrian foreign ministry, Hamburg, 5 Sept. 1895 in ibid.; and a note from the British embassy, dated Vienna, 2 Aug. 1913, in ibid.

[5] "Bericht des Central-Inspektors der k.k. Sicherheitswache in Wien über die Amtsthätigkeit derselben im Jahre 1874." MS. available in APD (Vienna). The outlay for security in Paris was actually higher still, because the figure did not include the cost of the Garde républicaine.

[6] Report by Carl von Boleslanski, Austrian consul general in Shanghai, 10 Mar. 1879, in HHStA (Vienna), Administrative Registratur F52, Karton 8, folder "Grenzsicherungsdienst."

[7] Dr. Oskar Dressler, "Das Urteil des New Yorker Polizeipräsidenten über die Wiener Polizei," in *Oeff. Sich.*, 2 Jhg., Nr. 21–2 (30 Nov. 1922), pp. 4–5; and Observations about the New York police by the Austrian ministry of interior (about 1909), AD 524 82/11, in HHStA (Vienna), F52, Karton 40, "Generalia 1885–1915. Parteisachen 1912–1919."

Commissioner of Police of the Metropolis for the Year 1909" consists of seventy-eight pages of entries that should delight the student of Edwardian England: It relates the number of runaway horses stopped by the London police and the number of offenses committed in royal parks like "furious riding, allowing dogs to run over flower bed, plucking flowers, and allowing motor car to emit visible vapour,"[8] but makes no mention of the concurrent worry of the British foreign secretary, Sir Edward Grey, over the breakdown of police order in tsarist Russia.

What borrowing from the police of other countries took place at the end of the nineteenth century was largely limited to scientific methods like fingerprinting for criminal identification, pioneered in Britain. Many new Balkan states after 1878 needed assistance in developing modern public administrations and institutions of law enforcement. Experienced police officials from Holland were assigned to Montenegro as instructors. International police administrations were also set up in the semi-colonial regions of the Near East, North Africa, and China, often run by the local European consuls who tried to impose a Western concept of public order with the help of native police. During the Franco-Prussian War of 1870–1, the French authorities in Algeria established a militia of all resident Europeans (French and other nationalities) presumably to guard against native troubles.[9] Constantinople was like many Chinese seaports subjected to a regime of capitulations under which the Turkish police could not interfere with the freedom of movement of foreigners without the approval and the presence of their consuls. Though in theory extraterritoriality was a temporary measure pending the evolution of police forces and law courts acceptable to the West, it appears that the element of foreign police rule prevailed over the element of foreign instruction. M. Lefoullon in Constantinople in the 1880s and Herr Kreitner in China during the 1930s served as much to show the French and the Austrian flag in contested regions of the world as they brought to them the benefits of modern police. When the Cairo police entered into direct communications with the police prefect of Paris in a matter concerning a case of white slavery (June 1914), the French ministry of foreign affairs interceded because Egypt was not a sovereign state but a country subject to capitulations: "Since our consuls in these countries are invested with juridical authority over French nationals, the local authorities must address themselves only to these consuls in all police matters that involve French nationals and their delinquencies."[10]

The Monaco Conference, 1914

How close did Europe at the turn of the century actually come to espousing an international policing system? There were three ways in which this term was understood: (1) International police as a multinational administrative body policing

---

[8] Folder, "Publikationen Gross-Britanien," in ibid.

[9] Swiss Bundesrath to Swiss legation in Paris, Berne, 17 Aug. 1870, in BA (Berne), Bestands-Nr. 21, Archiv-Nr. 501.

[10] Sûreté générale, 3e Bureau, to prefect of police, Paris, 8 June 1914, in APP (Paris), Carton B A/1693, "Polices étrangères."

places where local control did not exist or was inadequate (for example regulating merchant shipping on the Danube river or policing the international settlement in Shanghai); (2) international police as the enforcer of legal agreements between sovereign states and as the executor of international sanctions against delinquent states; and (3) police in the service of a future world government.[11] The first category existed mainly outside Europe. The second category, often associated with the doctrines of the legal theoretician Hans Wehberg, refers principally to military action short of war like intervention and reprisals by the European powers acting conjointly as the Concert of Europe (as in the blockade of Greece in 1886, the occupation of Crete in 1899, and in the punitive expedition against China in 1900).[12] The third category did give rise to the conference of Monaco in 1914, though we turn to a followup conference in Vienna (the International Police Congress in 1923) for the best formulation of its goals:

> The realization of the idea to create a region of states within which – despite [territorial] sovereignty and independence – one principle is recognized and put into practice: that no common crime committed within this region shall ever go unpunished as long as the perpetrator remains within its confines. Thus the aim is to correct a situation in which until now even capital crimes have repeatedly gone unpunished because of legal ambiguities and inadequate provisions for extradition.[13]

The *Premier Congrès de Police Judiciaire Internationale* opened in the Principality of Monaco on 18 April 1914. On its agenda were the discussion of ways to (1) expedite the apprehension of fugitives, (2) to improve the identification services throughout Europe, (3) to set up an international register for wanted persons and ex-convicts, and (4) to standardize the laws of extradition. Its practical achievements were modest: French was chosen as the language for international police communications, and a commission was set up to recommend to a future conference standardized procedures for police identifications.

Most interesting was the discussion of an "International Mobile Police Brigade" for executing "international arrest warrants" anywhere in the territory of the countries that would join in such an agreement. The proposal clearly exceeded what was politically attainable in Europe on the eve of the First World War. Robert Heindl, the famous German criminologist, later called the Monaco Conference "Euphoric dreams [*Frühlingsschwärmerei*] on the Côte d'Azur."[14] International police officials are still unacceptable, he wrote, even if their tasks are limited to pursuing common criminals because of the widespread fear of espionage and subversion. If only, Heindl wrote, one could at least have exempted police communications between countries from the cumbersome intermediary of

---

[11] Heinrich Mollmann, *Internationale Kriminalpolizei – Polizei des Völkerrechtes?* (Diss., University of Würzburg, 1969), p. 2.

[12] Hans Wehberg, *Theory and Practice of International Policing* (London, 1935), pp. 67–9.

[13] Internationale Kriminalpolizeiliche Kommission, *Die internationale Zusammenarbeit auf kriminalpolizeilichem Gebiet* (Vienna, 1934), p. 14.

[14] Quoted in Philipp, "Weltpolizei," p. 1146.

diplomatic channels! A symbolic beginning of direct contacts between national police forces may be seen in the formal notification sent by Police President von Borries of Berlin (1903–8) to the police chiefs of all the European capitals on assuming office, [15] and similarly the announcement of Arkadii Harting in 1905 on succeeding Rataiev as "Chief of the Russian Political Police Abroad" to the European police chiefs on whose collaboration he depended. [16] (After the First World War, the idea of police officials accredited to national police authorities in other countries gained much ground.)

The question whether to build a future "police international" on the neutral ground of administrative and criminal police collaboration, or else to found it on a common political goal such as the suppression of anarchism and Socialism – this was the problem facing the advocates of stronger police who wanted to ease Europe away from its traditional dependency on a military balance of power. The answer to this question depended on which countries were most likely to support what approach. For example Austria did not participate in the Monaco Conference though Hungary did. Also absent were Belgium, Denmark, Germany, Greece, Great Britain, Norway, and Sweden. Indeed, of the chief European powers only France, Italy, and Russia were represented in Monaco, the other European states were Bulgaria, Monaco, Romania, Switzerland, Serbia, and Spain. On the other hand Cuba, Guatemala, Persia, and San Salvador sent delegates. But if the domination of the Triple Entente at the International Criminal Police Conference was a drawback, [17] so was the alignment of the powers at the Rome Conference of 1898, whose subject was political police, and where the autocratic monarchies faced the liberal constitutional states of the West in a way that crossed their alignment along strategic military and diplomatic calculations.

International collaboration in political police work: The Rome Conference, 1898

General remarks

Modern criminology, which was represented by the delegates who attended the Monaco Conference, dated from the late nineteenth century. But its purpose, according to Marxist writers, was not to cure mankind of this social ill (for "bourgeois criminology" saw in crime an inescapable flaw in all human society) but to

---

[15] Notification of assumption of office by police president Borries in Berlin to the Swiss federal prosecutor, Kronauer, Berlin, 2 Jan. 1903, in BA (Berne), Bestands-Nr. 21, Archiv-Nr. 13879, "Deutschland 1885–1913."

[16] Hartwig to Staatsrat Brzesowski, section of political police in the Polizei-Direktion Wien, dated Paris, 30 Sept. 1905, in Hoover Inst., Archive of the Imperial Russian Secret Police, index no. Vf, folder 2, "Relations with Austrian Police."

[17] During the Second World War, a secret Nazi document sought to expose France's alleged long history of exploitation of international professional meetings for political purposes. See Combined Intelligence Objectives Sub-Committee, "Methods of Influencing International Scientific Meetings as laid down by German Scientific Organizations," item no. 24, file no. XXVIII-8, copy no. 138.

exploit crime as a justification for suppressing the proletariat by the police, the courts, and the prison system. These Marxist writers acknowledged that the new class of the proletariat in the nineteenth century was a principal source of urban crime, though from economic want and not from viciousness.[18] In the Marxist interpretation of history, capitalism, propelled by its inherent inner contradiction, was approaching its final crisis as the year 1900 drew near – a crisis marked by the formation of gigantic monopolies and growing working-class solidarity, of extremes in wealth and poverty, and by the extension of capitalist exploitation to overseas colonies. Later, from the perspective of the mid-twentieth century, Marxist historians detected in this period the beginnings of the Fascist doctrines of Mussolini, Hitler, and Pétain: new doctrines of chauvinism and militarism, and of racism (Cesare Lombroso in Turin, Hans Gross in Graz) advanced under the cloak of scientific criminology.

There was no Socialist police science with its own police philosophy prior to the Bolshevik revolution. Facing powerful and oppressive capitalist police machines the Socialist leaders before the First World War were better at criticizing the police of their days for its brutality and lack of enlightenment than at outlining their own plans for a "people's militia" in the workers' state of the future. They did not seem to wonder about the willingness of most policemen, whatever their social background, to serve the cause of the moneyed classes.

Before the twentieth century most police schooling took place not in classrooms but on the job in the streets. The average policeman obtained only a rudimentary idea of Socialism from his encounters with agitators at workers' meetings. His knowledge of anarchism was formed not by reading Kropotkin but the half-literate threats penned by bomb-throwers and arsonists. Even Goron, as director of the French Sûreté, had no explanation to offer for the sudden appearance – and subsequent disappearance – of anarchist outrages in France in the 1890s associated with the names Ravachol (alias François Koenigstein) and Valliant.[19] Some anarchist messages were brief and to the point, for example a letter received by a baker in the rue Nationale 47 in Paris, around 1892: "Monsieur, I notify you that if you don't price your bread at 80 centimes within 8 days I shall blow up your store with dynamite. Greetings from an anarchist of X/11."[20] Another letter, left in a public pissoir at the Esplanade des Invalides following Ravachol's execution, was more voluble though equally badly written:

The Anarchists hoped that the few violent demonstrations that have taken place (and which cost one comrade his head and others years of forced labor in exile) would draw

---

[18] Erich Buchholz, et al., *Sozialistische Kriminologie. Versuch einer theoretischen Grundlegung* (East Berlin, 1966), pp. 15–16.

[19] See letter by Goron, dated 23 Apr. 1892, in APP (Paris), Carton B A/1132, "Ravachol." On the other hand, the French police had little trouble penetrating anarchist circles with agents. See Marie-Joseph Dhavernan, "La Surveillance des anarchistes (1894–1914)," in Société d'Histoire de la Révolution de 1848 et des Révolutions du XIXe siècle, *Maintien de l'ordre et polices en France et en Europe au XIXe siècle* (Paris, n.d.), pp. 347–60.

[20] Available in APP (Pairs), Carton B A/1132.

attention to the principal cause (namely misery) that pushes man to this sublime madness, a madness which extinguishes in his heart all those secondary sentiments of "humanity" and leaves him with but the hope of a future Fraternity and also turns this [ie the Anarchist] into a monster in the eyes of people who are egoistic and indifferent and don't want to admit that it is they who have made him into what he is . . . – Long live Anarchism, which one day will rule mankind. Today we are 10, tomorrow 100.[21]

Pronouncements such as the above are easily dismissed as the ramblings of demented social outcasts. The police of the European states, however, could not afford to remain on the defensive when these anarchist attacks were directed against high-ranking state officials and ruling monarchs. Following the murder of Alexander II in 1881, there were fears of more attacks against European monarchs during the coronation of Alexander III in May 1883.[22] In 1893 there was a flurry of threats against Emperor Wilhelm II and the German chancellor, Caprivi (which the French police intercepted and swiftly conveyed to the Berlin police),[23] capped by an attempt to kill the commander of the Berlin uniformed police in 1895 and a dynamite explosion in Berlin-Moabit in 1898.[24] The French president, Sadi Carnot, was assassinated in Lyon in 1894, apparently in revenge for the death of Ravachol and Valliant,[25] and in 1898 the French and Italian police conferred through their consulates over the intricate connections between a bank robbery in Paris, the theft of dynamite from a salt mine in Switzerland, and a bombing outrage in Milan.[26]

On 10 September 1898 there occurred the tragic murder of Empress Elisabeth of Austria by the Italian anarchist Luigi Lucheni on the Quai Mont Blanc in Geneva, dealing one more blow to the unhappy Habsburg family so recently bereft by the suicide of Crown Prince Rudolf at Mayerling (1889). The assassination can accurately be termed the work of international anarchism as it was not intended to strike at the Austro-Hungarian monarchy. Lucheni had planned to murder Prince Henri d'Orléans who was living in Geneva; when the prince did not appear he decided to attack someone else from the ruling houses of Europe, and chance would have it that Empress Elisabeth was just then staying at the Hôtel Beau Rivage on a private visit.

The event caused an immediate clamor in all the European governments for international police countermeasures. It galvanized into action those who over the past decade had recommended some kind of international police organization to

---

[21] Found by an *officier de paix* in the 7e arrondissement on 21 Oct., 1892, this letter is available in ibid.

[22] Report signed "Loth," Geneva, 7 May, 1883, in APP (Paris), Carton B A/196, "Le Socialisme en Russie de 1872 à 1889."

[23] See communications in AN (Paris) F7 12905, "Anarchistes. Attentat de Sarajevo."

[24] Telegram, Bonnefois to "Figaro," Berlin, 6 May 1898, in ibid; and Hugo Friedländer, *Interessante Kriminal-Prozesse von kulturhistorischer Bedeutung* (Berlin, 1911), pp. 160–96.

[25] See internal year report of the Viennese police, "Die sozialdemokratische und anarchistische Bewegung im Jahre 1894," (Vienna, 1895), pp. 3–4, in APD (Vienna).

[26] See communications between French consulate in Zurich, French ministry of foreign affairs and police prefecture in Paris, 20 Sept. to 17 Oct., 1878, in AN (Paris), F7 12905.

strengthen the foundations of the European states by protecting every country's political order against violent upheaval. The chief question this raised was whether Europe by the 1890s had already reached the point where the sovereign states had become so closely linked to one another that their defense was now a collective necessity, no matter whether a particular regime under attack met the approval of the other nations or not. Did this mean the end of the Western dream of perpetual progress, so strong when the modern police arose in the early nineteenth century and for which the compartmentalization of Europe into separate states had been a useful vehicle for experimentation? Had the time come when the European countries had to settle for whatever political regimes they had evolved since the Congress of Vienna, even if this meant that the more "advanced" (read: democratic) states might have to accept a European order dominated by autocratic regimes?

Faced with a fundamental question that could affect the future of the European state system, most governments in 1898 responded to the outrage in Geneva with unusual promptitude. An international conference to combat anarchism was convened in Rome a bare three months after the death of the Austrian empress. It was attended by twenty-two European states including Turkey, and by December 1898 had laid down the foundations for an international network of police channels for rapid exchange of information on the activities of all known anarchists. As an instrument for the suppression of anarchism it was still rudimentary, but that may have been the condition for its widespread acceptance at that time. For what helped to make this step towards an international collaboration of political police successful was the absence of an acute sense of crisis in Europe. The murder of Empress Elisabeth saddened millions of Europeans but it did not put in question the survival of the Habsburg monarchy as would the assassination of Archduke Franz Ferdinand sixteen years later. There was no fear of imminent war because no one could possibly suspect Switzerland of harboring hostile intentions against Austria, as one suspected Serbia in 1914. And finally the Italian anarchist, Luccheni, resembled too much Ravachol, a man closer to a common criminal than a soldier in an underground war against the European order like Gavrilo Princip.

Though the antianarchist conference of 1898 took place in Rome, in the years following Italy did not assume a leading role in the campaign against political criminality. We must instead turn to the diligent efforts of the Vienna police, which monitored all international Socialist and anarchist developments from the 1890s to 1914, and to the concurrent Russian proposals of international disarmament and international police assistance against revolutionary activity of any kind. This should make us understand why the idea of collective police security in Europe failed so swiftly. With Germany committing itself to the Schlieffen Plan and Russia defeated by the Japanese in Manchuria and beset by open revolt at home, the military and diplomatic problems facing the European state system after 1900 were becoming too acute to be contained by the tentative police arrangements reached in Rome. The outbreak of the world war in August 1914 was triggered by an act of international criminality, which Europe was quite unprepared to deal with through concerted police action.

The position of Switzerland

The death of the Austrian empress in Geneva immediately revived the pressure by the Great Powers on Switzerland to curtail the right of asylum, which foreign political refugees had enjoyed on its territory since 1815. The Swiss government sought to placate foreign opinion by publicizing as far as was possible its police inquiry into the tragic event. The newspapers revealed that Elisabeth, wishing to travel incognito, had refused the detective escort offered to her by the Canton Vaud when she stayed in Lausanne for a few days before proceeding to Geneva.[27] An Austrian police councillor who arrived from Vienna was allowed to be present during the investigation of the Geneva police and given full access to all its findings.[28] Finally, the Swiss took immediate steps to assure the European governments of Switzerland's willingness to adopt sterner measures against anarchists on its territory. A German named Burgmayer who was overheard praising Luccheni's deed in Lausanne was promptly proposed for expulsion by the police of the Canton Vaud.[29] Switzerland, reported the French ambassador in Berne, M. Montholon, on 21 September, was anxious to anticipate foreign demands on it to change its domestic laws and its police procedures so as to avoid having to submit to an intervention by the powers. President Rüffy, he wrote, was meeting with the federal council to discuss new police measures that would close Switzerland entirely to the entry of more anarchists and place those who already were there under closer surveillance. The names of 120 to 130 known anarchists were also under review with an eye of expelling the most dangerous ones in the immediate future.[30] This, Rüffy had told Montholon, would be accompanied by efforts to expedite communications between the cantonal police forces in Switzerland and their counterparts in neighboring countries.[31]

Which neighboring countries? The Swiss quickly found that criticism of their asylum policy could come as readily from more distant countries in Europe as from neighboring states. At a reception given in the Burghof in Vienna on 18 September 1898, at which the Swiss minister, Alfred de Claparède, together with the representatives of twenty-two other governments offered his condolences to Emperor Franz Joseph I, it was the British ambassador to Austria, Sir Horace

---

[27] *Gazette de Lausanne* (supplement), 10 Sept. 1898.
[28] Geneva police to EJPD, 19 Sept. 1898, in BA (Berne), Bestands-Nr. 21, Archiv-Nr. 13907, Bd. I.
[29] Telegram, police of Canton Vaud to EJPD, Lausanne, 14 Sept. 1898, in ibid.
[30] Protocol of Bundesrath session, 22 Sept. 1898, in ibid.
[31] Telegram, Montholon to the Direction politique of the French foreign ministry, Berne, 21 Sept. 1898, in AMAE (Paris), Série C, administrative 1876–1907, Carton 24, Dossier 3, Sept–Dec. 1898, "Conférence internationale de Rome pour la défense sociale contre les anarchistes," hereafter cited as "Conférence internationale."

Rumbold, who unexpectedly had the harshest words to say about Switzerland. Claparède quoted him as follows in his dispatch home on 22 September 1898:

But my dear colleague, your Swiss police is a real scandal! It protects the anarchists, or else it is absolutely incapable of doing anything about them. With rogues like these you have to fall back on the punishment of the Middle Ages. Instead, Luccheni is better fed than an honest artisan. He is given things to read – *La Revue des Deux Mondes* – cigars, he is allowed to be interviewed. What is all this supposed to achieve? If you don't change your laws fast, your police system, you risk incurring an international intervention. In our country we also once had a police that wasn't too fabulous, but we have greatly improved it. You'll be in a jolly mess if people were to stage a military demonstration along your frontiers, and we also, because we have guaranteed your neutrality.[32]

The pressure on Italy

The saving grace for Switzerland was that after a week the Luccheni case was seen by most people as an international problem beyond Switzerland's responsibility. The Austrian foreign minister himself, Count Goluchowsky, talked to de Claparède on 18 September about the need for an "international police league" against anarchism. Switzerland, should change some of its laws to make possible the pursuit of anarchists "into their remotest hiding places," but he also thought Switzerland could do this without violating its democratic principles. Anarchists were not political dissenters, Goluchowsky said, but "wild beasts without nationality," a menace "not only to sovereign rulers but to all persons and all private property."[33]

The Swiss were furthermore in a better position to participate in international police collaboration than they were ten years earlier. Ever since the founding of the Swiss *Bundesanwaltschaft* (the federal prosecutor's office, which took charge of political police matters) following the Wohlgemuth affair of 1889, the Berne government had central files on all the anarchists living in Switzerland, recording them by name, place of birth, current address, and personal characteristics.[34] In 1892, during the hunt on Ravachol in France, the French minister of justice, M. Ricard, and the French prime minister, Loubet, had tried to organize a clandestine spy service to watch anarchists living in Switzerland. But the Berne government, on hearing this, was able to stop them by offering the French police all the information they wanted. The Swiss minister in Paris, Charles Lardy, had presented Switzerland's willingness for collaboration with the French police in an eloquent speech:

In my opinion MM. Ricard and Loubet are on the wrong path. To resort to such petty devices as organizing a clandestine spy service is risking embarrassment and is a sure

[32] Swiss minister to Vienna, Alfred de Claparède, to President Rüffy, Geneva, 22 Sept. 1898, in BA (Berne), Bestands-Nr. 21, Archiv-Nr. 14027. See also letter by the Swiss chargé d'affaires du Martheray to Rüffy, Vienna, 22 Sept. 1898, in ibid.

[33] De Claparède to Rüffy, Geneva 22 Sept., 1898, BA (Berne), Bestands-Nr. 21, Archiv-Nr. 14027.

[34] These lists of anarchists are available in ibid., Archiv-Nr. 14002.

way of getting nowhere in Switzerland. If we caught a French *mouchard* we'd treat him no differently than we treat *mouchards* of other countries. This breed is heartily disliked by the Swiss and we'll never tolerate them on our soil; all *mouchards* are anxious to earn their salaries and this easily turns them into agents provocateurs. After the Wohlgemuth affair France cannot possibly want to commit the same mistakes as Monsieur de Bismarck? – . . . If France wants information about a certain anarchist all it needs to do is to make a verbal request [to the Swiss legation in Paris] and this request will on the same day be sent to the federal prosecutor's office in a confidential manner. . . . We certainly do not insist on a formal procedure through diplomatic channels. In fact, we already are in daily communication with the Paris police and the ministry of interior regarding police information . . . But on no account let there be a French *mouchard* organization in Switzerland! Mutual help, yes. But no agents provocateurs, nor other agents in the pay of a foreign police![35]

Following bombing outrages in Barcelona and in the Chamber of Deputies in Paris in 1893, there had been talk about drawing up an international organization of police to combat anarchism. The idea came from Spain and France. England, Austria, and Germany all indicated an interest but were worried about the domestic repercussions which such an agreement might have. The British government, for example, whose participation was considered important because of the many political refugees in London, feared strong Irish opposition in the House of Commons.[36] This time it was the Austrians who proposed that there should be a quicker exchange of information between the police of different countries concerning anarchists.[37] The trouble was that there was no generally accepted legal definition and political interpretation of anarchism and every country had a different view on how anarchists should be dealt with. The Swiss were not anxious to be locked into a political police agreement with clerical–monarchical Spain,[38] while the French disapproved of the Swiss penal code which varied between the cantons and made no provisions for solitary confinement to stop political prisoners from spreading their ideas to other inmates. Nor did Switzerland condemn incorrigible anarchists to death or life-long penal servitude overseas.[39]

This is where matters stood when the tragedy in Geneva occurred. Less than a week after the murder, the Italian government came forward with a proposal for an international conference to take place in Rome before the end of the year. The official Italian invitation to all the European governments to attend an "International Conference in Rome for Social Defence Against Anarchism" went out on 29 September 1898. It asked that the delegations be made up not only of diplomats

---

[35] Swiss minister C. Lardy to federal department of foreign affairs, Paris, 17 May, 1892 *(confidentiel)*, in ibid., Archiv-Nr. 14026.
[36] Du Martheray to the Division politique of the federal department of foreign affairs, Vienna, 19 Dec., 1893, in ibid.
[37] Report by Swiss Legation in Vienna, 7 July, 1894, in ibid., Archiv-Nr. 13884.
[38] Lardy to Lacheval, department of foreign affairs, Paris, 2 Jan. 1894, in ibid., Archiv-Nr. 14026. The Swiss minister in Paris was instructed to speak to his Spanish colleague in an evasive manner about this project.
[39] Lardy to Lacheval, Paris, 4 July, 1894, in ibid.

but also "technical and administrative staff from the [ministries of] justice and interior," in other words, officials in charge of police affairs.[40] Ambassador Camille Barrère, who was to lead the French delegation, neatly summed up the Italian motive for playing host to a European conference:

Admiral Canevaro [the Italian foreign minister] makes no effort to hide the fact that he is above all concerned to relieve his country's responsibility towards Europe, a responsibility coming from the fact that many crimes in the name of anarchism have been committed by individuals of Italian nationality. But he knows the difficulties of reaching agreement on legal definitions and for arranging uniform legislation. He is inclined to think that only in the practical field of police work will an accord be possible. The countries that are most inclined to go beyond [technical police measures] are Russia, Austria-Hungary, and Germany.[41]

Indeed, of the twenty-two states that attended the Rome Conference between 24 November and 21 December 1898,[42] the three autocratic empires Austria-Hungary, Russia, and Germany accepted the invitation with the least hesitation.[43] The Swiss had the greatest qualms about attending, because the Italians at first wanted the Conference to agree on joint European measures against their country. The federal prosecutor, Bundesrat Scherb, seems to have argued against accepting the invitation, pleading Switzerland's ideological incompatibility with the conservative powers in Europe.

I cannot help but think that these international measures are intended to strike not only at the anarchists of deed, in other words, at criminals, but at all social-revolutionary elements who are seeking to change the established order in Italy or elsewhere. In that case we obviously cannot take part. The monarchical states have quite a different idea about [political?] freedom of movement [*Freiheit der Bewegung*] than we.[44]

When the Swiss federal council on 21 October finally voted to attend the Rome Conference the members comforted themselves that Switzerland was not going to be the only liberal country taking part and that unacceptable resolutions could be left to the stronger democratic powers to oppose.[45] France by then had announced that it would attend and the Swiss minister in Paris, Lardy, was assured that Paris no longer believed his country would be made the object of European reproaches. The attitude of the French was reassuring because of their broad political perspective. The former police prefect, Lozé, told Lardy that the Conference might serve to calm the governments that were still animated by the spirit of the Holy

---

[40] Circular, R. Ministero degli affari esteri, Rome, 29 Sept. 1898, in ibid.

[41] Report by Barrère to the foreign minister, Delcassé, Rome, 23 Nov. 1898, in ibid.

[42] The countries attending were Germany, Austria-Hungary, Belgium, Bulgaria, Denmark, Spain, France, Great Britain, Greece, Italy, Luxemburg, Monaco, Montenegro, The Netherlands, Portugal, Romania, Russia, Serbia, Sweden and Norway, Switzerland, and Turkey.

[43] Swiss minister Roth to the political department, Berlin, 25 Oct. 1898, in BA (Berne), Bestands-Nr. 21, Archiv-Nr. 14027.

[44] Unsigned comment attached to the official Italian invitation, but presumably written by *Bundesanwalt* Scherb, in ibid.

[45] Protocol of Bundesrath session of 21 Oct. 1898, in ibid.

Alliance. Foreign Minister Nisard said that in his opinion anarchism must be given enough time to mature into an organized party, as Communism had after 1848, making it easier to deal with politically.[46] In the meantime an international agreement directed against anarchist outrages would be useful, provided it was limited to the technical cooperation of national police forces and did not attempt to produce a conformity of domestic legislation in all the countries.

The Rome Conference, 24 November to 21 December 1898

When the Rome Conference opened on 24 November, it faced three tasks: (1) to define anarchism so as to make the advocacy and the practice of this doctrine a criminal offense throughout Europe; (2) to produce an international agreement on the treatment of anarchists by magistrates and police; and (3) to decide on technical arrangements between the appropriate authorities of the participating states to further the fight against anarchism.

Let it be said from the outset that of the three tasks, only the attempt to establish better exchange of police information between the capitals of Europe was to a limited extent successful. The final protocol of the Conference, in which anarchism was defined and proscribed as criminal, and the extradition of anarchists to their homeland agreed upon, lacked the power of enforcement because all the participating states were given the freedom following the end of the Conference to endorse or not to endorse the resolutions contained therein, or to endorse them with any qualifications and reservations they chose.

The definition of anarchism contained in the final protocol had first been proposed by the Russian ambassador Nelidov at the opening of the Conference. Its purpose was to eliminate acts of anarchism as offenses falling under the protection of political rights in certain countries. "Anarchism has no relation to politics," the final protocol read, "and cannot under any circumstance be regarded as a political doctrine. In the opinion of the Conference an anarchistic act is every act that aims at the destruction of any social organization by violent means. An anarchist is someone who commits an anarchistic act in the sense given above."[47] The definition of anarchism in the final protocol had doubtless the virtue of simplicity, but it was difficult to see how it could be applied equally to the many different situations facing the political police in Paris, London, Barcelona, Berlin, Belgrade, or St. Petersburg. The Austrian ministry of interior as early as 1894 had instructed the security organs throughout the monarchy to proceed on the still broader definition of anarchism as "that movement which seeks the destruction of all political and social order by direct *or* indirect means, with *or* without violence," and to regard as an anarchist "anyone who commits acts in furtherance of

---

[46] Lardy to the political department, Paris, 8 Nov. 1898, in ibid.

[47] Nelidov's draft is available in HHStA (Vienna), Administrative Registrature F52/9, Generalia 1877–1918, "Internationale Massnahmen gegen den Anarchismus."

anarchism, who supports its ideas or endorses them." At the same time, it specifically ruled out as "not belonging to anarchism . . . the supporters of social democracy or other social political doctrines."[48]

The difficulty of defining anarchism persuaded the Swiss government to reserve the right to decide independently from case to case what action it would consider as constituting an act of anarchism.[49] It prompted the English representative, Sir Philippe Currie, to defend the right of political rebellion by arguing that if anarchism referred to any violent action against a given social organization, it could be applied "to Socialism as easily as to a revolutionary action, as for example the substitution of a King for a Parliament, or of a Parliament for a King."[50] The French government also was under pressure at home to assume a position akin to Sir Philippe's. In the Chamber of Deputies in Paris, M. V. Dejeante interpellated the government on 24 November on the definition of anarchism:

The word 'anarchist' means something quite different when it is used by the government and when it is used by those who are governed. The word also changes in significance from country to country. . . . Were we not in France but in Russia, or Spain, or Italy we would be considered anarchists. And even in some parts of our provinces, if we expressed our doctrines people would not hesitate to call us anarchists.[51]

Dejeante then went on to ask whether the representatives of France at the Rome Conference would help to bolster the right to freedom of thought and expression by citizens against their governments, seeing that the conference would surely confer great powers of repression to the monarchies of Europe. He also asked what the French government intended to do to prevent police agents and anonymous informers from abusing their power over the fate of people whom they chose to label as anarchists.[52] At the Rome Conference Sir Philippe Currie was the most eloquent spokesman of liberalism. He explained that while anyone − whether from political motive or not − who committed murder or conspired to commit murder in England or abroad was susceptible to severe punishment under British law, "We do not in England place under police surveillance individuals against whom no charge of plotting a crime or inciting to a crime can be levied."[53] The final protocol took this into account, for the most sweeping legal changes for the suppression of anarchism which it contained were laid down only as recommendations:

[48] K.k. Min. d. Innern, z.Z.:2161/M.I. (1894), "Instruction für die politischen Bezirksbehörden, bezw. landesfürstlichen Sicherheitsbehörden betreff. die Überwachung von Anarchisten," in ibid.
[49] Ibid. [50] Ibid., p. 31.
[51] Extract from the record of the Chamber of Deputies, session of 24 Nov. 1898, pp. 2268–77, in AMAE (Paris), Série C, Carton 24, Dossier 3.
[52] Ibid. See also the French position since the 1830s on the right of political dissent as expressed by M. Dufaure, a recent minister of justice, in a speech on 2 May 1878: "la pensée qu'un réfugié politique pourrait être plus souvent un vaincu qu'un coupable," in *Journal Officiel de la République Française*, X (134), 16 May 1878.
[53] Ibid., pp. 40–1.

All anarchistic acts are extraditable if the crime committed is a crime under the penal code of the extraditing state and of the state requesting extradition; and in all cases involving an attempt at the life of a sovereign or of a head of state or members of their families.

The Conference hopes that all states will enact laws that prohibit the preparation of anarchistic acts (like bomb making), the organization of such acts, giving aid to anarchists, and public incitement to anarchism. Also prohibited should be anarchist propaganda in the army and the incitement of military personnel to insubordination for the purpose of promoting anarchism. Governments should seek to limit public knowledge about anarchism: there should be restrictions on the recounting of anarchistic exploits, and laws passed to permit the seizure of anarchist literature. Imprisoned anarchists are to be held in isolated cells. Judges should have the power to limit the freedom of anarchists to move between towns. Attempts at the lives of sovereigns or heads of state and their families are to be made capital offenses, but the execution of anarchists should not be held publicly. Anarchist crimes are to be treated like ordinary crimes without consideration of their motives.[54]

There were separate consultations in Rome among the specialists on police affairs of the countries attending: among them M. Viguié, in charge of the surveillance of anarchists in Paris, the chief of political police in Berlin, and the head of the political police in Basel, Herr Iselin. Their meetings took place behind closed doors and the content of these discussions is not recorded in the official minutes.[55] The final protocol laid down that:

Every country undertakes to keep the anarchists on its territory under strict surveillance and to establish a central office to this end. The central offices are to communicate to each other all useful information concerning anarchist activities.

All foreign anarchists are to be deported to their home states.

All states are to adopt the *"portraits parlés"* method of criminal identification.

The provisions relating to the police work of the participation countries were the easiest to put into practice because they could be implemented through administrative decree. It is true, international police contacts were nothing new, but because they were not new there existed established patterns of relationships and degrees of mutual trust to take into consideration. On this subject we have the opinion of the Paris police prefect on the eve of the Rome Conference, as reported by the Swiss minister to France, Charles Lardy:

The Prefect, Monsieur Charles Blanc, who once was director of the Sûreté, at the ministry of interior, thinks that defining anarchism in theory, or trying to suppress its activity by means of an international convention, is a waste of time. The only thing to do is to strengthen police surveillance in every country and not to believe anarchism dead simply because some time passes without new attacks. The existing laws in every country must be firmly enforced. All foreign anarchists must be expelled without much ado — as the French

---

[54] Document available in HHStA (Vienna), F52/9, Generalia 1877–1918.
[55] Swiss delegate Iselin to Bundesrath, Rome, 11 Dec. 1898, in BA (Berne), Bestands-Nr. 21, Archiv-Nr. 14027.

ministry of interior has the power to, by means of a simple order. Also all frontier police forces must be allowed to communicate with each other by telegraph and telephone to alert one another about anarchists who pass from one country to the other.

It seems that this is what in fact happens between the [French] police commissar in Annemasse and the police of Geneva, and also between police on the two sides of the Franco-Belgian frontier. In addition, the Spanish Government has so far voiced no objections to the French police maintaining a commissaire and a police staff in Barcelona to gather information about Spanish anarchists, seeing that in Spain anarchists and simple republicans are thrown in the same pot and that information provided by the Spanish police cannot be taken seriously. France also has informers in London. The police prefect assures us that there are none in Switzerland.[56]

The Rome Conference was over on 21 December 1898, and early in the new year most governments declared their adherence to the final protocols with only minor reservations. Turkey wanted to make sure that its agreement with Russia for the return of Armenians to Turkey would not be affected. Romania, like Switzerland, reserved the right to judge whether an individual on its territory was in fact an anarchist or not. The Swiss actually declined to sign the protocol altogether though they declared their willingness to support it, so that new legislation in keeping with the Rome Conference's recommendations would not legally constitute fulfillment of a treaty obligation incurred by Switzerland towards other countries. France signed with the enjoinder that the establishment of direct communications between the police authorities of Europe be kept under strict secrecy. "We see here some political difficulties since public opinion could interpret this agreement as tantamount to the establishment of a true international police service."[57] England's Sir Philippe Currie, despite all his skepticism, declared that Great Britain supported the goals of the Conference and recognized the existence of "an international duty to protect, as far as possible and by legitimate means, other countries besides the United Kingdom against the violent acts of anarchists."[58]

Austrian yearly reports on international anarchism

The Austrian government through the Polizei-Direktion in Vienna had systematically watched international Socialism and anarchism ever since two antianarchist laws had been passed in 1885 (mainly against criminals using explosives) and in 1886 (on the judicial competence of the courts in cases involving

---

[56] Minister Lardy to the political department in Berne, Paris, 8 Nov. 1898, in ibid. See also the message by prefect Charles Blanc delivered to the Swiss minister in Vienna, de Claparède, by his French colleague the Marquis de Revenceaux, in ibid.

[57] See Final Protocol, dated 21 Dec. 1898, in ibid.

[58] Conférence internationale, p. 40. On the effect of the Rome Conference on the behavior of various national police authorities, see Richard B. Jensen, "The International Anti-Anarchist Conference of 1898 and the Origins of Interpol," in *Journal of Contemporary History*, vol. 16 (1981), pp. 323–47.

anarchism).[59] Some of the yearly reports have been preserved in the archive of the Vienna police.[60] The first volume for the year 1892 announced that in the past twelve months the growth of the workers' movements had overshadowed other political events throughout Europe. Socialism had begun to make inroads in middle-class circles and among the peasantry, it said, and revolutionary Socialism had openly begun to challenge Christian Socialism. Interesting is the realistic assessment of the situation in Germany:

> The German Social Democrats are the exception. So recently only launched on a triumphant campaign of conquest, they have at this year's party congress in Berlin come to their senses and decided on a more moderate course. The overthrow of the existing social order is still on their books, but in practice they demand the realization of specific reforms which do not seriously endanger the structure of society.

By contrast Austria in 1892 experienced twelve cases of anarchist sabotage using dynamite charges. The year report also included news from Hungary, Switzerland, Scandinavia, Great Britain, France, Belgium, Holland, Spain, Italy, Russia, the Balkans, and the United States. In regard to Russia, the Polizei-Direktion noted the decline of the revolutionary organizations *Buntari, Semlya i volya, Peredel,* and *Narodnaya volya,* and a greater interest in pure Marxist teaching, among the Socialists. Among Russian academic youth at large, nationalism and anti-Semitism were said to be more in vogue than were Socialist ideas.

The 1893 report emphasized the international ties between the labor movements in Europe. The report for the following year was dominated by the murder of President Sadi Carnot, and in 1895 the Austrian officials actually believed that international Socialism had nearly run its course: "Various indications lead us to believe that the Socialist movement will soon have passed its peak. The employers are at long last organizing themselves and beginning to resist Socialist agitation." The report for 1896 is missing; but in 1897 the optimistic mood of the Austrian police still held up: "The streak of opportunism, which made its appearance in the socialist movement a few years back, has become still more prominent."

The year 1898, of course, was dominated by the murder of Empress Elisabeth by "that anarchistic monster" Luccheni, and by the calling of the International Conference in Rome for Social Defense against Anarchism. The Austrian *Centralstelle* was henceforth instructed to correspond directly with the central offices that were being established in the other capitals of Europe and to supply them with information about the anarchist movement on their request as well as on its own initiative.

The entry for 1899 had a sarcastic ring to it: "The collapse of the existing social order, prophesied by [Friedrich] Engels for the year 1900, and the creation of

[59] Karel Maly, *Policejni a soudni perzekuce delnicke tridy v druhe polovine 19. stoleti v cechach* (Prague, 1967), pp. 276–9.
[60] Yearly reports from 1892–1914, each entitled "Die sozialdemokratische und anarchistische Bewegung im Jahre . . . " (Vienna: Kaiserliche Hof- u. Staatsdruckerei, [year]), are available in APD (Vienna).

the social democratic state of the future did not come about." In 1900 the *Centralstelle's* attention was drawn to the creation of two organizations connected to the bourgeois pacifist and internationalist movement, the *International Bureau of Information and Initiative,* and the *Interparliamentary Union.*

From 1901 on the reports turned more pessimistic again. The American president, MacKinley, was murdered on 6 September 1901. Mass strikes involving unprecedented numbers of workers broke out in the less industrialized regions of Europe like Barcelona, Trieste, Lemberg, and among agricultural workers in eastern Galicia. The year 1903 brought the alarming success of the German Social Democrats at the Reichstag elections when no less than three million votes were cast for the SPD and eighty-one workers were returned as Reichstag members. The year 1904, in turn, was dominated by a renewed propaganda campaign against capitalism and militarism, the two chief pillars of the established order, all this in preparation for the general strike that was to usher in the violent seizure of power by the proletariat through anarchistic tactics.

While the Austrian yearly reports tell us about the Polizei-Direktion's seriousness of purpose and its willingness to serve in an international police front against world revolution, the entries are too sketchy and need to be complemented with the assessments by police officials in Rome, Paris, Berlin, and in particular by those in St. Petersburg. However, it seems as if the Rome Conference failed to persuade enough states to participate in a regular exchange of police bulletins on anarchism. The Austrian *Centralstelle* in 1914 had personnel files on 2,500 to 3,000 anarchists all over Europe,[61] but the reports from the other countries never dealt with more than a handful of individuals at a time. To judge by the collection of such reports that reached the Swiss prosecutor's office between 1898 and 1914, only France and Italy sent the other states monthly accounts about anarchistic meetings, publications, and other events inside their territories.[62] New Scotland Yard in London regularly acknowledged the receipt of the reports by other countries but did not issue reports on anarchists living in Great Britain. Romania sent only one report a few weeks after the end of the Rome Conference, in which it expressed more concern to please its powerful neighbors Russia and Austria-Hungary than fear for its own domestic security:

We have no knowledge of an anarchist center in Romania. It is possible that at various times anarchists who were expelled or hunted by the authorities of foreign countries have sought refuge in Romania. . . . The police has hunted down certain anarchists who were described as dangerous by the police of other states and forced them to leave the territory of the Kingdom when it was established that their presence could pose a threat to the internal or external security of the state, and when an interested state . . . has expressed a desire for such an expulsion.[63]

---

[61] Letter, Austrian minister of interior to Austrian minister of foreign affairs, Vienna, 12 Nov. 1914, 14915/M.I., in HHStA (Vienna), Administrative Registratur F52/9, Generalia 1877–1918.

[62] Documents available in BA (Berne), Bestands-Nr. 21, Archiv-Nr. 18031–4.

[63] Report by Ministerul de Interne, Directiunea Sigurantei Generale, Bucharest, 15 Jan. 1899, in ibid.

The Swiss folder contains no reports from Russia and only a few messages from the Berlin police concerning individual anarchists whose whereabouts had recently been located – and of others who, for mysterious reasons, the police considered as having "withdrawn" from the anarchist movement.[64]

There is a possible explanation for the paucity of the exchange of police bulletins after 1898 if we return to the history of the European state system and take note of the growing Russo-German rivalry for hegemony in Europe at that time. In the context of a struggle for mastery on the continent between these two empires the decisions reached at the Rome Conference were obviously far too paltry. In 1889 Russia began to prepare for a major reassertion of its foreign political goals in Europe and Asia. St. Petersburg decided on building the Trans-Siberian Railway and on revising its military commitments in Europe. Was the International Peace Conference in the Hague (1899) a way for Russia to gain more time for its long-range plans? At that Conference Germany, now similarly committed through the Schlieffen Plan to a daring military strategy against the Dual Entente, may have played the role of the spoiler because it anticipated being ready for war earlier than Russia. The tension was heightened between 1900 and 1902, when Italy and Switzerland were at loggerheads over the murder of King Humbert because Switzerland failed to suppress the propaganda work of Italian anarchists in Canton Ticino.[65] Germany and Russia thereupon took up the cause which the Rome Conference had barely succeeded to carry beyond its conceptual stage and pushed for a much more vigorous international police league than Admiral Canevoro had ever proposed: a league that would, if necessary, align the conservative powers against the Western democracies. Whether this Russo-German partnership was little more than a partnership of convenience until one of the two empires' military preparations were in place, or whether it was a sincere attempt to find in a police partnership an alternative to mutual war, is a question left unanswered because of the intervention of the Russian revolution of 1905.

The International Peace Conference at The Hague, 1899

The Russian invitation to all European nations to attend an International Peace Conference in The Hague to be held in May of the following year was issued on 24 August (n.s.), 1898 – one month before the Italian government called for an urgent conference in Rome to combat anarchism. As a result Monsieur Dejeante, speaking in the French Chamber of Deputies on 24 November 1898, could at one and the same time praise his government's acceptance of the Russian invitation and criticize its participation in the police conference in Rome. Indeed, some of the delegates to the Rome Conference also attended the event in the Hague, for

---

[64] For example, report by the police presidium, Berlin, to Swiss Bundesanwalt, Berlin, 27 Mar. 1911, Tagebuch-Nr. C.A. 621.11, in ibid. On the general inadequacy of the exchange of reports on anarchism, see also Bernard Porter, *The Origins of the Vigilante State. The London Metropolitan Police Special Branch before the First World War* (London, 1987), p. 122.

[65] For a survey of the political assassinations at the turn of the century, see Vladimir Dedijer, *The Road to Sarajevo* (London, 1967), passim.

example Léon Bourgeois of France (a former prefect of police and former prime minister), and Noury-Bey of Turkey (inspector and director general of the ministry of public works).[66]

The International Peace Conference was acclaimed by the partisans of the peace movement, which had raised its head as early as the outbreak of nationalist wars in the 1850s and 1860s. The Russian invitation came at an opportune time because of growing fears about the destructiveness of modern weapons including dum-dum bullets, submarines, and the prospects of future air war; and because colonial rivalries in Egypt and the Transvaal heightened international tensions in Europe. The one hundred delegates from twenty-six countries who attended gave warm praise to Tsar Nicholas II for his contribution to world peace.[67]

There were the skeptics also, notably the members of the German delegation to whom the very idea of mediation by a third power or legal arbitration in place of war amounted to an attack on the sacred principles of absolute sovereignty and national honor.[68] But this was well understood by pacifists like Bertha von Suttner, who knew that among the many high-ranking officials and military men she and other partisans of the peace movement cut a comical figure and were regarded as apostles of utopian visions. At the same time, von Suttner realized that only governments had the power to take effective steps to secure international peace. She also disapproved of the Socialists leaders who scoffed at the Conference because, in their doctrine, only a Socialist world could exist in peace, yet supported its work nonetheless for reasons of political calculation: Disarmament would make the capitalist states that much weaker against workers' uprisings.[69] Above all, there was skepticism about Russia's motive in calling the Conference: In the summer of 1898, had not General Kuropatkin, Finance Minister Witte, and Foreign Minister Count Muraviev discussed with Tsar Nicholas II Russia's great economic difficulties in keeping up with its rivals in the European arms race?[70] But in spite of all this, Bertha von Suttner saw value in the Conference because of the unprecedented publicity it provided the cause of peace.

Theoretically speaking, the idea of abolishing war complemented the idea of international police agreements. It meant abandoning the principle of national self-determination in favor of collective security and collaboration in civil administration. One lone supporter of such a transfer of responsibility was the British

---

[66] Bertha von Suttner, *Die Haager Friedenskonferenz. Tagebuchblätter* (Dresden, 1901), p. 94.

[67] All the European states were there except for those without military power: Monaco, San Marino, and the Papacy. There were also non-European states attending: China, Japan, Persia, Siam, the United States, and Mexico.

[68] Suttner, *Friedenskonferenz*, pp. 8–9; and Franz Carl Endres, *Der deutschen Tragödie erster Teil* (Stuttgart, 1948), pp. 43ff.

[69] Endres, *Tragödie*, pp. 21–2.

[70] William Hull, *The Two Hague Conferences and their Contribution to International Law* (Boston, 1908), p. 2. The German government was convinced that Russia's action was motivated by its difficulty in keeping up with the armament of the other powers. See, for example, Prince von Radolin to Chancellor von Hohenlohe, St. Petersburg, 26 Aug. 1898; and Count Münster to von Hohenlohe, Scheveningen, 17 July 1899, in *GP*, vol. 15, pp. 143–5, 354–8.

journalist Henry Wickham Steed, who in a lecture on the British Empire touched on the relationship between war and police order:

> By and large I would say for England that she represents today the strongest single tool in the service of world peace and civilization throughout the world. Yet within the British Empire itself, peace is maintained not on the basis of the Quaker principles of renunciation of force. On the contrary, it does rest on force – but on police force. Just as the medical doctor prevents smallpox by inoculating patients with diluted doses of this virus, so, I say, if you want to free the world from the scourge of war and militarism you must inoculate it with police. To replace soldiers with policemen, that's what we must do. Not to give up all force, which would be sheer fantasy, given what people today are like.[71]

By 1900 the concept of international police collaboration changed from the idea of helping all countries develop the same kind of objective and competent machinery of law enforcement to the idea that the police order which they enforced would also have to be compatible. Germany and Russia took the initiative to build a conservative police alliance with Austria-Hungary a strong supporter, and when they found the liberal states of the West reluctant to join them, they sought to confuse the Western camp by reopening the issue of Switzerland's alleged danger to European peace and security.

Plans for a reactionary police league, 1901–4

Shortly after the murder of the king of Italy, Humbert I, in 1900, the Italian legation in Berne demanded that the Swiss government prosecute a certain Bertoni, the author of an *Almanach des anarchistes italiens*. The Swiss courts, however, declared themselves incompetent and all the Swiss police could do was to confiscate the brochure.[72] The resulting dispute gave rise to a diplomatic break between the two countries as Rome insisted that the anarchists in the Swiss canton of Ticino – often with the encouragement of anarchists in America – were plotting more attacks against Italian domestic security.[73]

In November 1901, the Russian and the German governments agreed to help Italy to force Switzerland to changes its laws and its police organization. The Austro-Hungarian government concurred: In its view the situation in the Ticino was a permanent source of instability for all Europe.[74] The German minister to Berne, von Bülow, suggested that Switzerland should pass a law making punishable the mere glorification and incitement to anarchistic deeds; also that it should establish a central police bureau with the power to order cantonal police

[71] Suttner, *Friedenskonferenz*, pp. 197–8. The Englishman, Henry Wickham Steed, was violently denounced as a Russian agent by Count Münster in his report to von Hohenlohe, Scheveningen, 17 July 1899, in *GP*, vol. 15, pp. 355–6.

[72] "Traduction d'un projet d'instruction au Ministre de Russie à Berne (1902)," in HHStA (Vienna), Admin. Reg. F52/9, Generalia 1877–1918, folder 448rff.

[73] Austrian ambassador Freiherrr von Pasetti to the foreign minister, Goluchowski, Rome, 10 Dec. 1901, in ibid.

[74] Austrian minister, Count Kuefstein, to Goluchowski, Berne, 15 Nov. 1901, in ibid.

forces to proceed against anarchists. A memorandum was also handed to the American president, Theodore Roosevelt, by the ambassadors of Germany and Russia on 16 December 1901, urging the United States to join in international measures against anarchism.[75]

As may be expected, the French government was unhappy about a joint Russo-German demarche in the cause of international police collaboration: Was the Okhrana changing its strategy in Europe from partnership with France to partnership with Germany, now that Peter Rachkovsky had left Paris? Foreign Minister Delcassé informed the Russian ambassador that France saw no need to give its adherence to this protocol since it had no reason to want to change its existing laws.[76] In London, Lord Lansdowne listened to the proposal by the Russian and German ambassadors that his government expel all foreign anarchists living in Great Britain, then quietly explained that English public opinion would not support such a wholesale measure.[77] Even Romania was hesitant. Though it said it wanted to adhere to the proposal of Berlin and Petersburg, it had to consider Romania's constitution which provided for freedom of the press and public trials.[78] On 12 August 1902 the Russians and Germans also received a refusal from Italy, which said that the expulsion of all anarchists on Italian soil was impossible because most of them were Italian nationals.[79]

It is tempting to think that the unresponsiveness of England, France, and Italy may have prompted the Russian and German government to launch, together with Austria-Hungary, a full-scale diplomatic attack on Switzerland in May 1902, thereby associating their initial demarche once more with the old criticism of the Great Powers against Swiss liberalism.[80] The Russian minister in Berne delivered a note to the Swiss president reminding him that the Bertoni affair "affects the interests of all the monarchies of Europe" and that "Switzerland should remember its international obligation and its moral responsibility vis-à-vis the European states who, since 1815, have protected the neutrality of the Republic."[81]

The Swiss government did by December 1902 introduce a bill prohibiting the approval or the glorification of all anarchistic acts committed either in Switzerland or abroad that were punishable by a sentence in the penitentiary, but the bill met with much popular criticism as it was seen as an act of submission to foreign intervention. In May 1903 the bill was amended to replace the vague term "anarchism" with specific references to murder, robbery, arson, and attacks with explosives,"so as not to make a stage performance of *Wilhelm Tell* subject to criminal prosecution."[82] The three conservative powers were careful not to press

---

[75] Memorandum, U.S. Department of State, Washington, D.C., 16 Dec. 1901, in ibid.
[76] Telegram, Graf Wolkenstein to Austrian foreign ministry, Paris, 29 Nov. 1901, Nr. 9621, in ibid.
[77] Letter, Graf Deym to Goluchowski, London, 20 Dec. 1901, in ibid.
[78] Markgraf Pallavicini to Goluchowski, Bucharest, 20 Dec. 1901, in ibid.
[79] Freiherr von Pasetti to Goluchowski, Rome, 12 Aug. 1902, in ibid.
[80] Telegram, Austrian foreign ministry to Graf Kuefstein in Berne, Vienna, 21 May 1902, in ibid.
[81] "Traduction d'un projet d'instruction au Ministre de Russie à Berne," in ibid.
[82] Report, Freiherr von Heidler to Goluchowski, Berne, 21 May 1903, in ibid. Following the murder

the Swiss too hard, giving public opinion in Switzerland time to calm down. The new Swiss antianarchist law was finally ratified in 1906.

On 14 March 1904 a "Secret Protocol for the International War on Anarchism" was drawn up in St. Petersburg. It was immediately signed by Germany, Austria-Hungary, Russia, Sweden, Denmark, Bulgaria, Spain, Portugal, Romania, and Turkey. Luxemburg and Switzerland agreed to adhere to it but requested that it be done in a special form that would not involve them in legal difficulties of an internal nature: Thus the Swiss reserved the right to withdraw from it unilaterally at any time in the future.[83] As the Austrian ambassador to St. Petersburg reported on 2 February 1904: the Russo-German proposal for the surveillance of anarchism has been endorsed by all the neighbors of the two empires. "When Austria-Hungary joins, all of Eastern Europe will become a bloc of states consolidated in its fight on anarchism. As was to be expected, England, France, and Italy have given negative or evasive answers."[84] England's refusal was seen by the Austrian ambassador, Mensdorff, at the Court of St. James as an expression of its cynicism:

The English police no doubt watches the anarchists in this country, but it doesn't prevent them from leaving for the continent to commit some dastardly crime every now and again, and the police of the countries thus affected are not always forewarned. England so far has been spared anarchistic crimes. The freedom which it grants to the anarchists is a kind of insurance payment it pays for England's own immunity from attacks.[85]

In short the ideological division of Europe by the turn of the century was beginning to show itself in the various countries' alignments as police powers more readily than in their military partnerships as the Dual Entente and the Triple Alliance. Switzerland's ideological problem since the murder of Empress Elisabeth is best outlined in this report by Freiherr von Heidler, dated Berne, 8 January 1904:

To the Swiss an association with the three conservative great powers Austria-Hungary, Germany, and Russia may still be acceptable. But they can neither be proud of, nor enjoy, the idea of siding with Turkey, Serbia, and Bulgaria when the 'liberal' powers England, France, Italy, and America refuse to adopt the police measures outlined in the Protocol. The Swiss are particularly surprised by Italy's abstention. Italy poses enormous demands on Swiss compliance in matters of anarchism but is not willing to undertake major obligations itself or to make sacrifices of its own.

Finally, they don't like to keep secret an agreement tying Switzerland to governments like Turkey, Serbia, and Bulgaria.

The Swiss will end up accepting the protocol but only because they have committed themselves too far in the course of these negotiations.

of the Serbian royal family in June 1903, the Swiss wondered whether any expression of patriotism by a Serbian subject in Switzerland would now become an indictable offense. See Heidler to Goluchowski, Berne 23 July 1903, in ibid.
[83] Heidler to Goluchowski, Berne, 11 Apr. 1904, in ibid.
[84] Telegram, Graf Szapary to Aehrenthal, St. Petersburg, 2 Feb. 1904, in ibid.
[85] Graf Mensdorff to Goluchovski, London, 23 June 1906, in ibid.

And they have engaged in these negotiations to a large extent in the hope to redeem themselves from the stain of the bloody deed in Geneva.[86]

The Swiss government in 1907 finally accepted the St. Petersburg protocol of 1904 – but secretly, without informing the Bundestag and the cantonal councils and with the reservation that it should remain free to withdraw its consent at any moment in the future.[87]

The European response to the Russian revolution of 1905

General remarks

Shortly after the murder of Alexander II, a Swiss publicist, Victor Tissot, predicted that the future of Europe would be determined either by the politics of the working people of Berlin or by that of the peasant masses of Russia.[88] But as we shall see, the Berlin workers never became the spearhead of an international Marxist revolution, whatever certain French police spies thought during the turbulent "Gründerjahre" of the Bismarckian empire. Much class hostility had begun to abate after the fall of the anti-Socialist law in 1890. Tissot's prophecy of a revolutionary danger emanating from Russia, however, did become an alarming prospect in 1905, when that empire's ill-fated venture into Korea met with resounding defeat at the hands of the Japanese army and navy. The ensuing social disorders throughout the empire threatened to undermine the whole balance of power in Europe, not unlike the revolutionary unrest in the post-Napoleonic period upset the territorial arrangements of the Congress of Vienna. Only this time the danger came from Russia and not from France, and this time no Metternich organized a continental system to fight it. Worse, the police alliance pioneered by Russia, Germany, and Austria-Hungary, rather than assuaging the fears of revolution in Europe, contained the seeds of more incertitude inasmuch as a realignment of the powers into autocratic and democratic states would cut across the existing military arrangement of Europe into the Dual Entente and the Triple Alliance.

To be sure, all European governments valued Russia as the eastern bulwark of the continental equilibrium. "We have fared well with Tsardom for 180 years," wrote the German Chancellor Bernhard von Bülow on 30 March 1905. "Things will be very different with a Russian Republic."[89] Wilhelm II, watching in dismay Russia's military disaster in Manchuria, wanted to advise Nicholas II on how to suppress revolutions, and failing that, urge him to conclude peace with Japan

---

[86] Heidler to Goluchowski, Berne, 8 Jan. 1904, in ibid.
[87] Heidler to Aehrenthal, Berne, 7 Feb. 1907, in ibid. On Germany's and Russia's worry that the Austro-Hungarian Empire might disintegrate, see Chancellor Bülow to German ambassador Count von Alvensleben in St. Petersburg, Berlin, 15 Feb. 1905, in *GP*, vol. 22, pp. 11–12.
[88] Victor Tissot, *Russes et allemands* (Paris, 1882), passim.
[89] Letter, von Bülow to Prince Heinrich of Prussia, Berlin, 30 Mar. 1905, in *GP*, vol. 19, Part II, p. 417.

as speedily as possible since the sight of a European monarchy going down in defeat, he believed, would stir up rebellious Socialists and Nihilists everywhere else.[90] The Austrian ministry of interior banned a benefit evening scheduled for 26 February 1905, because the proceeds were intended for the Japanese Red Cross, even though the emperor's personal friend, the court actress, Katherina Schratt, had agreed to patronize that gala event.[91] And in London Sir Edward Grey, the British foreign secretary, spoke with sympathy in the House of Commons about "that terrible state of things" in Russia, where in less than one year 305 Russian policemen were murdered in a district staffed by only one thousand officials.[92]

It is of course true, that in all European countries, including autocratic Germany and Austria-Hungary, a public opinion had come into existence by the end of the nineteenth century, which no government could ignore any more. In Berlin, as much as in Vienna, philanthropists of the upper class like H. Coudenhove-Kalergi and pacifist writers like Eduard Fuchs and Alfred Kerr saw in the victory of the Japanese the triumph of culture over barbarity.[93] Fortunately, perhaps, for the German and Austrian governments the lower classes of Berlin and Vienna remained largely silent.[94] Not so in France and Switzerland. In France the violent passions of the Dreyfus Affair (1894–1906), kindled over an issue affecting the country's external security, were still very much alive. And in Switzerland, the past attempts by France and Austria, and more recently by Germany, Russia, and Italy, to interfere in its police sovereignty had given rise to a new determination to defend the Swiss people's freedom of speech.

---

[90] Note, Chancellor von Bülow on his audience with Wilhelm II, Berlin, 4 Feb. 1904, in *GP*, vol. 19, Part I, p. 62; and N. F. Grant, ed., *The Kaiser's Letters to the Tsar* (London, 1920), ch. XII. As an alternative, according to A. J. P. Taylor, the Germans in 1905 could have invaded Russia without difficulty. See his *The Struggle for Mastery in Europe, 1848–1918* (London, 1954), p. 427.

[91] Memo, Präsidium des k.k. Ministerium des Innern, Vienna, 7 Feb. 1905, P. Nr. 815/1905, in AVA (Vienna), Ministerium des Innern, Präsidiale, Karton 1982: "Polizeibefugnisse, Theater u. öffentliche Schaustellungen 1900–1918."

[92] Sir Edward Grey, *Speeches on Foreign Affairs, 1904–1914* (London, 1931), pp. 99–100. Figures on the number of police casualties in the Russian Revolution of 1905 differ from source to source. The last Okhrana chief, A. T. Vassilyev, cites 1,000 police killed in Russian Poland in 1905 in his *The Okhrana. The Russian Secret Police* (London, Bombay, Sidney, 1930), p. 87; while, more recently, Anna Greifman cites figures in the hundreds in her essay, "The Kadets and Terrorism, 1905–1907," in *Jahrbücher für die Geschichte Osteuropas* (Wiesbaden and Stuttgart), 36, Heft 2 (1988), pp. 248–67.

[93] See report on Ernst Reuter's lecture series, "Aus russischen Kerkern," in *Spandauer Zeitung*, 1. Beiblatt, Nr. 117, 20 May 1914; and letter of inquiry by Krassilnikoff to Henninger of the political police in Berlin, Paris, March 1918, in Hoover Inst., Archive of the Imperial Secret Police, index no. Vb, folder 1: "Relations with the German Sicherheit."

[94] Report by Wachtmeister Kemmenitz on a meeting at Restaurant Schloss Weissensee near Berlin, 22 Jan. 1906, to commemorate the first anniversary of "Bloody Sunday," in SPD Library (Berlin), Reg. d. Amstbezirks Weissensee, Acta Betreff. "Umsturzparteien und deren Agitationen," vol. I, 1894–1914. See also Carl E. Schorske, *German Social Democracy, 1905–1917* (Cambridge, Mass., 1955); Eduard Bernstein, *Die Geschichte der Berliner Arbeiterbewegung* (Berlin, 1907–1910), vol. III, pp. 160, 198; and Eberhard von Vietsch, *Bethmann Hollweg. Staatsmann zwischen Macht und Ethos* (Boppard a.R., 1969), pp. 63–4.

Switzerland and the Tiflis robbery, 1907

The Swiss police in 1905 had the good fortune that its government was not dependent on tsarist Russia, and that it had no direct responsibility for the preservation of the balance of power in Europe. When on 18 February 1905, the Russian minister to Berne, V. Jadowski, lodged a protest to the president of the Swiss Confederation because public collections were being held throughout the city to raise money for the victims of the civil disturbances in Russia (principally for the revolutionaries) his protest was politely but firmly rejected by the Swiss government.[95] Jadowski's irateness is easier to understand, however, if one considers that the chief of the police in Berne himself, Gemeinderat Guggisberg, belonged to the committee that organized this relief action. Guggisberg was the police chief who in the previous year had reacted with surprising nonchalance to information from the Russian legation that a Russian exile named Ilnitzky was threatening to kill Minister Jadowski. Instead of expelling Ilnitzky from Berne or placing him under constant surveillance, as the Russian legation had asked, the Berne police only questioned him after first showing him the letter from the Russian legation. Shortly afterward, Jadowski narrowly escaped an attempt by Ilnitzky to shoot him in the street. A passerby detained the gunman, but the policeman who later arrived merely asked him to report to the main police station in the afternoon. The French ambassador in Berne, as doyen of the diplomatic corps in Berne, proposed a joint demarche by the foreign envoys to demand better protection from the Swiss police.[96]

The phlegmatic behavior of the Bernese authorities was matched by the punctiliousness of the Genevan police whom the Russian government asked for help in connection with the robbery of the Russian Imperial Bank in Tiflis, Georgia, by armed revolutionaries, on 23 June 1907. Some 250,000 rubles in banknotes were stolen, but the serial numbers of these banknotes were known to the Russian police and communicated to the police of other countries.[97] On 18 January 1908, a Russian woman named Sarah Ravich was arrested by the police in Munich for trying to exchange some of the stolen money into German marks. Shortly thereafter the Swiss also detained several Russians who called at a villa owned by the same Sarah Ravich in Geneva. In February the Russian legation in Berne asked the Swiss government to extradite three of these men as suspects in the Tiflis bank robbery. But following consultations with the police in Munich, the Swiss refused because of what they called the "frivolity with which complicity in the

[95] Letter, Jadowski to Swiss president, Berne, 18 Feb. 1905, and the answer by the cantonal authorities of Berne, 21 Feb. 1905, in BA (Berne), Bestands-Nr. 21, Archiv-Nr. 14016.

[96] Report by French embassy on the attempt at the life of M. de Jadowsky, Berne, 13 June, 1904, in AMAE (Paris), correspondance politique, Nouvelle Série 1897–1918, Russie, Carton 80: "Protocole, Corps diplomatique et consulaire étranger 1896–1907."

[97] Notice in *Schweizer Polizeianzeiger*, 26 Dec., 1907, in BA (Berne), Bestands-Nr. 21, Archiv-Nr. 24650, Bd. 3. On the probable involvement of Stalin in this robbery, see Adam B. Ulam, *Stalin. The Man and His Era* (New York, 1973), pp. 89–90.

bank robbery is construed from the mere fact that these persons had been in contact with Ravich."[98]

The Swiss were equally reluctant to accede to the Munich police's request that the Genevan police examine the content of letters found in Ravich's mailbox. After considerable negotiations the EJPD finally instructed the Genevan officials to open the letters, but only in the presence of an independent witness, and to have their content translated into French only by someone "who had absolutely no connection whatsoever to the Russian legation or the Russian consulate."[99]

The scrupulousness of the Swiss authorities in matters of habeas corpus and postal privacy was surely admirable. But what seemed fitting in peaceful Switzerland did not necessarily apply to the chaotic conditions in Russia whose security was affected by Swiss actions. Looking back today, the historian may well ask whether Switzerland before the First World War gave due consideration to the enormous difficulties then besetting other European countries whose home security could no longer be ensured by domestic measures alone. The question is not whether Russia's brutal suppression of its students and workers at home was benighted or not, but whether the Swiss government was aware of a responsibility beyond the preservation of democracy and public order in its own territory. The Tiflis robbery was one bloody incident out of hundreds in a widespread revolutionary situation in Eastern Europe.[100] In Switzerland only one bomb exploded during that terrible year 1905, and that was an accident during an experiment someone conducted before a group of Russian students. More than half of the 3,784 foreign students at Swiss universities in 1906–7 were Russians and most of them were opponents of tsarism.[101] But the only difficulty they caused their Swiss hosts was that many of them used passports with false entries.[102] Were the Swiss guilty of complacency?[103]

The Franco-Russian police alliance in eclipse

In France the public reacted stronger to the events in Russia than in Germany or Austria-Hungary. Many people instinctively sympathized with the rebels even though they knew that their country was committed to an alliance with St. Petersburg. The police authorities played the role, in turn, of the enforcer of

[98] Letter, Bundesanwalt Kronacher to Bundesrat Forrer, Berne, 19 Feb. 1908, in BA (Berne), Bestands-Nr. 21, Archiv-Nr. 24650, Bd. 3..

[99] EJPD to Bundesanwalt Kronacher, Berne, 31 Jan. 1908, in ibid.

[100] "Vertrauliche Mitteilung betreff. Raub in Tiflis," Polizeidirektion Munich to EJPD in Berne, Munich, 27 Jan. 1908, in ibid.

[101] Swiss Bundesanwaltschaft to EJPD, Berne, 24 Jan. 1908, in ibid., Archiv-Nr. 14019.

[102] Letter, Département de Justice et Police of Canton Vaud to EJPD, Lausanne, 22 Jan., 1908, in ibid.

[103] It is interesting that the Swiss government in 1919 did initiate an inquiry to find out which Swiss officials in 1917 had permitted Lenin's trip from Zurich to Petrograd, given the dire consequences of that decision. See Willi Gautschi, *Lenin als Emigrant in der Schweiz* (Zurich, 1973), p. 282.

government policy, the protector of the people's democratic right to dissent, and sometimes – but increasingly less so – that of professional security men extending a helping hand to their Russian colleagues.

The protest meeting in France during 1905–6 numbered by the hundreds. Just on 18 February 1905 alone, there were demonstrations announced for twenty-one townships in response to "Bloody Sunday": in Lille, St. Etienne, Limoges, Dijon, Tours, Chartres, Auxerre, Clermont-Ferrand, Châlon-sur-Saône, Sotteville-les-Rouen, Belfort, Decazeville, Dunkerque, Le Havre, Mont-luçon, Sedan, Montceau-les-Mines, Périgueux, Chaumont, Cahors, and Epernay - thus, all over the interior of France, avoiding Paris, but not avoiding two harbors and three mining towns close to the Belgian frontier.[104] On 21 January 1906 a peaceful demonstration was permitted in Cherbourg;[105] On 11 February 1906 the police in Toulon tried to prevent a demonstration outside the Russian consulate and failed. The crowd outside the consulate called for a general strike in Russia to bring down the tsarist regime, for the abolition of all national frontiers, and the establishment of militias in place of standing armies. At a closed meeting afterwards, "the police detectives were recognized and were made to leave the hall."[106]

Perhaps the French police was inclined to be tolerant because many well-known intellectuals took part in the antitsarist movement, "people like Anatole France, Jean Jaurès, university academicians and bourgeois journalists."[107] Also, unlike in Vienna and Berlin, in France revolutionary Russian students participated in the demonstrations. At the *Maison du peuple* in Nancy, on 1 February 1905, thirty Russian students went on stage to sing revolutionary songs and to lead the audience in a rendition of the "Workers' International." A telegram to the Socialist leader Jean Jaurès asked his help to abrogate the Franco-Russian alliance.[108] In Grenoble members of the legislative and municipal council took part in a protest meeting on 9 February 1905, to denounce Nicholas II. Most meetings ended with resolutions that vilified tsarist Russia in the most vehement terms.[109]

A lot had changed in the relations of France and Russia since the conclusion of the Dual Entente ten years earlier. In France, the bitter quarrel over the Dreyfus Affair had made the memory of Sedan, Bismarck, and the Paris Commune seem that much farther away. A younger generation had entered public life, tired of being lectured to by its elders on the need for *revanche*, more aware than they of the social problems raised by industrial capitalism, and skeptical of Russia's com-

---

[104] See announcements of forthcoming demonstrations in *Humanité*, 18 Feb. 1905.
[105] Préfect de la Manche to commissaire de police in Cherbourg, 17 Jan. 1906, in AN (Paris), F7 125 19–20, "Révolution de 1905."
[106] Report by Commissariat Central de Police, Préfecture du Département du Var, Toulon, 12 Feb., 1905, in ibid.
[107] Report by agent "Albert," M/189, Paris, 4 Feb. 1904, in ibid.
[108] Report, *commissaire spécial de police*, gare de Nancy, 1 Feb., 1905, in ibid.
[109] For example, report by the prefect of Yonne to the Sûreté Générale in Paris, Auxerre, 30 Jan. 1905, on a resolution published in *Le Travailleur Socialiste*, in ibid.

mitment to help its French ally against Germany. Not only were French diplomats like Paul Louis in St. Petersburg, G. Bichon in Berne, Descos in Bucharest, and Thiébaud in Stockholm dismayed over the many envoys in the Russian foreign service with a personal liking for imperial Germany, [110] there were also recent signs of increasing cordiality between the Russian and the German police.

In 1902 Peter Rachkovsky, that partisan of the alliance with France, was replaced as head of the Okhrana's foreign agentura in France by Rataiev (1902–5), who after no more than two years was succeeded by Arkadii Harting (1905–9) and then by A. Krassilnikov (1909–17). Under Harting and Krassilnikov, excellent relations developed between the Russian agentura in Paris and the police presidium in Berlin, in particular with Polizeidirektor Dr. Wilhelm Henninger of the Prussian political police. The two agencies cooperated in the surveillance of Russian students in Munich, Darmstadt, and Hamburg, and of the Association of Russian Students in Berlin, which Henninger called "the most important Russian socialist-revolutionary organization in Eastern Europe." They worked together to interdict the smuggling of small arms from Belgium into Russia, to smooth the transport of prisoners across Germany to Russia, and to protect the lives of Russian dignitaries on their private visits to German health spas. Berlin also offered the Russians information from outside Germany: It sent St. Petersburg reports on Yekaterina Breshkovskaia's fund-raising trip to the United States (1904) and on the secret conferences of the Polish National Liga in Budapest and Vienna (1905). [111]

The French government had the more reason to worry about the rapprochement of Germany and Russia in matters of police because Germany at that time benefited from Russia's diversion of her energies away from Europe and into Manchuria and Korea. Playing the role of the good ally, the French government provided the Russian Baltic fleet with logistic assistance on its arduous journey to the Sea of Japan. But when the Russian warships in transit fired on British fishing vessels off the Dogger Bank on 21 October 1904, and French diplomacy had to work hard to bring about an amicable settlement between the two parties, it was Germany once more that offered assistance to Russia in case of conflict with England.

The Dogger Bank incident did not strengthen the Sûreté's faith in the Okhrana's allegiance to its French partner. It was bad enough that the shooting incident was probably provoked by a false report about Japanese torpedo boats in a Norwegian fjord emanating from Harting. Paléologue called it "the knavery of a

---

[110] See their reports in AMAE (Paris), Correspondance politique, Nouvelle Série 1897–1918, Russie, Carton 80: "Protocole. Corps diplomatique et consulaire étranger 1896–1907."

[111] See letter by Mahl of the Berlin police presidium to the department of police, Russian ministry of interior in St. Petersburg, Berlin, 31 Dec. 1904; and Police President von Hellmann of Posen to (not named), Posen, 30 Nov. 1905, in Hoover Inst., Archive of the Imperial Secret Police, index no. Vb, folder 1. But in December 1918, the Prussian political police burned most of the documents concerning its relationship with the Russian Okhrana. Albert C. Grzesinski, *Inside Germany*, trans. by Alexander S. Lipschitz (New York, 1939), p. 126.

low-down policeman [who] nearly caused a wholesale conflagration in Europe."[112] But Harting's act, if true, was consistent with information reaching the Sûreté about the Russian police's growing recklessness, which allegedly included arranging simultaneous attacks on the Russian imperial family in St. Petersburg and President Loubet in Paris so that France would take a harder line against Russian revolutionaries.[113] Perhaps the Russian security system was breaking under the strain of the enormous responsibility it bore as the tsarist regime's last line of defense. In Moscow and St. Petersburg the distinction between government agent provocateurs and rebels was becoming lost. In 1904–5, the tsar's uncle, Grand Duke Sergiei Alexandrovich and the minister of interior, Plehve, were killed by Ezno F. Azev, one of Rataiev's own Okhrana agents and at the same time a revolutionary.[114] In 1911 Prime Minister Stolypin was also murdered by a double agent, Bagrov.[115]

Matters were made worse when the long secret association of Sûreté and Okhrana finally became public knowledge in France. Since 1907 a Russian revolutionary "counter-police" under Vladimir Burtzev was active in Paris to expose the work of Russia's secret police in France. Burtzev, an escaped political convict from Siberia, was known since 1889 to the police in Western Europe as an agitator for open mass revolution in Russia.[116] Efforts by the French ministry of foreign affairs and by the Sûreté to expel Burtzev were blocked by Jean Jaurès who campaigned in the Chamber of Deputies against the Okhrana's foreign agentura: "The existence of this foreign police, without any responsibility and on occasion assisted by the French police, is a standing disgrace. I personally know French citizens who, on French soil, have been subjected to investigation and frisking by Russian police agents!"[117]

When Georges Clemenceau, as minister of interior, tried to disarm Jaurès with a bland assurance that the Russian police was no longer active in France – *"C'est déjà fait, Monsieur Jaurès!"*, the Parisian paper *Le Petit Journal*, on 17 July 1909, quite rightly asked: "But can one be rid of a foreign police if most of its agents are *French* nationals anyway, in the pay of that government?"[118] The editor of *Humanité* was more blunt: "Whom are you trying to deceive? Is not Monsieur Bint, the deputy chief of the Russian police and former assistant to Monsieur Harting, still in France, and still in charge of a team of *mouchards?*"[119]

[112] Maurice Paléologue, *Three Critical Years 1904–05–06* (New York, 1957), p. 148.
[113] Report by agent "Albert," AN (Paris), M/189, Paris, 4 Feb. 1904.
[114] Vladimir Dedijer, "A Guide to Infiltrators," in *New York Review of Books*, 25 Mar. 1971, p. 32.
[115] A. T. Vassilyev, *The Okhrana. The Russian Secret Police* (London, 1930), pp. 84–6.
[116] Report by Swiss Bundesanwaltschaft to EJPD, Berne, 30 Nov. 1903, in BA (Berne), Bestands-Nr. 21, Archiv-Nr. 14014.
[117] "La Police russe en France," in *Journal de Genève*, 18 July 1909.
[118] See clipping in APP (Paris), Carton B A/1693.
[119] "La Police russe en France. 'C'est fait!' De qui se moque-t-on?" in *Humanité*, 3 Aug. 1909. According to Richard J. Johnson, the Russian Agentura around 1904–5 employed 30 Russian "internals" and 40 French "externals" (*mouchards*). Richard J. Johnson, "Zagranichnaia Agentura: The Tsarist Political Police in Europe," in George L. Mosse, ed., *Police Forces in History* (London, 1975), p. 36.

The truth is that the French government could no longer control the presence of the Russian police in France or its activities. Since 1901 the French *Sûreté*, increasingly distrustful, assigned agents to observe the Russian police and commissioned confidential reports about it. A report dated 28 November 1901 is remarkable because of the sense of remoteness from the Okhrana agents in Paris that it conveys:

Monsieur Ratkowsky [sic] is the chief of the Russian police [in France]. He lives in Paris and has his office in the rue de Grenelle [the Russian embassy]. His power extends to all the towns in France and to many towns elsewhere in Europe. He has earned the title of excellency for assuring the safety of the Tsar during his last two trips abroad. He has at his disposal a large number of Russian and French agents and enormous sums of money. Among his French agents is a retired Sûreté official called Fernbach, who lives in a comfortable apartment in either 62 or 72, avenue d'Orléans, Paris VIIe. He receives 500 francs per month and reports to Ratkowsky daily between 3 and 5 p.m. The Russian emperor has given him a gold watch. – Manouiloff at the Russian embassy in Rome, and Popoff and Bourdonkoff at the Russian embassy in London perform similar functions to Ratkowsky's. The three men came to Paris last month to confer with Monsieur Ratkowsky.[120]

There was of course no alternative to France but to remain loyal to the Russian alliance even after – or perhaps especially after – 1905, however much Russia's prestige had declined because of the military debacle in Manchuria and the chaos in its cities. Another Sûreté report on the Okhrana, this one dated October 1913, argued the utility of associating with the Russian police – but not much more.

The Russian embassy has for many years maintained a service here whose purpose is to investigate and to watch trouble makers who are Russian nationals.
 The functionaries who run this service have always kept in touch, unofficially, with the Sûreté's Third *brigade de recherches*. In return we have on occasion asked for their assistance because there are items of intelligence which we cannot obtain without their intercession.
 Presently M. Krassilnikoff heads this special service at the Russian embassy.
 This functionary has several employees subordinated to him, among them M. Bitard-Monin. Generally, it is with the latter that we conduct our business.
 The information we provide to Bitard-Monin – incidentally, always by word of mouth only – exclusively concerns Russian revolutionaries and Russian anarchists in Paris.
 It seems useful that we should continue with this tradition, seeing that with our limited resources we could not ourselves provide an efficacious preventive surveillance over the many Russian revolutionaries and anarchists in our capital.[121]

[120] "La Police russe à Paris," report by Police Municipale *(confidentiel)*, dated Paris, 28 Nov. 1901, in AN (Paris), F7 12519–20.
[121] "Au sujet: Police russe," report marked "received" 29 Octo, 1913, in APP (Paris), Carton B A/1693.

4

War and revolution, 1914–1922

The assassination of Archduke Franz Ferdinand
in Sarajevo, 1914

General remarks

Every historian who has written on the causes of the First World War has included in his account a description of the assassination of the Austrian heir, Archduke Franz Ferdinand, and of his wife, the Countess Chotek, in Sarajevo on 28 June 1914. The motive for this double murder has not caused much disagreement. Contemporaries and historians alike have recognized it as the product of a sweltering feud between Serbia and the Habsburg monarchy dating from 1903. What the Austrian vice-consul in Niš reported about the views held among Serbian patriots in his town shortly after the double murder reflected prevailing opinion: Franz Ferdinand had to die because of his imminent succession to the Austro-Hungarian throne. Once becoming emperor, Franz Ferdinand was expected to attack Serbia forthwith because Russia, Serbia's great pan-Slav protector, would not be ready, militarily, to enter a war on its side for another five to six years.[1]

It follows that most historians of 1914 have also mentioned the police problem facing Austria at that time. What they have not examined is whether Austria's police service in 1914 was guilty of negligence and incompetence, or whether the security needs, particularly in the Balkans, were no longer manageable by the police of the European states working only within their own territorial jurisdictions.

The question of an Austrian police failure

Had the security for the Austrian heir and his wife at Sarajevo been sufficiently rigorous, and were the Austrians laying the blame on Serbia to cover the failure

[1] Austro-Hungarian vice consul in Niš to Berchtold, 20 July 1914, in HHStA (Vienna), 810 P.A.I. Liasse Krieg (früher Interna LXX), 1. Teil, "Attentat auf Erzh. Franz Ferdinand 28 Juli [sic] 1914," (hereafter: HHStA (Vienna), Liasse Krieg).

of their own police? On the basis of the fear and frustration expressed by Leon von Bilinski and General Oscar Potiorek, the civilian and the military officials responsible for Bosnia in 1914, it would seem that at least the authorities along the frontier of the Habsburg Empire were quite unprepared for the task of protecting so important and controversial a public figure. A letter by Bilinski to Potiorek, written under the immediate shock of the event, reflects fear and indecision, since he apparently did not know whether he should speak for the two of them or only for himself, leaving to Potiorek all the possible blame:

Had I been able to learn from Your Excellency's reports how inadequate our police is for the task at hand, the two of us [sic: I, for one?] obviously would have felt duty-bound to prevent this trip at all cost. I was frightened when I read the semi-official disclosure of the newspapers that the political police disposes of no more than 120 officials.[2]

The impression of helplessness is confirmed by the reminiscences of L. Stoichka, an official of the political police in Vienna, who in June 1914 belonged to a team of security experts detailed to Sarajevo as consultants to the local police. Stoichka found that the local chief of political police was inexperienced and incompetent, and worse, that the leading police officials in Bosnia had for years been afraid to inform their superiors in Vienna (including the emperor) of the widespread hostility toward Austrian rule among the mass of the population.[3] He and his colleagues were furthermore shocked when, shortly after the assassination the police of Sarajevo began to round up hundreds of suspects and had them stand against the wall in the courtyard of the townhall for hours on end, alternatively questioning them and beating them with fists and sticks. The police also allowed widespread looting by Croatians and Bosnians of Serbian-owned stores and homes.

We ventured to voice some objections to this manner of treating prisoners, which we had never seen before. Our objections were not appreciated. . . . Never in my life have I witnessed worse violence being done to human dignity. . . . So this is how during the past quarter century we have tried to win the love of this people for Austrian rule . . . We finally understood that what we were seeing was a punitive expedition wanted by the authorities, an expedition of the kind so-called cultured states launch against obstreperous natives in their colonies.[4]

A dispute over police rights and police competence

On 11 July 1914 Dr. Friedrich von Wiesner proceeded to Sarajevo on a three-day mission of inquiry. Wiesner was not a police official but a former judge and state

---

[2] Gemeinsamer Finanzminister R. von Bilinski to Landeschef Feldzeugmeister Potiorek in Sarajevo, Vienna, 3 July, 1914, in ibid., 2. Teil. Bilinski's apprehension may have been heightened by the fact that he personally had failed to follow up hints given to him by Serbian sources that Franz Ferdinand might face assassination in Sarajevo.

[3] L. Stoichka, "Das Attentat von Sarajevo im Jahre 1914 und seine wahren Ursachen," (typescript, n.d.) in AVA (Vienna), S.D. Parl. Klub 103, folder: "150 Attentat von Sarajevo."

[4] Ibid.

prosecutor, working as a councillor (*Sektionsrat*) in the Austrian ministry of foreign affairs. But since he was experienced with criminal cases he was dispatched to the scene in order to sift the police findings for evidence that might directly link the crime to the Serbian government. He was also asked to recommend demands that Vienna could justifiably present to Belgrade in the interest of better security in this region of the Habsburg Empire.

The Wiesner mission was not important in determining Foreign Minister Berthold's and Prime Minister Tisza's decision on war and peace — that decision was made in Vienna and Budapest on the basis of higher considerations of state interest. And yet, had Wiesner produced dramatic evidence of Serbian complicity, his mission might conceivably have influenced the course of events. Although detectives and criminologists could not offer scientific answers except to very technical questions — and even then still often proved fallible — at least the use of police findings to reach policy decisions (or to justify policy decisions to the public) had becoming much more acceptable by the turn of the century. What was needed was more trust in the accuracy and integrity of professional police work. The Wiesner report of 13 July 1914 was probably too careful to serve the immediate political purpose of the Austrian government. "Evidence dating from before the assassination does not show promotion of propaganda by the Serbian government," Wiesner wrote.

There is some material indicating that the Serbian government has tolerated this movement; it is scant but sufficient. The investigation of the assassination has yielded no proof that the Serbian government knew about it, helped in its preparation, or provided the weapons. There are not even grounds enough to suspect it. On the contrary, there are indications that rule out such complicity.[5]

So Wiesner had to be largely ignored. But unlike in the Dreyfus case in France (1894–1906) and the Friedjung case in Austria-Hungary (1908), no forged evidence was used in this investigation.[6] And Wiesner wrote his report knowing that what he had to say would not please his superiors. Like Stoichka he tried to respect individual rights and apply standards of legal truth which were fundamental to the principles of modern police.

In a similar display of professional correctness the police in Munich on 3 July returned confiscated posters in cyrillic print to Serbian students after a translation revealed that the text did not celebrate the murder of Franz Ferdinand but only appealed for donations to the families of Serbian soldiers killed in the last war.[7] However, there were others who insisted on "correct" judicial procedure for po-

---

[5] Handwritten document, available in HHStA (Vienna), Liasse Krieg, 2. Teil.
[6] In the Dreyfus case forged documents were placed by someone in the 2e Bureau in the file of the accused. In the Friedjung case, the defendant was the historian, Professor Heinrich Friedjung, who unwittingly had written an article denouncing Serbian parliamentarians on the basis of falsified evidence.
[7] Report by A.-H. minister to Bavaria Vecics, Munich, 4 July 1914, in HHStA (Vienna), Liasse Krieg, 2. Teil.

litical ends. *Stampa,* in Belgrade, came out with an article arguing – successfully, as it turned out – that because Princip was underage he could not be sentenced to death under Austrian law: "If the Austrian authorities have different information [as to his age] let them produce honest and believable witnesses, so long as their witnesses are not those 'life failures' [*verkrachte Existenzen*] who staff the Sarajevo police."[8]

The Austrians, in turn, distrusted the Serbian police from the very beginning of the crisis. On 30 June Dr. Wilhelm Ritter von Storck, the chargé d'affaires at the Austrian legation in Belgrade, had a stormy meeting with the secretary general of the Serbian ministry of foreign affairs, Count Gruic. In his report to Berchtold he offered this version of the interview:

I asked [Gruic] the obvious question what the Royal [Serbian] police had done, or is planning to do, in order to investigate the plot which reputedly can be traced back to Serbian territory. His answer was that until now the Serbian police had not concerned itself with this matter at all. I became indignant when my interlocutor asked me in a self-complacent [*süffisant*] tone, whether I wanted to submit an official request to this effect. I answered Herr Gruic with some heat "That I had received no orders from my government, but that I did not hesitate to ask him these questions because in my view the Serbian police had an elementary duty to undertake the measures that I was talking about." I told him once more that I, Herr von Storck, felt compelled to tell him, Count Gruic, that I was frankly dumbfounded at the thought that the Royal police might only do something following an official [Austrian] request.[9]

What results von Storck expected the Serbian police to produce is, of course, quite another matter; probably very little. A few days after his meeting with Gruic, he wrote to Berchtold (3 July):

I would still prefer to assume that we are only up against Serbian sloppiness [*Schlamperei*]. I would rather not think that Herr Pasic, who as the senior statesman now wants to take this matter in hand by himself, intended a hideous irony when he stood with me at the catafalk of our Archduke and assured me in a voice ringing with sincerity that Serbia henceforth would be just as concerned for the safety of foreign crowned monarchs as for its own. Have not the Serbs butchered their own last but one king?[10]

There was little prospect of police help from Serbia to curb the wave of terrorism in Bosnia, Herzegovina, and Albania, according to Storck, despite Pasic's promise to the diplomatic corps in Belgrade, that Serbia would now take steps to suppress anarchism by banning the export of arms and explosives. Storck wrote, "I would like to believe that the royal Serbian government had no knowledge of the murder plot. But a certain number of people did, people whom the Serbian police should have been watching. However, so long as you belong to the

[8] Report by A.-H. consulate in Mitrovitza, 5 July 1914, in ibid.
[9] Telegram, Legationsrat Wilhelm Ritter von Storck to Berchtold, Belgrade, 30 June 1914, in ibid.
[10] Letter, Storck to Berchtold, "Betreff. Staatspolizeiliche Unterstützung der k. u. k. Gesandtschaft durch die serbische Regierung," Belgrade, 3 July 1914, in ibid.

odbrana, you are safe from any importuning by the police."[11] In Storck's eyes the situation in the Balkans was unmanageable by methods of police and he wished for a swift military expedition against Serbia.[12] His superior, Minister Giesl, shared his doubts about the Serbian police as a guarantor of peace and order. On 12 July he warned about a possible popular outbreak against all Austrian subjects in Serbia. "Neither lives nor property are to be spared, houses are to be destroyed. Police and gendarmerie will presumably do nothing."[13]

Distrust of the Serbian police was not merely the personal prejudice of a few Austrian diplomats. At the Berlin Congress in 1878, the Western powers had all agreed that the Ottoman Empire needed foreign help to introduce modern methods of enforcing civil order in the Balkans. An incident during the Sarajevo crisis may be cited here for the lighter side that it throws on the police conditions in this region of prewar Europe: "For the past 24 hours," reported the Austrian legation in Centinje on 5 July 1914, "The King [Nicholas of Montenegro] has personally prevented a demonstration against Austria by forbidding all Montenegrian subjects to take part in such an action. In his patriarchal manner of ruling, the King himself has assumed *le policement des rues* – the policing of the streets."[14] The legation amplified this story the following day by describing how the king had personally held back a crowd of people outside the fence of the legation garden by sitting in his automobile and hitting out at the demonstrators with a big stick.

Could one possibly describe the difficulties between Austria-Hungary and Serbia as a dispute over policing rights and policing needs – the right of the Serbian kingdom to exercise police power independently on its territory, and the policing need of the Habsburg monarchy, where Bosnia could not be pacified without suppressing the irredentist elements operating from their Serbian sanctuary? If so, we are ready to enlarge our conception of "international police work" beyond the collaboration of border police for the suppression of banditry or the pooling of information to hunt down international swindlers and anarchists.[15] International policing might in the future require the standardization of police doctrine and police methods between countries whose security needs could no longer be provided by their respective police forces acting independently.[16]

---

[11] Letter, Storck to Berchtold, Belgrade, 9 July 1914, in ibid. Also Minster Giesl to the ministry of foreign affairs in Vienna, Belgrade, 17 July 1914, in ibid., concerning a member of the Serbian secret police who on that day was reported traveling incognito to Bosnia on a mission for the *Narodna Odbrana*.

[12] Letter, Storck to Berchtold, Belgrade, 1 July 1914, in ibid.

[13] Telegram, Baron Giesl to the ministry of foreign affairs in Vienna, Belgrade, 12 July 1914, in ibid.

[14] Message signed Hofrat Budisavljevic, of the A.-H. ministry of interior, as conveyed in a telegram by Bezirkshauptmannschaft Cattaro to Statthalterei-Präsidium in Zara, 7 July 1914, in ibid.

[15] Tagesbericht [of the foreign ministry], Vienna, 2 July 1914, in ibid.

[16] See telegram, Russia chargé d'affaires in Paris to Sazonov in St. Petersburg, Paris, 13/26 July 1914, no. 187: The German ambassador has informed the French minister of justice that Austria intends no attack on Serbian integrity. "Son seul but était d'assurer sa propre sécurité et de faire la police." René Marchand, ed., *Un Livre noir. Diplomatie d'avant-guerre d'après les documents des archives russes* (Paris, 1923), vol. 2, p. 278.

The charge of poor policing, incidentally, was not levied only by Austria against Serbia, but also vice versa. A leading Serbian daily *Politika*, on 1 July 1914 lambasted the Habsburg monarchy for the many inequities of its traditional police order:

> The cause of these murders [in Sarajevo] was not and is not Serbia, but a certain regime with a history of violent enserfment of entire nations, a history of the strangest legal court actions, and of ruthless attacks on the dignity and liberty of individuals. Not Serbia but the sufferings inflicted on state and nation by the police regime and terrorism of the house of Habsburg and its monarchy are the cause of all its woes.

How could Serbia be held responsible for the Carbonari movement of the early nineteenth century, the editors of *Politika* continued, and for the conspiracies against Austrian rule in Venice and Lombardy? Did Serbia bribe the Mexicans to shoot Emperor Maximilian? Were Serbs implicated in the deaths of Crown Prince Rudolf and Empress Elisabeth?[17]

The dispute between Vienna and Belgrade was not then described as a dispute over police jurisdiction, nor has it been so described in later historical literature. It consequently did not serve to advance the cause of international police collaboration. Austrian diplomats in Serbia undertook clandestine detective jobs in July 1914 that normally are regarded as highly unsuitable for officials in their positions. The Austrian consul in Uesküb (Skopje) volunteered to discover the name of a Serbian officer whose brother he said had trained the Sarajevo killers in revolver shooting. Dr. Storck was commissioned by the Austrian police post in Semlin to verify the identity of a Russian resident in Belgrade. Storck also hired a confidential agent to find out more about the *narodna odbrana* organization. The same agent and a local schoolmaster were given 100 dinars each for screening Serbian schoolbooks for anti-Austrian passages. Baron Giesl, the Austrian minister, undertook to find out particulars about two frontier guards mentioned in the Wiesner report as having allowed the killers to pass into Bosnia. He also tried to find out whether a shooting range existed in Topcida and the exact location of two cafés in Belgrade where the plotters had allegedly met. We must assume that the Austrian diplomats undertook these unusual tasks because they expected no help from the local police. The results of these inquiries were obviously intended to lend criminalistic support to an indictment of the Serbian government before world opinion. It would have justified the Austrian ultimatum of 23 July 1914, which included demands that clearly trespassed on the police sovereignty of a neighboring state, to wit:

> The royal [Serbian] government declares its disapproval and repudiation of any intention to interfere with the fate of people living in any portion of the Austro-Hungarian Empire. It recognizes as its duty formally to appraise all military officers, all civil officials, and the whole population of the kingdom of its intention henceforth to proceed with the greatest

---

[17] German translation of editorial in *Politika* (Belgrade, 1 July 1914), in HHStA (Vienna), Liasse Krieg, 2. Teil.

vigor against all persons who are guilty of such activities, activities that it will prevent and repress with every means at its disposal.

[Paragraph 5] It is ready to accept the collaboration in Serbia of organs of the Imperial and royal [Austrian] government in the suppression of the subversive movement directed against the integrity of the [Austrian] monarchy. [18]

These demands have often been criticized as overly harsh and clearly intended to provoke rejection by Serbia. Yet imposing a one-sided police tutelage over weaker neighboring states had been an Austrian practice since the days of Chancellor Metternich. Only a few years previously, the European powers had concurred in pressuring Switzerland to modify its police laws following the assassination of Austrian Empress Elisabeth. Metternichianism was furthermore not the only example Austria might cite in 1914 of foreign police operating on the territory of another state. What about the Okhrana in Paris? On 20 July, as the Austrian ultimatum was being delivered to Minister Giesl in Belgrade, the Austrian embassy in Paris received an urgent request to send Vienna a report on the Russian security service in France: "It would be most interesting for us to obtain authentic information concerning the existence of this foreign police agency, particularly in regard to the question whether [or not] it was established with the explicit consent of the French government." [19]

The memory of the recent revolutionary troubles in Russia and of Russia's leading role in promoting a conservative police alliance against subversion throughout Europe prompted Conrad von Hötzendorff on 26 July – two days before Austria declared war on Serbia – to propose threatening Russia with the abrogation of the police treaty of 1904.

I know that the imperial and royal ministry of foreign affairs is . . . bent on doing everything it can to prevent Russia's intervention in favor of Serbia and against [our] monarchy. For this reason I have the honor of drawing attention to a suggestion which has been made to me confidentially. It seems to me that it might influence the Russian government in the manner we desire. [The suggestion is] that we cancel the existing police treaty [with Russia]. There is no doubt but that it will be effective as a means of exerting pressure. [20]

Austria did receive spontaneous assistance from the police authorities of Italy and Germany, its partners in the Triple Alliance. The police of Turin and of Bonn sent notices to the Polizei-Direktion in Vienna about suspects who seemed to have known something about the Sarajevo assassination before 28 June. [21] The Berlin police raided the rooms of Serbian students in Charlottenburg and allowed the

---

[18] A copy of the Austrian ultimatum to Serbia, which was sent to Baron Giesl on 20 July 1914, is available in ibid.

[19] Telegram, ministry of foreign affairs to Ambassador Graf Szécsen in Paris, Vienna, 20 July 1914, in ibid.

[20] Letter, Conrad von Hötzendorff to Berchtold, Vienna, 26 July 1914, Evb. Nr. 2786, in ibid., 3. Teil.

[21] Telegram, A.-H. ambassador to Italy, von Merey, Rome, 2 July 1914; and A.-H. consulate general in Cologne, 29 June 1914, in ibid.

Austrian consul general to examine the confiscated materials.[22] Even Bulgaria sent a warning to Austria about information it had on a new secret society of assassins in Belgrade.[23] No encouragement, however, was forthcoming from France, Russia, and England. In Paris President Poincaré expressed France's condolences to Ambassador Szecsen on 4 July 1914. Poincaré said he was convinced that Serbia would show the greatest cooperation in the investigation of the murder and the prosecution of all accomplices. "No state could evade this responsibility."[24] But Poincaré's endorsement of the principle of international solidarity against terrorism did not prevent him from supporting Russia's unqualified support of the Serbian cause on his visit to St. Petersburg two weeks later. England also was noncommittal. In a conversation with the foreign secretary, Sir Edward Grey, on 17 July, Count Mensdorff emphasized that the aim of pan-Serbian propaganda was "to produce revolutionary movements inside territories that formed an integral part of the [Habsburg] monarchy. No state can accept this, no matter how peace-loving it is. Sir Edward agreed, but would not be drawn into an elaboration of this theme."[25]

The Austrian ultimatum was handed to Serbia on 23 July 1914. It was rejected by the Serbian government on 25 July, and on 28 July Austria formally declared war on Serbia. How the conflict between these two states quickly escalated into full-scale war between the two alliance blocs of Europe is a story many times told. It need not preoccupy us in this study, the less so as with the outbreak of war the police authorities in every country were swiftly subordinated to the command of the military.

The outbreak of the First World War

German mobilization

Of all the prospective belligerents of the coming war, Germany had the most elaborate mobilization plans. Germany depended on the *va banque* strategy devised between 1892 and 1905 by Count Alfred von Schlieffen, of quickly annihilating the French armies in a lightning invasion through Belgium before Russia could bring the full weight of its enormous manpower to bear against the Central Powers.[26] There could be no hitch in the clockwork execution of the German mobilization plan because it involved millions of soldiers and sailors, railway and postal employees, newspaper staff, and all the government officials from the imperial level down to the smallest townhall clerk. The fear of foreign agents

---

[22] Letter, Ambassador Szögyeny to Berchtold, Berlin, 9 July 1914, in ibid.

[23] Report from A.-H. military attaché to chief of Austrian general staff, Belgrade, 4 July 1914, Nr. 125, in ibid.

[24] Telegram, Count Szecsen to Austrian foreign ministry, Paris, 4 July 1914, in ibid.

[25] Letter, Ambassador Mensdorff to Berchtold, London, 17 July 1914, in ibid.

[26] See Gerhard Ritter, *Der Schlieffenplan* (Munich, 1956).

who might sabotage this operation reached a point bordering on hysteria in the month of August. A flamboyant admonition, issued to his men by the police director of Stuttgart, was swiftly passed on to the police administrations of all German towns.[27]

Policemen! The inhabitants are beginning to go crazy. Our streets are filled with old women of both sexes in pursuit of unworthy activities. Everyone sees in his neighbor a Russian or a French spy and believes himself duty-bound to beat him up – and also to beat up the policeman who comes to his rescue. . . . As far as we can determine, nothing – absolutely nothing – has so far happened that constitutes a threat to us. Nevertheless we seem to be living in a madhouse, and this at a time when anyone but a coward or a lazybones should be calmly going about his duties. . . . Policemen, keep your heads, continue to act like men and not like old women, don't be taken in, keep alert, do your duty!

Neither the police director of Stuttgart nor the police president of Berlin thought it necessary to alert his subordinates to the danger of socialist strikes against militarism and war. Shortly before Sarajevo, the Prussian ministry of interior had issued a new set of instructions banning the use of red flags or Polish national colors during street demonstrations as "contrary to good order."[28] After Sarajevo all this was forgotten as the workers flocked to the induction centers and the authorities quietly dropped the long-standing prohibition of Socialist literature inside army barracks. The Socialist paper, *Vorwärts,* called for workers' demonstrations against war on 28 July, just before Austria declared war on Serbia, but A. H. Kober's account of Berlin on the night of 31 July mentions only one lone workman climbing out of a gully in a deserted street to blaspheme those who had led the country into war.[29] The historian, Friedrich Meinecke, described 3 August as "one of the most beautiful moments in my life," so relieved he felt when the Socialists in the Reichstag voted in favor of war credits.[30] The same fear of workers' unrest had prompted the kaiser at the outbreak of war to proclaim a Burgfrieden among Germans of all classes. The police appeared to be the only ones in Germany not really worried about the workers' patriotism. Perhaps it had known all along about the existence of a de facto "Burgfrieden."

The workers of Berlin

Because the patriotism of the workers was essential for Germany's war effort in the next four years, and no less so for its survival in the face of Bolshevik sub-

[27] See "Polizeibericht," in *Die Polizei,* 11. Jhg., Nr. 11, 20 Aug. 1914, p. 273.
[28] "Verbot roter Fahnen, revolutionärer oder nationalpolnischer Abzeichen bei öffentlichen Aufzügen," in ibid., Nr. 7, 25 June, 1914, p. 166.
[29] Robert Scholz, "Ein unruhiges Jahrzehnt. Lebensmittelunruhen, Massenstreiks, und Arbeitslosenkrawalle in Berlin, 1914–23," in Manfred Galius, et al., *Pöbelexzesse und Volkstumulte in Berlin. Zur Sozialgeschichte der Strasse (1830–1980)* (Berlin, 1984), pp. 79ff.; and A. H. Kober, *Einst in Berlin* (Hamburg, 1956), p. 253.
[30] Friedrich Meinecke, *Erlebtes 1862/1919* (Stuttgart, 1964), p. 246; also his "Sozialdemokratie und Machtpolitik," in Friedrich Thimme and Carl Legien, eds., *Die Arbeiterschaft im Neuen Deutschland* (Leipzig, 1915), pp. 21–2.

version in 1918, a word must be said about the working-class movement in Berlin which Victor Tissot in 1882 had found so important for the future of Europe.[31] By the 1890s the fear of a workers' rebellion was largely gone. After the Rome Conference of 1898 the Berlin police presidium, as we have seen, even reported anarchists in Germany dropping out of the movement. Had not August Bebel, the chairman of the Social Democratic Party, himself dismissed the importance of that conference precisely because anarchism to him was irrelevant to the German workers?[32] Everyone knew that the German Socialist movement, because it was so self-assured, had no need to resort to violence, and because of its discipline was easily policed from outside.

The chief reason why the Berlin workers of the 1890s appeared very different from the discontented, sullen, and embittered rabble whom French police spies had seen in the 1870s was the improvement in Germany's overall standard of living. By the turn of the century good order in Berlin could be achieved by the application of all the classical methods of modern police, such as the exploitation of class rivalry in a society where rich and poor alike believed in success through individual initiative, or the introduction of new forms of control in the name of scientific progress and social reform. In addition, the fundamental Prussian police principle of the Burgfrieden was still effective in disciplining the lower classes. Their loyalty was ultimately secured by appeals to their pride in the fatherland and their distrust of Germany's jealous neighbors France, Russia, and England.[33]

But managing the workers was hampered by the existence of the short-sighted middle class and upper class and a very conservative church. The notion of the Berlin worker as "scornful, brutal, and uncompromisingly hostile" was still widely held by both burghers and nobility.[34] Had it been true, the Berlin police would have turned into a security service as ruthless as the tsarist police in Moscow and St. Petersburg. But knowing better, the police imposed no more than an irritating censorship on left-wing theatrical productions and literature, mild enough for the works of Max Kretzer, Gerhart Hauptmann, and Hermann Sudermann to score at least some modest success.[35] The vigorous Socialist campaign against church membership in the opening years of the new century, while it caused much alarm in court circles, was never seriously impeded.[36] Aside from

[31] See "Le Socialisme allemand," and "L'État moral de Berlin," in Victor Tissot, *Russes et allemands* (Paris, 1882).

[32] August Bebel, "Attentate und Sozialdemokratie," (Berlin, 1898), passim.

[33] Joseph Bader, *Jugend in der Industriekultur. Ihre Verhaltensweise zwischen Ideologie und Apparatur 1910–1933–1960* (Munich, 1962), pp. 69–70, 87.

[34] See for example Otto von Leixner, *Soziale Briefe aus Berlin* (Berlin, 1894).

[35] Samples of police-censored plays for the 1890s are available in the Social Democratic party (SPD) achive in Berlin. See also Siegfried Nestriepke, *Geschichte der Volksbühne Berlin* (Berlin, 1930), 2 vols.; and on the leniency of censorship, Otto Graf zu Stolberg-Wernigerode, *Die unentschiedene Generation* (Munich, 1968), pp. 74–75.

[36] On the antichurch campaign, see Bruno Violet, *Die Kirchenaustrittsbewegung* (Berlin, 1914); W. Ilgenstein, *Die religiöse Gedankenwelt der Sozialdemokratie* (Berlin, 1914); and Paul Piechowski, *Proletarischer Glaube* (Berlin, 1927).

noting down any attacks on religion during Social Democratic meetings – which did have a certain intimidating effect – there was no police interference with the "Socialist terrorism" waged against proletarian churchgoers. Vast rallies held by antireligious organizations in 1913 were left unmolested, and advertisements in the *Vorwärts* instructing its readers how to go about resigning their church membership were not suppressed. At the height of this anti-Christian campaign, a Berlin plumber named Bauer was arrested and fined 30 marks for distributing Otto Lehmann-Russbüldt's atheistic pamphlet, *"Der geistige Befreiungskrieg 1913."* Bauer appealed the sentence, which was reduced to 15 marks. When he appealed again, his sentence was further cut to 5 marks or one day in jail.[37]

The SPD and the trade unions had to fight for the allegiance of the rank and file, oftentimes in competition with one another, and to some extent in rivalry with institutions which in Marxist theory belonged to the enemy camp. Among these institutions were the municipal elementary schools and public libraries, where the workers found access to some of the education they yearned for, and the singing and athletic clubs and private allotment gardens (*Schrebergärten*), which the Socialists deplored as "petty bourgeois" but the workers cherished as a healthy form of family recreation.

All this should reaffirm the importance of individualism for effective police work in modern Western society. The Berlin workman was policeable because he did not behave as if he were a member of a collective. And the Socialist-run organizations he belonged to were policeable because they knew they could *not* count on their members' unquestioning class allegiance in a showdown with the authorities. Finally, the workers in Wilhelmine Berlin were policeable because they lived in one of the most exciting world cities at the dawn of a new age in which the future seemed to belong not to the traditional upper classes but to anyone who was young, keen, and adventurous.

Still, there is no denying that the Socialist Party in the years before the First World War won the sympathy of many workers through deft propaganda. One reason for its success was that it repeatedly could fool the Berlin police into treating the most innocent Socialist events as if they belonged to a vast plan to subvert all established society. The unsophisticated subaltern constables who were detailed to watch workers' rallies often misinterpreted the meaning of fiery Socialist slogans and banners.[38] Repeated police interdictions of popular cultural events sooner or later forced many law-abiding workers to choose between openly espousing the working-class movement or submitting to the petty chicanery of the police and the upper classes. The decision of so many in favor of Socialism was

---

[37] "Eine Bestrafung für Kirchenaustrittspropaganda," in *Das Monistische Jahrhundert*, 2. Jhg., Heft 6 (10 May 1913), p. 162.

[38] Samples of police reports about workers' rallies in the 1890s are available at SPD Library (Berlin). Friedrich Engels in 1884 very rightly called the police in Germany "the worst possible troops they could have sent against us." See Dieter Fricke, *Bismarcks Prätorianer. Die Berliner politische Polizei im Kampf gegen die deutsche Arbeiterbewegung, 1871–1898* (East Berlin, 1962), p. 67.

made that much easier by the fact that the SPD. refrained from using violence against the police and rather fought the authorities with printed sallies and ridicule. There were only a few violent encounters between police and workers at the turn of the century, the worst one in Berlin-Moabit in 1910, in the course of which one workman was killed. The ensuing investigation reprimanded the police for acting too hastily.[39] The police was the loser in 1893 also, when it arrested the seamstress Ottilie Baader, a well-known Socialist agitator, for incitement to violence, won its case in court, but then had to swallow the judge's slight to its intelligence: "The defendant may have meant 'spiritual weapons,' . . . but most of her audience was on the same intellectual level as the policeman, and *he* had understood her to say something different."[40]

In the last analysis the police had to endure the mocking scorn of the Socialists because their biting attacks were, in fact, official party disclaimers of revolutionary intentions, and that disclaimer was what really mattered in the end.[41] The passage below is from an editorial in the *Vorwärts* from the year 1908:

The grisly tale, that yesterday the unpatriotic characters in Rixdorf were about to seize power, that revolutionary armies were to march directly on Berlin and to subjugate the Reich capital, obviously had reached the Alexanderplatz [police headquarters]. Here the danger was met with the customary show of bravery. All the available men were called out to help smother the wicked plan of the Rixdorfers. They were very successful. They were so successful indeed, that any objective person could see that the warlike preparations of the police were quite unnecessary, and smile with disdain as if to say: Yes, watching unemployed workmen is easier than catching murderers.[42]

Still, the Socialist Party's inability to influence the workers' attitude toward the army was a measure of its limited hold over the rank and file. This did not change when Wilhelm II gave his notorious address to army recruits in 1891, in which he told them they had to obey him even if he ordered them to shoot at their own fathers and brothers – a veiled reference to the possibility of a workers' uprising.[43] This particular incident, loudly denounced by all critics of the Wilhelmine regime, was mainly thought to exemplify the emperor's political ineptitude and his childish boastfulness. Wilhelm's gaffe did not affect recruitment or influence army discipline. The workers, for example, gave little support to the Socialist platform of pacifism. When, in 1912, the German Social Democratic Party together with the British Labor Party called an extraordinary international Socialist congress in Basel it proved difficult to persuade the German labor unions to dispatch representatives to this congress. The Balkan wars and the naval rivalry

[39] Henri Moysset, *L'esprit public en Allemagne* (Paris, 1911), pp. 106–44.
[40] Ottilie Baader, *Ein steiniger Weg,. Lebenserinnerungen* (Berlin, 1921), pp. 38–9.
[41] On the absence of widespread fear of revolution, see also Robert W. Lougee, "The Anti-Revolution Bill of 1894 in Wilhelmine Germany," in *Central European History*, vol. XV, no. 3 (Sept. 1982), pp. 224–40.
[42] Editorial in *Vorwärts*, 6 Feb. 1908.
[43] Bernstein, *Berliner Arbeiter-Bewegung*, vol. III, p. 2.

between Germany and England, which alerted much of Europe to the danger of war, did not interest the common workers.[44]

The Prussian government nevertheless worried about the loyalty of socialist workers serving in the army. Three years after the fall of Bismarck's anti-Socialist law, the Prussian war ministry submitted a memorandum to the ministry of justice, proposing new measures for the suppression of revolutionary agitation in the military.[45] The war ministry's proposal was readily approved by the other cabinet members, including the Prussian minister of interior, von Eulenburg. Eulenburg proposed to extend the ban to the mere possession of Socialist literature by soldiers, but he also cautioned: "These prohibitions will not prevent the entry of Socialist influences in the Army. In view of the shortened time of service, the only effective way to proceed is to concentrate all efforts at maximizing the educational impact of military training on the rank and file."[46]

The difficulty was that soldiers off duty might unwittingly attend popular dances and other amusements sponsored by Socialist organizations. Consequently the army had to rely on the local police to inform it of social events that should be out of bounds to soldiers. Such restrictions were not thought unduly harsh in view of the very disciplined nature of military life in general. In fact, reminding the soldiers of their unconditional subordination to the king was considered the best counter-measure to the perfidious propaganda of the revolutionaries. This point was made again during a discussion of a revised penal code for the Prussian army in 1901, which attached special importance to the king's role as supreme judge in all disciplinary matters:

The soldier must know that his submission to the warlord's authority and protection is absolute. He must know that he can look to the king's mercy to alleviate a punishment lawfully meted out by a military judge but that may be too harsh. The royal power to confirm or to soften the punishment of a soldier strengthens the authority of the warlord and of military discipline in general.[47]

The confidence of the army that at the turn of the century it still could expect young industrial workers to submit unconditionally to their sovereign ruler by the grace of God may appear anachronistic, but it was on the whole vindicated by experience. Barring a few cases of mutiny by soldiers against exceptionally cruel officers, antimilitarism in Wilhelmine Germany was limited to the Social Dem-

[44] This correspondence between the Generalkommission der Gewerkschaften Deutschlands and the individual unions in 1912 is available in the SPD Library (Berlin).

[45] See von Kaltenborn, Prussian ministry of war, to the minister of justice, Dr. von Schelling, Rigi-First, 2 Aug. 1893, in GPStA (Berlin), Rep. 84a/2325, Acta d. Justiz-Min. betreff. "Massnahmen gegen das Eindringen von Umsturzbestrebungen in die Armee 1894–1914;" also Martin Kitchen, *The German Officer Corps, 1890–1914* (Oxford, 1968), p. 153.

[46] Minister of interior, von Eulenburg, to Schelling, St. Moritz-Bad, 14 Aug. 1893, in GPStA (Berlin), Rep. 84a/2325.

[47] Speech by Beckh (Coburg) in Reichstag debate of 4 Mar. 1901, as recorded in GPStA (Berlin), Rep. 84a/2352, Acten des Justiz-Min. betreff. "Die Kriminalstatistik für das Deutsche Heer und die Kaiserliche Marine."

ocratic Party leadership and to the editors of the satirical journal *Simplicissimus*. The exploits of a middle-aged cobbler named Wilhelm Voigt – a jailbird who in 1906 was denied a residence permit by the precinct police of several Berlin boroughs and ended up holding up the townhall of Berlin-Köpenick dressed up as an army captain – this exploit exposed the widespread commitment of the inhabitants of Berlin to militarism.[48] For the lesson of the "Captain of Köpenick" affair is not that it showed up the blind trust of civilians in any figure dressed up in martial array, but that the Berlin people, after laughing at themselves for having been so easily duped, took pride in the swiftness with which standing military emergency rules had gone into action.

In August 1914, seeing the war as one extraordinary and heroic moment rather than as a long and bitter endurance test between nations, prompted the police in the first weeks of the war to dispense with some normal procedures of law enforcement. To make up for the many routine matters that suddenly appeared unimportant, the police tried its hands at "morale-building." The police organized the purification of the German language of foreign idioms and purged bookstores of "trashy" adventure stories ranging from the memoirs of Casanova to the "*Rauhreitererzählungen*" of Theodore Roosevelt.[49]

Of particular interest were the efforts made to repatriate enemy aliens so they could take their place in the fighting forces of their home countries. This attitude was only the logical extension of the universal disapproval of military desertion by citizens of any nationality, which Europe upheld at least until the summer of 1914. In Berlin the police set aside a warehouse where foreigners could deposit their trunks for the duration of the war and in 1918 and 1919, many an ex-serviceman from the Italian, the British, and the French army did indeed find that his luggage had been kept safe for him.[50] In Alsace-Lorraine young men were leaving to join the French army – among them the well-known, anti-Prussian artist "Hansi" – and the Germans made little effort to stop them.[51] One French family at Rozerieulles, according to the French commissaire spécial at Longwy, was advised by the German police when the last train left for France if it wanted to go there before the frontiers were closed.[52] Similarly, General

---

[48] The complete dossier on Wilhelm Voigt in 1906 is preserved in the museum of the criminal police in Berlin. For a criminological comment on this case, see Dr. Erich Wulffen, *Verbrecher und Verbrechen* (Berlin, 1925), pp. 359–60; for a literary treatment, Carl Zuckmayer, *Der Hauptmann von Köpenick. Ein deutsches Märchen in drei Akten* (Berlin, 1930).

[49] Das Königliche Polizeipräsidium in Berlin, *Die innere Front* (Berlin, 1917), pp. 93–4. Also "Besprechung im Polizeipräsidium über die Fremdwörterausmerzung," in *Berliner Tageblatt*, 12 Oct. 1915, 1. Beiblatt.

[50] "Besprechung im Polizeipräsidium"; and Pietro Solari, "20 Jahre als italienischer Journalist in Deutschland," in *Berlin-Rom-Tokio*, Jhg. 1, Heft 2 (15 June 1939), pp. 60–2.

[51] J. J. Waltz (pseudonym "Hansi") was, however, placed on a German wanted list in 1915 for serving with French military intelligence helping to hunt down German officers. ADdBR (Strasbourg), AL 30 (131) "Acta betreff. den Zeicher Waltz (Hansi)."

[52] Report, *commissariat spécial* at Longwy to ministry of interior in Paris, Longwy, 31 July 1914, in AN (Paris), F7 12934, "Guerre de 1914, 24 juillet–1 août. Rappel des réservistes, mobilisation, arrestation d'étrangers."

Putnik, the chief-of-staff of the Serbian army, and his daughter were allowed by the Austrians to return to Belgrade from their vacation at Bad Gleichenberg. Traveling through Budapest on 26 July, they were detained on Conrad von Hötzendorff's urgings because Habsburg subjects were having difficulties returning from Serbia. But his advice to use Putnik as a hostage was not followed and the Serbian army chief and his daughter arrived home in time for the outbreak of the war.[53]

Austria-Hungary

While Germany needed full-scale national mobilization to launch its daring offensive through Belgium as quickly as possible, Austria-Hungary had to be thankful that its cumbersome multinational army could be readied for war at all. Because of the serious constitutional crisis in 1906 over the subordination to Vienna of the Hungarian *honved* army in case of war, Vienna had carefully negotiated an agreement with the Hungarian prime minister, Tisza, before taking a strong stand against Serbia during the Sarajevo crisis. But since there were no great offensives planned for the opening phase of the war, nor immediate enemy incursions expected, the level of police alertness in the Habsburg monarchy at the end of July was much lower than in Germany. It has been suggested that the Austrian military leaders may not have entered the war against Serbia and Russia so carelessly in 1914 had they known how much of their war preparations had been sold to the Russians by Captain Alfred Redl, the chief of the operations section of Austrian military intelligence. Redl was a spy in Russian service from 1901 to 1913. Shocked by the discovery of this treason case in high quarters the Austrian counter intelligence neglected to interrogate Redl before ordering him to commit suicide there and then. In the immediate war zone, Minister Bilinski on 6 July even rejected the idea of evicting all Serbian subjects from Bosnia as a military precaution: "Modern states today no longer apply such measures even against the nationals of enemy states in war time," he wrote to General Potiorek.[54] Our comment on Austria's war effort insofar as it affected police is therefore quite short.

If police vigilance there had to be anywhere, then in the Austrian hinterland was where the main political and economic effort for the war would have to be made. In Cisleithania the critical question was Czech loyalty, not least because of the important armament works in Bohemia. But, as is well known, the movement for Czechoslovak independence developed during the First World War largely along conspiratorial lines under the direction of a few outstanding poli-

[53] Telephone message from governor in Graz, as recorded by k.k. Ministerium des Innern, Staatspolizeiliches Bureau, Vienna, 4 July, 1914, in HHStA (Vienna), Liasse Krieg, 3. Teil.

[54] Notiz, Bilinski to Potiorek, Vienna, 6 July, 1914, in ibid., 2. Teil. The latest study of the Redl case is Georg Markus, *Der Fall Redl* (Vienna, 1984); but Robert Asprey, *The Panther's Feast* (London, 1959), is still the more through work. Also reliable is Istvan Déak, *Beyond Nationalism. A Social and Cultural History of the Austrian Officer Corps, 1848–1918* (New York, 1990), pp. 144–5.

ticians operating abroad. There was precious little that the Austrian police could have done to stop it. There was no significant national movement in Prague or among the Czechs in Vienna for the police to suppress because the mass of the Czech people remained docile and even moderately loyal to the Habsburg regime until the end of the war.[55] The "conspirators" abroad – T. G. Masaryk, Edvard Beneš, Vaclav Klofač, and others – were dangerous to the monarchy not because of their dreams of Czech independence but because they were making ready for the imminent collapse of the existing regime. The only way to stop the Czech independence movement was to save the Habsburg monarchy – and that in 1914 was far beyond the power of its police, if not beyond the power of all its executive departments together. Masaryk and Beneš employed some secret service ruses to go abroad for their political work and to keep in touch with the situation at home.[56] Their chief contact inside the Austrian ministry of interior was the Czech novelist J. S. Machar, who also was a member of the secret "mafia" organization.[57] In 1915 Machar was submitted to a house search by the political police in Vienna but the results proved unsatisfactory, largely because of the incompetence of the team of investigators. Only one of the Austrian detectives could read a little Czech. For five hours the men desultorily looked through Machar's books and papers for names they might recognize as belonging to "suspects": the French Czechophiles Louis Léger and Ernest Denis, the Czech national poets Jaroslav Vrchlicky and Jan Neruda. The farce ended when dusk fell and the chauffeur of the police auto outside came upstairs to say they had to get moving because their car had no parking lights. In haste the inspectors prepared to transport all the unread material to the Polizei-Direktorium and asked Machar to lend them an old suitcase and some string.[58]

German occupation policies in Belgium and Russian Poland

As we next turn to Germany's police performance during the First World War, our attention is drawn to the difference in its occupation policy on the western and on the eastern front. Once more we must distinguish between the police style applied to the settled urban communities of Western Europe (with their liberal, bourgeois, and legalistic minded inhabitants), and the policing style practiced in the vast rural plains of Eastern Europe where sparse population and fluid ethnic and racial frontiers invited undifferentiated coercion simply with soldiers. No

---

[55] Karl M. Brousek, *Wien und seine Tschechen. Integration und Assimilation einer Minderheit im 20. Jahrhundert* (Munich, 1980) pp. 26–8. Jaroslav Hasek's famous novel, *The Good Soldier Svejk*, trans. by Cecil Parrott (London, 1973), paints a devastating picture of the police chicanery in wartime Bohemia – devastating because of its obnoxiousness and its futility.

[56] On Masaryk and Beneš during the First World War, see in particular R. W. Seton-Watson, *Masaryk in England* (Cambridge, 1943).

[57] Brousek, *Wien und seine Tschechen*, p. 28.

[58] J. S. Machar, *The Jail. Experiences in 1916* (Oxford, 1921); also, Franz Brandl, *Kaiser, Politiker und Menschen. Erinnerungen eines Wiener Polizeipräsidenten* (Leipzig, 1936), pp. 221–2.

other country in this war was in control of as much enemy territory and for as extended a period of time as Imperial Germany. No other country was simultaneously involved in holding down hostile inhabitants in East and West. Together with the additional discovery that under extraordinary stress the German people would submit to very extensive restrictions on their freedom, Germany's war experience in 1914–18 may help explain the emergence of a regime twenty-five years later that we call totalitarian and which held much of the Continent between Paris and Warsaw under subjugation for almost four years. The extraordinary achievement of the Germans in mobilizing their civilian manpower for war production caused a German professor in 1915 to write with obvious pride:

Germany's system of free organization is scarcely known abroad. People smugly assume that all our organizations are derived from state coercion. Englishmen would never believe you if you told them that German trade unions surpass English unions in size and importance. The magnificent workers' organizations are rivaled by equally magnificent employers' organizations . . . Political associations like the Social Democratic Party, the Center Party, [and] the Agrarian League are extraordinary achievements. Since the outbreak of war free organizations in Germany have performed wonders in the field of finding people the right jobs, providing financial credits, distributing food supplies.

The picture of Germany abroad is that of a people drilled like soldiers and commanded by policemen. The political discipline of the Germans is explained by militarism and mindless subordination to authority. But how can a people as dully obedient as that also produce so many leaders who infuse its network of organizations with a pulsating life?[59]

In Belgium the Germans entertained the notion that, as in Alsace in 1870, their position as the new rulers might be assured for all times. They hoped for the support of the upper classes of Belgians who, they thought, would submit to German rule because they had a practical interest in good administration and surely also a high respect for German Kultur.

Belgian public opinion is split. Here and there we see changes to the better. The moral victory of the Germans and of Germandom is only softly admitted. But people sometimes talk more openly to Germans than to fellow Belgians. . . . The idea that the Germans will be driven out again is beginning to pale. . . . Sensible Belgians can read the signs of the time: the failure of the French offensive [in the Champagne], the situation in Eastern Europe, the economic might of Germany and the quality of German workmanship which demonstrates discipline and competence.

We can expect the public mood to improve as the economy revives and jobs become more plentiful. A smoothly running economy will help reconcile the population to the new situation.[60]

---

[59] Prof. Dr. Paul Eltzbacher, "Das Geheimnis der deutschen Organisationen," in *Die Woche*, 10 July 1915.

[60] Dr. von Sandt, Verwaltungschef bei dem Generalgouverneur von Belgien, "8. Verwaltungsbericht," (mimeo, 49 pages), pp. 1–3, in GPStA (Berlin), Rep. 84a/6207, Acten des Justiz Min. betreff. "Die Verwaltung der im Kriege 1914/ . . . besetzten feindlichen Gebiete (1914 bis 30. Juni 1915)."

An important role in advancing the normalization of life in occupied Belgium fell to the postal service which the Germans reorganized and improved. Many new post offices were opened on the district level to carry out the military censorship of the mails. "The collaboration of Belgian postal employees helps to acquaint the inhabitants with the character of German officialdom. We are happy when we can help out with personal problems that are mentioned in letters between prisoners-of-war and their families."[61]

Besides spying on civilians through the postal service, the Germans also introduced reforms in the morals police in Brussels and most other larger towns. The vice squad was reorganized along German lines under an experienced German police official and measures were introduced to fight prostitution and provide help to "fallen women." Thus Brussels was given eight vice police districts, each headed by a German police official assisted by a number of Belgian police. At the head stood a central morals police office [*Sittenpolizeizentrale*], staffed jointly by senior German and Belgian officials. "The Belgians work diligently and well," a contemporary report found. "Wherever there are sensible Belgians, they praise these police innovations and even the female persons who have been subjected to treatment express understanding and trust."[62]

Not counting the Belgian political police, which naturally disappeared when the occupation began, the morals police was the only department in the Belgian police administration where the Germans interfered. (Better morals police was also the principal reform introduced by the Germans in the police of Prague during the Second World War.) The Belgian police in 1915, like the French police in occupied France in 1940–4, was otherwise largely left to continue in its accustomed ways, seeing that its procedure was already tailored to the circumstances of the land. Besides, the Belgian police had kept excellent files which the German police greatly appreciated being able to use now for its own purposes. Only counterintelligence, security over vital communications, and frontier guard duties were entirely taken over by German personnel.[63]

We should add that the German authorities in Brussels were soon forced to concede that their report of February 1915 was overly optimistic. In May 1915, they were no longer so sure of the readiness of upper-class Belgians to collaborate. ("Their French education and cultural traditions make them blind and prejudiced against Germans.") Now the German hope was that the Belgian workers, until recently very hostile toward the occupier, would change their attitude in part because they needed the jobs which the Germans could give, and in part because they were surely more apt to be impressed by the austere severity of German military discipline.[64]

---

[61] Ibid., p. 10.   [62] Ibid., pp. 44–5.
[63] Report from Belgium dated 10 May, 1915, (mimeo, 86 pages, cover missing), in ibid., pp. 58–63.
[64] Ibid., pp. 2ff.

All the same, there seems to be no doubt but that German rule in Belgium required little resort to draconic force. To the Belgian population, a temporary acceptance of German rule was a matter of common sense since noncooperation entailed the risk of anarchy as metropolitan modern citizens will define anarchy – namely, the standstill of civilized life when postal and banking services, hospitals and schools, streetcars and order police, all cease to function.

In Russian Poland the German military authorities did not even bother to study public opinion, not to mention analyze the mentality of different sections of the population.[65] The Germans were in such dire need for the assistance of the few educated elements (landowners, managers of savings banks, clergymen) in the area between Bendzin, Sosnowice, and Dombrowo, that soon after their arrival they issued them permits to carry fire arms so they could help fight off bandits and Russian partisans. All Russian judges and all Russian municipal and rural police chiefs were evacuated when the Russian army retreated before the advancing Germans. Regular police service had ended though some towns had set up unarmed militias. There was no judiciary, and no postal or telegraphic service either. Private letters were given to German army drivers going west who, for a tip, would mail them from the first German town, a loss to the German political police in Poznan insofar as censoring letters was seen as a good source of information in wartime. The few social welfare institutions that were set up, such as the soup kitchens for the thousands of hungry Polish agricultural laborers, were not run by Germans because they could not speak Polish. The soup kitchens were run by Polish-Jewish students who – as a flabbergasted Herr von Brandenstein discovered on an inspection tour in February – were members of the Socialist Bund and used this activity to spread anti-German political ideas among the customers. Their great success in February 1915 was in organizing a Socialist meeting in Lodz attended by about five thousand people, among them Gustav Noske, the Social Democratic Reichstag deputy who was in Lodz as a war correspondent.[66]

The Germans in the First World War were thus faced in the West with situations in which modern police administration was a necessity of life to the inhabitants and served the invader to keep the population under control pending the outcome of the war. In the east the Germans faced a rural hinterland, where police meant little more than martial law imposed by battalions of mounted gendarmerie. Twenty years later the success of the Nazi regime merged these two police styles in one: First it established its ascendancy with displays of refined police skills, only to follow these up with brutal mass assaults at the point where

[65] Occupied Russian Poland was divided into a German and an Austrian area of administration. In the German area of administration the chief city was Lodz. The seat of the German civil administration was in Posen first; after May 1915, in Kalisch.

[66] "3. Verwaltungsbericht der Zivilverwaltung beim Oberbefehlshaber Ost," Poznan, 11 Mar. 1915, in GPStA (Berlin), Rep. 84a/6207.

the modern police in the West would have recognized the need for compromise and reform.

France

Mobilization. France did not suffer from popular spy fever in 1914. Nor did it, like Austria-Hungary, begin the war by temporizing. Like Germany, France had worked on its mobilization plans since the beginning of the 1890s, but unlike Germany it reckoned that military operations would begin on its home territory, in the *départements frontières* facing the northeast, the east, and the southeast. Making ready for war, therefore, had involved substantial collaboration between police and the army and navy in the last quarter century.[67] The special police watched all German military movements close to the French border; informers in Switzerland looked for any signs of German intentions to strike at France through the Jura mountains; and local police offices set up files on hundreds of French radicals and foreigners who might give assistance to a future invader. There were also arrangements for collaboration between police and soldiers against workers' disturbances during mobilization.[68] The French police preparations were so elaborate as to cause considerable self-confidence by 1914. Some of the precautions were actually found unnecessary in the tense days of July of that year, and the famous French offer to withdraw ten kilometers behind the frontier during the critical last days of diplomatic sparring (30 July 1914) was possible only because of France's defense preparations in depth.

The Dreyfus Affair of the 1890s was not yet forgotten, but we should remember that the betrayal of secret information to the Germans in large numbers had been the blight of France since the days of Taxil and Vézian in the 1870s.[69] German military intelligence kept a special staff of copyists and translators in Berlin just for the purpose of making available for analysis the constant flow of French military documents.[70] What made the Dreyfus Affair a national crisis was the realization that among France's intellectual avant-garde were men ready to place equality, truth, and justice for everyone higher than national patriotism. Like the Enlightenment philosophers in the eighteenth century, the defenders of Dreyfus sowed the seeds of change by exposing the shortcomings of certain national institutions, in this case the army. We may want to call them "precocious

---

[67] Circulaire, ministry of interior to all prefects, Paris, 9 Dec. 1895, in AN (Paris), F7 12584, "Surveillance des étrangers (1894–1899)."

[68] Jacques Aubert et al., *L'Etat et sa police en France (1789–1914)* (Geneva, 1979), pp. 111ff.

[69] The literature on the Dreyfus Affair is too abundant to be cited here, and almost every account includes a treatment of the police investigation it entailed. On Taxil and Vézian, see "Spies and Traitors in France," in Chapter 2.

[70] See handwritten confession of Helmut Wessel (alias "Kork"), former German army lieutenant, in 1903 under police arrest in Genoa, "Mémorial pour exposer les dessous politiques du gouvernement allemand concernant mon extradition," in AN (Paris), F7 12925, "Affaire Dreyfus. Lieutenant Wessel travaillant pour la police française."

revolutionaries," people who foresaw a future Europe beyond the divisive system of separate fatherlands. But their opponents, men like Maurice Barrès, who appealed to the French people's cultural nationalism and belittled rational intelligence as that *"petite chose à la surface de nous mêmes,"* could make at least as powerful a case.[71] As the historian Gerhard Ritter later wrote, the modern world had never known any pacifistic states before because pacifistic states had no chance of survival.[72]

To the police historian this affair is important not because it resulted in the transfer of French counter-intelligence from the ministry of war to the ministry of interior[73] (a step that had to be reversed when the First World War broke out) but because this great moral crisis of France could and did move towards a resolution – on a rational and objective basis – after the falsified document in the Dreyfus dossier (the "faux Henry") became public knowledge in 1898. Political passions subsided, even though slowly, when objective police evidence clearly proved Dreyfus's conviction to have been a miscarriage of justice.

With the Dreyfus Affair practically over by 1899, as if anxious to make up for its dangerous lapse in national alertness, France proceeded to reinforce its police defenses against the enemy across the Rhine. Since the Franco-Prussian War, all movement of German military personnel had been closely followed by the commissaires spéciaux in the French border towns. In 1905–6, when Russia's defeat in Asia prompted the beginning of the Anglo-French entente (and a German attempt to sabotage it by challenging French rule in Morocco) hundreds of military reports streamed into Paris from these strategical police posts along France's main railway lines. Belfort, to name just one commissariat near the German and Swiss border, reported on practice callups of German reservists in Mulhouse and about the disposition of German troops and guns down to the number of cartridges and provisions for each soldier in case of war. Every German reserve officer, Belfort informed Paris, who went abroad on private business now left behind the address of someone in Germany who would always know where he could be reached. More alarming, perhaps, Belfort also noticed a team of German officers in mufti who came to inspect the local railway station to assess the repair work that would be needed if the fort fell to a German attack after heavy combat.[74]

Police reports from Marseille kept track of the movement of German ships in the Mediterranean.[75] The commissaries facing the Swiss border watched German officers in Geneva, Clarens, Montreux, Vevey, and other Swiss towns to see if and when they were recalled to Germany to join their units. The commissaire spécial in Annemasse knew also of army depots under construction in

[71] Maurice Barrès, *Scènes et doctrines du nationalisme* (Paris, 1925), vol. I, p. 11.
[72] Gerhard Ritter, *Staatskunst und Kriegshandwerk* (Munich, 1954), vol. I, p. 13.
[73] Jacques Aubert and Raphaël Petit, *La Police en France. Service public* (Paris, 1981), pp. 105–6.
[74] See collection of reports by the *commissariat spécial*, gare de Belfort, for 1905–11, in AN (Paris), F7 12726, "Relations internationales – Allemagne – 1905–1911."
[75] For example, the report by Direction de la Sûreté Générale, Contrôle Général des Étrangers, Marseille, 22 Jan. 1906, in ibid.

Switzerland; he had information on meetings between foreign diplomats in Berne; and in 1906 he unmasked a German tourist living with his wife in a pension in Geneva as Major General Theodor von Berrer, chief of staff of the German 8th Army Corps, in Koblenz, and presumably engaged in military reconnaissance in Switzerland.[76]

In the years prior to the outbreak of the First World War, the Swiss caused the French some concern that they might be drifting into the camp of the Triple Alliance. The evidence, admittedly, was puny enough. French students who noisily protested the performance of a pan-German show at the Corso Theater in Zurich in June 1910 had been manhandled by the town police.[77] In 1914, the commissaire spécial at Pontarlier reported that German street signs were replacing the old bilingual French and German street signs in Berne: "Do not such changes tell us something about the way the German Swiss population feels about our country?"[78] On the eve of the war, French police observers were above all worried about the selection of Ulrich Wille as the commanding general of the Swiss army because of his reputation of sympathy for imperial Germany.[79]

France's most elaborate police effort in anticipation of war was the establishment of "black lists" (*carnets B*). They contained many Frenchmen who were deemed politically suspect (mainly Socialists and anarchists) and all foreigners who were thought to be security risks in case of war. The *carnets* were begun under Minister of War Boulanger in 1886, but only became important at the time of the Dreyfus Affair. Thus the ministry of interior by a decree of 27 August 1895 ordered prefects to report on "all aliens in France who might be of interest in connection to our national defense."[80] The work this represented was considerable, because every one of the over one million aliens in France had to be screened not once but screened anew every few years.[81] A questionnaire used by the police in 1906 for the review of the security status of aliens living in the department of Alpes-Maritimes was four pages long and contained twenty-nine questions. These questions included: Do the reasons for suspicion against him (the subject) still exist? Does he show an open interest in military matters? Is he seeking acquaintances with French military men and civil functionaries? Does he live close to a military fort, or a fortified place, or an arsenal? Do people suspect him of

[76] Report by *commissaire spécial* at Annemasse, 12 Feb. 1906, in ibid.
[77] Letter, French minister Comte d'Aunay to Foreign Minister Pichon, Berne, 6 June, 1910, in AN (Paris), F7 12727, "Relations internationales – Suisse – 1872–1915."
[78] Report by *commissaire spécial* in Pontarlier to Sûreté Générale, Pontarlier, 29 Mar. 1914, in ibid.
[79] Conversation with Hermann Böschenstein, Berne, 27 July 1973. Böschenstein examined the Wille family papers after the Second World War and found that Wille had indeed favored a Swiss alliance with Germany in 1914.
[80] Circulaire, ministry of interior to all prefects, Paris, 27 Aug., 1895, in AN (Paris), F7 12584.
[81] Statistics for 1895 show 1,207,500 persons registered as resident aliens in France. "Statistique des Etrangers établis sur le territoire Continental de la France, 30 juin 1895," p. 52, in AMAE (Paris), Série C administrative 1876–18, Numéro 85, C-24 intérieur, DR 2 "Etrangers en France 1893–1898."

espionage? Does he live within his acknowledged source of income? What do we know about his private conduct, his morals? Galtier-Boissière tells us that in July, 1914, the *carnets B* contained some three thousand names.[82]

A fourth police precaution taken in France, this one very shortly before the outbreak of war, was the creation of *gardes civiles,* or home guards. The initiative came in 1912 from the veterans' mutual benefit association (*Vétérans des armées de terre et de mer*), but the decision was made by the ministry of interior and the Sûreté Générale of the police prefecture in Paris after consultation with the prefects of departments.[83] The proposal was to establish a force of about 100,000 men who in case of war would protect France's railway lines against sabotage. The *gardes civiles* would set up road blocks in villages near railway lines, they would patrol the tracks in automobiles, and in strategic railway towns they would serve as auxiliary police.

The proposal was welcomed by the authorities inasmuch as the policing of the countryside had long been a source of worry to them. In rural communities local functionaries like village mayors and *gardes champêtres* were unreliable as agents of administrative police because they were agriculturalists mainly, poorly educated and badly paid.[84] The problem was aggravated by the fact that France since the 1890s depended more and more on foreign migrant laborers in agriculture and mining whose movements were difficult to check.[85] Finally, there had also been a number of attacks on express trains in France since the beginning of the century, notably the derailment of an express train near Dijon on 20 August 1902, and a threat in January 1911 to blow up trains between Paris and the Côte d'Azur carrying *"les grosses têtes parisiennes."*[86] (To what extent these incidents were caused by ecomomic discontent or by political motives, or simply by individual criminal behavior, was never fully cleared up.)

The ministry of interior and the Sûreté decided that the *gardes civils* would consist of volunteers between ages forty-five and fifty-five, who would have to pass a cantonal or departmental screening for physical and moral fitness. Wearing olive green armbands inscribed with the name of their commune and a service number, they would perform auxiliary police duties in teams of five men, armed with a revolver, a hunting rifle, or a sabre provided either by the commune or privately owned. Because they would be at the disposal of the Sûreté and the army for undisclosed missions, left-wing papers like the *Bataille Syndicaliste, Humanité,* and

[82] Jean Galtier-Boissière, *Mysteries of the French Secret Police* (London, 1938), p. 253. See also the small monograph by Jean-Jaques Becker, *Le Carnet B. Les pouvoirs publics et l'anti-militarisme avant la guerre de 1914* (Paris, 1973).

[83] Duxième Bureau of the Sûreté Générale to minister of interior, Paris, 2 Aug. 1912, in AN (Paris), F7 12840, "Projet de gardes civiles, 1913."

[84] Report by prefect of the département des Hautes-Alpes, Gap, 23 Oct. 1894, in AN (Paris), F7 12584.

[85] Circular, ministry of interior to all prefects, Paris, 13 Sept. 1893, in AMAE (Paris), "Etrangers en France 1893–1898."

[86] Letter, police of Oullins (département du Rhône) to Sûreté Générale, Oullins, 27 Jan., 1911, in AN (Paris), F7 12903, "Anarchistes en France et à l'étranger, 1892–1923."

Intransigeant complained that the government was recruiting old soldiers in preparation for civil war. To conservative critics, by contrast, the home guard had the dangerous potential of becoming the rank and file of a future commune.[87]

That there was more fear of open class war in France than in Germany is evidenced by the fact that a young fanatical patriot thought it necessary to murder the French Socialist leader Jean Jaurès on 31 July 1914 to prevent a general strike against mobilization. Galtier-Boissière asserts that without Jaurès's death, there would have been labor troubles in France. He also suggests that the Russian police in France may have organized this assassination.[88] In July 1914 the mine workers in Decazeville and St. Etienne (where strike actions happened to be in progress) were put under careful watch by the local authorities.[89] Small antiwar demonstrations actually took place on 28 July in Lorient, Limoges, Rouen, and Dijon, where many participants were Spanish and Italian workers.[90]

However, the French police did not ban antiwar demonstrations outright. In Belfort the military commander forbade a pacifist rally by Socialists because he feared that stirring up the working people would delay the evacuation of the seven thousand inhabitants which was about to go under way. The local police tried to calm the atmosphere by reminding the commanding general of the constitutional freedom of assembly in France and then discussing the situation directly with the Socialist leaders.[91] A peace rally in Toulouse was banned by the prefect, but in Paris and many other cities following the murder of Jaurès posters went up appealing to the workers' patriotism and calling for national concord.[92]

The political skill of the French authorities in this crisis is best expressed by three circulars issued by the ministry of interior to all the prefects of France and Algiers on 30 July, 1 August, and 2 August 1914:

30 July 1914: It is up to you what to do about public meetings. Generally you could tolerate socialist meetings which proclaim the wish for peace so long as the streets remain calm and they do not cause resistance to mobilization. All meetings of the CGT [Confédération générale du travail] or of anarchists that call for a general strike must be shut down. Your measures should fit local circumstances, and the state of mind and the character of the organizers.[93]

---

[87] *Commissaire spécial* of Nantes to Sûreté Générale, Nantes, 7 Sept. 1913, in AN (Paris), F7 12840. The decree of 7 Jan. 1914, which formally established the *gardes civiles*, attributed a civilian character to them and invested them in time of war with auxiliary police duties which would cease the moment their communities fell under enemy occupation.

[88] Galtier-Boissière, *Mysteries*, p. 253.

[89] Telegram 37620 23200, prefect to minister of interior and Sûreté, Rodez, 28 July 1914, 16:32 hours; and telegram, prefect of département de la Loire to ministries of labor, interior, public works, and war, 28 July 1914, 20:00 hours, in AN (Paris), F7 12934.

[90] See folder: "Meetings contre la guerre: manifestations" (28 July 1914), in ibid.

[91] Telegram 37582 22983, administration Belfort to ministry of interior, 28 July 1914, in ibid.

[92] Telegram, prefect to ministry of interior, St. Etienne, 1 Aug. 1914, 12:40 hours, in ibid.

[93] Telegram, ministry of interior to all prefects in France and Algeria, Paris, 30 July, 1914, 9855 W60/45, in AN (Paris), F7 12935, "Guerre franco-allemande. Instructions générales."

1 August, 1914: We have reason to trust all persons listed as political suspects on the *carnet B*. Do not arrest anyone in that category. Limit yourself to arresting aliens suspected of espionage.[94]

2 August, 1914: The current attitude of the syndicalists and CGT members allows us to give confidence to those who are listed on the *carnet B*. Do nothing more than keep them under discreet surveillance. As to the anarchists on the *carnet B:* as soon as mobilization is ordered act only when absolutely necessary against those who seem to constitute a genuine and acute threat. The others should merely be watched.[95]

The German response to the outbreak of the world war was another proclamation of Burgfrieden – of a truce between the unreconciled classes in its society. France was more fortunate in being able to elevate its principle of défense du territorie to a genuine *union sacrée* founded on a tradition of democratic pluralism.[96]

On the eve of the war France, incidentally, showed itself no less correct than the Central Powers in letting enemy aliens respond to their countries' call to arms. The French postal and telegraph service intercepted some messages which it presumed contained the mobilization orders for Germans and Austrians living in France, but in at least one instance the prefect of the department of Digne interceded because he thought France's international reputation would suffer if it became known that it had violated the sanctity of postal communications through unlawful confiscation.[97] On the night of 27 July the commissariat spécial at the Gare de l'Est in Paris reported 150 Germans and Austrians returning home on board the 21:05 train; among them one Czech house painter who had received a summons to call at the Austrian embassy, where he was handed the train fare and told to report home to fight. "Mr. Chaderal is Czech," wrote the commissaire spécial at Pontarlier through which the train passed. "Like nearly all his compatriots he is very anti-German and a great friend of our country."[98] But it would take until 1915 before the French authorities were ready to intercede with the Austro-Hungarian government's claim to the allegiance of its Slavic subjects.

The *Commission des Etrangers, 1915–17.* Between August and September 1914 the German Schlieffen Plan went awry. The Germans failed to execute the sweeping movement with their right wing to the west of Paris as originally conceived by Schlieffen that would have avoided the dense concentration of fortifications between Paris and the Belgian frontier. Instead the German armies advanced into the area east of the capital, where they were held up by the French and British armies in the heavily fortified region about Soisson, Reims, and Verdun. Here, for the next four years, the best crop of the young generation of Western Europe was bled white. Despite their great victory over the Russians at Tannenberg in

[94] Telegram, ministry of interior to all prefects in France and Algeria and to Gouverneur Général in Algiers, Paris, 1 Aug. 1914, 17:50 hours, in AN (Paris), F7 12935.
[95] Telegram, ministry of interior to all prefects in France and Algeria, Paris, 2 Aug. 1914, in ibid.
[96] A German tribute to the French *union sacrée* of 1914 is Hermann Platz, *Geistige Kämpfe im modernen Frankreich* (Munich, 1922), Part I.
[97] Report, prefect of département de Digne, 28 July, 1914, in AN (Paris), F7 12934.
[98] Report, *commissariat spécial*, Pontarilier, 27 July, 1914, in ibid.

August 1914, the Germans were forced from the beginning of the conflict to engage in that very continental two-front war which the Schlieffen Plan had been designed to avoid.

The city of Paris, still the most important nerve center of French national life, remained throughout the war within striking range of the German armies, who sometimes stood no further than eighty kilometers away. The fear that the home front might break under the strain was captured in a famous cartoon showing two French *poilus* telling one another, worriedly: *"Pourvu qu'ils tiennent!"* Although we cannot go into the details of French overall wartime policing, we should pause to consider the Paris police prefecture's effort to ensure the safety of the capital from internal betrayal by individual residents.[99] The work of the review board which examined the status of resident aliens in Paris reflected France's response to the political and social disintegration in Central and Eastern Europe during the war because it dealt chiefly with Russians and Austro-Slavs. It was a conservative and legalistic response compared to that of the German military authorities who faced the situation in Eastern Europe more intimately, their armed forces being in actual occupation of vast stretches of Russian Poland, the Ukraine, and Romania.

The commission des étrangers was established by a decree of the French ministry of interior on 28 December 1915. Headed by the director of the Sûreté, Monsieur Richard, its mission was to serve the ministry as a fact-finding body with advisory powers.

Article One: A special commission is instituted to examine the situation of all aliens residing in the département de la Seine who have received their residence permit because of their Russian or Italian nationality [i.e. as allies of France], or because of their [ethnic] identity as Turks, Poles, Czechs, Trentinos, Croatians, etc. (Alsace-Lorrainers are not included here) even though they are subjects of nations at war with France.

Article Two: Aliens of Russian and Italian nationality will receive summons by the Prefect of Police to appear before the commission. The commission will study the legal situation of each of them on the basis of their home country's military service laws.

Article Three: The commission will review the permission to reside in Paris of subjects of enemy countries who ethnically belong to certain national groups as described in Article One. With the advice of the Police Prefect, the commission will consult persons who can provide information useful to establish the precise national [read: political] status of such persons.[100]

Thus the French authorities by the end of 1915 were beginning to adjust to the complexity of modern total war, whose outcome could depend as much on the political opinions of the subjects of foreign countries as on the alignment

---

[99] Both Galtier and Daudet have made allegations about defeatism, if not actual collusion with the enemy, by the Paris police prefect Hennion, but without citing any documentary evidence. See Galtier-Boissière, *Mysteries*, p. 253; and Léon Daudet, *Magistrats et policiers* (Paris, 1935), pp. 111–12.

[100] See decree of 28 Dec. 1915, signed by the minister of interior, Malvy, in APP (Paris), Carton B A/896, "Guerre de 1914. Commission des étrangers."

of their governments. The difficulty of assessing the moral value to France and to Europe of a rebellious Russian or Italian or Czech or Hungarian subject may explain why the French ministry of interior invited the noted sociologist, Professor Emile Durkheim of the Sorbonne University, to become a member of the commission.

There were thirty to forty thousand Russians living in Paris in 1914. Many of them belonged to the antitsarist intelligentsia. In the first months of the war they were summoned to the police prefecture and, in a "menacing tone" (*un ton comminatoire*), urged to sign up either with the Russian or the French armed forces.[101] This was done in the belief that with the outbreak of war all domestic political grievances would be forgotten, and that the Russian exiles would be prepared to fight Germany either out of loyalty for their country of origin or their country of residence. Burtsev, for example, who had waged a long underground war against the Russian Okhrana in Paris, agreed in 1914 to return home and to urge his political followers there to support the Russian war effort.[102]

The overall situation, however, turned out to be more complicated. (Burtsev himself later deserted and returned to France.) Many Russian intellectuals in exile were Jews whose unwillingness to fight for their government had less to do with Russian foreign policy than with Russian domestic politics. There was much apprehension among the Russian students at the prospect of France delivering them as recruits to the very authority whose harsh rule had made them choose exile to begin with. Thousands of them now fled France for Spain and the United States, giving Germany the opportunity of accusing the French government of anti-Semitism, much to the dismay at the Quai d'Orsay.[103]

On the request of the ministry of foreign affairs the approach by the Paris police and the commission des étrangers was changed. All the students were to be asked simply why they had not joined the Russian army and why they did not think it their duty to do so. "To efface the poor impression made by the earlier convocations, it is important that henceforth no such convocations take place inside police commissariats."[104] Professor Durkheim was asked to study the problem of the Russian students' attitude to the war. In the session of 15 January 1916, he came out strongly in defense of the Russian colony. He reported that 3,393 Russian Jews in Paris had enlisted with the French Foreign Legion at the outbreak of war, and that another 8,000 had volunteered, though 57 percent of these were rejected as unfit. The decision to have the Russian students enlist in the Foreign Legion, however, had been a mistake, he said, because of the Legion's harsh discipline and

---

[101] The Russian mobilization law permitted Russian subjects in France to join one of the Allied armies. Letter, Russian ambassador Iswolsky to the minister of interior, Malvy, Paris, 22/24 Jan., 1916, in ibid.

[102] Typescript: "Abschrift eines Berichtes der K.K. Polizeidirektion in Wien vom 24. Aug. 1915 . . . an das k.k. Ministerratspräsidium," z.Z. 5090/M.P.-1915, in HHStA (Vienna), F 52, Karton 8, folder: "Anarchisten – Polizeiberichte."

[103] Minutes for session of 12 Jan., 1916 of the *commission des étrangers*, in App (Paris), Carton B A/896.

[104] Ibid.

its reputation of being the refuge of foreign adventurers. "In order to have another few hundred soldiers to send to the front, is it worth giving the Germans and Americans a pretext for calling France intolerant [towards Jews]? Is it worth making France appear to collaborate in the anti-Jewish persecution in Russia?"[105] Professor Durkheim's position earned him some grumbling from people who said he was in the pay of *"le Kriegs Ministerium allemand,"* but following a small mutiny by the Russians in the Foreign Legion, nearly all of them were transferred to regular French army units.

The commission des étrangers also dealt with Austro-Hungarian subjects, notably with the Czechs. The numbers involved were not so important but the good treatment accorded to the Czechs was significant. A very substantial number of them joined the French forces (no less than 600 volunteers out of a colony of only 1,600 Czechs living in France) where they were put in the prestigious French *chasseurs alpins*.[106] The commission des étrangers recognized the existence of a particular situation in Central and Eastern Europe where simple legal definitions of citizenship did not suffice. "In matters of national origin," the police prefecture admitted on 26 January 1916:

we have always held that we are not in the position to decide on the national origin of a person. This depends on a person's ethnic characteristics, his language and above all his accent and his pronunciation, which none of the functionaries of the police prefecture can determine. National origin is not established with legal documents. For example, to be Czech it is not enough to have been born in Bohemia, or necessary to have been born there. The police has had occasion to be reserved about the recommendations of the national committees, but never seriously to distrust them.[107]

There was a third topic that the French security services (though not the commission des étrangers) had to deal with: the resurgence of the Socialist Party's antiwar movement in Germany. Paul Louis, in a war publication in 1916, reported in some detail on the split that occurred in the German Social Democratic Party in 1915: the opposition inside the SPD. of the radical leaders Mehring, Ledebour, Zetkin, Luxemburg, and Liebknecht, and their recommendation of returning Alsace and Lorraine to France to speed up the conclusion of peace. He also spoke of the food situation in Berlin which he thought had reached a point comparable to the famine in Paris during the siege of 1870–1. According to him there were serious bread riots in Berlin and other German towns.[108] His view was supported by a report conveyed to the Sûreté by its intelligence post in Annemasse on 31 July 1916, and which we cite here as a sample of French wartime police intelligence on Germany:

[105] Lecture by Durkheim at the meeting of 26 Jan., 1916 of the *commission des étrangers*, in ibid.

[106] Ehrhard Preissing, *Die französische Kulturpropaganda in der ehemaligen Tschecho-Slowakei 1918–1939* (Stuttgart, 1943), p. 23.

[107] See general report on foreigners in France, dated Préfecture de Police, Cabinet du Préfet, 1er Bureau, Paris, 26 Jan. 1916, in APP (Paris), Carton B A/896.

[108] Paul Louis, *Les Crises intérieures allemandes pendant la guerre* (Paris, 1916), pp. 102–3.

Revolt is imminent in Berlin. Demonstrations were dispersed by mounted police. There are hundreds of wounded (women and children). In Cologne and Aachen there are 122 dead. There is open revolt in Frankfurt [am Main] where machinegun salvos were fired on crowds causing heavy casualties. In the evening public proclamations by orators assured the people the German armies would take Paris by 15 August, that peace would then be signed and that France would gladly submit to its terms. Three British prisoners working at the railway station were stoned by women who called them "satans." Women are committing suicide because they have received no ration cards for bread and lard for one week.

A large portion of the German population now knows that this war was not wanted by either France or England. The grumbling is swelling everywhere in the towns. Berlin is full of wounded people, there are sick beds everywhere even in the Town Hall. Everywhere people are demanding "Peace and Bread!"[109]

The reports of unrest in Germany, we now know, were quite inaccurate but they do represent the resurrection of police initiative by the end of the second year of war when the military stalemate on all fronts suggested that a solution to the military impasse might call for bold and innovative methods – not only in weaponry (airplanes, poison gas, tanks) but also in the field of police work. Russia's mounting military disaster in the East could not be reversed by French reinforcements, but the very complex international situation produced by Russia's long political crisis invited the reactivation of France's police involvement with the Russian revolutionary malaise from prewar days. Similarly, the heavy strain on the Habsburg monarchy produced the first French steps towards recognizing Czech national independence. The highly sensitive situation in Bohemia, where symbolic gestures of friendship for the Czechs could very tangibly affect the war capacity of Germany's principal ally, were an obvious invitation to the French security services to invest in them some of their means of exerting power.

Only the social situation in Germany seemed beyond the power of French intelligence to affect. The picture conveyed by Annemasse of war weariness on the brink of revolt suggests that French intelligence in Germany was unreliable. Military defeat was an essential precondition for a German surrender to the Allies, and the French were unrealistic if they banked on popular uprisings in Germany to end the war.

Switzerland

Surrounded by four great powers about to be engulfed in a continental war, Switzerland in July 1914 was also obliged to go on national alert, if only to protect its so vulnerable neutral status from being violated by any belligerent. The Swiss army was called up (*mise à piquet*) on 31 July 1914, only hours after general mo-

---

[109] Report, *commissaire spécial* of Annemasse, to Sûreté Générale, Annemasse, 31 July 1916, in AN (Paris), F7 12935. However, no such troubles are reported in the recent study by Thomas Lindenberger, "Berliner Unordnungen zwischen den Revolutionen," in Gailus et al., ed., *Pöbelexzesse und Volkstumult in Berlin*, pp. 43–76.

bilization was announced in Germany. [110] A special decree, "On the Preservation of Swiss Neutrality" (4 August 1914), placed the principal responsibility for this task on the military, the police, and the frontier guards. [111]

Two problems needed immediate solution: (1) How to suppress espionage by foreign agents on Swiss soil (and to a lesser extent, how to stop their war propaganda in Switzerland); and (2) what to do about deserters and draft evaders from belligerent countries.

The suppression of espionage was hampered by the absence of a national executive police force in Switzerland with the power to operate freely in all the cantons. The military police set up a *Detektiv-Abteilung* in Porrentruy to fight foreign espionage and requested the cantons to lend it some of their men as agents. [112] But the legal status of cantonal policemen operating on army missions in neighboring cantons remained a cause for countless disputes between the cantons throughout the war. Another cause of difficulty was that each canton faced only one of the belligerent powers and consequently saw only one aspect of the overall espionage problem in the country. Because Basel-Stadt was an excellent observation post for spying against Germany, only 19 of the 236 foreign agents who were caught by the police of Basel between August 1914 and January 1915 had worked for Germany, the overwhelming majority for France and its allies. This incurred the Basel police the criticism by the French – and by some Swiss citizens who sympathized with France – of breach of neutrality. [113] *Paris-Midi* published a polemic essay on the Basel police on 12 January 1915:

We are told that the police of canton Basel[-Stadt] does not hide its anti-French feelings. Armed with almost limitless powers, the Basel policeman knows he will always be covered by his superiors if he commits a scandalous blunder. Hence his arrogance, which he derives from the example set by superiors like inspector Müller and lieutenant Bloch. – What a strange fellow, that Müller! He looks like a German student down to the dueling scar on his unpleasant face. Müller is convinced that Germany will win the war. It is probably he who provides the Germans with their daily bulletins on what goes on here. [114]

The accusation of *Paris-Midi*, polemic though it was, must have been founded on some truth because, as the Basel police department reported to the political department (Foreign Ministry) in Berne on 28 August 1915, there were problems arising from the need for daily contacts and frequent mutual visits between police on the two sides of the German-Swiss frontier. Thus a German police inspector Fuchs, stationed in St. Louis (Alsace), often came to Basel to identify people who

---

[110] As reported by *commissaire spécial* at Morteau, 31 July 1914, at 19:30 hours, in AN (Paris), F7 12934.
[111] "Verordnung betreffend Handhabung der Neutralität der Schweiz," (4 Aug. 1914), in StA (Basel-Stadt), Politisches JJ2, "Weltkrieg 1914–18. Neutralität, Grenzverletzungen, Passwesen, Grenzkontrolle."
[112] Letter, Heerespolizei Kommando to Polizei-Inspektorat of Canton Basel-Stadt, Berne, 30 Oct. 1914, in StA (Basel-Stadt), Politisches JJ3, "Weltkrieg 1914–18. Spionage 1913–1916–1917."
[113] "Bundesrat Hoffmann über die Basler Polizei," in *Basler Nachrichten*, 5 Jan. 1915.
[114] "Comment la police bâloise pratique la neutralité," in *Paris-Midi*, 12 Jan. 1915, p. 1.

were particularly hostile toward Germany.[115] It is also true that police inspector Müller was in regular correspondence through 1916 with an *Oberleutnant* Hüglin of the German counterintelligence in Freiburg im Breisgau (*Abwehrstelle Süd*). Hüglin, for example, asked Müller in a letter dated 14 April 1916, to provide him with information on a French spy named Alphonse Meyer, "a French-Swiss Jew from La Chaux-de-Fonds," who allegedly was a courier for the French intelligence post at Annemasse.[116] In June 1916 Hüglin also asked Müller to help keep an eye on a Jewish shoe salesman in Basel, Salomon Geissmann. But it is also true that, though Müller ordered the famous Basel detective Vollenweider to investigate Geissmann, he admonished Hüglin: "Like Geissmann, many people in Basel speak French and are Francophiles. But they have a good right to their preferences and opinions and it simply won't do to treat them right away as spy suspects."[117]

Most of the espionage that could be done in Switzerland was low-level espionage: the scouting out of French and German troop movements close to the Swiss border. Some of this was done by local Swiss residents on walks in the countryside who saw a chance of earning themselves a small extra income.[118] However this kind of espionage lost much of its importance to the belligerents once the critical phase of mobilization was over and the fighting on the western front turned into a war of attrition. Some espionage continued, but in a novel form: foreign agents circulated among the interned deserters of the belligerent armies hoping to pick up information about the units from which they came.

Since 1871 the definition of "desertion" had become more difficult in Europe because universal military conscription had produced the new category of the civilian draft dodger and conscientious objector.[119] Switzerland, never sympathetic towards deserters, was particularly concerned during the First World War about foreigners of military age who wanted to sit out the fighting in the safety of Swiss asylum and at Swiss public expense. The *Berliner Tageblatt* quoted an unnamed Swiss source in 1916, as saying that: "Particularly insistent Swiss citizens have proposed that [Switzerland should] put these unstable characters into concentration camps [*Konzentrationslager*] where they would be put to hard labor under strict discipline."[120]

[115] Letter, police of Canton Basel-Stadt to federal political department in Berne, Basel, 28 Aug. 1915, in StA (Basel-Stadt), Politisches JJ3.
[116] Letter, Oberleutnant Hüglin, Abwehrstelle Süd, to Polizei-Inspektor Müller in Basel, Freiburg i.B., 14 Apr. 1916, in ibid.
[117] Letter, Polizei-Inspektor Müller to Oberleutnant Hüglin, Basel, 14 Apr. 1916, in ibid.
[118] Camille Decoppet, Militärdepartement in Berne, to cantonal governments of Berne, Solothurn, Basel-Stadt, and Basel-Land, Berne, 24 Oct. 1914, in StA (Basel-Stadt), Politisches JJ2.
[119] The famous Casablanca case of 1908 tried to reinforce the effectiveness of national armies by at least assuring governments of their jurisdiction over soldiers wearing their uniforms, whatever their nationality. See folder: "Tensions politique au moment de la proposition d'arbitrage au sujet des incidents de Casablanca. Déserteurs Français protégés par le Consul d'Allemagne – 1905–1911," in AN (Paris), F7 12726, "Relations internationales – Allemagne – 1905–1911"; and also L. B. Schapiro, "Repatriation of Deserters," in *BYB* (1952), pp. 310–24.
[120] "Das Asylrecht in der Schweiz," in *Berliner Tageblatt*, 18 Apr. 1916.

The chief difficulty Switzerland had with foreign deserters during the war was that all the frontiers around it were tightly guarded and to expel a political offender to his home state *or* to an enemy belligerent state would have violated its tradition of asylum. All deserters and draft dodgers were, however, forced by the Swiss military authorities to remain in a designated place and the local communities demanded from them a money deposit as bail. [121] A report by the police department of Basel-Stadt to the cantonal government on 15 September 1915 expressed frank hostility toward the foreign deserters in its city. There are 40 of them in Basel now, the report said, with their dependents 120 to 150. That number is growing daily and may soon reach 500 to 1,000. Most of them are likely to end up stateless at the end of the war.

Then it may be too late and we will have to keep them here, because to expel them will be regarded as "inhumane." Next, we will have to grant them citizenship too. We shall thereby experience a highly obnoxious increase [*höchst unerfreuliche Zunahme*] of our citizenry because it will largely consist of Galician and Russian Jews, in other words of elements which the Swiss people find very difficult to assimilate. What is more, these people will bear the stigma of deserters for the rest of their lives. [122]

In 1919 the police department of Basel-Stadt lost little time to inform its German, Austrian, Turkish, and Russian deserters that the time had come for all of them to leave Switzerland. They were given until 31 May to inform the police of their travel plans. Anyone with a record of prior convictions, or who had led an "unsolid" way of life, or fallen into destitution, would be deported without delay. [123]

Revolutions

Switzerland and the Bolshevik revolution 1917–19

Lenin's famous train trip from Zurich to Petrograd in April 1917, organized and financed by German military intelligence, ended the war in the east and changed the political course of Russia a bare six months later. This so successful German maneuver lent weight to the Allied notion that only international police intervention could be swift and versatile enough to stem – and perhaps even scuttle – the incipient world revolution now emanating from Russia. At a point where all the belligerent powers were strained to the breaking point, the survival of the European political order seemed to depend on preventing the Bolshevik revolution from engulfing the whole continent with a succession of coordinated uprisings in

[121] Territorialdienst, "Instruktion betreffend die Zuständigkeit der militärischen Kommandostellen und der kantonalen Polizeibehörden hinsichtlich der Behandlung der Deserteure und Refraktäre der kriegführenden Staaten," (Berne, 5 June 1915), in StA (Basel-Stadt), Politisches JJ3.

[122] Letter, Polizeidepartement Basel-Stadt to Regierungsrat Basel-Stadt, Basel, 16 Sept. 1915, in ibid.

[123] Polizeidepartement Basel-Stadt, circular letter to inhabitants who are foreign deserters, Basel, 15 Apr. 1919, in StA (Basel-Stadt), Politisches JJ6 (vol. 1), "Deserteure und Refraktäre, 1913–1916."

various strategical cities of Central and Western Europe. As the British military theoretician, J. F. C. Fuller, bluntly put it, Bolshevism could bring down the European structure of sovereign states by making physical warfare between them impossible simply by their refusal to respect the inviolability of the police domain of sovereign nations. Were not all international agreements ultimately enforced by the right of every state to resort to war? But could wars be fought if the belligerents sought to incite enemy soldiers to turn into social revolutionaries?[124]

The departure of the Bolsheviks from Zurich in 1917 took place with only the knowledge of Bundesrat Hermann Arthur Hoffmann, who then headed the Swiss political department and was in consultation with the German minister in Berne, and with the support of *Nationalrat* Fritz Platten, secretary of the Swiss Social Democratic Party.[125] It was not a formal decision by the Berne government. But Paris had feared for some time that Switzerland was gravitating towards a passive collaboration with Berlin. In a report by the Paris police prefect dated 1 August 1914, we read:

[We] have information that last Tuesday at a meeting of the Swiss general staff a participant declared France would surely be defeated by Germany in case of war, and that it would be in Switzerland's best interest not to resist a German march-through to invade French territory. His view was approved by the majority of the Swiss general staff, who declared that if France were to remonstrate with it, Switzerland could always claim that it had been unprepared for mobilization.[126]

French fears of a German collusion with Bolshevism, in which Switzerland might be forced into the role of reluctant participant, were laid out in a long Sûreté report dated 26 June 1918, titled "The Activities of the Representatives of Bolshevism in Switzerland." It described most Maximalists (Bolsheviks) as internationalist who had long lived in Germany, Switzerland, and in France. These Bolsheviks, the Sûreté contented, would have remained without significance had they not come under German influence.

Until that decisive moment you still could find in the Bolshevik ranks some representatives of the Russian tsarist police. We know that the tsarist government was always successful in penetrating the ranks of the revolution with devoted officials who worked inside as spies and *agents provocateurs*. The Germans first established their influence inside the Bolshevik circles by contacting these 'false Bolsheviks' [i.e. the tsarist secret police agents]. And from the moment when the whole Bolshevik movement became a department of German pro-

---

[124] J. F. C. Fuller, "The Changing Conditions of War," in *The Nineteenth Century*, May 1927, p. 687. It took the Soviet Union until 1933 to sign conventions with various European states and the United States in which it undertook not to support domestic rebellion in the territory of the other signatory powers. See Manuel R. Garcia-Mora, *International Responsibility for Hostile Acts of Private Persons against Foreign States* (The Hague, 1962), pp. 32–3, 107.

[125] Willi Gautschi, *Lenin als Emigrant in der Schweiz* (Zurich, 1973), pp. 256ff.

[126] Prefect of département de la Savoie, to minister of interior, Chambéry, 1 Aug. 1914, in AN (Paris), F7 12934.

paganda, the Bolshevik movement, under Berlin's direction, established relations with the reactionary and Germanophile party in Russia.[127]

Early in July 1918 French police agents were sent across the border to check out rumors about a mutinous movement in the Swiss army, going to every canton and investigating regiment after regiment, battalion after battalion.[128] This undertaking coincided with the discovery by the Basel police on 8 and 9 July of a political club which disposed of hidden caches of German-made hand grenades in the outskirts of the city. "This club is said to plan a revolution in Switzerland in order to spread it from there across the frontier into France and Italy," the French military intelligence reported to Paris.[129] On the same day, the French police in Annemasse reported the outbreak of disorders in Bienne (Canton Berne). Martial law was proclaimed, police, fire brigades, and troops were called out, and there was shooting in the streets.[130] The disturbances in Switzerland were interpreted by Italian naval intelligence – as conveyed by the French ministry of the navy to the Sûreté – as a Bolshevik strategy to use Switzerland as the funnel to spread Socialist and defeatist propaganda into France and Italy. The German spring offensive on the Western front was at that time still in full progress. "The Bolsheviks want to abandon Europe to the Germans for the time being, convinced that this is the only way to end the war and to begin the revolution. . . . To make propaganda in Germany for the time being will achieve nothing."[131]

Even assuming that there truly existed a conspiracy between the German military and the Russian Bolsheviks, the object of this partnership certainly vanished with the collapse of the German Western front and the conclusion of an armistice on 11 November 1918. Switzerland with its strategic location in the heart of Western Europe was no longer needed for sabotage operations against the Allied war effort. It also lost its importance to the Bolsheviks who now rather turned to the working class in the defeated German and Austrian empires as would-be allies. Switzerland did undergo a brief interlude of Communist unrest in the form of a general strike (the *"Landesstreik"* of 12 November 1918), but largely to serve as a diversion to cover the flanks of the Communist insurrections in Germany. The Communist movement in Switzerland in itself lacked the support of a strong working class. In a report in 1921 the Swiss federal prosecutor's office attributed the causes of the troubles in Switzerland exclusively to the proletarian unrest

---

[127] "Agissements des représentants du Maximalisme en Suisse," (secret report, 14 pages, received at Sûreté Générale 27 July 1918), in AN (Paris), F7 13506, "Le Bolchévisme dans le monde. Secours rouge international 1918–1932."

[128] Secret report on "anti-militarism" in the Swiss army, 8 July 1918 (received at Sûreté Générale, 13 July 1918), in ibid.

[129] Report, Etat-Major Général, 1er Section, "Information. Suisse: Propagande révolutionnaire," Paris, 15 July 1918, in ibid.

[130] Duxième Bureau-S.R., Annemasse, 22 July 1918, "Comte rendu. Appréciation hebdomaire [*sic*] des événements publics suisses du 8 au 14 Juillet 1918," in ibid.

[131] Report, minister de la marine to *commissaire Général* of the Sûreté Nationale, Paris, 13 Aug. 1918, in ibid.

elsewhere in Central Europe – to the Spartacist fighting in Berlin during the winter of 1918–19, the attacks on the German National Assembly in Weimar, the riots in Württemberg, and the short-lived Soviet republics in Bavaria and Saxony. It all culminated in an eight-day strike in Basel from 31 July to 8 August 1919. This time five persons died in Basel due to gunfire.[132] In Switzerland a number of individuals acted as revolutionary leaders: Jules Humbert-Droz in the French-speaking cantons, the German Socialist Willy Münzenberg in the German-speaking cantons (the Swiss expelled him in 1918), and Fritz Platten, the Socialist functionary who threw in his lot with the Communists in 1917.

Switzerland's part in the Bolshevik revolution was limited to the initial phase: the time prior to the end of the war, when the German imperial government had a certain interest in using social revolution to break down the resistance of its military opponents, and immediately following the armistice, when the Bolsheviks sought to divert attention from their attempt to extend the revolution to Austria-Hungary and Germany. Three consequences of the Swiss interlude interest us in anticipation of the police situation in Europe during the interwar years: (1) The firm steps taken by the Swiss authorities to prevent any recurrence of the disturbances of 1918 and 1919, if need be by military force; (2) Switzerland's readiness to join with other countries in police measures to combat Bolshevism; and, as a corollary, (3) Switzerland's alignment, for the first time since 1815, with all the major powers of Europe, in a common ideological front. We cite from the protocol of the federal government's "Commission for Defence Measures Against Revolutionary Movements" of 25 November 1918:

The Bolshevist movement receives its guidance and inspiration from Russia. It wants the violent overthrow of the bourgeois classes, destroy their rights and hold them under terror. Should Bolshevism triumph in Germany – and this could happen, especially if famine breaks out over there – we must be prepared for renewed troubles in our own country as well. But even without it, revolutionary disturbances remain a possibility in Switzerland.[133]

To prepare for more Communist troubles the Swiss government ordered close collaboration between the federal prosecutor's office, the military and cantonal police, the railways and the postal service. In February 1919, the Berne government went over the head of the cantonal authorities in Basel and ordered the local police to destroy a cache of 965 kilos of Bolshevik propaganda brochures. In April the Swiss army issued directives for the immediate militarization of the Federal Railways in case of another strike. In the same month, travel restrictions were

---

[132] Petition by Basel-Stadt to Bundesrat in Berne (1922), requesting waiving of repayment of federal expenses for the suppression of riots in Basel because the disturbances were caused by world-wide communist agitation. StA (Basel-Stadt), Politisches JJ8,4, "Weltkrieg 1914–18: Generalstreik Landesstreik 1919–1922."

[133] "Protokoll der Kommission zur Vorbereitung von Massnahmen gegen revolutionäre Bewegungen," 25 Nov. 1918, in BA (Berne), Bestands-Nr. 21, Archiv-Nr. 11855.

imposed on all Swiss citizens suspected of involvement in the international communist movement.[134]

There were also arrangements for collaboration with foreign governments. Had a Soviet republic been proclaimed in Basel in August 1919, the Swiss would have expected (and no doubt welcomed) French military intervention from Alsace.[135] An offer from Rome to send Italian policemen to Switzerland to help against Bolshevik subversion was declined by Berne on legal grounds,[136] but informally Swiss police officials now volunteered political information to the French police.[137] The *police spéciale* in Annemasse received a list of names, three pages long, of Bolsheviks in Switzerland who had personal ties to France.[138] The Lausanne police seems to have been particularly active in fighting Communism in Switzerland. The federal prosecutor's report in 1921 praised it for its vigorous campaign of expulsion against all foreign Communists.[139] Besides the French, there were officials in the British and the American legations in Berne who with the government's knowledge used confidential agents to observe Bolshevik activities in Switzerland.[140] The Swiss also tried the services of a Dutch private anti-Bolshevik detective bureau, the "Rotterdamsch Allgemeen Pers-Agentschap," which offered intelligence on the movement of Bolshevik agents throughout Europe.[141]

Austria and the Bolshevik revolution

With the collapse of the Hohenzollern and the Habsburg empires the focus of the international Bolshevik revolution shifted from Switzerland to the three new republics in Central Europe: Germany, Austria, and Czechoslovakia. The study of the police situations in Berlin, Vienna, and Prague after the First World War is the more interesting as all three capitals found themselves in this period at the height of their effectiveness as political centers. Controlling highly strategical states, they served as the stepping stones of European-wide revolutionary

---

[134] Instruction of the Bundesanwaltschaft to Basel police, 2 Mar. 1920, in BA (Berne), Bestands-Nr. 21, Archiv-Nr. 15882; instruction of Chef des Generalstabes to Schweizerisches Eisenbahndepartement, Berne, 5 Apr. 1919, in ibid., Archiv-Nr. 11865; and draft of Bunderatsbeschluss in Apr., 1919, in ibid., Archiv-Nr. 11870.

[135] See 1922 petition by Basel-Stadt to Berne concerning the monetary cost of repressing the Landesstreik, in StA (Basel-Stadt), Politisches JJ8, 4, "Weltkrieg 1914–18: Generalstreik Landestreik 1919–1922."

[136] Bundesanwaltschaft to EJPD, Berne, 20 Nov., 1918, in BA (Berne), Bestands-Nr. 21, Archiv-Nr. 13898.

[137] L/PT No. 245 S.B., "Au sujet du mouvement bolchéviste à Lausanne," Berne, 20 Nov. 1918, in AN (Paris), F7 13506.

[138] Report, "Bolchevistes en Suisse," *commissariat spécial*, Annemasse, 14 Mar. 1919, in ibid.

[139] Schweizerische Bundesanwaltschaft, "Le Parti communiste suisse" (19-page typescript, dated 13 Dec. 1921) in BA (Berne), Bestand 2. E 4001 (A), Aktenband 38b.

[140] Report, "Antibolschewistische Organisationen der französischen, englischen und amerikanischen Gesandtschaften in Bern" (1919), in BA (Berne), Bestands-Nr. 21, Archiv-Nr. 12038.

[141] Letter, Fritz Hodler of the Bundesanwaltschaft to Bundesrat Müller, chief of EJPD, Berne, 2 Sept. 1919, in ibid., Archiv-Nr. 12041.

movements during the interwar period. In 1918 Central Europe was crucial for the survival of the Bolshevik revolution and barely a decade later the same region and its three capital cities indispensable for the Nazi conquest of the whole Continent.

The strategy of the Bolshevik world revolution in 1918–24 can be followed on hand of police reports whose trail leads us from Basel to Vienna, from Vienna to Berlin, and from Berlin to Prague. Major Iselin, a Swiss military intelligence officer, reported from Vienna on 22 July 1919:

There is no real control in Poland, Bohemia, etc. Vienna is wide open to Communists and Bolsheviks. Everyone who is stirring up trouble anywhere between Moscow and Berlin finds his way to Vienna. All the money that flows into various pockets to pay for these salubrious deals is handled by Israelite bankers in Vienna. [142]

In an extraordinary demarche the Vienna police in 1921 confided to the Swiss legation its frustration with the weakness of the Austrian government:

Communist agitation has recently increased again. It has notably scored some success in the army, where 50 percent of the soldiers are deemed unreliable if not outright Bolshevik. There is more Russian money in circulation here than ever before. This eastern propaganda comes at a time when prospects of western help are diminishing. The Austrian government shows no resolution. [143]

Not only the Swiss but also Colonel Pageot, the French military attaché in Berne, had noted the shift in revolutionary activity from Switzerland to Austria. By 1919 he had more to tell Paris about conditions in Vienna than about events in Basel or Berne. [144]

Together with the shift eastward of the revolutionary crisis came the appearance of an anti-Semitic note in European police reports dealing with the Bolshevik problem. This included the reports emanating from Swiss and French sources. Major Iselin's dispatch, above, may be seen in this light, as well as the following warning of the Swiss consul in Kiev, which Dr. Heinrich Rothmund of the Swiss aliens police in Berne conveyed to his superiors in seeming agreement with its author:

More and more suspicious eastern elements are finding their way into Switzerland. He [the Swiss consul] says that nearly all these people travel on false passports. They are also without exception Jews from Hungary, Western Russia, and all the other eastern countries. They anticipate the imminent collapse of the wonders of Bolshevism and now seek a safe haven for themselves and their honestly earned possessions. The consul thinks people in Switzerland still have no idea what repulsive and dangerous rabble [welch' abscheuliches und gefährliches Pack] they are so thoughtlessly admitting into the country and permitting to move around freely. [145]

[142] Major Iselin, Nachrichtensektion, Armeestab, to Generalstabschef, Politisches Departement, and Zentralstelle für Fremdenpolizei, Berne, 22 July 1919, in ibid., Archiv-Nr. 15882.
[143] Report, Politisches Departement to EJPD, Berne, 11 Feb. 1921, in ibid.
[144] Colonel Pageot, Ambassade de France, to Ministère de la Guerre, Berne, 26 Apr. 1919, in AN (Paris), F7 13506.
[145] Dr. Heinrich Rothmund, Zentralstelle für Fremdenpolizei, Berne, 16 July 1919, in BA (Berne), Bestands-Nr. 21, Archiv-Nr. 14020.

A list in the files of the Swiss prosecutor's office, dated Berne, 24 December 1920, gave the names, the pseudonyms, and the race of all the members of the Soviet government: 50 persons from Lenin to Goukovsky, of which 42 were identified as "Jewish."[146] Similarly the stress on the Jewish character of Bolshevik leaders can be found in numerous French police reports from this period now stored in the *Archives Nationales.*[147] The practical consequence of this phenomenon may have been relatively minor at that time, but it should still be noted because it throws light on three aspects of the story of European police in the twentieth century: (1) The anti-Semitic prejudice in the French or Swiss documents may reflect the difficulty of modern police officials to apply their professional ethics of individual judgment and legal objectivity to social situations in Eastern Europe; (2) in the face of an international danger much graver than that presented by anarchism in the 1890s and so requiring much more intensive collaboration between police authorities, it may have offered the police of different countries the semblance of a common ideological ground (they did not necessarily share a common democratic conviction); and (3) it may also have played a tragic role in making the anti-Jewish police measures of the Nazis in the 1930s to some extent acceptable to the police of certain neighboring democratic countries. In the 1930s Dr. Rothmund was criticized for his alleged undue willingness in helping the Gestapo control the movement of Jewish refugees from Germany to Switzerland.[148]

The anti-Semitic attitude among the police in Vienna is frankly discussed in a biography of Hofrat Arnold Pichler, a senior Austrian police official at the turn from the monarchy to the republic, written on the basis of family papers by his son Franz. The specter of a "world revolution" apparently placed all the senior police officials in Austria under a permanent stress (*Dauerdruck*) because their social background and education made it difficult for them to understand – or to acknowledge – the genuine needs of the laboring classes for social improvements. The idea of a Jewish world conspiracy was to them a more persuasive explanation for the disturbances. Hofrat Pichler himself, so claims his biographer, was not anti-Semitic, though he shared the anxiousness of anti-Semites about the future of bourgeois civilization and Austrian officialdom. But there were outspoken anti-Semites in high places like the chief of the state police, Dr. Franz Brandl, who thought all Jewish colleagues in the Polizei-Direktion should be considered ipso facto "unreliable."[149] The son of a doorkeeper at the imperial ministry of foreign affairs, Brandl had worked himself up from the ranks since he entered the police in 1898. During the war he had worked in the department dealing with nationality questions and handled some espionage cases. When in June 1918,

---

[146] This list, stamped "Schweizerische Bundesanwaltschaft" and dated 24 Dec. 1920, is available in ibid., Archiv-Nr. 12036.

[147] See documents in AN (Paris), F7 13506.

[148] This point is also made in Hans Habe's study of the conference at Evian-les-Bains in 1938, concerning Jewish refugees. See Hans Habe, *The Mission* (New York, 1966), p. 155.

[149] Franz A. Pichler, *Polizeihofrat P. Ein treuer Diener seines ungetreuen Staates* (Vienna, 1984), pp. 33–34.

Johann Schober became police president, Brandl became his deputy and director of the state police. In 1933 he reminisced in a public lecture on Vienna's bout with Communism in 1918–19:

The impossible was made possible. Four thousand officials of the *Sicherheitswache* [the uniformed police of Vienna] contained an excited crowd of 200,000. We limited ourselves to arresting the ringleaders. Most of them were Russian or Polish Jews. . . . The detectives proceeded with much skill. I remember how Schober furiously shouted at one of the revolutionaries: 'You unpatriotic fellow!' What a picture: destructive internationalism face to face with earthbound nationalism. Schober couldn't understand why anyone would want to take racially pure human beings – God's finest achievement – and turn them into a hodge podge mass of mollusks.[150]

Fortunately for Austria, Vienna's alleged new vulnerability to coups d'états and its attraction for every revolutionary adventurer "between Moscow and Berlin" did not outlast the first few months of postwar turmoil. There were few serious clashes between police and demonstrators: The most serious ones occurred on 12 November 1918 and on 17 April and 15 June 1919. It quickly became apparent that Austria's international powerlessness following its collapse in October 1918 also protected it from the worst of the social conflict of postwar Europe. For without the prestige of its old dynasty, without its army, and with most of its old territory now separated from it, Austria could no more be expected to defend a revolutionary communist regime against the intervention of capitalist neighbors than could Kurt Eisner's Soviet republic in Bavaria or Bela Kun's Communist Hungary. The ultimate outcome of a communist coup in Austria would probably have been a right-wing dictatorship long before 1934. To the leaders of the Third International, Germany (whose military *renommée* was unbroken by the defeat) and Czechoslovakia (whose fighting potential was deemed to be considerable) – indeed, even China's vast human resources – appeared more important prizes to win than setting up a communist regime in Vienna.

Austria of course also had her police to thank for the prevention of a communist coup, her police which – rightly or wrongly – enjoyed an outstanding reputation for professional skill in the world. Hermann Oberhummer, the officious historiographer of the Vienna police, gave it almost the sole credit for Austria's escape from Communism in 1918:

Together with all the other administrative institutions of the defunct state, the Austrian Republic from its inception also took over its police. There never has been better proof that police is the heart of any state machinery than what happened in the first years of this republic. Austria's existence depended from one day to the next on the continued goodwill of the great and medium-sized powers; it earned trust because it stemmed the Bolshevik flood and maintained intact its security service squeezed between a Soviet Bavaria and a Soviet Hungary. This also explains why [the Austrian] police was not undermined by

[150] Franz Brandl, "Wien als Bollwerk gegen den Kommunismus. Die Kämpfe der Polizeidirektion gegen die Kommunisteninvasion im Jahre 1919," in *Deutschösterreichische Tageszeitung*, 17 May 1933, pp. 3–4.

the revolution, and was spared the various attempts in other countries of "democratizing the police."[151]

Another admirer of the police, Victor Germains, wrote in 1932: "The police have always played a very important part in Austria. In the days of the old empire, in combination with the church and the army, they were one of the most important props of the dynasty." In the transition from the monarchy to the republic, "they represented, so to speak, the point of balance between warring factions that were almost equally powerful."[152]

Austrian police historians since the end of the Second World War are less sure of the police's merits in 1918–19. Herbert Zima and Eduard Hochenbichler, in a history published by the Vienna Polizei-Direktion in 1969, cautiously speak of the difficulty of judging the wisdom of political decisions made fifty years earlier, adding defensively: "The Sicherheitswache itself was not to blame. As the executive instrument of the government it did its duty even at great sacrifice to itself."[153] The journalist Jacques Hannak in 1966, a vocal critic of Police President Schober, thought the credit for sparing Austria a Communist revolution in 1919 should go to the Austrian Social Democrats rather than to the police.[154] Franz Pichler very perceptively does not go into the question, whether the Sicherheitswache did or did not defeat the communist insurgents arms in hand. Rather, he asks how far the Vienna police went to purge its ranks and change its procedures and professional outlook in preparation for a new democratic age. The answer was: very little. In Austria, the police staff tended to adhere either to feudal–elitist views, in which case it remained monarchical (Schober and Arnold Pichler), or else to a "plebeian–elitist" school in anticipation of Nazism (Brandl and his associate Dr. Otto Steinhäusl, police president of Vienna in 1938–40). Franz Pichler sees Schober's police reforms limited to improvements of the police's fighting capacity in preparation for civil war (the Vienna street police grew from 4,500 in 1919 to 10,000 in the 1920s) and to political maneuvers aimed at removing the police from the control of the municipal government.[155] While the Viennese Sicherheitswache in 1918, like the old Berlin Schutzmannschaft, was now given the status of civil servants, unlike in Prussia, no police unions were tolerated in Austria after the war. The Austrian Social Democrats also failed to pay sufficient attention to the police, concentrating instead on penetrating the army with their adherents.[156]

[151] Hermann Oberhummer, *Die Wiener Polizei* (Vienna, 1938), vol. 2, p. 288.
[152] Victor Germains, *Austria of To-Day. With a Special Chapter on the Austrian Police* (London, 1932), p. 189.
[153] Herbert Zima and Eduard Hochenbichler, *100 Jahre Wiener Sicherheitswache 1869–1969* (Vienna, 1969), p. 54.
[154] Jacques Hannak, *Johannes Schober – Mittelweg in die Katastrophe. Porträt eines Repräsentanten der verlorenen Mitte* (Vienna, 1966), passim.
[155] Pichler, *Polizeirat P.*, p. 60.
[156] "Gleichberechtigung der Gewerkschaften der Wachbeamten," (typescript, dated 29 Aug. 1927), in AVA (Vienna), S.D. Parl. Klub/67, folder "43 Wr. Polizei 1927."

The dominating figure in Austrian police history for this period is Dr. Johann Schober, Vienna's police president from 1918 to his death in 1932, with only two brief interruptions when he assumed the post of chancellor (1921–2 and 1929) and vice chancellor plus foreign minister (1930–2). Unlike most police directors in the modern age, Johann Schober did not shun the political limelight. His ambition may have contributed to the conspicuous ascendancy of the police in the public life of the Austrian Republic, but his personal leanings toward monarchism and his contempt for the workers exacerbated the class conflict at a time when social reconciliation was badly needed in Austria.[157] For the catastrophic clash between workers and Sicherheitswache in Vienna on 15 July 1927, most of the blame today seems to devolve on Schober's order for the police to use force, and on certain officers who sanctioned the use of dum dum bullets (normally reserved for target practice only) when their men ran out of regular ammunition. That Schober, a few days later, staged a ceremonious demonstration of loyalty to his own person by the staff of the Polizei-Direktion reflects on his political character.[158] Worse, it injected the police into the political arena as an ally of right-wing German-nationalist politics instead of keeping it out of the political fray.

One source of Schober's considerable power was the extensive private and uncontrolled files he possessed on countless leading personalities. Even the political views of a well-known university professor in Vienna were looked into by a Bezirksinspektor who asked the waiters in certain cafés what newspapers the professor read there, and in what order.[159] Schober laid down that every political activity in Austria should be under police surveillance, including the behavior of police officials.[160]

SCHOBER'S CENTRAL INTELLIGENCE BUREAU

The world-wide Bolshevik scare, which coincided with a general crime wave throughout war-torn Europe, gave Austria the chance to assume once more the leadership in international police work. Schober still is best remembered abroad for founding the International Criminal Police Commission (ICPC) in 1923. During his tenure as police president of Vienna (which involved the presidency of the ICPC ex officio) he traveled to many international congresses and became well-known to the police leaders of many countries. Schober also encouraged foreign police authorities to send their officials on inspection tours or for training to Austria. Invitations went out to the Sûreté in Paris to visit courses in criminology at the Vienna University; Polish state police officials studied Austrian procedures in

[157] Both Hannak and Hochenbichler assert that Schober retained a clandestine loyalty to the fallen monarchy. See Hannak, *Schober*, pp. 74, 78; and Eduard Hochenbichler, *Republik im Schatten der Monarchie. Das Burgenland, ein europäisches Problem* (Vienna, 1971), pp. 49–50.
[158] "Sieg des Schober Terrors," in *Arbeiter-Zeitung*, 2 Mar. 1928.
[159] "Aufgaben der Wiener Polizei," in *Arbeiter-Zeitung*, 20 Apr. 1930.
[160] Gerhard Jagschitz, "Die politische Zentralevidenzstelle der Bundespolizeidirektion Wien. Ein Beitrag zur Rolle der politischen Polizei in der Ersten Republik," in *Jahrbuch für Zeitgeschichte 1978* (Vienna, 1979), p. 60.

1928; and in the early 1930's ten Chinese police cadets came for a year to learn every aspect of Austrian police administration. (One grateful cadet, later police president of Shanghai, changed his name to Yü "Shu-pin" in Schober's honor.)[161]

Less well known than the ICPC was the *Zentralevidenzstelle,* or *ZESt* (Central Intelligence Bureau) of the Polizei-Direktion in Vienna, officially founded in 1920. The *Evidenzstelle* could be regarded as a political counterpart to the ICPC, though much more limited in scope.[162] Like the ICPC it tried to be a professional police organization emphasizing objective intelligence gathering without directly applying executive police powers against individuals. Like the ICPC it emphasized contacts to foreign police authorities, though mainly with Austria's immediate neighbors. But it collaborated closely with the ministry of foreign affairs and also the ministry of war, since one of its tasks was to replace the Army's military intelligence service in the spirit of a comment by War Minister Dr. Julius Deutsch: "Today, even the most limited military action is much more costly than a timely scouting mission across the border."[163]

Much to Schober's disappointment, however, the *Evidenzstelle* was to remain practically inoperable throughout the 1920s, due to lack of money, equipment, and personnel. The chief intelligence agency of the new Austrian Republic could not have a service automobile of its own, and after 1923 was forced, for reasons of economy, to buy its foreign newspapers second-hand from Viennese cafés. When border guards near Marchegg in 1922 reported a sudden massing of Czech armed units on the other side of the frontier, the Polizei-Direktion in Vienna could not come up with the paltry sum of 100 Czech crowns to pay informers to take a look.[164]

Worse, the Evidenzstelle was responsible to three different government departments (interior, war, and foreign affairs) whose separate missions were difficult to reconcile on a tactical level. The war ministry on 11 December 1919 explicitly relinquished military intelligence work (formerly done by the Abteilung 1/N) to the new "central police intelligence bureau,"[165] but it was the foreign ministry, not the war ministry, which was given permanent representation on the staff of the *ZESt* to guard against any police interference with Austrian diplomacy.[166] When the war ministry in 1920 demanded the resumption of

---

[161] On the Polish visit, see "Das Eintreffen einer polnischen Studienkommission bei der Polizeidirektion Wien," in *Int. Oeff. Sich.,* Vienna, IV, Jhg. (1928), Nr. 19/20, pp. 16–18. For the Chinese cadets, see Polizeimajor Karl Schmutterer, "Unsere Berufskameraden in Hangchow," and "Aus unserer Studienzeit in Wien. Von zehn chinesischen Polizeioffizieren," in *Oeff. Sich.,* 13. Jhg., Nr. 12 (Dec. 1933), pp. 20–1; 22–3.

[162] Pichler, *Polizeihofrat P.,* p. 74.

[163] Letter, Deutsch, D.ö. Staatsamt für Heereswesen, to Oest. Staatsamt für Ausseres, Vienna, 20 Sept. 1920, in HHSta (Vienna), Liasse Oesterreich 26/I, Faszikel 439.

[164] Waldorff, Polizeidirektion Wien (Zentralevidenzstelle), to Bundesministerium für Inneres, Vienna, 4 Aug. 1922, in ibid.

[165] Deutsch to Staatsamt des Aussern, Vienna, 11 Dec. 1919, in ibid.

[166] See Deutschösterreichisches Staatsamt für Ausseres, "Zentralevidenzstelle bei der Polizeidirektion Wien. Errichtung," (1920), in ibid.

aggressive intelligence gathering in neighboring states Schober had to admit that he lacked the resources for such a mission. He suggested hiring civilians for secret missions abroad.[167] Consequently the army in 1923 dropped the *ZESt* and turned to the diplomatic and consular services for help when it needed information on foreign weapons research – light machineguns, pistols, hand grenades, tanks, and infantry camouflage. Only the Austrian diplomats and consular officials quickly complained about the unsuitability of combining diplomatic missions with espionage:

> The Spanish embassy in Brussels is currently acting as caretaker of Austrian interests in Belgium. We cannot possibly ask it to obtain confidential information on Belgian tanks. In Greece, the Austrian honorary consul has no secure means of communications to Vienna; he cannot convey sensitive military information. The Austrian representative in Copenhagen is also our envoy to Berlin. He spends most of his time in Berlin and is not in Copenhagen for long enough periods to establish the kind of personal relations necessary for obtaining military information.[168]

But in announcing the formation of the new intelligence agency to all Austrian diplomatic missions abroad, the Austrian foreign ministry itself had seemed confused. To the Austrian legation in Paris, the foreign ministry wrote:

> The new bureau at the police directorium in Vienna will record all political events and all political movements at home and abroad, analyze them, and make them available to all [Austrian] central and regional authorities. . . . The work of *ZESt* is not confined to the surveillance of individuals or movements which oppose the state. It does not constitute a political counterpart to the criminal police with its rogues' gallery and criminal file. *ZESt* will gather information on any and all political persons and movements, without distinguishing between their positive or negative attitude towards the state. Thus it will collect information equally on communist, monarchist, anarchist, Christian Socialist, and Social Democratic activities. The same neutrality applies to the study of politically active persons and political movements abroad, in particular in countries established on the territory of the former monarchy.[169]

The difficulty of this definition is that it deprived the officials of the Evidenzstelle of a target to work for (such as the protection of the Austrian Republic) and of an enemy to struggle against (such as international Bolshevism). Dr. Bernhard Weiss, who at that time ran the political police in Berlin, by contrast affirmed the similarity of the work of Prussia's criminal and political police: the one specialized on the defense of civil society, the other on the defense of the Republican constitution. As an experienced fellow professional Schober, in fact, concurred with Weiss that police work has to be anchored on a fundamental object of loyalty. In

---

[167] Schober, Polizeidirektion Wien, to Staatsamt f. Aeusseres, Vienna, 14 Aug. 1920, in ibid.
[168] Bundeskanzleramt (Auswärtige Angelegenheiten), to Bundesministerium für Heereswesen, Abt. 4, Vienna, 12 Feb. 1924, in ibid.
[169] Oesterreichisches Staatsamt für Ausseres, to all Austrian legations and consulates: "Aktivierung der ZESt. Uebernahme des offensiven Nachrichtendienstes," Vienna, 14 Aug. 1920, in ibid; and the same to Austrian mission in Paris, Vienna, 30 Aug. 1920, in ibid.

his original proposal to the Austrian chancellor Dr. Renner, dated 21 December 1919, Schober had formulated the object of the Evidenzstelle very carefully:

> On the basis of observations in recent months concerning certain individuals at home and abroad with left-wing and right-wing inclinations, whose intrigues are aimed at the violent and illegal overthrow of the conditions created by the Treaty of St. Germain on the territory of the former Austro-Hungarian Monarchy . . . [we need to establish] a tight organization of the police authorities of all succession states who maintain good relations to Austria. [170]

Schober immediately acted on this overall concept in the instructions which he issued on the same day to his subordinates in the Vienna police directorium. They were to prepare for renewing the kinds of contacts to foreign police headquarters which Austria developed in the wake of the Rome Conference of 1898 to fight international anarchism.

> The Polizei-Direktion Wien will establish contacts with the central police bureaus in other countries either through diplomatic channels or directly if this can be arranged by special agreement or on the basis of reciprocity. The Vienna police will provide relevant information to these foreign bureaus on request or on its own initiative and will seek to obtain similar information in return. It will in particular try to further direct intercourse between local [subordinate] police authorities in Austria and their foreign counterparts. [171]

Defending the political settlement of St. Germain was obviously much more functional as a definition of the Evidenzstelle's police mission, and the qualification of "good relations to Austria" a necessary reservation in case of political conflict with a neighboring state. But even Schober's more crafty statement was to prove unsatisfactory before long: applied to the pursuit of communist agents it facilitated cooperation with Berlin, Rome, Berne, and Helsinki. At the same time it did not earn Vienna the credit it had earned in the fight against nineteenth-century anarchists. Austria's anti-Bolshevik crusade was easily outdone by the parallel efforts of the Great Powers whose information services were well-funded, who had soldiers fighting Trotsky's Red Army, and whose relief missions in the famine areas deep inside Russia – so at least the Bolsheviks feared – traded train loads of food and medicine for military intelligence and political influence. Applied to the defense of the peace settlement of 1919, it raised the question which of the succession states was the least satisfied and would be the first to demand border revisions. Thus relations between Vienna and Prague became strained as Czechoslovakia in the twenties drew steadily closer to France, the principal champion of the new status quo, while Austria itself turned to Germany and was far less committed to the maintenance of the Paris treaties. In short, the direct coupling of professional international police work with the foreign policy goals of new

[170] Letter, Schober to Staatskanzler, Staatssekretär d. Innern, Staatsamt des Aeussern, and Landeshauptmann von Niederösterreich, Vienna, 21 Dec. 1919, in ibid.
[171] Schober, "Entwurf einer Instruktion für die Ueberwachung der an Umtrieben gegen den Staat beteiligten Personen," enclosed with the above in ibid.

states still undergoing a testing of their standing within the European balance of power was to invite serious difficulties.

From the mid-twenties on, the ministry of war resumed the conduct of military intelligence and the ministry of foreign affairs the collection of political intelligence abroad.[172] Gerhard Jagschitz, who in 1979 published an extensive study on the subject suggests that the Evidenzstelle may principally have served to provide political information for the extensive archive on important public personalities which Police President Schober kept – like J. Edgar Hoover in the United States – as protection for his own political power. If so, the agency's solid, old-fashioned bureaucratism prevented any chance of it growing into the kind of dynamic praetorian guard that served as power base for a Heinrich Himmler or Reinhard Heydrich, even had Schober nursed such ambitions. The ZESt at the Polizei-Direktion Vienna declined in the early 1930s when a new intelligence service was formed inside the chancellory of Engelbert Dollfuss, and in 1938 it was disbanded when Germany annexed the Austrian Republic.

The revolution in Berlin

Like the Habsburg monarchy the German Empire also had to undergo the difficult switch from autocracy to parliamentary democracy in a very short time, albeit without the same drastic loss of territory. In this study the German revolution interests us far more than the revolution in Russia, because the change in regime in Berlin proceeded along the lines of a "police" crisis instead of a protracted civil war and a military style conquest of power, thus more like the French revolutions of 1815 and 1830, in which the struggle for power centered on seizing the levers of government in the national capital. "Weak as it is politically," wrote a British journalist who visited Germany right after the Armistice, "the German governmental system is too strong police-ically to be overthrown by force."[173]

The German revolution of 1918 was a "police" revolution, and by and large a successful one, because there was no danger that the German Empire might dissolve into particularism, though it looked for a short while as if Bavaria might go the road of secession.[174] Arnold Brecht, a senior Prussian civil servant at that time, tells in his personal memoirs about proceeding by train on a lonely fact-finding mission to Munich in 1921 to see whether the government in Berlin could still count on the subordination of Munich.[175] (The telling point is that Brecht's train trip was sufficient to calm the fears of the Reich government. In fact, only the Munich police under Ernst Pöhner showed some disposition to enter politics on its own, rather like Schober's police in postwar Vienna, with whom Pöhner was

[172] Jagschitz, "Zentralevidenzstelle," p. 82.
[173] George Young, The New Germany (New York, 1920), pp. ix–x.
[174] "Weak as it is politically, the present German governmental system seems too strong police-ically to be overthrown by force." Ibid.
[175] Arnold Brecht, Aus nächster Nähe. Lebenserinnerungen eines beteiligten Beobachters 1884–1927 (Stuttgart, 1966), pp. 330ff.

in communication.)[176] As to class war, the Communist leaders in Petrograd knew that only a quick seizure of power in Berlin had a chance of success. Revolutionary armies were difficult to raise in so well policed a state as Germany. Furthermore, the Western powers were bound to intervene if Germany became embroiled in a long civil war. The German Red armies in the industrial regions of the Ruhr and in Thuringia were quickly annihilated by German troops and police with Allied blessing.[177] Communist emissaries like the young Ernst Reuter arriving in Berlin during the winter of 1918–19 with orders from Zinoviev and Lenin to prepare a workers' uprising found themselves quickly hunted from one place to the next, in great pains to hide a satchel of hand grenades or an army rifle from the prying eyes of other roomers or the landlady.[178] The Russian revolutionary, Karl Radek, was unexpectedly caught by Berlin city detectives when they raided a house in Kurfürstenstrasse in 1919, following a burglary at the Adlon Hotel.[179] The capture of Radek not only foiled an imminent communist plot but produced an important link between the Bolsheviks and the Reichswehr as Radek was visited in jail by the man who was to rebuild the German army after the war, General Hans von Seeckt.[180] It was not just the ubiquitous presence of the police that made preparing for civil war so difficult in Germany. There was also the suspiciousness of the population in town and country to reckon with, most of whom were opposed to a violent change in Germany's social fabric.[181]

We might add that a "police" revolution was the more appropriate for Germany as Berlin in the twentieth century was the kind of urban machine easily held to ransom by technically schooled saboteurs, as Curzio Malaparte described this technique in his 1932 study, *Coup d'Etat* – except that this tactic was never actually applied in this city. The Hohenzollern monarchy was not overthrown on 9 November 1918, by a careful plot such as Louis Napoleon would have prepared over many months with fellow conspirators. Instead the monarchy collapsed at home when the Burgfrieden doctrine with its one-sided emphasis on military success against outside foes became meaningless following the army's defeat on the Western front. Unlike in the occupied territories of Belgium and Russian Poland, security inside Germany had not been tight during the war.[182] When the news of

---

[176] Pichler, *Polizeihofrat P.* pp. 45–6.

[177] Johannes Buder, *Die Reorganisation der preussischen Polizei 1918–1923* (Frankfurt a.M. Berne, 1986), pp. 218ff.

[178] Among other descriptions, see Willy Brandt and Richard Löwenthal, *Ernst Reuter. Ein Leben für die Freiheit* (Munich, 1957), pp. 114–24.

[179] Buder, *Reorganisation der preussischen Polizei*, pp. 45–6. Hedda Adlon, *Hotel Adlon. Das Haus in dem die Welt zu Gast war* (Munich, 1955), pp. 145–68. The arrest of Karl Radek and Countess Treuberg was reported in *Vossische Zeitung*, 13 Feb. 1919 (morning and evening editions). On this occasion the criminal police detectives shared a reward of ten thousand marks offered by a private association, the *Vereinigung zur Bekämpfung des Bolschewismus*.

[180] Helm Speidel, "Reichswehr und Rote Armee," in V.f.Z.G. 1. Jhg., 1. Heft (1953), pp. 9–45.

[181] Richard Müller, *Der Bürgerkrieg in Deutschland. Geburtswehen der Republik* (Berlin, 1925), pp. 13–14.

[182] The Directorate of Military Intelligence, (British) War Office, *The German Police System as Applied to Military Security in War*, (1921), Part II, p.i.

Emperor Wilhelm II's abdication and his flight to Holland spread through the city on 9 November, the Imperial Palace, the Reichstag and the Rathaus, all the railway stations, military barracks and – last but not least – the police presidium on Alexanderplatz surrendered to the crowds of demonstrators without a fight. While Chancellor Max von Baden arranged for a caretaker government headed by the Socialist Friedrich Ebert to succeed him, Police President von Oppen telephoned the offices of the USPD (the Independent Social Democratic Party, which enjoyed a strong following among the Berlin workers) to ask for a replacement, then yielded his post to Emil Eichhorn, a veteran Socialist and trained metal worker.[183]

There was sporadic fighting in the streets of Berlin throughout the next three months, with government troops and Spartacists (the forerunners of the German Communists) in succession taking occupation of isolated public buildings or newspaper offices. None of these scattered operations seemed aimed at establishing a firm hold over the city and through it over the country as a whole. The police presidium was occupied by workers on 5 January 1919, but this powerful machine was something beyond what armed squatters knew how to use. The hilarious pen and ink drawings of Berliners during the street unrest of 1919 and 1920, which the German cartoonist Fritz Wolff published in contemporary newspapers – complete with a soldier escorting an *Oma* safely across no-man's-land and a revolutionary disappearing in a *pissoir* – were so telling because they entirely lacked the doctrinaire seriousness of Russian revolutionary art.

The technique of establishing a stranglehold over the city's vital services was not applied until the Kapp putsch in March 1920. However, on that occasion it was not used to seize political power in the country. It served the purpose of unseating the right-wing usurper government of Wolfgang Kapp and General von Lüttwitz. Malaparte acknowledged the success of the workers who thus paralyzed the Kapp government and brought it to fall in a matter of days.[184] According to him, the German Communist Party (founded in December 1918) thereupon trained squads in the 1920s to infiltrate and sabotage public utilities and police stations, moving them unnoticed among unsuspecting pedestrians in practice alerts, only the moment for a Communist coup never came.[185] After 1920 Berlin was well-protected by a reformed and greatly improved security police, the Schutzpolizei, equipped with automatic firearms and fast trucks, and enjoying considerable popular support among Berliners thanks to careful and imaginative public relations work.

Lastly, Berlin in 1918 escaped a Communist seizure of power because most workers had been willing after the fall of the anti-Socialist law to give the existing society a chance. Friedrich Stampfer, on 20 January 1918, underlined this in an

[183] Emil Eichhorn, *Meine Tätigkeit im Berliner Polizeipräsidium und mein Anteil an den Januar-Ereignissen* (Berlin, 1919), passim.
[184] Curzio Malaparte, *Coup d'Etat. The Technique of Revolution* (New York, 1932), pp. 126–9.
[185] Ibid., pp. 75–6.

editorial for the Social-Democratic paper, *Vorwärts*, in which he announced to his readers that Germany rejected the Russian road to democracy by way of a dictatorship of the proletariat. Germany, he said, would build her democracy on popular consensus without reference to class distinctions. "No other form of government is possible in a country where almost everyone reads a daily newspaper and shapes his political behavior according to his personal pocketbook."[186] Stampfer could not have better formulated the condition of a society ready for "modern police" rule: a society that is politically educated, down-to-earth rationalist, and individualistic in motivation.

THE BERLIN POLICE IN THE REVOLUTION OF 1918–19

Unlike in Vienna, no one in Berlin praised the old royal constabulary (the *Schutzmannschaft*) for saving the country from a Communist revolution. Germany's high level of urban industrial development, largely untouched by the war since all the fighting had taken place outside its frontiers, gave the civilian population an extra incentive to resort to self-policing during the Communist emergency. To these self-policing institutions we count the local civil guards (*Einwohnerwehren*) with two million members in all Germany, and the technical squads of engineers and skilled workers (*Technische Nothilfe*) whose job it was to keep city services running during public disturbances.[187] Not the police but seasoned trade union functionaries and factory stewards (*Obleute*) kept the restless workers under control and directed their strike actions against putschist elements of the extreme left and right.

The free-corps units which were created in December 1918 under General Ludwig von Maercker and with the sanction of the Ebert government had a more dubious record as police units. Their militarist mentality and tactics were often far too destructive to be used in the midst of a metropolitan city of four million inhabitants, however much apologists for Waldemar Pabst and the Garde Kavallerie Schützen Division might argue that the brutal murder of the Spartacist leaders Rosa Luxemburg and Karl Liebknecht (15 January 1919) was necessary to prevent a Communist revolution.[188]

In sum, the performance of the royal Schutzmannschaft in Berlin was unheroic. To be sure, in later years spokesmen for the police tried to excuse its abdication of responsibility in November 1918 by pointing to the "lack of leadership at the top," the "impossible odds they faced against immense crowds," and by claiming that the constables had been moved by the recognition that the time had come for Germany to espouse democracy.[189] The civil police eventually survived in Berlin not because it had served the city well during the troubles at the end of the war

---

[186] Friedrich Stampfer, "Demokratie und Revolution," in *Vorwärts*, 20 Jan. 1918 (Sonntagsbeilage).
[187] Directorate of Military Intelligence, *German Police System*, Part I, pp. 1, 16.
[188] On the brutality of the Freikorps and the Garde-Kavallerie-Schützendivision, see Müller, *Der Bürgerkrieg in Deutschland*, ch. 10.
[189] Hsi-Huey Liang, *The Berlin Police Force in the Weimar Republic* (Berkeley, 1970), ch. 2.

but because the Allies vetoed the paramilitary Sicherheitspolizei and insisted on the reconstitution of the old professional police.

Ironically, the ignominious failure of the old Berlin police in 1918–19 may have been the principal reason why the Schutzpolizei in the 1920s proved a much stauncher defender of democracy than the Vienna police of Johann Schober. (1) The civil police (both old and new) largely escaped involvement in the atrocities committed by both sides during the street fighting at the end of the war. (In Austria, the police in 1918 had fought against the workers and remained throughout the 1920s politically much more partisan on the side of reaction than in Prussia.) (2) After 1920, the civil police had to undergo a thorough reform to reestablish its credibility in the eyes of the public and – not being able to claim victory over the Communist insurgents – sought this recognition in bold proclamations of new democratic police principles and zealous displays of professionalism. The technical expertise was notably applied to the rationalization of office procedure inside police stations (the "Magdeburg reform") and criminalistic research, and this again reinforced the police's commitment to political neutrality.

By 1920 a new Schutzpolizei was ready to take over from the military the premier role as the executive instrument of the German state. The German army, reduced by article 160 of the Versailles Treaty to 100,000 men and limited to domestic pacification and border guard duty became an auxiliary to the modernized police because Germany henceforth could not found its police order any longer on "the primacy of foreign policy" and the need to subordinate domestic disputes to the exigencies of national defense.

The abandonment of Burgfrieden was facilitated in 1918–20 by the importance which most European governments attached to Germany as a bulwark against Bolshevism. A German offer to Switzerland in October 1919 for direct police communications between the two countries to fight Bolshevism in Central Europe was eagerly taken up by the Swiss minister in Berlin, von Planta. It provided among others for mutual visits by Swiss and German police officials and practical suggestions of police actions to take (*gegenseitige Anregung zu exekutiven Handlungen*). [190] A similar arrangement was in force between the police of Berlin and Vienna. The two authorities exchanged hundreds of messages through the Austrian legation in Berlin between February 1920 and June 1922 concerning individual communist couriers traveling in Central and Eastern Europe. [191]

Following the conclusion of the Rapallo agreement between Germany and the Bolshevik Russia (1922), Germany's immunity against Bolshevik subversion was by and large assured. Germany became one of Russia's most active trade partners. The political benefit of a reviving economy plus the rumor of 300,000 Russian

---

[190] "Frage wegen den Abschluss eines Abkommens zwischen der schweiz. und den deutschen Behörden untereinander um die Gefahr des Bolschewismus zu bekämpfen," (Oct./Dec. 1919), in BA (Berne), Bestands-Nr. 21, Archiv-Nr. 12039.

[191] See ninety-three exchanges between Regierungsrat Mayer (Vienna) and Staatskommissar für öffentliche Ordnung (Berlin), in HHStA (Vienna), Liasse Oesterreich, Faszikel 440.

grenades delivered to the German army were jocularly credited as a Bolshevik contribution to the suppression of Communism in Germany.

The Bolsheviks in Prague

By 1920, with Berlin pacified, it appeared as if Prague would become the alternative headquarters for Bolshevik activities in Europe: "Berlin has become too dangerous as a center," an internal Communist report read which the German gendarmerie intercepted on 1 April 1920, and which found its way to the French political police. "Consequently we must find another city to replace it that is easy to reach from Berlin. The close watch kept by the Berlin police could completely sever our contacts to Moscow."[192] What the Bolsheviks were up to in the Czechoslovak capital was summarized by the French Sûreté on 2 February 1921, as follows:

In Prague, which has become the center for all activities in Central Europe, the Soviet government maintains: (1) a mission charged with propaganda under Gillerson, to inform them on the political situation and on the success of Bolshevik propaganda; and (2) an economic mission to purchase whatever Russia lacks most (paper, sugar, and it is said also locomotives and rolling stock).[193]

Observations made by French diplomats in Prague in the subsequent months only reinforced the impression of Czechoslovakia's importance to Moscow following the failure of the Communist revolution in Berlin.

Berlin is the center of all secret agencies for Western Europe except Lithuania, Finland, Estonia and Latvia (which are directed from Reval).[. . . But] Prague is almost as important as Berlin as a center of propaganda. . . . Prague is important for Soviet couriers coming from Moscow. It is in Prague that they change into artists, simple workmen, or tourists, all well supplied by Moscow with money and instructions. To go from Prague to Paris the Bolshevik couriers follow this route: Prague, Leipzig (which is a control station), Stuttgart, Munich, Geneva, Lyon, Paris.[194]

That Czechoslovakia would fall to a Communist coup was probably not seriously feared by France. Of the three Central European capitals, Prague in 1918 had suffered the least civil strife. Not even the proclamation of independence from Austria on 28 October had caused serious violence, and when the small Czechoslovak Communist Party in 1920 tried to seize the building of the Socialist Party newspaper *Pravo Lidu* in an attempt at a political coup, it was evicted by the

---

[192] Letter by one Krazsni, Vienna, 24 Feb. 1920, as distributed by the Sûreté Générale, Contrôle Général des Services de Police Administrative, Service Spécial "Tchécoslovaquie," to M. Sicard and various French missions in Eastern Europe, in AN (Paris), F7 13486.

[193] Report, "Au sujet d'agissements de Kirdetsof (Dvoretski) et de B. Duchesne," 970-SCR-2/11, 2 Feb. 1921, in ibid.

[194] "Extrait d'un rapport des Affaires Etrangères, en date du 8 Nov. 1921, classé *à Propagande – Russie – 10–5*," in ibid.

Prague police without bloodshed.[195] The recent victory of the Czech national movement had doubtless rendered the new republic quite unreceptive to Communism, at least for a considerable time into the future. What bothered Paris more were the persistent efforts of the Bolsheviks not only to spy on Czechoslovak military strength but to turn the Czechs against their protector, France. Letters written by Karl Radek to the Czech Communist leaders Muna, Smeral, and Tuček which fell into the hands of the French police in October 1920, seemed to leave little doubt about the Bolsheviks' intentions:

You are on the right path and I want you to redouble your efforts to separate once and for all Czechoslovakia from the governments that support that infamous Treaty of Versailles. The Treaty of Versailles rests on 2 real powers: the bayonets of the French Army and the bayonets of the Polish Army. These 2 powers are the true danger, certainly not British capitalism or American capitalism. Every effort of the Third International must be directed to the destruction of French military power. The rest will follow by itself.[196]

A French Sûreté report, *"Au sujet de la Mission soviétique de Prague"* (1922) again emphasized the strategic military danger emanating from the activities of the Bolsheviks in Prague.

The new press bureau of the Soviet mission in Czechoslovakia is especially dangerous not to that country itself but to certain countries in Central and Western Europe. It is interesting to note that the press attacks in Prague against the French military mission and against French policies and French imperialism appear both in the [Czech] Communist papers and in German nationalist papers. This again shows that Russian Bolsheviks and German nationalists pursue the same goal and that they are allied in their hatred of the Entente, and of France in particular.[197]

French Sûreté concerns during the early twenties about the activities of the GPU (the Russian secret police) in Prague did however abate after 1924 when the Soviets dropped their agitation in Czechoslovakia in return for improved trade relations. In 1924 the conclusion of a Franco-Czech alliance stabilized the balance of power against Germany and the Soviet Union. The Czech police in that year not only arrested a "germano-bolshevik" named Serge Zhukovsky who had stolen Czech mobilization plans for the Reichswehr, it also caught seven members of Soviet espionage in Czechoslovakia whose manifold activities were said to have been aimed at an eventual Communist coup d'état in Prague.[198] The Czechoslovak government faced its toughest police problem not in the Bolshevik world rev-

---

[195] See "Blutige Zusammenstösse zwischen Arbeitern und Polizisten in Prag," in *Berliner Tageblatt*, 11 Dec. 1920, p. 2; and Gustav Fuchs, "Der Kommunismus in der Tschechoslowakei," in Ibid., 23 Dec. 1920, pp. 1–2.

[196] J.M.G./28 to Affaires Etrangères, Sûreté Générale, and (French) mission in Prague, "Au sujet d'une lettre de RADEK aux bolchéviques tchèques," Paris 4–5 Oct. 1920, in AN (Paris), F7 13486.

[197] "Au sujet de la Mission soviétique de Prague," (bonne source), No. 11414, S.D.R.-2/II, 1 Feb. 1922, in ibid.

[198] "Arrestation d'espions soviétiques en Tchéco-Slovaquie," P/9894.U., Paris, 4 July 1924, in ibid.; and "La Tchéka de Prague," P.9923.U., Paris, 10 July 1924, in ibid.

olution but in the national resentment of the German Bohemians who were included in the new republic against their will. Dr. Gustav Fuchs of the *Berliner Tageblatt,* a reporter not unsympathetic to the Czechs, wrote in 1920 that Beneš made a serious mistake when he decided to force three million German Bohemians to submit to laws that they would only accept under military duress – something incompatible with the relationship between fellow citizens.[199]

The International Red Cross in Russia

In the light of Switzerland's severe treatment of foreign deserters, we should mention the Red Cross Society, whose good work won Switzerland much deserved recognition abroad, and sometimes fulfilled functions akin to an international police in disaster areas.

Switzerland's mission as a country of political asylum in the nineteenth century had become compromised when "revolution" ceased to mean the fight for individual liberty as understood by a Locke, a Hume, or a Jefferson, but came to mean class war, terrorism, mass rebellion, and aspirations to proletarian dictatorship. In the twenty-five years before the First World War Switzerland's policy of asylum became too dangerous to uphold particularly in regard to political refugees coming from Eastern Europe and quietly fell into desuetude. Its place was taken by the International Red Cross inasmuch as this organization was better suited in the new era of world wars and permanent revolutions to give this small country a modicum of influence in state affairs.

The International Red Cross, founded in 1864 by the Genevan philanthropist Henri Dunant, had by 1914 developed national branches in almost all countries of the world. The Swiss ran two Red Cross societies: the International Committee of the Red Cross (ICRC) in Geneva and the Swiss Red Cross (*Schweizerisches Rotes Kreuz,* or *SRK,* founded 1882) in Berne, both of them staffed by Swiss citizens. The ICRC coordinated the work of the national Red Cross Societies throughout the world, while the Swiss Red Cross was the chief support of the Swiss army's medical services. As time went on, the Swiss Red Cross in addition became one of the principal instruments of the country's refugee policy, working together with the Swiss aliens police, and also its agency for humanitarian missions abroad.[200]

---

[199] Dr. Gustav Fuchs, "Das friedlose Tschechien," in *Berliner Tageblatt,* 24 Nov. 1920, p. 1.

[200] We have no evidence that a deliberate decision was ever made by the Swiss government to substitute for its former service of providing asylum to foreign democrats a new policy of disaster aid to other countries. Nor can we prove that the ICRC and SRK consciously saw their task as "police protection" for noncombattants as the European state system reached its destructive climax in the total warfare of 1914–18 and 1939–45. As historians, however, we cannot but note the neat coincidence in the breakdown of the one and the emergence of the other. Sad, but not altogether surprising, is the recognition that Switzerland's role as Europe's good Samaritan could have but a limited success given the enormous scope of the holocaust that befell the continent in midcentury. See also Peter Macalister-Smith, "Disaster Relief. Reflections on the Role of International Law," in *Zeitschrift für ausländisches öffentliches Recht und Völkerrecht,* 45. Jhg. 1. Heft (1985).

That the Red Cross performed policelike functions in the execution of its mission was officially never acknowledged by the society though it was in practice scarcely avoidable. True, the Swiss Red Cross had no need for any police machinery of its own as long as it served as an auxiliary to the Swiss army. The military provided all the necessary structure, organization, and discipline to take care of such needs. The First World War, however, shifted attention from the care for military casualties to servicing prisoners of war and civilian victims for whom the prerequisite for any relief was the imposition of some sort of order and control – in short, policing. (An international Red Cross agreement in 1906 had already given Red Cross personnel the right to carry arms for self-protection in danger zones.)[201] Thus the Greek Red Cross in 1921 joined the military in restoring order in Smyrna: It did general cleaning-up work, imposed compulsory inoculations, and rounded up stray children.[202]

Another potential "policing" function of the ICRC was monitoring combatants for infringements of the rules of war. The medical services that the Red Cross provided gave it some practical bargaining power to persuade belligerents to desist from the commission of war atrocities. This question came up with particular urgency in the Abyssinian War and in the Second World War.

In the First World War the Red Cross could rely on the principle of reciprocity to promote humanitarian treatment to prisoners of war. The police function of the Red Cross representatives was limited to inspection rights, but these were extensively used and included the examination of what punishments were administered to prisoners for infringements of camp rules.[203]

But the potential for actually assuming some executive police authority arose mainly in the devastated regions of Russia at the end of the civil war in 1921. In 1921–2, an estimated thirty-four to forty million people were prey to starvation and epidemics, leading to suicides, infanticides, depression, and apathy.[204] Because the Imperial Russian Red Cross had largely been run by members of the Russian aristocracy, its personnel was drastically purged in July and again in October 1917. By January 1918, a new Bolshevik Red Cross had been formed while the old Russian Red Cross continued to function with the counterrevolutionary White armies and abroad.[205] The representative of the old Russian Red Cross in Geneva was Dr. Georges Lodygensky. In a report to the International Russia Relief Committee (September, 1922) he argued that foreign Red Cross societies had been invited to go to Russia

in order to assist [the Russian Red Cross] in its work and, if necessary, to replace it in regions where it no longer has access . . . The work of these neutral foreign organizations in Russia is the more useful as they can more easily intervene in times of domestic troubles,

[201] Prof. Zorn "Das neue Abkommen über das Rote Kreuz," in *Die Woche*, 1907.

[202] Report by B. Patrikios and J. Athanassakis (Hellenic Red Cross), to Paul des Gouttes (ICRC), Athens, 5/18 Jan. 1921, in ASRK (Berne), J.II.15. 1969/7, Aktenzeichen 42.

[203] See collection of reports in ibid., Aktenzeichen 197: "Gefangenenlager 1914–1918."

[204] Hans von Eckardt, *Russia*, trans. by Catherine Alison Phillips (New York, 1932), p. 374.

[205] André Durand, *Histoire du Comité international de la Croix Rouge. De Sarajevo à Hiroshima* (Geneva, 1978), pp. 86–7.

and Europe and America will finally learn, through the testimonial of their own delegates, about the absurd and bloody horrors committed by the Bolshevik regime in Russia.[206]

Lodygensky's report was no doubt slanted with a political purpose. He asked the International Russian Relief Committee to press the Bolsheviks for the release of the patriarch of Moscow and of all the political prisoners in Russia, whose number he estimated at one million. Because the Committee was neutral, he added, it could demand that its aid be made available impartially to supporters and opponents of Bolshevism alike. The Italian and the Swedish Red Cross thereupon undertook steps to this effect, the Swedish Red Cross allocating 30,000 crowns for helping political prisoners.[207]

The Soviet Red Cross denied that it was responsible for the famine in Russia or that it had intervened with foreign relief missions. But it did admit that its missions served as advance parties for the government in its effort to establish its authority in the ravaged areas of the hinterland. The president of the new Red Cross society, Z. Soloviev, reported that his organization avoided duplicating the work of reconstruction of the Soviets but rather complemented it by "penetrating into regions which the government had so far failed to reach and by establishing institutions there which until then the government for various reasons had not been able to provide."[208]

Both the Soviet and the foreign Red Cross mission were obviously compelled to perform some executive functions in the territories where the famine raged. The German Red Cross reported from Moscow the outbreak of cannibalism among the starving inhabitants, accompanied by murder, and the confinement of persons found guilty of such acts to hospitals by German Red Cross personnel.[209] British and Swedish relief workers took it on themselves to appoint local inhabitants who appeared to them trustworthy for guard duty over supply stores, though they did rely on the Soviets for protection against major sabotage action and looting.[210] How far the International Relief Committee might have gone in exercising some spontaneous ad hoc policing functions had the Soviets not very suspiciously guarded against any usurpation of their political authority is difficult to say.[211] The Soviet Red Cross was itself accused of political activities abroad, for example of serving as cover for communist subversion in Czechoslovakia and of undertaking political intelligence work in Bulgaria and Switzerland.[212]

[206] Report by Dr. Lodygensky, second session of the Comité International de Secours à la Russie, Geneva, Sept., 1922, in ASRK (Berne), J.II.15. 1969/7, Aktenzeichen 113.

[207] Report by Hjalmar Cedercrantz, (Swedish Red Cross), in ibid.

[208] Report by Z. Solovieff (Russian Red Cross), "La Croix-Rouge russe dans la lutte contre la famine," in ibid., p. 13.

[209] German Red Cross, Russian Relief Section No. 362, "Tätigkeitsbericht Kasan," to Nansen Relief Mission in Moscow, Moscow, 24 Apr., 1922, in ibid.

[210] Report by M. Webster, "Save the Children Union," International Committee for Russian Relief, Riga, 28 Sept. 1921, in ibid.

[211] See paragraph 14 of the agreement between Dr. Friedjof Nansen and the foreign commissar Chicherin in Moscow, 27 August, 1921, in ibid.

[212] Letter, Serge Bagotzky, Russian Red Cross delegate to International Red Cross Commission, 17 Mar. 1924, in ibid.

A concluding remark

After the end of the civil war in 1922, in place of stirring up insurrections in Central Europe, Russia offered military help to revolutionary movements elsewhere in the world, notably to the Chinese revolutionaries under Sun-Yat-sen in Canton. The shift of attention from Basel to Vienna, from Vienna to Berlin, and finally from Berlin to Prague (and from there to Asia) intrigued observers like the pan-German writer from Bohemia, Hermann Ullmann:

As long as "European" Russia still formed part of Europe the center of Europe was anchored around three cities: Berlin (the political center), Prague (the strategic, geographical center), and Vienna (the historical center). If ever the border dividing Europe from Asia were to move westward – from the Urals to Poland's or Germany's eastern border – then Europe will have to find a new center in the Rhineland, probably anchored around Strasbourg, and Berlin will decline to a frontier town . . .[213]

The question which Ullmann raised in 1932 lost none of its acuity in the twenty-five years that followed. But how did he think Europe's borders would be held against the advance of Eurasia? George Young, a perceptive British journalist, warned in 1920 that Germany was being discouraged by three factors from assuming her important role against the East: the imposition of an untried system of democracy in Berlin, the assignment of three million Germans to Slavic rule (in Bohemia), and the Allied sanction against the merger of Germany with Austria.[214] Our attention in Chapter 5 will focus on the interlocking police situations in the Weimar Republic, the Austrian Republic, and in Czechoslovakia with its Sudeten German minority, which together spelled catastrophe for all Europe by 1938.

[213] Hermann Ullmann, *Flucht aus Berlin?* (Jena, 1932), pp. 102–3.
[214] Young, *The New Germany*, pp. 216–24.

5

~~~~~~

The threat of totalitarianism.
Nazi Germany's bid for
European hegemony

The prospects of democratization international police
collaboration after the war

The League of Nations

In a lecture on "The Ideal of the League of Nations and Police," in 1936, the police president of Vienna, Dr. Michael Skubl, commented on the common goal of the new world organization and the old institution of police. He traced their common pursuit of peace and order back to 1815 when, for the first time, the European powers agreed on the mutual recognition of each other's territorial sovereignty and their common need for security against domestic rebellion. He cited the steps towards more and more international police collaboration from the Congress of Vienna to the founding of the League of Nations, in particular the creation of the International Red Cross, the founding of the German Empire, the Rome Conference of 1898, and the Peace Conference in The Hague in 1899.[1]

The Covenant of the League of Nations was adopted in 1919. Given the wide range of political regimes brought together under the auspices of this world body, it should not surprise us that there were not many decisions reached at the political level of the assembly with direct bearing on police affairs. There were police situations arising from the refugee conventions adopted in the 1920s to deal with former Russian and Ottoman subjects in exile, and from the minorities treaties binding the succession states of Eastern Europe for which the League of Nations acted as guarantor.[2] A convention adopted in 1937 "For the prevention and punishment of terrorism" provided for international police collaboration in hunting down political assassins, however it was not put into effect.[3] There was also the

---

[1] "Völkerbundidee und Polizei," in *Oeffent. Sich.*, 17. Jhg., Nr. 1 (Jan. 1937), pp. 1–3.
[2] See Rudolf Levy, "Minorities and International Law," in Otto E. Lessing, ed., *Minorities and Boundaries* (The Hague, 1931).
[3] Manuel R. Garcia-Mora, *International Responsibility for Hostile Acts of Private Persons against Foreign States* (The Hague, 1962), pp. 102–3; and "The Convention for the Prevention and Punishment of Terrorism," in *BYB* (1938), pp. 214–16.

institution of the International Criminal Police Commission (ICPC) in 1923, but it carefully avoided becoming directly affiliated with the League. According to Skubl, "To incorporate the International Criminal Police Commission in the League of Nations would have been highly risky, perhaps even fatal."[4]

As is well known, the League of Nations remained largely ineffective during its short existence from 1919 to 1938 — substantial political agreement on any subject was found to be difficult to reach with so diverse a membership. At the same time the existence of this political forum was certainly useful, if only as a way of buying time pending the development of closer economic, social, and administrative ties from country to country and from continent to continent. The League wisely left the promotion of these ties to separate intergovernmental agencies which were only loosely attached to itself. There was notably the International Labor Office, founded in 1919, whose work was built on the conviction that international peace depended on the prevention of more Communist revolutions in Europe through the advancement of social justice.[5] Among the technical organizations attached to the League of Nations, we should mention the organization for communications and transit, the health organization, and the permanent advisory committees on opium and other dangerous drugs and on social questions, all of which served the cause of international police collaboration.

A conference to discuss the adoption of an international convention for the suppression of counterfeit currency was held at Geneva from 9 to 20 April 1929. Thirty-five states took part in this conference, which was called by the League of Nations, with the International Criminal Police Commission represented in an advisory capacity. Much of the discussion followed the pattern of prewar conferences on combating delinquencies that were considered a common menace to all states, like anarchism. M. Pella of Romania proposed ruling counterfeiting of currency a "common crime," to facilitate international extradition procedures.[6] As in the Rome Conference of 1898, the representative of Great Britain promptly objected to this in the name of the humanitarian principle of granting asylum to political fugitives.[7] While Italy, not surprisingly, foresaw great difficulty in executing an agreement that required the exchange of police information, Switzerland expressed reservations because the projected convention would require her to amend her legal code on the bidding of foreign powers.[8] New only was the presence of a professional police official, A. H. Sirks of the police of Rotterdam and also representing the ICPC, who advised that if a new international office to coordinate the fight against counterfeiting were to be established, it should be affiliated to "some important police organization."[9] Not new, however, was Hungary's request for the extradition of people's commissars who had served un-

---

[4] "Völkerbundidee und Polizei."

[5] E. J. Solano, *Labour as an International Problem* (London, 1919), p. 1.

[6] League of Nations, "Proceedings of the International Conference for the Adoption of a Convention for the Suppression of Counterfeit Currency, Geneva, April 9th to 20th, 1929" (Geneva, 1930), p. 53.

[7] Ibid., p. 58.   [8] Ibid., pp. 54–5.   [9] Ibid., p. 187.

der Bela Kun's Communist regime in Budapest in 1919.[10] Likewise, Liubimov of the Soviet Union, which by 1929 was anxious for the normalization of relations to the West, explained his government's interest in this conference by the losses the Soviet Union had suffered because of counterfeit rubles produced by anti-Bolshevik counterrevolutionaries abroad. Lone Liang for China recounted such a case from his recent experiences as a judge at the Supreme Court of Shanghai and used this occasion to plead China's case for the removal of consular jurisdictions and foreign concessions from Chinese soil.[11]

The International Criminal Police Commission (ICPC)

When the International Criminal Police Commission was founded in Vienna in 1923, the League of Nations was officially notified about the event and its assistance and collaboration solicited pending the successful development of closer technical collaboration between the police authorities of the ICPC members. The success of the ICPC in the first ten years of its existence can be measured by the large number of meetings that were held – Vienna and Berlin (1926), Amsterdam (1927), Berne (1928), Vienna and Brussels (1930), Paris (1931), and Rome (1932) – and by the many technical improvements initiated at these meetings to expedite the exchange of information and to standardize police procedures.

The greatest handicap of the ICPC, however, continued to be the problem of reconciling the ideal of promoting social peace and order throughout Europe with the political reality of national sovereign states. To promote the collaboration of police authorities exclusively in matters relating to common crime was almost impossible at a time when all Europe underwent great political turmoil. As Police President Skubl said in 1936, it is significant that the very first attempt at international police collaboration (at the Congress of Vienna) was after all directed towards matters of political police. "Except that politics is a dangerous ground on which to develop police ties across national frontiers. This is practicable only between countries that are closely allied."[12]

The ICPC's task of keeping out of politics was further made difficult by the fact that its most active supporters in the 1920s were states facing an uncertain political future, like Austria, Belgium, Czechoslovakia, the Kingdom of Serbia–Croatia–Slovenia, and the Weimar German Republic. France and England were not prominent participants, Soviet Russia played only a marginal role, and the United States belonged to other police associations whose activities were mainly in the Western Hemisphere. Thus a delegate from Belgrade, government Councillor Michael Bankovich in 1923 proposed police attachés as a permanent addition to the diplomatic corps in all the capitals of Europe. He began by describing his own activities as "a representative of my country's police authority" in Vienna before the First World War. In the interest of combating smuggling and "other material damage to my state," he said, he had kept every Serbian subject living in

---

[10] Ibid., p. 143. [11] Ibid., p. 64. [12] "Völkerbundidee und Polizei."

the Austrian capital under close surveillance and monitored all travel between Austria and Serbia. It is difficult not to consider Bankovich's role before 1914 as that simply of a spy, especially when he described his activities as "political and also preventive," hinting that he may have carried out some executive actions on Austrian soil.[13] To lend urgency to his proposal Bankovich spoke about the post-war phenomenon of numerous charlatans peddling fake state secrets from legation to legation, and about Austria's neighbors Italy, Hungary, Czechoslovakia, and Romania who already maintained police agents in Vienna.[14] But this only cast his proposal of creating police attachés in yet more political a light than the ICPC could possibly countenance.

Weimar Germany's police experiment with "défense du territoire"

The emergence in the 1930s of an utterly ruthless and ultimately self-destructive police apparatus from amid the German police establishment is the last major topic of this study. The Germans in the nineteenth century had not stood at the forefront of modern police development. Their yearning for national fulfillment in a German Reich made them rely mainly on diplomacy and war to attain their goals. But for more than a decade following the First World War their priorities had to be completely reversed. Disarmed and surrounded by suspicious victors and vigilant succession states, Germany was reduced to principal dependency on its police as the mainstay of its national defense; not to hold the German frontiers against an outside invasion, of course, but to promote a national solidarity that would make Germany immune to foreign subversion. To the Social Democratic politicians on whom national power was thrust in November 1918, this meant fostering reconciliation between the classes, promoting social justice and wellbeing, and aligning Germany with the democratic nations of Europe. Not unlike post-Napoleonic France, Germany now needed a police that concurrently shielded its domestic political life from foreign interference and submitted its social order to a parliamentary system of perpetual piecemeal reform and adjustment. Deprived of its Burgfrieden strategy through defeat in war Germany, in short, adopted the French police strategy of *défense du territoire*.

The police leaders of the Weimar Republic were conscious of their responsibility to give Germany's fledgling democracy a secure foundation in a few short years. They knew the difficulty of establishing the ground rules of democratic behavior in a society brutalized by four years of mass slaughter at Ypres and Verdun, shocked by the Bolshevik revolution, and aware of all the instruments of mass control which the new century had brought. Would a legal-minded and concil-iatory approach by the authorities be misunderstood as political weakness in an age when police forces could use armored cars and machine guns? Could a dem-

---

[13] Internationale Kriminalpolizeiliche Kommission, *Der Internationale Polizeikongress* (Vienna, 1923), p. 29.
[14] Ibid., p. 31.

ocratic police in Germany count on commanding authority after the Reich had recovered a measure of military capability and when voices would surely be heard once again calling for "silence in the ranks" pending the settlement of foreign issues? The professional civil police of the Weimar Republic for over a decade tried to secure Germany's road to democracy, only to succumb in 1932–33 to Nazi domination, part victim and part collaborator.

The rise of the Nazi police system in Germany influenced contemporary thinking about police in the West much more than the police dictatorship in Soviet Russia. What happened in Russia could happen in the West only if the West were to fall to Bolshevik rule. What happened in Nazi Germany, however, could happen in other European countries any time, even without Nazi conquest, through the erosion of the principles of social conduct that lie at the core of liberal bourgeois civilization. Today the terms "Gestapo," "SS," and "concentration camp" serve as warning cries about the abuse, aberration – indeed, delirium – that can befall the most advanced societies under severe social and political stress. The Cheka, the GPU, the KGB, or the gulag system, on the other hand, have in the West much more consistently been understood as specifically Russian or "Eurasian" phenomena.

That the Gestapo, the SS, and the concentration camps had roots in the history of modern police is borne out by the fact that many factors that brought about this terrible system between the two world wars had made their isolated appearance much earlier in the police history of Europe as described in previous chapters. There had been the idealism of German revolutionaries in the 1820s who sought an original new justification for state authority in virtuous and heroic self-sacrifice for the fatherland, and prophesied the coming of a future dictator in the midst of a national emergency. [15] We recall how Prussians and Austrians had found smaller, compact populations like the Alsatians, Belgians, or Czechs more easily policeable than Poles and South Slavs, whose hostility and uncooperativeness had prompted the arming of Austrian traders in the Balkans (1840s) and rural notables in the government of Posnan (1915), and the eviction of Polish Jews from Silesian towns and villages in disregard of their individual legal rights (1882).

What happened in Germany between 1933 and 1945 has served as a dire warning to the West because the Gestapo was so largely staffed by seasoned police officials. After 1945 these same Gestapo officials expected exoneration and pension rights because what they had done, as far as they could see, had been no more than regular police duty, admittedly under conditions of unprecedented severity. Under unprecedented conditions, they said, would not most

---

[15] The Nazis drew attention to this intellectual tie to the freedom fighters in 1813 by claiming that the swastika, a symbol of German Nordic culture, appeared also as the *Wenderkreuz* in Vater Jahn's gymnastic movement. This is mentioned in Dr. Rissom, "Mischehen im Licht der neuen Gesetzgebung," in *Zeitschrift der Akademie für deutsches Recht*, Nr. 1 (Jan. 1936), p. 8. Golo Mann in 1946 pointed out that Friedrich Gentz saw in the German nationalists of Jahn's generation advocates of the extermination of freedom of dissent. Golo Mann, *Secretary of Europe. The Life of Friedrich Gentz, Enemy of Napoleon* (New Haven, Conn. 1946), p. 268.

civil servants in most countries have abjured responsibility for the ultimate outcome of their actions and sought safety in a punctilious execution of immediate instructions?[16]

One clue for understanding the failure of the democratic police experiment of the Weimar Republic is Berlin, which in the early 1920s embarked on a period of exceptional social and intellectual daring. Unlike postwar Vienna with its shabby atmosphere of fading imperial grandeur, Berlin after the departure of the Hohenzollerns aspired to become a cosmopolitan "Weltstadt" renowned for its pioneering work in theater and movies, music, science, and social reform. The Berlin police, shaken as we have seen by its abject failure during the Spartacist unrest of 1918–19 and anxious to redeem itself by making a new start, became one of the city's many well-publicized experiments in modernization. The force was more than doubled to about 20,000 officials, three new training schools were opened in Brandenburg a.d. Havel, in Eiche, and in Berlin-Spandau, and a criminological institute founded in Berlin-Charlottenburg.[17] But Berlin's cultural and social experimentation in the interval between Kaiser and Hitler has also rightly been chastised as too eclectic, rootless, and unstable, torn like the city's inhabitants themselves were torn between frenzied activity and the corroding effect of unemployment, between the glamour of the Kurfürstendamm crowd and the silent underworld of crime and poverty around Schlesischer Bahnhof. It was a measure of the sickness of Europe between the two wars that the celebrated Berlin spirit of the twenties was admired as a "creative impulse" when almost all its goals were directed at negating old values.[18]

The police presidium published a popular series of books, all of them designed to herald the new concept of "The Police, Your Friend and Helper." Of particular interest were Ernst van den Bergh's philosophic treatise, Polizei und Volk: Seelische Zusammenhänge (Police and Nation: Their Spiritual Bonds) (1926), and Dr. Bernhard Weiss's, Polizei und Politik (Police and Politics) (1928). Van den Bergh's book celebrated the coming of age of the German people in 1918 and the redundancy of all further "police tutelage." Dr. Weiss boldly tackled the controversial question whether a secret political police is permissible in a parliamentary democracy, especially if it goes beyond controlling the behavior of individual persons and includes the policing of entire social groups and political movements. He boldly answered this question with a defiant "Sure it is!"[19]

[16] Bund deutscher Polizeibeamten e.V., "Die Geheime Staatspolizei. Ihre geschichtliche Entwicklung und Organisation, ihre Beamten und deren Rechtsstellung im Gesetz zu Artikel 131 GG und im Regierungsentwurf des Bundesbeamtengesetzes," (Kassel, 1953).

[17] "5 Jahre Preussische Polizeischule für Leibesübungen," in Die Polizei, 22. Jhg., Nr. 9, (5 Aug. 1925), pp. 269–70; and Willy Gay, Die preussische Landeskriminalpolizei. Ihre Errichtung, ihre bisherige und beabsichtigte Entwicklung, ihre Aufgaben (Berlin, 1928).

[18] For general descriptions of Berlin in the twenties, see Pem (Paul Erich Marcus), Heimweh nach dem Kurfürstendamm. Aus Berlins glanzvollsten Tagen und Nächten (Berlin, 1952); Friedrich Hussong, "Kurfürstendamm." Zur Kulturgeschichte des Zwischenreichs (Berlin, 1934); and Peter Gay, Weimar Culture. The Outsider as Insider (New York, 1968).

[19] Dr. Bernhard Weiss, Polizei und Politik (Berlin, 1928), pp. 99–100.

But how unreal at the same time the brilliant abstractions of van den Bergh's didactic police theories, how pessimistic Dr. Weiss's rebuttal to all criticism levied against political police work! Van den Bergh's theory that police reconciles the interests of nation and state, that it acts as the executive arm of state power and at the same time as the instrument of the people's collective conscience – that was an intellectual tour de force at best. It took much simple faith in the goodness of man to assume, as he did, that at the mere sight of uniformed police, the individual in the crowd is brought back to his own better self and relinquishes any political goals derived from personal selfishness.[20] By contrast, Bernhard Weiss's defense of political police as indispensable for the protection of any state, be that state democratic or not, reflected the sobriety of the seasoned police practitioner. The political policeman, according to Weiss, cannot go by public approval. He will never escape public vilification and might as well become hardened to all such attacks. (Which made it the more unbelievable that Weiss also insisted on policemen treating political offenders better than common lawbreakers because of their alleged altruistic motives and moral courage.)[21] But Weiss's skepticism was in tune with the tenor of contemporary social critics – of a Kurt Tucholsky and a Walther Mehring – whose essays in the *Weltbühne* portrayed man as essentially bad, murderous, dishonest, perverse, and vulgar.

The democratic principles propounded by the Prussian police leaders in the early twenties no doubt represented the honest convictions of the men who assumed leading positions in the Prussian ministry of interior and in the Berlin police presidium during the Weimar Republic. However, the democratic police theories were so easily introduced after 1918 not because they quickly proved their merits in the field but because in the turbulent first postwar years they did not have to be applied in practice.[22] Berlin in 1918–19 faced an extraordinary crime wave caused by a general slackening of moral restraints. There was fear of more Communist insurrections, thousands of firearms among the population had to be confiscated, conspirators and foreign spies rendered harmless, blackmarketeering and dope peddling suppressed. The sense of a return to normalcy did not come until the end of the inflation and the signing of the Locarno Pact (1925) and Germany's acceptance as a member of the League of Nations (1926) – in other words, not until the time when the Berlin police had completed the reorganization of its force and went public with its new democratic police philosophy.[23]

It is easy with historical hindsight to say that the democratic police experiment in Berlin was doomed to failure because its practical application in 1926 coincided

[20] Ernst van den Bergh, *Polizei und Volk–Seelische Zusammenhänge* (Berlin, 1926), pp. 6–7.

[21] Weiss, *Polizei und Politik*, pp. 2, 57, 60–1. For a balanced appreciation of Weiss, see Dietz Bering, "Isidor – Geschichte einer Hetzjagd. Bernhard Weiss, einem preussischen Juden zum Gedächtnis," in *Die Zeit*, 21, Aug. 1981, p. 6.

[22] Dr. Leopold Waber, "Polizei und Bevölkerung," in *Oeffent. Sich.*, 1. Jhg. Nr. 1 (20 Aug. 1921), pp. 4–5.

[23] See Friedrich Karl Kaul, *Justiz wird zum Verbrechen. Der Pitaval der Weimarer Republik* (East Berlin, 1953) for a detailed, though biased, accounting of political murders in the 1920s.

with the beginning of the Nazi campaign to conquer Berlin. But there was also a causal relationship between the success of the democratic republic and the onset of new troubles. *Because* Germany's survival after 1926 seemed assured, it could resurrect old foreign political goals requiring strong national leadership at the top. *Because* radical policies seemed feasible once more, the conservative legalism of the Republican police earned it no further credit after 1933. The Nazi police chiefs were to be at a psychological advantage when they proclaimed their will to use police power without any restraint for the building of a wholly new political order.

The Nazi dictatorship

The battle for Berlin

The battle for Berlin lasted five years, from 1927 to 1932. It pitted the Nazi Brownshirts against the Communist League of Red Front Fighters (*Rotfront-kämpferbund*, or *RFB*), and caught the police in the middle, seeking to restrain the two sides while maintaining the semblance of everyday normalcy in the capital. In the course of this civil war, the armed police (the Schutzpolizei, or Schupo, for short) was never forced to relinquish the field. The uniformed police was well equipped and well trained for combat, with special riot squads (Bereitschaften) held in readiness throughout the city, supported by heavy machine guns and a few armored cars. Only one major encounter with the Communist League of Red Front Fighters took place in May 1929.[24] On that occasion the police proved its absolute superiority in trained manpower and armament over any civilian opposition. As late as 1932 the Berlin police was able to close down the hundreds of Nazi strong points throughout the city in one well-coordinated operation of uniformed men and plainclothes detectives. Technically speaking, Berlin was as safe against armed insurrection as Paris was on the eve of the coup d'état of Louis Napoleon in December 1851.

And yet the police lost the battle for Berlin to the Nazis. It lost because the Brownshirts knew how to exploit the chief handicap of the government police, namely its democratic service instructions. These democratic rules were admirable in theory, but they applied to law enforcement in a democracy with an open and pluralistic society. Since Germany was only open and pluralistic but not democratic, the police was seriously hampered by its orders to respect the political freedom of all parties no matter how contemptuous they were of the republican constitution. The warring factions could not be pacified by displays of political

[24] Hsi-Huey Liang, *The Berlin Police Force in the Weimar Republic*, (Berkeley, 1970), pp. 106–8. A more critical view of the police is Eve Rosenhaft, "Working-Class Life and Working-Class Politics: Communists, Nazis and the State in the Battle for the Streets, Berlin 1928–1932," in Richard Bessel and E. J. Feuchtwanger, eds., *Social Change and Political Development in Weimar Germany* (London, 1981), pp. 207–36.

sagacity and threats of force. After 1927 it actually had to apply armed force continuously in daily sorties to separate the combatants in meeting halls, on city squares, and along their marching routes. And as the violence between Communists and Nazis continued month after month, the chance of the police building a public order based on moral consensus became ever more remote.

The defeat of the police did not arise from direct Nazi subversion. Most uniformed policemen were not politically minded enough to be drawn to the Nazi party (NSDAP). And being simple country lads, they were even less attracted to the proletarian doctrines of the German Communist Party (KPD). In this time of high unemployment they also had no wish to jeopardize their relative economic security as state officials with pension rights. But their resistance to Nazi efforts at fraternization weakened when it became apparent that only the storm troopers were ruthless enough to win the war against the Communists, not the Schupo, which never pressed its advantages beyond repelling an overt attack. Admittedly, some young patrolmen were confused by the paradoxical content of their political instruction. Why were Prussian civil servants forbidden to belong to the NSDAP but federal state officials in the railway administration or the postal service could march under the Hitler flag? Where was a policeman to draw the fine line between his obligation to remain politically neutral while on duty, and to stand up for his political conviction as a German citizen? Joseph Goebbels, Hitler's Gauleiter in Berlin, exploited the frustration of the lower ranking uniformed police by launching a campaign of ridicule against their highbrow superiors. Particularly effective was his crude anti-Semitic tirade against Dr. Bernhard Weiss, who headed the political police between 1928 and 1932. It elicited much secret merriment among Weiss's subordinates.

There were Nazi cells in the detective and in the political police departments (*Abteilung IV,* and *Abteilung IA*), where some individual officials secretly agreed with the Nazi analysis of current social ills. A handful of "Alte Kämpfer" served in the political police.[25] Certain detective inspectors (*Kriminalkommissare,* like Erich Liebermann von Sonnenberg, after 1933 promoted to head of the detective branch, and Otto Trettin, NSDAP member since 1932) in charge of theft, burglary, commercial swindles, criminal gangs (*Ringvereine*) and sexual delinquencies sympathized with the Nazi ideas on crime fighting.[26] Going far beyond Lombroso's anthropological theories, the Nazi theoretician, Friedrich von Rohden, recommended the compulsory castration of all alcoholics, epileptics, and imbeciles because of their supposed hereditary criminal propensities.[27] Another Nazi lawyer, Martin Knaut, proposed the extension of the concept of criminality from categories of social behavior to categories of mental attitude like "disloyalty,

---

[25] Interview, Regierungs- und Kriminalrat Paul Kuckenburg, Berlin, 16 Oct. 1962.
[26] Liang, *Berlin Police Force,* ch. 4.
[27] Friedrich von Rohden, "Aufbau des kriminalbiologischen Dienstes," in *Deutsches Recht,* 1. Jhg., No. 6 (Nov. 1933), pp. 184–6.

dishonesty, [and] lack of character [*Gesinnungslosigkeit*]."[28] A medical doctor in Munich, Dr. Friedrich Stumpfl, argued that all serious and recurring criminality was ultimately caused by spiritual dispositions inherent in race, which he used in defense of measures for racial purification in Germany.[29] In addition, a number of detectives like Arthur Nebe also joined the Nazi movement for reasons of political opportunism.

The number of policemen whom the Nazis dismissed as opponents of Fascism in 1933 was less than 500; but the number of secret partisans of their cause inside the police had probably counted no higher. Before long, some of them may even have come to regret their support of the Hitler party. In 1935 Trettin and Liebermann von Sonnenberg showed off the Gestapo's professional incompetence in 1935 during an investigation of an explosion at a munitions factory in Rheinsberg. While the Gestapo insisted to rule the catastrophe an act of sabotage, these two veterans of Abteilung IV, unfazed, managed to prove that the explosion was caused by a simple accident.[30]

The defeat of the Prussian police in 1932–3 was not caused by technical incompetence or political defection. In the last analysis it came about because of its pedantic commitment to legality. The Nazi victory at the polls on 24 April 1932 had destroyed the SPD majority in the Prussian Diet. Otto Braun, the Socialist Prussian prime minister, was compelled to stay on, presiding over a deteriorating situation without the mandate for energetic intervention. Attempts to stop the civil war by banning political demonstrations in the streets were countermanded by the Reich chancellor, Franz von Papen. When on 20 July 1932 President Hindenburg on the pretext of restoring order transferred the police to the command of Reichswehr generals he was acting within his constitutional powers. And because the suspension of the Prussian government and the change in the leadership of the Berlin police were legal under the Weimar constitution, the Prussian police force (with only a few exceptions like Schupo commander Heimannsberg) submitted to the fait accompli of the Papen putsch and carried out the new orders even when they contradicted the democratic principles of police established in the preceding decade.[31]

After the Second World War, Ferdinand Friedensburg, a former deputy police president, praised the Berlin police for its steadfast adherence to the principle of legality throughout the fourteen years of the Weimar Republic.[32] But if Friedens-

---

[28] Martin Knaut, "Schluss mit der restlosen Tatsachenaufklärung im Strafverfahren!" in ibid., pp. 183–4.
[29] Dr. med. Friedrich Stumpfl, "Kriminalität und Rasse," in ibid., 5. Jhg., 2. Heft (25 Jan 1935), pp. 31–4. See also the theories of the Austrian criminologist, Hanns Gross (1847–1916), in Wolfgang Stangl, "Bruchlose und abgebrochene Traditionen der österreichischen Kriminologie," in Herbert Leier et al., eds., *Vom Umgang mit dem Strafrecht. 10 Jahre Kriminologie in Oesterreich* (Vienna, 1982), pp. 16ff.
[30] I owe this information to Polizeiangestellte Grete Bomke (interviewed 1962), who took shorthand notes for the Berlin Kripo during the Rheinsberg investigation in 1935.
[31] Karl Dietrich Bracher, et al., *Die nationalsozialistische Machtergreifung* (Cologne, 1960), p. 39.
[32] Ferdinand Friedensburg, *Die Weimarer Republik* (Berlin, 1946), pp. 24–7.

burg was right, must we then not conclude that the attempt of the leaders of the Weimar Republic to impose democracy with police had been quixotic because democracy cannot be taught by instruments of duress? Inasmuch as the Germans had borrowed from the French police conception of "défense du territoire," had they not neglected three elementary factors that differentiated their situation from that of nineteenth-century France?

1. Germany lacked security abroad, a condition which even in France could erode democratic freedoms as was shown in the rise of French integral nationalism after 1871 and the hysteria of the anti-Dreyfusards in the 1890s.
2. Again unlike France, Germany possessed no balance between contending interest groups steadied and reinforced by a common culture, or by an institution that stood above party disputes like the now defunct monarchy.[33] The alternative of returning to a Burgfrieden strategy was always temptingly close at hand.
3. Berlin in the 1920s had reached the height of its effectiveness as a national capital comparable to that of Paris in France during the mid-nineteenth century. Only the police in the Weimar Republic did not use Berlin to build a coordinated police administration for all Germany comparable to the Sûreté in Paris. Though in 1923 a network of *Landeskriminalämter* was established as a clearing house for information on ordinary criminal police matters throughout the Reich, the LKA's had no executive powers and the original intention of extending this system to political police work was never carried out.[34]

Hitler in the 1920s emulated Louis Napoleon by setting his sights on the conquest of the capital, and once installed at the helm of the central government, surprised his opponents by using Berlin as a springboard to establish an unprecedented nationwide police dictatorship. In other words, the Weimar Republic had never been a police state in the way nineteenth-century France had. After 1933 Nazi Germany very quickly became a police dictatorship in which Göring and Himmler ruled a people unaccustomed to the methods of centralized police and quite at a loss how to go about resisting or evading such relentless powers.[35]

The Nazi police dictatorship

The Hitler period has raised three basic questions in historical literature: 1. Why was the Nazi regime welcomed with such apparent enthusiasm by the German

---

[33] For a good discussion of this point, see Robert Minder, *Dichter in der Gesellschaft. Erfahrungen mit deutscher und französischer Literatur* (Frankfurt, 1966), pp. 7–34.

[34] Regierungsrat Paetsch, "Die Errichtung der Landeskriminalpolizei im Rahmen des Polizeiwesens in Preussen," in *Die Polizei*, 21. Jhg., Nr. 20, 20 Jan. 1925, pp. 506–9; and Willy Gay, *Die preussische Landeskriminalpolizei, ihre bisherige und beabsichtigte Entwicklung, ihre Aufgaben* (Berlin, 1928).

[35] The German Resistance under Carl Goerdeler planned a return to the criminal procedure of the Weimar Republic and the denationalization of the police after the fall of the Nazi regime. Fabian von Schlabrendorff, *The Secret War against Hitler*, trans. by H. Simon (New York, 1965), p. 210.

public? And why did so many foreigners watch this German revolution with a neutral indifference bordering on approval? 2. Did the Nazi revolution make the Second World War inevitable? 3. Was the genocide in 1942–5 an integral part of the Nazi revolution?

To the historian of European police these same questions translate as follows:

1. How did the short period of almost perfect police control from 1933 to 1934 come about: by Nazi contrivance or by fortuitous circumstance? And how long could it have lasted without a steady succession of new orders and regulations ("*zwecks Frischhaltung des Polizeirechts*") to keep the same high pitch of public obedience from one week to the next? Was not the near unanimity of the German public on 30 January 1933 really unpoliceable in the long run?
2. Did the process of continued revision in police rules have to escalate to the point of total war (after 1943) because, barring a return to democracy, the maintenance of a domestic truce was possible only by turning Germany once more into a besieged fortress?
3. Lastly, the police historian must ask why the descent into limitless barbarity took place during the Second World War. To attribute the "Final Solution" to the need of keeping up the pressure of Burgfrieden discipline after the Germans had conquered most of Europe offers one possible explanation, but it is not satisfactory enough. Nor is a reference to the ferociously destructive racial ideology of Himmler's SS, who ran the extermination squads. The subject of our study, however, is not the SS but the modern police. The police forces in Germany and in German-occupied Europe provided low-level "order police," which included peripheral assistance to the SS and Gestapo like checking the neighborhood for unreported Jews and hunting down escaped prisoners. Why was there so little resistance from the old Prussian *Beamtentum* in Berlin or from the municipal police in occupied Paris, why did so many old officials despite serious misgivings suspend their independent judgment of right and wrong?

Gleichschaltung 1933–4

Berlin during the first weeks of Nazi rule was a picture of general acclamation for the new regime. The atmosphere of relief was hardly marred by the scattered reports about SA men, accompanied by police escorts, conducting mopping up operations in the few remaining pocket of Communist resistance. No iron curtain fell over Germany, there was no mass exodus by the defeated parties, and political conversation did not immediately come to a stop. By all accounts the torchlight parades in Berlin and in many other towns, the flag waving and the rapid spread of the Hitler salute were uncoerced. For the next year or two the uninhibited talk in the press about secret police or about famous artists (Willy Fritsch, Gitta Alpar, Gustav Fröhlich, and Marlene Dietrich) going abroad gave the superficial impression of public confidence bordering on insouciance.[36] Visits to concentration camps by distinguished foreigners like the Swedish explorer, Sven Hedin, were still permitted on request in 1936. A Norwegian major who was offered the same privilege by Hermann Göring in 1933, politely declined.[37]

The time from 1933 to 1934 can technically be called an ideal police situation because the wave of support, popular and widespread though it was, at no time threatened to deprive the government of its political initiative. Every institution and organization in the Reich, from the trade union to the university rectorate anxiously waited to be assigned its place in the great national awakening that was now beginning. At the same time the people's eagerness to serve the new regime was sharpened by everyone's private fears that something in their past might exclude them from membership in the national community (*Volksgemeinschaft*). The Nazis were past masters in the art of mesmerizing people with alternating demonstrations of generosity and brutality. The fire at the Reichstag building on 27 February 1933 followed only hours later by the rounding up of 4,000 to 5,000 Communists, Socialists, pacifists, and other political undesirables conveyed the impression of a police apparatus finally so well in control that its next move was unpredictable to the layman. The Prussian police under Prime Minister Göring and Police President von Levetzow, appeared to know exactly when to strike, where to strike, and how hard to strike. Physical violence, doled out in carefully measured portions, paralyzed the public more effectively than would have a protracted but indiscriminate rampage by political rowdies.

Gleichschaltung (as a procedure, the political coordination of the multifarious component parts in a society) is the goal of all absolutist or totalitarian regimes. It took decades in the Soviet Union because large portions of the old Russian society were first eliminated after 1917 as unusable under a Socialist order and the training of their replacements took many years. Also, the Soviet plan was to build a modern industrial society whose infrastructure had barely existed before the First World War. In the Fascist dictatorships of Southern and Central Europe the coordination of state, people, and political movement generally went much faster because the goals of the revolution in material terms were not set as high as in Lenin's or Stalin's Russia. Much of the Fascist program in Italy amounted to a mere change in symbols and political nomenclature, a redefinition of traditional arrangements, exhortations to greater efficiency, and outward gestures of adulation for the Duce. Gleichschaltung proceeded fastest in Germany because the inhabitants were well disciplined and highly literate, and because many private and public institutions in the Reich were penetrated by Nazi cells long before 1933. Ideological indoctrination (a slow-moving process) was less

---

[36] Ibid., pp. 102–3. Marlene Dietrich's stepfather was a grenadier lieutenant. Her actual father was a police officer. Otto Friedrich, *Before the Deluge. A Portrait of Berlin in the 1920's* (New York, 1972), p. 276.

[37] Sven Hedin, *Ohne Auftrag in Berlin* (Tübingen, 1949), p. 10; and Erich Gritzbach, *Hermann Goering. The Man and His Work* (London, 1939), pp. 36–7.

important in Nazi Germany than in Stalinist Russia; obedience to the Führer and subservience to Nazi rituals counted much more and could be achieved very quickly. The millions of party members and members of Nazi-run organizations (Hitlerjugend, Bund Deutscher Mädel, NS-Frauenbund, NSKK, and Reichsarbeitsdienst, to name but a few) could be held to discipline by fear of an anonymous denunciation, but better still by the countless small jobs they were given to perform, with an official badge or a cap to show and the seductive offer of just a shred of delegated police power, usable against fellow workers, office colleagues, or neighbors.[38]

Having said this we realize that the coming of the Nazi order infused German society with a dynamic energy which the new rulers could direct for a limited period of time only. Gleichschaltung (as a slogan, which implied vaguely the acceptance of authoritarian leadership in place of democratic decision-making by majority vote, cult of Germandom, and the exclusion of Jews) was liable to exhaust its hold over the minds of the people unless more substantial tasks were constantly added in justification for ever stricter discipline and closer control from the top. Winter relief for the poor, the reclamation of wasteland, and other public projects were one solution, especially since it went together with the enlistment of countless citizens in Nazi-led mass organizations. But insofar as membership in Nazi organizations brought with it the obligation to impose discipline on subordinates and nonorganized Germans, there was also the negative result of a dissolution of the bonds of private trust and friendship.[39]

The disintegrating effect of the Nazi revolution on German society after the first euphoric stage of Gleichschaltung was balanced by a new emphasis on professional compartmentalization (architect, jurist, soldier, farmer), and by the introduction of discriminatory laws for certain social categories, notably "professional criminals," Jews, and foreigners.[40]

Professional criminals, Jews, and foreigners

A drastic diminution in Germany's crime rate after 1933 (estimated at 60 percent within six months of the Nazi seizure of power) belongs to the proudest achievements of the Nazi police. By September 1933 the Berlin Kripo (criminal police) reported that the underworld gangs (Ringvereine) had virtually disappeared in the city, that the average rate of forty auto thefts per day in 1932 had been cut to

---

[38] By comparison, the Communist regime of East Germany after the Second World War found it much harder to impose its Moscow-inspired party doctrine on the inhabitants, and this failure in turn undermined discipline in the SSD and the Volkspolizei.

[39] On the danger of undermining the *Volksgemeinschaft* by inhibiting personal confidences between friends, see *Oberpostrat* Fritz's advice against postal censorship of private letters. Postrat Dr. Fritz, "Das Postgeheimnis im nationalsozialistischen Staat," in *Jahrbuch des Postwesens 1937* (Berlin-Friedenau, 1938), p. 188.

[40] This is not to denigrate the many political dissenters who were put in concentration camps, but whose story is much better known. Hannah Arendt, "Konzentrationslager," in *Die Wandlung*, III (1948), p. 319.

an average of two, and that not one single robbery with homicide (*Raubmord*) had been perpetrated.[41] The suppression of common crime albeit through ruthless measures produced the least criticism at home or abroad. Even well-known criminalists like Dr. Hans Schneickert joined in the general chorus of praise for the new regime which now discarded all scruples about invading the legal rights of "known criminals."[42] The service instructions for the auxiliary police (*Hilfspolizei*), which briefly saw service in 1933, informed the men that "The liberal idea, 'no punishment without a law,' is now replaced by the National Socialist principle, 'no punishable deed without punishment.' Today, no offender will go scot free merely because his action is not listed in the penal code."[43]

The presidential "Decree for the Protection of People and State" (28 February 1933), issued the day after the Reichstag fire, was the legal basis for two secret instructions by the Prussian ministry of interior providing for police supervision and preventive custody for professional criminals. By 1934 a police journal already reported some three hundred "habitual" or "professional" criminals in concentration camps.[44] Professional criminals were defined as persons who had committed more than three delinquencies from selfish motives that were each punishable by at least six months in prison or penitentiary, without a minimum of five years between each delinquency. Some of these criminals were given a chance at rehabilitation by submitting to close police surveillance while learning a useful trade. They had to observe an evening curfew and other restrictions on their individual freedom and duplicate keys to their lodgings were kept at the local precinct station to allow for unannounced control visits at all hours.[45] Preventive detention or surveillance was also applied to people who had committed especially grave crimes, to "asocial" individuals, and to people found to be living under assumed names.[46]

The Nazi legislation directed at the progressive exclusion of all Jews from German national life was quite a different matter. It began on 7 April 1933, with the "Law for the Restoration of Professional Officialdom," which led to the expulsion of Jews from all public service posts and most liberal professions. It reached a

---

[41] Report by Regierungsrat Johannes Thiele, Kripo Dept. at the Prussian ministry of interior, Berlin, 8 Sept. 1933, II B 2., in USDC (Berlin), files of the Ordnungspolizei (hereafter USDC (Berlin), Orpo files). The highway robbers Max and Walther Götze plied their trade very successfully in 1936–7, but their exploits were not glamorized in the press, and SS officers who fell victim to their attacks were court-martialled for "cowardice in the face of the enemy." Interview, Kriminalmeister Teigeler, Berlin, 11 Oct. 1962.

[42] Dr. jur. Hans Schneickert, *Einführung in die Kriminalsoziolgie und Verbrechensbekämpfung* (Jena, 1935), p. 54; and Kurt Daluege, *Nationalsozialistischer Kampf gegen das Verbrechertum* (Munich, 1936), p. 12. On the other hand, Nazi methods of crime fighting did draw the criticism of international penologists in 1935. See Benedict S. Alper and Jeremy F. Boren, *Crime: International Agenda. Concern and Action in the Prevention of Crime and Treatment of Offenders, 1846–1872* (Lexington, Mass., 1972), pp. 71–3.

[43] Otto Kämmerer, *Merkbuch für die Hipo* (Halle, 1933), p. 9.

[44] *Der deutsche Polizeibeamte*, Nr. 11 (1934), p. 405.

[45] Schneickert, *Einführung*, pp. 71–3.

[46] Dr. Werner Best, *Die deutsche Polizei* (Darmstadt, 1940), pp. 31–3.

temporary climax on 15 April 1935, with the "Law for the Protection of German Blood and Honor," which disqualified Jews from membership in the German nation (*Reichsbürgerschaft*).[47] The anti-Semitic legislation affected over half a million German fellow citizens, among them some of the country's greatest luminaries in science, business, the arts and the humanities. Foreign criticism of Germany because of these measures was strong and to some extent effective.[48] But as far as the regular police was concerned, up to and including the Kristallnacht of 9 November 1938, the new legislation did not require very much more than minor clerical work by precinct officers engaged in administrative duties. Certificates of Aryan descent in Berlin, for example, were not provided by the police but by the Reich ministry of interior, department of racial research (*Reichsstelle für Sippenforschung*).[49] The appalling violence done to Jews – from public humiliation in the streets to looting their stores and brutal beatings – was done by the SA and later by the SS and Gestapo.

In retrospect it is chilling to note how effectively and with what professional detachment the German uniformed police provided security to Aryan property adjoining Jewish shops during the pogroms launched by fanatic SA hoodlums.[50] The failure of these policemen to act more helpfully in the midst of this deep crisis of human civilization, when they were at the scene and had the organization, the training, and the equipment to interfere, is a most disheartening aspect to an already dismal record of contemporary European history. It cannot be explained by the long history of anti-Semitism in Central Europe, nor by the traditional obedience of German officialdom, because it is a phenomenon witnessed also in the behavior of local police in tsarist Russia, and during the Second World War in occupied France, Belgium, Norway, and elsewhere. It is a matter that historians may be less able to explain than anthropologists or social psychologists.

The persecution of Jews in Nazi Germany must nevertheless be mentioned in a history of European police because the racial laws contributed so much to the Nazi hold over the German people, even without strong participation by the professional police apparatus. The control arose from the penetration of the racial issue into all walks of life, because every family's ancestry came under scrutiny and every person was fitted into the new hierarchy of racial status, which now ranged from the full Aryan to the full Jew, with a complicated assortment of positions in between, each with its specific rights and obligations.

Worse, a person's Jewish qualities could be assessed by subjective assessments based on his or her appearance, character, and mentality. How spurious this was is well exemplified in the attempt at a stylistic and psychological comparison be-

[47] Dr. Rissom, "Mischehen," pp. 8–10.

[48] Alfred Wiener, "1. April 1933. Vom Judenboykott zum Boykott des Rechts," in *Die Zeit* (3 Apr. 1958).

[49] Scholz, Kommando der Schutzpolizei, S. lb. 6800/30.5, Berlin, 3 June 1936. Betr. "Polizeiliche Beglaubigung von Ariernachweisen," in LA (Berlin), Rep. 20, Acc 1968, Nr. 7763–7764.

[50] Richard Grunberger, *The 12-Year Reich. A Social History of Nazi Germany* (New York, 1971), p. 24.

tween letters written by German and by German-Jewish students killed in the First World War, which came out in 1936.[51] The arbitrariness of the decisions concerning a person's racial status based on their manner of thinking enormously enhanced the "policing" effect of the racial laws because it constituted a lurking threat directed against everyone.[52] There is some justice to Wickham Steed's comparison of Nazism to Anabaptism.[53] Just as the Anabaptists sought assurance of their spiritual salvation in their Christian behavior rather than vice versa, so a fanatical Nazi believer like Reinhard Heydrich sought assurance of his own racial purity in a willful and absolute endorsement of Nazi dogma. There is no stronger "police" hold on a people than self-induced ideological frenzy, but such police hold has no relationship to our concept of modern police anymore.[54]

Before the war foreigners were not harassed in Nazi Germany, but their distinct and separate place in German society was underlined by the heightened national consciousness in the country. The wearing of national flags as lapel pins by foreigners became fashionable. All contacts between Germans and aliens came under increasing state control, with fine distinctions made from one nationality to the next in accordance with Germany's shifting foreign political interests.

In the first year of Nazi rule the chief concern seems to have been reassuring foreigners that Germany had returned to domestic peace. The discrimination against Jews and the growing attention given to rearmament were played down. On 11 October 1934, the feuilletonist Adolf Stein still worried about the impression of violence Germany had made abroad during the twenties, with stories about daily street battles in the capital.

At the end of a North Sea cruise, a number of foreigners disembark with me in Germany: several Americans and Czechs, one Englishman, many Italians and Swiss, and quite a few Dutch people. A number of them look around with amazement in their eyes. – "Why, what's the matter?" – "Your policemen! They . . . have . . . no truncheons!" – "Ah yes. Well, ladies and gentlemen, there you have it. Let me present to you that brutal, that cruel Third Reich!"[55]

Stein blamed the troubles of the past on the immoderate policy of the Grzesinski police and glowed with pride at the so different image Germany presented since Hitler had become Reich chancellor. "Foreigners who at first listen to me with incredulous faces grow serious and interested."[56]

Foreigners from West European countries and Americans, not to mention diplomats, were treated with special consideration. The Berlin police presidium, the secret police office in Berlin (Gestapa), and all provincial police offices were

[51] As an example, see Dr. J. Mrugowsky, "Jüdisches und deutsches Soldatentum," in *Nationalsozialistische Monatshefte*, Nr. 76 (July, 1936), pp. 633ff.

[52] Germaine Tillon, *Ravensbrück* (New York, 1975).

[53] Henry Wickham Steed, *The Meaning of Hitlerism* (London, 1934), p. xviii.

[54] Shlomo Aronson, "Heyrich und die Anfänge des SD und der Gestapo (1931–1935)" (Diss., Freie Universität Berlin, 1967), p. 54.

[55] Adolf Stein [Rumpelstilzchen], *Nee aber sowas!* (Berlin, 1935), p. 5.   [56] Ibid., p. 97.

alerted by special circular from the ministry of interior on 18 October 1933 that the person and property of such foreigners had to be scrupulously protected against any molestation by SA patrols, who had repeatedly assaulted them for nothing more than failure to use the German greeting.[57] By decree of 14 June 1935, no foreigner could be arrested or his home searched without special authorization by Dr. Werner Best, the commander of political police for the *länder* (*Politischer Polizeikommandeur der Länder*) at the Gestapa, except in emergencies.[58] If foreigners attended public trials where political issues were discussed, the presiding judges were to alert the Gestapo.[59] By contrast, the police, since 1936, kept close watch on all Soviet citizens so that they could be placed under arrest at a moment's notice,[60] and the hundreds of Czech agricultural laborers, mainly women, who came to Germany for harvest work every year were submitted to individual security checks by the Gestapo.[61]

Particularly dramatic, of course, was the differentiation made in the good treatment of foreign citizens of German race (*Angehörige des deutschen Volkstum mit ausländischer Staatsbürgerschaft*) and the harshness towards Germans who were deprived of their citizenship for political reasons. As stateless persons the latter were slated for deportation and were held in concentration camps until their travel papers could be prepared.[62]

The distinct treatment accorded to aliens may be seen as an attempt to encourage mutual competition among them for German favors. But if the Nazi policy towards aliens was based on the classical formula "divide et impera," it did not succeed very well. Foreigners in high places whose good will was important to the Germans were too well educated and materially too secure to be bought. Those who were at their mercy like Polish, French, Hungarian, or Italian workers during the war may have quarreled between themselves over food rations and work assignments, but as conditions inside Germany grew steadily worse, they were united in a common hatred for their host country.

---

[57] Minister of interior to all Oberpräsidenten, Regierungspräsidenten, police president Berlin, Gestapo Berlin, and all Landespolizeiinspektionen, Berlin, 18 Oct. 1933, in BA (Koblenz), RSHA R 58/folder 1.

[58] Dr. Werner Best, Preuss. Geheime Staatspolizei, to all Staatspolizeistellen, Berlin, 14 June 1935, in ibid. This order was modified on 27 Nov. 1937: Only prominent foreigners were to be spared arrest and house searches, and the right to authorize such measures was transferred from Dr. Best to the Gestapa office Berlin. Circular, same to same, Berlin, 27 Nov. 1937, betrifft: "Festnahme von Ausländern," in ibid.

[59] Circular, Reichsminister der Justiz to Reichsgerichtshof, Volksgerichtshof, and all Oberreichsanwälte, Berlin, 29 Apr. 1938, in ibid.

[60] Circular, Geheime Staatspolizei to all Staatspolizei- u. Polizeileitstellen, Berlin, 7 Nov. 1936, in ibid. Also Dr. Karl Zechenter, *Kripo-Vademekum, Handbuch in Schlagwörtern für den kriminalpolizeilichen Dienst im Grossdeutschen Reich* (Berlin, 1943), p. 134.

[61] Circular, Dr. Best, Politischer Polizeikommandeur der Länder, Berlin, 29 July 1936 (Geheim), in BA (Koblenz) RSHA R 58/folder 1.

[62] Heinrich Himmler, Reichsführer-SS u. Chef der Deutschen Polizei, to all Prussian Regierungspräsidenten and the police president of Berlin, Berlin, 26 May 1937, betrifft: "Vollziehung der Ausweisungshaft in Konzentrationslagern," in ibid.

This may explain the efforts of the ministry of propaganda to concentrate on influencing foreign tourists who came to Germany on short visits only. The ministry of propaganda discreetly left much of this activity to local bodies like the Berlin tourist office and its special service to foreigners (*Deutscher Ausländer-Dienst e.V.*) and to a slew of cultural associations for the promotion of friendship between Germans and individual foreign countries.[63] In cooperation with the propaganda ministry, the Gestapa Berlin also ordered foreign exchange scholars to be treated with leniency, even if they expressed opinions in public that were hostile toward National Socialism. A circular letter by Gestapo chief Heydrich in 1938 explained that:

In almost every case the speaker had not thought enough about what he was saying. We must remember that these are foreigners who grew up and were educated in an ideological world [*Vorstellungswelt*] utterly different from ours.

Most of them cannot readjust their views in the short time they are in Germany, and while they certainly are guilty of tactlessness they are not necessarily enemies of National Socialism. It is more important that they not be provoked by police interference into becoming spokesmen against Germany on their return home.[64]

Ideological reschooling of the police

Gleichschaltung came to the professional police as to the rest of the German society in installments. In some *länder* like Mecklenburg (where Nazi sympathizers already predominated before 1933) it came easier; in Hamburg the police chief of Altona, Otto Eggerstedt, was sent to concentration camp; while in Berlin the process was accompanied by much ambivalence, fear, and frustration. Had the Berlin police at once been presented with a comprehensive Nazi police doctrine to be studied and then accepted in place of the old, a number of old officials might have refused to continue to serve. But an overall Nazi police doctrine was not discernible to most officials until 1936. Cautious, conservative, and legalistic as most of them were, they were disarmed by the piecemeal progress of Nazification in the field of domestic security.[65] The replacement of the democratic-minded leadership on 20 July 1932 had appeared legal, and so had the emergency laws that were issued in the weeks following Hitler's appointment as Reich chancellor. The sweeping arrest of members of left-wing parties seemed justified by the current insecurity, or were tolerated because all the rougher and questionable operations were left to the armed SA and SS formations of the Nazi party. (The Berlin police in 1848 and 1918 also preferred to await the outcome of a political tug of

---

[63] Circular, Reichsminister für Volksaufklärung und Propaganda, to all Reichspropagandaämter, Berlin, 16 July 1938, betrifft: "Ausländerbetreuung," in ibid.

[64] Heydrich, Gestapa, Rundschreiben betr. Kommunistische Propaganda durch ausländische Austauschlehrer, Berlin, 5 Dec. 1938, in ibid.

[65] On the successful application of this piecemeal method in submitting civil servants, the judiciary, and the army to the Nazi Party police, see Brian Chapman, *Police State* (New York, 1970), p. 61.

war before resuming its regular order service.) The SA, SS, and members of the war veterans' organization (Stahlhelm), who by a decree of the Prussian ministry of interior (22 February 1933) were enrolled in an auxiliary police force (Hilfs-polizei, or Hipo) against the "the continued left-radical, and particularly Communist, threat to public security" were not expected to last beyond the period of consolidation of the new regime. They were in fact disbanded before long because their brutal behavior confirmed the rumors that many Hipo men had criminal records.[66] Besides, the French government in May objected to this expansion of Germany's paramilitary armed formations.[67]

Seemingly extraordinary and temporary were also Göring's instruction on 21 February 1933 regarding the use of firearms by police ("the activities of all organizations hostile to the state will have to be checked by the most ruthless means. The police who in the exercise of their duty make use of their firearms will be assured my protection regardless of the consequences") and hopefully the violence committed against the Jews.[68] The harsh measures taken against professional criminals were deplored by only a small number of seasoned Kripo detectives.

The ambivalent attitude of the police toward the Nazi revolution is also explained by the turmoil inside the police presidium as the entire staff underwent a review during February and March 1933. Everyone's attention was diverted from the situation in the streets to the hundreds of transfers, demotions, and dismissals that took place in all the departments of the police. The purges were carried out by fellow officials sitting on extraordinary review commissions, and their decisions were based on a mixture of political, professional, and personal evaluation in which subjective factors played a not insignificant role. Was then a purge victim to blame the Nazi government for his demotion or the rancorous disposition of a colleague whom he had offended at some point in the past?[69]

But the real force behind the Nazification of the German police service was the SS and SD. While the brown-shirted SA (*Sturmabteilungen*) had mainly acted as the political army of the Nazi Party during the civil war, the SS (*Schutzstaffeln*) was the Party's police arm, designed for swift action against individual political enemies rather than for open combat. Now it was more needed than before 1933. The SS furthermore had an intelligence organization of its own, the SD (Sicherheitsdienst), which enforced loyalty within the SS.

As the SS and SD grew in power and set out creating *Sonderkommandos* to strike at all opponents of Nazism, they constituted a challenge to the old political police

---

[66] There were clashes between professional police and SA units when the latter proceeded with their new "police" duties with excessive brutality. Joe Heydecker and J. Leeb, *Der Nürnberger Prozess. Bilanz der Tausend Jahre* (Zurich, 1958), p. 137.

[67] AA to Reich minister of Interior, II F 1370, Berlin, 15 May 1933, in USDC (Berlin), "Polizei. Verschiedenes;" and report on Hitler's Reichstag speech of 17 May 1933, in AMAE (Paris), Série Z Europe 154, "Propagande ennemie, des Alliés de la France."

[68] On the difficulty of foreseeing the ultimate dimension of the anti-Semitic policy in 1933, see Edward N. Peterson, *The Limits of Hitler's Power* (Princeton, N.J., 1969), p. 11.

[69] Liang, *Berlin Police Force*, pp. 165ff.

(Abteilung IA) who either had to join forces with them or leave the field to these newcomers.[70] The political police had of course undergone the most stringent political review of all departments at the Alexanderplatz. The remaining Abteilung IA commissars, some of whom survived on the strength of their good work in the investigation of the Reichstag fire, were then reconstituted on 26 April 1933 as the Prussian *Geheimes Staatspolizeiamt* (Secret State Police Office), or Gestapa. It was still a department of the Berlin police presidium, but in effect it now took orders directly from the Prussian ministry of interior. The Gestapa thus became the branch of the old professional police that served as the chief link for the coordination of the old police apparatus and the new Nazi order. In the spring of 1934, the Gestapa offices throughout Germany were centralized under Heinrich Himmler as deputy chief of secret police.[71]

On 30 November 1933 the Gestapa was removed one step further from the old police when it was transferred from the jurisdiction of the Prussian ministry of interior to the office of the Prussian prime minister and its offices were moved from the Alexanderplatz to the Prinz-Albrecht-Strasse.[72] The next step was another diminution in the power of the police presidium: the Gestapa in Prinz-Albrecht-Strasse on 10 February 1936 extended its duties to include criminal police work as well. On 28 August 1936 it officially assumed the new title *Geheime Staatspolizei,* or Gestapo.

Having lost the political police and portions of its authority in criminal affairs, the Berlin police was left with the Schutzpolizei as its strongest remaining asset, strong notably because of the formidable fighting power of its riot brigades (*Bereitschaftspolizei*). But on 1 August 1935 a decree transferred the Bereitschaftspolizei wholesale to the regular German army.[73]

The ideological reschooling of the professional police was also taken in hand in 1936, though again in easy stages. It was now laid down that all police officers were in the future to be recruited from the ranks of the SS, and all future police rookies would have to be members of the NSDAP.[74] The Nazi idea of police mission now became better known. Göring wanted the Gestapo to be absolutely obedient to his orders because the police was to him the instrument for the creation of a dynamic new order, not the enforcer of established laws. "We want men who obey blindly and can shoot straight," he was quoted as saying.[75] Hans Kehrl expressed this principle more tactfully in a book on German police history: "In an authoritarian state, the defense of the state is taken much more seriously. Our new state will not, like the Weimar regime, wait to suppress attacks against its

---

[70] Hans Buchheim, *Die Organisation von SS und Polizei im NS-Staat* (Duisburg, 1964), p. 29; and Heinz Höhne, "Das ist die Mentalität eines Schlächters," in *Der Spiegel,* 29 Apr. 1985, pp. 29–32.

[71] A very useful account is the monograph by Edward Crankshaw, *Gestapo* (New York, 1957).

[72] Bernhard Vollmer, *Volksopposition im Polizeistaat* (Stuttgart, 1957), pp. 9–10; and Hannah Arendt, *Eichmann in Jerusalem* (New York, 1963), p. 32.

[73] "Die Preussische Landespolizei, 1933–1935. Ein Rückblick anlässlich ihrer Ueberführung in das Heer am 1. August 1935," (mimeo, 35 pages), in USDC (Berlin), "Polizei. Verschiedenes."

[74] Helmuth Koschorke, ed., *Die Polizei – einmal anders!* (Munich, 1937), p. 157.

[75] Hans-Jürgen Köhler, *Inside the Gestapo. Hitler's Shadow over the World* (London, 1940), pp. 16, 34.

integrity until it is nearly too late. It will strike at any resistance, any sign of subversion."[76]

Indeed, every opposition to the national movement was now declared criminal. This included attacks on the National Socialist movement as much as attacks against the German Reich. Political crimes were no longer, as under the republic and in many democratic countries in the nineteenth century, honored as springing from idealistic motives but execrated as "the worst of all crimes."[77]

Werner Best, who was the chief legal authority of the Gestapo, elaborated on the duties of the German police in the service of the Nazi revolution by laying down three basic principles: (1) The police never acts illegally or contrary to the law so long as what it does corresponds to the rules laid down for it by its superiors – up to the highest level of leadership; (2) the essence of police is: taking care of whatever the government wants to have taken care of; and (3) whether the leadership's orders to the police are right or wrong is not a juridical question but a historical question. Mistakes committed by the leadership are punished by fate, through national misfortune, revolution, and defeat.[78]

A Swedish journalist during the Second World War, Arvid Fredborg, wrote that "The National Socialist regime rests on two solid pillars. One is the German police, the other is the Party with its various organizations, foremost among them . . . the SS."[79] This is probably quite true, because the German police, though we may see in it a professional corps trapped into serving a regime whose ideology violated its ethical principles, continued to perform its services without demur for twelve years. Had it fully submitted to the Nazis or was it just biding its time? How long can civil servants bide their time without becoming fully compromised? Fredborg's American colleague, Louis P. Lochner, wrote in 1941 that there were "thousands" of holdovers from the Republican police, whose minds he said had not been twisted in spite of incessant political instruction. These men, he thought, would make reliable policemen again after the fall of the Nazi regime.[80] But, writing after the war, the historian Dietrich Bracher credited the few cases of police officials refusing to obey Nazi orders to personal character only, not to political motives or professional integrity.[81]

Austria

The Nazification of the Austrian police will be discussed, below, in connection with the tenuous relationship between the Austrian and the Czechoslovak security

---

[76] Hans Kehrl, "Die Polizei," in *Die Verwaltungs-Akademie. Ein Handbuch für den Beamten im natio-nalsozialistischen Staat* (Berlin, ca. 1938), vol. II., p. 8.

[77] Roger Diener, "Das System der Staatsverbrechen," in *Deutsches Recht*, 4. Jhg., No. 14 (25 July 1934), p. 331.

[78] Best, *Die Deutsche Polizei*, p. 20.

[79] Arvid Fredborg, *Behind the Steel Wall. A Swedish Journalist in Berlin 1941–43* (New York, 1944), p. 227.

[80] Louis P. Lochner, *What About Germany?* (New York, 1942), pp. 227–9.

[81] Bracher, *Machtergreifung*, p. 439. See also references to Willi Lemke and Walther Wecke in Liang, *Berlin Police Force*, pp. 171–3.

forces during the 1930s. Some of the main differences between the Austrian and the German police's relationship to Nazism, however, must be mentioned here. The fundamental difference between the rise to power of the Hitlerites in the Berlin police and in the Vienna police is that in Berlin the conversion to Nazism amounted to a capitulation; in Vienna it came much closer to the attainment of a long-term goal. The events in Berlin were more complicated and more dangerous because what happened there was the surrender of thousands of highly trained civil servants who, bewildered and frustrated, in a critical moment (1932–3) gave up on democracy and then were left with no ideological conviction to their name. The Viennese police had never seriously attempted to establish a democracy in Austria after the First World War; the ascendancy of the Nazis in the Polizei-Direktion in the 1930s was a development long foreseeable. But the Viennese police for that very reason retained a larger measure of self-confidence and more control over how it wanted to interpret National Socialism – namely, as a continuation of an authoritarian tradition going back to the Schönerian nationalism of imperial days if not further back still. Perhaps this is why the Prussian policemen in 1945 were more apt to disclaim having held any true Nazi conviction under Hitler. In retrospect it was hard for them to understand how they could have fallen for his fantastic program twelve years earlier. The Austrian civil servants after 1945 did recognize that their ideology – like Japanese nationalism – no longer fitted in a world ruled by the Western Allies and the Soviet Union. But they did not feel obliged to apologize for their old beliefs either, which after all had been with them since the ancien régime.

The Austrian police was from the beginning of the twenties far more engaged on the side of right-wing extremism than its German counterpart. The reason for this must largely be found in the precarious situation of the Austrian Republic, which induced many government officials after the war to wish for a radical political change in the foreseeable future, be that in the direction of international socialism, union with Germany, or a Habsburg restoration. Political tensions were much higher inside the Viennese police in the postwar years than in the Berlin police. Many more lower-ranking Austrian policemen belonged to the militant Socialist Party, but they were quickly weeded out after the fateful clash between Sicherheitswache and organized workmen outside the justice department, in Vienna on 15 July 1927. At the same time the higher echelons under the administration of Johann Schober had largely leaned towards Christian Socialism and monarchism. Following Schober's death in 1932, the officials with Fascist leanings (Austro-Fascist, Heimwehr, or else Hitlerite Nazi) were in the lead: Dr. Michael Skubl, Benno Breitenberg, and others.[82]

The year 1934 brought not only the consolidation of Hitler's regime in Germany. In Austria the Socialist workers were suppressed in a brief but bloody civil war in February, followed by a Nazi putsch attempt that resulted in the death of

---

[82] Elisabeth Winkler, "Die Polizei als Instrument in der Etablierungsphase der austrofaschistischen Diktatur (1932–1934) mit besonderer Berücksichtigung der Wiener Polizei," (Diss., Vienna University, 1983), pp. 17–18.

Chancellor Dollfuss. Seven policemen were put on the wanted list.[83] Formal investigations were eventually begun against three leading police officials: Breitenberg, Steinhäusl, and Leo Gotzmann. (Breitenberg's charges were dropped; Steinhäusl and Gotzmann amnestied in 1936.)[84]

Following the unsuccessful Nazi putsch, Austria introduced a new constitution, which converted the republic into an authoritarian Fascist state. The new constitution replaced the democratic principle of popular sovereignty ("people and ruler are one") in favor of the restoration of clear divisions between leader and followers, rulers and ruled.[85] But what made the coming of Fascism so interesting in the Austrian case was that unlike in Germany where the police lost much power to the Nazi Party security forces, in Austria the police was invested with *more* power so that it could spearhead the coming new order. On 10 May 1933, three months after Hitler became German chancellor, a new oath of loyalty to the government – but not to the Austrian constitution – was exacted from the Vienna police to secure its obedience in case a coup d'état from above was needed.[86] And in the following year, State Councillor Adamovich, speaking to a police audience, openly praised the new constitution of 1934 for permitting the legislative "to empower the administrative authorities to issue decrees with the effect of changing existing laws. . . . The administrative authorities, *notably the police*, are thereby given the means to make general disposition, if necessity calls, that deviate from, or bypass, existing legislation."[87]

Nazi Fifth Columns in Central Europe

The Nazi regime was popular at home in its first two years not only because it put an end to years of political trouble and rampant criminality, but because it promised to restore Germany's freedom of action as an equal partner in the international community. From the moment Hitler assumed the chancellorship he set his aims at denouncing the Treaty of Versailles. In 1933 Germany withdrew from the Disarmament Conference and from the League of Nations. In March 1935 it restored compulsory and universal military service. Thus Germany's apparent return to a picture of internal peace under Nazism – the cherished attainment of a *"konfliktlose Gesellschaft"* – was accompanied by her resumption of a posture of bellicose confrontation towards the other powers of Europe.

Such a dramatic change in the military weight of one country traditionally prompted counter-actions by the other members of the European balance of

[83] Dr. Weiser, Polizeidirektion Wien, Vienna, 17 Jan., 1935 (Pr. VI IV-931/35), in Beilage in der *Oeffent. Sich.*, 15. Jhg., Nr. 2, Feb. 1935.

[84] Franz A. Pichler, *Polizeihofrat P. Ein treuer Diener seines ungetreuen Staates* (Vienna, 1984), p. 114.

[85] Polizei-Oberkommissar Dr. Dr. Hermann Roeder, "Der Durchbruch zum autoritären Ständestaat," in *Oeffent. Sich.*, 15. Jhg., No. 1 (Jan 1935), p. 7.

[86] Winkler, "Die Polizei als Instrument in der Etablierungsphase der austrofaschistischen Diktatur," pp. 120–1.

[87] Staatsrat Prof. Dr. Ludwig Adamovich, "Verfassung 1934 und öffentliche Sicherheit," in *Oeffent. Sich.*, 15, Jhg., No 1, (Jan. 1935), pp. 6–7. Italics mine.

power. The "risk" of a hostile coalition had worried the Wilhelmine empire in the 1890s when it set out to raise Germany to the level of a world power. The same risk faced Hitler's Germany when it set out to challenge the distribution of forces laid down at the Paris peace conferences by boldly rearming on land, on sea, and in the air.

But in the view of Generaloberst Hans von Seeckt, the founder of Germany's postwar Reichswehr, a revision of Germany's position in Europe by military means held out little promise. He deplored the French military preponderance since 1918 not because it was French but because, in his view, in the twentieth century any kind of military foundation to the European order threatened the economic well-being of the whole Continent and permanently undermined peace.[88] Consistent with this interpretation of Germany's dilemma in a Europe where war operations were no longer tenable yet a military way had to be found to break down the fatal stranglehold of French hegemony, von Seeckt as early as 1923 had supported clandestine cooperation between the Reichswehr and the Soviet Red Army.[89] Ten years later he shifted his attention to China, which by then was on the threshold of becoming a modern state with a national government, while Soviet Russia was plunged into the turmoil of collectivization and the consolidation of Stalin's dictatorship. To Seeckt as much as to a number of other leading German military men, industrialists, bankers, and diplomats, the best strategy was to expand the geographical dimension of the balance of power beyond the European Continent to include countries that might be willing to side with Germany, like China. He responded with reservation to attempts by men like E. Ledeberg and Dr. Lodgman von Auen, leaders of the Sudeten German minority in Czechoslovakia, to draw him into their conspiratorial work against the Prague government next door.[90] But in 1933 and 1934 he willingly undertook two arduous voyages to Nationalist China.

This is not the place to dwell on the strategic speculation behind German military missions outside Europe, which in the twenties were dispatched to Argentina, Chile, Peru, Bolivia, Russia and, after 1928, finally to China. But it is interesting that the German military in the 1930s showed little enthusiasm for undertaking a direct breakout of the encirclement by France and her allies in Eastern Europe. In a new war, Germany had to expect to face yet larger numbers of opponents than in 1914, sustained by far more abundant resources. Since 1934 the French encirclement was furthermore reinforced by new military agreements linking France with Czechoslovakia and the Soviet Union, and there was reason to assume that in another European war Britain once more would be on France's side. The Wehrmacht respected the excellent progress made since 1918 by the

---

[88] Pencil notes taken by Alexander von Falkenhausen during his conference with von Seeckt in Munich on 14 Aug. 1931, in BA-MA (Freiburg i.B.), Nachlass Falkenhausen, China Box 1.

[89] E. H. Cookridge, *Gehlen. Spy of the Century* (New York, 1971), p. 24; and Hans W. Gatzke, "Russo-German Military Collaboration during the Weimar Republic," in *American Historical Review*, LXIII, No. 3 (Apr. 1958), pp. 565–7.

[90] See correspondence 1923 in BA-MA (Freiburg i.B.), Nachlass Seeckt, N247/171.

French and the Czech military in building up the Czechoslovak armed forces. With a seasoned war industry as base, the Czech defenses included good tanks, a respectable air force, and by the mid-1930s modern fortifications along the border with Germany built on the model of the Maginot line.[91] Unless the military encirclement of Germany disintegrated because of French domestic turmoil or a French involvement in the Spanish Civil War, Germany's best means to neutralize her potential opponents was to use against the weakest ones among them that unorthodox weapon of international warfare that dictatorial police states can better use than democracies: demoralization through propaganda, subversion, and terrorism.[92]

Different kinds of agents were readily available to the Nazi regime for this purpose. They ranged from regular diplomatic and consular staff to the officials of cultural organizations catering to Germans settlers living abroad. To proselytize among German settlers abroad, the old Pan-German *Verein für das Deutschtum im Ausland* was since 1933 effectively superseded by the *Volksdeutscher Rat* led by General Karl Haushofer and his son Albrecht Haushofer. For purposes of terrorism or to prepare German settlers to support an invading German army, the agents were mostly members of the Gestapo, the SS, and SA, and functionaries of the Nazi Party branches abroad. These latter were the NSDAP *Landesgruppen*, under the supervision of the Party's *Auslands-Organisation* (AO) directed by Ernst Bohle, which ostensibly worked only among Reich Germans. When difficulties arose with foreign governments, as in Czechoslovakia where the Nazi party was outlawed in 1933, the Germans worked through native Fascist parties with identical programs (in this case with the Sudeten German *Heimatfront*) whose connections to Germany were carefully hidden.[93]

It is difficult to recognize the work of the Nazi agents abroad as genuine police work in the way we have defined the mission of the modern police. Though they produced some measure of "control" over the ethnic Germans in a given country through administrative organization and the manipulation of individual persons, their purpose was not the amelioration of the society in which their subjects lived

---

[91] Charles-Henri, *The Czecho-Slovak Army*, trans. from the French by L. L. Pendleton (The Army War College, Washington D.C., March 1929), passim; David Vital, "Czechoslovakia and the Powers, September 1938," in *Journal of Contemporary History*, Vol. I, No. 4 (1966), p. 45; and Gert Buchheit, *Der deutsche Geheimdienst. Geschichte der militärischen Abwehr* (Munich, 1966), pp. 117–18.

[92] On the basically defensive position of the German military, see Hans-Adolf Jacobsen, *Nationalsozialistische Aussenpolitik 1933–1938* (Frankfurt a.M. 1968), pp. 420–1. Also Ronald M. Smelser, *The Sudeten Problem 1933–1938. Volkstumpolitik and the Formulation of Nazi Foreign Policy* (Middletown, Conn., 1975), pp. 178ff. But in the Swiss experience, German military espionage in Europe (*Abwehr*) was more professional than Gestapo and Nazi Party operations. Agents of the latter were often corrupt and not above cheating native informers out of the monetary rewards they were promised. *Bericht des Chef des Generalstabes der Armee an den Oberbefehlshaber der Armee über den Aktivdienst 1939–1945* (Berne, n.d.), pp. 479–93.

[93] "Henlein sprach in Wien," in *Deutsche Allgemeine Zeitung*, 6 Mar. 1941, p. 5. The British government protested against the AO because of what London regarded as an illegal exercise of sovereign powers on British soil. See Public Records Office (London), FO. 371, 20741.

but rather to set the stage for its conquest and subjugation. Their methods were not those of civil police in a state ruled by law, since they included brutal intimidation and assassination. We must mention them here mainly because the countries in which the Nazis operated in this fashion were democracies whose sole defense against infiltration were their conventional modern police authorities. Our chief interest is to enquire how well the democratic police authorities acquitted themselves in this unprecedented contest with the police of a totalitarian dictatorship.

The use of diplomats to watch German émigrés in Paris, unbecoming though it was by the ethics of conventional diplomatic usage had, as we know, a certain precedence in the activities of the tsarist Russian embassy in the nineteenth century. (The French embassy in Berlin under François-Poncet also engaged in intelligence work under the aegis of an old Parisian journalist.)[94] Besides, the Germans were not the only ones to spy on expatriate countrymen in Paris. Since the First World War Paris had become Europe's principal place of refuge for political exiles from many countries. The largest number of dissidents came from Fascist Italy, the next largest from Bolshevik Russia. Experienced in such problems as the French police was, it apparently managed to satisfy the Germans before 1933 that in the interest of peaceful relations between France and the Weimar Republic, no sanctuary was offered to Germans whose activities constituted a danger to Germany's national security.[95] But since the coming of Hitler a large number of anti-Nazi refugees had arrived in Paris. The German embassy in Paris admitted, in a letter dated 15 October 1934, that it was unhappy about the "criminal" tasks it was directed to carry out by the German police ("*die inneren Behörden*") in Berlin. It thought the Gestapo underestimated the ease with which information could be collected among refugees. "There are very few people among them who like Germany so much that they will tell us what they know without payment."[96]

Because of the unenthusiastic performance of Germany's diplomats as police agents, the Gestapo and SS sent their own men to Paris some of whom successfully posed as Jewish émigrés and sowed suspicion and fear inside the German exile community.[97] A French police report in 1933 noted that Gestapo agencies were secretly being established under the direction of a Professor Georges von Meczaros in Strasbourg, Innsbruck, Prague, Karlsbad, Warsaw, Danzig, Copenhagen, Brussels, Antwerp, London, Rome, and Moscow.[98] At the German

---

[94] André François-Poncet, *Souvenirs d'une ambassade à Berlin* (Paris, 1946), pp. 5–8.

[95] Polizeimajor A. L. Ratcliffe (Berlin), "Paris als Sammelpunkt politischer Flüchtlinge," in *Oeffent. Sich.*, 12. Jhg. Nr. 6 (June 1932), p. 2.

[96] Deutsche Botschaft to Herr von Bülow, Paris, 15 Oct. 1934 (Geheim!), in CDJC (Paris), folder: CLXXXIII-2.

[97] See, for example, report of an unnamed SS-Scharführer just returned from a scouting mission to the Paris Exposition, dated Berlin, 13 July 1937, in ibid., folder: CD XXXVII-7.

[98] Typed note, dated Berlin, 4 July 1933, in APP (Paris), Carton B A/1693, "Polices étrangères," folder: "Police allemande à Paris."

embassy in Paris some forty staff members were replaced by new personnel in 1934, and the French police assumed that all of them were Gestapo agents.[99]

Among the cities selected for special Gestapo missions, Prague was probably the most important one from the point of view of Germany's strategical interests. Germany's best chance to overcome France's military preponderance in Europe lay in undermining the defenses of the three small countries that bordered it on the south and southeast: Switzerland, Austria, and Czechoslovakia. Of these three, Czechoslovakia was the most defiant opponent of Nazism on ideological grounds, yet at the same time the one most vulnerable to infiltration, because of the three million Sudeten Germans living along its strategic border with Germany.

1937: The turning point

There came a critical moment in the second half of the thirties when the balance-of-power strategy which Hans von Seeckt and like-minded notables such as Göring, Hjalmar Schacht, and Generals Blomberg and Reichenau supported on a Eurasian scale was abandoned in favor of dismantling neighboring Czechoslovakia through subversion. A premonition of what was to come was the failure of a scouting mission by Albrecht Haushofer and Maximilian Count zu Trautmannsdorff to Prague in 1936, which sought to detach Czechoslovakia from the French alliance system through a ten-year nonaggression pact.[100] When, in the summer of 1937, Japan invaded China, Germany was forced to decide how seriously it was interested in China as a potential Far Eastern partner. To help China meant gambling on an investment that could take another decade or two before it produced tangible results. Japan, on the other hand, though the Germans had no reliable hold over it, offered Berlin the hope of immediate military support from outside Europe should warlike complications arise in East Central Europe.[101]

One reason why Hitler in 1937 thought he could destroy Czechoslovakia was France's failure to challenge Germany's remilitarization of the Rhineland in 1936 despite Polish and Czech offers of military assistance. Hitler doubted the strength of the Franco-Czechoslovak alliance, and for good reason. The relationship between the two countries had been fraught with small but persistent disagreements, so that in the end too much reliance was placed by both sides on technical

[99] Préfecture de Police, Direction des Renseignements et des Jeux, to prefect of police, Paris, 23 Jan. 1934, in ibid. Police attachés were introduced into German embassies abroad only during the war by an agreement between Ribbentrop and Himmler dated 8 Aug. 1941.

[100] Smelser, *Sudeten Problem 1933–1938*, ch. 7; and František Moravec, *Master of Spies. The Memoirs of General František Moravec* (New York, 1975), pp. 96–9. Unlike his father, Karl Haushofer, Albrecht Haushofer sympathized with China and opposed Hitler. He was liquidated by the SS as a resistance fighter in April 1945.

[101] There is an unconfirmed story told by Carl Marcus, who in the thirties worked for Kurt Jahnke's secret diplomatic service in Berlin, that explains the decision in favor of subversion against Austria and Czechoslovakia in terms of the rivalry between Göring and Reichenau on the one hand and Himmler and Ribbentrop on the other. See Hsi-Huey Liang, *The Sino-German Connection* (Assen, 1978), pp. 122–4.

cooperation in military matters alone.[102] Yet France's cultivation of Czechoslovakia as a military partner for the encirclement of Germany was based on several miscalculations:

1. As long as Germany during the 1920s dropped the *Burgfrieden* strategy for Foreign Minister Stresemann's "fulfillment policy" and something resembling the police strategy of "défense du territoire," to push Czech military preparations beyond a certain point seemed unwarranted if not outright provocative.

2. When Germany after 1933 resumed its old Burgfrieden strategy it used infiltration and subversion against the small countries Austria, Czechoslovakia, and Switzerland which to interdict required coordinated police measures on their part in place of (or at least in addition to) military defences.

3. The crucial test for the feasibility of developing such coordinated police measures against Germany were the steps taken by Austria and Czechoslovakia after the war towards mutual assistance in questions of internal security. Unlike Switzerland, these two newly founded republics were highly vulnerable to Nazi irredentist propaganda. Police collaboration, moreover, was technically easier in their case since they had both belonged to the Cisleithanian half of the Habsburg Empire and the old administrative substructure was still in place. But, of course, the very fact that the Weimar Republic posed no threat to either Austria or Czechoslovakia minimized the chance of much progress in the cooperation of their respective security forces before 1933.

4. Police work on the tactical level depends on close adjustment to local customs and administrative practice. The Austrian police system, which was largely continued by the new regime in Prague, was surely more than adequate to meet all Czechoslovakia's tactical police needs. With special attention given to the frontier police it would seem reasonable that Czechoslovakia could use the old security personnel and still apply the French strategy of shielding its territory against foreign interference while promoting the democratic evolution of its domestic political life. But should not the French have understood that Czech parliamentary democracy was doomed to failure in the absence of military security, and that Czechoslovakia could not be secure – no matter how many French officers served in Prague and how excellent the Skoda guns – as long as the military thinking of the Republic remained consonant with the passive concept of "défense du territoire"? Given Czechoslovakia's size and location, with Bohemia practically surrounded by unfriendly states and Prague within range of German and Polish bombing planes, should its police strategy not rather have aspired to emulate eighteenth-century Prussia's concept of Burgfrieden?

[102] On the French commitment to help Czechoslovakia exclusively in matters of external defense, see letter by Derby, British embassy in Paris, to Foreign Minister Pichon, Paris, 27 Feb. 1919, in AMAE (Paris), Série Z Europe 1918–1929. Techécoslovaquie 12. "Section des renseignements militaires."

There is no easy answer to these questions. Without democracy Czechoslovak independence would have been meaningless to many of its most ardent supporters. Without a peaceful foreign policy in Prague, the League of Nations would have had that smaller a chance of success. And a policy of "défense du territoire" might have worked had the "territoire" in question gradually been extended to include neighboring Austria and perhaps Hungary and Switzerland, through better collaboration between their respective internal security services.

The fall of the Sudetenland and the failure of collective police security

General remarks

During a luncheon in 1937, Winston Churchill said to Shiela Grant Duff, an Englishwoman who sympathized strongly with Czechoslovakia, that Germany could still be contained and the peace of Europe preserved if the European powers around it would stand firm and – by rebuffing Hitler's foreign adventures – bring him down by provoking an internal explosion. "An explosion of some sort is inevitable in Germany," Churchill said: "If Germany is sufficiently tightly encased by a strong alliance system . . . the explosion will be inside Germany and get rid of this gang. A military revolution would at least put people in power who could be spoken to, who would understand what they could do and what not, and who would hesitate at crime."[103]

It was unfortunate for Czechoslovakia that Churchill at that time was still a lone voice crying in the political wilderness. Most historical studies in the last half century have confirmed Germany's lack of military readiness in 1938 and, though not with the same confidence, the possibility of an army coup against Hitler. And yet we must ask what chances Switzerland, Austria, and Czechoslovakia had in holding out against Germany's expansionist drive. As links in the encirclement of Nazi Germany these three countries were from the military point of view quite unequal. Austria was the weakest, its army at best ready for border skirmishes with Czech or Hungarian troops. Switzerland was strong only in defense against a German attempt at permanent subjugation, but probably incapable of stopping a German march-through from Basel to Geneva. Czechoslovakia was well prepared to resist a land attack from across the German border but not an attack that also came through Austrian territory plus Poland and Hungary, and not if the Sudeten German areas were to rise in rebellion. The shortcomings in their defenses were in each case compounded by their respective police dispositions. Austria could hardly fight a German invasion if its highest police authorities flirted with Nazism, as they did since 1933. Switzerland could not be counted on assisting Austria and Czechoslovakia against the inroads of Nazism if

[103] Shiela Grant Duff, *The Parting of Ways. A Personal Account of the Thirties* (London: Peter Owen, 1982), p. 159.

its police leaders preferred to ignore what happened there and to tolerate Nazi activities on Swiss soil so long as they remained reasonably inconspicuous. In the Czechoslovak case the chief problem was that the democratic principles of modern police were out of place in a small country with disproportionately long frontiers to defend and with a newly constituted multinational population lacking a tradition of solidarity. The police situation of Switzerland, Austria, and Czechoslovakia could, however, have been much better had they agreed on some measure of mutual police assistance: had Switzerland not dissociated itself from the growing crisis throughout east-central Europe, and had Austria and Czechoslovakia collaborated in defense of their sovereign independence against subversion from Germany.

Switzerland

Switzerland was less inviting a target for Nazi subversion than the untested succession states Austria and Czechoslovakia. But its eventual success in evading Nazi occupation altogether may simply have been because after the fall of Vienna (1938) and Prague (1939), Hitler had no more need to take Berne. And yet, Swiss independence in 1937 mattered if the Hitler regime was to be denied every possible chance for expansion. Besides, Switzerland's strategy is instructive for our study, as throughout the nineteenth century this country had often had to deal with foreign police operating clandestinely on its territory.[104]

In the European crisis of 1937–8, Switzerland's attitude toward Nazi Germany was influenced by three recent or concurrent experiences: (1) Its direct confrontation with Communist subversion in 1918; (2) the memory of past disputes with Italy (1898, 1902), rekindled since the establishment of Mussolini's fascist regime in 1922; and (3) the stress exerted on its neutrality since 1936 by the Spanish Civil War as numerous foreign and some native volunteers daily traveled along Swiss railway lines to join up, often recruited by the Spanish republican legation in Prague.

The cumulative pressure of the international crises of the mid-1930s must have been exceptionally trying to Switzerland. Therefore, if its old stratagem of quietly yielding to strong outside pressure could hold Nazi penetration into Switzerland within tolerable limits, so much the better. Besides, the politics of the Nazi regime in Berlin were not entirely alien to the thinking of some Swiss police officials. There had been Swiss police officials in 1918–19 who concurred with the thesis that the Bolshevik revolution was a Jewish plot.

When, in 1936, the Swiss Freedom Committee (*Schweizerisches Freiheitskomittee*) under the presidency of Dr. Kronauer openly opposed the government ban on

[104] The following passage is largely based on Swiss EJPD documentation. Hans-Adolf Jacobsen's treatment of German–Swiss relations in his *Nationalsozialistische Aussenpolitik 1933–1938* (Frankfurt a.M., 1968), pp. 509–17, concentrates more on German documents concerning Swiss newspapers and parliamentarians who were anti-Nazi, which casts Switzerland in a somewhat different light.

Swiss citizens fighting in the Spanish Civil War the committee was investigated by the EJPD. The resulting police report reflected the ideological leanings of certain individuals in the Swiss police. It described the committee as officially neutral but in fact closely linked to the Communist and Socialist parties and antimilitarist. It also insinuated that it was run by Jews. Dr. Kronauer was called "a wild agitator [*hemmungsloser Kämpfer*] with an enormous need for prestige. He will use any means to attain his goals." The character of the other leading figures on the committee were said to be sufficiently revealed by their names: Oprecht, Rosenbaum and Rosenbusch. "No further comment is necessary. [*Kommentar überflüssig, usw.*]"[105]

The Swiss authorities disapproved of helping the republican government and the International Brigades on the grounds that should Franco's Nationalist Party win the Civil War, it would blame Switzerland for having supported the legitimate regime. This surprising interpretation of the legal duties of third powers in a civil war took the Swiss so far as to deny medical help to the republican government, arguing that such help would amount to rendering military assistance as it would free more government manpower for combat duty.[106] In its anxiousness to keep out of the Spanish Civil War the Berne government on 28 December 1936 ordered a police investigation in every canton to find out the names of all citizens who had clandestinely left for the Spanish theater of war or who might be planning to do so, and to ferret out all secret recruiting stations. The postal services were asked to help because the volunteers in Spain were all expected to be writing home at Christmas time as well as to receive parcels from their families.[107]

The Swiss police in the thirties was also needed to deal with Italian consular officials who were spying on anti-Fascist countrymen in Switzerland. The Italians were not a great problem however, because their activities resembled the kind of infractions of Swiss sovereignty which often took place in the nineteenth century. Italian Fascism lacked the dynamic and expansionist threat that contemporaries perceived in world Communism and in Nazism. Swiss independence was not put in question by Rome, and Berne did not worry about domestic support for the Duce. One major issue was the contention by the government in Rome, in 1929 and in 1930, that the Italian delegation to the League of Nations in Geneva was

---

[105] Letter signed Weber, to Bundesrat, dated 29 Aug. 1936, in ibid.

[106] EJPD to Schweizerischer Bundesrat, Berne, 13 Aug. 1935, C.8.151: "Verbot der Teilnahme an den Feindseligkeiten in Spanien," in ibid.; and "Neutralitätsbegriffe im roten Basel," in *Basler Nachrichten* (19 Aug. 1936). Switzerland did, in 1937, send a Red Cross convoy to Madrid to evacuate women and children from the besieged city, reminiscent of the succor that Basel offered Strasbourg during the siege of 1870. On the other hand, the argument that medical help amounted to war help was not invoked by the Swiss government when the Swiss Red Cross sent teams of doctors and nurses to German front-line hospitals in Russia during the Second World War. See "Switzerland and the Red Cross in the Second World War" in this chapter.

[107] Circular letter, BA to the "obersten Polizeibehörden der Kantone," No. C.8.150, Berne, 28 Dec. 1936, in StA (Basel-Stadt), Str. & Pol. D3, 1936-1028; "Spanischer Bürgerkrieg. Verbot der Teilnahme an den Feindseligkeiten in Spanien – Flüchtlinge – Sigg – Birk Rudolf."

the target of an assassination plot by Italian anarchists. The Swiss prosecutor's office (*Bundesanwaltschaft*, or BA), after consulting the French and Belgian police, concluded that the Italian fears were unfounded. It used the occasion to present to the EJPD a statement on the problem of foreign police activities in Switzerland in which the current Italian demands were placed in the context of the country's traditional policy on political asylum.

The steps taken by the Italian legation are ultimately designed to eliminate the antifascist centers in Switzerland. . . . Any sizable collection of antifascists in Switzerland is of course a danger to our external security because it incites the foreign state concerned to invigilate its citizens here. . . . Therefore the federal council in former times used to expel foreign revolutionaries if too many sought refuge in Switzerland, because their numbers threatened our security by giving foreign states a cause to attack us. . . . Later, political refugees were expelled only if they mounted attacks on other countries from Swiss soil. . . . Switzerland has granted many Italian antifascists asylum, as has France, England, and the United States.

Should the Italian government take umbrage at our moderation in the exercise of our power of expulsion, we should remind it that Italy owes Switzerland thanks for the asylum it granted Italian refugees during the time of Austrian rule. We cannot in any event keep the antifascists in Switzerland under close surveillance because we lack a strong political police . . . [108]

Fortunately for the Swiss BA, it had no overt evidence of Italian police spies operating inside the Confederation. At the same time, the Swiss success in warding off Italian police incursions with conventional diplomatic maneuvers may have made it that harder for the Berne government to find an effective way of interdicting the Nazi movement in Switzerland.

To illustrate the Swiss government's difficulty in regard to the Hitler movement, we may cite its concern as early as the spring of 1932 over German citizens in Swiss border towns wearing the Nazi party uniform. There was no law on the books concerning foreign party uniforms, and an outright ban against such displays seemed excessive because of the particular circumstances prevailing in most border towns. In Basel, for example, the German Reichsbahn maintained a railway station (the Badischer Bahnhof) on Swiss territory where German railway police since the late nineteenth century had done duty in their uniform and wearing guns. Since the mid-1920s there had been Nazi meetings in the hall above the buffet of that railway station, guarded by twenty-five to thirty young German storm troopers who, however, always took pains to cross into Germany for training and drill. After 30 January 1933, the Badischer Bahnhof flew the swastika flag, much to the annoyance of the local Swiss inhabitants, but it was difficult to know exactly when and where to draw the line because the German national flag had been tolerated at the station before. Could Switzerland now discriminate between Germany's state flag and the flag of its ruling party?

---

[108] BA report to EJPD, Berne, 16 Jan. 1930, in BA (Berne), (Handakten Häberlin), E 4001(a)1, Aktenband 39, IX, "Fascistischer Spitzeldienst in der Schweiz."

Another problem was that the German Nazis in Switzerland were always careful to limit their overt activities to agitation among German and Austrian citizens, knowing that this would by and large shield them from Swiss legal intervention as long as there was no proof of coercion or intimidation. The Nazi student organization in Switzerland, the *Vereinigung deutscher arischer Studierender*, entertained an "information service" whose purpose was to see to the proper political indoctrination of students and professors of German nationality. [109] The German Nazis could confine their activities to their fellow citizens without diminishing their effect among the Swiss population for there were enough native sympathizers who proselytized among the general public. The existence of Swiss Nazis, in turn, served to inhibit strong government intervention because of Switzerland's tradition of political freedom. Three indigenous Nazi parties existed by 1935: (1) The *Volksbund* (also known as *Nationalsozialistische Schweizerische Arbeiterpartei*, or NSSAP); (2) the *Bund Treuer Eidgenossen Nationalsozialistischer Weltanschauung* (BTE); and (3) the *Eidgenössische Soziale Arbeiterpartei* (EPT). [110]

In 1932, when in Czechoslovakia the government took legal steps against the Sudeten German *Volkssport* movement and in Germany the Prussian government banned the SA and SS, the Swiss, also, were ready for energetic steps against the Hitler party. The federal prosecutor on 14 April of that year ordered the Zurich police to interrogate the two principal Swiss Nazi leaders Ernst Höflinger and Theodor Fischer, and allowed it to search their homes for evidence that they were taking orders from the NSDAP headquarters in Munich. Similar steps were prepared against the Swiss Nazi leader Kraull in Lausanne and the German *Landesgruppenleiter* Wilhelm Gustloff in Davos. The federal prosecutor submitted a first report on the NSDAP in Switzerland on 6 June 1932, whereupon two German citizens were expelled from the country. [111] But in 1932 the Nazis were wise enough to meet the Swiss authorities halfway, promising not to violate any Swiss laws and to open their files to Swiss police inspection on demand.

The volume of Nazi activities among Germans and Austrians living in Switzerland jumped immediately after Hitler came to power in 1933. The number of local party offices (*Ortsgruppen* of the NSDAP, *Standorte* of the Hitler youth) multiplied quickly, and by 1935, the membership of the NSDAP in Switzerland was estimated at 5,000. [112] At the same time the NSDAP renewed its assurances to Switzerland that its neutrality and independence were in no way imperiled; the

[109] Basel police to EJPD, Basel, 23 Aug. 1933, in ibid., E 4001(A)1, Aktenband 42.
[110] On the Nazi activities at Badischer Bahnhof, see letter, Gemeinderat Riehen to Regierungsrat Basel-Stadt, Riehen, 17 Mar. 1933; and letter, police department of Basel to Regierungsrat Basel, 19 Apr. 1933, in StA (Basel-Stadt), Politisches EE15,1, "Fascismus, Nationalsozialismus, Fronten 1920–1945.". A fairly objective general report written after the war is "Bericht des Regierungsrates über die Abwehr staatsfeindlicher Umtriebe in den Vorkriegs- und Kriegsjahren sowie die Säuberungsaktion nach Kriegsschluss," a report to the Grosser Rat of Basel-Stadt, 4 July 1946, in ibid.
[111] Bundesanwaltschaft, "Die Hitlerpartei in der Schweiz," (Berne, 6 June 1932) (typescript, 16 pages), available in BA (Berne), (Handakten BR Häberlin) E 4001(A)1, Aktenband 42.
[112] See Session of Swiss Nationalrat, 3 Apr. 1935.

Swiss authorities, so it appears, were only too anxious to take these assurances at face value. Rudolf Hess, the deputy Führer, jovially told Swiss journalists in Berlin that Switzerland did not figure in the Nazi plans for a future "Grossdeutschland" (point one in the NSDAP program of 25 February 1925), but he did, on 24 April 1935, administer over the radio an oath of "unconditional loyalty and obedience" (*unverbrüchliche Treue und unbedingter Gehorsam*) to Hitler and his designated representatives, which all Nazi Party members in Switzerland had to swear at an appointed time while standing erect in their homes before their radio sets. Once more the Swiss allowed themselves to be diverted into a technical discussion over the legality of this most unusual procedure. The police chief of the canton of St. Gallen, Regierungsrat Keel, vehemently opposed it (but then he was a Socialist and a committed anti-Fascist) while the EJPD chief, Johannes Baumann, in the Bundestag session of 3 April argued that such an action did not violate Swiss sovereignty. All the same, he admitted that an oath to a foreign leader, even when taken long distance over the air waves, constituted a spiritual bond that could create a conflict of loyalties in case of war between Germany and Switzerland. He therefore insisted that Gustloff should hand him a full list of everyone who would take the oath. The extraordinary caution of the EJPD is best expressed by Dr. Heinrich Rothmund, then chief of its police section, who on 5 June 1935 wrote to his superior, Bundesrat Baumann:

We do not in any way underestimate the danger of the National Socialists. Obviously they try at present to show themselves as a loyal and lawful organization so as to benefit as much as they can from such behavior. Once they possess more power, they will without hesitation strive to fulfill their more far-reaching goals, using whatever methods will suit the political situation. We agree with the federal prosecutor's office that during its "legal" phase we cannot take any radical steps against the Nazi movement and must content ourselves with the use – negatively – of every available tactical means to slow its development. One way we can do this is to make sure that [the Nazis] *are given absolutely no grounds to claim that we treat them with any less favor than we treat other foreigners . . .* [113]

What Baumann and Rothmund missed, but *Regierungsrat* Keel did not, was that the Nazi oath was significant not because of a possible future war with Germany but because of a very real campaign of terror that was already taking place throughout Central Europe, executed by Nazis who had vowed unquestioning obedience to their leaders. By the spring of 1935 there had been, among others, the murders of Professor Lessing and the engineer, Formis, in Czechoslovakia, the assassination of Chancellor Dollfuss in Vienna, and the kidnaping of the journalist, Berthold Jacob, in Basel. [114] Of course, only the Jacob case took place in Switzerland, and most of the Nazi terror then and in the following years was concentrated in Austria and Czechoslovakia.

---

[113] Letter, Rothmund to Baumann, Berne, 5 June 1935, No. P. 32039/R., in BA (Berne), Bestand 4001(B) 1970/187 (Handakten BR Baumann), Karton 3. Italics mine.

[114] For a chronicle of Nazi terrorism between 1933 and 1935 abroad, see *Das braune Netz. Wie Hitlers Agenten im Auslande arbeiten und den Krieg vorbereiten* (Paris, 1935).

Let us acknowledge that in the Jacob case the Swiss government acted with firmness and dignity. The émigré journalist, Berthold Jacob, was kidnaped by the Nazi agent Hans Wesemann and his accomplices in Basel on 9 February 1935. By lodging a complaint with the International Tribunal in The Hague, Switzerland eventually forced Berlin to return Jacob to Swiss territory. Switzerland also reaffirmed its political independence in the case of the murder of the Nazi *Landesgruppenleiter* Gustloff by a Jewish student in Davos on 4 February 1936. It refused to extradite the assassin, David Frankfurter, to Germany and insisted that he stand trial before a Swiss court of law.

But at the same time the Swiss government in 1936 forbade the publication by the Reso-Verlag in Zurich of Helmut Klotz's book, *Der neue deutsche Krieg*, as too provocative, factually inaccurate, and too disrespectful toward the Hitler regime.[115] As far as supporting anti-Nazi publications was concerned Switzerland's attitude contrasted sharply to the decided anti-Nazi position taken by the Czechoslovak government, as was noted by a private Swiss organization called the Bernese Action Committee for Spiritual Home Defense (*Berner Aktionsausschuss für geistige Landesverteidigung*). Its president, Otto Meyer-Lingg, in 1935 petitioned the federal government to borrow a leaf from the Czechoslovak law for the defense of the republic (1923). His lengthy petition may be summarized as follows.

In the nineteenth century Switzerland granted political freedom to everyone – to friends and opponents of democracy alike. "This political neutrality caused no problems because what antidemocratic tendencies there were had no more than curiosity value." However, things had greatly changed during the last twenty years. Powerful influences were now at work, emanating from countries that never had known the meaning of democracy at all. The number of antidemocrats in Switzerland may still be small, but today even small numbers can exert much power thanks to the new element of mass propaganda.

The author then described the propaganda methods which so effectively had sabotaged democracy in certain countries adjoining Switzerland. "Unrestrained defamation of the authorities and of select groups in the population. . . . The stirring up of envy and ill-will. . . . Excitement of primitive instincts. . . . " The police is ultimately checkmated by such propaganda devices, whereupon the antidemocrats resort to street riots until the average burgher, in distress, yearns for a dictatorship to restore order.

Until today only one country has understood how to infuse its laws for the defense of the state with a truly democratic spirit, and that country is the Czechoslovak Republic.

The Czechoslovak law of 19 March 1923, paragraph one, states that: Whosoever tries forcibly to alter the constitution of the Republic, particularly in regard to its independence, unity, and its democratic-republican form . . . commits a crime punishable by 5– 20 years penitentiary, and in particularly grievous cases, by life-long penitentiary.

---

[115] Session of Swiss Bundesrat, 10 Nov. 1936, as recorded in BA (Berne), Bestand 4001 (B)1970/187 (Handakten BR Baumann), Karton 4.

Understanding that social peace is the necessary precondition of democracy, the Czechoslovak law also states in paragraph fourteen, section 2:

Whosoever publicly incites to acts of violence or other forms of hostile action against select groups of the population, identified by nationality, language, race, religion, or atheism . . . commits a delinquency punishable by prison arrest of one month to one year. A similar sanction also applies to the incitement of hatred against individual members of such minorities.[116]

The difference between the Swiss and the Czechoslovak response to the Hitler regime in Germany was not based on a difference in their perception of Nazism as much as on a difference in how they understood democracy. The Swiss were long accustomed to acting alone as the custodians of principles of freedom unique to their mountain republic. The Czechoslovaks, more idealistic than politically schooled, were convinced that a peaceful European order was only possible if democracy prevailed equally in every country. Both had understood the coming of Hitler as a threat to their independence. But while Czechoslovakia immediately began arming its borders and formed military alliances with France and the Soviet Union, Switzerland, mindful of its neutrality, contented itself with creating a small political police and discussing hypothetical defense questions.

The Gustloff case, indeed, momentarily brought Switzerland to the brink of outlawing the NSDAP. The *Bundesanwaltschaft*, always politically more farsighted than the EJPD, submitted the following recommendation to Bundesrat Baumann on 17 February 1936, ten days after the murder in Davos. Its recommendation made three basic points:

1. The Gustloff case is closed and Switzerland must now decide what to do should Hitler send a replacement.

   It is our considered opinion that we cannot tolerate another *Landesgruppenleiter* [in Switzerland] who functions as the diplomatic envoy of a foreign political party. Nor do we want to have a foreign party headquarters here with a staff of party bureaucrats. In any event, it is likely that a German minister who is also a Nazi Party member will act as the Party leader for the German colony here, just as the Italian diplomats [since 1922] have acted as party functionaries for the Italian colony.

2. There will be National Socialists in Switzerland as long as there is a National Socialist regime in Germany.

   As long as there are National Socialists in Switzerland they will band together and organize, so that – in accordance with their ideology – they can draw their compatriots [in Switzerland] into direct involvement with the political changes in Germany.

   This brings us to the heart of our problem concerning National Socialism. National Socialism does not want to be a political party. It wants to be a national movement with claims to absolute (totalitarian) authority. This claim to absolute authority is an assumption not even realized in Germany. But it has justified the relentless struggle in Germany to bring it closer and closer to actual fulfillment (*vide* propaganda ministry!). Therefore the need for the dual institution of state and party.

---

[116] Letter, Otto Meyer-Lingg to Bundesrat, Berne, 18 Nov. 1936, in ibid.

3. The above describes a situation that we are powerless to change. The best we can do is to draw the consequences by taking steps that will minimize the threat to the security and integrity of our country.

(a) There must be no political clashes in Switzerland between Swiss and Germans.

(b) We may want to consider banning all foreign political parties. But the difficulty would be that we then would also need to ban the Third Communist International, the Second Socialist International, and the Universalita di Roma [the Fascist International founded at Montreux] plus various national movements of Eastern European minorities seeking to upset the Paris peace settlement. Some of them have Swiss members – do we want to deprive them of their right of political association?

(c) Whatever Switzerland decides to do, it will need a stronger police to enforce what legal measures the country adopts against these powerful but secret political organizations. [117]

Both Czechoslovakia and Switzerland at about the same time decided to strengthen their political police to meet the danger they faced from Nazi Germany – except that the Czechoslovak political police was given much more aggressive an assignment. Switzerland passed a law instituting a federal political police (the *Bundespolizei*) by a "Law for the Protection of the Security of the Confederation," dated 21 June 1935. Unlike the political police founded in 1889, this one was to be directly at the disposal of the federal prosecutor, not of the prosecutor's office. New also was that the federal police was to work closely with cantonal police authorities, wield some executive powers, and receive some modern equipment (automobiles). Less encouraging was the modest size of its projected personnel (twelve to twenty-two persons) and the curious insistence that for reasons of prestige its leading officials would have to be "men who are in the position to hold suitable social receptions in their homes." Finally, there was the slow and deliberate pace with which its first chief, Colonel Jaquillard of the police of the canton of Vaud, proposed to go about initiating the work of his new force. In a note, dated 12 April 1935, Jaquillard offered these thoughts about the Swiss police that was supposed to checkmate the tactics of the Gestapo, the SS, and the SD:

In all police matters psychological factors play a very important role. . . . A newly formed police . . . can never achieve very much, because it still lacks [moral] authority – unless, that is, "chance" happens to come to its aid. It needs time to adapt itself. It must expect reverses brought about by *malchance*. So we must begin by avoiding all cause for negative criticism and all appearance that such criticism may be founded on good reasons. Publicity must be avoided, and all actions by the federal police must be as securely founded in law as possible.

Because of Switzerland's comparative inexperience with political police work, Jaquillard's first practical recommendation was a tour of study with the police forces of Paris, Brussels and . . . Vienna, seemingly unaware of the rapidly

[117] Report by BA to BR Baumann, No. C.2.1., Berne, 17 Feb. 1936, in ibid., Karton 3.

changing political situation in the Austrian police toward Fascist authoritarian rule.[118] In retrospect, the historian wonders whether Monsieur Jaquillard was the right man to take on opponents as ruthless as Göring, Himmler, and Heydrich.

To conclude our discussion of Switzerland, we must return to the question of how it intended to meet the threat of German military aggression in Europe. Between 1936 and 1940 a dispute took place between the federal government and the cantonal government of Basel-Stadt over the question whether the police of Basel should take part in the active defense of the city in case of invasion, with the Basel police strongly in favor of abstention from combat. The matter was only settled at the outbreak of the Second World War, when, paradoxically, the Basel police yielded to the federal government by agreeing to fight with the Swiss army, while Berne reached the decision not to defend Basel at all on account of its too close proximity to the German border.[119] The Swiss also discussed a project of dotting Europe with neutral zones of refuge for civilians and wounded soldiers under the protection of the International Red Cross and the duties of Red Cross personnel under enemy occupation in time of war.[120]

The Swiss reaction in 1937 and 1938 to the mounting Nazi pressure against Austria and Czechoslovakia was disturbing. The Swiss aliens police apparently sought to safeguard Switzerland against Nazi covetousness by dissociating the country as much as possible from the situation developing in Eastern Europe.[121] This required constraining Switzerland's Fascist movement, because a Fascist Switzerland like a Fascist Austria might have suggested to Berlin a willingness on its part to be annexed to the Greater German Reich. But it also required that Switzerland not be the kind of hotbed of anti-Nazism as Prague had become since 1933, to give Berlin no pretext for intervention. Dr. Heinrich Rothmund expressed this in a recommendation in 1938 concerning the Austrian Jewish refugees in Switzerland:

We learn that a substantial number of Austrians (or former Germans, now living in Austria) – most of them Jewish – now reside in hotels and boarding houses in Switzerland. Most of them entered this country before the reintroduction of obligatory entry visas [by Switzerland, on 1 April 1938], and, surprised by the recent events, do not dare return to their homeland. It is urgently required that the aliens police establish the identity and the whereabouts of all these foreigners as quickly as possible and that it arranges their repatriation or their departure to different countries. We repeat: The situation has changed to our detriment. The pressure on Eastern Jewry to emigrate has greatly increased, and not only in Austria. But our capacity to receive newcomers has never been so

---

[118] Note by Jaquillard, dated 12 Apr. 1935, in ibid.

[119] "Verwendung des Polizeikorps im Kriegsfalle," in StA (Basel-Stadt), Str. & Pol. D3, 1936-904.

[120] See "Switzerland and the Red Cross in the Second World War," in this chapter.

[121] See Swiss refusal to offer Czechoslovakia assistance in a political treason case in 1934: EJPD to Justizdepartement of Basel-Stadt, Berne, 12 Feb. 1934, Ref. Nr. R. 1592 Sch., in StA (Basel-Stadt), Straf-7, Polizei-Acten P8, "Requisitionen und Citationen fremder Behörden in Criminalfällen überhaupt, 1827–1936."

limited, and it is becoming very difficult to make these people leave again. We expect that other West European countries will also progressively shut their doors in the face of this migratory wave.[122]

In 1938, a Bundesrat Müller made a memorable speech in protest against the Swiss government's lack of responsiveness to the plight of the Jews seeking to flee from Germany and Austria, memorable also because its opening line resembles words Heinrich Himmler used in a notorious anti-Semitic speech on 4 October 1943, but for the opposite end:

Everyone knows a Jew whom he'd just as soon send packing to Timbuctoo, if not to Palestine. Still, private dislikes, however un-Christian, are not illegal and they are not dangerous to the person concerned. Things are different when a state directs its hostility toward Jews in general and uses all the coercive instruments at its disposal against them. What the Third Reich does in this regard is too horrible and too despicable for me to describe in this assembly with the words that it deserves.

Things have in recent days taken a turn for the worse. My interpellation may soon be redundant because, if the threats that we have heard are put in practice, all the Jewish men, woman, and children in Germany will soon be killed by the Aryan supermen. This of course would solve our problem over Jewish immigration and our government could breathe a sigh of relief.

But I will not withdraw my interpellation. I will use this opportunity to point out that our aliens police, while not acting under German influence, seems to think largely along the same lines as the new Germany. Our police gives the appearance of having abandoned its independence of decision and to model its behavior, however unconsciously, after that of the German model. It thereby opens itself to the charge of subservience to the Third Reich.[123]

Austro-Czechoslovak police relations in the 1920s

At a conference in Prague between the Austrian chancellor, Dr. Renner, and the Czech foreign minister, Dr. Beneš (10–23 January 1920), the two politicians concurred that their countries needed each other's assistance in a number of police matters. Thus, because both countries were threatened by Hungarian irredentism they would profit from sharing their intelligence resources concerning Hungary's intentions. Next, domestic peace in Austria, according to Renner, required that a satisfactory solution be found in regard to the Sudeten German question in Bohemia. At the same time a number of political trials in Czechoslovakia de-

---

[122] "Flüchtlinge aus Österreich," circular, the chief of EJPD Baumann to all cantonal police authorities, Berne, 8 Apr. 1938, Nr. 210, in BA (Berne), Bestand 4001 (B) 1970/187 (Handakten Baumann), Karton 2, folder 22/6: "Flüchtlinge und Emigranten" (1935–1940).

[123] Interpellation Müller-Biel, session of Swiss Nationalrat of 9 Nov. 1938, in ibid., folder 22/6. For Himmler's address to the SS in 1943, see Wather Hofer, ed., *Der Nationalsozialismus. Dokumente 1933–1945* (Frankfurt a.M., 1957), p. 114: "Und dann kommen sie alle an, die braven 80 Millionen Deutschen, und jeder hat seinen anständigen Juden. Es ist ja klar, die anderen sind Schweine, aber dieser eine ist ein prima Jude."

pended for their satisfactory outcome on Austria's willingness to give Czech officials access to confidential court records in Vienna.[124]

A general accord was reached at the end of this conference, but the climate between the two governments had not genuinely warmed. Although Renner readily agreed to release the Austrian files, it should be remembered that a similar request from Prague in December 1918 had been acceded to with considerable ill feeling. The Austrian ministry of foreign affairs in that bitterly cold winter of 1918 had urged compliance with the Czech wish because Austria urgently needed coal deliveries from Bohemia, adding cynically: "We should have the less objection to this transaction as the files contain various documents that are apt to cause rifts inside the Czech camp."[125]

In spite of mutual dislike, particularly on the part of the Austrians, who saw their reduction from Empire to a small succession state as a degradation they owed largely to Czech "treason" during the war, the two countries concluded a political treaty on 16 December 1921. Paragraph four of this treaty concerned security matters. The two contracting parties undertook not to tolerate on their territories any military organization whose aim was detrimental to the external and domestic security of the other. More particularly, the two states undertook to assist one another in foiling all plans and all attempts at restoring the Habsburg state or the Habsburg form of government be these undertaken in the realm of diplomacy or internal politics. Finally, to implement this agreement the pertinent authorities of both countries (i.e. their police forces) were to collaborate directly in the suppression of all conspiratorial activities directed towards such goals.[126]

While the agreement of 1921 represented the beginning of what could have developed into effective Austro-Czechoslovak collaboration, both sides in the following years continued to regard themselves as ultimately dependent not on each other's assistance but on the European-wide balance of power, in particular on a reconciliation between France and Germany.[127] Had Prague and Vienna sought the protection of the same great power things might have been easier; it was bound to lead to difficulties when Austria increasingly placed its hopes on fusion with a rehabilitated German Reich while Czechoslovakia drew steadily closer to France. By 1926 the rapid growth of Czechoslovakia's military strength on land and in the air caused the Austrians some anxiety about their future relations to their Czech neighbors as equal partners. In that year the police commissariat in Wiener-Neustadt alerted the Polizei Direktion in Vienna that it had information about a Czechoslovak plan to march on Vienna in case chaos broke out in Austria

[124] "Prager Verhandlungen auch Entrevue Dr. Renner mit Dr. Beneš vom 10.-13. Jänner 1920 in Prag," in HHStA (Vienna), NPA (Neues politisches Archiv), Karton 415, Liasse Tschechoslowakei I/III Geheim folder 1–417.

[125] Deutschösterreichisches Staatsamt für Heerwesen to Staatsamt des Aeussern, Vienna, 18 Dec. 1918, in ibid., Liasse Oesterreich 26/I, Faszikel 439.

[126] "Entrevue Masaryk/Hainisch, Hallstadt, 10. Aug. 1921," in ibid., NPA, Karton 415, Liasse Tschechoslowakei I/III Geheim, folder 1–419, fols. 53ff.

[127] "Der Besuch Dr. Beneš' in Wien am 4. u. 5. März 1926, " in ibid.

over a threatened strike by postal and telegraph workers, and that in the event of an invasion the Czech general staff hoped for assistance from the Czech colony in Vienna.[128] By 1928, in a meeting held in Prague between Dr. Beneš and the Austrian chancellor, Ignaz Seipel, we discern for the first time a note of melancholic resignation. The two men spoke about their hopes for peaceful progress and at the same time admitted their inability to influence the course of European politics.[129] The advent in the following year of a world-wide economic crisis and the rise of Nazism in Germany and Austria finally put an end to the tentative collaboration of the two small succession states, whose contribution to the containment of German expansionism was to be needed exactly when their attempt at mutual assistance broke down.

Austro-Czechoslovak police relations in the 1930s

The Vienna police leaders in the 1920s closely followed the work of their colleagues in Berlin in matters of crime fighting, organization, and discipline. Besides the obvious advantage that Austrian police officials could read German texts on criminology and criminalistics, there may also have been the interest to see how the German republican regime dealt with the problem of political armies of the right and left seeking to enforce their preferred political systems with propaganda of violence. Austria's own task of balancing the National Socialist storm troopers, the Socialist *Schutzbund,* and the government's own police, gendarmerie, the army, and the *Heimwehren* was rendered more difficult by the fact that Nazi, Socialist, and Communist elements were much stronger inside the Austrian police ranks than they were in the Prussian police during the Weimar Republic.

Whether or not the Viennese police in the thirties worked for an eventual merger of Austria and Germany is difficult to say. But in the same period that German criminologists debated the pros and cons of the death penalty an article in the Austrian journal *Der Panther* pleaded in favor of capital punishment, chiefly because of the continued use of this penalty in the German Reich:

Legal alignment [*Rechtsausgleichung*] with the German Reich has become a political slogan for Austria. The legal reform work which has proceeded over the last few years in both Germany and in Austria, and which has occasioned a number of bilateral conferences, has served the cause of cultural Anschluss between the two countries. If Austria were now to persist in the abolition of the death penalty our goal of full legal compatibility [between Germany and Austria] would become unattainable in one very important aspect.[130]

---

[128] Bundes Polizei Kommissariat Wiener-Neustadt to Polizeidirektion Wien, Wr. Neutstadt 18 Jan. 1926, in ibid., Liasse Oesterreich 26/I, Faszikel 439.

[129] Unterredung Aussenminister Dr. Beneš-Bundeskanzler Dr. Seipel in Prag am 13. und 14. Februar 1928. Aufzeichnungen," in ibid., NPA, Karton 415, Liasse Tschechoslowakei I/III Geheim, folder 1-417.

[130] E. S. Cyhlar, "Wiedereinführung der Todesstrafe," in *Der Panther,* 25 Apr. 1931. The death penalty had been abolished in Austria in 1919. Hermann Baltl, *Oesterreichische Rechtsgeschichte* (Graz, 1986), p. 273.

Following the death of Johann Schober in 1932 and Hitler's appointment as German chancellor in 1933, the leadership in the Vienna police took a sharp turn to the right. The Polizei Direktion was now headed by Dr. Franz Brandl and Dr. Michael Skubl. In an interview given to the press on 21 January 1933, Police President Brandl announced that he had no intention of disciplining any of his subordinates who participated in Nazi rallies. [131] On 31 March 1933 the Socialist Republikanischer Schutzbund was dissolved, soon followed by the banning of the Austrian Communist Party. [132] These developments caused immediate concern to the Jewish citizens of Austria, but not enough to suggest to them the need for special protective measures. Instead, the Austrian Jewish *Verband* in June 1933 passed a formal resolution against the formation of any kind of armed self-defense corps and proclaimed its complete trust in the Austrian state's police executive. Were not the Hitler movement and the Steirischer Heimatschutz also banned by the government on 20 June 1933? [133]

Vienna's maintenance of a "juste milieu," on which the Austrian Jews – and like them the Czechoslovak government in Prague – counted, barely survived for another year. The first step in the direction of a right-wing authoritarian state was taken in February 1934, when the *Heimwehr* leaders Emil Fey and Rüdiger Ernst Count Starhemberg, heeding a suggestion by Mussolini to suppress the Austrian Socialists with military force ("the better, later, to put an end also to the National Socialists") [134] attacked the strongholds of the Viennese workers in the outskirts of the capital, resulting in a civil war in which artillery was used at close range against workers' housing. To illustrate the brutality with which the military executed its auxiliary assistance to the police, we quote from the subsequent report of the Austrian defense ministry:

There will always be situations when the residents of a building will fail to obey an order to come out, mostly because they are prevented from doing so by the insurgents inside whose own houses are elsewhere. This must not deter the commander of a military unit from opening artillery fire at the prescribed moment. . . . The effectiveness of artillery bombardment largely derives from its protracted impact on the morale of insurgents, on their leaders' will to resist. Sections of the population which are hostile but have remained on the sidelines feel intimidated by gun fire that can be heard from far away. The detonation of artillery projectiles, the crash of broken windows, the crunch of falling masonry and tiles, and the noise of splintering timber produces widespread fear, especially at night. [135]

---

[131] Interpellation by Franz Schattenfroh in the 183rd session of the Austrian Bundestag, 31 Jan. 1933, in AVA (Vienna), S.D. Parl. Klub/67, folder 43: "Polizei und Gendarmerie."

[132] "Parteibetätigunsverbote," in Max Weiser, ed., *Das Polizeirecht der Jahre 1933 und 1934* (Vienna, 1935).

[133] AVA (Vienna), S. D. Parl. Klub 103, folder: "151 Juden."

[134] H. R. Knickerbocker, *Kommt Krieg in Europa?* (Berlin, 1934), p. 55.

[135] Bundes-Ministerium für Landesverteidigung, "Erfahrungen anlässlich der Assistenzleistungen zur Unterdrückung der Aufstände im Jahre 1934," (mimeo), pp. 5–10, available at KA (Vienna).

"The fighting . . . produced a shock effect in Czechoslovakia," reported the Austrian minister to Prague, Dr. Ferdinand Marek, on 20 April 1934, following a conversation with Foreign Minister Beneš. *Lidové Noviny* published an account on 1 March 1934 under the title, "Soldiers March Through the City," which depicted Vienna after the fighting as lying at the mercy of an arrogant *soldateska* holding down a despondent population. The writer of this article was Jan Stránský, the son of *Lidové Noviny's* owner, Rudolf Stránský. Ten weeks after the article appeared, Jan Stránský was arrested by the Austrian police and it took Beneš's personal intervention to secure his release and expulsion from Austria.

Though the Austrians had clearly acted with disproportionate severity to a pessimistic but by no means inflammatory article, it was the Czechs who subsequently took steps to repair the damaged relations between the two governments. To Minister Marek, Dr. Beneš promised that he would try to persuade Czech newspaper editors henceforth to exercise greater discretion in their lead articles.[136] When in August of that year anti-Austrian posters appeared in the Czech town of Schluckenau with slogans like "Black Terror in Austria!" and "Cannons Against Workmen!," the Czech police immediately confiscated them and launched an investigation.[137]

Many Austrian Socialists after the February fighting sought sanctuary in Czechoslovakia while arms and leaflets were smuggled to Austrian workers from Bohemia.[138] This was consistent with the Prague government's policy in the early years of Nazi power to permit subversive operations by exiled German Socialists (the Sopade) against the Hitler regime from posts along the German–Czech frontier. The German government countered this with official protests and clandestine Gestapo activities in Czechoslovakia. This Austrian government, officially neither Nazi nor intent on subverting the independence of Czechoslovakia, entered into negotiations with Prague which, unlike the threats from Berlin, to some extent succeeded in eroding the Czech resolution to resist the rising tide of fascism in Europe. Thus in early July 1934, there was talk in the papers about a "police pact" between Austria and Czechoslovakia to curb illegal frontier crossings: the Czechs were to turn back all Austrians seeking to enter their territory without Austrian exit visas and the Austrians to stop Sudeten Germans seeking to evade their military duty in Czechoslovakia.[139]

The spectacular murder of Austrian Chancellor Engelbert Dollfuss on 25 July 1934 during a bungled Nazi attempt to seize power, in which important figures of the Vienna police (Police President Dr. Seydl, Vice Police President Dr. Skubl,

---

[136] Marek to Dollfuss, Prague, 24 Mar. 1934, in HHStA (Vienna), NPA/824 Liasse Tschechoslowakei, folder 117ff.

[137] Hügel report to Egon Berger-Waldenegg, Prague, 31 Aug. 1934, in ibid., folder. 150ff. Schluckenau, however, is situated along the Bohemian frontier with Germany, not with Austria.

[138] As samples, see report by Gestapa – II 1A2, Berlin, 8 June 1934, in BA (Koblenz), R58/10 folder 1; and report by same of 13 May 1938, in ibid., R58/494 folder 1.

[139] Austrian legation in Berlin to Egon Berger-Waldenegg, Berlin, 4 July 1935, Zl. 177/Pol., in HHStA (Vienna), NPA/824 Liasse Tschechoslowakei, folder 201ff.

and Hofrat Steinhäusl) were implicated, heightened the tension between Prague and Vienna. The coup d'état was occasioned by Dollfuss's decision to discharge the current director of public security in the Austrian ministry of interior, Major Emil Fey, and to replace him by Staatssekretär Carl Karwinsky. [140] The coup dealt a severe blow to the prestige of the Vienna police. Following the disclosure of the names of the participants, Police President Michael Skubl came out with a loud protestation of contrition:

Something terrible, monstrous, unimaginable has happened: officials of the Viennese Sicherheitswache, officials of the Sicherheitswache on active duty, have taken part in this mad *putsch,* this senseless attack on the federal chancellery, in order to overthrow a legitimate government and to proclaim a new government in the place of this legitimate one. Officials of the Sicherheitswache, to whom we have preached time and again to keep out of politics. . . . [141]

(We note that this disclaimer carefully avoided calling the would-be new government "illegal," or denouncing the putschists' goal of bringing about an Austro-German merger.)

There was of course no chance for Czechoslovakia to derive advantage from the disgrace of the Vienna police. In the absence of a democratic regime firmly ensconced in Austria, an authoritarian Austrian Republic independent of Nazi Germany was still better than a Nazi Austria allied or merged with the German Reich. In August 1934 Austria adopted a new constitution that removed the country from the ranks of Europe's democracies and once more restored the powers of the security forces. [142]

Despite their own continuing allegiance to democratic principles of government, the Czechs in the late summer of 1934 and in the spring of 1935 joined with the Austrians in more discussions of security along their borders. But clearly, Prague and Vienna were beginning to deal now as neighbors belonging to opposite camps rather than as partners with a common interest in defending their independence against Nazi Germany. In the long run their ideological incompatibility made police collaboration next to impossible. "The direct association of Czechoslovak and Austrian frontier officials . . . ," an Austrian report from 1935 read, "seems to work only in regard to cases of smuggling National Socialist propaganda and terrorist materials. However, this is the kind of smuggling that has now ceased for some time. When it concerns the interception of propaganda material by left-wing parties it seems ill-advised for us to notify the Czechoslovak authorities." [143]

---

[140] Staatssekretär a.D. Carl Karwinsky, "Vor 20 Jahren. Ein Beitrag zur Geschichte des 25. Juli 1934," (typescript in possession of Eva Dollfuss, Vienna).

[141] "Ansprache des Leiters der Polizeidirektion Wien Dr. Skubl anlässlich des Hauptrapportes der Sicherheitswache am 1. September 1934," in *Offentliche Sicherheit,* 14. Jhg., Nr. 9 (Sept. 1934), p. 18.

[142] Polizei-Oberkommissar Dr. Dr. Hermann Röder, "Der Durchbruch zum autoritären Ständestaat," in ibid., 15. Jhg., Nr. 1 (Jan. 1935), p. 7.

[143] Bundeskanzleramt, "Dienstzettel an die Abteilung 13 pol.," G.D. 325.221-St.B./35, Vienna, 26 Apr. 1935, in HHStA (Vienna), NPA/824, Liasse Tschechoslowakei, folder 192.

Beneš, reverting to a principle that he already followed in the late twenties, namely that negotiations with little hope for concrete results are better than no negotiations at all, thereupon tried to broaden the talks between Czechoslovakia and Austria by the inclusion of Hungary in what he hoped would slowly become a merger of the three countries' separate national interests without any specific solutions in mind. "We shouldn't be in such a hurry to fix our relationship on paper in the form of statutes and institutional agreements," he told Dr. Marek on 2 May 1935. "As in the case of the Little Entente, we could let things develop slowly, organically, by holding periodic conferences, possibly by creating some common institutions." Only by May 1935, with Germany openly rearming, Beneš's political situation had weakened to the point where such tentative projects carried little persuasive power. In the same conversation with Marek, Beneš made one dramatic concession: "If such conferences and agreements were to come about," the Austrian diplomat reported the Czech foreign minister as saying, "he would also seek, in consultation with us, to reform the [Czechoslovak] law of asylum and subsequently take steps to curb the activities of Austrian émigrés [in Czechoslovakia]."[144]

Following 1935, the relations between Austria and Czechoslovakia were increasingly dominated by such events as the return of the Saar to Germany, the Italian invasion of Abyssinia, and the reoccupation of the Rhineland by the German army. Insofar as all of these events enhanced the prestige of the Third Reich they emboldened Austria, by then practically a parallel Nazi state to Hitler's Germany, to take an imperious stand toward Prague. A Czechoslovak film in 1936 that glorified the Czech declaration of independence in 1918 as a "bloodless revolution" and also praised the Socialist uprising in Vienna in 1934, was censored on Austrian demand.[145] And in the following year, when world attention was drawn to the outbreak of large-scale hostilities in the Far East, the Austrian government made ready to denounce the old treaty of cultural exchange, signed in Prague in 1920, in particular the part concerning the sharing of Austrian state archives for police purposes. In this matter, the Austrian federal chancellery and foreign ministry (BKA [AA]) took the position that

The Prague Agreement was forced on the Austrian government in a time of great economic distress by threats of suspension of sugar and coal deliveries. . . . Granting Czechoslovak representatives free access to all the archives of the old monarchy gave rise to a situation tantamount to a Czechoslovak archival occupation of Austria. The Czechoslovak government thereby obtained copies of the most secret documents of the Austro-Hungarian government, whose content it published . . . much to the detriment of the prestige of the Austro-Hungarian Monarchy and consequently also of today's Austria. . . . The BKA (AA) is waiting for the first opportunity to denounce the Prague Agreement, and all other archival treaties which are incompatible with Austrian sovereignty and Austria's interna-

144 Marek to Berger-Waldenegg, Prague, 2 May 1935, Zl. 222/Pol., in ibid., folder 183.
145 Report by Marek, Prague, 27 Feb. 1936, in ibid., folder 246ff.

tional position. Under no circumstances will it permit this treaty [the Prague Agreement of 1920] to be reactivated. [146]

We have cited this document less because of its political importance – it counted little in the political high stakes of the years 1937 and 1938 – but because it signaled the end of a short-lived but curious experiment in administrative police collaboration at the end of the First World War. Beneš's proposal of a Czechoslovak, Austrian, and Hungarian merger of national interests in 1935 was only a feeble reminder of an internationalist mood by then almost forgotten.

How close Czechoslovakia came to capitulating to Austria is best illustrated in the success of Austria's remonstrations against the Czechoslovak National Defense Law of 1936. This law permitted the Prague government in a time of national emergency to impose tight controls on all industrial enterprises that it deemed important to the country's security. Austria, like Germany, was immediately worried about possible Czech attempts to nationalize strategical industries in Czechoslovakia and to remove Germans and Austrians from employment in such enterprises. But the Austrians also knew that Nazi Germany alone was more than capable of interdicting any such Czech moves with threats of massive retaliation. Marek called on his German colleague in Prague, Freiherr vom Stein, on 22 July 1936, and subsequently could report, rather smugly, to his government in Vienna:

Everything is ready in Berlin: There are complete lists of the names of all Czechoslovak citizens in Germany and all their property. At the first move by the Czechoslovaks against Reich property in the border regions [the strategic Sudeten German regions facing Germany] retaliatory measures against Czechoslovaks in Germany will go into effect. I draw your attention to this insofar as this has a bearing on our threatened citizens [in Czechoslovakia]. [147]

After this Czechoslovakia had very little freedom of movement left. Its every opposition to the Austrian drift to the right only furthered the rapprochement between Berlin and Vienna. The *Pražské Noviny* of 10 November 1937 came close to admitting Czechoslovakia's impotence when it argued in an editorial titled "The Truth About Austria":

The Czechoslovak press has too long accepted the political standpoint of the Austrian émigrés, which was colored by the events of 1934 – worse, by the inclusion of fantasy, ill will, and lies. We should rather look at the truth from the standpoint of Czechoslovak interests.

---

[146] Bundeskanzleramt, "Bemerkungen des Staatsarchivs zu event. Kulturabkommen mit Tschechoslowakei," (Vienna, 13 May 1937), in ibid., Folien 580–1.

[147] HHStA (Vienna), NPA/Karton 415, Liasse Tschechoslowakei 7/1 Geheim. Germany in 1936 imported 1,600 Czech women workers for agricultural labor. Each one of them was checked out by the Gestapo for her political reliability. See Rundlerlass Dr. Best, Berlin, 29 July 1936, in BA (Koblenz), Reichssicherheitshauptamt R58/folder 1. On the eve of the Sudeten crisis, the Gestapo took into custody 400 Czechoslovak citizens in Germany to use as hostages in case the Prague government tried to suppress the Henlein party. See Woermann, AA, to German legation in Prague, Berlin, 16 Aug. 1938, as quoted in Vaclav Kral, ed., *Die Deutschen in der Tschechoslowakei 1933–1947. Dokumentsammlung* (Prague, 1964), p. 310.

The present leaders of Austria are doing their best for their country. They are fighting for its independence against the relentless attacks of German nationalism and Hitlerism. The émigrés, by persisting in their negative attitude towards the Vienna government, undermine Austria and abuse the asylum granted to them by Czechoslovakia.[148]

With their country a mere six weeks away from Anschluss with Germany, the Austrians succeeded in January 1938 in emasculating the Czechoslovak National Defense Law by forcing major concessions from the Prague government as described in this report by Dr. Ferdinand Marek:

Subject: Negotiations regarding the [Czechoslovak] National Defense Law in relation to other pending questions abut the treatment of Austrians in Czechoslovakia. Top Secret.

The Czechoslovak delegation was headed by Dr. Fiedler. The discussion was hampered by the absence from the Czech delegation of representatives of the ministry of defense. The Czech delegates had discussed their position with the ministry of defense where the violent opposition of certain generals to any concessions to Austria was finally overruled by the Minister of Defense himself. The Czech delegation is now willing, confidentially, to assure the Austria delegation that Austrians will be treated with the same rights [sic] as other foreigners, if not better still. Czechoslovak authorities which are charged with the execution of this law will treat all cases where the law affects Austrian citizens with the greatest goodwill and with consistent concern for their economic needs. All intercessions by the Austrian legation in such cases will be treated with utmost expeditiousness.

After we had signed the protocols and the documents, I told the Czech delegation in my farewell speech that our agreement would be useless unless the spirit that had accompanied the talks . . . was also imparted to the lowest level of the local government and served them as guidelines. The Czechs agreed to give special notification to the presidents of all provincial governments [*Landesämter*].[149]

Three months later, following the departure of the last Austrian chancellor, Kurt von Schuschnigg, an American journalist observed Viennese policemen grinning to one another as large Nazi crowds shouted "Sieg Heil!" and "Ein Volk, ein Reich, ein Führer!" In the Kärntnerstrasse, policemen were already wearing swastika armbands. "So they've gone over too!"[150]

Czechoslovak resistance to Nazi subversion

The Czech attempt to placate Austria until the very eve of the Anschluss should not mislead us into assuming that Czechoslovakia's opposition to the rising power of Nazism in Central Europe crumbled at an early stage. On the contrary, Ger-

---

[148] From *Pražské noviny*, 10 Nov. 1937.
[149] Marek to Guido Schmidt, Prague, 31 Jan. 1938, Zl. 31/Pol., in HHStA (Vienna), Liasse Tschechoslowakei I/8 Geh.-31/1 geh. (Folien 418-601). Before the negotiations began, the Czechs were asked by the Austrians to replace two members of their delegation who were Jewish. The Czechs complied. On Germany's counter measures to the Czechoslovak defense law, see U.S. Department of State, *Documents on German Foreign Policy, 1918–1945*, Series D, vol. II, pp. 92–3.
[150] William L. Shirer, *Berlin Diary. The Journal of a Foreign Correrpondent 1934–1941* (New York, 1941), p. 100.

man police files at the federal archive in Koblenz will indicate that the Czechoslovaks not only put up a strong resistance against the pressure of Nazi agents, but also that their many concessions to Austria were probably based on the hope that Austria – democratic or authoritarian – could still be prevented from joining forces with the German Reich.

Czechoslovakia's police defenses against Nazi subversion went into action before even Hitler assumed the chancellorship in Berlin. The Nazi movement in Germany and its supporters in Czechoslovakia constituted so serious a threat to its democratic constitution and its national independence that in 1932 the government decided on a public trial of seven renegade Sudeten Germans belonging to a Fascist organization called the *Volkssport*.[151] No wonder that from the very beginning of the Hitler regime the Czechoslovak Republic became the target of a vehemently hostile propaganda campaign.[152] Aware that Czechoslovakia was likely to be the first target of renewed German military power, Czechoslovakia's "police defense" took the form of an aggressive espionage service, directed by Colonel František Moravec, which scored some important successes in 1935–6.[153]

Not unlike the Swiss, the Czechoslovaks appealed to world opinion by denouncing in the press the incursion of Gestapo agents on assignments as kidnapers and assassins. The number of these attacks was not very high, but they were sufficient in this small country to produce an atmosphere of terror. Best known were the murder of the Jewish professor from Hamburg, Theodor Lessing, in Marienbad in 1933, and two years later the killing of Rudolf Formis an engineer, who was operating a clandestine radio station outside Prague.[154] An editorial concerning the murder of émigrés in Czechoslovakia in the Czech paper *A-Zet* was quoted by the German legation in Prague in early September 1935, as follows:

> Not too long ago, every country still tacitly recognized the need for international security – no special treaties were required for that. A police official could go to any country and expect to be treated with respect and to receive swift assistance in the performance of his functions. Now this has changed. From the moment that a member of the Gestapo assumed command of an auto in Rosenthal which took the murder squad to assassinate engineer Formis, this gentlemen's agreement between the police of different countries was wiped out in half of Europe.[155]

And just as the Berne government after the Berthold Jacob kidnaping in 1935 founded a federal political police, so the Prague government established a new

---

[151] See the reports of the Austrian minister in Prague, Dr. Marek, to Chancellor Dollfuss, Prague 22 Sept. to 7 Oct. 1932, in HHStA, NPA/824 Liasse Tschechoslowakei, folder 36ff.

[152] One of the principal propagandists was Dr. Karl Viererbl, whose anti-Czech articles appeared in the *Nationalsozialistische Monatshefte* and in such polemic publications as Hans Hagemeyer, ed., *Europas Schicksal im Osten* (Breslau, 1939).

[153] Moravec, *Master of Spies*, pp. 33ff.

[154] See the émigré publication, *Das braune Netz*. On Formis, see also Hans-Jürgen Koehler, *Inside the Gestapo. Hitler's Shadow Over the World* (London, 1940).

[155] RSHA, Hauptabteilung III, Berlin, 3 Sept. 1935, Tgb. Nr. A 30685 III 3 A/914/35, "Verhaftung von '4 Gestapo-Agenten' in der Tschechoslowakei," in BA (Koblenz), R58/380, folder 1, "Zwischenfälle an der Č.S. Grenze."

state police in June 1935 to fight the inroads of Gestapo agents in the German émigré community in Czechoslovakia. At first meant to be modeled on the old Prussian political police, the Abteilung IA, the Czechs switched to the French pattern of an elite frontier police designed for the protection of a democratic state territory against foreign incursions. The new police sent agents on political scouting missions abroad, especially to Germany. It monitored all border incidents and studied their possible political significance for transmission to a central office in Prague. All its officials belonged to the Czech ethnic group and were specially trained for use in domestic surveillance as much as for foreign espionage. [156] Local police posts and army posts along the frontier were instructed to provide executive assistance. The Czech state police scored a few successes in bringing to trial Gestapo agents like Gerhard Berthold and his wife Martha in 1935, and another Gestapo agent code-named "W" in 1936. But such successes occurred only during these early years of Nazi rule, when Berlin was still anxious to ingratiate itself with international public opinion. [157]

Unlike the Swiss the Czechs went out of their way to offer asylum to militant opponents of Hitler's regime, more than half of them Jews and many of them Communists and Social Democrats. The German Social Democratic Party, driven out of its home country, established a new headquarters in exile here, under the new name of Sopade. "The authorities in Prague present the émigrés with no difficulties of any note," reported the German legation to Berlin. "Superior Police Councillor Dr. Benda of the Prague police has officially stated that there was no cause to deny these refugees asylum in Czechoslovakia. Anyone is welcome here provided he respects all the laws of the Republic." [158] The point was emphatically repeated by Deputy Foreign Minister Kamil Krofta at a reception for foreign journalists in June 1933:

Czechoslovakia is willing to offer asylum to political émigrés from Germany as long as they refrain from all activities that are likely to disturb the relations between Germany and Czechoslovakia. Under 'activities' [Krofta] understood such things as planning political assassinations, forming secret societies, etc. Reich German émigrés will however not be prevented from openly expressing their political views in Czechoslovakia, nor from criticizing conditions in their homeland. [The Czech government] will not object to the émigrés publishing newspapers so long as they abide by the press laws of this country. [159]

Czechoslovakia's most remarkable contribution to the European-wide resistance to Nazism was in fact its open support for the Sopade's propaganda campaign against Hitler's regime, which the Sopade intended to conduct from frontier posts [*Grenzsekretariate*] all around Germany located just inside France,

[156] Unsigned report dated Berlin, 23 Feb. 1937, "Die Geheime Staatspolizei der Tschechoslowakei," in ibid., R58/10, folder 1.
[157] Dr. Werner Best, Geheimes Staatspolizeiamt, Berlin, 7 July 1936, B.-Nr. II 1 A 4/283/36, Betr.: "Verhaftung eines Beamten des Geheimen Staatspolizeiamtes in der Tschechoslowakei," in ibid.
[158] Report by agent Scheffler on émigrés in Prague, dated Berlin, 2 June 1933, in ibid.
[159] Dr. Koch to AA, Prague, 17 June 1933, in ibid., R58/484, folder 1.

Switzerland, Denmark, Belgium, England, Sweden, Norway, and above all Czechoslovakia.[160] The headquarters of the exiled German Social Democratic Party in Czechoslovakia was in Prague-Karlin, Palackého třida 149/24, third floor, and throughout 1933 to 1938 the Sopade maintained from six to twelve frontier posts in Bohemia. Most of them were in the north along the German border between Graslitz and Jägerndorf.[161] The strategy of this undertaking was described in a summary report by a Nazi confidential agent in 1934 as follows:

The first goal of this new organization is to train people who are ready for any sacrifice and any deed. Courageous and determined, they are to struggle for the conquest of power in Germany. Consequently they are trained to be as self-reliant as possible; it is not intended to build yet another mass organization. [In the view of the Sopade] all contacts to national organizations must be maintained and secured, especially contacts to the police, the Reichswehr, and other authorities. . . . The ideological basis for this mission and its goal is the Proletarian Revolution and the conquest of power by the proletariat. . . . All anti-Fascist groups inside Germany must receive our moral and material support. Outside Germany, émigrés of all parties including dissident Nazis must be collected into a common cause whose purpose is the solidarity of all revolutionary anti-Fascists under the leadership of the Sopade and the general acceptance of its new program.[162]

It is true, that in the five years of its existence in Bohemia the Sopade never developed enough strength to go beyond gathering intelligence inside Germany and engaging in some scattered propaganda work against the Sudeten German Heimatfront of Konrad Henlein.[163] The Sopade orders to its infiltrators in 1934 for so-called subversive activity amounted to little more than polling public opinion about the Nazi regime. "How satisfied are the workers? How satisfied are the middle classes – would they support a revolution if their material conditions became worse? What are the political opinions of the civil servants, police officials, railway officials? Do we still have contacts to local city governments, police, Gestapo, army command posts?"[164] Unlike the illegal German Communist Party (KPD), whose agents planned the murder of Gestapo agents and who repeatedly engaged German border guards along the Czech frontier in firefights, the Sopade's strategy was aimed at a general propaganda war with planted articles in *Le Temps,* the London *Times,* and the *Basler Nachrichten.* For the Eleventh Conference of the International Penal and Penitentiary Commission in Berlin, 1935, the

---

[160] This list of countries is based on a report about the first general meeting of the Sopade's *Grenzsekretäre,* held in Paris on 8–11 Mar. 1939 by which time however the Sopade was already evacuating Czechoslovakia. See ibid., R58/488, folder 1, "Grenzsekretariate in Č.S.R."

[161] Report by "S3" dated Berlin, 20 July 1936, in ibid., R58/484, folder 1; and report by Stapo Nürnberg-Fürth, August 1937, in ibid., R58/494, folder 1.

[162] "Anordnungen zur Durchführung des revolutionären Programms der Sopade," in Brauer, German legation, Brussels, to AA, Brussels, 3 Feb. 1934, in ibid., R58/484 folder 1.

[163] Sudetendeutsche Heimatfront, "Weisung No. 16 [. . .] an alle Ortsleiter," Eger, 8 Mar. 1934, in Kral, ed., *Die Deutschen in der Tschechoslowakei,* p. 66.

[164] "Anweisungen an die Organisationsleiter der Sopade betreffend Durchführung von Zersetzungsarbeiten," Brauer, German legation, Brussels, to AA, Brussels, 15 Feb. 1934, in BA (Koblenz), R58/484, folder 1.

Sopade prepared a highly informative report on conditions in Nazi prisons and concentration camps[165] and published the names of Gestapo agents abroad who were working out of German diplomatic missions.[166]

Ultimately there was to be an assault on the Nazi regime in a propitious moment more or less along the lines of Churchill's "implosion" idea, to be triggered by a crisis such as nearly developed during the remilitarization of the Rhineland in 1936. On that occasion, the Sopade drew up a seven-page report triumphantly announcing that it had recently found the majority of the German people opposed to the prospect of another European war: "This situation must affect the tactics of the Sopade: war must be avoided, and the [Nazi] system brought down by fostering a rigid resistance [to German expansion] by all the other nations which then will present Germany with a foreign political crisis that will lead to a domestic political crisis."[167]

The revolutionary zeal of the Sopade was not matched by a like belligerence on the part of the Czech hosts, to be sure. The Czech police leaders provided the Sopade offices in Prague with special protection and also listened to Albert C. Grzesinski, the deposed Socialist police president of Berlin and former Prussian minister of interior, who toured Europe in 1935 hoping to form a Socialist alliance against Hitler.[168] Following the German march into Austria and the first Czechoslovak mobilization in May of 1938, the Czech army enlisted the Sopade's help for military reconnaissance across the German border and at police stations small arms were available for Sopade men should war break out.

And yet the Czechs were careful to keep their support of the Sopade within the limits of reason and moderation. Czech gendarmerie, more alert often than German frontier guards, were known to have arrested illegal frontier crossers of the KPD and Sopade and to have fined them for unauthorized possession of arms. The Sopade leaders, in turn, knew that the freedom of action they enjoyed in this democratic republic could vanish overnight should a cabinet crisis bring a more right-wing government to power and that their *Grenzsekretariate* would be lost if the Czech army decided not to defend the mountains along the German border.[169] In January 1938 the German government finally succeeded in pressuring the Czech government into withdrawing its protection from the German Socialist newspaper *Neuer Vorwärts*, which moved to Paris.[170] Following the

---

[165] Vorstand der Sozialdemokratischen Partei Deutschlands (Sitz Prag), "Entwicklungstendenzen im deutschen Strafvollzug. Denkschrift an den 11. Internationalen Kongress für Strafrecht und Gefängniswesen," in ibid. See also Alper and Boren, *Crime: International Agenda*, pp. 70–3.

[166] Zentralorgan der deutschen Sozialdemokratischen Arbeiterpartei in der tschechoslowakischen Republik, "Die Organisation der Gestapo" (Prague, 4 Sept. 1935), in CDJC (Paris), folder CD XLVI-69.

[167] Anonymous seven-page report on the Sopade's reaction to the Rhineland crisis, in BA (Koblenz), R58/484, folder 1.

[168] RSHA, Dezernat II 1 A 2, reports by agent "S4," of 9 Jan. and 16 July 1935, in ibid.

[169] Report by Kriminal-Kommissar Sattler, Berlin, 8 Apr. 1935, probably based on information by "S4" in ibid.

[170] Franz Osterroth, ed., *Biographisches Lexikon des Sozialismus* (Hannover, 1960), p. 298.

fateful Munich Conference and on the eve of the German occupation of Bohemia and Moravia, the Sopade was evacuated with the assistance fo the Czechoslovak Red Cross.[171]

In the end the Czech resistance to Nazi subversion failed because the terror actions of the Gestapo in this small country were devastatingly effective: The clandestine radio transmitter of Rudolf Formis, once destroyed, was never replaced. From 1935 on, more and more émigrés sought asylum in countries further away from the reach of the German police. Worse, the Czechs found next to no support in their police war against Nazism from fellow democracies or from allies. A request in 1934 for judicial help to the Swiss aliens police – in connection with the investigation of a Sudeten German accused of treason – was turned down because of its political nature.[172] Three years later, a well-intentioned warning by the Czech press attaché in Berlin to a Swiss diplomat about the subversive activities of Dr. Bibra at the German legation in Berne was suppressed – Dr. Kappeler, the Swiss diplomat in Berlin, happened to be a Nazi sympathizer.[173] While Czech intelligence did benefit from the private help of Swiss army Colonel Masson, the military intelligence services of France and the Soviet Union, Czechoslovakia's principal allies against Germany, turned out to be uncooperative.[174] Attempts by the Prague government to move German political émigrés out of strategic places like Prague, Brno, and the frontier districts adjoining Germany drew a public protest from Thomas Mann.[175]

The betrayal of Czechoslovakia on the European diplomatic front in September 1938 is a story often told. The abandonment of Czechoslovakia on the police front between 1933 and 1938 has not been told, probably because the existence of this front has not received the same attention by historians. Nazi Germany together with the Soviet Union in the thirties operated on the international stage with the use of police power not available to the democracies: It had a powerful party machine with extensive police capabilities at home and abroad, reinforced by propaganda means that in other countries were still kept in private hands.[176] During the Munich Conference the Czech police surrounded the German legation to prevent the German military attaché from communicating to Berlin any strategic

---

[171] "Sopade verlässt Prag. Auch eine Folge der weltpolitischen Ereignisse," in *Prager Montagsblatt*, 14 Mar. 1939.

[172] See EJPD to Justizdepartement of Canton Basel-Stadt, Ref. Nr. R. 1592 Sch., Berne 12 Feb. 1934, in StA (Basel-Stadt), Straf-7, Polizei-Acten P8.

[173] Alice Meyer, *Anpassung oder Widerstand: Die Schweiz zur Zeit des deutschen Nationalsozialismus* (Frauenfeld, 1965), p. 40; also interview with Hermann Böschenstein, who at that time was correspondent for the *Basler Nachrichten* in Berlin, Berne, 1974.

[174] Moravec, *Master of Spies*, pp. 94–5, 103.

[175] Thomas Mann, "Letter to Karel Čapek," in Richard and Clara Winston, eds., *Letters of Thomas Mann* (New York, 1971), pp. 267–8.

[176] To combat the Nazi fifth columns the democracies needed a ruthless police minister like Joseph Fouché. Erwin Faul, "Hitlers Ueber-Machiavellismus," in *V.f.Z.G.*, 2. Jhg., Heft 4 (Oct. 1954), p. 363.

information he might have on Czech defenses.[177] It suggests that in the last analysis Czechoslovak security in the 1930s did, after all, depend mainly on the army and air force.

The beginning of the Second World War

The next challenge to the modern police – whether or not it could justify its methods and principles in the age of mass politics – came when totalitarian rule descended on the democratic countries of Europe in the wake of military conquest. The German Wehrmacht marched into Prague on 15 March 1939. It occupied Denmark and Norway, the Low Countries, and France in the spring of 1940. At first glance, the historian of the Second World War is wont to say that the encounters between modern police and totalitarian police in 1939 and 1940 ended in disastrous defeat for the former. The police officials of the democracies were forced into humiliating collaboration and over the months and years until V-E Day showed signs of moral abdication. And yet, their very submission may have had still more corrupting an effect on the Nazi police who, by amassing unlimited power over millions of defenseless foreign subjects, sank to the basest level of human depravity, especially in Eastern Europe.[178] We limit our discussion to two occupied countries in the first two years of the war, whose police situation has already been treated in this book and end with a note about the "police power" of the Swiss Red Cross.

The Protectorate of Bohemia and Moravia, 1939–45

When Germany occupied Czechoslovakia on 15 March 1939, no state of war existed between the two countries and the Wehrmacht did not enter Prague as a belligerent occupation army. Because Bohemia and Moravia were legally incorporated as a protectorate in the Reich without war, the German police and other German domestic state institutions from the outset took part in assuming control in Prague.[179] German and Austrian police officials arrived after only four weeks of orientation on the history and geography of Bohemia and Moravia, the local administrative system, some information on public figures in Prague and Brno, and on the national character of the inhabitants.[180] Maintaining order in the streets of Prague posed no problem since the Czech policemen remained on duty

---

[177] Alfred Vagts, *The Military Attaché*, (Princeton, N.J., 1967), p. 77.

[178] For reference to corruption in the Gestapo in occupied Poland, see, for example, Jan Karski, *Story of a Secret State* (Boston, 1944), pp. 186, 194, 254.

[179] Hans Umbreit, *Deutsche Militärverwaltungen 1938–1939. Die militärische Besetzung der Tschechoslowakei und Polens* (Stuttgart, 1977), pp. 30ff. Brian Chapman attaches importance to this arrangement in which he sees a breach of international law and a capitulation by the German Wehrmacht to Himmler's political police. Chapman, *Police State*, p. 77.

[180] Pol.Batl. V/1, Prague, 26 Apr., 1939, "Ausbildung und Stoffplan für die Zeit vom 1.-28.5.39 (4 Wochen) . . ." in BA (Koblenz), R70/Böhmen und Mähren/1.

and the population, deeply dejected ever since the Munich Conference of the previous year, was largely passive and compliant.[181] Prague society nevertheless continued to be suspect to the Germans who viewed it as imbued with "a democratic civilization, a spirit of Geneva, a Jewish tradition of intellectual palaver in downtown cafés."[182] For the "thought control" of the Czech population, the use of the old police was indispensable because of the difficult language barrier. But many Sudeten Germans were recruited as vigilantes for the German security authorities.[183]

German police supervision in the Protectorate was regulated by a decree of September 1939, whose essential provisions were:

The government of the Protectorate retains some measure of police sovereignty in Bohemia and Moravia. Consequently there will be a German and a Protectorate police operating side by side. . . .

The chief of the German Kripo [criminal police] supervises the work of the Czech Kripo and the Czech gendarmerie. He tries to standardize procedures [between the German and Czech police].

The German police authorities have the right and the duty to call on the assistance of the Protectorate police in relation to specific cases and to issue orders to individual members [of the Protectorate police].

All communication between the two police forces is in German.

Should the Czech police find it necessary to extend an investigation into the territory of the *Altreich* [i.e. Germany in her 1937 frontiers] it must do so through the German police in Prague or Brünn [Brno]. The Czechs are not permitted to contact the police in the *Altreich* directly.[184]

Unlike in occupied France, where the German army rather than the SS and Gestapo was in charge of overall security between 1940 and 1942, no consideration was given in the Protectorate to the "natural duty" of the Czech police to stand up for the needs of the local population. Instead, the Czech police was expected to give unconditional priority to German Reich interests, as was reaffirmed in a decree on 19 November 1941, signed by the president and prime minister of the Protectorate government, Hacha and Krejči.[185] While the French

---

[181] Heinrich Himmler is said to have admired the Prague police for its professional behavior on the day the German Wehrmacht marched into Prague. Walter Schellenberg, *Memoiren* (Cologne, 1959), pp. 58–9.

[182] Dr. Otto Krieg, "Die Wahrheit über Deutsche und Tschechen. Eindrücke einer Reise nach Prag," in *Die Woche*, 29 Jan. 1941, pp. 16–19.

[183] Kral, ed., *Die Deutschen in der Tschechoslowakei*, p. 32.

[184] "Verordnung über den Aufbau der Verwaltung und die Deutsche Sicherheitspolizei im Protektorat Böhmen und Mähren vom 1. September 1939" (Reichsgesetzblatt I, S. 1681), with Anlage 2, 4, 7, in BA (Koblenz), R70/Böhmen und Mähren/5.

[185] "Regierungsverordnung vom 19. Juni 1942 . . . über Disziplinarmassnahmen gegen politisch unzuverlässige öffentliche Bedienstete," in *Sammlung der Gesetze und Verordnungen des Protektorates Böhmen und Mähren* (1942), pp. 1455–6, in ibid., R70/Böhmen und Mähren/3. President Beneš in exile made a radio broadcast to Czechoslovakia, in which he freed all Czech soldiers, police, and gendarmerie from any obligation of obedience to the Nazi authorities. Edvard Beneš, *Memoirs. From Munich to New War and New Victory, 1918–1945* (London, 1954), p. 114.

police under the German occupation was allowed much autonomy in style and procedure (in the interest of preserving its effectiveness in the native social milieu) the Protectorate police was ordered to adjust itself to the police doctrines of the Nazi Reich. The liberal practice of allowing policeman some margin of discretion and the sanctity of individual rights were discarded.

All rumors abut punishable acts *must* be investigated by the police in accordance with paragraphs 160 and 163 of the St.PO. [Order for Criminal Prosecution]. Since the interest of the community has absolute priority before the interest of the individual and since all guardians of public order must report everything they know without any concern for their own personal interests, policemen are duty-bound to report even breaches of the law in which they themselves are criminally involved. [186]

In an overall report on the reform of the nonuniformed Protectorate police between 1 July 1942 and 31 March 1943, SS-Standartenführer Dr. Weinmann stressed improved criminal–technical methods, better arms and ammunition, new badges and a more efficient filing system, and "reform in police thinking."

In regard to juvenile delinquency, the old police was allowed to deal with each case on its own merits and often left accusations of moral delinquencies by school teachers against pupils to the disciplinary procedure of the schools. The same adherence to the Jewish-liberal *Weltanschauung* is manifest in the old police's attitude toward prostitution. Now all this has been replaced with sterner measures. Recidivists are now assigned to treatment by the preventive police.

To be sure, the Czech police had been purged, but according to Weinmann only twenty-three "inefficient and unreliable officials" were dismissed by 1943. Another 450 positions were slated for elimination in the coming year. At the same time, six Czech police officials were rewarded for their extraordinary services. One inspector second class who was wounded in a battle with political criminals was promoted to inspector first class. The Germans themselves policed the concentration camps at Biechowitz, Hradischko, Königgratz, Miroschau, and Plan a.d. Lanitz in Bohemia, and at Hodonin, Mährisch-Ostrau-Witkowitz, and Theresiendorf in Moravia. [187]

It might be argued that the removal of twenty-three detectives from the Prague police by 1943, or the punishment threatened in Hacha's and Krejci's decree of 19 November 1941 (which ranged from reassignment to retirement or dismissal) was not very severe. Likewise, there has been much comment on the astonishing laxity in security surrounding the person of Reich Protector Heydrich, who was killed by Czech parachutists on his way to work in May 1942 while riding in an open car with only his driver as bodyguard. [188] When one reads the instruction for the

---

[186] "Vorläufige Geschäftsordnung der deutschen Kripo – Kripoleitstelle Prag, K 10-104-02/ 15.5.1941," in BA (Koblenz), R70/Böhmen und Mähren/5.

[187] Der Generalkommandant der nichtuniformierten Protektoratspolizei, SS-Standartenführer Dr. Weinmann, "Tätigkeits- und Erfolgs- (Ergebnis-) Bericht für die Zeit vom 1.7.1942 bis 21.3.1943," ST. I - 10 - 108 - 02, in ibid., R70/Böhmen und Mähren/8.

[188] On the murder of Reinhard Heydrich, see Rudolf Ströbinger, *Das Attentat von Prag. Was wusste*

German criminal police in case of a general alert in Prague, one is made to think of the comical atmosphere in J. S. Machar's recollections of a house search in 1915 and of Karel Čapek's homespun detective stories set in the Prague of the 1920s:

Kriminalleitstelle Prag
K 10-105-10/15.5.1941
How to alert the German criminal police at night

1. In case of unusual happenings, telephone calls to Director, Deputy Director, and Chief of the Inspection.
2. Every [German] criminal police official who does not have a telephone connection or does not live in a place that can be reached by telephone must provide a house key so he can be reached at night. This house key must have a label on which must be written the official's family name, Christian name, official rank, his city district, street, street number, and floor. Key and label must be firmly attached to each other by solid string.
3. All keys must be deposited in a cupboard in the office of the alert service.
4. In case of alert, a Czech-speaking [German] official drives in a car from one city district to the next. In each city district he wakes up the first detective he can reach, who then goes on foot to wake up all the other detectives in the district and orders them to report to headquarters while the Czech-speaking official proceeds by car to the next district.
5. During the time when the Czech-speaking official is inside the house of the official whom he must wake up, the driver must be sure to stay with the service automobile and see to it that it is not damaged by any person in the street.[189]

The air of provincialism surrounding the German police operation in Bohemia and Moravia does not diminish the horror of German rule during the Protectorate period, which was marked by the murder of hundreds of Czech notables, the savage annihilation of the village of Lidice, the deportation of thousands of Jews, and the sufferings of the inmates of Theresienstadt.[190] The optimal size of the Czech nation for police control made it particularly vulnerable to blackmail by hostage taking. During the German attack on Poland in September 1939, notable Czechs were seized by the Germans to ensure that no disturbances broke out that could interfere with military operations north of the Protectorate.[191] And following the assassination of Heydrich in May 1942, it was possible for German and Czech police to use traditional methods of detective work to search the whole city of Prague house by house to apprehend the Czech paratroopers who had killed him.[192]

Heydrich? (Landshut, 1977); and Stanislas F. Berton, "Das Attentat auf Reinhard Heydrich vom 27. Mai 1942. Ein Bericht des Kriminalrats Heinz Pannwitz," in V.f.Z.G., 33. Jhg., Heft 4 (Oct. 1985), pp. 668–707.

[189] KPLST Prag, K10 - 105 - 10/15.5.1941: "Alarmierung der Kriminalbeamten," in ibid. Karel Čapek, the well-known Czech author, wrote *Tales from Two Pockets* (1928) to encourage public sympathy for the police.

[190] On the destruction of Lidice, see report by Horst Böhme, Office of the Reichsprotektor, Prague, 12 June, 1942, in Kral, ed., *Die Deutschen in der Tschechoslowakei*, p. 480.

[191] Moravec, *Master of Spies*, p. 163.

[192] Berton, "Das Attentat auf Reinhard Heydrich," p. 683. Vojtech Mastny calculates that by 1942, the Germans ruled Bohemia's and Moravia's 250,000 administrative employees with less than 2,000 German officials. Vojtech Mastny, *The Czechs under Nazi Rule. The Failure of National Resistance* (New York, 1971), p. 201.

But the point we want to make is that, given the small size of the Czech nation and the long-standing contempt for them by German racists in Bohemia and Austria, they faced a very real threat of being altogether annihilated. In one of his luncheon conversations during the war, Hitler said,

Of all the Slavs, the Czech is the most dangerous because he's a worker. He has a sense of discipline, he's orderly, he's a Mongol more than a Slav. . . . To put it briefly, the Czechs are a foreign body in the midst of the German community. There's no room both for them and for us. One of us must give way. [193]

At the funeral for Heydrich, Hitler warned President Hacha that unless the Czech people gave full support to the Reich in this war, the whole population would be deported. [194] Public loudspeakers blared out the names of the hostages who were shot to the accompaniment of marching music. [195] In light of this terrible threat the passive submission of the Czech civil servants under the occupation is difficult to criticize. The Germans did not depend on them to police the Czech people as they depended on the French police to control France – the Czech people were to them truly expendable. It was demoralizing for the Czechs to be denied Allied assistance in May 1945, when they, like the Parisians before them, took up arms to fight for their liberty but were told from London to wait for the arrival of the Red Army. It brought back the memory of the betrayal by the Western democracies at Munich. During the interval from 1945 to 1948, though the Masarykian republic was briefly restored and Dr. Beneš reinstated as president of the Czechoslovak Republic, the Czechoslovak people could not recover their old love for Western democracy. Quietly, the Czechoslovak Communist Party took over the leading positions in the Prague police and by February 1948 was able to establish a people's democracy in a bloodless coup d'état.

German army control of occupied France, 1940–2

The image of the police in occupied France is less sad than that of the police in the Protectorate. For Czechoslovakia the war was lost by 1938, before it had even begun. In 1939 the Czech police watched helplessly as the Bohemian people returned into servitude after a mere twenty years of independence. For France the war in 1940 was not over. The struggle continued overseas as much as on its own territory in a daily contest of will between vanquished and conquerors, with the French police seeking to maintain a delicate modus vivendi. Indeed, the police in occupied France had a classical function to perform: to mediate between contesting parties in an ongoing political struggle, during which it had to protect the civilian society to the best of its ability. (Pétain's *révolution nationale* was not expected to survive the devastation of the war, whoever emerged as the victor.) [196]

---

[193] *Hitler's Secret Conversations, 1941–1944* (New York, 1961), p. 237.   [194] Ibid., pp. 520–2.
[195] Ursula von Kardorff, *Berliner Aufzeichnungen aus den Jahren 1942 bis 1945* (Munich, 1962), p. 148.
[196] Robert O. Paxton's study, *Vichy France: Old Guard and New Order, 1940–1944* (New York, 1972), raises the question of whether a substantial element of the French political establishment may not have actively sought a partnership role for France in a new order headed by Nazi Germany. But

How well the French police acquitted itself of this function is, of course, another matter. But the reply given after the war by the police prefect of Paris between 1942 and 1944, A. Bussière, is worth considering: "Make a comparison between France which had a government and Belgium and Holland which had no government in power!"[197] Bussière's point was that the survival of France in the war had depended very much on the availability of good police organization – if not French, then German. Keeping up French police morale under foreign occupation was important for the future. Maybe this explains the importance attached by the French police to a large-scale raid mounted on Marseille's old quarter in 1943 as described by Jacques Delarue, the well-known commissaire de police, Resistance hero, and historian. Carried out at great cost by 12,000 French police and scores of German plainclothes detectives from Berlin, the point of this operation seems mainly to have been a public demonstration of French police alertness and efficiency. It was a useful way also of strengthening the French police's hand in its uneasy partnership with the German police.[198]

Against this one must consider that France was not an easy country for the Germans to control without French police collaboration. Though there were many small-time traitors in France and some prominent intellectuals who sympathized with Fascism, there was no consolidated bloc of inhabitants like the Sudeten Germans of Czechoslovakia, who voluntarily rallied to the Führer for political reasons. Nor was the French people a small nation, like the Czechs, who could be destroyed through mass deportation.[199]

The German occupation of France lasted just over four years. The Paris police prefecture recovered much of its prewar prestige during the dramatic days of August 1944, when 162 of its officials gave their lives in the gallant Parisian uprising against the Germans.[200] How much or how little the French police contributed to the Allied victory in the war is not at issue here. There were resistance fighters who served in the French police and used their access to security information to help the underground.[201] But let us not forget that fighting a war against a foreign enemy is not integral to the modern police's mission. The French police should rather take pride in the implicit compliment paid to it by the Germans, inasmuch as the latter dared not entrust to it the task of hunting down

even so, there is a fundamental difference between French demands for a place in a new Europe and Czech doubts after 1938 about their own fitness for independent statehood.

[197] A. Bussière, in Hoover Institution on War, Revolution, and Peace, *France during the German Occupation, 1940–1944. A Collection of 2929 Statements on the Government of Maréchal Pétain and Pierre Laval*, trans. by Philip W. Whitcomb (Stanford, 1957), vol. I, p. 550.

[198] Jacques Delarue, *Trafics et crimes sous l'occupation* (Paris, 1968), pp. 235ff.

[199] Strasbourg, evacuated by the French in 1939, could not be used by the Germans until hundreds of French civil servants and the city's archives were brought back. Albert Brodbeck, "Umbau und Aufbau einer Stadt. Das Beispiel Strassburgs," in *Deutsche Allgemeine Zeitung*, 6 Apr. 1941, Beiblatt, p. 2.

[200] Confédération nationale des policiers anciens combattants et résistants, *Pages d'histoire 1939–1945. Les Policiers français dans la résistance* (Paris, 1964), pp. 75–7.

[201] For example, "Honneur et patrie," "Police et patrie," and "Front populaire de la police," cited in Hoover Institution, *France during the German Occupation*, p. 550. See also Robert Aron, *Histoire de la libération de Paris* (Paris, 1954), p. 384.

French resistance fighters. The fight against French patriots was rather left to new organizations recruited from the criminal underworld (Henri Lafont's "French Gestapo,") and to Fascist paramilitary forces like the "Milice Française," founded in 1943 by Joseph Darnand, Bousquet's successor in the ministry of interior.[202]

This leaves us with one last question to examine, the French police's part in the deportation of some 76,000 Jews to Nazi extermination camps. It has been calculated by historians of the Holocaust that the vast majority of these Jews, perhaps as many as 90 percent, were rounded up by French police and not by German police and that this work was done by them with a grim indifference.[203] Was this not an instance in which the police officials should have refused collaboration for reasons of professional ethics? Milton Dank has made the observation that in the absence of strong anti-Semitism in France the Germans had to offer economic incentives to the native Jew catchers which, if true, would throw an alarming light on the moral fiber of French officialdom under the occupation.[204]

But did the Germans in the Second World War see the French police in such a somber light? When the German armies overran France in May and June 1940, they relied on conventional rules of war to define their rights and duties as occupation authorities.[205] They saw the task of police best performed by local officials in individual contact with the population. They took this traditional position of an occupation authority in opposition to the Nazi police rulers and held to it until the summer of 1942; in Belgium still a little longer. The situation later changed with the outbreak of war in Russia and the beginning of the mass extermination of Jews throughout Europe.

This section is based on documents originating from the German military administration's departments for justice and police (*Gruppe Justiz im Verwaltungsstab, Kommando Ic,* and *Gruppe Polizei*) during the first two years of the occupation. They suggest that the basic principles of modern police work still found support among German military and civilian officials outside the SS and Gestapo apparatus at a time when the Holocaust was already beginning. There were no attempts during the tenure of Generals von Vollard-Bockelberg, Streccius, and Otto von Stülpnagel as military commanders in France to introduce Nazi principles to the French police. It may be argued that the three commanders assumed this attitude for reasons of expediency because they needed the support of the regular French police. But these documents also suggest that professional soldiers and professional policemen shared a view of the world that adhered closer to the nineteenth-century concept of a Europe composed of separate, legally defined, po-

---

[202] Milton Dank, *The French against the French. Collaboration and Resistance* (Philadelphia, 1974), pp. 205–17.

[203] Ted Morgan, "The Barbie File. The 'Butcher of Lyon' Goes on Trial Tomorrow – as Do France and America," in *New York Times,* Magazine Section, 10 May 1987, p. 28.

[204] On Hitler's cynical explanation in 1942, that the French police was grateful for the strong support it received from the Germans in the execution of its duties – unlike from the French government before the war, see Lucien Steinberg, *Les Allemands en France, 1940–1944* (Paris, 1980), p. 141.

[205] Henri Michel, *Paris allemand* (Paris, 1981), pp. 58–9.

litical states than to the apocalyptic visions of the Nazi fanatics. The German invasion of France in 1940 had, after all, brought back memories of battles fought seventy years earlier, reminders that the French Republic had been in existence since Bismarck and Moltke had led the Prussians at the battle of Sedan. In the rural communities of France in 1940, there were still public criers alerting the inhabitants to major events, and in Dijon the German authorities again imposed fines (ten million francs this time) on the whole town as punishment for a sniper shot fired at a German officer in December 1941. (And German officers were still "correct." The money was punctually returned to the city eleven months later, when the culprit was found.)[206] Once more there were *francs tireurs* recruited by the French gendarmerie this time to go after flyers and parachutists with hunting rifles and dogs. After the armistice, the German *Reichskriminalamt* in Berlin sent lawyers to help the Luftwaffe's judicial courts decide the fate of fifty-three such *gardes territoriaux*. The lawyers' recommendation was for leniency because the *gardes* had done no harm to the few Germans they had captured.[207]

The use of civilians as hostages is the principal problem discussed in the documents we cite here. A high-ranking official, Ministerialrat Balz of the German military administration, was particularly insistent that the hostage system be understood as an extraordinary police measure justified only in time of war. An occupation force cannot wield police power on the assumption that a community of interest and a moral bond exist between rulers and ruled, he explained, least of all in a war between politically mature nations. Furthermore, a foreign invader does not possess enough knowledge to provide order police as well as can local officials. Unless a military occupation force is fully supported by the police of the vanquished state, most international lawyers, according to Balz, would argue that it has no alternative but to apply wholesale retaliatory measures against a recalcitrant population. The only moral requirement is that it must give the public sufficient advance notice of its intentions before resorting to such punitive action.

Hostages, according to Balz, were thus persons taken from the local population who vouched with their lives for the obedience which the population at large legally owed the occupation authorities. The destiny of the hostages was thereby placed in the hands of fellow citizens. Consequently no hostages should be executed in retaliation for attacks that took place before the public warning was issued and before the hostages were taken into custody.[208]

Shortly following Hitler's decision in May 1942 to transfer responsibility for suppressing sabotage in occupied France from the army to the SS, the German

---

[206] "Rückzahlung der der Stadt Dijon wegen eines Anschlages auf einen deutschen Offizier auferlegten Busse von 10 Millionen Franken 1942," in BA-MA (Freiburg i.B.), RW 35/311.

[207] Der Militärbefehlshaber in Frankreich, Verwaltungsstab, Abteilung Verwaltung, Paris, 31 Mar. 1941, Vju 831c. 471/41. Betrifft: "Festnahme französischer Staatsangehöriger," in ibid., RW 35/307.

[208] *Min. Rat.* Balz, "Geisel-Frage," (Neugefasstes Referat in Vju 299 42g. (typescript, 10 pages), in ibid., RW 35/308, Militärbefehlshaber Frankreich, Verwaltungsstab, "Vorbeugungs- u. Sühnemassnahmen zur Bekämpfung der Sabotage; Abwehr von Attentaten, Geisel-Frage 1941–42."

military authority in occupied France submitted a report, fifty-eight pages in length, under the title "Preventive and Retaliatory Measures of the Military Commander in France to Combat Sabotage in France." The document is remarkable for its undisguised preference for conventional over ideological war; for its endorsement of the French police and its commitment to defend French interests first; and for its rejection of Hitler's hostage policy on the grounds of individual conscience. The following is a summary of this report, whose style of expression we follow as closely as possible.[209]

This war differs from other wars because it is ideological. National-Socialist or authoritarian states are at war with Bolshevism and with parliamentary democracies. As a result the civilians in this war feel they have a duty to resist the occupation forces in their country, in particular if this resistance receives encouragement from outside the occupied territory. There is sabotage not only of military objectives but sabotage of economic life and systematic subversion of the peaceful cohabitation of the population and the occupation forces.

Since the outbreak of war between [Soviet] Russia and Germany these acts of sabotage have grown in severity. The German authorities have replied by resorting to sterner measures: hostage taking and deportations. By a special decree of 15 August 1941, the Military Commander [Otto von Stülpnagel] declared all activity in support of communism as equivalent to "aiding the enemy." Four days later (19 August 1941) the French government was asked to order its police to hand over all cases involving communists to German military tribunals. (This second decree was canceled after the French established special political tribunals of their own by a law of 7 September 1941.)

The Communists in France thereupon set up an 'Organisation spéciale' (O.S.) to fight the German occupation forces, the French government, and the French police. Its ultimate goal is to create a Red People's Militia and to establish a Soviet France after Germany has been defeated by England and Russia.

The creation of the O.S. means that the Germans no longer face individual saboteurs but an organized and centrally led opposition. The shootings on 21 August 1941, of a German naval officer at the métro station Barbès-Rochechouart and of a noncommissioned officer at the métro station Bastille were assumed to be Communist attacks. The military commander ordered the taking of hostages and issued a proclamation to the population on 22 August 1941. In the following months 471 hostages were executed.[210] This gave the enemy an opportunity to denounce Germany for its alleged relapse into barbarity and to vilify the military commander as 'Stülpnagel the butcher.'

But we must remind the outside world that the French government is committed to Germany by an armistice agreement in which it undertook not to carry out any hostile operations against the German Reich and to ensure the loyal collaboration of all French authorities in the occupied territories of France.

We recognize that the French government has basically abided by this agreement. French authorities in the occupied territories have frequently remonstrated with the German authorities, but this was so because the French authorities sought to protect the interest of the French people rather than German interests, '*which was only natural, and in fact was their*

---

[209] "Vorbeugungs- und Sühnemassnahmen des Militärbefehlshabers in Frankreich zur Bekämpfung der Sabotage in Frankreich" (typescript, 58 pages, 1942), in ibid.

[210] Ibid., p. 13.

duty.'[211] Otherwise there have been few difficulties, generally speaking. The French authorities cooperate with the German occupation and the sabotage actions they both are fighting are directed against the French as much as against the German authorities.

In view of the above, French officials (from prefects and mayors down to the small functionaries) were considered by the Germans as unsuited to be used as hostages. Nor was there much point in seizing noted lawyers or doctors because Communist saboteurs are indifferent to their fate.

The Germans therefore decided to use as hostages individuals from among the thousands of French persons already arrested for anti-German activities. Communists in French prisons were also declared liable to be used as hostages in the hope of discouraging attacks on German personnel.

Unlike Communists, partisans of de Gaulle in London are largely exempted from this hostage policy because the Gaullists are engaged in a military battle with Germany and not in a revolutionary struggle against the existing social order. Only if future attacks clearly reveal a military objective will Gaullists also be used as hostages, for they are "the carriers of the truly military will to resist."[212]

Some hostages have been Jews. But they were seized as hostages only if they were known for their hostility toward Germany or if they were communists.

On 7 September 1941, after three Communists were executed in retaliation for the murder of a German soldier, the Führer ordered that the ratio of retaliation be greatly increased. Unless the murderer of this one soldier was quickly found, 50 other hostages were to be shot. He also ordered that the murder of the next German soldier be punished by the immediate execution of 100 hostages.

The military remonstrated that such a policy would play into the hands of the saboteurs by poisoning the atmosphere between the German occupation authorities, the French government, and the French people. The military commander informed the Führer on 15 January 1942, that he would execute hostages only if an attack on German military personnel has resulted in death or was otherwise very serious. He also said that executions would be delayed sufficiently long to give police investigators a reasonable chance to bring in the individual culprits. "I cannot proceed to mass executions because I consider such actions inappropriate in the light of the overall situation, their likely effect on the French people and on our relationship to France, and finally because I cannot reconcile them with my conscience or my responsibility to history.[213]

In June, 1942, the Führer answered this by transferring the suppressive work in France from the military commander to a higher SS and police leader [Karl-Albrecht Oberg].

The report included high praise for the French police which, albeit slowly, had become quite efficient in assisting the German army in preserving basic order in France. "If nearly half of all saboteurs between 21 August 1941 and 14 March 1942 have been caught (46 culprits for 109 attacks) this has largely been thanks to the energetic efforts of the French police."[214] The report ended with a statement of regret that the military standpoint in this matter (how to preserve order in occupied France) had not been accepted. "To handle the French situation according to a preconceived strategy centrally directed from the Reich has not proven feasible."[215]

[211] Ibid., p. 25; my italics.   [212] Ibid., pp. 30–1.   [213] Ibid., p. 49.
[214] Ibid., p. 53.   [215] Ibid., p. 58.

The most disturbing element in the above report is, of course, the reference to the 471 executions within a short time, especially if they affected innocent civilians rather than underground resistance fighters who had volunteered to risk their lives for their cause.[216] Balz at one point frankly admitted that "We have no interest at all in relieving the French people of their nightmare on account of the hostages. At least not as long as we have no clear assurance that the majority of the population takes part in preventing crimes against the occupation forces and helps in apprehending the culprits."[217]

The question is whether under the extreme condition of war the German occupation troops should be given any credit at all for at least exercising their hostage policy with a certain amount of restraint – in Belgium, for example, General von Falkenhausen applied a ratio of 5 executions for every German who was killed rather than Hitler's 100, and took the victims as far as possible from among imprisoned resistance fighters awaiting a certain death sentence rather than from civilians at large.[218] Finally, we should also list some basic points adopted by the German military administration toward the French police in 1940–2:

1. The French police is most effective when it is given to understand that we trust it to fulfill its obligation. There should be no unnecessary interference with French police autonomy and with its responsible execution of its task.[219]

(Thus the Germans confirmed the principle of police work as demanding local initiative and responsibility.)

2. Local disagreements between German and French officials are inevitable, but on the whole no serious difficulties have arisen over the use of French police organs by the German authorities. Of course we must be careful how far we trust the French police. It happens to be the only French authority that can seriously threaten the occupation forces, be it through passive resistance or active opposition. Therefore our task is clear: the French police must remain strong enough to maintain good surveillance over the French population and if need be to hold it in check, without at the same time making us responsible for its behavior in the eyes of the French people. The French police must also be strong enough not to need any German military support and yet be denied a true military capacity of its own. To this purpose the Garde Républicaine Mobile was disbanded by the Germans, but the communal police and gendarmerie were strengthened.

---

[216] At the final reckoning in the Nuremberg trial, the French prosecution presented a list of approximately 30,000 hostages shot during the war in twenty-one leading French cities, including Paris. See Edward Crankshaw, *Gestapo* (New York 1957), p. 161.

[217] Letter, *Min. Rat.* Balz to Dr. Werner Best, Paris, 24 Oct. 1941, in BA-MA (Freiburg i.B), RW 35/308.

[218] Summary of Maître Botson's defense plea in the war crimes trial against Alexander von Falkenhausen in Brussels (1950–1), in ibid., Nachlass Falkenhausen, Box: BT; and "Le procès von Falkenhausen," in *Le Soir*, 5 Jan. 1951.

[219] Circular, Dr. Werner Best, "Die Aufsicht über die franz. Polizei im besetzten Gebiet, hier Zusammenfassung der allgemeinen Grundsätze," Paris, 14 Mar. 1942, V pol. 220/463/42, in BA-MA (Freiburg i.B.), RW 35/340.

(Thus the principle of proportionality in all forms of police work was also applied to the relationship between the German control authorities and the French police.)

3. We have no interest in reorganizing or reforming the French police on the German model even where the German model is better.

(There never has been an accepted standard for comparing the quality of national police forces against each other, except in technical methods. The Germans during the war did help the French police with tapping telephones. What technical improvements in organization took place during the war, Delarue tells us, should not be assumed to have political significance.)[220]

4. Can the French police be entrusted with the execution of tasks which exclusively serve German interests? In some smaller tasks like confiscating a French book, yes. Otherwise only in missions where the French government has an interest also: traffic control, crime fighting, and the suppression of Gaullism and Communism.

(This assessment of the French police's trustworthiness is surely interesting because it was so guarded – and yet was considered as satisfactory.)

Finally, the Germans paid their respects to the famous French police spéciale, whose qualities they remembered from the days of Louis Napoleon and the Schnaebelé affair of 1887:

5. The French police spéciale before the war was a political intelligence service par excellence. It was well-trained for monitoring public opinion and political trends in the *départements* and it disposed over valuable archives and files. Because their number is relatively small, they can be watched with special care.

(Why were the commissariats not abolished? Were the Germans here paying tribute to an old and respected adversary?)

Switzerland and the Red Cross in the Second World War

The Swiss situation was quite different from the French one because Switzerland was spared enemy occupation throughout the war. There is no need for us to study the policing of its society between 1939 and 1945. This small country, already so well ordered on a democratic basis in peacetime, could rely on the people's heightened sense of patriotic solidarity after 1939 to forgo any thought of special wartime police.[221] The number of aliens who arrived in Switzerland because of

---

[220] See Jacques Delarue, "La police sous l'occupation," in *L'Histoire,* No. 29 (Dec. 1980), p. 9.

[221] An internal Swiss government report at the end of the war, *Bericht des Chef des Generalstabes der Armee an den Oberbefehlshaber der Armee über den Aktivdienst 1939–1945* (Berne, n. d.), p. 491, makes scant reference to police, except to mention some turncoat Swiss policemen who served the Gestapo in German towns close to the Swiss border.

the fighting did not much exceed 100,000. Distributed throughout all the cantons, they were easily kept under surveillance by local police.[222]

What makes Switzerland interesting to us in the Second World War is, rather, the use the Swiss made of the International Red Cross (IRC), and especially of their national Red Cross organization to reinforce their external security. To make our point we must reiterate that the Swiss Red Cross (SRK), whose peacetime strength was about 10,000 doctors, nurses, and employees,[223] was in 1939 still closely linked to the Swiss Confederation. According to the SRK statute, Section III, paragraphs 41–3, the SRK's chief purpose was to serve as an auxiliary to the Swiss army's medical service. It received funds and supplies from the Swiss government, which, in return, could through the military department control its activities. In case of war the SRK came under complete army command and a SRK director, the Red Cross chief surgeon (*Rotkreuz-Chefarzt*) was appointed by the federal government. (State control was believed to ensure that the Red Cross served humanitarian ideals, which would not be the case if the society were run on commercial concepts of efficiency.)[224] The same close relation between the state and the nation Red Cross chapters existed elsewhere in Europe too. In Italy the Red Cross worked with the Voluntary Militia for National Security, and in Romania with the ministry of interior and King Carol's Fascist youth organization, *Straja Tarii*.[225]

In Switzerland the moral crisis of Europe was less keenly felt than in occupied France or Czechoslovakia. The war was largely externalized as a contest between neighboring territorial states in whose political cause to inquire was no business of the Swiss. By the end of the Second World War, the Swiss reluctantly recognized that Europe had entered a new age in which the competition of objective "state interests" had given way to wars between mutually incompatible ideologies. Reluctantly, the Swiss Red Cross in its postwar accounting admitted having helped some countries for reasons of subjective sympathy: Finland in 1940, "so far away yet so close to our hearts!"; France in 1944, "because of the traditional amity of our two states and the many personal friendships among our people"; and Greece in 1942, "because Switzerland is always interested in a small nation that bravely stands up against a powerful oppressor."[226]

---

[222] According to an EJPD report in February, 1945, 104,683 persons in Switzerland counted as foreign émigrés or refugees: 7,500 émigrés, 31,775 refugees, 188 miscellaneous aliens in internment, 2,258 escaped prisoners of war, and 905 German and Italian deserters. EJPD, Polizeiabteilung, Flüchtlingssektion, "Zusammenstellung über die in der Schweiz anwesenden Emigranten und Flüchtlinge. Stand vom 1. Februar 1945," (mimeo, 2 pages), in ASRK (Berne), J.II.15. 1969/7, Aktenzeichen 92: "Justiz- und Polizeidepartement 1942–1947."

[223] Oberstlt. Denzler, "Aufruf an die Bevölkerung" (Bundesfeierversammlung 1937), (typescript, 3 pages) in ibid., Aktenzeichen 13.

[224] SRK, "Die Aufgaben des Schweizerischen Roten Kreuzes," (Berne, 16 Feb. 1948), in ibid.

[225] "L'Organisation italienne des services de secours rapide en cas de calamité publique," (mimeo, 12 pages, 29 Jan. 1937), in ibid., Aktenzeichen 101; and Dr. Marosin, "Rapport de la Croix-Rouge roumaine sur son oeuvre en faveur des réfugiés polonais en Roumanie," (16 Apr. 1940), in ibid., Aktenzeichen 75, "Réunion des non-belligérants 1940."

[226] "Rapporte SRK," (typescript, 87 pages, n.d.), in ibid., Aktenzeichen 92, folder 98, pp. 41–52.

But before the Second World War the Swiss Red Cross still thought in terms of objective territorial warfare. The most poignant expression of this concept was the proposal of the International Red Cross Committee to establish neutral zones as a way to limit the damage inflicted by war on civilian society. Modern war was seen as a scourge because of its mounting material destructiveness, not because war is the wrong way to solve international disputes. The causes fought for by either side were not weighted on their ideal merits.

Henri Dunant, the founder of the Red Cross in the 1860s, had been the first to think of establishing "oases of humanity" in the midst of war, territorial enclaves immune from hostile action where the wounded and sick would find refuge and medical aid. [227] The subject came up for discussion in a Red Cross conference in 1929 but concrete proposals were not forthcoming until October 1936. A conference on the subject of "A Project for the Creation of Sanitation Towns and Villages" was attended by delegates from eleven nations: Germany, Belgium, France, Britain, Hungary, Italy, The Netherlands, Romania, Czechoslovakia, Yugoslavia, and Switzerland. [228] Germany, France, and Czechoslovakia endorsed the idea in principle. All delegates, however, saw in them insuperable technical problems, notably the problem of how they should be policed. Who would guarantee that they would not secretly be used for military purposes? Professor de la Pradelle of France came up with the remarkable suggestion that the medical doctors attending the sick and · wounded should double as police inspectors. ("Since they will be living in the *ville sanitaire* in order to perform the medical functions that will be entrusted to them, they would have no difficulty at all in learning everything that passes in them.")[229]

With the outbreak of war and the fall of France in 1940, Switzerland's greatest concern became dissuading the Germans from occupying the country. The SRK repatriated thousands of interned French soldiers (with destination to their individual home towns, to make it less likely that the Germans would put them in prisoner-of-war camps) but its officials were under strict orders not to extend any individual help to refugees from France, to guard against personal involvement on their part with the fate of particular victims, and to preserve the SRK's absolute neutrality in the war. [230] However, relief supplies were rushed by the *Cartel suisse de secours aux enfants victimes de la guerre* and the *Secours suisse* to French internment camps throughout 1939 and 1940, many of them holding Jews from Germany and war orphans. [231]

Although we respect the generosity of Swiss relief work in the war, our attention must center on Swiss Red Cross's activities accompanied by some form of

---

[227] Oberst H. Remund, "Hilfsaktion und Rotkreuz-Grundsätze," (typescript, 5 pages, ca. 1946), in ibid., Aktenzeichen 13.

[228] See folder: "Villes sanitaires 1936," in ibid., Aktenzeichen 187.

[229] Protocol of talk by Prof. de la Pradelle, France, at the meeting of 15 Oct. 1936 in Geneva, in ibid.

[230] Conversation with Dr. Nicolas Burckhardt, retired IRCR official, in Basel, 18 Aug. 1984.

[231] See report on French internment camps for civilians shortly before the war, in ASRK (Berne), Aktenzeichen 320, "Berichte 1941–1943 Frankreich. Allgemeines Internierungslager."

"police function." One of the most interesting documents in this regard is an order issued by the *Rotkreuz-Chefarzt* Colonel Redmund, "Directives on the activities of the local Red Cross Chapters in case of war, as adjusted to the latest military situation," (18 December 1941). Paragraphs 3 and 4 were instructions on how the Swiss Red Cross should act in a city that had fallen to an enemy.[232]

3. The chief task of the Red Cross is to provide medical aid to the wounded. This service may also be provided by the sanitation corps of the approaching occupying power, but there is no assurance that this will happen. The Swiss Red Cross will in any event offer medical aid to the wounded and request the permission from the commander of the occupying force to this effect.

   There will be danger of unexploded bombs and shells, and the problem of countless people who have no shelter. But our chief concern will be to rescue the children. We must give absolute priority to the care of children. What recently happened in one French *département* must not happen in Switzerland: in that *département* out of 22 homes for expectant mothers and young children, prepared by the French Red Cross, 17 were ordered by the civil authorities to be put aside for old people, the incurably sick, and for the mentally ill. As a result, thousands of children died, whose survival was essential for the future of their country. *This kind of false humanitarianism is a sign of decadence. In fact, this is not humanitarianism at all, but a sin against the natural, healthy life instinct of the nation.*

4. The Swiss Red Cross must be ready to run registration centers to record the refugees and homeless for which it will need stores of writing material, telephones, and maps. *All information so gathered must be passed on to the occupation authorities on request.*

It is not clear whether the above reference to the "decadence" of the French civil government and the "healthy life instinct of the nation" represented Dr. Redmund's personal view or an unwitting leaning toward *völkisch* ideas. There are grounds, however, to worry abut the kind of information the Nazis would have "requested" from the local Swiss Red Cross organization in return for granting it permission to cater to the sick and wounded.

In the case of the Swiss Red Cross's decision to send medical teams to the German side of the Eastern front in 1941–3, the political motive of winning the Nazi government's continued indulgence of Switzerland's neutrality and independence is difficult to ignore. Officially, the reason for these missions was to give Swiss army doctors first-hand experience with treating wounds inflicted by the new weapons used in this war. The excuse for sending doctors and nurses exclusively to German field hospitals was that the Soviet or Allied front lines were inaccessible from Switzerland. However, we also find in a report in 1944 the admission that sending these teams was meant "as a kind of compensation to Germany for the children's relief missions [in 1939–40] which had mainly benefited France."[233] The agreement between the SRK and the German Wehrmacht was,

232 Oberst Remund, SRK, "Orientierung über die Tätigkeit der Zweigvereine im Kriegsfall entsprechend der gegenwärtigen militärischen Lage." (18 Dec. 1941), in ibid., Aktenzeichen 15, folder 16: "Hilfsmassnahmen bei Bombenschäden," 1941–3. Italics mine.

233 "Règlement für die Teilnehmer der Aerzte- u. Schwesternmission organisiert vom Komitee für

moreover, negotiated by Hans Frölicher, the Swiss minister in Berlin, who understood his mission to be the appeasement of the Nazi leaders even at the expense, if it had to come to that, of his own personal reputation at home.[234]

A total of four medical missions went to the Eastern front: to Smolensk (October 1941–January 1942), to Warsaw (January–April 1942), to Riga (June–September 1942), and to Stalino-Rostov-Kharkov (November 1942–March 1943). Some of the Swiss doctors, including Oberstdivisionär H. Bircher himself, who organized the undertaking, could be suspected on the basis of their reports to have sympathized with Nazi Germany to the extent, at least, of admiring the fighting spirit of the German soldiers and their enthusiasm for the Third Reich.[235] But there were also Swiss doctors and nurses who returned home deeply perturbed by what they had seen, notably the mistreatment of Russian prisoners by the SS, the fact that Russian wounded as a rule were denied medical help, and the rumor that German doctors used serum made from Jews and criminals in concentration camps deliberately infected for this purpose.[236]

We have no doubt that the Swiss doctors and nurses had no chance to interfere with what Nazi atrocities they witnessed on the Russian front, even though the contributions by these highly qualified teams (each of them 70 strong) must have been very valuable to the Germans. But the failure of the Swiss to make better use of the Red Cross to alleviate the sufferings of the European Jews does raise some questions. Was the moderation of the Swiss a part of the price that they had to pay for Switzerland's freedom, or were the Swiss really standing so far apart from the moral conflicts tearing asunder the fabric of Western civilization?

By the accounts of the Swiss Red Cross after the end of the war, some 20,000 inmates of German concentration camps were rescued by it, under difficult and sometimes dangerous circumstances.[237] There had been three visits by the International Red Cross to German concentration camps in 1935 (one was by Karl J. Burckhardt to see the pacifist and Nobel-prize winner Carl Ossietzky at Esterwegen KZ), and one visit in 1938. The visits were not very effective because legally these camps fell outside the range of the IRC's competence, the inmates being German nationals held in a German penal institution. Besides, the Nazi government placed restrictions on visits by outsiders "for reasons of national security."[238] In 1938 a Society to Aid Jewish Emigration (*Hilfsverein für jüdische Auswanderung*) in Zurich officially asked the Swiss Red Cross to inspect the sanitary conditions in the German camps and was given this soothing reply:

Hilfsaktionen unter dem Patronat d. SRK," (Berne, 9 Oct. 1941), in ibid., Aktenzeichen 136; "1. & 2. Ostfrontmission. Personelles."

[234] See Hans Frölicher, *Meine Aufgabe in Berlin*, (Berne, 1962), pp. 53–4.

[235] H. Bircher, "Drei Monate an der Ostfront," in *Allgemeine Schweizerische Militärzeitung*, 90. Jhg., No. 9 (Sept. 1944), pp. 654–720, in ASRK (Berne), Aktenzeichen 136, folder 137.

[236] See report by Hauptmann Arnold, Kommandant of the Second Swiss Medical Mission, dated Davos, 24 Apr. 1942, in ibid., Aktenzeichen 133; "Ostfrontmission – Rapporte 1941–1943."

[237] Ibid., "Rapporte SRK," Aktenzeichen 92, folder 98, pp. 6–7.

[238] Durand, *Histoire du comité international*, pp. 501–2.

The German Red Cross is quite capable on its own to undertake sanitary controls in concentration camps. A foreign Red Cross society will obviously never be granted permission to do this. But we have been assured that we can receive news about individual relatives or friends of émigrés now living in Switzerland if we submit personal details concerning them.[239]

In order to help the camp inmates, both the International Red Cross and the Swiss Red Cross decided on the bureaucratic approach as the only one likely to produce some results, however modest. Sometimes it was possible to obtain the freedom of single individuals on the basis on an international convention, for example prisoners of war from countries that had ceased to exist, and civilian hostages.

Without openly provoking the detaining authorities the International Red Cross was able to reach the prisoners by indirect routes. It could ask for news about particular individuals, it could send them letters and parcels, and with patience one small measure of protection after another could be extended to the inmates without risking a total breakdown in communications [with the Nazi authorities]. But this took much time and much discretion. The result was that public opinion was left unpersuaded [by our efforts]. The Red Cross's silence was taken for indifference, its patience for passivity.[240]

However, one of the most vocal charges came not from the uninformed public at large but from the Yugoslav Red Cross in 1947. The Yugoslav Red Cross charged that the International Red Cross in Geneva had (1) not been neutral in the war (for example it had extended recognition to the independent state of Croatia); (2) had done nothing about the concentration camps, not even protested publicly when atrocities must have been observed during Red Cross visits to such camps; and (3) had given an attestation of "generally satisfactory" to the German prisoner-of-war camp Stalag VIII B even though one third of its 300,000 inmates died from overwork in mines and factories and another 40,000 died from mistreatment. "The IRC should not have kept silent about conditions it found in certain camps 'in order not to make things worse.' On the contrary, going public would have been better because even Fascists fear the pressure of public opinion."[241]

Had the Swiss Red Cross officials during the war given up too easily? One must remember that already before the war the Swiss had not been very forthcoming toward Jewish refugees seeking asylum. During the war a substantial number of refugees in Switzerland were confined in camps where the atmosphere was deliberately kept harsh. This applied not only to those whom the aliens police classified as "criminal and asocial elements," but also to deserters and escaped prisoners of war, and to people who fell under the jurisdiction of the poor police because of their indigence. Foreigners who had come in violation of Switzerland's

---

[239] Dr. med. Ed. Denzler, Rotkreuzchefarzt, to Hilfsverein für jüdische Auswanderung, Zurich, 21 Jan. 1939, in SSRK (Berne), Aktenzeichen 188; "Flüchtlinge, Emigranten 1939, 1946."

[240] André Durand, *Histoire du comité international de la Croix Rouge. De Sarajevo à Hiroshima* (Geneva, 1978), p. 502. For the International Committee of the Red Cross's performance during the war, see Jean-Claude Favez, *Das Internationale Rote Kreuz und das Dritte Reich. War der Holocaust aufzuhalten?* (Zurich, 1989).

[241] Yugoslav Red Cross to ICRC (n.d.), in ASRK (Berne), Aktenzeichen 74, "C.I.C.R."

aliens law were kept under specially austere conditions "to discourage them from staying in our country." We cite two excerpts from the "General Principles" enunciated at a Swiss Police Conference on the refugee problem, held in October 1940:

Harsh treatment cannot be avoided. Our compassion for the individual refugee must be subordinated to the interest of our country.

It would be ideal to give every individual refugee his personal due, but in practice this is impossible. Instead we try to persuade these people to return voluntarily to their home countries. We urge them to make peace with their countries and to go home, *even at the risk of incurring some form of punishment.*[242]

At the height of the war, in December 1942, the following categories of would-be refugees were turned away from the frontiers by order of the EJPD with, presumably, the enjoinder to accept what punishment was in store for them in their home countries:

For a person to be recognized as a political refugee, it is not enough that he disagrees with the political regime of his country. This person must also directly be wanted by the authorities of his country for oppositional political activity. For example, a Frenchman who says he supports de Gaulle is a political fugitive only if he can demonstrate that this fact is known to the [Vichy] Government and that he personally is being sought for Gaullist activities. A German who is a Social Democrat or a trade unionist is not a political refugee until he persuades the Swiss authorities that he is wanted for anti-regime activities. Frenchmen who have been brought to Germany as forced laborers are not political refugees and must be turned back at our frontier. The same applies to other foreigners who now work in Germany, whether voluntarily or under duress. *Persons who flee only because of racial persecution should not be regarded as political refugees in the sense of this Directive. {Flüchtlinge nur aus Gründen der Rassenverfolgung sind nicht als politische Flüchtlinge im Sinne dieser Weisung zu betrachten.}*[243]

Switzerland's refugee policy in the Second World War has become a matter of much debate since the publication of documents and accounts on this subject during the last ten years by Swiss historians and publicists like Bonjour, Häsler, and others. In 1985, a police commander of the canton of St. Gallen, Paul Grüninger, dismissed during the war for having allowed refugees into the country by falsely dating their entry into Switzerland prior to 18 August 1938, was posthumously rehabilitated. "The good of saving human lives," it was now recognized, "outweighs the misdemeanor of falsifying documents and breaking federal laws."[244] Our intention here is not to criticize or to defend Switzerland's refugee policy

[242] E. Scheim, "Referat über die Handhabung der fremdenpolizeilichen Internierungen," (typescript), Konferenz der Kantonalen Polizei-Kommandanten, Sitten, 11/12 Oct. 1940, in BA (Berne), Bestand 4001 (B), 1970/187 (Handakten Baumann), Karton 2, folder 22/3. Italics mine.

[243] EJPD, Polizeiabteilung, "Weisung über Rückweisung oder Aufnahme illegal einreisender Ausländer," (mimeo, 3 pages, Berne, 29 Dec. 1942), in ASRK (Berne), Aktenzeichen 92, "Justiz- und Polizeidepartement 1942–1947." Italics mine.

[244] "Fall 'Grüninger': Fluchthilfe war Hauptgrund für seine Entlassung," in *Basler Zeitung* (14 Feb. 1985), p. 9. On Switzerland in the Second World War, see Edgar Bonjour, *Geschichte der schweizerischen Neutralität* (Basel, 1970), vols. 3, 4, and 5; on the refugee problem, Alfred A. Häsler, *Das Boot is voll. Die Schweiz und die Flüchtlinge, 1933–1945* (Zurich, 1967).

during the war but to point to the existence of a certain "moral" police power in the community of European states in the Second World War, which this small neutral country possessed to a unique degree and decided to use very cautiously.

Perhaps we should balance the picture we have drawn of Switzerland during the perilous years when it was totally surrounded by Axis powers by crediting it for its equally neutral attitude in 1945, when most of Europe was celebrating the Allied victory over Nazism. Switzerland was one of the first countries to extend humanitarian help to the defeated German people. A Swiss team of International Red Cross officials toured Germany in March and April 1947.

In Frankfurt [am Main] our delegation was concerned about the current critical attitude of the American occupation forces, who disapprove of the relationship between the International Red Cross Committee (CICR) and the German civilian internees. The Americans have criticized the CICR for not doing enough to help the inmates of the concentration camps [during the war] who had been civilian internees and so outside the jurisdiction of the International Red Cross. Now the Americans will not let Red Cross inspectors see the camps where they keep the German civilian internees. In these camps thousands of Germans who are suspected of Nazism await the ruling of special courts. Some of these internees are subjected to intolerable living conditions. Thus in Darmstadt, some inmates were put up in tents throughout the winter, which resulted in numerous serious illnesses, and there have also been stories of mistreatment.[245]

Writing as head of the Swiss chapter of the Red Cross, Colonel H. Remund gave his views on the attitude he believed the SRK should take towards the suffering people in occupied Germany:

In the spring of 1946 there took place a large "People's Collection for Freedom," whose proceeds were intended to benefit solely those who, during the war, had politically opposed the regime in power [in Germany]. However, as we look at the enormous misery of the people in the wartorn countries, we ask: Have we the right to provide special treatment to those who distinguished themselves by their political fight against tyranny and to neglect those who cannot produce evidence of political resistance during the recent war? What about the children of those who had worked for the tyrants and are now dead: don't these children also need our help? The Red Cross must not sit in judgment. We must cut the causal chain linking one evil to the next. Children must not be made to pay for the misdeeds of their parents. The Red Cross must reject all efforts to make it deny aid to the German people in its present distress.[246]

[245] Dr. H. R. Oeri, "Bericht über meine Reise nach Deutschland vom 25. Mai 1947 bis 3. Apr. 1947," in ibid., Aktenzeichen 131. "Deutschland 1946–1950."
[246] H. Remund, "Hilfsaktion und Rotkreuz-Grundsätze."

Epilogue

Our study ended with Europe's descent into the catastrophe of the Second World War. The swift surrender between 1939 and 1940 of many democratic states to the German Wehrmacht, and in June of 1941 the onset of the titanic struggle between the totalitarian empires of Hitler and Stalin, closed a period of one hundred years of progress toward more civilian police rule in Europe and better police collaboration among its various nations. With the exception of Great Britain, all the European countries served by liberal police systems had shown themselves too weak to resist Hitler's furious assaults. They were liberated because of the endurance of the Soviet Union – the one continental power Germany failed to subvert with fifth columns – and by overseas intervention from America and the Commonwealth nations of the British Empire.

True, in 1945 the Western Allies restored the liberal foundations of modern police administration in their occupation zones of Germany and Austria. But many of the social conventions and cultural habits on which modern police power had relied in the preceding century were now gone. For example, class war: Who in Western Europe still talked of "working-class solidarity" or "bourgeois respectability?" Or else national patriotism: Who continued to believe in *"dulce et decorum est pro patria mori"*? Ten years after the war the English writer, Rebecca West, discovered that military bravery as a virtue had become "dowdy," whereas betraying state secrets in the public eye had unaccountably acquired an aura of sophistication – a shamelessness Dreyfus would not have understood and Redl never admitted to.[1]

After 1945 Western Europe gradually ceased to be a collection of separate parcels of inhabited land, each one so policeable because of its complicated social compartments at home and its clearly defined frontiers to the outside.[2] In one of

---

[1] Rebecca West, *The New Meaning of Treason* (New York, 1965), p. 251. Likewise, the French president Georges Pompidou was once reported to have expressed a "sophisticated disdain" for the self-righteousness of the Resistance: "La résistance m'agace." See Jean Améry, "Wider die Rehabilitierung der Barbarei," in *NZ am Wochenende*, Basel, 13 Mar. 1976, p. 1.

[2] Countries as different as France and Hungary henceforth proposed to prosecute offenses against

C. P. Snow's novels a Cambridge don is heard speaking mournfully about the disappearance of privileges derived from skin color, upbringing, and private inheritance.[3] His regrets should have extended to the decline of national allegiances – by citizens to their countries and by governments to their nationals.[4] Back in 1929 the city council of Basel had scarcely dared wonder whether it was really obliged to intercede on behalf of one of its burghers, a Swiss Communist being tortured in an Italian jail, or could leave him to be bailed out by Moscow.[5] Today the idea of a government rescuing one of its private citizens, no matter how disreputable he may be, on the Palmerstonian principle of *"civis Romanus sum,"* is more likely dismissed as either old-fashioned or too expensive.[6] As far as the European Continent is concerned, with the Western countries in the process of forming a confederation and their neighbors to the east abandoning state socialism, a country's success depends more on economic power than national solidarity. A prominent legal scholar, Hershel Lauterpacht, argued after the Second World War about the need for greater attention to police problems under international law: (1) International law should assume more responsibility for regulating "in detail the life of its individual members [i.e. the states] *in its internal aspects"*; and (2) international law should recognize that there is a limit to a state's right to independence. "To assert any such right would be to suggest that for an independent state to pass from the condition of independence to that of dependence necessarily involves a moral loss."[7] The Helsinki agreement of 1975 was a step in that direction because by guaranteeing the inviolability of each other's frontiers, the signatory states rendered police sovereignty to a large extent obsolete as a precondition of territorial defense. International criticism of police violations of human rights in any of the signatory states, consequently, has become much more acceptable.

Writing the history of police in the second half of the twentieth century must be left to researchers who in the coming decades will have access to many more sources than we have today, including the mountains of records amassed by the East European ministries of interior between 1945 and 1989. For this study the collapse of the police states of the Warsaw Pact is too close to be viewed without

their national security wherever in the world they were perpetrated. Manuel R. Garcia-Mora, *International Responsibility for Hostile Acts of Private Persons against Foreign States* (The Hague, 1962), pp. 166–9.

[3] C. P. Snow, *The Affair. A Novel* (New York, 1960), p. 84.

[4] On the importance of national loyalty to keep civil servants in line, see Walter Fredericia, "Muss Nationalismus unmoralisch sein?" in *Die Zeit*, 28 June 1951, p. 4.

[5] See debate in the Grosser Rat of Canton Basel-Stadt on 14 Mar. 1929 (interpellation Bodemann), in StA (Basel-Stadt), Politisches EE 15, 1: "Faszismus, Nationalsozialismus, Fronten 1920–1945." "Die schweizerische kommunistische Partei hätte also vielleicht die russische Regierung anfrangen können, ob sie nicht etwas tun könne für einen Mann, der in Italien politische Funktionen im Auftrage der russischen kommunistischen Partei ausübte."

[6] Pitt Cobbett, *Cases and Opinions on International Law* (London, 1909), Part I, p. 201.

[7] L. Oppenheim, in Sir Hersh Lauterpacht, ed., *International Law. A Treatise* (New York, 1955), vol. I, p. 249, italics mine; and idem, "Brierly's Contribution to International Law," in *BYB* (1955–6), p. 7.

distortion and bias. But we would be negligent if in this Epilogue we did not record the fact that totalitarian police — the principal alternative to modern police civilization — has already suffered two major setbacks: one in mid-century, when Hitler's Third Reich was defeated, and another at the end of this century. Concerning the first setback, the end of Gestapo rule, we may already venture a few conclusions by describing the situation in Berlin from the terrible last year of the Second World War through the building of the Berlin Wall in 1961.

Berlin in the cold war

There was no reason why the dissolution of the Nazi police system in 1945 should have been regarded by contemporaries as conclusive evidence for the unviability of totalitarianism as an enduring form of government. It was simpler to attribute the end of Gestapo and SS rule in Europe to the military defeat of the Third Reich, in reaffirmation of a pessimistic view already heard under the Second French Empire — and eighty years later again in Germany — that powerful police dictatorships are irremovable by domestic insurrection and can only be brought down by military force from outside. It explains the behavior of certain elements of the German resistance who sought contacts to foreign governments and after 1939 were disposed to assist the Allied armies to hasten the downfall of Hitler.[8] But to hold this view is to disregard the steady erosion of the French emperor's powers throughout the 1860s, long before the battle of Sedan. It means playing down the prognoses of chaos for Hitler's Grossdeutsches Reich through internal disputes and bureaucratic mismanagement even had the Nazis defeated England and the Soviet Union. Admittedly, it took the popular revolutions of 1989 to prove that given enough time, dictatorships can and do disintegrate through sheer mediocrity, without foreign invasion. It is ironic that whereas in the 1930s waging war against dictatorial regimes had seemed the only way to defend democracy, in the atomic age, precisely because in Europe armed conflict between fully mobilized nations has become inconceivable, police dictatorships — be they the regime of Khrushchev and Brezhnev in the USSR, or that of Ulbricht and Honecker in East Germany — have been deprived of their principal rationale.

In 1933, fourteen years after Versailles, Hitler could still use the German people's wish for a restoration of military sovereignty to justify the establishment of his dictatorship. And after the battle of Stalingrad he could scare them with the threat of a Russian invasion to impose his absolute will over them. "Total war was declared by 1943," wrote General Georg Thomas in 1945, one of the few surviving military figures of the German resistance against Hitler: "All along the front the [police] terror was increased in order to whip up the maximum of fighting spirit among the troops. Party and Gestapo spies appeared in commando

---

[8] Harold C. Deutsch, *Verschwörung gegen den Kreig. Der Widerstand in den Jahren 1939–40* (Munich, 1969), p. 155.

posts where none had been seen before. . . . The number of denunciations and arrests rose astronomically."[9]

Only in Western Europe could the German occupation authorities control their conquests by playing on the traditional sectarianism of French, Belgian, or Luxemburgian inhabitants. In the east the German occupation authorities simply applied physical coercion, indiscriminately, over uncounted masses of Slavic and non-Aryan people, condemning them by the millions to forced labor, resettlement, subjugation, and eventual extermination.[10] Instead of adapting their police rule to local conditions, the Nazis recruited local collaborators as auxiliary guards the better to enforce the will of Berlin. Instead of building police authority on the performance of public services they based it on the desperate scramble for physical survival which they unleashed among a terrorized population.[11] Police work of this order, for which the cold-blooded killing machines (Einsatzgruppen) of the SS, supported by certain elements of the Gestapo and by native mercenaries had to be used, does not belong to the history of modern police except as a warning about how disastrously the barbarity of total war can disorient and corrupt individual police officials.[12]

Coincident with the beginning of the "Final Solution of the Jewish Question" in 1942, the assassination attempts against Adolf Hitler steadily grew in number.[13] Most of them originated in the highest circles of the German army and civil government. Coincidence in timing does not, of course, mean that there was a direct causal relationship between the Holocaust and the resistance.[14] The resistance was made up of elements ranging from the far left of the political spectrum to the extreme right and included besides selfless idealists like Carl

---

[9] Georg Thomas, "Die Opposition," (MS. Falkenstein, 1945), courtesy Walther Döhner.

[10] Gerhard L. Weinberg, *World in the Balance. Behind the Scenes of World War II* (Hanover, 1981), p. 19.

[11] Raphaël Lemkin, *Axis Rule in Occupied Europe. Laws of Occupation, Analysis of Government. Proposals for Redress* (Washington D.C., 1944), p. 24. On the brutality of German occupation policy in Eastern Europe, the classical study remains Alexander Dallin, *German Rule in Russia 1941–1945. A Study in Occupation Policies* (London, 1957). See also Arno Mayer, *Why did the Heavens Not Darken? The 'Final Solution' in History* (New York, 1989), passim; and Franz Neumann, whose *Behemoth. The Structure and Practice of National Socialism* (New York, 1963), made an early point about the German need for fanaticism in a war against Russia.

[12] A good example in point is Arthur Nebe (1894–1945), an early Nazi supporter in the Berlin police during the Weimar Republic, head of an Einsatzkommando in Russia during the war, and in 1944 the man responsible for shooting fifty recaptured British POWs – and yet one of the conspirators against Hitler. Hans Bernd Gisevius, *Wo ist Nebe? Erinnerungen an Hitler's Reichskriminaldirektor* (Zurich, 1966). More critical of Nebe is Werner Rings, *Advokaten des Feindes. Das Abenteuer der politischen Neutralität* (Vienna, 1966), pp. 64–8; and the deposition of Nebe's own translator in Einsatzkommando B, Andreas von Amburger, dated Mossburg, 27 Dec. 1945, in USDC (Berlin), Acta Nebe, document 12.

[13] Dieter Ehlers, *Technik und Moral einer Verschwörung. 20. Juli 1944* (Frankfurt a.M., 1964), p. 12; and Günther Weisenborn, ed., *Der lautlose Aufstand. Bericht über die Widerstandsbewegung des deutschen Volkes, 1933–45* (Hamburg, 1953), passim.

[14] See Hannah Arendt's complaint, that the conspirators "were motivated exclusively by their conviction of the coming defeat and ruin of Germany," and not by the fate of the Jews, in Hannah Arendt, *Eichmann in Jerusalem* (New York, 1963), p. 91.

Goerdeler and Adam von Trott zu Solz, *völkisch* nationalists like Friedrich Wilhelm Heinz and opportunists like Arthur Nebe. What links the Holocaust to the plots against Hitler's life is that the first was the symptom of a political regime that was losing control over the course of events and sought escape in blind destructiveness, the second a spontaneous revolt against this very breakdown in political sanity. Assassination had never played an important role in German political life before the twentieth century. If the *feme* murders by right-wing extremists in 1919–22 were warning signs about a German Burgfrieden unraveling into civil war, the blood purge of 1934 (Röhm putsch), the assassinations by the Gestapo of émigrés abroad, together with the many plots to kill Hitler between 1938 and 1944 were proof that Germany was becoming an ill-policed society, increasingly prone to violence, reminiscent of tsarist Russia in the nineteenth century. Accounts of the unsuccessful attempt to overthrow Hitler on 20 July 1944 bear some resemblance to chronicles of the Decembrist uprising in St. Petersburg in 1825. Both tell about the ineptitude of idealistic rebels too well brought up to act with sufficient ruthlessness; about the silence of a population untrained for political action; and describe the Byzantine response of autocratic regimes gloating over the confessions of the conspirators, exacting atrocious revenge, and ending up being undermined by their own suspiciousness and rancor.[15]

Another symptom of the breakdown in public security was the stories circulated in Berlin after 1942 about strong points everywhere in the capital where SS and Gestapo men were waiting to quell popular insurrections.[16] Both the existence of hidden machinegun nests in apartment houses and of preparations of popular uprising have never been proved. To the very end of the war some desperate Berliners kept asking why the workers of the old labor movement did not use the growing chaos in the city to rise in revolt. Was Berlin too firmly policed after all? We think it was not. More likely, fear of imminent Russian conquest and of foreign retribution for the crimes of the Nazi regime, together with the people's strong social discipline and endurance in the face of adversity (that quality that had made the Germans so policeable for centuries) gave the Nazis in 1944–5 one last – if very provisional – hold over the city.[17]

In the light of events in 1989, having seen how demonstrators in Leipzig, Dresden, and East Berlin easily overthrew Erich Honecker's albeit much milder dictatorship, one is tempted to speculate about the loss of moral integrity by any

[15] Ehlers, *Technik und Moral*, pp. 161–2; and Thomas, "Die Opposition," p. 18. Also John Wheeler-Bennett, *The Nemesis of Power. The German Army in Politics* (New York, 1954), p. 669.

[16] Examples of this rumor can be found in Paul Hagen, *Will Germany Crack?* (New York, 1942), p. 147; Louis P. Lochner, *What About Germany?* (New York, 1942), pp. 236–7; Howard K. Smith, *Last Train from Berlin* (New York, 1942), p. 163; and Avid Fredborg, *Behind the Steel Wall* (New York, 1944), p. 54. Ursula von Kardorff wrote in her diary in 1944: "Wie Giftpilze haben die Gestapo-Stellen sich in allen Vierteln angesiedelt." U. von Kardorff, *Berliner Aufzeichnungen aus den Jahren 1942 bis 1945* (Munich, 1962), p. 213.

[17] "Es ist schwer zu sagen was grösser war: die stille Anständigkeit [dieses] Volkes . . . oder der unbeugsame Wille, den Hals aus der Schlinge zu winden." Editorial in *Christ und Welt*, 8 May 1952; also Kurt Ihlenfeld, *Stadtmitte* (Witten, 1964), pp. 82–3.

police endowed with excessive power. Corruption can set in when police power goes unchecked for too long because the population is submissive while the police is extravagantly supplied with arms and equipment – as was the case in the German Democratic Republic between 1953 and 1989. It equally afflicts a police that is granted unlimited power to commit violence, as was the case in wartime Germany. The latter however mainly applied to German police in the occupied countries, particularly in the east, not to the ordinary police and the lower ranks of the Gestapo at home.[18] As long as precinct constables were needed for everyday "low police" services they could count on some measure of appreciation by the population. True, the rapidly deteriorating situation also overtaxed its technical discipline and resources. In Alsace, German field police had to give names, blood group, and addresses of their parents and siblings to guarantee their continued loyalty to superior orders.[19] In 1942 it took the Berlin police one year to process a simple application for a residence permit. Notifying the next of kin of a victim in a motor accident took thirteen months.[20] But with defeat in 1944 drawing ever nearer the police, in its growing helplessness, became more like fellow victims of the other inhabitants of this dying city, not their watchdogs. Ursula von Kardorff describes Friedrichstrasse railway station in the last year of war as a veritable melting pot of nations and races: Russian prisoners in padded jackets, Danes and Norwegians with very blond hair, Frenchwomen chic even in prison garb, Poles with hatred in their eyes, and pitiful Italians shivering in the cold. The Reich Germans circulating among them were detectives of the Berlin city police – and they were scared.[21] One Gestapo interrogator allowed a young woman to spare her mother grief by sending her a postcard made to look as if it were mailed in Switzerland.[22] Another Gestapo employee, Hertha Schulz, assigned to guard the Belgian princess, Elisabeth Ruspoli, in 1943, made friends with her prisoner during one night of heavy bombing, in which the two women were forced to run for hours with their suitcases through the burning streets of Berlin seeking shelter in local police stations.[23]

Of the three cities that played an important role in our study of international police problems in the twentieth century – Vienna, Prague, and Berlin – Berlin underwent the most interesting democratic resurrection after the war. Berlin's fate

---

[18] On the corruption of Berlin police president Count Helldorf, see Richard Grunberger, *The 12-Year Reich* (New York, 1971), p. 102; and Bella Fromm, *Blood and Banquet* (New York, 1942), p. 280. On the corruption of German police in Poland, see Jan Karski, *Story of a Secret State* (Boston, 1944); and Tomasz Szarota, *Warschau unter dem Hakenkreuz,* trans. from the Polish (Paderborn, 1985).

[19] Telephone message, Bez.-Hauptmann Liersch, Gendarmerie-Kreis Molsheim, to "Alle Gendarmeriedienststellen der Kreise," 16 Dec. 1943, in NA (Washington), T-175, Roll 13.

[20] Smith, *Last Train from Berlin*, p. 163.

[21] Kardorff, *Aufzeichnungen*, pp. 220–1.

[22] Christabel Bielenberg, *Ride Out the Dark* (New York, 1971), p. 129.

[23] Letter, Hertha Schulz to Alexander von Falkenhausen, 12 Aug. 1947, in BA-MA (Feiburg i.B.), Nachlass Falkenhausen, Box: Ruspoli. That there were decent boys also among the guards at Sachsenhausen KZ is attested to in S. Payne Best, *The Venlö Incident* (London, 1949), pp. 71–2.

was so different from that of the other two cities because of its continued importance in international politics. Situated deep inside the Soviet occupation zone of Germany, it nevertheless was jointly controlled by all four occupation powers. By 1946, because of the rapidly deteriorating relations between the Western Allies and the Soviet Union, the city split into West Berlin (consisting of the American, British, and French sectors) and East Berlin (the Soviet sector, which after 1949 doubled as the capital of the German Democratic Republic). Divided Berlin became the object of intense rivalry in the ensuing Cold War, each half of the city stamping its own capitalist or communist image on the reconstruction of public buildings and business streets, on its shops and factories, its schools, newspapers, radio, and popular recreation. Each side resorted to a cat-and-mouse game of propaganda, counter propaganda, and intimidation in which police played a central role. Three major Cold War crises focused on Berlin: the Berlin Blockade (1948–9), the East German uprising (17 June 1953), and the erection of the Berlin Wall (13 August 1961). And since, during the next forty-five years, no one could be sure that Berlin would not again become the capital of a unified Germany, neither East nor West was ready to relinquish its position in the city.

The police problem in Berlin between 1945 and 1961 was to a large extent conditioned by the ease with which the inhabitants during these years could travel between the western and the eastern sectors of the city. The sector boundaries were not closely guarded except along the major thoroughfares and in the inner city. Pedestrians and passengers on city trains and subways could move from the districts Charlottenburg to Prenzlauer Berg or from Treptow to Neukölln without going through border controls, though they did run the risk of spot checks for identity papers, especially in the Soviet sector. There were also cases of politically wanted persons being kidnaped in the western sectors by the Soviet NKVD and the East German state security service (Staatssicherheitsdienst, or SSD – more recently nicknamed the "Stasi").[24]

Because of this freedom of movement everyone in Berlin could see how differently democracy manifested itself in east and west, and in general the comparison heavily favored the west – to judge by the ceaseless flow of thousands of people arriving in West Berlin's refugee camps. The Stalinist police dictatorship east of the Brandenburg Gate bore too close a resemblance to the crude despotism of the Third Reich at the close of the war: a militarized political police, gigantic slogans and the portraits of leaders covering the facades of war ruins, public loudspeakers blaring out marching songs, uniformed youths shouting and clapping in unison, and for the older inhabitants indoctrination booths (Aufklärungslokale) at street corners. If we call the West Berlin police in the late 1940s and in the 1950s "democratic" as no police force in this city had ever been democratic before, we

---

[24] A notorious case was the abduction of the lawyer Dr. Walter Linse from his home in West Berlin on 8 July 1952 by agents of the Staatssicherheitsdienst, as reported by Dr. Johannes Stumm in HICOG, *Information Bulletin* (Dec. 1952), pp. 21–2.

mean that there existed during these years an unprecedented political consensus in
the western sectors between the guardians of public order and the local inhabitants. Vehement rejection of communism (and Nazism), particularly at the time of
the Berlin Blockade, made for a simpler and stronger bond than a joint endorsement of democracy could ever have, as older police officials who remembered the
Weimar Republic well knew. The Cold War also forged solidarity inside the police. In the 1920s Dr. Weiss would never have asked his subordinates to collect
political intelligence in their off-duty hours as could the police chiefs of district
Tiergarten after the Berlin Blockade: "Because we have detectives and employees
of the administrative police whose homes are . . . in the eastern sector, we can
carry out intensive intelligence operations [against the Communists]. In particular, we can determine the strength and the intentions of communist agitators."[25]

True, the West Berlin police was held to democratic reconstruction by the Allied occupation authorities. The American, British, and French commanders who
took over West Berlin in June 1945 had at first contented themselves with so-
called police sector assistants (Polizeisektor-Assistenten) as liaison to the city-wide
police under Police President Paul Markgraf, a Soviet appointee. By July 1948,
however, the differences between the Allies and the Soviets over police appointments and police assignments[26] had led to an open rift and to the creation of a
separate West Berlin police force with headquarters in the American sector.[27] The
Americans, in particular, were interested in introducing German civil servants to
the American idea of political association based on voluntarism, in contrast to the
Hegelian state idea with its propensity to suppressing dissent.[28] To them democratic police meant decentralization, deconcentration, and demilitarization.

Yet given the utter discredit of Germany's previous regime, the relations between the Allied occupation forces and the German local police were marked by
a surprising measure of mutual trust and respect, reinforced by the shared hard-
ship of the Berlin Blockade (1948–9). In all essential matters the Allies maintained a legal controlling function: They had the right to question all personnel
appointments and promotions in the Berlin police. They had the overall supervision of all operations and offered the German police advice and admonitions on

---

[25] Polizei-Inspektion Tiergarten to Kommando der Schutzpolizei, PI Tg.-Tgb. Nr./50GB, Berlin,
30 Mar. 1950, in LA (Berlin), Rep. 20, Acc. 2200, Nr. 7854. Soon thereafter, however, all staff
members and employees were ordered to move to West Berlin for safety reasons.

[26] Karl Heinrich, in 1933 a victim of the Nazi purge inside the Berlin police and reintegrated in the
police force as commander of the Schutzpolizei right after the fall of the Third Reich, was placed
in a labor camp by the Soviet authorities in August 1945 without explanation, where he died three
months later.

[27] A good summary account is Walter Krumholz, *Berlin-ABC* (Presse- u. Informationsamt, Berlin,
1968), pp. 491–4.

[28] J. F. J. Gillen, *State and Local Government in West Germany, 1945–1953. With Special Reference to the
U.S. Zone and Bremen* (Historical Division, Office of the Executive Secretary, HICOG, 1953), p.
73; and Hans J. Wolff and O. Gönnewein, *Die Gestaltung des Polizei- und Ordnungsrechts in den
einzelnen Besatzungszonen. Verhandlungen der Tagung der Deutschen Staatsrechtslehrer zu München am 20.
und 21. Oktober 1950* (Berlin, 1952), pp. 183–7.

their performance.[29] But insofar as there was a clear separation of functions between the Allies and the Germans there was also an implied understanding that they depended on one another for the performance of a common task. The Allies limited their policing to security work around military installations (supported by subordinate German police) and to occasional spot checks on public thoroughfares. In a dragnet operation against blackmarketeers the Allies would use their military units to seal off a given terrain but leave the filtering of the crowd to German officials. On special holidays when massive disturbances from the Communist side were expected, the Allies lent the German police their army vehicles but otherwise stayed well out of sight. In the absence of any resistance to the Allied occupation by die-hard Nazis or right-wing nationalists in the style of the freecorps fighters of 1918, the Allies and Germans lost no time in recognizing their common interest in restoring civil order and producing that political solidarity among the West Berliners which proved so valuable in defeating the Soviet blockade of Berlin in 1948–9. (The absence of a comparable social discipline among the anti-communist inhabitants in Prague earlier that year may have contributed to the success of the Communist coup in Czechoslovakia.)

The West Berlin police was a trusted partner of the Allies. At the same time it did not shoulder the ultimate responsibility for Berlin's security. The Allied intelligence services reserved the right to interrogate all East German refugees and Communist deserters before they were questioned by German police. American, British, and French garrisons provided military protection in case of a full-scale attack. When in 1950 and 1954 the Communist youth organization, Freie Deutsche Jugend, sent thousands of youngsters into West Berlin on Whitsuntide day with instruction to cause disturbances by hoisting Communist flags, firing off rockets filled with propaganda leaflets, and challenging pedestrians to political debates, the West Berlin police did not close the border. Instead, the young people were let in provided they could be split into small groups. Reception centers staffed by civilian volunteers waited on them with refreshments, conversation, and counter propaganda and both events ended peacefully. Though the West Berlin police since 1952 maintained mobile brigades (Bereitschaftspolizei) to deal with major disturbances, the future of the city was clearly in the hands of the policy makers in Washington, London, Paris, Bonn, and Moscow.[30]

George E. Berkley once said that to think of democratic police as founded on a consensus between police and public is paradoxical, since the police's work really begins at the point where consensus breaks down.[31] But in the case of the Berlin

---

[29] For a general discussion of Allied occupation rights, see Institut für Besatzungsfragen, Bürgerrechte und Besatzungsmacht. Eine Übersicht (Frankfurt a.M., 1951).

[30] Polizei-Inspektion Charlottenburg to Kommando der Schutzpolizei, Org.Abtlg. - Pl.Ch. - I.B. - 52.05/50GB., 30 Mar. 1950, Betr.: "Massnahmen der Pol.-Insp. Charlottenburg für das Pfingsttreffen der FDJ," in LA (Berlin), Rep. 20, Acc. 2200, Nr. 7854; and police sector assistant (British), Schupo, to the inspector general, Public Safety Branch, British Military Government, BS/S61.10 ref. no 1208/54GB, Berlin, 4 June 1954, in ibid., Rep. 20, Acc. 2200, Nr. 7861.

[31] George E. Berkley, *The Democratic Policeman* (Boston, 1969), p. 2.

police adjustment to a democratic role after the war came that much easier precisely because the common front of public and police against the Communist threat next door justified the prolongation for nearly another twenty years of behavior in accordance with the old Burgfrieden principle: to the West Berlin police (as much as to the Volkspolizei in East Berlin) the chief enemy of society still stood outside its territory, except that this time the military burden to hold him at bay was left to foreign soldiers.[32]

During these two decades of confronting Stalinism, the de-Nazification of the West Berlin police proceeded with relatively little fanfare. Although the Nazi police leaders were definitely gone, many lower-ranking veterans from before 1945 had reentered the service side by side with newcomers. Insofar as some of them had stood on the periphery of the Nazi cult and had once belonged to the unthinking mass of small fellow travelers, they were trusted not to exert any deleterious influence.[33] The Western Allies, unlike the Russians, made no attempt to root out the cause of German Fascism by far-reaching intervention in the social fabric of their occupation zones. On the contrary, consistent with the spirit of modern police principles they wanted de-Nazification "to serve the welfare of the governed," that is, of the German people, and bring about the democratization of political life with minimal disturbance to the society. One of the American worries was how to avoid the formation of a large group of malcontents, that is, of former Nazis denied all avenues of self-improvement, since this would pose a potential menace to social peace.[34] De-Nazification was rather used as an opportunity to demonstrate democracy's commitment to impartial, legal procedures and respect for individual rights. As the U.S. High Commissioner for Germany, John J. McCloy, explained in a letter to Mrs. Eleanor Roosevelt, who in 1951 had written an article asking "Why are we freeing so many Nazis?":

I feel I can say I followed a principle which I believed was based on a distinction between actions taken for reasons of military security and those based on furtherance of Nazi racial and political objectives. . . . The people whose sentences I reviewed were not imprisoned for being Nazis, but for specific offenses against law or humanity. . . . We do believe that Nazism was morally bad. But you would not maintain that because a man was a Nazi he should be ineligible for clemency when convicted for other offenses.[35]

---

[32] Hendrik Bussiek, *Die real existierende DDR. Neue Notizen aus der unbekannten deutschen Republik* (Frankfurt a.M., 1985), p. 44. True, the West Berlin police in 1952 also set up heavily armed units for local emergencies, the Bereitschaftspolizei.

[33] On the tolerant attitude of the West towards "kleine Mitläufer," see Ernst Müller-Meiningen, Jr., *Die Parteigenossen. Betrachtungen und Vorschläge zur Lösung des "Naziproblems"* (Munich, 1946), which was published under U.S. military government license. See against this the Communist accusation that Nazi war criminals were serving in the West Berlin police: Nationalrat der Nationalen Front des demokratischen Deutschland, *Strauss und Brandt mobilisieren die SS. Drahtzieher der Revanchehetze um Westberlin* (East Berlin, 1962), pp. 71–100; and idem, *Braunbuch. Kriegs- und Naziverbrecher in der Bundesrepublik* (East Berlin, 1965), pp. 93–4.

[34] John G. Kormann, Historical Division, Office of the Executive Secretary, "U.S. Denazification Policy in Germany" (HICOG, 1952), chaps. II, III.

[35] Letter, McCloy to Eleanor Roosevelt, 12 Mar. 1951, reprinted in HICOG, *Information Bulletin* (May, 1951), pp. 11–12.

When the police in Berlin-Charlottenburg proceeded to de-Nazify the local residents by investigating everyone listed in a district honor roll of the NSDAP, the Allied military authorities encouraged them to act with leniency. A British review of three cases, dated 14 January 1946, for example, read:

1. Konrad Huse. Failing to report Party membership. In this case, it appears the only proof that he was a party member is a letter written by him to the chancellery of the Führer. This may be sufficient proof in itself, but in my opinion it is not. You can bring this case before the German courts on the evidence available, but unless you are able to support the letter with other evidence, the case is very weak.
2. Ernst Rummel. Failing to report Party membership. This case appears to offer no difficulties insofar as proof is concerned, and the man can be brought before a German court.
3. Else Tillack. Failing to report Party membership. Where is the evidence in this case that this person was a member of the Party? I cannot see any.[36]

Encircled by a menacing Stalinist regime on all sides that united the population and its German and Allied security authorities into a close community of faith and interest, West Berlin after the war offered the world a brief glimpse of practical international police collaboration within a very circumscribed piece of territory. This was a heartening achievement following so closely on a devastating world war in which some European police organizations had gone berserk. Not until the wall went up in 1961 did the situation in Berlin change again. With the danger of open conflict between East and West becoming very remote, West Berlin ceased to be the beleaguered outpost of the Cold War in Europe. Its society, increasingly giving way to its inherent pluralistic interests, became rent by economic and ideological disputes not unlike those known to policemen in Paris, London, Rome, or Berkeley (California). Unable to rely anymore on universal acceptance of one public interest (to remain free of Stalinist rule) the police was henceforth called on to improvise social compromises from day to day in the style of the free-market democracy which thirty years later – after the revolution of 1989 – all the East European authorities are beginning to face as well.[37]

When five Warsaw Pact countries invaded the Czechoslovak Socialist Republic on 20–1 August 1968 in defense of their common pattern of government, the world

---

[36] Military government Charlottenburg to Herr Vorwerk of F.S. Section, department of registration of former members of the NSDAP, Berlin, 14 Jan. 1946, (7 VBK), Char/17104/PS/, in LA (Berlin), Rep. 20, Acc. 1968, Nr. 7763-7764. Original in English. A dissenting voice was André Siegfried, who thought Nazism expressed the inherent political character of the Germans. André Siegfried, "Conférence d'ouverture du stage de l'A.M.F.A." (faite en Sorbonne). (Pamphlet used by French occupation forces in Germany in 1945, courtesy Louis Séverin.)
[37] "Befehl und Gehorsam – das geht nicht mehr," in *Der Spiegel,* 5 Feb. 1973, pp. 38–57. A vivid account of clashes between students and police in Charlottenburg is provided by Joseph Wechsberger, in "Letter from Berlin," in *The New Yorker,* 27 June 1970, pp. 69–72. On the stabilizing effect of the Berlin Wall, as recognized by the West, see Karl-Heinz Janssen, "Preussens Gloria, Deutschlands Elend," in *Die Zeit,* 21 Aug. 1981, p. 1.

was given notice that the people's republics of Eastern Europe, under the leadership of the USSR, represented a distinct state system within the larger international world order. Reminiscent of the Metternich system 150 years earlier, the Warsaw pact countries reconfirmed the classical view (in this instance defined as the "Brezhnev doctrine") that states committed to collaboration must share a common political ideology. Just as in the early nineteenth century a relationship founded on trust was deemed possible only between legitimate monarchies, and later between sovereign states duly recognized as such under international law, so in the mid-twentieth century the victory of world socialism was seen as dependent on all the progressive countries subscribing to the banner of Leninism–Stalinism.

As we know, the Metternich system was crushed in 1848 not by military armies, but by government incompetence, indifference toward popular discontent, and by the police's failure to anticipate the impact of telegraphs and railways on the politics of the common people. Likewise the collapse of the East European regimes in 1989 can be attributed to long years of bureaucratic pedantry and to miscalculations concerning the importance of television news and the computer revolution in the rest of the world, and once again not one enemy soldier fired a shot.

No Westerner visiting the Socialist countries in the last forty years could help but be astounded by their vehement insistence on the sanctity of territorial sovereignty. Every foreign traveler was reminded of it by the ubiquitous police surveillance in railway stations and in hotels, the heavy armament of the police, the military drill for young boys and girls, and the paranoid inspection of every vehicle at the frontier. This so visible cult of armed strength brought home to all outsiders the Socialist governments' commitment to fight the imperialist West and to train their people as soldiers of a future socialist civilization. The German Democratic Republic, together with the Czechoslovak Socialist Republic, both directly facing NATO forces in West Germany, were of critical importance for the military defense of the Eastern bloc.[38] From the Western view, however, the situation did not call for conventional military posturing with emphasis on holding strategic defense lines. To avoid a military showdown over the capitalist or socialist orientation of Central Europe, the West instead preferred to keep Germany divided into separate occupation zones for an indefinite period of time and merely to advance the principles of democracy and free enterprise in its own sphere of influence.[39]

Over the next three decades the Western policy turned out to be doubly successful. Not only did the Soviet and the East German governments fail to match

---

[38] Memorandum by Vjacheslav Dashichev of the Institute for the Economy of the Socialist World System, Moscow, 18 April 1989, as reported in "Enormer Schaden für Moskau," in *Der Spiegel*, 44. Jhg., Nr. 6, (5 Feb. 1990), pp. 142–58.

[39] Reiner Eger, *Krisen an Oesterreichs Grenzen. Das Verhalten Oesterreichs während des Ungarnaufstandes 1956 und der tschechoslowakischen Krise 1968. Ein Vergleich* (Vienna, 1981), p. 14.

the economic prosperity achieved by the Bundesrepublik under Konrad Adenauer and Ludwig Erhard, they redoubled their efforts to strengthen their armed forces and to tighten their police control throughout the GDR at great economic cost.[40] When the machinery of the East German Staatssicherheitsdienst was finally brought to a standstill by popular insurrection, the public discovered that East Germany had in proportion ten times the police surveillance of the German Federal Republic: 85,000 full-time secret police officials plus 109,000 paid informers (not counting the many civilian spies pressed into involuntary service). The police control of the German Democratic Republic was technically far more complete than that of the Third Reich, though mercifully, casual talk in public places was not as carefully controlled as were press publications. There was also the significant difference that in East Germany the political police did not draw additional psychological power from the commission of mass murder. The Staatssicherheitsdienst (or Stasi) was feared and hated for its brutality, arbitrariness, and remorseless snooping, but it was not galvanized by fanaticism like the SS. There were not even gulags and mass purges as in Stalinist Russia, and there were no extermination camps.[41]

And still we must count the Stasi in the category of totalitarian institutions, and so in conflict with the standards of modern police. What the East German police lacked was support by a constituency freely and positively responding to it as to civil servants subordinate to a government dependent on popular approval. Not even the ordinary police in East Berlin – the people's police (Volkspolizei, or Vopo) – could claim to enjoy popular trust. In the early postwar years many Vopos were young men, seventeen or eighteen years old, inducted into police service against their will and full of resentment against daily political indoctrination. On the average four to five Vopos deserted to the Western sectors every day.[42] But the main weight of popular dislike was concentrated on the secret police whose work was identified with the inflexible politics of the ruling Socialist Unity Party (Sozialistische Einheitspartei, or SED). As a member of the Institute for Social Sciences attached to the central committee of the SED admitted in the spring of 1990, following the collapse of Communist rule in the GDR:

---

[40] Günther Braun, in Kölner Stadtanzeiger, 3 Feb. 1990; and "Schild und Schwert der Partei (I)," in *Der Spiegel*, 5 Feb. 1990, p. 51.

[41] By comparison, Nazi Germany, with twice the population of the GDR, had 45,000 Gestapo officials and 100,000 paid informers. Walter Nelson, *The Berliners. Their Saga and Their City* (New York, 1969), p. 115.

[42] "Eine Armee von Deserteuren?" in *Die Zeit*, 19 Apr. 1951, p. 2; "Why 'Vopos' Desert," in HICOG, *Information Bulletin*, Aug. 1951, pp. 59–61; and "Vopo Fugitives Describe Bad Camp Conditions," in ibid., Feb. 1953, p. 22. However, after reunification of Germany in 1990, the West Berlin police found it possible, and even necessary, to absorb the majority of the lower- and middle-ranking officials of the East Berlin Volkspolizei into its ranks, albeit subject to a process of individual screening and extensive professional and political retraining. Georg Schertz, "Vereinigung der Polizeibehörden. Herausforderung bei der Integration zweier Polizeibehörden aus Berliner Sicht." Lecture delivered at the Polizei-Führungsakademie Münster, 1 Oct. 1991.

Did we make the mistake of embarking on a socialist plan that can work only with Socialist human beings long before we actually produced such socialist human beings? Did our leadership fail to see that our people was still pluralistic? There is a parallel between our history and the history of the Roman Catholic Church. We also made our ex-cathedra pronouncements. Only the Catholic Church very wisely never forgot that its believers were nothing but ordinary sinners. We did not.[43]

The ideological program of the SED was wrong because regimenting the people of East Germany for forty years as if preparing for total war had been palpably unwarranted almost from the beginning. The Western powers repeatedly showed they would not "roll back" the Iron Curtain by military force even when serious domestic crises inside the Eastern bloc offered tempting opportunities for attack.

The SED program was wrong because it could not bring about a Socialist society.[44] Had not the modern police in the nineteenth century earned its acceptance by the townspeople in large part by providing them with tangible public improvements like street cleaning, food inspection, and crime fighting? The massive desertion of young and highly trained East Germans to West Germany throughout the forty years of the GDR was prompted by endemic economic and social stagnation. When the prospect of a communist world revolution and wars of liberation became ever more remote the police regime of the GDR reminded Western reporters less of Gestapo rule than of Latin American dictatorships: the Stasi were just as self-indulgent, as corrupt, and as exploitative.

The East German police state failed, finally, because it was not sufficiently in command of its task. Barracked Volkspolizei served with Soviet troops under Soviet officers.[45] The imposition of Russian police traditions on the service directives of police throughout Eastern Europe since 1945 had the effect of alienating the public and isolating the Communist police in Poland, Hungary, East Germany, and Czechoslovakia from the moral world of their constituencies: public confessions, denunciations of family members, and mindless recitation of political slogans had for centuries worked in Russia, where the police of Peter I, Catherine II and Stalin had never acted as mediators between state interest and popular wishes but solely as the coercive instrument of change decreed from above, intolerant of the people's resistance to new ideas.[46] The East German police was also not in control because it had no way of maintaining the necessary secrecy over its operations. Thanks to modern technology the individual police officials in East

---

[43] Interview, Prof. Harry Nick, Akademie für Gesellschaftswissenschaften beim ZK der SED, Berlin, 12 Mar. 1990.

[44] Bundesministerium für gesamtdeutsche Fragen, "Bericht über den Aufbau der Volkspolizei in der sowjetischen Besatzungszone (Stand Frühjahr 1951)," (MS., Bonn, 1951); and particularly Harwig Lüers, "Das Polizeirecht der DDR. Aufgaben, Befugnisse und Organisation der Deutschen Volkspolizei" (Diss. University of Cologne, 1973), pp. 19, 39–40, 53.

[45] Horst Duhnke, *Stalinismus in Deutschland. Die Geschichte der sowjetischen Besatzungszone* (1955), pp. 363–8.

[46] " 'Unser Volk wird schon zu lange belogen . . . ' Brief eines Prager Sicherheitsoffiziers an Parteichef Gustav Husak," in *Der Spiegel*, 17 May 1971, pp. 104–6.

Germany had reason to believe that all their actions were continuously recorded by private and state intelligence services in the West.[47] Fear of personal retribution has been cited as one reason why so many Stasi officials fled to the West in November 1989, bringing with them documents in exchange for immunity from prosecution.

We must, of course, not forget that the collapse of the police states in Eastern Europe was largely made possible by the changes in the Soviet Union since 1985. Mikhail S. Gorbachev's perestroika destroyed the myth of the Communist world revolution. The relaxation of the Soviet dictatorship unleashed a stampede of East Germans seeking refuge in West Germany. And true to the behavior of all police forces in times of political overhaul, by the summer of 1989 the East German political police began to straddle the situation between the ruling power and the insurgent people. Still using abusive language to describe the defectors (as a token of continued loyalty to the regime), the Stasi urged the central committee of the SED and the GDR government to accept the fact that the mass exodus to the West could not be stopped. "The large numbers who are leaving hurt us. No matter what miserable specimens [*miese Drecksäcke*] they all are, they do represent manpower that we cannot afford to lose."[48] The Stasi did not recommend that the frontiers be sealed tighter or that demonstrators be dispersed by brute force. Ever since Gorbachev in the fall of 1989 indicated that Soviet Russia no longer stood behind East Germany, Erich Mielke, the minister of state security, and his close associates knew that the regime they had served so long was doomed. In 1992, some former officials of the East German ministry of state security claimed that the 1989 revolution was supported by the secret police acting independently against the Communist party, in a desperate attempt to keep control of a deteriorating situation.[49]

The paralysis of the SED regime in turn opened the door to democratic change in neighboring Czechoslovakia. Czechoslovakia under Communist rule between 1948 and 1989 had continued to display its "optimal" quality for police control. There was "divide and rule": workers isolated in their factories, peasants in their villages, and intellectuals in their libraries, their common interest represented only by the bureaucracy that purported to be indispensable for their coexistence. There was secrecy and fear, and there was myth: the myth of the Communist Party line that everyone knew to be untrue but pretended to believe, and the still

---

[47] At the height of the Cold War, such work was undertaken in West Berlin by organizations such as the Kampfgruppe gegen Unmenschlichkeit, the Untersuchungsausschuss freiheitlicher Juristen, the Vereinigung der Opfer des Stalinismus, and the Freie Vereinigung der Volkspolizisten.

[48] Ernst Mielke at a Stasi conference, 31 Aug. 1989, as documented in Arnim Mitter and Stefan Wolle, eds., *"Ich liebe euch doch alle!" Befehle und Lageberichte des MfS Januar-November 1989* (Berlin, 1990), p. 134.

[49] Wanja Abramowski, "Politischer Anspruch und alltägliche Wirklichkeit in der Arbeit des MfS," paper given at 2. Arbeitstagung des Unabhängigen Historikerverbandes e.V., Berlin, 12 Jan. 1992.

more frightful myth about an omnipresent police surveillance, with the capacity of paralyzing all individual self-confidence, so well portrayed in Vaclav Havel's play, "Largo Desolato" (1984).

At the same time, Czechoslovakia's police optimality also made possible the success of counter-myths to challenge the existing state police power. Jan Palach, a student who burned himself to death on 16 January 1969 in protest over the Soviet invasion, became the symbol of popular defiance overnight. In 1989, the Czechoslovak state security discovered that its nymbus broke the moment the people learned about the events in Leipzig, Dresden, and East Berlin and ceased to be afraid. By 17 November the country was in full revolt. By December, the Communist regime in Prague could depend on no more than 2,000 to 3,000 policemen to defend it.[50] The history of the Communist police in the Eastern bloc, just like the history of police in the European state system since the time of Metternich, must ultimately be studied in a multistate context.

In our conclusion we have quickly surveyed the years from the end of the Second World War to the eve of the twenty-first century. At the outset of this period, George Orwell's novel, *Nineteen Eighty-Four* (1948), sounded a warning bell about the world of absolute police control into which we seemed to be heading despite Hitler's recent defeat. The book was a warning much heeded in the West and banned from the bookshelves in the Communist East. Since 1983, however, Orwell's novel has been publicly discussed in Soviet periodicals. Today the Soviet Union has disappeared and the KGB is being dismantled.[51] Were Orwell alive today he probably would still caution us that our world is headed toward extensive police control, for we must have such control to keep the wheels of our supertechnology going, to fight off erratic outbursts of terrorism, to curb ecological pollution, and to manage the migration of hungry populations. But he might well add that we can take comfort from having seen Hitler's Third Reich fall in ruins and millions released from Russian labor camps in the course of de-Stalinization. Franco's Fascist Spain has disappeared and Soviet tank crews have been immobilized by civilians in the streets of Budapest (1956) and Prague (1968). Most dramatically, we have seen in November 1989 the rout of police dictatorship in one communist country after the other, sent packing by popular exasperation with bureaucratic brutality, inefficiency, and economic mismanagement. The danger that police power will be abused continues to exist, but we have reason to believe that people can bring down such tyranny if they really want to.[52]

---

[50] Interview with Valtr Komarek, "Die Machtmafia wurde nervös," in *Der Spiegel*, 25 Dec. 1989, p. 101.

[51] Raymond G. McInnis, "George Orwell's Nineteen Eighty-Four in the Communist World," in *East European Quarterly*, XXI, No. 3 (Sept. 1987), pp. 345–53.

[52] For an interesting observation on the vulnerability of police machines to the challenge of free-minded individuals, see Andrei Amalrik, *Notes of a Revolutionary*, trans. by Guy Daniels (New York, 1982), pp. 15–6.

List of archival files consulted

Archive de la Préfecture de Police, Paris

Carton A A/419	"Police de Paris . . . Inspection générale de la Navigation et des Ponts" (1815–16)
Carton A A/420	"Evènements divers 1830"
Carton A A/433	"Coup d'état 1851"
Carton A A/434	"2ème Empire. Attentats et complots"
Carton B A/195	"Socialisme en Allemagne 1871–89"
Carton B A/196	"Le socialisme en Russie de 1872 à 1889"
Carton B A/323	"Allemagne 1877–86"
Carton B A/878	"Séliverstoff"
Carton B A/896	"Guerre de 1914. Commission des étrangers"
Carton B A/923	"Gambetta année 1880"
Carton B A/924	"Nétchaièf, Russe coupable d'assassinat politique"
Carton B A/953	"Bazaine, Maréchal de France"
Carton B A/1023	"De Cyon, Elie"
Carton B A/1287	"Tchernischewski, Tourgeneff"
Carton B A/1329	"Attentat du 13 mars 1881 contre Alexandre II"
Carton B A/1132	"Ravachol"
Carton B A/1510	"Mouvement Bonapartiste"
Carton B A/1644	"Général Boulanger"
Carton B A/1693	"Polices étrangeres. Police allemande à Paris (1892–1934)"
Carton B A/1703	"Dossier Schwartzkoppen"

Ministère des Affaires Etrangères, Archives diplomatiques, Paris

Série C administrative 1876–18. Numéro 85 C-24 intérieur, DR "Etrangers en France 1893–8."

. Numéro 86 C-24 intérieur, DR "Anarchistes 1892–8. Conférence internationale de Rome pour la défense sociale contre les anarchistes."

. Numéro 87 C-24 intérieur, DR "Anarchistes sept.–dec. 1898."

Correspondance politique, nouvelle série 1897–1918. Russie, Carton 80: "Arrestations et expulsions 1896–1917."
Série Z Europe 1918–1940. Tchécoslovaquie 12–155. "Section des renseignements militaires."

Centre de Documentation Juive Contemporaine, Paris

CD XLVI-69. SPD report on Gestapo in Prague (1935).
RSHA report on Gestapo surveillance of German émigrés in Paris.
Files on Germans who opposed Nazism.

Archives nationales, Paris

F7 12428	"Agissements bonarpartistes 1871–1891."
F7 12519–20	"Révolution russe de 1905."
F7 12521	"Organisation révolutionnaire russe à l'étranger."
F7 12584	"Surveillance des étrangers 1894–9."
F7 12587	"Notices individuelles d'étrangers. Inscriptions au Carnet B."
F7 12566	"Relations Allemagne."
F7 12644	"Notes sur l'espionnage en général."
F7 12548	"Circulaires 1887–1907." Confidential instruction to border police in case of mobilization for war.
F7 12649	"Catastrophes, inondations, accidents, 1907–10."
F7 12710	"Evènements 1848–51."
F7 12726	"Etrangers: Contrôle Général."
F7 12727	"Relations internationales–Suisse–1872–1915."
F7 12751	"Alsace-Lorraine 1923–5."
F7 12840	"Projet de gardes civiles" (1913).
F7 12865	"Action Française. Mort de Philippe Daudet."
F7 12903–4	"Anarchistes en France et à l'étranger, 1892–1923."
F7 12905	"Anarchistes. Attentat de Sarajevo."
F7 12925	"Affaire Dreyfus. Leutnant Wessel travaillant pour la police française."
F7 12934	"Guerre de 1914."
F7 12935	"Guerre franco-allemande" (1914).
F7 13486	"Tchécoslovaquie 1920–6."
F7 13506	"Le bolchévisme dans le monde. Secours rouge international 1918–32."

Archives départementales du Bas-Rhin, Strasbourg

3 M (54)	"Police Générale. Contrôle de l'esprit public 1836."
AL 87 (3289)	"Feindselige Handlungen gegen deutsches Militair und deutsche Beamte, Excesse, Alarm-Nachrichten" (1872).
AL 87 (3920)	"Ruhestörung, Renitenz, Ausweisung" (1870).
AL 87 (2160)	"Beschwerden über die Polizei-Verwaltung und deren Organe" 1889–1905.

AL 87 (2142)	"Schutzmänner in Strassburg (1873–1907)."
AL 87 (4812)	"Die Berichterstattung über wichtige ungewöhnliche und Aufsehen erregende Ereignisse (1870–1918)."
AL 87 (400)	"Socialdemokratische Umtriebe 1871–93."
AL 87 (453)	"Verbrechen und Vergehen 1870–84."
AL 29 (11)	"Die Verhaftung des französiscen Polizei-Kommissars Schnäbele und das Verhalten des Pol. Kommissars Gautsch bei derselben" (April 1887).
AL 30 (131)	"Zeichner Waltz (Hansi), 25. April 1910."
AL 102 (11)	"Weill, Georg, geb. 17. Sept. 1882."
AL 30 (109)	"Die Verhaftung des Polizei-Inspektors Wohlgemuth in der Schweiz 23 April 1889–6 Dez. 1889."
AL 30 (102)	"Die französische Grenzpolizei (1887)."
AL 30 (77)	"Ueberwachung deutschfeindlicher Agenten und Kundschafter (1911)."
AL 132 (25)	On Zabern affair, 1913.
AL 121 (801)	"Situation et pensions des gendarmes alsaciens-lorrains ayant servi dans la gendarmerie allemande (1920–3)."
AL 121 (847)	"Organisation générale des services de police d'Alsace-Lorraine 1919–25."
AL 98 (281)	"Evacuation 1939–40."

Archives départementales du Haut-Rhin, Colmar

4 M 28	Rapport des commissaires de police spéciaux de Sant-Louise et de Delle 1854–70.
4 M 197	Passage par la France de réfugiés expulsés de Suisse et dirigés vers la Grande Bretagne et les EU 1834–55.
4 M 241	Feuilles de signalement suisses 1859–66.
1 Z 139	Commissaires et agents de police 1814–70.
1 Z 289–29	Ressortissants français et étrangers 1801–70.

Haus-, Hof- u. Staatsarchiv, Vienna

Deutsche Akten, alte Reihe 103 alt 40. "Central Untersuchungs Commission 1819."

Administrative Registratur F52. "Politische Flüchtlinge 1835–45" / *Central-Polizei-Blatt,* 1853 / Austausch / Fremde Polizeibeschwerden / Deutsche politische Flüchtlinge / Schubwesen 1880 / Prostitution 1870 / Russ. pol. Insurr. 1863 / Grenzsicherungsdienst 1884 / Arbeiter / Anarchisten – Polizeiberichte / Beschwerden 1896–1918 / Parteisachen 1912–1919 / Polizeiwesen Marokko / Postwesen 1862–54 / Staaten-Deutschland."

Faszikel 810. Politisches Archiv I, Liasse Krieg (früher Interna LXX), 3 Teile. "Attentat auf Erzh. Franz Ferdinand 28. Juli [*sic*] 1914."

Liasse Oesterreich 26/I, Faszikel 439. Annexation of South Tyrol by Italy, 1919. Agreement with Prague on sharing Austrian archives. Schober's Political and Military Intelligence Service 1918–35.

Faszikel 440. Police cooperation between Vienna and Berlin 1920–3; Hungarian deserters 1924.

Neues Poltisches Archiv. Karton 415, Liasse Tschechoslowakei I/III geh. folders 1–417; I/8 geh. 31/1 folders 418–601; 7/1 geh.

Liasse Tschechoslowakei folders 36–665.

Karton 614, Liasse Ungarn II4–9/14 geh.

Liasse Personalien geh. K-P (Waldemar Pabst).

Liasse China, Faszikel 596. Austrian police instructors for China 1928–33.

Allgemeines Verwaltungsarchiv, Vienna

Ministerium des Innern, Präsidiale. Karton 707. On Militär Polizeiwache, 1851.

Karton 710. "Sicherheit, Gendarmen, 1875–82."

Karton 1968. On coalminers' strike in Kladno, 1900.

Karton 1982. "Polizeibefugnisse, Theater u. öffentliche Schaustellungen 1900–18."

Allgemeine 192/a. On protection of telegraph lines 1848–69.

Präsidiale 19/4. Karton 362. On deserters, 1848–69.

Karton 690. On 1848–53: espionage; compensation for damages in civil war; army–police relations along border; foreign subjects seeking to join Austrian army.

Präsidiale 20/9. Karton 1986. On Kladno miners' strike, 1900.

S.D. Parl. Klub/44, 61, 67, 103. Socialist documents from the 1920s on party affairs, Communism, the Republikanische Schutzbund, the police, particularly the fighting in Vienna on 15 July 1927.

Kriegsarchiv, Vienna

KA. Nachlassammlung, sign. B/126, Nr. la, folders 117–26, (Max Ronge). Documents on military assistance to police, Feb. 1934.

Archiv der Polizei-Direktion, Vienna

Miscellaneous papers, handbooks, instructions.

Geheimes Preussisches Staatsarchiv, Berlin

Rep. 84a/8034	"Die Bestrafung der Duelle" (1822).
Rep. 84a/2234	"Die Militärpflichtigkeit der Ausländer" (1822–84).
Rep. 84a/11603	"Das Verfahren der Civilbehörden bei einer etwa eintretenden feindlichen Invasion 1840–60."
Rep. 84a/11604	"Das Verfahren der Civilbehörden bei einer etwa eintretenden feindlichen Invasion 1866–1919."
Rep. 84a/8552	"Die bei den Polizeibehörden entstehenden Kosten für Ausmittelung und Verhaftung von Verbrechern" (1852–57).
Rep. 84a/574	"Die Verwendung preussischer Justizbeamten in den occupierten französischen Landestheilen 1870–1."

Rep. 84a/6126   "Die Auslieferung der Ausländer die in einem fremden Staat Verbrechen begangen haben und an ein drittes Gouvernement ausgeliefert werden sollen (1823–1934)."

Rep. 84a/6151   "Die Auslieferung politischer Verbrecher (1881–1928)."

Rep. 90/1885   "Das Gräfliche Haus Henckel von Donnersmarck Bd. I."

Rep. 84a/2325   "Massnahmen gegen das Eindringen von Umsturzbewegungen in die Armee. 1894–1914."

Rep. 84a/2352   "Die Kriminalstatistik für das Deutsche Heer und die Kaiserliche Marine, 1900–2."

Rep. 84a/6207   "Die Verwaltung der im Kriege 1914/ . . . besetzten feindlichen Gebiete (1914 bis 30. Juni 1915)."

SPD Library, Berlin, Zietenstrasse 18

Registratur des Amtsbezirk Weissensee, "Acta spec. betreff. Umsturzparteien und deren Agitationen 1894–1914."

Landesarchiv, (West) Berlin

Polizeipräsident Berlin. Theaterzensurexemplare (1892–1902).

Political cases tried before the Preussisches Oberverwaltungsgericht, 1923–33.

Rep. 58. Political cases tried before the Landgericht Moabit, 1929–50.

Rep. 20, Acc. 1968, Nr. 7763–7764. Concerning the issuance of Aryan passes by the police, 1936.

Rep. 20, Acc. 1236, Nr. 6959. Registration of former members of Nazi Party, Berlin-Charlottenburg, 1946.

Rep. 20, Acc. 1151, Nr. 7158. Creation of Polizeisektorenleiter, 1946.

Rep. 20, Acc. 2200, Nr. 7861. Police measures in anticipation of demonstrations in the Lustgarten, 1948.

Rep. 20, Acc. 2200, Nr. 7854. Police preparations for the FDJ-Pfingsttreffen, Mar. 1950.

Rep. 2, Acc. 927, Nr. 31–93. The Kemritz case, 1951.

Rep. 2, Acc. 2200, Nr. 7862. Police protection of Rundfunkhaus in British sector, 1953.

Rep. 20, Acc. 2200, Nr. 7858. Police preparations for Weltjugendfestspiele, 1951.

Zeitgeschichtliche Sammlung Nr. 6607/1–55. "Major Karl Heinrich."

Bundesarchiv, Aussenstelle Frankfurt a.M.

The following files were consulted, all dealing with the events of 1848–9:

DB 54/33, 35, 36, 37.
DB 56/1, 42.

Bundesarchiv-Militärarchiv, Freiburg i.B.

N16/14–15. Nachlass Helmuth Graf von Moltke (1800–91).
N43/110. Nachlass Alfred Graf von Schlieffen (1833–1913).

N78/17. Deutsch-Südwestafrika. Hottentotenaufstand (1907).

Militärbefehlshaber Frankreich. RW 35/306. "Handhabung der polizeilichen Strafgewalt, 1940."

RW 35/307. "Festnahme französischer Staatsangehöriger. Gardes térritoriaux."

RW 35/308. "Vorbeugungs- u. Sühnemassnhamen zur Bekämpfung der Sabotage, Abwehr von Attentaten, Geisel-Frage 1941–2."

RW 35/320. "Verordnung über die polizeiliche Strafgewalt 1942."

RW 35/311. "Rückzahlung der der Stadt Dijon wegen eines Anschlages auf einen deutschen Offizier auferlegten Geldbusse von 10 Millionen Franken 1942."

RW 35/312. "Sammelverordnung zum Schutze der Besatzungsmacht, Vorbeugungs- und Sühnemassnahmen bei Angriffen auf die Besatzungsmacht, 1942–3."

RW 35/313. "Anzeigepflicht für Aerzte usw. über Personen, die Schusswaffen- oder Sprengstoffverletzungen aufweisen." (1944).

RW 35/340. "Franz. Verwaltungsstellen."

RW 35/617. "Zusammenarbeit mit dem höheren SS u. Polizeiführer in Frankreich."

Bundesarchiv, Koblenz

Akten des Polizei-Präsidiums zu Berlin. NS 26/Vorl. 1368: On Captain Walther Stennes. NS 26/Vorl. 1970. On Horst Wessel.

Reichssicherheitshauptamt, R 58/376: On state of emergency 1923.

R 58/744. On KPD insurrection in Berlin, 1 May 1929.

R 58/10 folder 1. Gestapa reports on émigrés in Prague, 1933.

R 58/380 folder 1. "Zwischenfälle an der C. S. Grenze" (1935).

R 58/484, folder 1. On Czechoslovak policy of asylum, 1933.

R 58/488, folder 1. On "Grenzsekretariate in C.S.R." (1936).

R 58/494, folder 1. Nuremberg Gestapo spying on SOPADE in Prague, 1937.

R 58/687. Anti-Nazi leaflets addressed to police, 1933–7.

R 58/590. Report on captured Sûreté files by RSHA in Paris, 1941–2.

R 58/806. Report on Gestapo agent "Kosak," 1939.

R 70 [Böhmen und Mähren] 1, 3, 5, 8, 16. On training of German police for duty in Czechoslovakia, 1939; Czechoslovak police law, 1922; German criminal police in Protectorate; reorganization of Czech police, 1942; Gestapo in Protectorate; interrogation of captured Gastapo official, 1945.

Politisches Archiv, Bonn

Abt. IA. Europa Fasc. 1, Nr. 11. "Aufstand in Paris. Krieg 1870/71."

Abt. IA B.c.81 Vol. I. "Nachrichten von politischen und Polizei-Agenten über Verhältnisse in Frankreich" (1870s).

Europa Generalia 82 Nr. 8. "Die Sozialdemokratie in Oesterreich-Ungarn" (1884).

Abt. IA. Frankreich Nr. 113 (Generalia). "Das Französische Spionagegesetz." Vol. I (1886).

Berlin Document Center (West Berlin)

NS-Party membership files of police officials.

RUSHA files.

SS files.
ORPO files.
Polizei-Verschiedenes.

Bundesarchiv, Berne

Bestand 21 (Polizeiwesen 1848–1930)

20612	Organisation der Eidg. Polizeiabteilung 1911–30.
20803	Reorganisation der Zentralstelle für Fremdenpolizei 1919.
14088–	
14021	Tätigkeit russischer Polizeibeamter in Genf 1879–1909.
19893	Angebliche russische Polizeiagenten in Zürich 1889.
13894	Indiskretionen des Polizeihauptmanns Fischer in Zürich, 1888.
8475	Verhaftung des Wohlgemuth 1889–92.
13897	Anarchisten-Ueberwachungsdienst in der Schweiz durch die italienische Regierung 1914.
12038	Antibolschewistische Organisationen der französischen, brit., u. amerikanischen Gesandtschaften 1918.
13898	Französische Polizeikommissare in der Schweiz 1918–20.
19899	Mühlfriedel, Hubert, deutscher Polizeikommissar in der Schweiz 1929–30.
15773	Auskunftgesuch der franz. Gesandtschaft über Tibaldi 1870.
13905	Demonstrationen nach der Ermordung Kaisers Alexander II.
13907	Ermordung der Kaiserin Elisabeth 1898.
13909	Attentat auf russischen Gesandten Jadowsky 1904.
14395	Bombenattentat auf Lonzawerke 1915–22.
15872	Anwerbung von Schweizern für die Fremden-Legion 1919.
15871	Warnung vor Eintritt in die Fremden-Legion 1922.
14441	Schmähschriften gegen Napoleon III 1850–66.
14456	Agitation von italienischen Flüchtlingen 1899.
9826	Verteilung revolutionärer Drucksachen an russische Kriegsgefangene 1916.
15882	Vernichtung von bolschewistischen Drucksachen in Basel.
14524	Strafverfahren gegen Bertoni wegen Verherrlichung anarchistischer Verbrechen 1906.
14502A–	
14502B	Verbreitung des "Sozialdemokraten" in der Schweiz.
15683	Entwurf zu einem Auslieferungsvertrag 1883.
12039	Abkommen mit deutschen Behörden betr. Bekämpfung des Bolschewismus 1919–20.
24626	Auslieferungsvertrag mit Frankreich 1869.
24624	Unterhandlungen mit Deutschland und Oesterreich betr. die Auslieferung wegen politischen Verbrechen 1885–7.
24650	Auslieferungsvertrag mit Russland 1873, Verfolgung der Täter des Banküberfalles in Tiflis 1872–1910.
24656	Auslieferungsvertrag mit der Tschechoslowakei 1935.
11847	Gefährdung der inneren Sicherheit der Eidgenossenschaft, Massnahmen gegen Ausländer, boschewistische Umtriebe 1918–19.

12043	Bürgerwehren, Werkdienst, Vaterländerischer Verband zur Bekämpfung des Bolschewismus 1914–23.
12042	Entente internationale contre la IIIe Internationale.
14008	Demonstration von Russen in der Schweiz 1905.
15708	Wanderverbot für preussische Handwerksgesellen nach der Schweiz 1849–70.
13929	Schweizerische Gesandtschaft Berlin über sozialistische Bewegung 1878–1902.
19879	Kontrolle und Ueberwachung politisch verdächtiger Personen 1883–1910.
13800	Kontrolle politisch tätiger Ausländer 1881–98.
13801	Kontrolle ausländischer Gemeinverbrecher 1899–1917.
13999	Aus Preussen ausgewiesene Sozialisten 1879–85.
14008	Russen in der Schweiz 1879–1909.
10558	Bolschewistische Umtriebe der Dadaisten in Zürich 1919.
10353	De facto Beziehungen mit der Sowjetunion 1917, 1937.
14027	Internationale Konferenz in Rom 1898–1912.
15771	Nachforschungen über böhmische Beseda 1870–1.
21845	Asylgesuch von Kossuth.
20871	Kollektivmassnahmen gegen die Schweiz wegen Asylpolitik (Sozialistengesetz) 1878–81.
21870	Angriffe Russlands gegen die schweizerische Asylpolitik 1879–81.
20873	Anschuldigungen von Bismarck gegen die schweizerische Asylpolitik 1884.
41	Schreiben des französischen Gesandten betr. Flüchtlinge in der Schweiz 1849–51.
57	Abordnung von General Dufour nach Paris.
2/755	Unruhen in Frankreich 1848–53.
2/8	Flüchtlingspolitik der Schweiz 1852.
85	Polenaufstand 1863, polnische Flüchtlinge in der Schweiz.
80	Deutscher Krieg 1866, Kompagnie hannoveranischer Soldaten.
125	Pariser Commune-Aufstand von 1871.
27/13345– 13402	Internierung der Bourbaki-Armee.
20864	Deutsche und französische Deserteure 1870–1.
27/13925	Deserteure, Refraktäre 1914–18.

Bestand 2 (*Auswärtige Angelegenheiten, 1848–95*)

614	Stellung und Kompetenzen der fremden Konsuln 1853–89.
610	Depeschengeheimnis der ausländischen Vertretungen 1895.
475	Grenzkorrekturen gegen Frankreich, Abtretung des südlichen Elsasses und Hochsavoyens an die Schweiz 1870–1.
494	Aufenthalt und Durchreise von Militärpersonen der kriegführenden Staaten durch die Schweiz 1870–1.
499	Blockade von Paris 1870–1.

| 4001 (A) | Handakten BR Häberlin 1920–34. |
| 4001 (B) | Handakten BR Baumann 1935–40. |

Staatsarchiv, Canton Basel-Stadt

EE4	Politische Flüchtlinge in der Schweiz 1815–33.
EE8	Louis Napoleon Bonaparte 1838.
FF4, 1	Eidg. Politische Polizei betr. Vereine, Flüchtlinge usw. 1849–50.
GG5	Deutscher Krieg, Hannoversche Flüchtlinge 1867–8.
N1	Polizeikorps: Bekleidung, Bewaffnung (1869).
EE12, 1	Sozialisten – Anarchisten – Politische Polizei 1878–84.
N6	Detective 1874–1918.
JJ2	Weltkrieg 1914–18. Neutralität, Grenzverletzungen, Passwesen, Grenzkontrolle.
JJ3	Weltkrieg 1914–18. Spionage 1913–17.
JJ6	Deserteure und Refraktäre 1913–1916–1921.
JJ8, 4	Weltkrieg 1914–18. Generalstreik Landesstreik 1919–22.
JJ8, 2	August 1919.
EE15, 1	Faszismus, Nationalsozialismus, Fronten 1920–45.
P8	Requisitionen und Citationen fremder Behörden in Criminalfällen überhaupt 1827–1936.
D3 1935–1028	Spanischer Bürgerkrieg. Verbot der Teilnahme.
D3 1931–1419	Pass- u. Dokumentenfälscherwerkstätte.
D3 1936–904	Verwendung des Polizeikorps im Kriegsfalle 1936–40.

Archiv des Zentralsekretariates des Schweizerischen Roten Kreuzes, Berne

Bestand J.II.15

144	Aerztemission (Deutschland) 1945–6.
42	Konflikt Italien-Aethiopien 1936.
75	Agence Centrale des Prisonniers de Guerre 1929–47.
15	Neutralisierung von Städten Zonen u. Ländern 1949.
43	Verwundetenaustausch 1914–18.
119	Westfront Belgien, Holland 1944–5.
120	Belgien 1944–6.
320	Frankreich. Internierungslager 1940–3.
91	Politisches Departement 1940–50.
92	Justiz- und Polizeidepartement 1942–7.
131	Deutschland 1946–50.
40	Displaced persons.
188	Flüchtlinge, Emigranten 1939–46.

198   Deutsche Kriegsgefangene 1915–16.
197   Gefangenenlager 1914–18.
100   SRK Tätigkeitsbericht 1939–45.
113   Nachkriegshilfe Russland (Nansen).
114–15   Russland 1922–3.
116   Spanien 1937–42.
133–8   Ostfront 1941–3.

Hoover Institution on War, Revolution and Peace. Archive of the Imperial Russian Secret Police (Okhrana)

European and Other Outposts in General. Index Numbers IIb, IIe, Va, Vd, Vf, and VIIc (relations with French, German, and Austrian police, 1890–1914).

Index